TOWARD A LAW
OF GLOBAL
COMMUNICATIONS NETWORKS

COMMUNICATIONS

George Gerbner and Marsha Siefert, Editors
The Annenberg School of Communications
University of Pennsylvania, Philadelphia

TOWARD A LAW
OF GLOBAL
COMMUNICATIONS NETWORKS

The Science and Technology Section
of
The American Bar Association

Edited by ANNE W. BRANSCOMB

Longman
New York & London

Executive Editor: Gordon T. R. Anderson
Production Editor: Pamela Nelson
Text Design: Thomas Bacher
Production Supervisor: Eduardo Castillo
Compositor: Graphicraft Typesetters, Ltd.
Printer and Binder: Interstate Book Manufacturers

Toward a Law of Global Communications Networks

"The Right to Communicate Under International Law," by Mark B. Feldman has
appeared in the *International Lawyer* and *Transnational Data Report.*

Library of Congress Cataloging in Publication Data
Main entry under title:

Toward a law of global communications networks.

   (Annenberg/Longman communications books)
   Bibliography: p.
   Includes index.
   1. Telecommunication—Law and legislation—Addresses,
essays, lectures. 2. Information networks—Law and
legislation—Addresses, essays, lectures. 3. Communica-
tion, International—Addresses, essays, lectures.
I. Branscomb, Anne W.   II. Series.
K4305.6.T69 1985   343'.0994   84-7902
ISBN 0-582-28530-5   342.3994

86 87 88 89 9 8 7 6 5 4 3 2 1

PREFACE

This book constitutes the contribution of the American Bar Association Science and Technology Section to World Communications Year. The various chapters represent a wide diversity of views (neither comprehensive nor exhaustive, but insightful) concerning international information networks in both public and private sectors, multinational companies, government agencies, and nonprofit institutions.

The participants in the project are members of the International Information Networks Committee of the Communications Law Division of the ABA Science and Technology Section. They include practicing attorneys and consultants who were recruited because of their expertise or who volunteered because of their special interest in the subject matter. Their papers were presented in 1982 and 1983 at a series of three conferences sponsored by the ABA and funded through the ABA Education Fund by contributions from many corporations including Control Data, Mobil, Exxon, International Business Machines, Citibank, American Telephone & Telegraph, Comsat, General Electric, and Xerox. These conferences were part of the educational component of an ongoing research project on the legal impact of the emerging technologies of computers and satellites on the global information marketplace.

To that extent the book does not represent a finished project but a progress report designed to encourage others interested in the subject to pursue their own research and thought processes more diligently.

The papers are varied in style and format. They describe avenues of inquiry rather than formal conclusions of the professionals involved. Similarly, any opinions in the papers generally represent the views of the author and not the formal position of any institutions they may serve professionally.

The objectives of this research project are threefold: to educate the members of the Bar about changes in the communications environment in which information is being exchanged internationally; to study the legal impact of new technology on commercial transactions, diplomatic relations, and transportation systems across international borders; and to assist the participants in telecommunications policy development.

The first conference focused on the manner in which information is transferred across national boundaries. Participants identified the types and uses of some of the international information networks employed by industry and government and, in some instances, the types of restrictions of international data flows they had experienced. Participants in the second conference explored the applicability of contemporary legal principles to the issues of law and policy that had been identified during the first conference. Participants examined the ramifications of applying existing tenets of criminal and various civil bodies of law (most notably property, contract, and tort) to problems that arise in international telecommunications. The effect of disparate attitudes among countries toward such issues as privacy, international trade, and cultural sovereignty upon emerging policies treating the free flow of data across the national borders formed a crucial part of the discussion. The third conference provided an opportunity to unify and update the information gathered thus far and to form some conclusions.

CONTENTS

INTRODUCTION

With the advent of computers and satellites, the international information marketplace has grown enormously. Moreover, the global communications environment seethes with emerging legal and policy issues concerning the transfer of information across national boundaries. This collection of essays is offered as resource material which attorneys, government officials, corporate executives, and public policy students may draw from, both for general background about the rapidly developing trade in information products and services and for identification of some of the emerging legal and policy issues.

The book consists of an Overview and three general sections: *The Global Communications Environment, Global Information Users and Information Transfer Systems,* and *Emerging Legal and Policy Issues in Global Information Flow.*

The Overview (Branscomb) offers a description of the current system of transnational information transport, a history of the concern about transborder data flows, and a brief analysis of the major legal issues of current concern.

THE GLOBAL COMMUNICATIONS ENVIRONMENT

This section addresses the impact of computer communications upon the technological environment (Pelton), the economic environment (Brown) and the political environment (Ganley) in which transnational information transfer takes place. It also covers both the historical development (Goldey and Kincaid) and current issues facing communications systems providers and users. A common theme in all the papers in this section is a basic philosophical dichotomy between the United States and the rest of the world over the ownership and control of communications systems.

Political and social issues are very evident in video communications (Dunham and Hering), in the delicate issues raised by direct broadcast satellite short wave radio proposals (Read) and in transnational advertising (Pri-

moff). Social subsidy and bureaucratic issues are apparent in the traditional telephone (Goldey) and record carrier areas (Kincaid). Clearly, the development of Integrated Services Digital Networks—ISDN's—(Rutkowski) will be heavily influenced by whether private competitive service providers are allowed to enter and exit "inside" the system. In the satellite area, an equivalent issue is whether orbital slots should be freely available or obtained by prior consent of the underlying countries. Taken together, the papers in this section offer reasons why the United States has adopted a competitive model for its treatment of communications facilities and demonstrate how the United States is consistent in its approach with its individualistic philosophy.

The papers raise critical questions regarding whether the international institutions developed to support traditional voice and record communications systems can evolve to meet the challenges of technological change (Rutkowski, Kincaid), or the political challenges from the developing countries (Goldey, Kincaid).

GLOBAL INFORMATION USERS AND INFORMATION TRANSFER SYSTEMS

Several layers of enhanced service providers have developed to bridge the gap between providers of basic communications conduits and the ultimate users. The issues facing the providers of computational and data base facilities (Beach & Marks) and specific services such as legal retrieval data bases (Taylor) are quite similar. Both are concerned with providing a cost effective network, usually based on private lines for high density routes (Beach & Marks). The availability of these cost effective networks is uncertain, however, inasmuch as many Post, Telephone and Telegraph Administrations (PTTs) are advocating the adoption of usage sensitive networks. Providers and users also face possible restrictions due to differing local laws. Any system containing data on individuals must consider the application of national data protection laws (Beach & Marks) on data originating in, transiting through, or destined for a country.

In addition to the issues facing any provider of basic communications conduits, enhanced service providers may have to deal with extensions of these issues or with entirely different issues. For example, legal retrieval systems raise interesting questions of liability in situations where no assurance exists of the completeness or timeliness of the data base itself (Taylor). The U.N. provides services such as data collection and standardization and a forum for multinational discussion of information control issues (Dizard). Various U.N. member countries have differing attitudes regarding the role of the U.N. in resolving problems in transborder data flows depending on the vantage point and domestic policies of the countries.

The papers in this section reveal that, from the user's perspective, information networks are integral to corporate operations (McCann, Czelen, Schaefer), government and educational institutions (Ramsay, Timlake, McCredie), and not-for-profit organizations (Solomon, Taylor). These networks are increasingly international in scope, and they vary widely to respond to the specific needs of individual users. Some networks are fixed, while others must be highly flexible to accommodate constantly shifting markets and the availability of raw materials (Czelen). Communications and data processing systems that most effectively bridge time and distance promote operational efficiencies and rapid market exploitation. In fact, communications and information networks, when put to innovative use, have created new profit centers for some users, particularly in the service industries. Operations management has become a critical function for international information networks (McCann, Schaefer, and Ramsay).

Some industries have been fundamentally altered by the inclusion of telecommunications technologies. Other sectors merely have become dependent on them for effective management. Nevertheless, despite evident technical diversity, all kinds of users share the same concerns and are subject to similar constraints on their communicating freedoms. All are vulnerable to emerging international laws and regulations that inhibit, by volume or kind, the flow of information across national boundaries. As a consequence, while the papers in this volume vary widely in their approach, they indicate that users' concerns cluster around eight general areas: access to services and facilities, reliability, flexibility to control facil-ities, unrestricted flow of information, cost effectiveness, security, privacy, and liability for error. Although the significance of these issues varies with a user's perspective and position, each paper discusses this range of issues in some form. Proposed solutions likewise vary, and this raises critical national public policy issues.

Nondiscriminatory access to international communications facilities is particularly critical to international commercial competitiveness (Czelen, McCann, and Schaefer), reflecting the increasing importance of access to information. Energy information flows, for example, transmit information about markets that are constantly shifting as hydrocarbon reserves around the world become exhausted. The competitive edge of a company or of a group of companies may depend on access to better, more accurate information delivered more quickly over secure facilities (Czelen).

In this instance, the critical issue of government subsidization is raised. The U.S. government currently possesses unmatched capabilities for gathering information worldwide. Such data collection capability can be viewed as a tool of economic expansion and control. Oil companies have access to information of critical reserves through earth-sensing satellites (Czelen) operated and controlled by the U.S. government. Some countries have attempted to respond to this activity by asserting property rights over their air space. Other users have argued that standards, protocols, and tariffs have been adopted in foreign countries specifically to hinder domestic market penetration by the United States and other countries (Beach and Marks, McCann).

A marked difference exists between privacy and security in the minds of some users (Ramsay, McCann, Schaefer). Privacy pertains to personally identifiable records, while security is appropriate for commercial information or legal persons. Many corporations have responded to increased concern over the protection of personal privacy, both at home and abroad, by developing internally effective corporate policies (Schaefer, McCann). Self regulation of this type has been adopted as the official position of the United States in international fora such as the OECD and the Council of Europe (Yurow). Other users have argued that heavy investment in international systems and in methods of official accounting for use are necessary to protect personal privacy.

Security is of primary importance to virtually all users. In some foreign countries, the security of corporate transactions is covered under privacy regulations (Schaefer). Governments are particularly sensitive to this requirement, but a diplomatic communicator may enjoy certain privileges not available to commercial and private users (Ramsay). For example, diplomatic transmissions are inviolable and must be transmitted without delay. Similarly, diplomatic archives also are inviolable. No such assurance is provided for a private communicator, whose operating and market activities may depend on secure transmissions.

EMERGING LEGAL AND POLICY ISSUES

Every issue already identified as significant to users and providers has legal ramifications and could be recast as a legal issue. In this section, nine areas of concern about transborder data flows are explored. These papers are intended to provoke further thought about how to apply existing legal concepts, principles, and methods of negotiation to the developing computer/communications arena. They are not meant to represent the most significant or the most inclusive legal areas. Rather, the papers provide an approach toward the possible resolution of predictable problem areas before those areas become major obstacles to the flow of information.

The application of four areas of established law— patent, trademark, trade secrets, and copyright—to the problem of protecting intellectual property is explored (Miller and Blumenthal). Who has protectible legal rights in computer stored and manipulated information? What is a derivative work? How are authorship and fair use defined when computers are used?

As far as the applicability of established law is concerned, the authors conclude that of the four areas identified, copyright law offers the best possibility of extension to meet the needs for protection of data in both national and international spheres. Recent case law seems to have positively influenced the U.S. Patent Office to begin to issue patents to computer programs that meet the tests of patentability. Thus, this area of the law can be expected to afford a greater possibility of protection for some types of intellectual property contained in computer programs than it has in the recent past (Miller and Blumenthal).

Basic provisions of the data protection laws of eight European countries are identified; U.S. privacy law and countries' responses to other countries' laws are discussed (Yurow). These responses may lead some governments to place even more restrictions on the flow of

personal data into, out of, and through their countries. This concern led the United States to take an active role in the Organization for Economic Cooperation and Development's (OECD) effort to draft an international agreement to harmonize national data protection laws. The agreement became known as the Guidelines Governing the Protection of Privacy and Transborder Flows of Personal Data. In it, economic and cultural concerns about the flow of personal data and the extension of privacy protection laws to legal persons are reviewed.

Experiences with implementing the General Agreement on Tariffs and Trade (GATT) over the past 30 years are explored to identify those factors proved to be problem areas with regard to international trade in goods (Herzstein). The author theorizes that, although the GATT rules themselves are not particularly helpful to the service industries, the lessons learned in working through these problem areas could be applied to similar areas as they emerge in the international information flow sector.

Three difficulties that had to be overcome in the process of facilitating global trade in goods are identified— economic restraints that distort trade, "technical" barriers to trade such as those contained in a country's internal regulations, and the inhibitory influences on its trade of a country's national industry policies. As far as the international flow of data is concerned, economic restraints have not yet become so entrenched that they are a significant problem. However, both technical barriers and a country's individual national industry policies, as they now exist and as they are developing, are potentially serious blocks to the flow of information (Herzstein).

The elements of basic computer contracts as well as international aspects of computer law are examined (Nycum). A checklist of considerations to be addressed by a U.S. concern doing computer-related business abroad is provided. A survey of court opinions dealing with standing, choice of forum, and choice of law questions in transborder data flow contract and tort claims is given (Smiddy).

Criminal liability within an electronic environment is explored (BloomBecker). Studies of "computer crime" in several countries is reviewed and questions are raised concerning the desirability or likelihood of reaching international agreement on definitions of criminal behavior.

The papers in this section that more specifically address policy issues raise concerns ranging from worldwide international relations between multinational corporations and nations to more specific and local issues such as United States domestic communications regulatory policy. This broad range of topics illustrates the scope of policy issues that nations must face and resolve, the breadth of the effects that may result, and the difficulties an organization may face when doing business in the world communications arena.

The relationships between multinational corporations and various host nations, based predominantly on issues of sovereignty, are explored (Glasner). One point of view advanced is that multinational corporate activities are perceived as inherently antinationalistic and that their international information flows are therefore construed to strike against national sovereignty. To counteract this effect, lesser developed countries (LDC's) are attempting to control the data flows of multinational corporations into and through their territories. The value of uninhibited flow of information as a policy base is analyzed. A coherent national United States policy built upon market protections is advocated.

Three legal aspects of international broadcasting—establishing broadcasting facilities, regulating broadcast content, and jamming, or electronic interference—also are addressed in an earlier section (Read). Jamming is discussed in detail; the point of view advanced is that current international legal systems justify jamming by a state in situations where extraterritorial transmissions disturb national airspace, threaten national security, or threaten domestic values. International law is seen as unrestrictive and permissive regarding the activities of a state within its own boundaries. Jamming of broadcast transmissions for political purposes is likewise discussed.

The lack of coherence in U.S. informatics regulatory policy is discussed (Roth). One reason may be the wide distribution throughout the government of power in this field. Political and business forces are likewise fragmented. The result is that market forces in telecommunications are seen as being permitted to run their course.

Finally, the applicability of international law to transnational communications is explored (Feldman). First, the current claim of a right to communicate under international law is discussed. Several other international legal principles are analyzed and an implicit balancing of rights against tested responsibilities is presented.

Taken as a whole, the papers in this book offer a first effort in defining the legal and policy issues that need to be resolved by the participants in the global information marketplace. By this pioneering effort, the contributors to the book hope to stimulate readers to offer their own analyses of these issues and thus contribute to a public dialog. A diligent search for underlying principles upon which agreement can be reached will provide a stable and predictable legal environment in which the international exchange of information electronically can flourish.

TOWARD A LAW
OF GLOBAL
COMMUNICATIONS NETWORKS

OVERVIEW

Global Governance of Global Networks

ANNE W. BRANSCOMB

INTRODUCTION

The Information Society

Transborder data flow, the transfer of computer readable information across national borders, has become a matter of international concern. With the marriage of satellites and computers, groups as diverse as religious organizations and terrorist bands can transfer in microseconds vast amounts of the world's accumulated knowledge simultaneously to users around the globe. The politics and economics of information access are complex. The impact of the new technologies may disrupt relationships between nation-states and their nationals, whether individuals or corporate entities. For example, as computerized information systems facilitate international trade and financial transactions, multinational businesses are proliferating. Indeed, improved transborder data flow facilitates global contacts of all varieties as users form their own distributed computer networks[1] and employ them for their own purposes. The ability of users to pursue both eleemosynary and criminal purposes is greatly enhanced. Whether individual users of international systems will achieve their goals, either good or evil, will depend upon the policies and practices adopted by nation-states. Individuals, groups, or organizations may influence the accommodation of the legal system to the new technological environment only if they understand which goals are desirable, the values that are at stake, and the options that are available. This chapter reviews the current global ferment in policy directives concerning transborder data flows and projects the options that individuals, organiza-tions, and governments might choose to attain their objectives.

The position of the United States is changing in the world debate on global governance. In 1945 the United States provided the leadership to establish the United Nations as an international forum for the discussion of human rights and the minimization of armed conflict. In 1962 the United States led the world into an international satellite system, INTELSAT. Despite its traditional stance of encouraging worldwide cooperation on information technology, however, the United States seems in-creasingly unready, unwilling, and even unable to lead the world community into an international system of information exchange that maximizes shared use of information resources.[2] As the United States sees its leadership position eroded by strong competitors in the international information marketplace, the pendulum of American opinion on these policy questions swings in the opposite direction towards information protection-ism, information independence, and even information indifference.[3]

Information is the lifeblood that sustains political, social, and business decisions. Power resides in those entities that control the communications system and consequently the gathering, processing, distribution, and storage of information. In primitive societies the individuals who controlled information and information exchange stored the data in human brains and distrib-uted it in face-to-face encounters over which they had exclusive control. In these societies the death of one who possessed a learned brain was the loss of a human library.

ANNE W. BRANSCOMB ● Ms. Branscomb is a lawyer and organized the group which produced this book while serving as chairman of the Communications Law Division of the American Bar Association Science & Technology Section. She has served as a member of the United States Department of Commerce Technical Advisory Committee and as an advisor to the Department of State and Office of Technology Assessment of the U.S. Congress.

"Recorded history" emerged with the technology of writing on stone, papyrus, or paper. Since the time of Marco Polo or earlier, merchants have circled the globe in search of gold, spices, and other precious cargo. Monks have established monasteries in the far corners of the most remote and inaccessible places to carry their version of the truth to the heathens. Chinese bureaucracies, Roman soldiers, Greek philosophers, American moviemakers, and Japanese television manufacturers all have pursued a global marketplace in both manufactured goods and information products. As a result, today tourists and bankers alike enjoy the benefits of a worldwide communications system. In the modern world electronic brains gather, store, and distribute vast amounts of information. Satellites circling the globe can place an electronic eye over a third of the earth's surface, collect information, and deliver it to any other spot on earth instantaneously. The coupling of computers with advanced communications systems can merge voice, image, text, and symbols to render obsolete the customary legal distinctions that people have used to govern the delivery of information by telegraphy, telephone, television, or newsprint.

The very existence of information technology is threatening to nation-states. A satellite "footprint"[4] has great difficulty honoring national boundaries. The beam can remain within the national territorial limits only over land masses that are geographically isolated, like Australia, or vast, like the Soviet Union or the People's Republic of China. Computers do not question the motives of their masters. Thus, information wars are brewing over how governments and private industries will develop these computerized information systems and what kinds of political and social systems will evolve in response to their existence.

The United States has a great stake in the heated debate over transborder data flow. As a developer of both satellites and computers, it still leads the world in the manufacture of telematics hardware.[5] The United States also is the world's largest supplier of data bases for the distribution and management of information. Yet, strong competition threatens the country's superiority. Japan, for example, has established a goal of becoming an "information society" by the end of the 1980s. Moreover, potential competitors like Canada and France see telematics as a major source of economic strength. Smaller countries view the telematics infrastructure as crucial to their own economic development plans for industrialization. Thus, the health of the American econ-

omy is at stake. American foreign investment is far greater than that of any other nation state ($190 billion in 1979).[6] Much of this investment is in service industries, such as MacDonald's and Colonel Sanders, which are as popular in Japan as in the United States. United States-based consultants travel the globe offering advice on manufacturing projects that may be receiving capital and other input from both domestic and foreign sources. Transborder data flow has become indispensable to the very existence of transnational enterprise and to the currently flourishing global marketplace. The service sector of the American economy alone employs more than half the nation's workers and contributes over a third of its exports. Services—especially information services—are the most rapidly growing economic sector both domestically and abroad. In addition, American consumers' insatiable appetite for imported goods has made the United States less self-sufficient that it once was. Thus, transborder data flow may be essential to national survival in an increasingly interdependent global economy.

Two futurists who have examined the potential impact of computer technology on the world have developed similar visions of the characteristics of an information society. Yoneji Masuda has observed that such a society amplifies the mental power of humans while it minimizes their physical labor. In addition, an information society transforms the exchange economy into a synergistic economy in which society pursues social goals through voluntary exchange of information rather than geographically-based communities. This society maximizes self-actualization and self-fulfillment rather than physical acquisition of durable goods, increases participatory democracy and social feedback mechanisms, and promotes "a spirit of globalism, a symbiosis in which man and nature can live together in harmony."[7] Exactly ten years after Masuda presented his ideas, Harlan Cleveland pronounced his notion of desirable goals for an information society. He observed that an economy based upon abundant, synergistic, energy-conservative information resources should encourage spreading of benefits rather than concentration of wealth, maximization of choice rather than suppression of diversity, and planning in collegial and participatory decisionmaking about shared social goals.[8] These visions of social structure and goals differ from the competitive market model that Americans have valued throughout their history. Although the competitive market is entirely appropriate for an industrial society based upon a mass market and consumer choice in an ever expanding economy, this traditional model may be entirely inappropriate and counterproductive for an information society in a globally interdependent economy in which citizens must share both resources and decisions about their allocation.

Definitions

Variations in the definitions that commentators have ascribed to the term *transborder data flows* contribute to the confusion in current discussions. No ambiguity exists in the definition of *transborder*, which means across national political boundaries, or *flows*, which means movement. No consistent construction, however, exists for the term *data*. According to the dictionary, data are "something upon which an inference or an argument is based or from which an intellectual system of any sort is constructed." Data basically are the raw material from which people develop information and knowledge. The current primary concern in discussions of transborder data flow, however, clearly is about computer-generated information. People have transported data across geographical boundary lines in many forms and by many means for centuries. Therefore, all data presently in existence cannot be of concern; rather, debate centers around a specific kind of data that specific types of transmission systems transport. Many descriptions of this data exist. For example, Fishman speaks of "electronic movement of data between countries."[9] Turn discusses "transmission over computer-communications systems of automated data to be processed and stored in foreign data processing systems."[10] Eric Novotny discusses "units of information coded electronically for processing by one or more digital computers which transfer or process the information in more than one nation-state."[11] Pool and Solomon refer to "computer communications networks . . . digitalized transmission enabling voice and data to be handled in a single mixed stream of data."[12] Antonelli speaks of "international flow of computer data."[13] Documents of the Intergovernmental Bureau for Informatics discuss "transmission of data over telecommunications circuits."[14] Lemoine defines transborder data flow as "international information trade in a computer-generated and machine-readable format."[15] This definition includes all computer-to-computer, computer-to-human, and human-to-computer communication.

The Bing report, unlike other works on the subject, addresses the ambiguities in definition. Most other writings merely assume that the reader understands the problem well enough to ignore the definitional difficulties. Bing includes in his report on legal issues all transport of "data," which means "any representation of information" over "telecommunications"—defined by the International Telecommunications Union as wire, radio, optical, or other electromagnetic means. Bing, however, limits his discussion to "all computer services capable of accepting written material" including electronic mail, information retrieval, teledocuments, and data processing. This definition excludes voice and image transmissions.[16]

No doubt exists that the new ferment about transborder data flow has arisen from the convergence of computer technology, which stores and processes information, and communications technology, which permits rapid dissemination of this information to all parts of the globe by satellite, undersea cables, or conventional radio. The various definitions of transborder data flow fail to discriminate with respect to the type of transmission; some descriptions include the transport of computer tapes across national boundaries by conventional transportation methods, such as an individual taking the tape by commercial air carrier. Definitions in the work of Mark Feldman and David Garcia are representative of a flexible, expansive approach:

> Man's rapidly developing ability to transfer information across national boundaries has become a crucial component in our increasingly integrated world economy. The advent of the computer has revolutionized man's capacity to process and store information. Simultaneously, man's capacity to transmit information has been dramatically increased by a variety of telecommunications innovations, including increasingly effective cable transmissions and orbiting satellites. Together, these two technologies have resulted in a transborder data flow (TDF) essential to expanding international economic development.[17]

Interesting and complex legal issues arise in the context of the marriage between computer technology and satellite technology, in which scientists can merge voice, image, and text into a single system with a digital bit stream and thus render obsolete the traditional legal principles that have separated telephony, telegraphy, television, post, and personal delivery. For example, passport regulations and travel permits that governments use to facilitate or inhibit transborder information flows that require personal travel may be totally inadequate to regulate participants who may see and hear each other as well as deliver documents through a computer printout in their various locations. Moreover, laws that traditionally have governed the delivery of messages sent by postal services may be unsatisfactory in protecting the delivery of information by microwave or satellite circuits from electronic interception.

This chapter's examination of the development of the international system of information exchange limits its inquiry to transnational transport of computer-processed and machine-readable digital data via electronic transmission. This definition includes voice, image, characters, and other symbols transported by satellite, microwave, cable, or conventional radio in a converged digital bit stream that does not discriminate between types of communications services. These delivery systems now are called integrated services digital networks (ISDNs). The last part of the chapter examines the legal environment in which these networks currently are developing.

A Taxonomy of Information

In addition to the problem of definition, another difficulty in understanding the issues related to transborder data flow is that the information in transit is not all of equal value. For example, yesterday's news is not worth much on the information market, but financial information about potential mergers or acquisitions may have great value to persons who discover the facts first. That sixteenth century Augsburg bankers published the first European newspaper was no accident.[18]

A huge variety of information is available for distribution. Governments spend mammoth amounts of money to keep secure some information, such as the technical specifications of nuclear weapons. Public and private groups, in contrast, seek to disseminate without charge information concerning, for example, health care aid to pregnant women in developing countries. Profit-seeking enterprises distribute a wide variety of other types of information. For example, an active international marketplace now exists for scientific and technical information as well as for entertainment and news products. Licensing of United States patents is as active as the marketing of its manufactured goods, and the international market for American movies, television programs, books, and magazines is quite strong. Publishers of *Reader's Digest* distribute 41 editions of the magazine throughout the world in 17 languages; Dow Jones now publishes a Hong Kong edition of the *Wall Street Journal* directly by satellite. *Time* magazine is available in 191 countries. Viewers throughout the world watch Holly-wood movies, and American television programs are as well known in foreign capitals as Chase Manhattan, Citibank, and American Express.

Clearly, a taxonomy of information is necessary to sort out the legal issues that arise from information flows across national borders. The legal environment in which the "hot line" between the Kremlin and the White House operates is very different from the one in which a hurricane alert system works. To avoid catching information in which a high priority exists for flow without legal constraints in the same legal net designed to control information in which nation-states have a legitimate interest, one must examine separately the legal environment of each type of information flow. Such taxonomy would include at least 11 types of information.

1. Personal
2. Political
3. Scientific and technical
4. Strategic and military
5. Health, safety, and environmental
6. Economic
7. Financial
8. Management
9. Educational
10. Religious and moral
11. News and entertainment

GLOBAL GOVERNANCE OF INTERNATIONAL INFORMATION TRANSPORT BY ELECTRONIC MEANS

Territorial imperative and natural geographical boundaries inhibited the transport of information in primitive societies. Nevertheless, a system of respect developed early for the personal integrity of the messenger bringing information from other cultures or tribes. Although some Greek rulers reportedly cut out the tongues of messengers bearing bad tidings, this policy was self-defeating, because it stifled the flow of reliable information that rulers could use to make decisions rationally. From this background, the tradition has developed that personal representatives of nation-states possess an immunity from the application of local laws.[19] Messengers physically transporting information through the territories of other nation-states may travel unmolested unless a host nation shows that the messengers are violating the trust that the state has granted by using their presence to promote activities inimical to the interests of the host nation.[20] Oswald Ganley has pointed out that

> information has always traveled by the fastest or most convenient means for communicating it, whether that be by speaking, yelling, smoke signaling, beating drums, sending a runner with a message, entrusting a note to a packetboat or the pony express or a carrier pigeon, posting or flashing lights, writing, printing and distributing books, newspapers, and magazines, or making use of the postal system.
>
> Whether the information was spoken, or handwritten, or printed with ink, or recorded on wax, film, or magnetic tape, the purpose has always been the same: To take whatever information was available and convey it to someone for social, informative, entertainment, educational, financial, commercial, political, or military ends. In this sense, nothing has ever changed.[21]

The immediacy, bulk, and complexity of the information that modern "messengers" can carry across national boundaries by cable or satellite interconnected data networks has changed, however. A substantial body of international law has developed concerning the transport of information in written documents through the mails. The earliest governmental response, the Universal Postal Union, began in 1878 to negotiate and develop acceptable protocols for the posts.[22] Agreements promulgated bilaterally and through the efforts of the World Intellectual Property Organization have protected proprietary rights in published works.[23] This chapter, however, restricts its review to international and intergovernmental efforts that concern transport of information by electronic means.

An international legal system for electronic transport of information grew out of the frustration of telegraph operators having to hand-carry telegraphic messages from a telegraph terminal in one country across the border to a telegraph terminal in a neighboring country. This arrangement could result in distortion, loss, or interception of the messages. Frustration and widespread awareness that the technology was available to deliver messages from source to user without this delay resulted in the creation of the International Telegraph Union in Paris in 1865. The treaty that established the union granted participating nations the right to correspond by telegraph, provided for protection of the secrecy of the transmissions, and established uniformity in tariffs and regulations.[24] Article 2 of the treaty, however, reserved the right of nation-states to stop any telegram that they considered dangerous to national security or contrary to the law, public order, or good morals of the receiving country.[25] Although the United States no longer recognizes this mandate for state censorship, the provision remains part of the union's regulations.[26] After plenipotentiary meetings that all signatory nations attended in Paris in 1865, Vienna in 1868, Rome in 1871–1872, and St. Petersburg in 1875, the advent of the telephone in 1876 prompted the International Telegraph Union to add another "T" to its name and become known as the International Telegraph and Telephone Union.

A separate organization developed in 1903 to regulate the use of radio technology.[27] This negotiating body was a response to the monopolistic practices of the Marconi Wireless Company. Marconi negotiated contracts to install equipment only in ocean-going vessels that agreed to refuse to communicate with vessels that Marconi had not equipped.[28] Concern that this monopolistic practice might endanger the safety of maritime transportation prompted international cooperation to establish safety regulations. Coastal and ship stations thereafter "bound [themselves] to exchange wireless telegrams reciprocally without distinction of wireless systems adopted by such stations."[29] Signatory nations could reserve the right to ignore this requirement provided one or more coastal stations in their territory remained subject to the obligation. Eighteen of the 27 nations signing the treaty did not make any reservations and 21 countries signed compulsory interconnection agreements for ship-to-ship transmissions. Compulsory obligation to install radio transmitters and receivers followed shortly after the disastrous sinking of the Titanic, in which many passengers might not have lost their lives if vessels in the vicinity had been listening to their radios.[30]

By 1932, nations began to realize the advantages of merging radio, telephone, and telegraph functions into a single agency, and the International Telecommunications Union (ITU) emerged. In 1947 the ITU became a part of the United Nations.[31] The ITU essentially is a cooperative venture among nations that provides a forum for negotiating agreements which facilitate the flow of information across national borders by electronic means. The ITU also serves as an administrative means for identifying and recording users, their frequencies, and their purposes. Perhaps the organization's major contribution is in the development of international technical standards through which technicians can interconnect different operating systems into a global network.[32]

The ITU has been primarily a forum for participants from technical backgrounds to address the resolution of technical issues. Lawyers and politicians rarely have made appearances in the many conferences and consultative committees through which the ITU functions. The United States' 67 member delegation to the World Administrative Conference in 1979 included only two lawyers, and the only participant there with sufficient political skills to function effectively in an international political arena—the American Ambassador to the United Nations Special Agencies in Geneva—had responsibilities to numerous other agencies.[33] Increasingly, however, the decisions that the technical representatives make have political and legal consequences of great significance. Political considerations more often motivate the requests of member nations as the Third World countries seek greater access to the global communications systems. Concerns over access are part and parcel of the larger effort of Third World nations to establish a new economic order and a more balanced distribution of the world's resources.[34] The Third World is waging this effort in the United Nations General Assembly, in UNESCO,[35] and in the ITU.

In the ITU context the struggle has meant a rejection of the "first come, first served" principles under which nation-states merely initiated services and recorded them for all to see within the International Frequency Registration Board. Developing nations are applying increasing pressure to allocate frequencies according to equitable formulae, and two of the three world regions already have allocated geostationary orbits for direct broadcast satellites. The United States forestalled the planning exercise for satellite allocation for the North and South American Region 2 until 1983 in the hope that it could circumvent the exercise. The United States also claimed that a priori planning would result in inefficient use of the spectrum.[36] However inefficient early allocation may be, the Third World nations—which wield substantial power in the ITU because of the rule by majority vote—may find this planning an expedient way to obtain control over resources of economic value. Third World governments might then lease or negotiate away these information resources for technology transfer or capital investment in their own telecommunications infrastructure.

The ITU continues to work because,[37] without it, global electronic communication could not function. Participation is completely voluntary; the organization has no sanctions to enforce compliance and no mandate to develop operational services. Indeed, the ITU may not have sufficient resources to do more than set the agenda for training and consulting services for developing countries, although the organization has undertaken a very ambitious project in its World Year of Communications: Development of Communications Infrastructures, focusing the world's attention upon the necessity of providing these advisory services to all nations. Upon taking office the new Secretary General of the ITU called the world telecommunications network "the largest machine in the world ... a marvel of the century ... including 550 million telephones, 560 million television receivers, 1.4 million telex terminals, thousands of data networks and other special-purpose transmission systems."[38] Yet 90% of these installations serve only 15% of the world's nations. Secretary General Butler has made it his goal to see that the ITU becomes a tool for expanding the global network to include more of the underserved:

> Communication is an inexhaustible resource, an ever-growing technology which can greatly enhance the use of all the earth's resources, natural, human and economic ... the harmonious and well-balanced development of an ever-closer knit world communications network is a major historical event in keeping with the emergence of a collective awareness among mankind as a whole ... no one should any longer be isolated from the national or international community. Communications should be a right and not a privilege.[39]

Secretary General Butler's statement is more a political tactic than a legal argument, although a growing sentiment exists that the right "to receive and impart information" contained in the Universal Declaration of Human Rights[40] should become more than a mere exhortation to the world's conscience. To turn the ITU's essentially neutral forum into a politically charged battleground for the determination of power structures or the development of legal principles would likely jeopardize its value as a device for formulating the technical standards upon which the very existence of the global network now rests. Thus, partisans who tamper with the ITU or press upon it substantial new responsibilities do so at their peril. Technical innovations in themselves are beginning to overwhelm the capacity of the present bureaucracy; the increasing number of special conferences scheduled for the next few years and the decreasing time between world administrative conferences are evidence of this problem.[41]

THE GLOBAL SATELLITE SYSTEM FOR INFORMATION TRANSPORT—INTELSAT

The international satellite system known as INTELSAT is a major component in the international infrastructure for transborder data flow. INTELSAT provides a common carrier satellite service to 170 nations; its transponders[42] transmit two-thirds of all international message traffic and virtually all live transborder television. The system's primary use is to transmit telephone traffic. INTELSAT is an intergovernmental agency with 108 participating member nations, second only in size to the international organization ITU, which has a membership of 160.[43] Treaties, conventions, or executive agreements govern the relationship between the participating members.[44] INTELSAT was the godchild of COMSAT, an organization set up under the Communications Satellite Act of 1962[45] to build a global satellite system. The global system has grown from 11 original participating member nations in 1964, whose use of world telephones constituted 85% of all telephone traffic. Long the leader and largest investor in the system, COMSAT now only has 23% ownership in INTELSAT.[46]

Satellite service INTELSAT has grown at a 25% per annum rate from 240 telephone circuits in 1964 to 60,000 today.[47] The price of leasing a full circuit has dropped from $64,000 to $9,360 per annum.[48] Today, the top users include newly industrialized countries (NICs) like Brazil, Venezuela, Nigeria, Saudi Arabia, the Oil Emirates, and the member nations of the Organization for Economic Cooperation and Development (OECD).[49] Although the heaviest use and financial support still comes from the developed nations, the vast majority of participants are developing countries.

The global satellite system has revolutionized the flow of communications traffic. Before the system, communications traffic traveled internationally by point-to-point cable facilities;[50] undersea cables interconnected only the wealthiest, most developed countries. Cables are not obsolete because they provide reliability, redundancy, and security of transmission. The satellite service, however, provides multipoint rather than point-to-point transmission services. Since the system is distance and volume insensitive, small users do not suffer a penalty of higher tariffs, [51] and large and powerful nation

users have no inherent advantage over the smaller and economically less developed countries.

Each country maintains its own national system and controls its own interconnection to the global system. Furthermore, a sovereign state may only curtail its own access to the system. Thus, INTELSAT is an independent, accessible global network open to all nations that choose to participate. Participants are not subject to the disruption of service at the whim of individual nations, unless, of course, a nation chooses to shoot down the satellite.[52] While the system is vulnerable to the few states that currently have the capacity to destroy satellites in orbit, the political consequences of such an action make it unacceptable public policy for any nation state.

Commentators have described INTELSAT as the most successful international organization and as an international organization that actually works.[53] The system has not escaped criticism, however. Some of the less developed countries and less affluent users in developed countries have claimed that INTELSAT's low-powered, high-orbit satellites require expensive, high-powered satellite saucers to gain access to the system, and thus exclude the poorer users. The Public Interest Satellite Association[54] in the United States has lobbied successfully for allocation of frequencies that could accommodate lower-powered, low-cost saucers.[55] Yash Pal, executive secretary of the UNISPACE Conference and former director of the Indian SITE Education Project, has urged a system of lower powered orbiting satellites, which might better suit the financial capabilities and informational needs of the developing nations.[56]

INTELSAT has responded to the criticisms of developing and less affluent users by establishing a "low-density telephony service" designed particularly to meet the needs of the Pacific Island nations.[57] The organization also has planned new business services to provide small, lower cost ground terminals for public and corporate users. These terminals will utilize five- to eight-meter earth stations installed at the users' places of business rather than large feeder satellite antennae that presently interconnect to the public networks. INTELSAT does not intend to allow potential competitors to overwhelm it; "eventually all communication services can be provided by INTELSAT in the framework of the global integrated services network."[58]

Thus, INTELSAT sees itself as a major—if not sole—supplier of transnational information transport by satellite, and it is moving rapidly to meet the changing needs of users at both the high end and low end of the financial spectrum. The system is organizing to provide new telecommunications services, such as video conferencing; aeronautical, maritime, and land mobile services; business data; and possibly remote sensing data and direct broadcasting.[59] Nonetheless, INTELSAT recognizes that no international monopoly could or does exist, as long as alternative channels of communication via surface mail, undersea cables, or radio broadcasting continue to be viable.

The very existence of the INTELSAT system has facilitated greatly the transfer of information across international boundaries and proliferated the transfer of voice, video, and data communications. By 1986 INTELSAT expects to have satellites in orbit that are capable of transmitting the entire contents of the *Encyclopaedia Britannica* or its equivalent across the face of the globe 20 times every minute, for the equivalent of 28,000 *Encyclopaedia Britannica*s a day.[60] Clearly, the system provides a critical part of the infrastructure for transborder data flow.

GLOBAL NETWORKS OF TRANSBORDER DATA FLOW

A number of systems have developed for international exchange of a tremendous variety of data. Some of these systems make use of INTELSAT as their means of transmission; others utilize cables and more traditional means. A review of several of these systems illustrates the wide range of data types that flow through global networks. An analysis of the legal issues concerning transborder data flow requires an awareness of the environment in which each of these global networks functions.

Navigational Systems—MARISAT/INMARSAT

One of the earliest recognized needs for satellite communications was for navigation. Maritime Satellite Communications (MARISAT) is a service that COMSAT General Corporation of Washington, D.C. originated in 1976.[61] Three satellites[62] provide links to ships at sea with interactive communications capability, to computer networks and data bases. Not only does MARISAT meet navigational needs by satellite, but also seamen may make telephone calls. Ships may send telex transmissions and establish linkups with personal data bases;

these data bases include computer games, electronic mail, and educational routines. Jacques Cousteau's famous research vessel *Calypso*, after 18 months of access to MARISAT, reported that both scientific and personal contacts have been greatly facilitated: "It has changed our life on board ship."[63]

Today INMARSAT has taken over the three MARISAT satellites and also is leasing transponder space from INTELSAT. INMARSAT has 37 member countries. The United States, the Soviet Union, the United Kingdom, Norway, and Japan hold the largest investment shares in the organization. Olof Lundberg, director of the new system of INMARSAT, described its value and potential as follows:

> INMARSAT services mean that ships can be as easy to reach as offices on shore, and this can have a dramatic impact on the way they are managed, as well as on the quality of life enjoyed by ship's crews, and, most important of all, safety of life and property.... The potential for growth of mobile satellite communications is enormous. The world's merchant fleet consists of over 70,000 ships. The number at present fitted for satellite communications is about 1,000.[64]

Financial Data

Not surprisingly, the banking industry has been most active in developing transborder data links. Indeed, in one of the earliest air travel data linkups, a Rothschild banker organized a private carrier pigeon service, which enabled him to obtain a competitive advantage in marketing securities through access to information about the defeat of Napoleon at Waterloo.[65] The reasons for the banking industry's interest in transborder data flow are apparent. Because banking is a system of mediation between borrowers and lenders of money, it is an information industry in which money itself is information and the information content of all money transactions is high. The success or failure of a banking transaction depends largely upon the parties' knowledge about the political and economic environments in which the lending transactions take place. Thus, financial data carries considerable market value, and its successful use depends upon the speed and accuracy with which bankers can deliver it.

Most major banks now have worldwide networks for their own internal use and are interconnected through a special dedicated network.[66] Huge amounts of financial information still cross national boundaries by post, telex, and telephones but, increasingly, banking institutions transfer raw data in machine-readable form in a stream of electronic signals recognizable only by a computer. Continental Illinois National Bank and Trust Company has been one of the leaders in establishing international data links. As early as 1980 Continental's European branches were transmitting computerized transactions data over leased lines to a central processing unit installed in Chicago. The branches were providing customers worldwide with their daily banking needs through a computer in the United States.[67]

Citibank's GLOBECOM, a network of leased lines that reach overseas branches in over 100 countries, is typical of today's banking networks. The GLOBECOM system passes more than 300,000 transmissions per month through computer switches in London, Bahrain, Hong Kong, and New York. Chase Manhattan Bank's private communications network reaches out from a cable and wireless computer in Hong Kong and an RCA computer in New York to branches in Piraeus, Rio de Janeiro, Jakarta, and other parts of the globe. Indeed, a global system of monetary exchange operates 24 hours a day.[68] Bankers perceive the efforts to inhibit the flow of information internationally as inimical to their business interests. Large international institutions in particular fear that measures which governments intend to limit transfer of other types of information will have a restrictive impact upon banking networks as well. According to a Citibank executive:

> Since the digital information flowing in cables or moving through space will be, in effect, a single, homogenous stream, it will become increasingly impossible to maintain any of the traditional distinctions between transmissions carrying news, entertainment, financial data or even personal phone calls. This intermixing of data will make it impossible to pass laws restricting the transmission of one kind of information without impinging on all the others. Efforts to impede the flow of capital must inevitably lead to restrictions imposed on the flow of information and vice versa.[69]

In contrast, governing elites fear that the international movement of financial data will make it easier for banks and other international business institutions to escape the application of national laws regulating and taxing money transactions because these organizations will be able to manipulate electronically the situs of their funds.

This fear has some validity. Banking institutions have threatened the very existence of the national money markets in their efforts to control national currencies in the same international trade transactions that gave rise to the Eurodollar. Experts have estimated that approximately one trillion dollars has found refuge in a stateless pool of investment capital of "supermoney."[70]

Although transborder data flow has contributed to international trade, some critics believe that the use of new technology information transfer increases financial instability by disrupting the influence of nation-states, either individually or collectively, over the international monetary system. Thus, critics see an alteration of the balance of power not only between international financial institutions and their national governments, but also between small and large banking institutions. As larger institutions gain the ability to install sophisticated computerized information systems, they will obtain a competitive advantage over smaller banks that cannot make transfers as easily. Moreover, large institutions, which have access to an international information market when they deliver ancillary financial data and services—such as Chase Manhattan's economic data and econometric modeling services, which estimates show grossed $2.5 billion in 1978 and are growing at a 30% annual rate—have an advantage over smaller banks.[71]

Thus, banking rapidly is becoming globalized. Two international financial data systems reportedly are interconnecting their services: CIDEL, which links 51 countries from headquarters in Luxembourg and handles stock transactions, and SWIFT, which links 21 countries from headquarters in Belgium and handles interbank transactions. VISA International President Dee Hock has warned bankers that events will overwhelm them if they remain rooted in past practices, because in the future banking institutions will deliver their services to customers wherever the customers happen to be.[72]

Resources Management

Remote sensing of the earth is another area in which the availability by satellite of computerized data about a nation outside another nation's territorial boundaries causes concern to policymakers. For some years the nation-states that lead the world in space technology commonly have been known to operate spy satellites but this type of practice is acceptable and only disturbs ruling elites when it becomes public, for example, when the pilot of the American U2 spy plane crashed over

Soviet territory.[73] Nevertheless, some theoretical ferment has developed over whether these observational craft are violating air space and whether the satellites are operating with the peaceful purposes required by the Treaty of Principles Governing the Activities of States in the Exploration and Use of Outer Space, Including the Moon and Other Celestial Bodies.[74] Some commentators argue that strategic reconnaissance should not be permissible except by the consent of the photographed country.[75] Arguably, however, the maintenance of a system of nuclear stalemate contributes to the benefit and is in the interests of all countries, and nations should encourage it as long as the satellite photography causes no detriment to the photographed country. Technologically, most countries could not possibly exert national control over the space that extends above their territorial boundaries. The ability to control this space, however, one day might lead to greater wealth if space explorers are able to mine the resources of planets light years away. Hence, the notion of control by nation-states over space may have a certain attraction in the long term.

The most controversial type of data recovery by satellite has been remote sensing of the earth's resources. LANDSAT 1, which the United States launched in July 1972, LANDSAT 2, launched in January 1975, and LANDSAT 3, launched in March 1978, orbit the globe about 575 miles above the earth and carefully scrutinize the planet in sections about 100 nautical miles wide. Photographs that LANDSAT cameras obtain can identify objects less than 100 yards in size. Within an 18-day period the satellite can map the entire face of the globe—a rather startling economy compared with the years that Captain Cook spent mapping the Pacific Islands. In addition to gathering data extremely rapidly, LANDSAT produces accurate information and can prove, for example, that maps of the Amazon River were miles off course in the jungle areas of Brazil. Moreover, image processing through a computerized system of color correlation permits careful differentiation of certain features from others.

The speed, accuracy, and detail of the LANDSAT data production has suited it to many purposes. Users of the system can estimate crop acreage of wheat fields in the United States to an accuracy of 95%. The system has facilitated regional planning in the Philippines by producing images of the Manila metropolitan area from 1972 to 1976 for comparison. A 54% increase in residen-

tial construction and a corresponding decrease of 85% in forested areas provides dramatic confirmation of the rapid urbanization of the Philippines. In Pakistan the government used LANDSAT data to select promising sites for copper exploration. LANDSAT has greatly improved water resources management by allowing experts to monitor the monsoon rains to anticipate and thus diminish their adverse consequences.[76]

LANDSAT transmits the raw data it has gathered to the Earth Resources Observation Systems (EROS) Data Center, which the United States Geological Survey operates at Sioux Falls, South Dakota.[77] EROS processes the remote data and makes it available to purchasers all over the world at prices based upon reproduction costs. Although the prices of processed LANDSAT information are not negligible, they are modest compared to the research and development costs for the system itself, which developed as an offshoot of the United States investment in space technology.[78] The Reagan administration already has announced its intention to turn the processing of LANDSAT data over to the private sector. The current market for LANDSAT products is quite small, however, about six million dollars annually, whereas estimates of the cost of operating the system range from one to ten billion dollars over a 10-year period. Although the American private sector would find such profit prospects unattractive, the French government has moved toward launching its own remote sensing satellite.[79]

Some nations have developed their own capability to receive and process the information directly from the LANDSAT satellite without the help of EROS. For example, the Brazilian Institute de Pesquisas Espaciais possesses its own processing unit. This unit has issued reports on oceanographic data, forestry and agronomy data, geographic data (including soil use, urbanism, and environmental impact), and geological data.[80]

Not all nations have been equally eager to use the EROS data, and many governments have questioned whether any nation has a legal right to sense via satellite the territorial area of a sovereign nation without its consent. Technically, a nation-state would have difficulty prohibiting the space photography of its land mass because the technologically capable states merely could ignore a nation's legal restriction. Switching the satellite's camera lenses on and off at the request of the states below would be difficult, especially in areas where the nations are in close proximity. Furthermore, the sensing itself is harmless; the use to which the data is put creates the problems.

Nation-states that are technologically unable to process LANDSAT data or financially unable to buy EROS information have been especially critical of the system, which they believe disadvantages them. Many Third World nations feel unprepared to compete with the activities of nonnational business organizations that seek to develop natural resources or buy the crops of these countries. Outsiders with access to EROS data may know more about the Third World nations than the nations do themselves. Yet, in early negotiations only Brazil claimed to require the consent of the state that the satellite sensed prior to photographing.[81] Even more controversial is the right of the sensed state to obtain the information related to its land mass or to require prior consent to dissemination of the data to third parties.[82] Whether or not a sensed nation can or should control the sensing, clearly it has an undeniable right under international law and traditional concepts of territorial sovereignty to control the natural resources found within its territorial jurisdiction.[83] The USSR claims that nation-states have an inalienable right to control both their own natural resources and information concerning such resources.[84] The Japanese, however, have taken the position that remote sensing is not equivalent to taking the natural resources of another nation.[85]

The United States, which practices what it preaches on the issue of the right of sensed nations to control the flow of information about their territories, has made the data that it has collected from LANDSAT equally available to all nations. Without the ability to analyze the data, however, access is not equal. Many nations are becoming increasingly sensitive to vulnerability created by their dependence upon foreign sources for information about their own resources. If these nations permit their economies to become dependent upon satellite imagery, they may question the wisdom of permitting the service to remain indefinitely under the control of a single nation—the United States.[86] In the current American setting of budget cuts, however, increased United States investment in remote sensing is unlikely to benefit developing countries.

The continuing investment of developed nations in their own domestic satellites doubtless will cause the legal questions about remote sensing satellites (RMS) to proliferate as more countries become capable of receiving and processing satellite images. The historical practice of the United States has been to transfer governmentally developed research capability to the private sector when the activity has become economically viable. The resolution of legal uncertainties, however, is necessary before private investors will commit their capital to developing the potential of RMS data for all users around the globe, both public and private.[87]

Some regional or global system of RMS data management and collection might be a solution to the legal problems that arise in this area. Surprisingly, approximately 120 nations, two-thirds of which are from the developing world, are investing substantial sums of money to develop computerized capability to utilize RMS data, with little concern over the legal threat to the right to receive the data from its source—a United States controlled, NASA launched satellite system. Apprehension about the consequences, however, may be the source of a suggestion by a committee of the National Research Council that the American government should "declare soon that remote sensing systems constitute, in effect, an international public utility destined for international governance."[88]

Science and Technology Information—ARPANET, TELENET, CSNET, and VNET

Scientists consider uninhibited exchange of information across national boundaries to be essential to their work. Transfer of data subjects new discoveries and theories to the scrutiny of peers in other laboratories for verification or disproof. Scientific knowledge is cumulative—each scientist learns from the work of others. Open access to information stimulates creativity as scientists compete to be first in publishing research and discovering new areas of inquiry. Because no single country has a monopoly on scientific talent, communication among research scientists is international. Scientists historically have transferred scientific and technological information by hand, through oral communication, or through the mails by publication of scientific findings in journals. Scientists distribute and read over 2000 scientific journals. The essential transnational nature of these publications is evident: American authors write only 37% of the articles that appear in these journals. Moreover, American researchers frequently cite foreign research results.[89]

Despite the desire of scientists to maintain free transfer of information, governmental interest in restricting information for national security purposes is increasing. This part of the chapter focuses on the types of restrictions and regulations that the United States government places upon the transborder flow of scientific data. The United States government restricts transfer of scientific information to protect national security interests in five ways: (1) classification restricting access; (2) export control; (3) restrictions upon acceptance of federal funds; (4) voluntary agreements; and (5) control of foreign visitors. The categories of information eligible for classification include "scientific, technological, or economic matters relating to the national security" and "cryptology."[90] A specific exemption exists for "basic scientific research information not clearly related to the national security."[91]

Transborder transfer of security information occurs under a system that international agreements established through the Coordinating Committee for Multilateral Export Controls. The committee is a voluntary organization for the consideration of trade controls on exports to the Warsaw Pact Countries and the People's Republic of China. The group consists of all the NATO countries except Iceland and Japan. Only its member nation-states, however, can implement its decisions.[92]

The federal government may restrict transfers of unclassified technical data under an export control system that consists of the Export Administration Act (EAA)[93] and the Arms Export Control Act (AECA).[94] The Export Administration Regulations (EAR),[95] promulgated by the United States Department of Commerce, implement the EAA, which governs the export of information that has both military and civilian applications. The EAA authorized export controls to further national security, foster foreign policy, or protect the domestic economy from a drain of scarce materials.[96] The EAR controls "technical data."[97] An export of this data occurs whenever one of the following events takes place: an actual transmission of data out of the United States, a release in the United States with the knowledge that the data will be shipped out of the country, or a release abroad.[98] The International Traffic in Arms Regulations (ITAR)[99] of the United States Department of State effectuate the Arms Export Control Act, which addresses exports with strategic value. Any export of technical data requires prior approval and a license by the Office of Munitions Control in the Department of State.[100] No distinctions exist among various export destinations, except for Canada, to which this requirement does not apply.

Although the categories of data transfer that are subject to ITAR are narrower than the categories that the EAR cover, the ITAR controls are broader reaching because of their geographical sweep. Both sets of regulations provide criminal and administrative remedies to punish violators of their rules.[101]

To export technical data the EAR requires that the exporters either obtain a general license[102] or a validated license.[103] A general license is analogous to an exemption; it is effective automatically by force of regulation without an application or document authorizing the export. The general license is available for "data that have been made generally available to the public" through publications "that may be purchased without restrictions at a nominal cost or obtained without costs or are readily available at libraries open to the public" or through "open conferences."[104] The license is also available for scientific data that is not directly and significantly "related to design, production, or utilization in industrial process."[105] A validated license, in contrast, authorizes a specific export of data. The Office of Export Administration of the Department of Commerce issues the validated license in response to a letter of application and an explanation from the proposed exporter.[106]

In 1981 the Office of Export Administration processed over 71,000 applications for validated licenses and denied about 9,000.[107] Most of these requests were from industrial firms. Apparently, increasing control of technical data exports will result from changes in the agency's control system and from a growing concern in the intelligence community that these exports contribute to the competitive disadvantage that the United States is experiencing internationally.

In response to fears that America is losing its competitive advantage, United States' policy is moving toward more sophisticated controls on transborder flows of technological data. In 1976 a Defense Science Board task force proposed that the export control system should shift its focus from the products themselves to the technology that is critical to design and manufacturing capability.[108] The report recommended that the export control system should place primary emphasis on (1) array of design and manufacturing knowledge, (2) "keystone" manufacturing, inspection, and test equipment, and (3) products requiring sophisticated operation, application, or maintenance ability. The task force concluded that the American lead in critical technological areas was becoming increasingly difficult to preserve but that the United States could maintain its advantage in two ways: first, by denying the export of technology when it represented revolutionary rather than evolutionary advances, and second, by strengthening the export control laws in the United States and allied nations.

In 1979 Congress incorporated into the EAA the defensive technology export policy that the task force had recommended. Congress directed the United States Secretary of Defense to develop a list of militarily critical technologies; the list now covers a broad spectrum of technologies, including many with nonmilitary applications.[109] The Arms Export Control Act and the ITAR regulations control export of strategic information.[110] The Secretary of Defense's list includes a category for "technical data" pertaining to the listed items. Like EAR, ITAR defines the term "technical data" to include "any technology which advances the state-of-the-art or establishes a new art in an area of significant military applicability in the United States."[111]

The United States government can regulate the transmission of technical data by means other than statutory controls. As a major source of funds for university research the government apparently can impose restrictions on grant recipients to prevent communication of technical data. These restrictive stipulations in contracts may inhibit severely the free flow of transborder data from university and industrial research laboratories. This inhibited flow could impede the movement of information that scientists and researchers consider essential and limit the global interaction that stimulates innovation throughout the world.

Monitoring the flow of data from university research centers to ascertain whether to apply the various regulations is particularly difficult. Laboratory researchers create data flow networks using high speed data links, such as the ARPANET, a computer system that the United States Department of Defense developed in the early 1970s and funds as an experimental computerized environment for researchers on Defense Department contracts.[112] The original purpose of ARPANET was to promote load sharing among expensive computers at universities, but the system soon became the test-bed for electronic mail and data exchange. TELENET, another computer system, had its origin in ARPANET concepts and provides packet switching services internationally.[113] Today TELENET and its competitor, TYMNET, provide the communications support for a wide variety of information services through which scientists communicate internationally.

Other computer networks also transmit research data across national lines. In the United States, the National Science Foundation is funding the rapidly growing CSNET,[114] which will connect to ARPANET and inevitably seek connection to information networks in other countries. Scientists working for corporations use proprietary networks for research and development collaboration internationally. For example, the IBM Corporation's internal computer system, VNET, reportedly connects over 800 computers in 26 countries using leased lines for interconnection.[115] Not only does data exchange occur over this network, but also researchers can use it to collaborate on research and development. Data flow networks may make the conventional concepts of export control for technical data difficult to apply when the same idea emerges concurrently from scientists in several countries.

Other Global Networks

A number of other global data networks function today. These networks transmit a variety of data, which recipients desire for a broad spectrum of purposes. A brief survey of these networks, combined with the foregoing examination of the major avenues of transborder data flow, reveal the different settings in which legal issues concerning data transport can arise.

The weather satellite, NIMBUS, operated by the National Oceanographic and Atmospheric Administration, provides pictures of global geology, with the result that weather fronts can be plotted and hurricane watches can be organized, to warn of meteorological disasters. The morning television news has changed radically with the advent of "real time" satellite pictures, which permit forecasters graphically to analyze on television monitors the rain clouds and sunshine. No inherent reason other than cost exists to prevent these weather pictures from being available worldwide via satellite directly to any point on the globe. The World Weather Watch uses some of the largest and most sophisticated computers in operation.[116]

Another significant use of remote data recovery is a system called Remote Continual Verification (RECOVER). RECOVER is an international system of electronic devices that the 110 member nations of the International Atomic Energy Agency currently are installing at 672 facilities.[117] The system's primary surveillance devices detect hazards to safety in the use of nuclear installations, and report to a central computer console in Vienna. Data transport occurs over hardwired dedicated lines, radio frequency transceivers, and data overlay on existing electric power lines. Scientists designed RE-COVER to be reliable under adverse environmental conditions, timely in its reporting capability, simple, safe, and operable without human assistance.[118]

The entertainment and informational uses of satellite systems are proliferating, primarily through the use of domestic satellites or by interconnections through the INTELSAT system. The global impact of instantaneous, worldwide distribution of television signals was most dramatic during the moon landing on July 20, 1969, only one week after the INTELSAT system became operational. Transmitting pictures for 22 hours of uninterrupted coverage required the cooperation and teamwork of four countries and one interstellar body. Following transmission of the picture from the surface of the moon to the space tracking station in the Red Center of Australia, the image went via INTELSAT to Jamesburg, California, then by NASA radio relay to Houston, Texas, from there via a Pacific satellite to Tokyo, via an Atlantic satellite to Goonhilly Downs in the United Kingdom, and from there by the Eurovision network to participating national networks. A truly global audience, estimated at 538 million, watched.[119] Global audiences like this one now have become commonplace. Global weddings, as well as global funerals, take place with growing frequency. In addition, an estimated two billion viewers watched the 1984 Olympics.[120]

Other networks connect remote habitations with each other and with the rest of the world. For example, the PEACESAT network in the South Pacific involved the most extensive use of satellites. It operated in the South Pacific where islands are widely dispersed and separated by large bodies of water. The Indian Satellite Instructional Television Experiment (SITE), the Canadian CTS, and the American ATS 3 and ATS 6 satellites have successfully demonstrated educational and medical uses of communications in remote villages in India, Alaska, and the northern territories of Canada.

Although educational users of satellite systems are in an earlier stage of development than other users, educational uses are not primitive. Although computer-based education is developing slowly in the United States, the systems have great potential for international networking between both developed and developing countries. The PLATO system of the Control Data Corporation (CDC) is one of the earliest educational prototype systems and among the most powerful. Permitting individualized instruction of a very sophisticated and highly interactive nature, the PLATO terminals are useful on site for everything from remedial education in schools to flight simulation for apprentice pilots. CDC also operates a network of more than 50 learning centers in cities around the United States and trains professionals around the world in a variety of specialties at its Institute of Advanced Technologies. CDC maintains very specialized data processing services for a broad range of scientific and engineering applications through its CYBERNET data base services, which are available throughout the United States and Canada and in 24 other nations. CDC is a full service remote data processing service and provides access to a complete range of specialized remote transactions, including credit verification, stock brokerage, computerized ticket purchases (TICKETRON), television viewing habits (ARBITRON), employment opportunities (CYBERSEARCH), bookkeeping for credit unions (FOCUS), and a global technology data base (TECHNOTEC).

CDC, however, like other remote data processors, has encountered difficulties in numerous countries in obtaining private leased lines to serve its remote customers worldwide. A variety of reasons motivate these refusals, including the desire of some nations to keep control of all data services and resulting revenue, and a national telematics policy to preserve data processing services for a local entity or nationally controlled subsidiary. Such policies may not be in the refusing nation's best interests, however, as Stephen Beach, associate general counsel for CDC, has observed:

> Those countries that seek to impose barriers beyond legitimate self-interests will fence themselves in as well as keeping others out. They will not obtain the world's technology or the data bases of information which they seek.[121]

EMERGING GLOBAL LEGAL ISSUES

Privacy

As personal data increasingly has found refuge in the memory banks of large computers, concerns about the accuracy, accessibility, and use of this information have grown rapidly both in the United States and abroad. The United States has been the leader in enacting legislation to protect the privacy interests of individuals in personal data. Congress passed the Privacy Act of 1974,[122] followed by the Freedom of Information Act,[123] the Fair Credit Billing and Reporting Acts,[124] and, more recently, the Right to Financial Privacy Act.[125] Privacy legislation embodies principles of openness and disclosure about the existence of data banks, and protects the rights of individuals to obtain, challenge, correct, or expunge inaccurate information. The Privacy Act of 1974 mandated the creation of a Privacy Protection Study Commission which conducted a major analysis of privacy policy.[126]

Since the mid-1970s when European countries began to follow the American lead in protecting privacy interests, international organizations have noted that a patchwork quilt of different national laws—allegedly protecting the privacy of their nationals—could wreak havoc with the internal personnel management and information flow of transnational companies.[127] A recent count shows that thirteen nations have passed privacy protection statutes, and five more nations have similar legislation pending. As the number increases, international desire to harmonize these laws is becoming stronger.

The Organization for Economic Cooperation and Development (OECD) and the Council of Europe (CoE) have initiated efforts to develop guidelines[128] for harmonization of privacy protection laws among their member nations. The provisions and force of the two groups' guidelines differ. Whereas the CoE Convention on privacy legislation is legally binding on signatory nations, the OECD Guidelines are voluntary. Little difference in effect may result, however, because both contain ineffective sanctions. The CoE Convention is narrower and more specific than the OECD guidelines. It covers only automated data base information, while the OECD guidelines cover both automated and conventionally stored information. Both sets of standards cover the public and private sectors; in contrast United States legislation addresses primarily federal agency, educational, and credit records of individuals.[129]

None of the rules discussed above protects the privacy of corporations, although several national legislative enactments do cover data banks operated by corporate entities. Surprisingly, not all transnational companies welcome protection of corporate informa-

tion. Because a substantial part of a corporation's strategic planning may depend upon information about its corporate competitors, a company could suffer a disadvantage if its competitors could obtain access to this data.[130]

The CoE Convention contains several safeguards for transborder data flow that balance the privacy protections which otherwise might inhibit the movement of information. First, the Convention prohibits signatories from disallowing transnational flows *solely* upon the grounds of privacy protection. Second, it admonishes member nations not to create obstacles to transborder data flows that exceed requirements for privacy protection. Third, the convention requires members to take reasonable steps to ensure uninterrupted and secure transit of data through member countries. Last, the rules urge nations not to obstruct transborder data flow unless the domestic legislation of another nation does not provide equivalent privacy protection and hence no danger exists of circumventing that country's laws. The Convention forces thusly a harmonization of national privacy laws.[131]

A prime motivating force behind the CoE efforts to preserve transborder data flow freedom and equalize national privacy laws is the knowledge that the European Economic Community's (EEC) largest unexploited opportunity is to develop the combined market of its member states to provide a competitive environment equal to or better than the one that historically has been available to large corporations in the United States. Thus, the harmonization of privacy legislation is part of the community's attempt to expand the "teleinformatics" industry to provide a foundation of economic growth and development in the region.[132]

Criminal Action

Because banks have been at the forefront of computerization and traditionally have attracted embezzlers and other avaricious and enterprising individuals, financial transactions, not surprisingly, have become the target of computer pirates. The most notorious case is that of *United States* v. *Rifkin*, which concerned an international interbank transfer. Rifkin was an employee in the "wire room" of Security Pacific National Bank of Los Angeles. The wire room is the hub of a computerized system that transfers two to four billion dollars of funds every day. By manipulating this system, Rifkin successfully transferred $10.2 million through the Irving Trust Company in New York to the Wozchod Handels Bank in Zurich, Switzerland, and later reduced the proceeds to the contents of an ashtray overflowing with Russian diamonds. Rifkin was apprehended, tried, and sentenced to eight years in federal prison, despite a plea by his attorney that the authorities should permit this computer genius to remain free as a consultant to businesses that needed his expertise to devise security systems which other computer thieves could not invade electronically.[133]

Society has not punished all acts of computer piracy as it did Rifkin's crime. Unauthorized invasions of computerized systems have outdistanced the attempts of American legislators to keep up with the technological opportunities for criminal behavior. As recently as 1974 only 42% of the states had effective legislation prohibiting theft of computer software and only 24% had legislation concerning theft of computer time.[134] In addition, the press tends to glorify the actions of computer thieves. Perpetrators of this type of crime have been successful in establishing themselves as advisers to the very institutions from which they have taken computer time, or altered or pirated data.[135] Students at prestigious academic institutions who have engaged in this behavior have found their actions condoned and even applauded. At the Massachusetts and California Institutes of Technology "student pranks" have demonstrated students' ability to break through the data security of banks and obtain access to the computerized switching systems of the long lines of the American Telephone and Telegraph Company. A competitor of the company which provided the magnetic storage technology used by BART, the San Francisco mass transit system, advertised for young computer wizards who could break into the computer code and obtain tickets without payment. They succeeded and BART had to bear the additional expense of installing countermeasures. This incident raises interesting legal issues of unfair competition—for which a court might assess compensable damages—and of ill-conceived if not actually illegal behavior by the parties that encouraged students to gain uncompensated access to the computer system.

As micro and minicomputers proliferate and interconnect over various information transport systems, the opportunities for embezzlement of electronic funds in the process of transfer, piracy of proprietary signals or services, and deliberate damage to persons or property

from the alteration of data will increase exponentially. To ensure a global environment in which the transfer of data can take place securely, without alteration or diversion between users, legislatures must develop laws prohibiting computer crimes. These laws must be compatible and enforceable regardless of the locus of the crime, because the embezzlement, distortion, destruction, or otherwise unauthorized use of data may occur in outer space or within a radio frequency band at high altitudes where sovereign rights and responsibilities may be very cloudy indeed.

Contract and Tort Liability

Together, contract and tort liability are one of the most volatile and interesting areas for legal development in the transborder data flow field. No great body of case law on tort liability in the transborder data flow area yet exists, but the potential for unintentional torts increases as people use computers more widely both at home and abroad.[136] For example, computers can cause physical damage: malfunctioning systems can endanger medical patients; erroneous input or processing can injure credit ratings, endanger air transportation, or unleash a debt collector against a citizen whose payments are timely.[137] One court has awarded damages of over $200,000 for unfair competition stemming from unauthorized remote access to a data bank.[138]

Some business organizations potentially may become liable for failure to use computer services—technological "nonfeasance"—in addition to misuse of these services. This situation would be comparable to the cases holding tugboats negligent for not using their radios. International regulations that require ships at sea to have available radio transmitters and to keep their receivers open on a specified channel to ensure the safety of all navigable vessels[139] also are analogous; the failure of a crew to use these transmitters would be negligence.

Another basis of litigation may be the defendant's reliance upon a computer when human judgment should have intervened. In an unforgettable Ford Motor Credit Company case a computer error caused the company to repossess an automobile that belonged to a customer who had been making his payments quite promptly.[140] As electronic videotex and teletext begin to provide traditional news and information services directly to home terminals, opportunities for tortfeasance, such as defamation or libel, will arise. The problems will be especially thorny as distributed networks permit increasingly large numbers of entrepreneurs access to the information distribution system worldwide. Questions about insurability and risk assessment in a global information environment containing a multiplicity of user networks may inhibit the development of such a diverse information marketplace. Liability is far simpler to assess within a system in which corporations and public networks assume responsibility for the content of the information as well as for the management of the information transport system.

Proprietary Rights in Information

> Is information on the international level an intellectual asset which belongs to the whole of humanity or is it also a marketable asset?[141]

In economic terms, data flow obviously will slow down if no market value exists for the offered information products and services. Because the monetary value of information is of key importance in the market, a clear delineation of the rights in intellectual property is necessary when the international marketplace is concerned. Unfortunately, substantial misunderstanding and disagreement may arise about the value of information. The economics of information is a new and underdeveloped discipline, although some scholars have made notable efforts to remedy that situation.[142]

Historically, a paradox has existed between the promotion of progress through wide dissemination of knowledge and the protection of the economic interests of those who contribute to the development of new knowledge. The founders of the United States recognized this conflict of interests, and the Constitution purports both to "promote the Progress of Science and useful Arts"[143] and to protect the proprietary rights of artists, writers, and inventors through a system of copyright and patent protection. Thus, one strand of United States policy long has recognized the contribution of the free flow of ideas to innovation and productivity. This causal relationship has not escaped the notice of developing countries,[144] which may desire a freer flow of data into their hands. Determining the kind of information flows that government should refuse to inhibit and the costs associated with technology transfer is troublesome in a global context.

The question of the applicability of the present system of copyright, patent, and trademark protection to the new forms of information also is disconcerting. Substantial evidence exists that legal distinctions developed for the printing press and the copies imprinted in a permanent form simply do not protect adequately the interest of participants in the dynamic electronic environment. New rules may be necessary when "authors" are in various locations contributing their intellectual input either simultaneously or consecutively into a "work product" that may never be fixed or permanent.

Professor Pool and Mr. Solomon have noted the difficulties associated with protecting proprietary rights in electronic information:

> First, liability is incurred neither at input nor at output, but within the computer network. Second, what protects the author or publisher is physical control of the text for there is no count of its reproduction once it is out of his hands. Third, a billing system operated by the network is necessary if fee collection is to be easy. Without that there is too much red tape in making arrangements for occasional access. Fourth, once the publisher's text has been read by someone else, evasion of royalty payments is quite easy because the reader can store the text in his computer and do whatever he wants with it. Computer copying is even easier than photocopying.[145]

Observing that "every reading of computer output requires the regeneration of it, every reading is a printing," Professor Pool and Mr. Solomon warn that traditional legal protection may not be adequate to protect proprietary rights in information. The peril, they note, is particularly great in the new international trade environment in which "information in a pure form is one of the newest private industries." These scholars, however, see premature conventions or legislation as impediments to innovation in the development of information systems and suggest that the wiser course is to consider the legal problems of transborder data flow primarily as international issues. Thus, the priority concerns in legal development should be to delineate what constitutes computer fraud, abuse, negligence, and breach of contract, and to provide mechanisms through which such grievances may be redressed.[146]

Ownership of and Access to Information
Another thorny legal question concerns the ownership or right to lease transmission systems and the right of

the owner, lessor, lessee, or user of the system to control the content of the message transmitted. Historically, legislation in the United States has segmented different types of transmission services and endowed each one with a distinct regulatory system. At least seven models of regulation for various data transmission systems exist. The continued usefulness of any of these models or their hybrids as transborder data flow becomes increasingly sophisticated is uncertain. Lawmakers may radically change or even discard some of these models. Nevertheless, the following paradigms provide necessary starting points in the development of the legal environment for transborder data flow.

1. The print media is a virtually unregulated system. No licensing of entry into the print media is tolerated under the first amendment.[147] No right of reply exists, and no right of access is legally enforceable to the printed page or to the newspaper columns.[148]

2. Broadcasting is a regulated system in which the government licenses radio broadcasters to transmit on a given frequency. The broadcasters must monitor the content of their transmissions for certain objectionable material. The regulations also require them to be trustees of the public interest, to ensure that broadcast content is fair, and to permit individuals as well as groups to reply to personal attacks and questions of public controversy.[149] Nevertheless, no mandatory right of access to the broadcasting system exists, except for candidates for federal office.[150]

3. For telephony the government has applied a common carrier policy,[151] in which the carrier must accept all messages without censorship or carrier interference except in the cases of obscenity or personal harassment.[152] A virtual monopoly at the national level and a regulated monopoly at the local level traditionally have controlled the transmission of vocal messages. The recent deregulatory actions of the Federal Communication Commission and pressure from the antitrust division of the Department of Justice, however, have led to a more open competition in the interstate voice message transmission system, with only the local operating company retaining a monopoly.[153]

4. For magazines, newsletters, and direct mail soli-

citations the system is in part regulated and in part free of regulation. The postal service is a common carrier but the contents of the publications that the postal service transmits are not subject to regulation unless the material is pornographic or so personally offensive that recipients may prohibit delivery by filing a special form with the local post office.[154]

5. Record carrier services have been an oligopoly. Western Union has provided the domestic telegraph services, and a group of five international carriers have divided the international traffic through authorized gateways that interconnect to the domestic public switched network.[155] Telegraphy has operated under mandatory common carrier principles, and has permitted no censorship or monitoring of the content. In recent years, however, telegraph and international telex services have become more competitive. Western Union now may provide international services, and the international record carriers may have direct access to domestic customers without going through an authorized international gateway.[156]

6. A hybrid regulatory system operated traditionally for cable television.[157] A common carrier policy applied to some of the early leased channels. Hence, the channels had to broadcast nearly all material without censorship unless the contents were obscene or harassing. The locally originated channels, in contrast, followed the broadcast model, and the pay services, a third form of cable television, operated on the model of the print media. The courts, however, recently have questioned the authority of the Federal Communications Commission to make decisions about ownership of and access to cable systems. Consequently, authorities at the city or state level now must make these decisions.[158]

7. Satellite services operate under an "open skies" policy domestically[159] and through a quasi-monopoly carrier, INTELSAT,[160] internationally. The difficult legal problems in satellite services arise in video publishing of text on the television screen either by broadcast or by telephone. Major questions, of course, concern which model of ownership and access applies to these services. Within the ISDNs that digitalize and transmit all

the different satellite signals in a single bit stream, the problem is particularly acute. Typologies that relate to allocations of different frequencies are very awkward to apply to satellite transmissions. If broadcasters provide text from the satellite transmission—the system called teletext—government could regulate this service according to the broadcast model. If the telephone company provides the text—videotex— then a common carrier system of regulation might be most appropriate. No model, however, is obviously best either for teletext or for videotex.[161] Prestel, a videotex service in the United Kingdom, operates on the print model; hence information providers have complete control over satellite messages that they transmit by the telephone system. Broadcasters in this country, in contrast, tend to claim control over text imbedded in their transmissions, even though the Federal Communications Commission could allocate the service to a different owner and operator for the purpose both of ownership and of control over the message.[162] The distinction is most problematic in a situation in which a newspaper provides the service over a broadcast or telephone system, because the newspaper is operating only as an information provider through a cable, broadcast, or telephone system rather than as the distributor of information in its traditional print mode.

The legal status of newspapers as information providers and owners of the new technological systems of delivery is unclear. Nor have lawmakers determined what rules should apply to remote computer service vendors that operate videotex services over private leased lines. The unanswered questions become even more difficult if the sources of the information provided through the electronic data service originate simultaneously from newspapers, broadcasters, and common carriers, as well as from independent information providers that have had no previous history with any of the currently recognized service modes.

An Emerging Legal Right to Communicate

Interest is growing in the idea of establishing a legal right to communicate across national boundaries—a right that would be independent of national authorities. This legal right would be tenuous at best, however, because no legal forum exists in which to adjudicate it, and no independent authority exists to enforce it. At present, the protection of basic human rights, including the right to communicate, falls under the protective cover and responsibility of the nation-state to which the citizen who claims such rights has allegiance. Nevertheless, some hopeful signs have appeared that basic human rights may become universally recognized and litigable in courts other than those of the nations in which derogation of the rights occur.[163]

Several international intergovernmental documents recognize rights to communicate freely across national boundaries. The oldest document is Article 19 of the Universal Declaration of Human Rights, which states:

> Everyone has the right to freedom of opinion and expression; this right includes the freedom to hold opinions without interference and to seek, receive and impart information and ideas through any media and regardless of frontiers."[164]

An American court has acknowledged that the declaration has universal validity and that the right is exercisable in a court of law other than a court of the nationals who claim the right.[165] Sixty-nine nations have entered into treaty obligations under the International Covenant on Civil and Political Rights,[166] a document that contains wording which is almost identical to the language of the Universal Declaration of Human Rights.[167] In addition, the ITU, has recognized "the right of the public to correspond by means of international services of public correspondence."[168] Various treaties of friendship, commerce, and navigation have established the rights of nationals of treaty countries reciprocally to "communicate freely with other persons inside and outside such territories by mail, telegraph, and other means open to general public use."[169]

The organizations and nation-states that have recognized the right to communicate, however, generally have intended to accord this right to members of the public for public correspondence and to journalists for dispatching their stories to the print, audio, or video media. Whether the signers of these statements intended the right to extend to the transfer of information via computer for commercial or other purposes is not clear. Authorities certainly could read the words of international documents to imply this electronic-age meaning.

Furthermore, the interests of major trading nations dictate establishment of these rights in the interests of a healthy global economy. The likelihood of an unambiguous declaration of the right to electronic communication, however, is small; even if organizations and nation-states recognized the right they would clothe it in so many exceptions and ambiguities that any nation-state desiring to do so could easily circumvent its enforcement. The ITU regulations,[170] for example, reserve the rights of member nations to suspend services or to interfere with specific transmission if security, public order, or morality dictates.[171] Furthermore, the Universal Declaration of Human Rights permits curtailment of the right to receive and impart information if other, higher, human rights are in jeopardy or if considerations of "morality, public order, and the general welfare in a democratic society" carry higher priority.[172]

Notwithstanding the current state of international law with respect to the enforceability of human rights, international public opinion is a powerful deterrent to aberrant behavior. New telecommunications technologies may advance the state of the law. They make national boundaries more permeable. Audio and video recorders become an eye or ear for the world beyond. Arthur C. Clarke puts great faith in the ability of satellite communication to reform human conduct:

> The very existence of the myriads of new information channels, operating in real-time and across all frontiers, will be a powerful influence for civilised behaviour. If you are arranging a massacre, it will be useless to shoot the cameraman who has so inconveniently appeared on the scene. His pictures will already be safe in the studio five thousand kilometers away; and his final image may hang you.[173]

Although the communication rights that international groups recognize admittedly are tenuous, nevertheless, including transborder data flow within the purview of these rights is preferable to the present lacuna in international law in which nation-states seem to see transborder data flow regulations as within their power to enact. As Feldman and Garcia have noted, the friendship, commerce, and navigation treaties that recognize a right to exchange information do not include a right to operate communications facilities within a country. Thus, these treaties provide no help in guaranteeing access to leased lines to establish data processing services that the state-operated ministries of posts,

telephones, and telegraph (PTTs) do not offer.[174] This lack is a source of major concern for both service providers and major transnational corporations that use transborder data flow.[175] Furthermore, a right to transmit transborder data flow over the public switched network of a host country would depend upon exclusion of these data services from the the the definition of "domestic communications." Domestic communications are transmissions that a nation-state deems sensitive and excludes from both reciprocal "national treatment" and from most-favored-nation treatment.[176] The United States has suffered for over a decade from the problems inherent in trying to rid its regulatory processes of the distinction between computer and communications services.[177] This distinction has resulted in the more recent dichotomy between basic (traditional and regulated) and enhanced (computerized and unregulated) services.[178] Fortunately, for transnational companies, substantial movement is occurring in some of the more developed nation-states to open up computerized "enhanced" communications services to competition.[179] If the competition includes nonnational service providers, a more open international market for transborder data flow could develop.

Nonetheless, the absence of international and domestic law on the subject forbodes substantial arguments and litigation until the formulation of some internationally recognized principles. A great need exists to develop a taxonomy of information that will establish priorities among types of information for the application of either a regulatory or a free access mode. Uninhibited access would apply to international communications facilities, but the taxonomy would grant a lower priority to information whose very sensitive nature indicates the necessity of substantial controls. The former class would include internal transborder data flow within transnational companies, private correspondence of individuals, diplomatic correspondence, journalistic reports, and health and weather data. The latter, more restricted, class would contain strategic, intelligence, and criminal data. The most problematic categories of information are the ones that highlight transnational variations in public morality and relate to the transfer of technology. For example, although established procedures exist in other countries for rejecting foreign films such as *E.T.*, that are palatable to general audiences in the United States but offensive in other nations,[180] no technical method exists for accommodating these concerns when the information is transmitted in a merged digital bit stream.

Concepts of Territoriality

Legal concepts that concern different types of geographical areas vary considerably. For example, the law of the sea historically has opened maritime areas to all compatible users; the law of physical land masses, however, has developed with a basic concept of territoriality.[181] Laws concerning air space have been a compromise between land and sea law,[182] but the line between territorial exclusivity and shared use in airspace remains unclear. Some legal commentators have urged the use of the Von Karmann line, the threshold beyond which dynamic lift no longer is maintainable.[183] The point at which a space satellite can sustain a stationary orbit or the point of gravitational neutrality would be equally valid, however, as would the distance beyond which a nation-state cannot shoot down an object flying over its territory. This "shooting range" concept would be equivalent to the three mile territorial limit beyond which the high seas became common property. The three mile limit, which is based upon the distance that a cannon could propel a cannonball,[184] became technologically outmoded with the development of aircraft. Obviously, the concepts applicable to define shared and owned air space are as varied as the imagination of legal scholars.[185]

The Final Acts of the 1979 World Administrative Radio Conference (WARC) passed a resolution guaranteeing "in practice for all countries equitable access to the geostationary satellite orbit and the frequency bands allocated to space service."[186] This admirable goal raises questions about the legal definition of "equitable access." Also, assuming that an agreement on such definition might be reached, how could such access be guaranteed? This resolution considerably exceeds the admonition to member nations of Article 33 to keep in mind that radio frequencies and orbital parking places are limited natural resources which should be "used efficiently and economically so that all countries . . . may have equitable access."[187]

Equitable access is more nearly defined as fairness than as exact equality, although another WARC 1979 resolution admonished the ITU administration to consider that "all countries have equal rights" to space.[188] Thus there is ample room for confusion concerning

whether access to space for the purposes of communication should be the basis of a common ownership of space, a fair allocation of services on the basis of need and technical ability, or some absolute property right in a portion thereof.

None of these concepts of territoriality helps very much to establish rights in information that is in transit through the radio magnetic spectrum to and from a geostationary satellite 22,300 miles out in space.[189] In addition, the present jurisdictional scheme perhaps underestimates the functional changes that have accompanied the growth of large economic enterprises which operate transnationally. Most of the jurisdictional aspects of territoriality operate under national systems of justice. Interestingly, a law of merchants existed in the Middle Ages, which transcended territorial boundaries and preceded the historical development of the nation-state as a powerful political entity. An examination of the manner in which the *lex mercatoria* of the medieval merchants functioned may be useful to determine its potential applicability to today's growing global networks.[190] In a world in which the annual income of some transnational companies exceeds the gross national product of many nations, parallel systems of governance may provide guidance in the development of an open telecommunications system in which messages can flow freely from enterprise to enterprise, institution to institution, and person to person. A Japanese legal scholar suggests:

> In the administration oriented economic law field, we must also realize that the adherence of ego-influenced exercises of sovereignty will only further confusion and confrontation in a world of interdependence.[191]

PERSPECTIVES

The legal issues that this chapter addresses are only a few of the many questions concerning transborder data flow that are emerging in various national, regional, intergovernmental, and international fora. For example, some legal theorists propose to tax the flow of information by measuring the bit stream or the value of the information that it contains.[192] This plan is probably no more ridiculous than taxing telephone calls, metering telephone rates, or valuing business telephone services more highly than residential, but the proposal clearly is threatening to free trade practices and inimical to First

Amendment values. Other theorists argue for absolutely unfettered flow of information, whether by newsprint or by electrons.[193] This view fails to consider the many ways in which all nation-states alter the flow of information to suit their political, military, and economic strategies.

Determining the appropriate legal restrictions and freedoms for transborder data flow is a difficult task. Critics at either end of the spectrum fail to reach satisfactory conclusions on this issue. Proponents of a highly regulatory regime[194] doubtless are premature, because even if the components of a regulatory scheme were obvious, we would not know where or how to establish it. On the other hand, uncompromising advocates of "free flow" are out of touch with reality.[195] Most of the world simply will not accept this practice. The United States has no sanction with which to force other countries to apply a facsimile of the First Amendment. Moreover, other nations consider the notion of freedom of speech to be a peculiarly American policy that most benefits American information products and services.[196]

Consequently, legal skirmishes in a multiplicity of legal arenas are inevitable, and all interested parties must attempt to work out the rules under which information societies in an interdependent global economy will function. Whatever the results, unfettered competition among private corporate entities clearly will not produce an international free marketplace in information. The competitors in this marketplace by no means are all private, and the interests at issue span public, private, and governmental sectors. To achieve a workable system, nations of the world must combine hybrid policies when expediency dictates, cooperate when cooperation is mandatory, and compete when the virtues of competition are apparent, as in the stimulation of innovation.

The complexities of transborder data flow negotiations, litigations, and arbitrations—as well as the exhortations to conscience and equity—are almost incomprehensible. The positions that each party takes in disputes or negotiations will depend upon the particular perspective of the proponent. Available, reliable, accurate, and low-cost access to a variety of options in information services may be of high priority to an individual. A multinational bank, in contrast, will require high-speed, secure, private line service to specified locations and access to the public network for the delivery of financial information services to its customers. An ethnic or religious group may want direct access

to its members without interference by governmental entities. A government, however, will put a higher priority on gateway nodes, which provide a high level of access control; deposit of data bases in its own country's files; use of locally produced hardware and software; and the availability of encryption keys to protect its national security interests and encourage development of its own information economy.[197] A government also may desire to control the content of traffic through its territorial boundaries by reviewing applications and licensing only the interests that coincide with its national priorities.

Proponents of a global perspective might argue for sharing spectrum resources and expediting and giving high priority to social service systems that are available to all countries. Thus, people who look upon themselves as "citizens of the world" favor information systems that provide environmental monitoring, weather predictions to help prevent disruptions and loss from hurricanes and typhoons, and that protect against terrorism, encourage law enforcement, expedite land use planning, and facilitate pestilence control. A global system of information management would put high priority on ISDNs, which would guarantee to businesses, institutions, and individuals anywhere on the network the world's collective knowledge at their fingertips. This integrated network ideal is like the "Networks for Knowledge" program that President Lyndon Johnson espoused shortly before he announced his intention not to seek another term of office in 1968.[198]

An acquaintance with the varied objectives of competing interest groups makes it easy to understand the policies that the different nations espouse currently in the global dialogue about the New World Information Order (NWIO).[199] Those countries, notably Sweden,[200] with the greatest concern about their societies' vulnerability to data stored outside their national boundaries are pursuing national policies to ensure information independence. Countries like Japan[201] that perceive the opportunities of a large information marketplace are following strategies to give themselves the economic capability to create their own hardware and software for marketing to the rest of the world and, consequently, to strengthen their own economies. Countries that are vigorously pursuing national telematics policies include France[202] and Brazil.[203] Nations that perceive themselves to be too small to develop the computer capability within the confines of their own national boundaries are working to combine their economies to compete more effectively. The harmonization policies that the European Economic Community (EEC) has espoused are an example of this type of joint action.[204]

Canada is a leader in concern about cultural sovereignty. Living in close proximity to the United States, Canadians have developed a deep awareness about the loss of cultural identity and control over their own information resources. Canada has developed transborder data flow policies in a number of fields including the print media, motion pictures, direct broadcasting satellites, and computers, and it has served as a model for many countries seeking national telematics policies.[205]

Other organizations and their nation-state members advocate liberal information trade policies. The 37 member nations of the Intergovernmental Bureau of Informatics (IBI) are active in formulating the policies of reciprocity, in which more information will flow between developed and developing nations.[206] Major ferment has occurred within UNESCO over issues such as "balanced information flow," the licensing of journalistic endeavors, and the transfer of information technology to the developing nations.[207] International businesses within the International Chamber of Commerce are pursuing a policy of liberalization; they are favoring international trade in information products and services and urging the availability of private leased lines for the development of special purpose data networks.[208]

Only a policy in favor of greater international cooperation in the development of global information resources seems to lack advocates.[209] Like the United States, where the proliferation of special interest lobbying groups makes it difficult to identify the collective public interest, in the international arena, a locus of responsibility is difficult to find for ascertaining global interests that may override rather than coincide with legitimate national concerns. While a surplus of lawyers is available to represent corporate, nonprofit, and governmental clients, no active bar represents the global common interest.

Daniel Bell, who has labored long and hard to understand the social problems that the onslaught of the new information technologies have precipitated, has stated:

> Today we have an international economy, but the political units are national political units; and the relationships are unstable. We have centrifugal and centripetal forces. We have an international economy, but also a new international division of labour which is re-making and re-working the entire world economy . . . .
>
> Then the national state has become too big for the small problems of life and too small for the big problems of life . . . .
>
> We must try to think in terms of how one can bring all these matters together in some intellectual coherence, in some intellectual framework, that allows one to think of society not in terms of gadgets, because it is not gadgets which will change society, but modes of thought.[210]

Ample opportunities will arise in the days and years to come for lawyers and public policy analysts to propose some coherent global alternatives for rationalizing the legal environment in which electronic transfer of information across national boundaries occurs. The proliferation of networking across such boundaries will not abate. A number of alternatives are available to lawyers:

1. They may follow the developments in such diverse arenas as the IBI, UNESCO, CoE, OECD, and the ITU and either react to adverse circumstances affecting their clients or take a leadership role in expounding policies that favor their clients.
2. They may respond only in particular circumstances in which their clients face litigation and thereby contribute in an ad hoc manner to the developing body of law of international networks.
3. They may anticipate the legal problems that their clients and their nation may face and devise working hypotheses concerning such diverse legal questions as tort liability, conflicts of law, criminal liability, and property rights.
4. They may develop national legislative strategies or national teleinformatics policies to improve their own country's position in the global competitive environment.
5. They may develop strategies for a global system of information transport and global sharing of information resources.

Transborder data flow rapidly is becoming an integral part of the infrastructure that links societies globally.

That this data flow will continue to increase in importance is certain. Less clear, however, is how the United States and other nation-states will respond to the changes that transborder data flow and the global links it inevitably provides will bring. This chapter concludes with a list of 20 principles that may serve as guides for development.[211] These principles rest on the ideal that an information transport system which optimizes the opportunities for personal and national interaction will serve best the world community of nations.

1. *Availability.* This concept concerns the physical existence of telecommunications systems to serve global needs. Availability not only implies the existence of telecommunications facilities, but also actual channel space and operational readiness to receive and transmit messages, whenever and wherever users desire.

2. *Accessibility.* According to the Japanese this concept is even more inclusive than availability—it implies guaranteed use for those who would like to claim the right.

3. *Authenticity.* This principle concerns the ability to rely upon messages stored, transmitted, or processed through electronic systems to establish legal rights and obligations.

4. *Compatibility.* This principle assumes that technical systems can be interfaced.

5. *Diversity.* This principle assures users access to a choice of telecommunications services and information systems.

6. *Efficiency.* An economic goal espoused in most national policies, this principle means that the telecommunications system should be cost effective for its intended purposes.

7. *Equity.* Users should share both rights and responsibilities.

8. *Insurability.* This concept concerns the ability to assess risks and obtain insurance against unforeseen and uncontrollable events and circumstances that disrupt service or impose loss upon users.

9. *Integrity.* This goal is message clarity and accuracy, which permits the assurance that users receive their messages without error.

10. *Interactivity.* This principle is the potential for immediate response in real time.

11. *Interoperability.* This concept implies more than mere "plug compatibility." Interoperability concerns protocols for access to, through, and across various public and private networks, so that no one arbitrarily can exclude users from the global system.

12. *Literacy.* Telecommunications systems should be "user friendly" and not inhibit use by non-professionals.

13. *Property.* This principle addresses guaranteed protection of recognized exclusivity rights in personal information. These rights include the right to privacy and the right to release or withhold information about oneself as well as corporate rights to protect information transport that is necessary to internal operations and/or is a commodity in trade, the right to reward for intellectual productivity, and the right to cultural sovereignty.

14. *Reciprocity.* All users should have the same access to telecommunications services and products as most-favored nations.

15. *Redundancy.* Under this principle if one information transport system breaks down, an alternative channel is available.

16. *Reliability.* Regularly established and uninterrupted service should be available.

17. *Security.* This principle concerns the protection of data from disclosure or misuse and the assurance that the intended recipient and no one else receives messages.

18. *Transparency.* The user should not confront apparent inconsistencies in operating systems or equipment.

19. *Universality.* This is the ultimate goal of integrated services digital networks (ISDNs) and the final extrapolation of availability, interoperability, and transparency.

20. *Vulnerability.* Users should have assurance that interdependence is mutual and dependencies are reliable. They should be reasonably certain that access is available to information stored in remote data bases in times of crisis or national or personal peril.

In summary, the time is ripe for a new level of statesmanship in the governance of global communications networks. What is needed is less naysaying about their potential for abuse and a more diligent effort to achieve their positive benefits for the global family of nations.

NOTES

1. A distributed computer network facilitating communication among numerous users relies on the implementation of an organizational pattern that links the users' terminals and local computer equipment, the transmission facilities, and usually one or more central computers. Such networks are used for many purposes (e.g., to support local transactions and keep the information consistent with information in other computers at remote locations). Typical applications are airline reservations, retail point of sale transactions, credit verification, electronic funds tgransfers, teleconferencing, cooperative research, and shared creative efforts. See, *e.g.*, S. HILTZ & M. TUROFF, THE NETWORK NATION: HUMAN COMMUNICATION VIA COMPUTER (Reading, Mass.: Addison-Wesley, 1978).

2. For a discussion of the benefits that the United States might reap by leading the world community into an international system of information exchange, see address by Arthur C. Clarke to the United Nations Committee on Disarmament, August 31, 1982), *reprinted in* CONG. REC. E4307–09 (daily ed. Sept. 21, 1983) (statement of Rep. Brown).

3. Indeed, the most recent U.S. policy analysis evidences both myopia and paranoia. See STAFF OF NATIONAL TELECOMMUNICATIONS AND INFORMATION ADMINISTRATION, 98TH CONG., 1ST SESS., United States LONG RANGE GOALS IN INTERNATIONAL TELECOMMUNICATIONS AND INFORMATION: AN OUTLINE FOR UNITED STATES POLICY xi, xii (Comm. Print 1983) [hereinafter cited as NTIA report], which is the best available historical documentation of current United States policies and organizational problems although it makes little mention of any responsibilities the United States might have to help develop and maintain a global system of telecommunications.

4. A satellite footprint is the area on the earth's surface covered by the satellite's beam.

5. D. SCHILLER, TELEMATICS AND GOVERNMENT 148 (Norwood, N.J.: Ablex, 1982); NTIA Report, *supra* note 3, at 156, "estimates for the telecommunications equipment market in 1987 indicate a U.S. market of about $34 billion and a world market of just under $60 billion."

6. D. SCHILLER *supra* note 5, at 108.

7. Y. MASUDA, THE INFORMATION SOCIETY AS POST-INDUSTRIAL SOCIETY (Bethesda, Md.: World Future Society, 1981).

8. Cleveland, *How Leaders Must Change in the Information Age*, Christian Sci. Monitor, Feb. 16, 1981, at 27, col. 1.

9. Fishman, *Introduction to Transborder Data Flows*, 16 STAN. J. INT'L (1980).

10. PAC. TELECOM. COUNCIL CONF. PROC. Jan. 1980, at I-D, 31.

11. Novotny, *Transborder Data Flows and International Law: A Framework for Policy Oriented Inquiry*, 16 STAN. J. INT'L 143–44 (1980).

12. Pool & Solomon, *Intellectual Property and Transborder Data Flows*, 16 STAN. J. INT'L 114–15 (1980).

13. C. ANTONELLI, TRANSBORDER DATA FLOWS AND INTERNATIONAL BUSINESS 5 (Paris: Organization for Economic Cooperation and Development, June 2, 1981).

14. INTERGOVERNMENTAL BUREAU FOR INFORMATICS, ISSUES ON TRANSBORDER DATA FLOW POLICIES (Rome: Documents on Policies for Informatics, SPIN—230 Green Series, Sept. 1979).

15. Lemoine, *Transborder Data Flows*, INFORMATION SYS. MAG., Spring 1979, at 30.

16. J. BING, P. FORSBERG, AND E. NYGAARD, LEGAL ISSUES RELATED TO TRANSBORDER DATA FLOWS (Paris: Organization for Economic Cooperation and Development, June 2, 1981)(hereinafter cited as Bing Report).

17. Feldman & Garcia, *National Regulation of Transborder Data Flows*, 7 N.C. J. INT'L. & C.R. 1 (Winter 1982).

18. Hamelink, *Banks' Control and Use of Information*, 5 TRANSNAT'L DATA REP. 21 (1982).

19. Vienna Convention on Diplomatic Relations, Apr. 18, 1961, arts. XXVII, XXIX, 23 U.S.T. 3227, 3239, 3240, 500 U.N.T.S. 95, 108, 110.

20. 18 U.S.C.A. § 2511 (3), *repealed by* Foreign Intelligence Surveillance Act of 1978, Pub. l. 95-511, 92 Stat. 1797 (1978), *replaced by* Exec. Order No. 12,333, 46 Fed. Reg. 59,941, 59,941 (§ 2.5) (Dec. 8, 1981).

21. O. GANLEY, THE U.S. AND INFORMATION RESOURCES: INTERNATIONAL IMPLICATIONS 15 (Cambridge, Mass.: Harvard University Press, 1980).

22. The UPU originated under provisions of the Treaty of Berne of 1875 and operated under the Universal Copyright Convention signed by the United States on September 16, 1955.

23. The World Intellectual Property Organization began under a convention that 51 nations signed in Stockholm (1967) and now includes 88 nations.

24. The International Telegraph Convention of Paris, May 17, 1865, 9 Recueil des Traites de la France 254.

25. 56 Brit. & Foreign St. Papers 294. See Glazer, *The Law Making Treaties of the International Telecommunications Union through Time and Space,* 60 Mich. L. Rev. 269, 271 n. 12 (1962).

26. Final Protocol to Telegraph Regs., Nov. 29, 1958, art. 85, 10 U.S.T. 2611, 2613, T.I.A.S. No. 4390.

27. An international convention established the International Radiotelegraph Union in 1906. Berlin Radiotelegraph Convention, Nov. 3, 1906, 37 Stat. 1565, T.S. No. 568. The organization remained in existence until 1932, when the newly born International Telecommunications Union absorbed its functions.

28. Glazer, *supra* note 25, at 274.

29. *Id.* at 275.

30. *Id.*

31. International Telecommunication Convention, Oct. 2, 1947, 63 Stat. 1399, T.I.A.S. No. 1901, 30 U.N.T.S. 316. *See generally* D. Leive, International Telecommunications and International Law: The Regulation of the Radio Spectrum (1970); G. Codding, Jr. and A. Rutkowski, The International Telecommunication Union in a Changing World (1982).

32. The most recent examples relevant to TDF are the x.25 interface standards for packet switched networks and the efforts to produce an international standard for videotex services.

33. William vanden Heuval, Deputy Chief of the United States Mission to the European Office of the United Nations and Other International Organizations.

34. G.A. Res. 3281, 29 U.N. GAOR Supp. (No. 30) at 40, U.N. Doc. A/9030 (1974).

35. S. MacBride, Many Voices, One World, Report by the International Commission for the Study of Communications Problems (New York: UNESCO, 1980).

36. The electromagnetic spectrum is a continuous range of frequencies "from the longest known electrical wave to the shortest cosmic ray." C. Sipple, Data Communications Dictionary (1976), 132.

37. *See generally* Robinson, *Regulating International Airwaves: The 1979 WARC,* 21 Va. J. Int'l L, Fall 1980.

38. Inaugural Address at the Pacific Telecommunications Conference, Jan. 16, 1983.

39. *Id.*

40. G.A. Res. 217, 3 U.N. GAOR, U.N. Doc. 1/777 (1948).

41. For example, the ITU will be holding conferences over the next several years on high frequency radio bands (1984 and 1986), the uses of geostationary satellite orbits, and the planning of space services (1985 and 1987). For a complete list of conferences, see NTIA report *supra* note 3, at 56–59.

42. "The equipment which receives a signal, amplifies it, changes its frequency, and retransmits it is called a transponder." Martin, *supra* note 32, at 281. Communication satellites typically contain several transponders.

43. The ITU recently has grown from a relatively small association of developed nations into the world's largest intergovernmental organization, because of the influx of membership from the less developed nations. See Rutkowski, *The 1979 World Administrative Radio Conference: The ITU in a Changing World,* 13 Int'l Law. 289, 298 (1979).

44. *See* J. Pelton, M. Perras, & A. Sinha, INTELSAT, The Global Telecommunications Network (Honolulu: Pacific Telecommunications Conference, Jan. 1983) [Hereinafter cited as J. Pelton].

45. 47 U.S.C. § 701, *et seq.*

46. INTELSAT, *1980 Annual Report* 6 (1981).

47. J. Pelton, *supra* note 44, at 16, 21.

48. *Id.* at 16, 47.

49. The OECD, established in 1961, promotes the economic and social welfare of its member states; members include Australia, Austria, Belgium, Canada, Denmark, Finland, France, the Federal Republic of Germany, Greece, Iceland, Ireland, Italy, Japan, Luxembourg, Netherlands, New Zealand, Norway, Portugal, Spain, Sweden, Switzerland, Turkey, the United Kingdom and the United States.

50. Point to point communication facilities pass information incrementally from one station to the next. Thus to send a message from location A to D requires transmitting the message from A to B, B to C, and C to D. With a multipoint network the message might be sent from a central point via different paths to several destinations simultaneously, but with a satellite system the central message may be distributed simultaneously to all points on the surface of the globe within view of the satellite beam which have an appropriate satellite receiver.

51. With fiber optical cables the high speed and fidelity required by data communications may be

available equally by land and undersea installations but not to mobile sites.

52. *See* M. Goldey, *infra,* chapter 4. It has been reported that discussions were held in the State Department during the Iranian hostage crisis of methods of withholding television service from Iran to the United States. See *No Go for Satellite Sanctions Against Iran—A Presidential Proposal to Cut Off Iran's Access to the Satellites of Intelsat Has Been Quietly Shelved,* SCIENCE May 18, 1980, at 685.

53. J. PELTON, *supra* note 44, at 8.

54. The Public Interest Satellite Association (PISA) is a public interest group whose purpose is to conduct research on the use of satellites for public purposes and to lobby for legislation favoring use of satellite technology to benefit the broadest number of people possible.

55. W. McGRAW, TOWARD THE PUBLIC DIVIDEND (New York: Public Interest Satellite Association, 1977); A. Horowitz and W. Thomas, The Unexplored Option: Critical Choices for Public Telecommunications, 1977–2000 (A working paper prepared under the auspices of the Public Interest Satellite Association); for a discussion of the negotiations and claims of various national delegations concerning space options, see generally Robinson, *supra* note 37, at 18–28.

56. Address on the Occasion of the Award of the International Marconi Fellowship, The Hague (June 12, 1982).

57. See K. Imakita, How Regional Satellite Communications Should Be Arranged in Terms of Pacific Telecommunications, Pacific Telecommunications Council Seminar (June 7, 1982).

58. Joseph Pelton, Pacific Telecommunications Conference, in response to questions (January 18, 1983).

59. These goals for expanded service are consistent with INTELSAT's primary objective of "efficient provisions, technologically and economically, worldwide satellite communications." Snow, *INTELSAT: An International Example* 30 J. COM. 147, 155 (1980).

60. J. PELTON, *supra* note 44, at 17.

61. The members of the MARISAT joint venture include COMSAT General Corp., RCA Global Communications, Inc., Western Union International, Inc., and ITT World Communications, Inc.

62. For technical information about the three MARISAT satellites (named MARECS, MARISAT, and MAROTS) see M. BROWN, COMPENDIUM OF COMMUNICATION AND BROADCAST SATELLITES: 1958 TO 1980, (1981), 47–58.

63. "On Line (in Orbit) with MARISAT," SOURCEWORLD 5.

64. *Maritime Communications Gets Boost from Inmarsat System,"* COM. NEWS, April 1982, at 40.

65. Hamelink, *supra* note 18, at 21.

66. A dedicated network of this nature combines several specific communication circuits allocated solely to the specific bank's transmissions. C. SIPPL, *supra* note 36, at 123.

67. *International Data Flow: Hearings before the Subcomm. on Government Information and Human Rights of the House Comm. on Government Operations,* 96th Cong., 2d Sess. 112–39 (statement of Robert E. Walker, Vice President and Associate Corporate Counsel, Continental Illinois National Bank and Trust Co.).

68. Hamelink, *supra* note 18, at 24.

69. Will Sparks, Citibank Vice-President, The Flow of Information and the New Technology of Money, Address at the Conference on World Communications, Annenberg School of Communications, Philadelphia, Pa., at 7 (May 1980).

70. Hamelink, *supra* note 18, at 27.

71. *Id.* at 23, 27.

72. *Visa Warns Bankers over New Technology,* 5 TRANSNAT'L DATA REP. 28 (1982).

73. For a contemporary discussion of the U2 incident and its international implications, see Wright, *Legal Aspects of the U-2 Incident,* 54 AM. J. INT'L L. 836 (1960).

74. Multilateral treaty, Jan. 27, 1967, United States-Great Britain: U.S.S.R., 18 U.S.T. 2410, T.I.A.S. No. 6347, 610 U.N.T.S. 205.

75. See Goedhius, *Some Recent Trends in the Interpretation and Implementation of Rules of International Space Law,* 19 COL, J.T.L. 213 (1981).

76. Umali, *Landsat: Uninvited Eye,* PERSPECTIVES (Honolulu, East-West Center magazine), Winter 1980, at 12–21.

77. Waldrop, *Imaging the Earth (II): The Politics of Landsat,* SCIENCE, Apr. 2, 1982, at 40, 41. For a discussion of the data collected by EROS and its uses, see Bylinsky, *ERTS Puts the Whole Earth under a Microscope,* FORTUNE, Feb. 1975, at 117.

78. The annual expenditure of the National

Aeronautic and Space Administration is approximately $6–7 billion; NOAA estimates the cost of operating Landsat alone at approximately $1–10 billion over the next 10 years; the cost of a single map from EROS is about $45. According to a recent estimate, EROS could derive only about $6 million in income annually. Waldrop, *supra* note 77, at 40–42.

79. *Id.* at 40, 41.

80. Letter from Rene Antonio Novaes, head of the Remote Sensing Department of the Conselho Cientifico e Tecnologico, to author (Nov. 24, 1981).

81. U. N. Doc. A/AC 105/122 at para 3 (1974). For a discussion of legal problems related to sovereignty, see generally Comment, *Earth Resources Satellites: A Puzzle for the United Nations,* 16 HARV. INT'L L.J. 648 (1975).

82. Umali, *supra* note 76, at 16.

83. Comment, *supra* note 81, at 650.

84. Proceedings, Report UN/AC 105, paras. 4–5 (1973).

85. Umali, *supra* note 76, at 16.

86. U.S. National Academy of Sciences (NAS), Ad Hoc Committee on Remote Sensing (1977).

87. Bylinsky, *supra* note 77, at 130.

88. NAS, *supra* note 86.

89. U.S. NATIONAL SCIENCE BOARD, SCIENCE INDICATORS 1980 at 16–18 (1981).

90. Cryptology in this context covers "all aspects of code work. . . ." J. BAMFORD, THE PUZZLE PALACE: A REPORT ON AMERICA'S MOST SECRET AGENCY 29 (1982). Cryptology includes both the making and breaking of codes and currently is of great importance to national security institutions needing the latest application of scientific and technological theories to carry out their eavesdropping and code-breaking operations. Cryptographic protection of communications transmission via satellite relies on the use of computer scrambling devices called cryptographic interference units (CIU). Each use of the satellite system connects at an access point termed a network security center. All transmissions pass through a CIU; only properly authorized locations on the system thereafter may receive the communication. See F. KUO, PROTOCOL AND TECHNIQUES FOR DATA COMMUNICATION NETWORKS 369–429 (1981). Interception of the satellite beam is feasible; the reception is worthless, however, unless a cryptoanalyst is able to break the code. BAMFORD, *supra,* at 32–281. Thus the restriction of access to a nation's cryptologic

information is of highest priority for national security.

91. Exec. Order No. 12, 47 Fed. Reg. 14,874 (1982). *See generally* NATIONAL ACADEMY OF SCIENCES, SCIENTIFIC COMMUNICATION AND NATIONAL SECURITY (Washington, D.C.: National Academy Press, 1982).

92. The United States established the Consultative Group-Coordinating Committee in 1945 to impose an embargo on shipment of strategic technologies from the allied nations to the Eastern bloc. COCOM's functions include preparing an international list of embargo items, processing requests for exceptions to the export list, and consulting on export control enforcement. T. ECKERT, THE TRANSFER OF U.S. TECHNOLOGY TO OTHER COUNTRIES: AN ANALYSIS OF EXPORT CONTROL POLICY AND SOME RECOMMENDATIONS 16–17 (Princeton University Center of International Research, Monograph No. 47, 1981).

93. 50 U.S.C. § 2401 et. seq.

94. 22 U.S.C. § 2778.

95. 15 C.F.R. § §368.1–399.2

96. 50 U.S.C. § 2402.

97. 15 C.F.R. § 379.1.

98. *Id.* at § 379.1(b).

99. 22 C.F.R. § § 121.01–130.33.

100. 22 C.F.R. § § 125.20–24 (1982).

101. 15 C.F.R. § 379.3(a); 50 U.S.C. § § 2410(b) and (c).

102. Two types of general export licenses are available; the general license GTDA, which covers "technical data available to all destinations," 15 C.F.R. § 379.3; and the general license GTDR, which covers "technical data under restrictions," 15 C.F.R. § 379.4.

103. 15 C.F.R. § 379.2.

104. 15 C.F.R. § 379.3(a); willful violations of the export regulations subject corporations to penalties of five times the value of the export up to a million dollars and for individuals $250,000 or as many as 10 years in jail, 50 U.S.C. § 2410(b); but administrative remedies are the more often imposed penalties involving seizure, or forfeiture, or loss of export import privileges, 50 U.S.C. § 2410(c); an aggressive effort on the part of the Departments of Commerce and Treasury, called "Project Exodus," has increased enforcement of the regulations.

105. 15 C.F.R. § 379.3(b)(1).

106. 15 C.F.R. § 379.5.

107. NATIONAL ACADEMY OF SCIENCE, *supra* note 91.

108. U.S. DEPARTMENT OF DEFENSE SCIENCE BOARD TASK FORCE ON EXPORT OF U.S. TECHNOLOGY, AN ANAL-

YSIS OF EXPORT CONTROL OF U.S. TECHNOLOGY—A DOD PERSPECTIVE (1976) (popularly called the Bucy report).

109.   32 C.F.R. § 159.21 (1982).

110.   22 U.S.C. § 2778.

111.   22 C.F.R. § 125.01.

112.   Newell & Sproull, *Computer Networks: Prospects for Scientists,* SCIENCE, Feb. 12, 1982, at 843; International Conference on Computer Communications, PROCEEDINGS 273, Oct. 27, 1980.

113.   Crocker, Healner, Metcalfe, & Postel, *Function-Oriented Protocols for the ARPA Computer Network,* 40 AM. FED'N INFORMATION PROCESSING SOCIETIES CONF. PROC. 271, (1972).

114.   *See* McCredie and Timlake, *infra.,* chapter 14.

115.   *See* McCann, *infra.,* chapter 11.

116.   The World Weather Watch originated in a U.N. General Assembly Resolution (XVI-1972), passed in 1961, which asked the World Meteorological Organisation (WMO) to set up a worldwide meteorological service to ensure that all WMO members would receive timely meteorological observations and processed data. The WMO is one of the most successful examples of global cooperation, involving 147 member nations banded together in 1947 to monitor weather on a worldwide basis. Designated a U.N. specialized agency in 1951, the WMO has 3 world centers (Washington, D.C.; Moscow; and Melbourne), 23 regional centers, and about 750 national centers. 6 INTERMEDIA, April 1978, at 14.

117.   The International Atomic Energy Agency (IAEA), established in 1957, promotes the use of atomic energy for peaceful purposes and ensures that its offices do not further any military purpose. The agency is an autonomous international organization within the United Nations System. IAEA, 20 YEARS INTERNATIONAL ATOMIC ENERGY AGENCY 1957–1977, at 1–9 (1977).

118.   Newell & Sproull, *supra* note 112, at 635–640.

119.   Washington Post, July 20, 1979, at C-1, 3.

120.   J. PELTON, *supra* note 44, at 31.

121.   Non-Tariff Trade Barriers—U.C. Response, paper presented at the American Bar Association annual meeting (Aug. 10, 1982).

122.   Pub. L. No. 93-579, 88 Stat. 1561, 5 U.S.C. § 552a (1976).

123.   5 U.S.C. § 552 *et seq.*

124.   15 U.S.C. § § 1631, 1637, 1666, 1666(a).

125.   Pub. L. No. 95-630, § § 1100–1122, 92 Stat. 3697 (codified in tits. 12 and 31 of the U.S.C.)

126.   *See* PRIVACY PROTECTION STUDY COMMISSION, PERSONAL PRIVACY IN AN INFORMATION SOCIETY (1977).

127.   HOUSE COMM. ON GOVERNMENT OPERATIONS, INTERNATIONAL INFORMATION FLOW: FORGING A NEW FRAMEWORK, H.R. REP. NO. 1535, 96TH CONG., 2D SESS. 18 (1980).

128.   The CoE proposed the *Convention for the Protection of Individuals with Regard to Automatic Processing of Personal Data,* 3 TRANSNAT'L DATA REP, no. 6, at 17 (1980). The OECD put forth the *Guidelines Governing the Protection of Privacy and Transborder Flows of Personal Data,''* 4 TRANSNAT'L DATA REP., no. 1, at 45 (1981).

129.   The membership of the two groups is quite similar. CoE has 20 members, only 3 of which—Cyprus, Luxembourg, and Malta—are not members of OECD as well. Of the 24 members of OECD, only 6 are not in the European Economic Community (Australia, Canada, Finland, Japan, New Zealand, and the United States); OECD AT A GLANCE (1982). Every nation in the two groups has privacy legislation or is considering recommendations for legislation by privacy commissions. *See* Patrick, *Privacy Restrictions on Transnational Data Flows: A Comparison of the Council of Europe Draft Convention and the OECD Guidelines,* 21 JURIMETRICS J. 405, 406–08 (1981). *See also* Coombe, *Multinational Codes of Conduct and Corporate Accountability: New Opportunities for Corporate Counsel,* 38 BUS. LAW., Nov. 1980, at 17.

130.   Maisonrouge, *Regulation of International Information Flows,* 1 INFORMATION SOC'Y, no. 1, at 17, 22 (1981).

131.   Patrick, *supra* note 129, at 417.

132.   Ramsey, *Europe Responds to the Challenge of the New Information Technologies: A Teleinformatics Strategy for the 1980s,* 14 CORNELL INT. L. J. 237, 245 (1981).

133.   Becker, *Rifkin, A Documentary History,* 2 COMPUTER L.J. 471 (1980).

134.   D. PARKER, S. NYCUM, & S. OURA, COMPUTER ABUSE (Stanford, Cal.: Stanford Research Institute, 1975).

135.   Becker, *The Trial of a Computer Crime,* 21 JURIMETRICS J. 421, 429 (1981).

136.   How the American judiciary will adapt its tort principles to cases concerning electronic funds transfer is unclear. In EVRA Corp. v Swiss Bank Corp.,

673 F.2d 951 (7th Cir. 1982), the Seventh Circuit of Appeals considered a case in which Swiss Bank Corp. failed to transfer $27,000 that an Illinois bank had telexed, intending the money to be payment for the lease of a vessel. The District Court held that Swiss Bank Corp. had been negligent in its failure to make the payment and assessed damages of $2.1 million, 522 F. Supp. 820, 829, 835 (E.D. Ill. 1981). The Seventh Circuit reversed, noting that the plaintiff should have known "that messages sometimes get lost or delayed in transit . . . even when all the banks are using reasonable care" 673 F.2d 957. The sharp disagreement between the district and circuit courts in this case highlights the potential for a conflict in the circuits as more of these cases arise. *See also* Greguras, *Corporate Electronic Fund Transfers: Increasing the Stakes*, 5 TRANSNAT'L DATA REP. 31 (1982).

137.   R. BIGELOW & S. NYCUM, YOUR COMPUTER AND THE LAW 136 (Englewood Cliffs, N.J.: Prentice-Hall, 1975).

138.   Ward v. Superior Court, 3 C.L.S.R. 206 (1972).

139.   Agreement for the Promotion of Safety on the Great Lakes by Means of Radio, December 19, 1978, United States-Canada, 30 U.S.T. 2523, T.I.A.S. No. 9352.

140.   Ford Motor Credit Co. v. Swarens, 2 C.L.S.R. 347, 447 S.W.2d 533 (Ky. Ct. App. 1969) ("Trust in the infallibility of a computer is hardly a defense. . . .").

141.   Lemoine, *supra* note 15.

142.   ECONOMICS OF INFORMATION AND KNOWLEDGE (D. Lamberton ed., Penguin, 1971); K. Arrow, *The Economics of Information,* in THE COMPUTER AGE: A TWENTY YEAR VIEW (M. Dertouzos & J. Moses eds., Cambridge, Mass.: MIT Press, 1979); F. MACHLUP, PRODUCTION AND DISTRIBUTION OF KNOWLEDGE (1962); Wunderlich, *Property Rights and Information,* 412 ANNALS 80 (1974); O'Brien & Helleiner, *The Political Economy of Information in a Changing International Order,* INT'L ORGANIZATIONS 445–70 (Autumn 1980).

143.   U.S. CONST. art. I., § 8.

144.   Feldman, *Commercial Speech, Transborder Data Flows and the Right to Communicate under International Law,* 17 INT'L L. 87, 87–88 (1983).

145.   Pool & Solomon, *supra* note 12, at 121.

146.   *Id.* at 123, 133, 137–38.

147.   Lorain Journal v. United States, 342 U.S. 143 (1951). Associated Press v. United States, 326 U.S. 131 (1945).

148.   Miami Herald Publishing Co. v. Tornillo, 418 U.S. 241 (1974).

149.   47 U.S.C. § § 301, 315. *See generally* F.C.C. v. Pacifica Found., 438 U.S. 726 (1978) and Red Lion v. F.C.C., 438 U.S. 726 (1978).

150.   47 U.S.C. § 312(a)(7). C.B.S. v. D.N.C., 412 U.S. 94 (1973).

151.   Traditionally, a common carrier is "one who undertakes for hire to transport the goods of those who choose to employ him from place to place. He is, in general, bound to take the goods of all who offer . . . when he receives the goods, it is his duty to take all possible care of them in their passage, make due transport and safe and right delivery of them . . . at common law, a carrier . . . is in the nature of an insurer. . . ." Niagara v. Cordes, 62 U.S. 7, 22 (1858).

152.   47 U.S.C. tit. II, § § 201, 202, 223.

153.   Consent Decree in United States v. American Telephone and Telegraph, Civil Actions Nos. 74-1698, 82-0192, 82-0025, Jan. 8, 1982; Modification of Judgment, Aug. 24, 1982, U.S. District Court for the District of Columbia. *See generally* PRACTICING LAW INSTITUTE, AFTER THE AT&T SETTLEMENT, THE NEW TELECOMMUNICATIONS ERA (1982).

154.   Rowan v. U.S.P.O., 397 U.S. 728 (1970). 39 U.S.C. § 4009, Pub. L. No. 91-375; U.S.C. § § 3008, 3010.

155.   47 U.S.C. § 222 (1976), *amended by* Record Carrier Competition Act of 1981, *repealed by* Pub. L. No. 97-30, 95 Stat. 1690 (1982).

156.   58 F.C.C.2d 250, 254 (1976); F.C.C. Docket No. 19660; *see generally* D. SCHILLER, *supra* note 5, at 157–68. *See also in re* Regulatory Policies Concerning the Provision of Domestic Public Message Services by Entities other than Western Union Telegraph Company and Proposed Amendments to Parts 63 and 64 of the Commission's Rules, 75 F.C.C. 2d 345, 382 (1980), and *Hearings on S. 271, The International Record Carrier Competition Act of 1981; Before the Subcommittee on Communications of the Senate Committee on Commerce and Science,* (1981).

157.   47 C.F.R. § 76, 37 Fed. Reg. 3252 (Feb. 12, 1972) 36 F.C.C.2d 143 (1972).

158.   Midwest Video v. F.C.C., 517 F.2d 1025 (8th Cir. 1978), *aff'd,* 440 U.S. 689 (1979).

159.   *In re* Establishment of Domestic Communications Satellite Facilities by Non-governmental Entities, 35 F.C.C.2d 844 (1972).

160. *See infra.*, Section III.

161. Neustadt, Skall, & M. Hammer, *The Regulation of Electronic Publishing*, 33 FED. COM. L.J. 331 (1981).

162. *Id.* at 367.

163. *See* Filartiga v. Pena-Irala, 630 F.2d 876, 883–85 (2d Cir. 1980) in which the United States Court of Appeals for the Second Circuit held that "deliberate torture perpetrated under color of official authority violates universally accepted norms of the international law of human rights, regardless of the nationality of the parties. Thus, whenever an alleged torturer is found and served with process by an alien within our borders [the Judiciary Act] provides federal jurisdiction." *Id.* at 878.

164. G.A. Res. 217, 3 U.N. GAOR, U.N. Doc. 1/777 (1948).

165. *See supra* note 163.

166. Art. 19, G.A. Res. 2200, 21 U.N. GAOR Supp. (no. 16) at 52, U.N. Doc. A/6316 (1966). U.S. adherence is not fully established since the Senate has not yet ratified the President's signature. *See* L. Henkin, *Rights: American and Human*, 79 COLUM. L. REV. 405, 423–24 (1979).

167. The pertinent language in the covenant is: "Everyone shall have the right to freedom of expression; this right shall include freedom to seek, receive and impart information and ideas of all kinds, regardless of frontiers, either orally, in writing or in print, in the form of art, or through any other media of his choice." International Covenant on Civil and Political Rights, G.A. Res. 2200, 21 U.N. GAOR Supp. (No. 16) at art. 19 (2). *See* Feldman, *supra* note 144, at 87–90. "The author believes a right to communicate already exists under international law that embraces . . . transborder data flows."

168. ITU Convention, Oct. 25, 1973, Malaga-Torremolinos, 28 U.S.T. 2495, T.I.A.S. No. 8572.

169. Treaty of Friendship, Commerce and Navigation, Oct. 29, 1954, United States-West Germany, art. II (4), 7 U.S.T. 1839, 1842, T.I.A.S. No. 3593.

170. *See* ITU Convention, *supra* note 168, at art. 19.

171. See text accompanying notes 24 and 25.

172. G.A. Res. 217-3 U.N. GAOR, at art. 29, U.N. Doc. 1/777 (1948).

173. Beyond the Global Village, Address on World Communications Day, United Nations, New York, (May 17, 1983).

174. M. Feldman and D. Garcia, *supra* note 17, at 8–10.

175. W. Fishman, *supra* note 9, at 14–15. *See also infra*, Beach and Marks, chapter 10.

176. M. Feldman, *supra* note 144, at 94.

177. The F.C.C. defined "basic computer services" as a "pure transmission capability over a communication path that is virtually transparent in terms of its interactions with the customer supplied information." 77 F.C.C.2d 384; 420 (1980) (Second Computer Inquiry); 84 F.C.C.2d 50 (1980) (Reconsideration Order); 84 F.C.C.2d 512 (1981) (Further Reconsideration Order).

178. The F.C.C. defines "enhanced services" to be "all services offered over common carrier transmission facilities used in interstate communications, which employ computer processing applications that act on the format, content, code, protocol or similar aspects of the subscriber's transmitted information; provide the subscriber additional, different, or restructured information, or involve subscriber interaction with stored informaion." Procedures of Implementing the Detariffing of Customer Premises Equipment and Enhanced Services, 89 F.C.C.2d 694, 694 n.1 (1982) (Second Computer Inquiry).

179. E.g., the United Kingdom and Japan, particularly. TELECOMMUNICATIONS POLICY COUNCIL (Japan) A VISION OF TELECOMMUNICATION IN THE 80S (August 1981).

180. CBS Evening News, Jan. 19, 1983.

181. *But see* the Antarctic Treaty, 12 U.S.T. 794, T.I.A.S. No. 4780, 402 U.N.T.S. 71.

182. *Compare* Convention on International Civil Aviation, Dec. 7, 1944, art. 6, 61 Stat. 1180, T.I.A.S. No. 1591, 15 U.N.T.S. 295, 3 Bevans 944 ("The contracting States recognize that every State has complete and exclusive sovereignty over the airspace above its territory.") *with* Treaty on Outer Space, Jan. 27, 1967, United States-United Kingdom-U.S.S.R., art. 2, 18 U.S.T. 2410, 2413, T.I.A.S. No. 6347, 610 U.N.T.S. 205 ("Outer space, including the moon and other celestial bodies, is not subject to national appropriation by claim of sovereignty, by means of use or occupation, or by any other means."). States have exclusive sovereignty over their land territory, but no State has sovereignty over the open sea.

183. *See, e.g.*, Glazer, *supra* note 25, at 291–93.

184. Baty. *Three Mile Limit*, 22 A.J. Int'l L. 503 (1928).

185. M. MCDOUGAL, H. LASSWELL, & I. VLASIC, LAW

AND PUBLIC ORDER IN SPACE 193–359 (1963)

186.   Resolution B.P. Final Acts of WARC 1979.

187.   1973 Plenipotentiary responding to WARC 1971 Resolution Sp. 2-1.

188.   *See* Memorandum of Martin A. Rothblatt to members of Working Group B, Space Advisory Committee to the Federal Communications Commission (Mar. 17, 1982).

189.   An accepted principle of international law does exist, however, stating that sovereign states have a right to object to transgression of their territory by offensive radio waves through protest or jamming. Estep & Kearse, *Space Communications and the Law* 60 MICH. L. Rev. 873, 876 (1963).

190.   For scholarly discussions of the Lex Mercatoria, see SANBORN, ORIGINS OF THE EARLY ENGLISH MARITIME AND COMMERICAL LAWS (1930); Teetor, *England's Earliest Treatise on the Law Merchant,"* 6 AM. J. LEGAL HIST. 178 (1962).

191.   Sono, *Sovereignty, This Strange Thing: Its Impact on Global Economic Order*, 9 GA. J. INT'L & COMP. L. 549 (1979).

192.   *E.g.*, A. Madec, *Economic and Legal Aspects of Transborder Data Flows*, OECD Doc. EST I/ICCP 80.26 (1980), *cited in* Eger, *The Global Phenomenon of Teleinformatics: An Introduction*, 14 CORNELL INT'L L.J. 209 & N. 26 (1981).

193.   I. POOL, TECHNOLOGIES OF FREEDOM (Cambridge, Mass.: Harvard University Press, 1983); Theberge, *UNESCO's New World Information Order: Colliding with First Amendment Values*, 67 A.B.A. J. 716 (1981); L. Susman *The Western World and the Third World's Challenge*, in CRISIS IN INTERNATIONAL NEWS POLICIES AND PROSPECTS 17–20 (Richstad & Anderson eds., 1981).

194.   F. Hondius, *The Legal Regulation of Information and Data Processing*, INT'L INST. COM. ISSUES COM., no. 2, at 29 (1978); Groshan, *Transnational Data Flows: Is the Idea of an International Legal Regime Relevant in Establishing Multilateral Controls and Legal Norms?*, 15 LAW/TECHNOLOGY 1 (1982); Bing report, *supra* note 16.

195.   Brussels Mandate, An Alliance for World Communications and Information, Minutes of the London Meeting (June 15–16, 1978).

196.   A. SMITH, THE GEOPOLITICS OF INFORMATION, HOW WESTERN CULTURE DOMINATES THE WORLD (New York: Oxford University Press, 1980); D. SCHILLER, COMMUNICATIONS AND CULTURAL DOMINANCE 39–40 (White Plains, N.Y.: International Arts and Sciences Press, 1976).

197.   Encryption is the encoding of a signal so that interceptors are unable to understand the transmission without the "key" that deciphers the code. For further discussion of the science of cryptology, see *supra* note 90.

198.   *See* Gardner, *Selling America in the Marketplace of Ideas*, N.Y. TIMES MAG., March 20, 1983, at 63.

199.   "The 'New World Information Order' has been heralded by the United Nations Educational, Scientific, and Cultural Organization (UNESCO) as an attempt to facilitate the free flow of information and condemned by journalists as a step toward legitimizing government control and censorship of the press." Theberge, *supra* note 193, at 714. *See also* Christol, *International Satellite Communications and the New Information Order*, 8 SYRACUSE J. INT'L L. COM. 321 (1981). The N.W.I.O. idea has emerged gradually through UNESCO conferences; it is a policy that promotes development of national communications infrastructures, as opposed to private sector control of communications. THEBERGE, *supra* note 193, at 716.

200.   MINISTRY OF DEFENSE (Sweden) THE VULNERABILITY OF COMPUTERIZED SOCIETY (1979), Freese, *The Vulnerability of Computerized Society*, 5 TRANSNAT'L DATA REP. 21 (1982). COMMISSION ON NEW INFORMATION TECHNOLOGY (Sweden) NEW VIEWS: COMPUTERS AND NEW MEDIA—ANXIETY AND HOPES (1979).

201.   MASUDA, *supra* note 7; RESEARCH INSTITUTE OF TELECOMMUNICATIONS AND ECONOMICS, A VISION OF TELECOMMUNICATIONS IN THE EIGHTIES (1982).

202.   S. NORA & A. MINC, REPORT ON THE COMPUTERIZATION OF SOCIETY, BOARD OF FINANCIAL EXAMINERS TO THE PRESIDENT OF FRANCE, 20 JANUARY 1978 (Cambridge, Mass.: MIT Press, 1980).

203.   Brizida, *The Brazilian Transborder Data Flow Policy*, 4 TRANSNAT'L DATA REP., no. 3, at 19 (1981).

204.   *See* Ramsey, *supra* note 132, at 283–84.

205.   CONSULTATIVE COMMITTEE ON THE IMPLICATIONS OF TELECOMMUNICATIONS FOR CANADIAN SOCIETY, CLYNE REPORT (1979); Ostry (Deputy Minister of Communications), *Telecommunications in Canada: Today, Tomorrow and Next Week?,"* 4 INTERMEDIA. July 1979, at 6; O. Ganley, *Political Aspects of Communications*

and Information Resources in Canada, 1 Information Soc'y, no. 1, (1981), at 79.

206.   *See* Declaration of Mexico on Informatics, Development, and Peace, June 22–23, 1981; *See also* Intergovernmental Bureau for Informatics, *supra* note 14.

207.   S. McBride, *supra* note 35.

208.   International Chamber of Commerce, Commission on Computing, Telecommunications and Information Policies, Working Party on Telecommunications, The Liberalization of Telecommunication Services—Needs and Limits (March 1982).

209.   The major exception is the very substantial investment in both time and money in the development of the INTELSAT global system of information transport. The World Communication Year, initiated by the ITU, may also be a major thrust in the direction of fomenting interest in global perspectives.

210.   D. Bell, The Matching of Scales, The Louis G. Cowan Lecture of the International Institute of Communications (London, 1979).

211.   Although the author has developed these principles independently, a surprising similarity exists between those enunciated in this chapter and the principles espoused by Licklider and Vezza. *Compare Branscomb, Principles for Global Telecommunications Systems,* in World Communications: A Handbook 185 (G. Gerbner & M. Siefert eds., New York: Longman, 1984), first enunciated in Toward a Global Communications Policy for an Interdependent World, paper given at the Annenberg Conference on World Communications, Decisions for the Eighties (May 12–14, 1980); *with* J. Licklider & A. Vezza, *Applications of Information Networks,* 66 Proceedings IEEE, November 1978 at 41.

PART I

THE GLOBAL COMMUNICATIONS ENVIRONMENT

CHAPTER 1

THE TECHNOLOGICAL ENVIRONMENT

JOSEPH N. PELTON

In the fourteenth century, Peking was the world's largest city and, as such, was some 50 square kilometers in area. Thus, one could reach the opposite extreme of the city by taking an 8-kilometer hike or, in effect, walking less that 5 miles. The transportation systems of the twentieth century have of course created vast urban amoebas spanning hundreds of miles. The need to move people and things at great expense, at inefficient speeds, and with high levels of energy consumption, is typical of "developed societies" of this century. As energy costs continue this upward surge, communications options that allow ideas and information to compensate or substitute for physical transportation will doubtlessly become more and more important (see Figure 1.1). Advanced communications technologies, such as satellites and fiber optics, which allow the transfer of information at less cost, will of course strengthen this trend (see Figure 1.2).

Certainly, the last few centuries have brought enormous changes in how we live, work, and communicate, and advances in communications have prompted much of the change. Figure 1.3 shows that we can send a one-page message some 10-million times faster than we were able to do a few hundred years ago.

There is, of course an important correlation between new service requirements and new transmission capabilities. Figure 1.4 suggests that electronic telecommunications represent an exponential growth curve in terms of both service demand and transmission

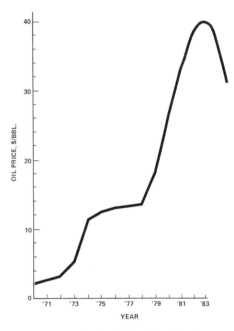

FIGURE 1.1 Cost Trends for Petroleum

capability. Faster transmission rates seem to stimulate higher levels of service needs, and vice versa.

There are also very important correlations between telecommunications and economic development (see Figure 1.5). Conversely, there seems to be a negative

The views expressed in this article are those of the author and are not intended to reflect the official views of the International Telecommunications Satellite Organization (INTELSAT).

JOSEPH N. PELTON ● Dr. Pelton is currently the director of strategic policy of the International Telecommunications Satellite Organization (INTELSAT). He has been involved in satellite applications since 1965. He served as managing director of the executive board of the U.S. Council for World Communications Year 1983.

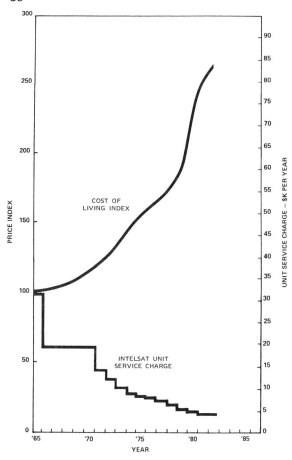

FIGURE 1.2

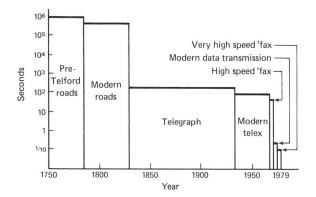

FIGURE 1.3 Progress in Telecommunications

correlation between manpower involved in agriculture versus economic prosperity, as measured in telephones per capita (see Figure 1.6). This is true for several reasons, including the relatively higher economic productivity levels for industry and manufacturing, the strong multiplier effect resulting from investment in telephones, the low level of use of technology and telecommunications in traditional farming, and especially the low economic yield of labor-intensive agriculture.

Finally, before trying to make some sense out of this maze of facts and figures, let's examine Figure 1.7, which shows a correlation, or rather, a noncorrelation between the cost of robotics device operation in industry versus the cost of labor in industry. This graph indicates that robotics are already remarkably more cost effective than U.S. workers, in terms of cost per hour. Perhaps more surprisingly, this graph shows that in the foreseeable future the same results will also be true for so-called "labor-cheap" countries such as Taiwan, the Republic of Korea, Malaysia, Brazil, and the like.

What then do all these facts and figures mean, when considered as a whole? Let's reflect upon some key facts: (1) the cost of automation and intelligent robotics industrial production is dropping; (2) the importance of telecommunications and information services is increasing, as reflected in both investments and employment levels; (3) the cost efficiency of information and telecommunications is growing at an exponential rate in contrast to most other services and products where the cost is being driven upward with inflationary cost spirals. This contrast is particularly noticeable when comparisons are made to the economics of conventional energy production and labor-intensive enterprises; and, finally, (4) the patterns of international investment, the rise of multinational enterprises, and the cost efficiency of worldwide global networks all indicate the development of a global economic enterprise based upon geographic decentralization and functional distribution of effort across national lines, even though the hub of centralized management and policy control may be located halfway around the world.

In short, the world of global talk and global think is arriving in a big way—at least for a significant proportion of the world's population. The current and perhaps growing gap between those who inhabit the world of the electronic future and those who do not could well become a dangerous one. In the 1950s the developing countries, with two-thirds of the world's population, had

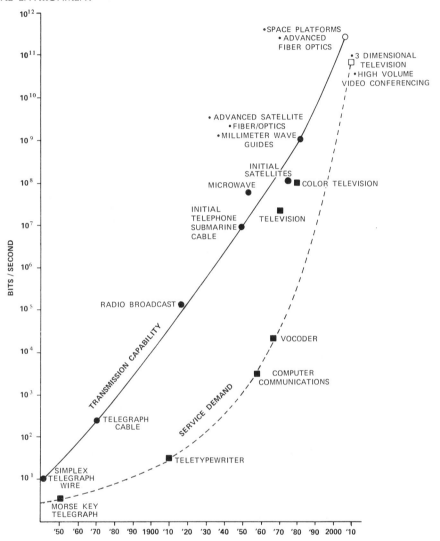

FIGURE 1.4 150 Year Look at Development of Telecommunications (Service Demand vs. Transmission Capability)

over 30 percent of the world trade; today that proportion has shrunk to 17 percent. Should this trend continue, then the problem of an "information and communications gap," as defined in terms of trade, could become increasingly troublesome.

If current patterns of technical development and global trade continue, we can expect to see (1) the rapid emergence of global computer-communications networks and robotics as two of the most key elements in world economic activity; (2) a rise in technological underemployment and skill loss in an increasing number of countries, with legislative reactions not far behind; (3) long-term conversion from conventional petrochemical energy sources to technology-intensive recyclable energy sources or "smart" energy production (this should also serve to promote the growth of newly

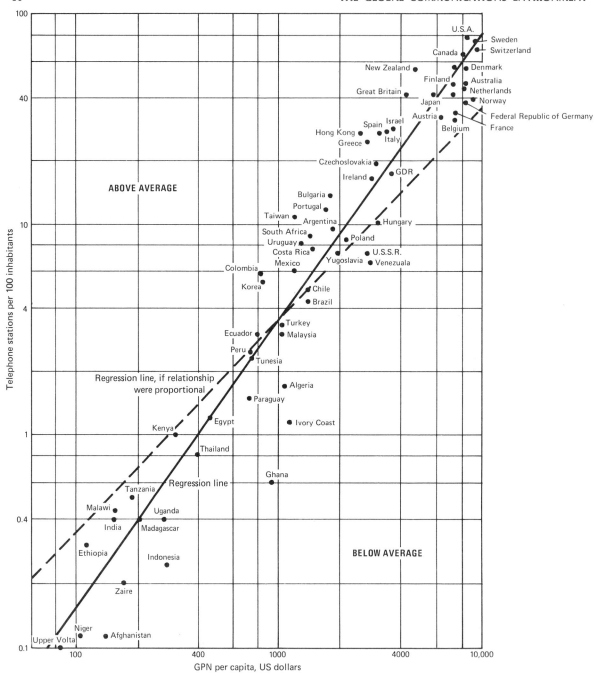

FIGURE 1.5   Correlation of Telephone Stations and GNP: Status as of January 1, 1978

AGRICULTURAL ACTIVITY AS PERCENTAGE OF TOTAL GNP	CORRESPONDING TELEPHONE DENSITY
70%	2% or Less
50%	10% or Less
Less than 2%	Up to 70%

FIGURE 1.6

emerging gigantic "telecomputerenergetics" enterprises); and (4) growth of technology enclaves around resource-rich areas (perhaps we will even see the emergence of extraterritorial floating island enclaves operated by multidestinational enterprises.[1]

Current technology trends suggest that the entire fabric and structure of society—in terms of how we work, live, and relax—is changing. The design and functions of our cities, the decisions as to where industry is located, the process by which we manufacture products, the way we grow food, how services are offered and distributed—the very nature of our lifestyles will all be dramatically affected by what might be called our "future electronic environment."

But the future electronic environment does not necessarily apply to everyone. It is far from clear the extent to which modern electronic communications and energy technology will impact upon the standard of living and societal paths for developing, in contrast to developed, countries. Figure 1.8 shows the startling contrast that exists between the Organization for Economic Cooperation and Development (OECD) member countries and the rest of the world. If we were to assume that the "global village" consisted of 1,000 people, 125 would live in the OECD countries. We would find that, of the remaining 875 villagers, over 500 would suffer from malnutrition. The "other" 875 villagers would also have access to only 15 telephones and a handful of main-frame computers. The cost of upgrading telephone service for the remainder of the global village in order that it would be comparable to OECD standards (at $2,000 per installed telephone line) would be a staggering $8 trillion, or almost equivalent to the total gross national product of the world for almost a year.

Clearly, enormous shifts in economic investments would have to occur if indeed the entire world were to become a global electronic village. There is, of course, an important subsidiary question: What are the economic, social, and political implications if the new electronic environment being created for the affluent "first world" is largely isolated from the trends toward

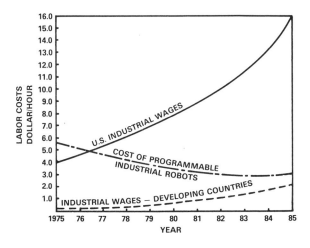

FIGURE 1.7 Human Labor vs. Robots

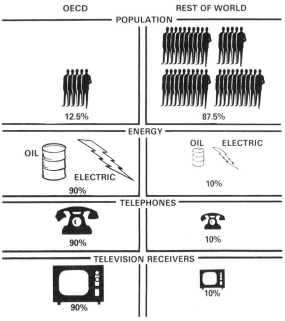

FIGURE 1.8 Global Village: 1981

economic and technical progress in the so-called Third World countries? Let's focus, for the purpose of illustration, on the pace of change for the world at large, as contrasted to the U.S.

Let's briefly review how things were in 1964, how they are today, and how we might find them in the year 2000. Figure 1.9 shows us a picture of quite remarkable change, especially in the field of communications. Over the 36-year period international communications capabilities will have increased a thousand fold.

In 1964 the highest capacity transoceanic communications facilities were the TAT-3 cable across the Atlantic and the TRANSPAC cable across the Pacific Ocean. Each had a total capacity of only 138 3-KHz telephone circuits and indeed had only been in operation a few years. It is surprising to some that the first

Atlantic telephone cable was laid as recently as 1956— less than 30 years ago.

The era of commercial satellite communications began in 1965. In that year the initial U.S. defense communications satellite system and the Soviet Molniya domestic communications satellite system were both deployed in medium-orbit operation. More significantly, however, the first INTELSAT satellite (*Early Bird*) was launched in April of that year. *Early Bird* doubled telephone capacity between the U.S. and Europe and for the first time enabled live television transmissions to occur. Thus, 1965 marked the birth of the age of global television. Not as well understood is the fact that "the age of supertribalization" also began from this time as well. Certainly, the rapid flow of electronic information at low cost and with high reliability serves to create a

FIGURE 1.9   The U.S. and the World: In the Years 1964, 1982, and 2000

INDICATOR	1964	1982	2000 (Projected)
Population (World)	3,100 Million	4,300 Million	6,000 Million
Population (U.S.)	190 Million (6.0%)	235 Million (5.5%)	290 Million (4.8%)
Electrical Power (World)	3,000 Billion Kwh	8,500 Billion Kwh	24,000 Billion Kwh
Electrical Power (U.S.)	1,100 Billion Kwh (36.1%)	2,250 Billion Kwh (26.4%)	4,600 Billion Kwh (19.1%)
Telephones (World)	175 Million	475 Million	1,630 Million
Telephones (U.S.)	80 Million (45.7%)	175 Million (37.1%)	422 Million (25.9%)
World Transoceanic Telephony Service*	678 Voice Circuits	40,000 Voice Circuits	Equivalent of 2,000,000 Voice Circuits
U.S. Transoceanic Telephony Service*	330 Voice Circuits (48.7%)	9,200 Voice Circuits (23%)	175,000 Voice Circuits (21.8%)
Individual Submarine Cable Capacity	128 Telephone Circuits	4,000 Telephone Circuits	150,000–200,000 Telephone Circuits
Individual Satellite Capacity (International)	240 Telephone Circuits (1965)	12,000 Telephone Circuits Plus 2 Color TV Channels	100,000–300,000 Telephone Circuits

*In operational full-time service

more unified and uniform world. Cultural differences, language barriers, national marketing strategies, and almost everything else are enormously influenced by electronic global communications.

Through the global satellite communications system, global TV has become a reality. Five hundred million people watched the moon landing in 1969 and a billion people saw at least some part of the 1976 Summer Olympics in Montreal. In 1984, perhaps 2 billion people saw the Los Angeles Olympics. Similar dramatic shifts have occurred in the field of computers during the same time period. Growth in the memory capability of computer disk storage devices has averaged over 50 percent per annum, growing from 5.4 trillion terabytes of memory in 1975 to 100 trillion terabytes in 1982. By the mid-to-late 1980s, the U.S. computer industry will be manufacturing sufficient quantities of processors, memory and logic circuits to be able to produce a mainframe computer for one out of every two Americans. Obviously, this is not going to be the case. Instead, we will see dozens of microprocessors hidden inside mass consumer goods, such as television sets, toys, automobiles, household appliances, security systems, etc. Recently, an enterprising British group even announced the invention of an "intelligent brassiere." This is a personal body temperature monitoring device that aids in the use of the rhythm method of birth control. I'll not explain further how it operates.

The principal focus for our purposes, however, should be on host mainframe devices tied into communications networks that can support a large number of mini- and microcomputers. Figure 1.10 shows the rapid growth of mainframe computers and computer chip capacities, even on a logarithmic scale.

The combination of computer and advanced communications networks today represents the leading edge of technology and, as such, is seen by many as a threat and an assault on traditional values. Discussion of this topic therefore must consider the subjective as well as objective aspects of the field. Tariff policies, copyright protection, patent and date rights, technical standards, trade agreements, etc.—all of these subjects and more, as they relate to computer communications networks, must be seen in a broader aspect. The issue of whether or not there should be a 7 or 8 bit companding law or whether TDMA systems should be plesiosynchronous or not can mean millions of dollars of profit or loss. Commercial advantage, market protection, regional in-

terest, and more are frequently involved in "technical decisions." An attempt to broadly categorize some of the key conflicting values in a technologically "modernizing" world is provided in Figure 1.11.

If the pattern of change has seemed rapid in the past, the future prospects seem even more challenging. To appreciate the nature of our changing world, let's look at the dimensions of the world of global talk, as measured by digital communications or bits per second. Thirty to 40 bits per second is equivalent to one word per second. Most people, therefore, talk at a rate of around 100 bits per second, when measured in terms of written text.

Figures 1.12 and 1.13 show us the changing dimensions of our "electronic world." An advanced communications satellite or fiber optic system can today send a billion bits of information a second; today's fastest computers can also process data at this rate as well. Sending data at a gigabit/second (which is 50 times the capability of 20 years ago), it should be noted, is the equivalent of transmitting the complete *Encyclopaedia Britannica* six times a minute.

But this is just the early stages of the digital communications revolution. In another 20 years, today's capabilities will seem like a snail's pace, as data transmission rates of perhaps 100 gigabits per second are realized. But let's scale these data rates to human dimensions. A typical fairly literate person processes about 650,000,000 words, or about 20 billion bits of information in a lifetime. If we equate 20 billion bits to a Typical Information Use Per Lifetime (TIUPIL), we find that an INTELSAT VI satellite scheduled to be launched in 1986 could transmit 9 TIUPIL in a minute. Going a step further into the future, let's assume that a global network of 10 satellites were available in the year 2000 and that each we capable of transmitting at 100 gigabits per second and thus a system capability of a terabit per second were available. This network could send 31.5 quintillion bits of information, or 2.62 GHIUDs per year—a GHIUD, incidentally, is Global Human Information Use Per Decade.

Other than the obvious answer that these calculations are somewhat between far-fetched and mad, what does this suggest? My own answer is first that communications in the year 2000 will be largely machine-to-machine—perhaps more than 90 percent so. Specifically, you will see computer-to-computer communications, or even artificial intelligence-to-artificial intelligence, as the primary means of information relay and storage.

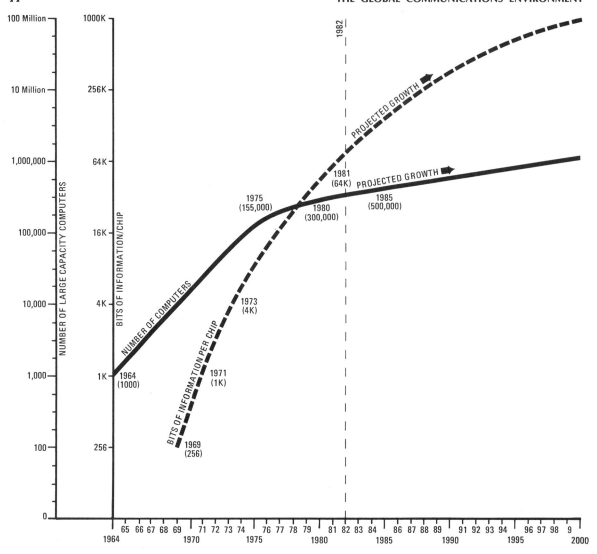

FIGURE 1.10   Computer Trends: 1964–2000

Secondly, we will have to cope with an enormous information overload problem. Personal computers that act as mailman, secretary, librarian, and file clerk will be necessary for coping with information diarrhea. The British Library's ASK program and the new computer program dubbed the "Last One" are perhaps a significant step in developing the essential software.[2] The protection of personal privacy will be, of course, extremely difficult to achieve in such an environment.

What then is the pattern that we can see for the future electronic world, in terms of new developments, as well as significant problems to be solved? As Leonard Marks, former director of the U.S. Information Agency, put it:

> Global electronic networks . . . will pose realistic questions about information flow and cultural integrity . . . . These networks will move massive amounts of information through high-speed circuits across national bound-

Centralized Standards	vs.	Diversity; Multiple Alternatives; Frequent Need for Standards Conversion
Efficiency (measured in maximum economic yield per year)	vs.	Inefficiency; Economic Waste; Redundancy; Survival Margin; Beauty and other Subjective Values
Exponential Growth in Size and Complexity of Human Industrial Systems	vs.	Long Term Survivability; Human Scale; S-Curve Type Economic Expansion
Very Large and Increasing Global Population	vs.	Shrinking or stable Global Population
Open, Competitive Markets and Global Society	vs.	Protected Markets, Protected Cultures
Mathematical/Rational	vs.	Emotional, Altruistic and Subjective Values
Universal Systems (Large, highly integrated systems with centralized control and management)	vs.	Non-Universal Systems (Small systems and subsystems with "coordinated," "democratic" or "negotiated" controls, rules or decision-making)

FIGURE 1.11   Opposing Value Systems for a 21st Century Technological World

FIGURE 1.12   Dimensions of Global Talk I
— Kilobit (10^3 Bits/Second)
— Megabit (10^6 Bits/Second)
— Gigabit (10^9 Bits/Second)
— Terabit (10^{12} Bits/Second)

FIGURE 1.13   Dimensions of Global Talk II

Medium Speed Data Channel	9.6 Kilobits/Second
Digital Voice	50 Kilobits/Second
Teleconference Channel	3 Megabits/Second
Digital TV	40 Megabits/Second
Advanced Communications Satellite	1 Gigabit/Second
TIUPILS	20 Gigabits/Second
HOLOVISION	1 Terabit/Second
GHIUDS	12 million Terabits/Second

aries. Moreover, they will be effectively beyond the reach of the traditional forms of censorship and control. The only way to "censor" an electronic network moving . . . 648 million bits per second is literally to pull the plug. The international extension of electronic mail transmission, data-packet networks and information-bank retrieval systems in future years will have considerably more effect on national cultures than any direct broadcast systems.[3]

Alvin Toffler foresees a coming revolutionary transition that he calls the "third wave of the industrial age." This image is, I believe, a misleading one. Rather, it would seem that we are riding a mounting tidal wave of change. We are living in an age of rapidly increasing "future compression." Problems and issues related to our new technologies are listed in Figure 1.14.

Indeed, if we were to view the 5-million-year history since Australopithecus man as being one single supermonth, the results would be startling (see Figure 1.15).

FIGURE 1.14   Developments by the Year 2000 and the Problems They Pose

DEVELOPMENTS	POTENTIAL ISSUES
1. Higher Transmission Rates (up to 100 gigabits per second using laser and millimeter wave communications satellites, space platforms, advanced digital modulation and compression techniques).	a. Information overload. b. Obsolescence of equipment/depreciation schedules. c. Centralization vs decentralization (both geographic and functional).
2. Rapid Growth of New Video Services & International Business Communications Networks (videoconferencing, high resolution TV, multiple rastered TV, dedicated corporate networks for all forms of communications).	a. Congestion of orbital arc in geosynchronous orbit. b. Satellite proliferation. c. Obsolescence of earth segment equipment. d. Limited system interconnectivity and network breakdowns. e. Developing countries' demands for New World Information Order. Reforms to status quo. Perceived extravagance in face of unmet needs of third world. f. Increased national trade protection in telecommunications area. g. National telecommunications monopolies' resistance to external "competition" and to customer-premise services. h. Emergence of electronic crime as a major problem (e.g., data banks, embezzlement, espionage).
3. Rapid Growth of Robotics and Artificial Intelligence in Global Industries Connected by Computer Networks. High-Speed Machine-to-Machine Communications.	a. Technological unemployment, underemployment, and skill loss. b. Redefining of economic values of work. New work ethics. c. National political resistance to automation within developed and developing countries. d. Personal privacy. e. Man-machine interface; psychological feelings of personal worth. f. Sabotage and terrorism. g. Questioning of Industrial Age values.
4. Development of New Telecity and Extraterritorial Corporate States (e.g., free trade zones, such as in Sudan; floating, docked industrial units in offshore ocean locations; space platforms; moon colonies).	a. Redefinition of roles and fiscal responsibilities of corporations and governments. b. Force of international and national laws for extraterritorial bodies, oceans, polar regions and subterranean areas of earth. c. Status and financing of new urban infrastructure, e.g., transportation, computer and communications networks; power and energy; utilities; etc.
5. Continued/Perhaps Increased Economic and Technological Gaps Between Developed and Developing Countries.	a. War, terrorism, sabotage. b. Appropriate role of media and information flow. c. Appropriate international investment and marketing strategies. d. Need for new institutions and greater need for international law with effective sanctions.
6. Major challenges to Economic Growth and Prosperity Posed by the Limits of Earth Resources, Environment and Ecology. The "S-Curve" Limits of Growth.	a. Effective strategies for space and the oceans. b. Relationships among countries, particularly developed, vis-a-vis, developing. c. Relationships among international agencies, governments and multinational enterprises. d. Effective incentives for "recycling economy" and conservation.

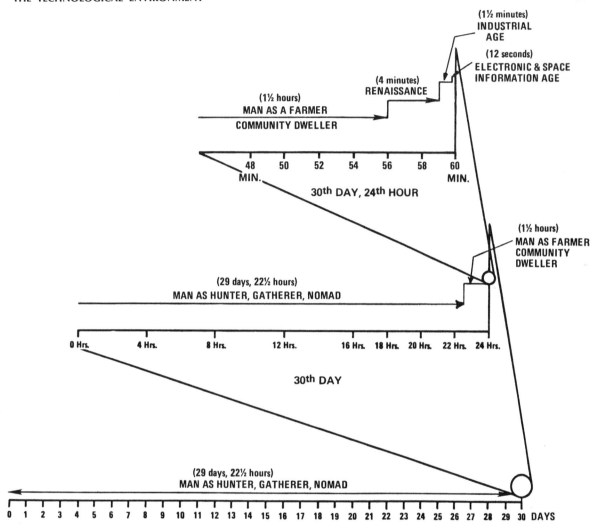

FIGURE 1.15 History of Man Depicted as a Supermonth

Only at 9:30 p.m. on the last day of the month did man discover agriculture and invent the city. At 11:56 p.m. comes the Renaissance and the creation of scientific knowledge. This is the time of creation of what Pierre Theilhard de Chardin characterizes as the "noosphere—the age of scientific knowledge." The age of electronic computers, space travel, satellites, and television represents only the last 12 seconds of the supermonth. within the next 60 seconds of supermonth time (or the interval from now until the 22nd century), the scope of change that mankind will experience will be stupendous, rewarding, frightening, and awe-inspiring. Perhaps we will see within this time the emergence of a new intelligent species. The only thing that is certain is that the issues raised by our technological and social development should be sufficient to keep a very large number of legislators and attorneys actively employed for some time to come.

NOTES

1.   For further information on the above projections, see J. Pelton, Global Talk (Alphen aan den Rijn, The Netherlands: Sitjthoff & Noordhoff, 1981). Also *see Artificial Islands Could Help Third World,* New Scientist, Nov. 26, 1981, at 603.

2.   ASK stands for "Asynchronous State of Knowledge." This is a computer program designed to allow a researcher to "discuss" his research needs with a computer, allow the computer to diagram the problem and ask clarifying questions, conduct a search of literature, and then help explain and interpret the results. See N. N. Belkin & R. N. Oddy, Design Study for an Anomalous State of Knowledge (ASK) Based Information Retrieval System (The British Library, 1981). For information about the "Last One," an English-instructable computer program that prepares basic utility-type computer programs through human commands, see *A Terminal Case for Programmers,* New Scientist, Aug. 13, 1981, at 410.

3.   L. Marks, International Conflict and the Free Flow of Information in Control of the Direct Broadcast Satellite, Values in Conflict 66 (Palo Alto, Cal.: Aspen Institute Program on Communications and Society, 1974).

Chapter 2

COMPUTERS AND THE INFORMATION INDUSTRY

RONALD W. BROWN

The late Professor Ithiel de Sola Pool of MIT once posed the provocative question: "Should anyone be concerned with what goes on between consenting computers?" For a variety of reasons, the answer to this question is emphatically *yes*. One of these reasons is that communication between consenting computers will be an essential requirement of the "office of the future."

The office of the future—which is in fact emerging today—can be seen as an "integrated services digital network[1]" (ISDN; see Figure 2.1) in which voice, text, image, and data information will be sent and received in digital form in one network. As described by Phillip Whittaker of Satellite Business Systems, the office of the future is characterized by word processing and text editing systems, with remote terminals in a communications network, with computers talking to computers at megabits per second, with video conferencing networks bringing people together quickly and conveniently to solve problems and to make decisions regardless of physical location. In such an office, there are a range of new, accessible management information systems enhancing the efficiency of modern business operations.

However, for computers to communicate effectively in this office, and for the office to exist internationally, significant technical, legal, and regulatory policy questions will first have to be resolved.

In the technical area, two major international standardizing bodies for telecommunications, the International Telecommunication Union's (ITU) International Telephone and Telegraph Consultative Committee, and the European Conference of Post and Telecommunications, have groups studying principles and guidelines for ISDNs. Also, the American National Standards Institute has 19 subcommittees working on various standards for computerized information systems like those that will be needed in the office of the future. In the legal and regulatory areas, Congress, the Federal Communications Commission, and the courts, continue to focus on the rules of competition that will affect what will be provided by whom in the office of the future.

Communication between consenting computers may also be vital to the development of what Hans P. Gassman, head of the Information Computer and Communications Policy Division in the Organization for Economic Cooperation and Development Secretariat, describes as "information entrepreneurs, marketing information products and services," in something called "data trade." AT&T Information Systems is a new entrant into data trade, reported to have started up with $40 million in assets. AT&T stated in full page newspaper ads that it "intends to do for data what Alexander Graham Bell did for voice." Only time and the marketplace will measure the impact of data traders like AT&T Information Systems in expanding and developing our new information frontier. For now, it is interesting to note that Gassman believes computer linkage and communications networks used by data traders will, like

RONALD WELLINGTON BROWN • Mr. Brown is staff counsel, consumer products and services, at the world headquarters of ITT Corporation.

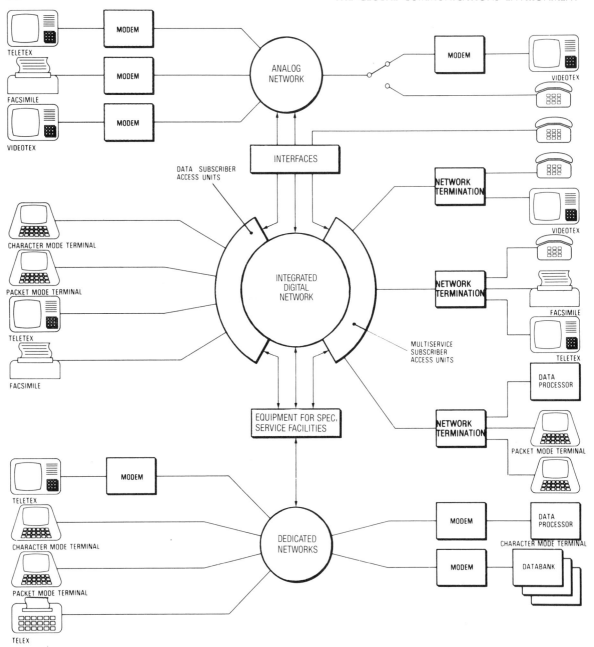

FIGURE 2.1 Information Delivery in an Integrated Services Network

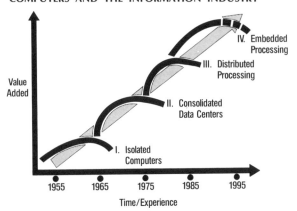

FIGURE 2.2   Technological Change

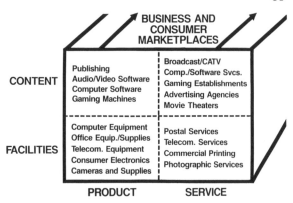

FIGURE 2.3   The Information Industry Today Embraces What Used to Be Many Separate Businesses

waterways, roads, and other historical transportation systems, provide important infrastructures for economic growth and development. Recent Booz Allen & Hamilton research seems to echo Gassman's words in describing our present information industries.

Mr. Harvey L. Poppel, a senior vice-president and director of this major consulting firm's information industry practice, has written extensively on the emerging information society; he defines the information industry upon which such society is based as including those firms which not only produce information, but those which also produce the facilities to process, store and distribute it. As of June 1982, AT&T, IBM, GTE, Eastman Kodak, Phillips, Matsushita, ITT, Xerox, Bell Canada, and RCA were identified by Booz Allen as the top 10 firms in the information industry. These firms generated annual information revenues of more than $145 billion, just under one-fourth of the global total for revenues of the information industry.

There are three characteristics of the information industry which are of interest. First, a technology called "embedded processing" binds the industry together (see Figure 2.2).[2] Embedded processing is nothing more than a form of applied information technology. The office of the future operating in an ISDN environment is one example of the use of embedded processing. An automated banking machine is another example. In its simplest form, this technology combines science, technology, and engineering with management techniques used in information handling and processing to produce information products and services. The last stage of

embedded processing will, according to Poppel, enable those who work in such an electronic environment to exchange information through computerized information systems and have access to electronically stored information regardless of a person's geographic location. Thus, embedded processing in an ISDN environment may provide the technological equivalent of Article 19 of the Universal Declaration of Human Rights, whose text is as follows:

> Everyone has the right to freedom of opinion and expression; this right includes the freedom to hold opinions without interference and to seek, receive and impart information and ideas through any media and *regardless of frontiers*. (Emphasis added.)

Second, the information industry, according to the Booz Allen research, integrates what formerly constituted many separate businesses (see Figure 2.3).[3] Note that the content output of the industry ranges from book publishing to audio/video software and computer applications software. Facilities output ranges from postal services to telecommunications services and photographic services. In some areas, however, product or service outputs are becoming alternative marketing choices.

Where existing legal protections extend to trade in products but not to trade in services, there may be legislative pressure to extend that protection to cover information services. For example, revised S. 2094, the Reciprocal Trade and Investment Act of 1982,[4] and approximately 12 bills introduced in the House of

Representatives, recognized and in part attempted to correct the disparity in legal protections applicable to goods and services in international trade. Much of this legislative activity attempted to clarify or expand the President's authority under Section 301 of the Trade Act of 1974[5] to take retaliatory action, if he determined that a foreign nation's trade practices were unjustifiable, unreasonable, or discriminatory. S. 2094 mandated two primary negotiating objectives with respect to trade in services, foreign direct investment and high technology products. Those objectives were (1) reduction or elimination of barriers to, or distortions of, international trade and services, and (2) the development of internationally agreed upon rules, including those for settlement procedures. In addition, the definition of what constituted a barrier included an express provision in S. 2094 covering restrictions on the transfer of information or on the use of data processing facilities within a country. Another example under Section 301 is worth noting.

Since Section 301 of the Trade Act came into force, 31 investigations have been initiated of which 14 cases are still pending. Of the pending cases, the only one which has produced presidential action under the Trade Act was the one which directly involved international communication of information. In that case, U.S. broadcasters filed a petition concerning Canadian Bill C-58, which amended Canadian tax law to deny tax deductions to Canadian taxpayers who purchased advertising services from U.S. broadcasters if those advertisements were directed at Canadian markets.

Finally, the Booz Allen research into the information industry indicates that this industry is not highly concentrated. The top 10 firms account for only 25% of the world market, and U. S. firms constitute 60 of the top 100 information industry firms worldwide (see Figure 2.4).[6]

It is also important to understand the convergence of communications and computer technology, which contributes to the electronic environment in which the office of the future will be operating. In an advertisement[7] in the *Financial Times* (see Figure 2.5), Dr. Koshi Kobiyashi, chairman of the board of the Nippon Electric Company in Japan, described communications, computers, and microelectronics as the three major foundations of information technology underlying the growth of the information industry and emerging information societies. Just as computers and communications are merging into what is now often called telematics, Dr.

U.S.	60
JAPAN	17
GERMANY	8
U.K.	5
FRANCE	4
ALL OTHERS	6
	100

FIGURE 2.4 Where Are the Top Firms?

Kobiyashi believes that there will be something called "a unified structure of software and hardware, with the result that software will be treated like intellectual merchandise." Obviously, such merchandise could become another commodity in "data trade."

Dr. Kobiyashi believes that we also should be concerned with the dialogue between consenting computers because what they are capable of achieving depends upon their software. These software systems instruct the computers what to do. It has been projected that in the five-year period between 1981 through 1986, expenditures in the U.S. information services market, which includes such software products, is expected to grow from $3.6 billion to $15.2 billion, with an average annual compound growth rate of 33%.

Forms of legal protection for applications software, for computer utility programs, for data bases and information technologies of this expanding information marketplace will become increasingly important for lawyers and their business clients to understand. However, before technical and legal barriers are erected which may impede the development of global communications, it is imperative that a thorough examination of the issues arising from the information marketplace be made.

What has gone on between consenting computers has produced a strange progeny—transborder data flow (TDF). TDF is electronic transmission of personal or nonpersonal information across political boundaries for processing or storage in and retrieval from computer files. The complexities of TDF might lead one to think of TDF as an ugly child. Drawing on that analogy, the ugly child might say, "Well, if you had a computer for a mother, telecommunications for a father, trade and

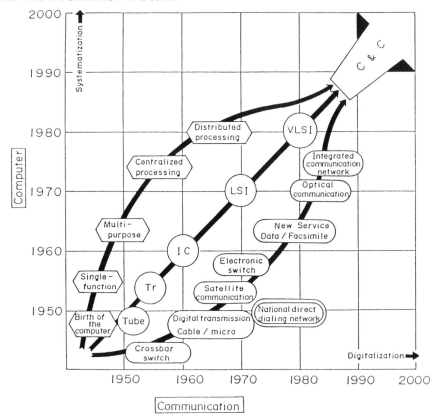

FIGURE 2.5

economic issues for a midwife, and something called a 'legal regime' as an obstetrician, you'd be not only ugly, but confused and perhaps misunderstood too." The appearance of this ugly child will improve when we understand what we are looking at, its function, genesis, and development. We will then be able to appropriately facilitate the increased exchange of information between consenting computers in an information society; a task worthy of the attention of lawyers and government officials concerned with extending the benefits of such exchange throughout the world.

NOTES

1. 56 ELECTRICAL COM. no. 1, (1981) at 10.
2. Booz Allen & Hamilton, Inc., 1 INFORMATION INSIGHTS 2 (1982).
3. *Id.*
4. S. 2094 (REP. No. 483), 97th Cong., 2d Sess. (1982).
5. 19 U.S.C. 2411(a).
6. Booz Allen & Hamilton, Inc., 2 INFORMATION INSIGHTS 1 (1982).
7. FINANCIAL TIMES, June 1, 1982, at 9, col. 1.

CHAPTER 3

INFORMATION EXCHANGE AS COMMUNICATIONS TRADE

OSWALD H. GANLEY

INTRODUCTION

Communications are becoming increasingly important both directly and indirectly as a factor in international trade, because of their abundance, their pervasiveness, and the speed with which they can be disseminated. The convergence of information technologies together with the fundamental structural changes which are occurring between and among the information industries is leading to increased international complexities.[1] Various groups are calling for a new international legal regime to deal with escalated flow of information internationally.

Is trade in information unique from other types of trade? If not, is consideration of such a legal regime justified, necessary, or even desirable?

This paper suggests a number of ways in which trade in information might be examined in an effort to determine its similarities to and differences from "ordinary" trade. In an attempt to shed light on this complicated issue, information trade items are broken down into the conduits by which they are transmitted, the content they contain, the formats in which they appear, the hardware from which they are made, and the functions they serve.

To dramatize the importance of information, a Swedish parliamentarian is reported to have proclaimed, "If Karl Marx were alive today he would not have written

Das Kapital, he would have written *Die Information*."[2] Numerous figures have been used to describe its economic importance:

> It is calculated that over the period 1965–1975, the share of information-related goods and services increased from 13 to nearly 20 percent of total OECD exports of goods and services, and from 17 to 30 percent of OECD trade in finished manufactures.[3]

The accompanying U.S. Department of Commerce chart (Figure 3.1) shows trade in services, which contains a great deal of trade in information services.[4] Not all information trade is services, and not all services are in information. But the lines on the chart are quite typical of what is happening in this dynamic area. According to a report prepared for the U.S. Departments of State and Commerce and the U.S. Trade Representative, foreign revenues of the U.S. services sector amounted to about $60 billion in 1980.[5] This is nearly two-thirds that of exports of U.S. capital equipment and about equal to U.S. exports of all food and consumer goods for that same year.

Multiple international legal and other issues are already emerging and creating difficulties in these information-related areas of trade. These issues can be expected to grow and become more complicated in

An earlier version of this paper was present at the International Networks Committee, American Bar Association, Mt. Kisco, New York, March 29, 1982. It was published by Harvard's Program on Information Resources Policy, December, 1982, [P-82-11]. (Reprinted by permission.)

OSWALD H. GANLEY • Mr. Ganley is executive director at the Program on Information Resources Policy. He teaches at Harvard's John F. Kennedy School of Government. A former career foreign service officer, he is currently a consultant to the under secretary of state and an advisor to the U.S. Council for International Business.

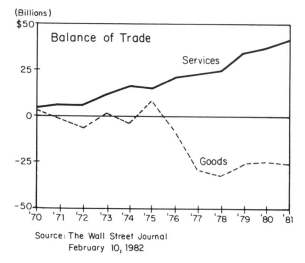

(Billions)

Source: The Wall Street Journal
February 10, 1982

FIGURE 3.1

art has advanced rapidly across a wide range of these items. Almost overnight, new types of equipment, new systems, and new things that can be done with them have emerged. Thus, all sorts of previously nonexistent possibilities have been made accessible for the needs of trade.

Convergence
The second change is in the convergence of telecommunications and information technologies with each other, both of which have been fundamentally changed by the advent of computers. These technologies are operating in unison, or as parts of completely integrated systems, thus permitting new kinds of interactions to take place.

Merger
The third change is a structural one that is taking place within and among industries. First, all U.S. industries are beginning to rebuild their basic infrastructures, grounding them on electronic computer-based technologies. For example, the steel industry and the automobile industry are switching to robotics as a means to control production processes; financial institutions are transferring funds electronically and other business operations are being managed by computer-based systems. Citibank and Exxon, who were not previously involved in telecommunications services or information products, are quickly moving into this rapidly growing field.[6] Thus, the lines of separation between various industries are becoming less distinct.

Pervasiveness
The fourth change is the growing pervasiveness of information-related devices in every area and every walk of life. Such devices are fast reaching individuals in all nations, not just in the industrialized parts of the world. Tape cassettes and long-distance dialing are in the hands of revolutionaries the world over. Everybody, globally, is seeing at least some of the same films and the same television shows. Computers are making their way into farmhouses just as did their predecessors—telephones, radios, and television sets. Individuals worldwide will very soon—governments willing—be able to have windowsill receivers for direct broadcasting by satellite television. INTELSAT now has 108 signatories, 78 of them from the Third World. Thus, almost any nameable business, industry, government, or military

future years as national and international economic systems become increasingly information-intensive. Legal and other systems must be updated to cope with these changes if orderly trade is to continue and expand. This makes it imperative to determine what, if anything, is basically different between trade in information-related products and services and trade in other goods and services. To make such a determination requires that the really different be distinguished from what merely seems different.

This paper does not attempt to accomplish such a comprehensive task. It does, however, lay some groundwork and give some descriptions which could be helpful in determining where such an investigation could usefully begin.

FROM OLD-FASHIONED TO NEW COMMUNICATIONS AND INFORMATION— QUANTITATIVE CHANGES

Seven simultaneously occurring changes are altering trade in information products and services in a fundamental way.

Abundance
The first of these changes is a massive move from scarcity to abundance in information products and services. Within less than two decades, the state of the

organization is becoming increasingly involved and will be required to address these new policy issues as related to their interests.

Speed

The fifth change is in the speed of dissemination that can be seen in data trade. The speed of the transportation system for information is unequalled by existing transport systems for any other commercial product.

Decentralized Management

The sixth change is seen in how international business is transacted. Managerial control of multinational business is changing in character in response to growing capability for immediate access to worldwide information. Management now has more of a choice of whether to centralize or decentralize control, for instance. More kinds of information are becoming trade items themselves, with certain companies offering only information for sale. The choice of trade items thus grows steadily wider. New forms of financial exchanges now permit the conversion of one type of asset to another, which in turn leads to new marketplaces created especially for handling these kinds of deals.[7] There are many instances of this sort, all of them indicating that there is growing flexibility and at the same time growing complexity in both trade in information products and services, and in general trade, as a consequence of the introduction of these new electronic devices.

Globalization

The seventh change is that these new electronic technologies are permitting other types of trade and trade infrastructures to go global. Many facets of trade are now operating beyond the traditional national controls, so deep international concerns have in many instances been aroused.

Whether these shifts in abundance and convergence, in the activity, grounding, and crossovers of industries, in the pervasiveness and the speed of dissemination, and in the changes in managerial operations and national control represent anything more than quantitative changes remains to be examined. If the communications changes are merely quantitative—then relatively slight modifications of the basic existing legal arrangements that act to facilitate trade might suffice. If what we are seeing is merely an economic sector that is much more dynamic and in a greater state of chaos across a far wider percentage of its whole than is the case for the more traditional sectors, then precedents may be found in the older sectors from a time when they, too, were in their infancy. Thus we might avoid the necessity for any wholesale changes.

Quantitative changes, when sufficiently exaggerated, do tend to become qualitative, however. Judging when they have reached this point is difficult, but, nonetheless, necessary.

QUALITATIVE ASPECTS OF COMMUNICATIONS AND INFORMATION THAT MIGHT MAKE THEM DIFFERENT FROM OTHER TRADE[8]

When information products and services are items of trade, there may be up to five qualitative facets that could make that trade more complicated than the ordinary trade item counterparts.

The first facet that may be different is the *conduit*—the physical channel—which has been put in place and through which the product, in this case, information, can be transported. Electronic conduits include the transmission systems associated with satellites, computer communications, and traditional forms of telecommunications such as telegraphy, telephony, and broadcasting.

The second facet that may be different from other trade items is the *content*—the information the medium contains. This includes things like news, financial and other data, various forms of entertainment, advertising and its close relative propaganda, and the computer software and the information embodied in chips.

The third facet that may be different is that the information content is often displayed in unique physical forms. This is called *format*, and can be ink on paper, pictures on a video tube, sound from a speaker, information on a computer display, magnetized computer tapes, punched cards, bits composed of zeros and ones, impulses over a telecommunications line, broadcast waves, photocopied material, facsimile, etc.

The fourth facet is the facilitating *hardware*—the actual information-gathering or information-transport system involved. This can be telephone and television sets, computers, microphones, typewriters, remote sensing equipment, earth stations, transistor radios, cables, telephone lines, and the physical space satellites.

The fifth facet that may be different is the specific *function* to which the conduit, content, format and hardware are dedicated. This may be broadcasting, publishing, data transmission, spying, remote sensing, etc.

Conduits

All trade items have conduits. But the first difference that can be seen between electronic conduits and regular trade conduits is that the former occupy an area that has traditionally been held close by the sovereigns of individual countries. With rare exceptions, the telecommunications system is owned by the state and regulated in the interest of national security. There are usually severe restrictions on foreign procurement and foreign ownership. Many other transport systems, especially airlines and railroads, are often state-owned and heavily regulated, of course.

The second difference to be noted is that while the conduit for the ordinary trade item is a truck or a ship or a train, the conduit for much information today is some sort of electronic transport system. Trucks can carry anything—including information in the form of books, or computers or other communications and information hardware—but a telecommunications system can only carry information as image, sound, data, or text. Thus, there is an intimate relationship between information trade and the conduit by which it travels that does not exist with other types of trade.

A third difference is with the emergence of new electronic conduits, the unit cost for information trade items is relatively cheaper than the cost of transport for many conventional goods.

A fourth difference is the increased speed and volume of trade in data processing services and information products. Global political questions have emerged that are more complex than for more conventional items of trade.

With the introduction of satellites and their attendant ground stations, the U.S. moved from a telecommunications system which linked a few nations bilaterally, to a situation involving global dispersion of information through outer space. Instead of a link to London, Paris, and Tokyo, satellites beam from anywhere to everywhere. By advancing the state of the art the U.S. has achieved instant global involvement.

This global involvement means that the U.S. must be concerned about (1) questions of cultural identity and the national sovereignty of 150 nations, (2) the competing military and civilian needs and the races between the superpowers, (3) the problems of the haves and the have-nots, and (4) new tensions with its best trading partners—the other industrialized nations of the world.

Content

A major difference between the general trade item and the information trade item is that content is about something. It is composed of ideas. It may be ideas expressed as art, or as financial data, or as scientific or engineering information, or it may be advertising. It may be about the financial situation of some individual or some company or some country. It may concern domestic defense or domestic economics. It may include proprietary secrets. Or it may be of privacy concern to natural or to legal persons. Content may on the one hand be less concrete and more difficult to define than the usual trade item, and on the other hand, more politically flammable. Similar problems are, of course, encountered with any trade item that appears to threaten national security.

Content may be overt propaganda. Or it may embody unwanted cultural information. When previously isolated parts of the world are exposed to unaccustomed content, there is often trouble. Content is responsible for the heated discussions on free flow of information—especially concerning the rights of the news media—in the United Nations Educational, Scientific, and Cultural Organization (UNESCO).[9] Content was responsible for the discussions and eventual development of guidelines on personal privacy in the Organization for Economic Cooperation and Development (OECD).[10]

Content is one of the major new and expanded items being traded today and often has enormous value—not just to the private trader but also to states. For many communications and information items—films, TV programs, books and magazines—the value of content has been determined and the trade is already regularized in some way. Difficulties arise with the newer, more nebulous forms of trade, such as that in data communications, where the value of content varies widely and is difficult to fix. Whether this really makes it different from other trade, and whether there is some inherent reason why content cannot or should not be subjected to concrete valuation, is questionable.

Where markets are well developed for specific items, value can be more readily determined. But, for instance, in intracorporate information systems, or for financial transactions, value is harder to assess. The question is how to determine value for a somewhat less concrete product like information or where a market has yet to be defined. More important, perhaps, is to anticipate the consequences of placing a value on such goods and services that is in many ways arbitrary. This is especially important since the basis for arbitrary determination is likely to vary from country to country, but probably not more so than for more general trade items, where numerous precedents can be found.

The issue is not just whether a customs or a similar authority is properly equipped to place a value on content of an electronic nature or on similar items of trade. In a mechanical sense, the Customs Valuation Code under the General Agreement on Tariffs and Trade (GATT) provides for a valuation principle or transaction value, with an agreed upon series of alternate valuation methods. The fundamental question involved is whether it is appropriate for content to be included in the valuation for customs and tax purposes at all.

To sum up content, it embodies ideas, it is often politically very sensitive, it can arouse fears and cultural irritations, and thus it may be a target for restrictions that are politically inspired. When content is valuable it is vulnerable to taxes and tariffs, the appropriateness of which may be difficult to determine. The market imperfections that presently exist in the area of content would seem to be even greater than for most general trade items, wheat or oil, for example.

Format

The dominant information format until three decades ago was ink-on-paper, i.e., the print media. At the time of the 1934 Communications Act, sound (telephone, records, etc.), optical/mechanical light projection (film), and radio broadcasts existed, but print was still the main way to go. Since that time, electronic formats have virtually taken over but the U.S. is still operating within a legal framework designed for the print media. Such legal anomalies can be seen, for instance, in the way the courts have interpreted the rights and limitations of the electronic and print media in the *Tornillo* and *Red Lion* cases.[11]

Newspapers need not provide space for reply but the electronic media must provide access. The chairman of the FCC, Mark Fowler, is now suggesting that with the abundance of radio and video stations and the advent of cable TV, there is no longer a need for a mandated right of reply in broadcasting such as existed during an era of scarcity.

When formats change, problems of protection of intellectual property become acute. Ithiel de Sola Pool

has an excellent discussion of the problems encountered when moving from book publishing—where a certain number of identical copies are produced in one locale—into the computer area where material is both transmitted and modified.[12] Who owns such computer-modified material and how the owner holds onto his rights are two of the questions that must be addressed here.

Even if there are rules for the game there are problems of enforcement. If means are available to tape-record in private homes from privately-owned televisions or stereo sets, who is going to put a stop to it? If a dish antenna strong enough to pick up any satellite transmission is available, who is going to keep the public from listening or viewing? If dry copiers are available that are fast enough and economical enough to reproduce printed material, who is going to control such reproduction? If someone wants to use tape cassettes or long-distance dialing for revolutionary activities, or to intercept telephone conversations in transit, a big enforcement problem is bound to ensue.

In sum, there are many new problems emerging concerning how to devise and enforce regulations and protect intellectual property where technologies such as those involving formats are rapidly changing.

Hardware

Information hardware is perhaps most closely related to ordinary trade. It is bought, sold, and transported in individual pieces just like regular items of trade. Yet it cannot be divorced from the problems encountered with conduit, content, format, and function, since the component parts of information transport systems are often a highly protected national market which the PTTs consider a part of their state monopoly. There are also stringent U.S. restrictions on the sale of computer and telematics hardware to the Soviet Union, because of its dual capability for both civilian and military uses.

Function

Function combines everything—the content, the format, the conduit, and the hardware—and puts them to work. Here differences are more complex. Traditionally, certain formats have been handled by certain industries. Publishers printed books and distributed them. That was their function. Television broadcasters distributed video programs. Newspapers printed the news and ran classified ads. Banks took care of checks and exchanged currency. Each group had its own set of regulators, but separation of function is no longer so crystal clear or compartmentalized.

The casual TV viewer doesn't know whether the show is being broadcast over the air, delivered by cable, played from a video cassette or a video tape. The show may be coming from Timbuktu or from across the street. Except in subscribing or paying for service, the audience doesn't care. But the television broadcaster cares. His suppliers care. And especially, the regulators care. For here you have put your foot right in the regulatory mess. There are 116 government agencies and departments which regulate U.S. business, 20 of which are new since 1970. At least 15 are concerned with information transport systems or information products and services.

The Wall Street Journal now transfers its material from New York electronically to be printed in Hong Kong, as well as in other cities domestically. Here we have a print medium using the electronic medium, but operating under different rules. The New York Times Publishing Company, McGraw-Hill, Time, Inc., Gannett, and the Times Mirror Co., have direct mail, film, TV programming, cable, broadcast, or data base services. Increasingly, the major companies are becoming multimedia information providers. Banks are offering all kinds of electronic financial services, while many non-banking industries such as Sears Roebuck and Merrill Lynch are offering the traditional services previously offered by banks. IBM, through its partnership with Aetna and COMSAT in Satellite Business Systems (SBS), is providing telecommunications services. AT&T is not only processing and delivering its telephone services using computer-assisted techniques, it is becoming an information provider through its call-in recording service and proposes to do so through electronic yellow pages.

It is over the electronic yellow pages that battle lines are being drawn. If these pages are converted to an easily updated electronic format, the yellow pages might cut seriously into the daily newspaper revenues from classified ads. Newspapers are also concerned that dominant carriers such as AT&T through its new subsidiary AT&T Information Systems not be permitted to publish information over their own monopoly transmission lines.

The recent settlement of the AT&T antitrust case permits the reorganized Bell system to move more freely into the computer and data processing (enhanced) services area. The consent decree has caused a major shakeup in the whole U.S. telecommunications industry,

for it gives AT&T the legal freedom to move from strictly providing conduits to being able to offer content. AT&T will thus be allowed to expand its noncommon carrier functions.[13] IBM, meanwhile, will be breaking into the traditionally regulated realm of telecommunications services. As deregulation decreases functional restrictions, legal complications and confrontations may increase rather than diminish.

LEGAL AND OTHER IMPLICATIONS

On close examination of these separate factors, it may be found that what falls outside the existing trade framework is just a facet or two. Or it may be that an area which still appears intact has actually been so skewed by new circumstances that it is, in fact, no longer workable. It may take only one facet to provide the legal loophole to get around an otherwise adequately covered area, and that may be good or bad, depending on the perspective. It may be that one facet provides most of the stumbling blocks or can be used to frustrate or unwarrantedly restrict the others.

However this may be, we know that a combination of dramatic changes has already led us to an attempted rewrite of the 1934 Communications Act. It is forcing us to reconsider the Equal Time and Fairness Doctrines. It has stirred up the controversy over conditions for renewal of radio and television licenses. It brought about Computer Inquiries I and II, and the 1982 AT&T Consent Decree. To a certain extent, it has led to the dropping of the IBM antitrust suit. It has prompted many problems in UNESCO, caused discussions over prior consent, and is involving more and more of OECD's time. This is what, in 1979, stopped WARC from being a once-in-every-two-decades event, and spawned numerous conferences to be held over the next five years.

This is just the beginning. More and more problems will arise. The U.S. will be confronted in the future with an increasing number of issues related to information trade policy with over 150 countries that differ radically in political and economic ideology. These countries are at many stages of development and have many varying and often conflicting interests, wants, and needs. They also have different approaches to the law. There are, therefore, many questions to consider:

1. To what extent is ordinary trade law applicable to trade in information services and products?

2. How can the common law approach of the U.K., Canada, and the United States be reconciled with that of Europe, which is steeped in civil law traditions, or that of tribal societies whose systems are rooted in natural law concepts?

3. How is the European omnibus approach reconcilable with the U.S. preference for dealing with instances of demonstrated abuse?

4. Can the trend toward increasing competition within the telecommunications industry in the U.S., U.K., and Japan be reconciled with those who would bring the whole data processing industry under a government owned or regulated umbrella?

5. Are present concepts of choice of law and conflicts of law adequate to cover information transport in international distributed networks?

6. Does admiralty law have concepts, such as innocent passage, or international free ports, which could be applied to global networks?

7. How can laws that hinder international trade in information products and services be identified, analyzed, harmonized and/or dispensed with if unnecessary or undesirable?

8. Should major structural disruptions in the international labor market be addressed?

9. Will concern for regularizing the legal environment inhibit technological innovation?

10. Is the legal approach appropriate? Are more political, trade, and economic negotiations more pragmatic and flexible than established legal principles?

Various parties within the context of the OECD, and especially the New World Information Order advocates, are suggesting, even demanding, new international regimes. This appears to mean writing whole new rules for the game. What are the U.S. interests here? A logical argument could be made that this is a new area, so make new rules. But is it more advisable to follow the present U.S. approach, that is, to go on a case-by-case basis and make changes as necessary? We should remember that the U.S. *de facto* wrote the "old" rules, as a result of initial market domination. These *de facto* rules are pragmatic applications of the free trade institutional order drawn up in GATT, the IMF, and the World Bank during the post-World War II era. Should the U.S. now begin thinking in terms of formalizing international rules for trade that would formally extend this free trade tradition to cover the changed technological conditions?

More than anything else, many U.S. businesses are seeking a way to bring about the certainty and foreseeability that would permit rational planning and encourage capital investment. They also seek a framework in which their strong trading position can be maintained. The question is how this can best be accomplished. In the short term it may seem to be more in the U.S. interest to proceed case-by-case, although this reduces the U.S. to an *ad hoc* reactive position. Unless a strong case can be made that trade in information services and products is radically different from other types of trade, and unless it can be shown that information has a universally recognizable quality, it would be advisable to exercise extreme caution before entering into broad negotiations such as led to the Law of the Sea conferences.[14]

CONCLUSION

Newness, abundance, high speed, political sensitivity, all-pervasiveness, global involvement, impingement on sovereignty, economic attractiveness, potential for military use, and regulatory crossovers are just a few of the current changes in the information field which produce both opportunities and conflicts with which no country in the world is presently prepared to deal in a political, economic, or legal sense.

The structural, economic, employment, political, social, and military forces set loose by the technologies are the same in all advanced countries. They will rapidly become so in developing nations as well. The drama unfolding in the U.S. on the future of the telecommunications industry will probably be played with equal noise, emotion, and rancor in all of the world's nations. The curtain is rising, not falling, on these struggles in these multiple jurisdictions that will ultimately shape information trade in the global marketplace.

Acknowledgments

Special thanks are due the following persons who reviewed and commented critically on previous drafts of this study. These persons, however, are not responsible for or necessarily in agreement with the views expressed herein, nor should they be held accountable for any errors of fact or interpretation.

Jonathan Aronson	Roger L. Levien
Ronald A. Bamberg	Herbert E. Marks
J.D.M. Davies	D. Verne Morland
Harry B. DeMaio	Dante N. Piccone
Donald V. Earnshaw	E. Laurence Povich
William D. English	William H. Read
Richard D. Harris	Teresita C. Schaffer
Penelope Hartland-Thunberg	Joan E. Spero
	Raymond Vernon
Norman M. Hinerfeld	Robert Wedwick
Meheroo Jussawalla	Jane H. Yurow

NOTES

1.   O. Ganley & G. Ganley, To Inform or to Control? The New Communications Networks 3.9 (New York: McGraw-Hill, 1982).

2.   E. Ploman, *The Communications Revolution,* Editorial in Intermedia, Sept. 1981.

3.   H. P. Gassman, *Is There a Fourth Economic Sector?* 113 OECD Observer, Nov. 1981, 18–20.

4.   All data on services trade are very incomplete and of dubious accuracy. Existing data should therefore be considered as indicating trends only.

5.   Economic Consulting Services, Inc., The International Operations of U.S. Services Industries: Current Data Collection and Analysis, Final Report (Washington, D.C., June 1981) (prepared for the U.S. Departments of State and Commerce and the Office of the U.S. Trade Representative). Foreign revenues are comprised both of exports and of income from foreign affiliates.

6.   J. McLaughlin with A. Birinyi, Mapping the Information Business (Cambridge, Mass.: Program on Information Resources Policy, Harvard University, Publication P-80-5, July 1980).

7.   United Nations Economic and Social Council, Commission on Transnational Corporations, 7th Session, Geneva, August 31–September 14, 1981; On the Effects of the Operations and Practices of Transnational Corporations, U.N. Doc. E/C.10/87 (July 6, 1981).

8.   B. Compaine, A New Framework for the Media Arena: Content, Process and Format (Cambridge, Mass.: Program on Information Resources Policy, Harvard University, 1980).

9.   *See supra* note 1, at 71.

10.   *Id.* at 83.

11.   Miami Herald Publishing Co. v. Tornillo, 418 U.S. 241 (1974). Red Lion Broadcasting Co. v. F.C.C., 395 U.S. 367 (1969).

12.   I. Pool and R. Solomon, *Intellectual Property and Transborder Data Flows,* 16 Stan. J. Int'l L. 113–39 (1980).

13.   H. Geller, The New Telecommunications Act as a Regulatory Framework, presentation at the Conference on Regulation and New Telecommunications Networks, Arden House (June 2–4, 1982) U.S. Department of Commerce, National Telecommunications and Information Administration, Major Telecommunications Policy Proposals, (Washington, D.C.: GPO, May 5, 1982.)

14.   L. Ratiner, *The Law of the Sea: A Crossroads for American Foreign Policy,* Foreign Aff. 1006 (1982).

CHAPTER 4

INTERNATIONAL VOICE COMMUNICATIONS

MICHAEL J. GOLDEY

BACKGROUND

The early transoceanic cables were used for telegraph transmissions. In 1915 AT&T transmitted the first transatlantic voice communications via overseas radio. In 1921 voice service to Cuba via cable was initiated. In 1927 voice service to Europe was offered commercially when AT&T and the British Post Office[1] established a direct, high-frequency (HF) radio link between New York City and London. The initial cost was $75.00 for three minutes.

In 1956, AT&T, with the British and Canadians, laid the first transatlantic telephone cable, TAT-1. This facility made reliable, low cost transatlantic *voice* communications possible.[2] The voice bandwidths could be used for transmission of data or facsimile at high speeds, or subdivided (i.e., multiplexed) into telegraph grade circuits for use in the provision of public message telegraph service, telex, and leased telegraph circuits. In 1959 the FCC authorized both AT&T and the international record carriers (IRCs)[3] to provide the recently developed alternate voice-data (AVD) service. In 1964, in the *TAT-4* decision[4], with certain limited exceptions, the FCC created a voice–record dichotomy in the provision of international services by ruling that only the IRCs would be authorized to furnish leased AVD and SVD (simultaneous voice–data) circuits. Thus, AT&T, in co-operation with its foreign correspondents throughout the world, has provided message telephone service (MTS) and voice-only private line circuits from the United States mainland to overseas points,[5] while IRCs have provided record service and AVD/SVD private ' line services,[6] except that as a secondary or permissive use all carriers can provide international "dataphone-type" services.[7]

This policy was reviewed in CC Docket No. 80–632, which eliminated the voice/record dichotomy in December 1982 by holding that AT&T should be authorized to provide any international data service, and the IRCs any international voice service, without restriction.[8] Additional United States carriers are also entering the international market.[9]

The Hawaiian Telephone Company provides international and interstate services to Hawaii. It jointly provides with AT&T all those services AT&T is authorized to provide between Hawaii and the United States mainland. In a like manner, All American Cables and Radio, Inc. (AAC&R) and ITT Communications, Inc.-Virgin Islands (ITT-CIVI), both ITT subsidiaries, jointly provide with AT&T overseas circuits for telephone message service, and leased circuits for voice-only use, from Puerto Rico and the U.S. Virgin Islands, respectively.

To provide international voice services, AT&T must negotiate with its foreign correspondents, the PTTs, regarding the facilities to be utilized or constructed, and concerning the divisions of revenues from international traffic. The FCC is involved with certain of these aspects of international communications by exercise of its facility application powers under Section 214 of the Communications Act of 1934 and its supervision of tariff (i.e., collection) rates.

MICHAEL J. GOLDEY ● Mr. Goldey is an attorney for the New York Telephone Company in New York ·City.

OVERSEAS MTS AND THE FOREIGN PTTS

In contrast with domestic interstate MTS, where both terminals are under the jurisdiction of the FCC, one terminal of overseas MTS is under control of another nation, and when the facilities utilized transit several countries they may be under the control of several nations. The overseas section of AT&T Tariff F.C.C. No. 263 lists over 200 separate points to which overseas MTS service is offered and the rates that apply for calls billed in the United States.

The PTT entity of any nation generally responsible for the provision of overseas MTS and for service negotiations is usually referred to by AT&T as its "correspondent."[10] Typically, there are formal bilateral service agreements between AT&T and its correspondents and between each pair of foreign countries for international communications. Because of private ownership of telecommunications in the United States and multiple United States international carriers, the bilateral agreements with regard to telecommunications to and from the United States are between foreign governmental or quasi-governmental entities—the PTTs—and separate privately owned common carriers—historically only AT&T and the IRCs, but more recently other United States carriers, including Western Union and Satellite Business Systems.[11]

In addition to membership in the ITU and the CCITT, countries may participate in regional telecommunications organizations, some of which have been organized by the CCITT to prepare and recommend policies applicable to particular geographical areas.[12]

The AT&T–PTT service agreements set forth the conditions under which service will be provided between AT&T, representing the contiguous 48 states,[13] and the correspondents for the other countries. Typically, the agreements identify the types of MTS services to be established (e.g., station-to-station, person-to-person, collect, credit card, reduced rate periods), procedures both parties will follow in accounting to each other for the revenues collected in their respective countries, and technical parameters for facilities, equipment, and service. In general, each entity agrees to provide at its own expense the necessary facilities, switching equipment, and terminal equipment to link overseas traffic to its domestic telecommunications system in a timely and efficient manner, while AT&T and each correspondent share equally in the costs and engineering responsibilities for the facilities, equipment,

and circuits required for traffic between the two countries. Typically, each entity provides half the overseas facilities,[14] and thus shares half the revenues from overseas service.

One advantage to the United States public of the arrangements of AT&T with its correspondents for the provision of overseas MTS is that it provides a framework for PTTs to accept the use of collect and telephone credit card service by United States customers overseas, because AT&T has agreed to remit appropriate payment for such calls, even though most PTTs deny use of this service to their own customers.[15] Use of credit card and collect calls from overseas have often afforded United States customers the convenience of billing international calls to home numbers and the means to avoid the high surcharges some foreign hotels impose on outgoing calls.[16]

FACILITIES USED FOR OVERSEAS MTS

The United States public switched network, utilized by AT&T and Independent Telephone Companies (ITC) to provide MTS and WATS, in 1980 consisted of over 415,000 long distance intercity circuits, serving over 109 million telephones. Of these, for international MTS, approximately 50 percent are capable of dialing overseas points directly, while approximately 90 percent can reach an overseas point via their local operator or an International Originating Toll Center (IOTC). The remaining U.S. telephone subscribers can reach overseas points via an International Operating Center (IOC) operator.

By mid-1981, there were over 16,000 direct circuits overseas for MTS.[17] These circuits carried overseas both-way message volumes of 205 million in 1981,[18] with 50.6 million outgoing mesages from the U.S. going to International Direct Distance Dialing (IDDD) points— i.e., these calls were completed from the U.S. by direct subscriber dialing without operator assistance.

The needs of long distance and international MTS dialing in the United States are met by switching and circuit arrangements that employ a hierarchical network configuration and automatic alternate routing within the United States to provide rapid and accurate connections while making efficient use of telephone plant.[19] Both domestic and international calls traverse this domestic network until the point where they are separated by the international portion of an appropriate switching machine. Beyond that point, domestic calls with interna-

TABLE 4.1 Percent of INTELSAT
Investment Shares by Country

COUNTRY	% INTELSAT INVESTMENT SHARES*
United States	23.05
United Kingdom	13.80
France	6.02
Germany	3.49
Australia	3.47
Japan	3.06
Brazil	3.05
Saudi Arabia	2.89
Canada	2.87
Italy	2.62

* 8 INTELSAT Annual Report 4 (1981).

tional destinations are routed over an international portion of the public switched network, guided by international signalling[20] and codes, to an international facility and on to the destination country.

Because international MTS message volumes to and from the United States are so high, AT&T is the largest user of satellite circuits; it currently uses approximately 10,750 INTELSAT satellite channels[21] in the provision of international telephone service to 206 countries worldwide. The investment shares of a country in INTELSAT is based on its use of the system and generally bears a close relationship to the number of INTELSAT satellite channels it uses. In March, 1984, COMSAT owned approximately 23 percent of INTELSAT.

Approximately 66 percent of AT&T's international circuit requirements are provided via the international satellite system; the remainder is on cable. Circuit multiplication equipment has been used to derive additional circuit capacity from existing cables. INTELSAT will be introducing a satellite circuit multiplication system.

Since United States earth stations to do not see the Indian Ocean satellite, MTS satellite circuits to that region are presently routed via a trans-Atlantic cable and access the Indian Ocean region satellite from a European earth station.

In determining how many circuits are needed and what facilities will be utilized for MTS international traffic to a particular country, proposed network configurations are evaluated in terms of service reliability,

economics, international comity, and regulatory policies. Service reliability means the robustness of any particular facility configuration in providing service of a given quality over time. Due to the large number of circuits to many countries utilized for United States–overseas MTS, there are substantial service reliability risks. Service reliability is directly dependent on the route diversity, media diversity, redundancy, and restoration capability available in a service configuration.

Route diversity is the provision of two or more independent routes (e.g., multiple cables) between countries; route diversity obviously prevents a facility failure on one route from blocking all calls. Media diversity is the provision of transmission links via different transmission technologies, permitting the advantages but suffering the defects of the different characteristics of each medium. For example, satellite circuits generally have a much higher rate of interruption than do cable circuits, but failed cable circuits have historically taken longer to repair, even though service is generally quickly restored.

Redundancy is the planned provision of facility capacity intended to be used for restoring working service and for future growth. There obviously can be no restoration of failed services without the availability of redundant facility capacity. The steady growth of international MTS over the past decade and as projected through the next decade has required long-range planning for redundancy and growth.

Cost considerations are obviously also important in the evaluation of alternate facility configurations. Costs are influenced by (1) the distance between the points to be served, (2) the level of demand between the two points, and (3) the end links required to extend the high capacity facility (e.g., from the satellite earth station or the cable landing point).

In the case of relatively short distances and high demand (such as for international MTS traffic between the United States and Europe), cable costs are lower than satellite facility costs, due in part to the significantly longer lifetimes of undersea cables as compared to satellites, and the increased circuit capacities which have been developed since the 1960s for both new and old cables.[22] As the distance between international MTS service points increases (such as between the United States to countries in the Pacific Ocean region), satellite channels have proven to be generally less costly, especially with low message volume.

International comity is a major factor influencing

selection of facilities for international MTS. National objectives, future plans, security requirements,[23] economic status, political influence, and other factors all play a part and affect decisions for reasons other than economics.[24]

The FCC's regulatory policies also influence selection and use of facilities. Circuit allocation formulas can force facility distribution in one direction or another without consideration of service reliability, economics, or international comity. Regulatory delays in the facility planning and approval processes in the past[25] have been sharply reduced in recent years.

For example, the FCC took a major step toward improving long-range planning with the implementation of a consultative planning process, which was successfully used in developing a long-range 1985–1992 facility plan for the North Atlantic Region,[26] and in the Pacific Region planning process for 1981–1995, which was initiated by the FCC in May 1981.[27]

CURRENCY REGULATION

United States common carriers, like all domestic industrial/commercial enterprises involved in international trade, must comply with the currency, blocked account, licensing, and trade regulations issued by the Office of Foreign Assets Control, Department of the Treasury. These include the Foreign Assets Control Regulations,[28] the Transaction Control Regulations,[29] the Cuban Assets Control Regulations,[30] the Foreign Funds Control Regulations,[31] and the Iranian Assets Control Regulations.[32]

There are some exemptions to these regulations and special licensing arrangements utilized with regard to the purchase or importation of "films, tapes and other news material ... by news gathering agencies ... without restriction as to method of payment ...."[33] Regulations specifically address telephone and telegraph service between the United States and Cuba and use of common carrier satellite services from Cuba for news.[34]

ELECTRONIC SURVEILLANCE OF INTERNATIONAL MTS CALLS OUTSIDE THE UNITED STATES

Electronic surveillance of international voice conversations transmitted over MTS facilities occurring outside the territorial boundaries of the United States is not regulated by Title III of the Omnibus Crime and Safe Streets Control Act of 1968 (18 U.S.C. Sec. 2510 *et seq.*).[35] If United States law enforcement or intelligence personnel merely accept information derived from electronic surveillance by their foreign counterparts, that information may be used, divulged, and admitted into evidence in federal courts, without restriction.[36] Even where the surveillance outside the United States may have violated foreign law, the admissibility of any derived information in the United States apparently would not be affected,[37] unless "the circumstances of the foreign search and seizure are so extreme that they 'shock the judicial conscience'...."[38]

Thus, international MTS calls, such as those between Canada and the United States, if intercepted in Canada, can be used as evidence in a United States court. *United States* v. *Cotroni*, 527 F.2d 708, 711–12 (2d Cir. 1975). The legislative history and specific language of Title III make it clear that Congress intended to regulate unlawful interceptions occurring *within* the United States. The place of interception and the parties involved in making the interception are the relevant factors, not the fact that an interception occurred. *United States* v. *Tirinkian*, 502 F. Supp. 620 (D. N.D. 1980).

United States intelligence personnel may lawfully intercept international MTS (or voice-grade private line) communications only in extremely limited circumstances. On December 4, 1981, President Reagan signed Executive Order 12333,[39] regarding United States Intelligence Activities, including those of the F.B.I., C.I.A., and other agencies. Pursuant to Sec. 2.5 of the executive order, the attorney general can approve the use for intelligence purposes, *within* the United States or against a "United States person"[40] *abroad*, of any technique for which a warrant would be required if undertaken for law enforcement purposes, provided that he has determined that there is probable cause to believe that the surveillance technique is directed against a foreign power or an agent of a foreign power.[41]

FOREIGN INTELLIGENCE SURVEILLANCE ACT OF 1978[42]

The FISA represents an exclusive charter for the conduct of *domestic* electronic surveillance intended to gather foreign intelligence information—i.e., the nonconsensual acquisition of *all* domestic radio and wire communications (50 U.S.C. Sec. 1801 (f) (1)–(3)) and the use of *any surveillance device* in the United States for acquiring information, even where reasonable expectations of privacy and a warrant would be required for law enforcement purposes. The FISA thus filled a lacuna left by Title III of the Omnibus Crime Control and Safe Streets Act of 1968 (OCCA), which was limited to "aural acquisition" and had expressly disclaimed any intention that it or Section 605 of the Communications Act limited the constitutional power of the president, if any, to protect the national security,[43] by electronic surveillance within the United States.[44]

A lacuna still exists as to the constitutional power of the president to utilize electronic surveillance *outside* the United States—e.g., from ships at sea and in neighboring and foreign countries—to protect the national security. Congress made it clear that the FISA only addressed the acquisition of national security and foreign intelligence information by electronic surveillance *within* the United States, and did not address the question of the constitutional power of the president to conduct electronic surveillance of a U.S. person abroad without a court order.[45] As noted, *supra*, Executive Order 12333 of December 4, 1981, United States Intelligence Activities, appears to provide a framework for executive branch electronic surveillance outside the United States.[46]

Prior to enactment of the FISA, and in the absence of legislation, the Supreme Court had reserved decision on the question of the applicability of the Fourth Amendment warrant requirement to national security electronic surveillances. Neither *Katz* v. *United States*, 389 U.S. 347, 358 n. 23 (1967), nor *United States* v. *United States Dis. Court* (*Keith*), 407 U.S. 297, 322 (1972), resolved fundamental constitutional questions regarding claims of an inherent presidential power with regard to activities of foreign powers or their agents.[47] The executive branch for years has acted on the belief that the purposes of and authority for national security intelligence gathering are fundamentally different from those of domestic law enforcement. The former is concerned with international diplomacy, foreign relations, and national security affairs, while the latter is concerned with the civil and criminal laws.[48] Accordingly, there has been extensive warrantless electronic surveillance by the executive of foreign governments and their agents for national security purposes.[49] These are usually, and may have to be, expressly, authorized by the president

through the attorney general.[50] At times, due to the state-secrets privilege, even the existence of such surveillance may be a matter as to which a court may not inquire.[51] The government argued prior to FISA that Section 605 of the Communications Act did not apply to domestic wiretaps authorized by the attorney general and conducted for purposes of gathering national security information,[52] and some lower federal courts agreed.[53]

Now, by the FISA, Congress has attempted to balance the president's power to conduct foreign affairs and the Fourth Amendment's warrant requirements. The FISA significantly limits the warrant exception suggested and approved by the lower federal courts. Without delving into its detailed provisions, under the FISA, after attorney general approval, application is made to a specially designated Foreign Intelligence Surveillance Court, 50 U.S.C. Sec. 1804(a), for orders to conduct electronic surveillance within the U.S. where there is probable cause to believe that the target of the surveillance is a "foreign power" or an "agent of a foreign power" (an agent may be a United States person).[54] The application to the court must certify that the information sought is foreign intelligence information that cannot be obtained by normal investigative techniques. 50 U.S.C. Sec. 1805(a)(7). Only where a United States person is the target is the judge authorized to examine the substance in addition to the form of the certification. 50 U.S.C. Sec. 1805(a)(5). If the certification is complete, the issuance of the court order is mandatory. Additional "minimization procedures" protect United States persons' privacy from accidental warrantless surveillance and from the unnecessary acquisition, retention, and dissemination of nonpublicly available information, 50 U.S.C. Sec. 1801(b).

Two exceptions to the FISA general warrant requirement are when the surveillance is authorized by the president and certified by the attorney general (1) as being directed exclusively at official foreign-power communications, and (2) as acquiring technical intelligence from premises controlled exclusively by said foreign power. 50 U.S.C. Sec. 1802(a)(1)(A).

As evolving FCC policies permit additional carriers to offer domestic and international services, it is likely that such carriers may have to adopt adequate procedures to respond to both Title III Omnibus Crime Control Act and FISA wiretap warrants where carrier assistance is required, as well as to FISA requests involving exceptions to the warrant requirement.[55]

SECTION 606 OF THE COMMUNICATIONS ACT—CONTROL AND SUSPENSION OF OVERSEAS COMMUNICATIONS IN TIME OF WAR OR NATIONAL EMERGENCY

Nation states, in the exercise of their sovereignty, periodically close their borders and may attempt to close the borders of other nation-states to commerce in goods and commodities, to people, and to telecommunications. For example, in December 1981, in conjunction with its exercise of martial law, Poland cut off all public international telecommunications links (e.g., overseas MTS, overseas telex) and suspended public use of its internal telephone system; in September 1982 the Soviet Union required operator intercession by ending direct-dial calls in and out of the country.

It is to be expected that all nation-states, including the United States, will take such action as they deem appropriate in time of war or national emergency to regulate telecommunications so as to deny information to the enemy, conserve resources, and support national policies.

Section 606 of the Communications Act of 1934, 47 U.S.C. Section 606, War Powers of President, authorizes the president to exercise certain authority (1) during a war (Sec. 606(a) and (b)), (2) upon proclamation "that there exists war or a threat of war, or a state of peril or disaster or other national emergency" (Sec. 606(c)), and (3) upon proclamation "that there exists a state or threat of war involving the United States" (Sec. 606(d)). Pursuant to 47 U.S.C. Sec. 606(c) and Sec. 606(d), presidential authority may be asserted to suspend telecommunications service within the jurisdiction of the United States, and to use or control, respectively, any radio or wire facility or station.[56]

During World War I, by Joint Resolution of July 16, 1918, c. 154, 40 Stat. 904, Congress authorized the president, when necessary for national security or defense, to supervise or take possession, and control and operate, any telegraph, telephone, marine cable, or radio system. The postmaster general operated these facilities on behalf of the president. *See Dakota Cent. Telephone Co.* v. *State of South Dakota ex rel. Payne*, 250 U.S. 163 (1919); *Commercial Cable Co.* v. *Burleson*, 255 F. 99 (D.C.N.Y. 1919), *rev'd on other grounds*, 250 U.S. 360 (1919).

Prior to the United States' entry into World War II, due to actions by the European combatants, there were interruptions of cable communications between the United States and Italy, Germany, France, Belgium, and Holland,[57] as well as disruption or suspension of radiotelegraph service to Poland, Czechoslovakia, Norway, Denmark, Iceland, France, Belgium, and Holland.[58] The Federal Communications Commission noted that the "content" of international messages was "dependent upon the restrictions placed by the administration or agency operating the foreign end of the circuit" and that communications often were completed by "rerouting of traffic via devious routes and additional restrictions."[59]

By December 1941, the interruption of all direct cable service to the continent of Europe had occurred, except for the United Kingdom, Eire (Ireland), and the Azores,[60] and by rule the FCC had banned all amateur radio in the United States and required that all international record carriers keep files of originals of all messages.[61]

Shortly after the United States entered the war in December 1941, all service to Berlin, Rome, and Tokyo was suspended under 47 U.S.C. Sec. 606. Subsequently, radiotelephone service to Java and the Philippines was discontinued.[62] The Pacific cable was operated to Hawaii and Midway only.[63]

The president's wartime authority under Sec. 606(a) of the Communications Act was delegated early in the war[64] to the Board of War Communications. The board promulgated various orders to ensure that communications essential to the national defense and security would have preference and priority,[65] and, under Sections 606(c) and (d), it directed the use, control, or closure of radio and wire communications stations and facilities.[66] Control and censorship of telecommunications from the United States to certain overseas areas became common.[67]

It would not be unexpected that existing international satellite, cable, and radiotelephone communications may similarly be subject to exacting United States governmental regulation in time of war or threat of war. Obviously, the scope of the war may affect the type and extent of governmental regulation. During the Korean and Vietnam conflicts, and the Cuban missile crisis of 1962, generally communications to only those countries were subject to increased control.

Throughout the past three decades, unsettled conditions in overseas areas have often led to temporary or permanent suspension of service and to changes in serving arrangements to overseas areas.[68] However, nothing comparable to the massive telecommunications disruptions of World War II has occurred, due to the localized scope of the conflicts, the location of key facilities outside the war zones, and the sheer redundancy of alternative telecommunications facilities. In an era of cable, terrestrial radiotelephone, satellites, and other technologies, control and/or interruption of international communications during time of war can be expected to be significantly different from the World War II experience.

In any major conflict, new and sophisticated methods of communications facility interdiction are likely to be used against the new and old communications technologies. Satellites can be destroyed or jammed; undersea cable can be cut or destroyed. Rigorous censorship and control of communications can be expected from any nation with the resources and capability for the job. In this connection it should be noted that pursuant to the Foreign Intelligence Surveillance Act, 50 U.S.C. Sec. 1811, the president may authorize electronic surveillance without a court order otherwise required by the FISA to obtain foreign intelligence information, for up to 15 days after declaration of war by Congress.[69]

The FCC does not publicly detail its activities relating to the national defense, largely due to their classified nature, and Section 4(j) of the Communications Act of 1934, 47 U.S.C. Sec. 154(j),[70] which "in effect, enjoins the Commission from publicizing information affecting the national security."[71] Of course, private entities, including carriers, are similarly constrained by operation of laws relating to classified information.[72]

THE FOREIGN MISSIONS ACT OF 1982—SUSPENSION OF COMMUNICATIONS SERVICE TO FOREIGN MISSIONS IN THE UNITED STATES

The Foreign Missions Act of 1982 (Title II of Public Law 97–241, Sec. 201–213, 96 Stat. 273, to be codified at 22 U.S.C. Sec. 4301–4313), became effective on October 1, 1982. It is intended to afford the Department of State effective leverage to prevent the growing imbalance between the treatment of U.S. embassies and missions abroad and that provided to missions of foreign governments in the United States.[73] The Secretary of State is empowered to enforce reciprocity by restricting benefits, privileges, and immunities of foreign missions in this country as an incentive to obtain equitable and non-discriminatory treatment for U.S. missions and personnel in the foreign territory.[74]

The definition of "benefit" in Section 202(a)(1)(B)[75] includes the provision of "public utilities services—e.g., telephone service. Section 211[76] makes it unlawful for any person—e.g., the telephone company—to make available any benefits to a foreign mission if the transaction is prohibited by the Secretary of State pursuant to the Foreign Missions Act.

Providers of public utility services appear to receive adequate protection under the Foreign Missions Act for any restrictions on, termination of, or refusal to provide service to foreign missions pursuant to direction of the Secretary of State. Section 208 (b) of the Foreign Missions Act, 22 U.S.C. Sec. 4308 (b), provides that

> Compliance with any regulation, instruction, or direction issued by the Secretary under this title shall to the extent thereof be a full acquittance and discharge for all purposes of the obligation of the person making the same. *No person shall be held liable in any court or administrative proceeding* for or with respect to anything done or omitted in good faith in connection with the administration of, or pursuant to and in reliance on, this title, or any regulation, instruction, or direction issued by the Secretary under this title. (Emphasis added.)[77]

In addition, under Section 204, foreign missions can be required to comply with any terms the Secretary of State prescribes as a condition to receiving any benefits from "any entity providing public services" (e.g., a telephone company), including the requirement that the foreign mission waive any recourse against "any entity providing public services ... in connection with any action determined to be undertaken in furtherance of this title."[78]

SUSPENSION OF INTERNATIONAL COMMUNICATIONS BY THE UNITED NATIONS OR INTELSAT

Under the United Nations' Charter, the Security Council can decide, pursuant to Article 39, to recommend action under Article 41[79] to impose a complete or partial interruption of international communications to a country to give effect to a Security Council decision. Under Article 49, all members are mandated to mutually assist one another in carrying out the measures. It is believed that such interruption of international communications has never been recommended by the Security Council, even where it has recommended other types of economic sanctions against a country.

The fundamental documents regarding the establishment and organization of INTELSAT—the "Agreement" and the "Operating Agreement" of August 20, 1971—appear to stress the principle that satellite communications are to be universally available on a nondiscriminatory basis. Unlike the United Nations Charter, there is no recognition, in the INTELSAT Agreement or the Operating Agreement, of an organizational prerogative to expel or partially suspend or completely interrupt satellite communications to any country for any reason. Thus, while the U.N. may "punish" a party for its military, diplomatic, political, or economic transgressions, INTELSAT apparently cannot. There does not appear to be, at present, any process within INTELSAT to affect a member state's use of international satellite communications facilities for activities unrelated to INTELSAT.[80] A country's use of INTELSAT facilities apparently can be affected only for failure to comply with an obligation established under the INTELSAT Agreement or Operating Agreement, and binding arbitration utilizing "generally accepted principles of law" are intended to resolve any such controversies.

NOTES

1. Outside the United States, private operation and ownership of telecommunications facilities is the exception. Control of postal, telegraph, and telephone services has generally been consolidated in a single centralized governmental entity, the PTT (Postal, Telegraph, and Telephone organization). The PTT, with responsibility for construction, operation, and regulation of each nation's telecommunications services, may be (1) a government administration or ministry, (2) a public corporation under the authority of a government department, or (3) operated by a private corporation, controlled and/or partially owned by the government. International telecommunications policies and issues are affected by differences between the United States–private ownership and PTT—public ownership approaches.

2. TAT-1 was retired at midnight on November 27, 1978.

3. AT&T, 27 F.C.C. 113 (1959). The major IRCs are Western Union International, RCA Global Communications, ITT World Communications, FTC Communications, and TRT Telecommunications.

4. AT&T, 37 F.C.C. 1151 (1964).

5. In the *Dataphone* decision, the FCC authorized the use of international MTS for the transmission of data on a secondary basis. *See* AT&T, 75 F.C.C.2d 682 (1980) (File No. I-P-C-12, Docket No. 19,558, *aff'd. sub nom.* Western Union Int'l v. FCC, 673 F.2d 530 (D.C. Cir. 1982).

6. The *Datel* decision removed the restriction on voice traffic over IRC facilities to the extent that voice traffic would be allowed as a permissive or secondary use. *See* Western Union Int'l, 76 F.C.C.2d 166 (1980) Docket No. 19,558, *aff'd. sub nom.* Western Union Int'l v. FCC, 673 F.2d 539 (D.C. Cir. 1982).

7. In 1960, DATAPHONE® data sets were introduced as a permissive use of the public switched domestic MTS voice network. Today, any customer with appropriate equipment (e.g., facsimile scanners, teletypewriters, or data sets, attached either electrically or acoustically to the voice telephone network) may send data, facsimile, or other hard copy communications by means of an ordinary telephone voice circuit. *See* 75 F.C.C.2d 682, 683 (1980).

8. Overseas Communications Serv., 84 F.C.C.2d 622 (1980) (Notice of Proposed Rulemaking); 92 F.C.C.2d 641 (1982) (Report and Order).

9. For example, while primarily a domestic satellite carrier, Satellite Business Systems (SBS) has been authorized to provide international service. 88 F.C.C.2d 195 (1981); 88 F.C.C.2d 258 (1981); FCC 82–422 (released Oct. 1, 1982). Pursuant to the Record Carrier Competition Act of 1981, Pub. L. No. 97-130, 96 Stat. 1687, Western Union has been authorized to provide international record services. Western Union Tel. Co. (File No. I-T-C-82-228 et al.), Memorandum Opinion Order, Authorization and Certificate (released Dec. 30, 1982).

10. A "correspondent" is defined "as being any entity which has agreed to provide specified overseas communications services with AT&T." All Am Cables & Radio, Inc., 70 F.C.C.2d 824, 833, n.8 (1979).

11. United States common carriers participating in international communications are influenced, of course, in their decision-making by United States governmental policy, and by actions of the International Telecommunications Union (ITU), a United Nations agency, and the International Telegraph and

Telephone Consultative Committee (CCITT), in whose activities they may actively participate.

12. For example, the CEPT (Telephone Committee of the European Conference of Postal and Telecommunications Administrations).

13. AT&T is authorized by the FCC to provide telecommunications services within the 48 contiguous United States and the District of Columbia and from these states to the rest of the world.

14. For satellite circuits utilized for overseas MTS, AT&T leases from COMSAT circuits from the United States earth station to the satellite, while the correspondents each provide the matching circuits from the satellite to their domestic earth stations. For transoceanic cables utilized for overseas MTS to and from the United States, generally circuits are assigned jointly to AT&T and its foreign correspondents as owners. Each owner is considered as having the assignment of an undivided interest in a "half-circuit" on an end-to-end basis for the length of the cable system—i.e., longitudinally from one end of the cable system to the other end.

15. Analogies may be drawn to the use overseas by United States residents of travelers checks, as well as of charge or credit cards such as American Express, VISA, MasterCard and bank credit cards. In each case, there is an underlying agreement to remit appropriate payment.

16. AT&T credit cards are honored by approxpimately 140 countries for calls back to the U.S.; they cannot be used for calls between foreign countries. Collect calls back to the U.S. are permitted by approximately 150 countries.

17. Approximately 10,500 satellite, 5500 cable.

18. International MTS message count to and from the United States is small compared to the total interstate and intrastate MTS message count of 9.2 billion for 1978. International MTS traffic demand is projected to grow at a high rate.

19. Few of the overseas correspondents—i.e., national telephone and telegraph administrations providing the foreign circuits used to complete international MTS calls—have telecommunications networks comparable to those in the United States in terms of rapidity, accuracy, and efficiency.

20. CCITT No. 5, to be replaced by CCITT No. 6.

21. COMSAT Circuit Status Report to FCC—full-time circuits in operation as of February 28, 1982.

22. Introduction of lightwave (digital fiber optics) submarine cable, because of its high circuit capacity without using the radio spectrum, could affect the relative use of satellite and cable communications for international MTS traffic. Long-range international planning for the Atlantic Region includes a fiber optic cable in 1988.

23. In FCC Docket No. 18,875, regarding North Atlantic facilities, the FCC rejected COMSAT's opposition to the holding of a top secret briefing on national defense matters, 44 R.R.2d 607 (FCC 78–755), and attended the briefing. See 69 F.C.C.2d 1232 (1978) (FCC 78–756).

24. As has been demonstrated in proceedings before the FCC, there often is a wide divergence of opinion regarding the economics of satellite v. cable facility configurations. *See, e.g.,* FCC Docket No. 18,875.

25. In FCC Docket No. 18,875, regarding planning for the North Atlantic region, the proceedings took eight years. *See* Overseas Communications, 30 F.C.C.2d 571 (1971) (Statement of Policy and Guidelines); 62 F.C.C.2d 451 (1976) (Further Statement of Policy and Guidelines); 67 F.C.C.2d 358 (1977) (Report, Order and Third Statement of Policy and Guidelines), *partial recon.,* 70 F.C.C.2d 348 (1978) *modified,* 71 F.C.C.2d 1090, (1979), *further modified and adopted,* 71 F.C.C.2d 71 (1979); Policies for Overseas Communications, 73 F.C.C.2d 326 (1979).

26. CC Docket No. 79–184, Policies for Overseas Common Carrier Facilities, 73 F.C.C.2d 193 (1979) (Notice of Inquiry); 76 F.C.C.2d 522 (1980) (Second Notice of Inquiry); 82 F.C.C.2d 407 (1980) (Notice of Proposed Rulemaking); 84 F.C.C.2d 760 (1981) (Report and Order).

27. CC Docket No. 81–343, Facilities to Meet Pacific Telecommunications Needs, Notice of Inquiry, FCC 81–243, 46 Fed. Reg. 31,286 (June 15, 1981); Notice of Proposed Rulemaking, FCC 82–206, 47 Fed. Reg. 21,868 (May 20, 1982); Report and Order, FCC 82-513, 47 Fed. Reg. 57,040 (Dec. 22, 1982).

28. 3 C.F.R. pt. 500.

29. 3 C.F.R. pt. 505.

30. 3 C.F.R. pt. 515.

31. 3 C.F.R. pt. 520.

32. 3 C.F.R. pt. 535.

33. *See* 3 C.F.R. § 500.562 (Korea, Viet Nam,

Cambodia); 3 C.F.R. § 515.546 (Cuba).

34.   3 C.F.R. § 515.542 provides:

Communications

(a)   All transactions of common carriers incident to the receipt or transmission of mail between the United States and Cuba are hereby authorized.

(b)   All transactions incident to the use of satellite channels for the transmission of television news and news programs originating in Cuba by United States news organizations are hereby authorized.

(c)   Specific licenses may be issued on a case-by-case basis for transactions incident to the receipt or transmission of communications between the United States and Cuba, other than communications covered by paragraph (b) of this section. Specific licenses are generally issued for such transactions as entry into traffic agreements to provide telephone and telegraph services, provision of services, and settlement of charges under traffic agreements.

35.   United States v. Tirinkian, 502 F. Supp. 620 (D.N.D. 1980); Stowe v. Devoy, 588 F.2d 336 (2d Cir. 1978), cert. denied, 442 U.S. 931 (1979).

36.   The Fourth Amendment would appear to apply, however, if such surveillance is conducted by or at the behest of or in any way initiated, supervised, controlled, or directed by United States law enforcement personnel. See Berlin Democratic Club v. Rumsfeld, 410 F. Supp. 144, 154 (D.D.C. 1976); United States v. Toscanino, 500 F.2d 267, 280 (2d Cir. 1974). However, a nonresident alien has no standing to sue civilly in United States courts for surveillance by United States officials which occurred overseas. Berlin Democratic Club at 153.

37.   United States v. Controni, 527 F.2d 708, 712 (2d Cir. 1975); People v. Nicoletti, 84 Misc.2d 385, 390, 375 N.Y.S.2d 720, 725 (Niagara County Ct. 1975); State v. Ford, 499 P.2d 699 (Ariz. 1972). Suppression of the evidence or of the fruits of the evidence would not be considered to act as a deterrent, in such cases, to unlawful state action, as is the case when United States personnel are directly involved in the unlawful activity. But cf. United States v. Phillips, 479 F. Supp. 423, 435–38 (M.D. Fla. 1979), which held that if the interception was affirmatively established as unlawful under the foreign law at the place of interception, then the fruits of the interception could not be used against a participant in United States courts.

38.   Stowe v. DeVoy, 588 F.2d 336, 341 (2d Cir. 1978). It would appear unlikely that mere wiretapping or electronic surveillance by foreign officials in their territory, without more, would induce a federal court in the exercise of its supervisory powers to require exclusion of the evidence so seized.

39.   46 Fed. Reg. 59,941 (Dec. 8, 1981) 3 C.F.R. 200 (1982).

40.   Definition includes a United States citizen and a permanent resident alien. See § 3.4(i), 46 Fed. Reg. at 59,954, 3 C.F.R. at 215.

41.   46 Fed. Reg. at 59,951. In addition, it is provided that "Electronic surveillance, as defined in the Foreign Intelligence Surveillance Act of 1978, shall be conducted in accordance with that Act, as well as this Order."

42.   Pub. L. No. 95-511, § § 101–301, 92 Stat. 1783, codified at 50 U.S.C. § § 1801–1811 (Supp. IV 1980).

43.   See 18 U.S.C. § 2511(3) (1970), repealed by FISA. FISA amended 18 U.S.C. § 2511(2) by adding § 2511(2)(f), which provides that OCCA's procedures and those of FISA shall be "the exclusive means" by which electronic surveillance and the interception of wire or oral communication may be conducted within the United States.

44.   See S. Rep. No. 95th Cong., 604, (Nov. 15, 1977), reprinted in 1978 U.S. Code Cong. & Ad. News 3908, 3914–3916.

In defining "electronic surveillance," FISA intentionally used the word "acquisition" rather than the OCCA "aural acquisition" (see 18 U.S.C. § 2510(4)). Accordingly, nonverbal communications may be obtained under FISA court orders—e.g., data transmissions, dial tones by use of a pen register, and other forms of nonvoice communications.

45.   See S. Rep. No. 95th Cong., 701, (Mar. 14, 1978), reprinted in 1978 U.S. Code Cong. & Ad. News 3976.

46.   See text accompanying notes 40 to 42.

47.   In Zweibon v. Mitchell, 516 F.2d 594 (D.C. Cir. 1975) (en banc), cert. denied, 425 U.S. 944 (1976), the Fourth Amendment warrant requirement was held applicable to a wiretap of a domestic organization (Jewish Defense League) that was neither the agent of, nor acting in collaboration with, a foreign power.

48.   See Civiletti, Intelligence Gathering and the

Law: Conflict or Compatibility, 48 FORDHAM L. REV. 883, 886 (1980).

49. *See, e.g.,* United States v. Humphrey, 456 F. Supp. 51 (E.D. Va. 1978); United States v. Stone, 305 F. Supp. 75 (D.D.C. 1969) (wiretap to gather foreign intelligence information); United States v. O'Baugh, 304 F. Supp. 767 (D.D.C. 1969) (wiretap of foreign embassy).

50. United States v. Kearney, 436 F. Supp. 1108 (S.D.N.Y. 1977); United States v. Ehrlichman, 546 F.2d 910, 935 (D.C. Cir. 1976), *cert. denied,* 429 U.S. 1120 (1977) (unauthorized break-in); United States v. Giordano, 416 U.S. 505 (1974) (court-ordered Title III Omnibus Crime Act wiretaps invalid since applicaion approved by Assistant to rather than by Attorney General personally).

51. *See* Jabara v. Kelley, 476 F. Supp. 561, 557–78 (E.D. Mich. 1979) (NSA intercepts may involve the state secrets privilege and require dismissal); Halkin v. Helms, 598 F.2d 1 (D.C. Cir. 1978) (state secrets privilege sustained with respect to mere fact of interception of foreign telegraphic communications by NSA); Halkin v. Helms, 690 F.2d 977 (D.C. Cir. 1982) (same, with respect to CIA activities during period 1967–1974); Salisbury v. United States, 690 F.2d 966 (D.C. Cir. 1982) (FOIA and Tort Claims Act actions against government seeking records concerning intercepted communications; NSA use of state secrets privilege and affidavit that disclosure of the mere fact that plaintiff's communications had been intercepted would compromise national security required dismissal). *Cf.* United States v. Brown, 484 F.2d 418 (5th Cir. 1973) (*in camera* examination of wiretap logs by court—scope, location, subject, and duration of foreign intelligence surveillance not revealed).

52. United States v. Stone, 305 F. Supp. 81 (D.D.C. 1969). In addition, between 1945 and 1975, NSA and its predecessor agencies obtained from commercial cable companies copies of most international cables sent abroad from the United States. *See* Salisbury v. United States, 690 F.2d 966, 969 (D.C. Cir. 1982); S. REP. NO. 755, 94th Cong., 2d Sess., bk. III, 765–76.

53. United States v. Stone, 305 F. Supp. 82 (D.D.C. 1969). United States v. Humphrey, 456 F. Supp. 51 (E.D. Va. 1978); Jabara v. Kelley, 476 F. Supp. 561, 576 (E.D. Mich. 1979); United States v. Brown, 484 F.2d 418 (5th Cir. 1973), *cert. denied,* 415 U.S.

960 (1974); United States v. Butenko, 494 F.2d 593 (3rd Cir. 1974), *cert. denied sub nom.* Ivanov v. United States, 419 U.S. 881 (1974).

54. United States v. Falvey, 540 F. Supp. 1306 (E.D.N.Y. 1982), held that FISA on its face and as applied to United States persons of Irish ancestry acting as agents of a foreign power (the IRA), did not violate the First, Fourth, or Sixth Amendments, and that evidence of criminal activity uncovered during lawful FISA electronic surveillance was admissible in a subsequent criminal trial. *See* 18 U.S.C. § 1806, which specifies the procedures required for the use of any evidence obtained or derived from electronic surveillance under FISA in a criminal proceeding. *Ex parte* and *in camera* determinations of the legality of FISA electronic surveillance, without an adversary hearing, was upheld in United States v. Belfield, 692 F.2d 141 (D.C. Cir. 1982).

55. Common carriers properly directed (*see* 50 U.S.C. § 1802(a)(4) and § 1805(b)(2)(B)) or authorized to render assistance under either FISA or OCCA, are protected from liability in connection with their cooperation. Such carriers also are precluded from disclosing even the existence of *legal* wiretaps "or the device used to accomplish the interception or surveillance," and must adopt adequate security safeguards to protect all information.

Title II of FISA amended Title III of OCCA, 18 U.S.C. § 2511(2)(a)(ii), which now provides that communication common carriers are "authorized" to render facilities, information, or technical assistance under Title III (interception of wire or oral communications during OCCA criminal investigations) and under FISA (electronic surveillances) only if they obtain a court order or an appropriate Attorney General certification. However, if a facially valid court order or certification is obtained, "no cause of action shall lie in any court" for the carrier's limited technical role in the form of providing technical assistance and facilities to government personnel. The carrier's reasonable expectation of legality should also preclude the possibility of any liability for statutory or constitutional violation, even if the court order or certification were later found to be defective. *Cf.* Smith v. Nixon, 606 F.2d 1183, 1191 (D.C. Cir. 1979).

56. It should be noted that § 606(c) is addressed to *radio* communications while § 606(d) addresses *wire* communications, and that § 606(c) appears to

grant the President powers under a wider set of circumstances. A proclamation under § 606(c) may involve *"public peril or disaster or other national emergency"* in addition to "war or threat of war." The reasons for the differences in language are not clear.

The President issued a proclamation of "national emergency" in Exec. Order No. 12,170, on Nov. 14, 1979, in accordance with the National Emergencies Act, 50 U.S.C. §§ 1601 *et seq.*, with regard to the situation in Iran (*see* 44 Fed. Reg. 65,729, (Nov. 15, 1979), thereby invoking the International Emergency Economic Powers Act, Pub. L. No. 95-223, 50 U.S.C. §§ 1701, *et seq.* Although this act permits the President to regulate and prohibit most commercial transfers, foreign exchange, currency, securities, and other transactions with a foreign country, pursuant to 50 U.S.C. § 1702(b), it does *not* grant the President "the authority to regulate or prohibit, directly or indirectly—(1) any postal, telegraphic, telephonic, or other personal communication, which does not involve the transfer of anything of value. . . ." The legislative history of Pub. L. No. 95-223 in 1977 U.S. CODE CONG. & AD. NEWS 4540, does not discuss § 1702(b)(1). The President, however, would appear to retain power under § 606(c) of the Communications Act to suspend *radio* communications during any "national emergency."

57.　6 FCC ANN. REP. 41 (1940).

58.　*Id.* at 109. There is no indication in the FCC reports that any of these interruptions were due to the exercise of powers under 47 U.S.C. § 606.

59.　*Id.* at 108.

60.　7 FCC ANN. REP. 1, 16 (1941).

61.　*Id.* at 2.

62.　8 FCC ANN. REP. 20 (1942).

63.　9 FCC ANN. REP. 34 (1943).

64.　Exec. Order No. 8964 (Dec. 10, 1941), and Exec. Order No 9089 (Mar. 6, 1942).

65.　For example, domestic telegraph messages of congratulation or felicitation were banned by a Board order.

66.　11 FCC ANN. REP. 90 (1945).

67.　For example, international radiotelephone communications were restricted by Board Order No. 19, issued Sept. 30, 1942, which provided as follows (*see* 8 FCC ANN. REP. 20–21 (1942)):

1.　Nongovernmental business radiotelephone calls between the Unted States and Great Britain shall be permitted subject to the prior approval thereof from the Office of Censorship. No personal radiotelephone calls shall be permitted between the United States and Great Britain.

2.　No nongovernmental business or personal radiotelephone call shall be made to or from any foreign point outside of the Western Hemisphere other than Great Britain unless such call is made in the interest of the United States or the United Nations and unless an agency of the United States Government sponsors such call and obtains prior approval therefor from the Office of Censorship; PROVIDED, HOWEVER, That this provision shall not apply to American press calls or radio broadcast programs, or to such other press calls and radio programs as may be specifically approved by the Office of Censorship.

3.　No calls of any nature, over the radiotelephone circuits under the jurisdiction of the United States, no matter where such calls may originate, unless sponsored and approved as provided in paragraph (2), shall be permitted to, from, or on behalf of, the following thirteen countries: Egypt, Finland, France, Iceland, Iran, Ireland, Latvia, Lithuania, Portugal, Spain, Sweden, Switzerland, and Turkey.

4.　Personal calls other than those prohibited in the foregoing paragraphs may be completed between two points in the Western hemisphere.

68.　*See, e.g.,* 15 FCC ANN. REP. 108 (1949) (China) and the first paragraph in the text after note 56, *supra.*

69.　House Conference Report No. 95–1720 (Oct. 5, 1978) indicates that 15 days was considered adequate time for Congress to consider any appropriate amendment for the wartime emergency. *See* 1978 U.S. CODE CONG. & AD. NEWS 4063.

70.　The last sentence of 47 U.S.C. § 154(j) provides: "The Commission is authorized to withhold publication of records or proceedings containing secret information affecting the national defense."

71.　*See, e.g.* 16 FCC ANN. REP. 24 (1950), and the Commission's orders regarding the holding of a top secret briefing on national defense matters in Docket No. 18,875, *Overseas Communications,* 44 R.R.2d 607 (FCC 78–755, released Oct. 26, 1978) and 69 F.C.C.2d 1232 (FCC 78–756, released Oct. 26, 1978).

72.　*See, e.g.,* 18 U.S.C. §§ 793–794, 798.

73.　The provisions of the act may be extended

by the Secretary of State to any public international organization or to official foreign missions thereto. 22 U.S.C. § 4309.

74.   *See* S. Rep. No. 329, 97th Cong., 2d Sess. (1982), *reprinted in* 8A U.S. Code Cong. & Ad. News 714 (Oct. 1982). *See also* S. Rep. No. 283, 97th Cong., 1st Sess. 1–4 (1981).

75.   22 U.S.C. § 4302(a)(1)(B).

76.   22 U.S.C. § 4311.

77.   Section 208(b) thus appears, at minimum, to afford public utilities protection before any court or regulatory agency in the United States.

78.   The waiver provisions of Section 204—22 U.S.C. § 4304—would appear intended to afford public utilities protection both domestically and in foreign and international tribunals when they act in conformance with the Foreign Missions Act.

79.   Article 41 of the Charter of the United Nations reads as follows: "The Security Council may decide what measures not involving the use of armed forces are to be employed to give effect to its decisions, and it may call upon the Members of the United Nations to apply such measures. These may include complete or partial interruptions of economic relations and of rail, sea, air, postal, telegraphic, radio, and other means of communication, and the severance of diplomatic relations."

80.   To permit the freeze-out of a country, apparently the INTELSAT agreement first would have to be amended by two-thirds of the members present at an INTELSAT Assembly of Parties followed by a vote to suspend the country's use of INTELSAT satellites. *See* Broad, *No Go for Satellite Sanctions against Iran—A Presidential Proposal to Cut Off Iran's Access to the Satellites of INTELSAT Has Been Quietly Shelved*, 208 Science, May 16, 1980, at 685.

CHAPTER 5

THE RECORD CARRIER INDUSTRY

SANDRA K. KINCAID

The purpose of this paper is to provide, for those who are unfamiliar with it, an overview of the United States record communications industry, including its history, the facilities used, the services provided, the regulatory and standard-setting organizations which have evolved, and some of the legal problems which have occurred over the years.

INTRODUCTION

Record service is communication which produces a permanent replica or "hard copy" of the transmission and includes telegraph, telex, facsimile, and data transmission. Record service originated in the 1830s with the telegraph, with traffic initially sent by overhead wires and eventually by undersea cables. In the 1890s, Guglielmo Marconi developed radio transmission of telegraph signals. In the 1930s transmission by high frequency radio waves, or microwaves, was developed, and this eventually led to satellite communications in the 1960s.

The first telegraph company in the United States was Western Union, followed during the late nineteenth and early twentieth centuries by such companies as American Telegraph and Cable Company, Commercial Cable Company, All America Cables and Radio, Inc., Commercial Pacific Cable Company, De Forest Wireless Telegraph Company, United Wireless Telegraph Company, Radio Corporation of America, Mackay Radio and Telegraph Company, Federal Telegraph Company, Globe Wireless, Ltd., U.S. Liberia Radio Corporation, Press Wireless, Inc., and the Postal Telegraph Company.

In the 1950s, telex service was introduced, and grew rapidly, outstripping telegraph service by 1970. From the 1960s until the late 1970s, the record market consisted of only six carriers. The Western Union Telegraph Company had a monopoly of domestic telex and telegraph traffic, and international telex and telegraph service was provided by Western Union International, Inc., ITT World Communications, Inc., RCA Global Communications, Inc., TRT Telecommunications, Inc., and FTC Communications, Inc.

This stable situation began changing in the 1970s as new carriers such as Satellite Business Systems, Southern Pacific Communications Co., GTE Telenet, TYMNET, RCA Americom, and American Satellite Corporation, emerged to provide specialized and value-added services. Another source of change was the Federal Communications Commission (FCC), which began by allowing, and then encouraging, the entry of new carriers to compete with the American Telephone and Telegraph Company (AT&T) and the traditional record carriers.

The legal issues in the industry over the years have arisen in connection with such matters as the "public interest" of insuring good quality nationwide and worldwide telecommunications services, monopoly versus competition, undersea cable landing rights, exclusive agreements with foreign countries, policy and technical cooperation with other countries, rate regulation, facilities planning, activation and termination, and accessibility by new entrants to bottleneck facilities of other carriers, among others.

The views expressed in this paper are those of the author and do not necessarily reflect those of ITT.

SANDRA K. KINCAID ● Ms. Kincaid is staff counsel for the ITT Corporation communications group of companies, which includes the record carrier ITT World Communications, Inc., and devotes much of her time to practice before the Federal Communications Commission.

Length limitations necessarily preclude anything but a very broad picture of how some of these legal problems arose and how they were dealt with by the industry and by the U.S. government.

THE BEGINNINGS OF THE TELECOMMUNICATIONS INDUSTRY

Record service could be said to have begun in the 1830s when Samuel J. B. Morse began his experiments leading to telegraphy.[1] In 1838, Morse, with Alfred Vail, developed a workable telegraph and by 1843 Congress passed the Telegraph Bill which provided $30,000 to build a telegraph line from Baltimore to Washington, D.C. On May 27, 1844, the first "record" message, "What hath God wrought," was sent 40 miles between Baltimore and Washington.

Morse demonstrated the feasibility of submarine telegraph cables in 1842, and by 1850 short distance underwater cables were in operation in the United States. The first transatlantic cable was completed in 1858. A message of 90 words took 16½ hours to transmit. The cable failed shortly after it was inaugurated and never worked again. The first permanently successful transatlantic cable went into operation in 1866. By the 1870s rates were $100 for 20 words, but by the 1880s they had fallen to 50¢ a word, and by the 1890s rates were as low as 12¢ a word as rate wars among the various carriers followed the introduction of each new transatlantic cable.

In 1896, Guglielmo Marconi demonstrated the practical application of transmission of telegraph signals by radio and in 1897 the British Marconi Company was founded. The first transatlantic radio signal was received in 1901; by 1917 regular transmissions were made during World War I between the United States and its Western European allies; by 1920 regular commercial transatlantic radiotelegraph message service had commenced. High frequency radio signals were bounced off the troposphere, 6 miles up, for short-distance communication, or off the ionosphere 30 miles up for longer distances. This use of high-frequency radio signals eventually led to the first satellite in 1962. Commercial service via satellite began in 1965.

The "voice" telecommunications industry began in 1875 when Alexander Graham Bell invented the telephone. In the same year the Bell Telephone Company was organized in New Haven.

The first voice transatlantic radio communication was not completed until 1915, and it was not until 1927 that commercial transatlantic radio voice service began. The first cable dedicated to transatlantic voice service (TAT-1) did not become operational until 1956.

The first United States record company was The Western Union Telegraph Company, which built the first telegraph line between Baltimore and Washington, D.C. in 1844.

The British dominated the transatlantic cable networks in the early years. The first two transatlantic cables laid by a U.S. company, the American Telegraph and Cable Company financed by Jay Gould, did not become operational until 1882, and Western Union leased both these cables.

Other U.S. international telegraph companies began appearing toward the end of the nineteenth and beginning of the twentieth centuries. In 1883, the Commercial Cable Company was formed with the financial aid of the *New York Herald* to improve press communications. This company laid two cables between Nova Scotia and Ireland in 1884.

All America Cables and Radio, Inc. also entered the field in the 1880s to develop service between the United States, the West Indies, and Central and South America.

The Commercial Pacific Cable company laid a cable between Hawaii and San Francisco in 1902, and extended that cable to the Philippines in 1903.

The radiotelegraph was first used for ship-to-shore traffic and the dominant U.S. company was the British-controlled American Marconi Company. The De Forest Wireless Telegraph Company of America was organized in 1903 to compete for Marine radio traffic from the Atlantic and Gulf coasts, and later the Great Lakes.

The Federal Telegraph Company was incorporated in 1911; and the Tropical Radio Telegraph Company, a subsidiary of the United Fruit Company, was incorporated in 1913.

During World War I, for reasons of national security, the U.S. Navy took control of all radio facilities in the United States. After the war, the government encouraged General Electric to organize the Radio Corporation of America (RCA), which was incorporated on October 17, 1919. RCA subsequently developed the radio patents which had belonged to General Electric, AT&T, Westinghouse and others; after it purchased the assets and patent rights of the American Marconi Company, its only serious competitor was Mackay Radio and Telegraph

Co. Mackay began operations between San Francisco and Honolulu in 1927 with stations acquired from the Federal Telegraph Company. It expanded its radio circuits across the Atlantic and Pacific, but was limited in its ability to compete for radio record traffic by the exclusive agreements negotiated by RCA with various foreign governments.

In 1922, Press Wireless, Inc. was set up by three American newspapers to receive news from Britain via a station in Halifax, and in 1929, it was officially organized to perform services for all the press.

Industry growth in general was hampered in the 1920s and 1930s by problems with interconnection between overseas and domestic carriers and with securing agreements with foreign correspondents. Western Union refused to handle domestic delivery for RCA until 1931, when it finally agreed, but only if RCA paid the maximum cable-zone rate per word, regardless of the class of traffic.

During the 1930s, there was talk of consolidating radio and cable services to take care of the problems of underutilization, lack of adequate inland connecting services, meeting foreign competition, and exclusivity in that different carriers served different areas of the world, and were either cable or radio carriers.

Mergers in the 1930s, as well as the increasing use of radio facilities by cable carriers as backup facilities, took care of some of the problems.

GOVERNMENT REGULATION OF THE RECORD INDUSTRY

Government regulation began in 1910 when the Interstate Commerce Commission was given jurisdiction over the record carriers and the voice carriers. But the ICC was so involved with railroad expansion that it generally ignored regulation of the telegraph and telephone industries.

Because of British domination of the transatlantic cable networks in the early years, the U.S. government became involved in submarine cable landing rights during the latter half of the nineteenth century. In 1921, Congress formalized government authority by passing the Cable Landing Act, vesting in the president authority to grant, deny, condition, or revoke submarine cable landing licenses.

In 1927, Congress established the Federal Radio Commission to, among other functions, allocate trans-oceanic radio frequencies. This commission set an important precedent by taking the position that radio frequencies should not be granted for private use, but only on a public utility basis.

Globe Wireless, Ltd. and U.S. Liberia Radio Corporation were formed as a direct result of this commission action, in order to preserve assigned radio frequencies for their respective parent companies, The Dollar Steamship Co. and Firestone Rubber.

The Communications Act of 1934 established the Federal Communications Commission to insure that all common carrier services were available to the public upon reasonable request; that rates were just, reasonable, and on file with the commission; that carriers submitted annual and other reports; that carriers kept their records and accounts in prescribed forms; and that any construction, acquisition, and operation of new lines, or discontinuance of existing services, was done only with the authorization of the commission.

In the landmark Oslo case, 2 FCC 592 (1936), the FCC grappled with the problem of carriers holding exclusive agreements to handle all telegraph traffic to a given country by either cable or radio, holding that competing radio circuits could be authorized to points served only by cable, and additional radio circuits could be authorized to a point already adequately served by radio or cable if rate reductions could be expected to result.

During World War II, the FCC authorized additional circuits to 41 countries at the request of the Defense Communications Board, and after the war, from 1945 to 1951, authorized additional competing circuits on its own initiative. Also, before the war, Britain had required all traffic to points where the British held exclusive franchises to be routed via the United Kingdom or an Empire point closest to the country originating the message. After the war, in partial consideration for U.S. loans, the British abandoned this policy, and by the Bermuda Agreement, allowed U.S. companies to establish direct circuits to several countries. This agreement was later extended to allow direct U.S. circuits to many Commonwealth countries.

Before World War II, two companies, Western Union and the Postal Telegraph Company, handled most domestic telegraph traffic, but by 1943, Postal Telegraph was near bankruptcy and Western Union was operating at a loss. Because of the war, Congress wanted to insure a viable telegraph service, and therefore authorized the merger of Western Union and Postal Telegraph, in effect giving Western Union a monopoly of the mainland U.S., Canada, and Mexico telegraph service (47 U.S.C. Sec. 222). As a condition of the merger, Western Union had to divest itself of all its international telegraph operations, develop a formula to distribute unrouted, international telegraph traffic to all the international telegraph carriers, and establish procedures for the division of revenues with these carriers for that traffic. The remaining international record carriers were given authority to handle telegram pick-ups and deliveries in the coastal or "gateway" cities where their operations were based.

The 1950s and 1960s saw unusual facility and traffic growth in both the record and voice industries. In the 1950s, telex service was introduced, beginning a rapid growth which led to telex outstripping telegraph service by 1970. After the first transatlantic voice cable, TAT-1, was laid in 1956, overseas telephone calls more than doubled. The international record carriers (IRCs) also used this cable for record traffic by leasing circuits from AT&T. By the end of the 1950s, an additional cable was needed, and TAT-2 was put into service in 1959. TAT-3 was installed in 1963.

When it came time to build TAT-4, both Mackay and AT&T applied to the FCC to construct the cable. In the decision authorizing AT&T to construct TAT-4, the FCC for the first time permitted the international record carriers to become joint owners of cables rather than being restricted only to leasing circuits from the carrier granted the application to build the cable.

When applying for authorization to build this cable, AT&T also asked to broaden its authorization so that it could provide alternate voice data (AVD) service. The international record carriers strongly opposed this request and the FCC agreed with the IRCs, protecting the IRCs by limiting AT&T to providing voice services. It was the position of the FCC that AT&T's entry into the record service market would divert business from the smaller record carriers and might put the IRCs out of business altogether.

The powers and duties of the FCC were expanded by the Communications Satellite Act of 1962. This act provided for the establishment of a commercial communications satellite system and gave the FCC authority to insure that authorized carriers would have nondiscriminatory access to the satellites and earth stations, that cost savings made possible by use of the satellite system were reflected in the rates of the common carriers, and that no additions to the satellite system would be made unless required by the public interest, convenience, and necessity.

The Communications Satellite Corporation (COMSAT) was set up as a private company to serve as the U.S. operational participant in the global satellite system. The FCC originally limited it to the role of a carriers' carrier, primarily for the purpose of providing satellite circuits to carriers which offered telephone and telegraph message, telex, and leased circuit services to the public.

The international organization established to coordinate use of the satellite system was the International Telecommunications Satellite Consortium (INTELSAT), a partnership of owners. COMSAT is the U.S. representative to INTELSAT and a member of the governing body. COMSAT was the original system manager. Other countries are represented by government postal and telegraph agencies or companies similar to COMSAT. Nonmember countries are permitted to use satellites by leasing circuits.

INTERNATIONAL COOPERATION

International telecommunications technical and policy problems have been dealt with through an organization originally founded in 1865 as the International Telegraphy Union, and now functioning as an agency of the United Nations called the International Telecommmunications Union (ITU).[2]

Countries are members of the ITU and participate in its activities. ITU headquarters is in Geneva, Switzerland, where facilities are available for frequent international meetings. The ITU consists of four major functioning elements: the General Secretariat, the International Frequency Registration Board (IFRB), the International Radio Consultative Committee (CCIR), and the International Telegraph and Telephone Consultative Committee (CCITT).

The General Secretariat of the ITU consists of six departments: personnel, finance, conferences and common services, computer, external relations, and technical cooperation. Each department is operated by an international staff drawn on a rotating basis from member countries.

The IFRB handles registration, approval, and assignment of transmission and broadcast frequencies worldwide and resolves cases of interference between member countries.

The CCIR deals with the technical and operating aspects of radio communications, including point-to-point, mobile services, and television broadcasting.

The CCITT deals with all aspects of planning and operation for telephone, telegraph, and data transmission.

The ITU Administrative Council meets every few years to make resolutions and decisions on the operation of the ITU itself.

The CCIR and CCITT operate on four-year cycles offset by two years, so that every two years one or the other is holding its fourth year Plenary Assembly, usually in Geneva, at which officers are elected for the next four years; various reports, recommendations, and amendments are considered and approved by vote of the attending countries; and study groups and working committees are created to deal with specific problems and prepare recommendations to be voted on at the next Plenary Assembly. The study groups are staffed by telecommunications professionals from member countries who meet several times each year. Each group's recommendations and reports are published and circulated among the member countries to be formally approved at the next Plenary Assembly.

The proceedings and adopted recommendations of each Plenary Assembly are issued in a series of printed books with recommendations classified by letters of the alphabet. Series V, for example, contains recommendations for data transmission standards for public-utilized telephone networks. Recommendation V.24 sets out the standards for the interface between a computer terminal and a modem. Series X contains recommendations for public data networks. Recommendation X.75 deals with interconnecting packet networks. No carrier or country is bound by these recommendations. Compliance is voluntary.

In most other countries of the world, telecommunications is handled by the government on a noncompetitive basis. A single agency usually has the responsibility for providing telephone, record and data service, mail, and broadcasting. These agencies are usually referred to as "foreign administrations" or PTTs (for Postes, Telephonique et Telegraphique).

The U.S. participants in the various functions of the ITU are drawn on a voluntary basis from the existing international carriers which, until recently, consisted of only AT&T for voice service and five IRCs for telex, telegraph, and private line data service. U.S. policy has been formulated in an informal way, by consensus of the carriers, the FCC, the State Department, and the Executive Branch.

THE CURRENT TELECOMMUNICATIONS INDUSTRY

The telecommunications industry developed a configuration in the 1960s which remained stable for approximately 20 years.

RCA was created as a private company under government auspices after World War II, and was the dominant international telegraph carrier for many years.

Western Union finally divested itself of its ocean cable system in 1963, as required by the legislation permitting it to merge with Postal Telegraph. Western Union International, Inc., a wholly separated company, took over Western Union's international cables and operations; and The Western Union Telegraph Company had an exclusive monopoly of all domestic telegraph and telex traffic.

In the 1960s, the International Telephone and Telegraph Company acquired and consolidated assets of All America Cables and Radio, Inc., Mackay Radio and Telegraph, Globe Wireless, Inc., and the Commercial Cable Company, to form ITT World Communications, Inc. (ITT Worldcom).

These "big three" (RCA Global Communications, Inc., Western Union International, and ITT Worldcom) shared the international record market with two small carriers, TRT Telecommunications, Inc. (formerly Tropical Radio), and FTC Communications, Inc. (formerly French Cable).

During the 1960s and 1970s, AT&T provided international voice service, five IRCs provided international record service, and Western Union provided domestic record service.

The services offered by the IRCs are telegraph, telex, and private line. Telegraph messages are filed with Western Union or the IRCs, sent by cable or satellite and delivered by messenger or by phone, with a confirmation copy put in the mail.

Telex service consists of subscriber-to-subscriber conversations where the sender types a message on a teleprinter, the message is transmitted at 66 words per minute over a world-wide switched network and, typically, an unattended teleprinter at the other end switches itself on, identifies itself by sending an "answer-back" to the calling party, types out the message on paper fitted into the printer, and switches off.

Private line circuits can be leased from the record carriers to handle traffic at various speeds and are charged for at a fixed rate per month, as opposed to telegraph, which is charged for by the word, and telex, which is charged for by the minute. A voice grade channel can be subdivided to provide several telegraph speed channels, or it can be used alternately for voice and data (AVD), or simultaneously for voice and data (SVD).

Today these basic services have become very sophisticated with many add-on features. ITT Worldcom, for example, still provides basic telegram and telex service, but today telex customers can also get such add-on features as multiple-address, single-text, automatic retry, store and forward, Easy Call (use of a single character for dialing frequently-called numbers), departmental billing, fractionalized billing, and Databridge (which accepts telex input from data processing systems, word processors, intelligent terminals and tape/diskette transmission units, and provides code and protocol conversion).

Timetran, the ITT Worldcom outbound store-and-forward service, provides retry, delivery confirmation, conversion to telegram if the telex machine is not functioning after a certain number of retrys, and multi-address, common text to up to 50 overseas correspondents. Insure, the inbound ITT Worldcom store-and-forward service, holds messages until the customer calls for them, or delivers them immediately or over a specified time range.

Datel is a data service provided over appropriately conditioned lines, utilizing the customer's telephone to originate or terminate calls. This service is available to 22 countries.

Leased channel service is available to ITT Worldcom customers between the U.S. and approximately 100 countries. The ARX (Automatic Retransmission Exchange) allows customers to put together their own private leased channel networks. The customer is connected to the ARX switch at a port and can route traffic over one line to any one of several dedicated private lines or access the international telex or telegram network.

ITT Worldcom also provides international facsimile service, marine telegraph service to and from ships at sea, and Universal Data Transfer Service (UDTS), an international packet-switched data communications service for users who do not have their own private networks. This service can be used to access data bases, or to transmit information.

However, the IRCs and Western Union are no longer the only carriers of record or data traffic. In recent years, four other types of domestic U.S. carriers have been authorized by the FCC to carry data traffic: telephone companies, specialized common carriers, value-added carriers, and satellite carriers.[3] During the late 1950s, the telephone switched network began to be used for data and, until the mid-1970s, data traffic flowed through the same channels as voice traffic. Today, most data traffic is generated by computers and it is still carried over telephone lines, but now there are communications networks designed especially for data.

Telephone companies such as AT&T provide such data services as switched, unconditioned, voice-grade lines through Direct Distance Dialing (DDD); Wide Area Telecommunications Service (WATS) and Dataphone; leased analog lines under Series 100, 2000, 3000, 8000; and an all-digital network, Dataphone Digital Service, offering speeds of 2400, 4800, 9600 and 56 kilobits per second. 1.544 megabits per second is offered only from point to point.

Specialized carriers such as Satellite Business Systems provide an advanced satellite communications system to serve business and government organizations. SBS provides for digital, integrated transmission of voice, data, electronic mail, and video teleconferencing, and seeks to take care of the total communications needs of large users over dedicated facilities, private network services through the shared use of facilities, and low-cost, intercity voice service for smaller users.

Southern Pacific Communications Co., another specialized carrier, has provided private leased line service since 1974 and now offers service designed to accommodate voice, data, facsimile, telemetering, control, alarm, and other dedicated special services. Its services include full-period, dedicated tie lines, foreign exchange service (reach a remote telephone exchange by dialing a local call), satellite channels, voice plus data over the same tie line, data channels, multipoint channels, facsimile systems, traffic analysis, Dataport electronic mail, and Sprint, a low-cost, distance telephone service.

MCI and ITT's United States Transmission Systems are other specialized carriers offering services similar to Southern Pacific.

Value-added carriers include GTE TELENET, TYM-NET, UNINET, and facsimile carriers such as Graphnet.

GTE TELENET was formed in 1972 and was the first value-added network to receive FCC authorization. It provides a tariffed nationwide packet switched communications service between computers and a variety of terminals. It also provides leases, turnkey data network systems on a lease or purchase basis, and TELEMAIL, an electronic mail service in the United States and to 37 other countries, with input from data terminals, word processors, and telex machines.

TYMNET originated in 1969 to deliver remote computing services within Tymshare Incorporated. Other organizations began making requests for networks to connect their own computers and terminals and TYMNET became a wholly owned subsidiary of Tymshare in 1977, providing a public packet data network accessible by local phone calls from 270 domestic areas and 35 overseas areas. Packets can contain characters from multiple users and charges are based on the number of characters transmitted, the transmission speed, connect hours, and peak or off-peak traffic. International access to U.S. computers is accomplished via the IRCs. Other services offered by TYMNET include ONTYME Electronic Message Network Service for intracompany messages by subscription or turnkey systems permitting the storing and retrieving of messages; NEWSTYME Electronic News Distribution permitting subscribers to instantly access a publication or electronic news service; and TYME-GRAM to meet the first class U.S. mail needs of large customers. Messages from business customers are sorted by zipcode and transmitted over the TYMNET network to processing centers in 30 areas where the messages are printed, inserted into TYME-GRAM envelopes, and delivered to the post office for next day delivery.

UNINET is a similar service, provided by United Telecommunications since 1981.

Satellite carriers include COMSAT, Western Union, RCA Americom, American Satellite Corporation, and Satellite Business Systems.

They provide end-to-end satellite communictions services. American Satellite, for example, provides leased circuits with the circuits connected to ASC central offices by means of other carriers' facilities, the signals are then multiplexed into groups for transmission, usually by microwave to an ASC earth station, then to a satellite, and back down by the same type of route. ASC also provides specialized network services such as digitized voice, computer-to-computer data, high speed facsimile, high fidelity audio (broadcast), teleconferencing, and electronic mail.

Western Union, via its Westar satellites, also provides private line voice service, AVD, two-way, point-to-point data traffic, full time video channels, full duplex wideband data traffic, occasional video channels, and inter-carrier analog transmission.

It is important to note that all of these new entrants into the telecommunications market are providing only domestic U.S. service. International access to TYMNET and TELENET is via the IRCs. The "frontier" of the international market has only recently begun to be tested by potential new entrants.

MODERN TELECOMMUNICATIONS FACILITIES

The facilities used by all the domestic carriers and the IRCs for record or data traffic are wire pairs in open wires, cables, coaxial cables, radio systems, microwave radio systems (using the high end of the radio frequency range), undersea cables, waveguides (metal tubes which serve as paths for high-frequency radio waves), and fiber optic cables with lasers or light-emitting diodes.

The common carriers offer three broad categories of channels for leased circuits: narrowband (subvoice-grade), voice grade (voiceband), and wideband. The greater the size of the channel, the faster it can transmit data and the higher the number of bits it can handle. The rates for leased lines are generally based on the transmission speed. The narrowband channels allow the transmission of 45 to 150 bits per second and are used for telegraph traffic and low-speed data terminals. Voice-grade channels allow the transmission of 1800 to 2400 bits per second, although 9600 bits per second can be handled with special conditioning. Wideband is used for the transmission of 500,000 bits per second or higher.

A time-division multiplexor (TDM) divides a channel into time slots or subchannels. Signals from several information sources are transmitted one at a time so that no two pulses occupy the same time interval.

A frequency-division multiplexor (FDM) defines subchannels by frequencies. it does not rearrange the data, but converts incoming data from each terminal into one or two frequencies in each subchannel.

Transmission circuits are either simplex, permitting

traffic to go only in one direction from the transmitter to the receiver; half-duplex, with a transmitter and receiver at either end, but traffic can move only in one direction at a time; and full duplex, allowing transmission in both directions simultaneously.

Data signals are either analog or digital. Analog was the original method for transmitting both voice and data and it was not until 1975 that digital transmission systems began to be offered in the United States. Computers and data terminals generate signals in two discrete voltage levels to represent 0 or 1. A digital signal wave has peaks and valleys with square edges, whereas an analog wave has rounded peaks and valleys. The analog wave must be amplified periodically as it travels over long distances to its destination, but a digital signal can be regenerated at each repeater. Amplification will pick up and pass on any distortions to the waves, whereas regeneration results in a dramatic reduction in errors. Digital multiplexing also allows more channels to be derived, providing high-quality service. Of course, if the local loop, or line from the subscriber to the digital carrier, is analog, that signal must be converted to digital at the originating end and back to analog at the terminating end, reducing the benefits of digital transmission.

The narrowband channels are used for telex, remote metering, signaling, and supervisory control. Voice-grade channels are used for telephone systems and data sent at speeds of 300 of 9600 bits per second. Wideband channels are used for computer-to-computer traffic, terminal-to-computer traffic, and network trunk lines.

Switched services are provided over a carrier's network of lines. Subscribers are connected to one or more switching nodes connected to a backbone of trunk lines linking the population centers. Low-speed switched service networks include those for telex and Western Union's TWX; voice-grade switched service networks include those for telephone, Direct Distance Dialing, WATS, and private lines; and wideband networks are used for high-speed data services and facsimile.

Private or leased lines are totally dedicated to one customer who has the sole use of that circuit and can use it whenever he likes and condition it as he likes. A private line can go from point to point, or be interconnected to form a private network. The customer is usually connected to the leased circuit by local loops supplied by the local telephone company. As noted above, private lines are available at different speeds of transmission and the monthly rates are related to the speed of transmission.

The packet-switching carriers, such as GTE Telenet, Uninet, and TYMNET lease lines from other carriers and organize these lines into nationwide networks by using minicomputer-based controllers, switches, and interfacing devices. The user leases an access port or dials in over the telephone network and the carrier organizes the data into packets of up to 128 characters, then routes the packets digitally at high speeds through the network to domestic and international locations. TYMNET makes up packets with traffic from multiple users. The IRCs also provide international packet-switched services.

Emerging new applications include electronic mail, electronic fund transfers, teletex (telex formatted as a letter), teletext (printed information transmitted to home television sets adapted with decoders), videotext (computerized information systems transmitted to home television sets), and video teleconferencing.

Public digital data networks are being developed in Europe, Japan, and Australia. Existing or about-to-commence networks include the Nordic Data Network for Denmark, Finland, Norway and Sweden; Transpac for France; Datex for West Germany; RETD for Spain; PSS for the United Kingdom; Euronet for ten European countries; DDX for Japan; and MIDAS for Australia (which interconnects with TYMNET and Telenet in the U.S.).

FCC RESTRUCTURING OF THE TELECOMMUNICATIONS INDUSTRY

The FCC was, at first, reluctant to change the status quo in the telecommunications industry, particularly as far as AT&T was concerned, but under court pressure, it finally allowed the interconnection of non-AT&T terminal devices to the Bell system, *Hush-a-Phone Corp.* v. *United States*, 99 U.S. App. D.C. 190, 238 F.2d 266 (D.C. Cir. 1956), then local connections to Bell for competing intercity telephone services, *Bell System Tariff Offerings*, 46 FCC2d 413 (1974), aff'd sub nom. *Bell Telephone Company of Pennsylvania* v. *FCC*, 503 F.2d 1250 (3rd Cir. 1974), cert. denied, 422 U.S. 1026 (1975).

In 1969, MCI's Section 214 application was granted by the FCC to construct a line of microwave towers between St. Louis and Chicago to provide point-to-point private line services (*MCI*, 18 FCC2d 953 (1969)); and in 1971 the FCC authorized the entry of entities other than telephone and telegraph companies to offer specialized services as common carriers (*Specialized Common Carrier Services*, 29 FCC2d 870 (1971), aff'd sub nom. *Washington Utilities and Transportation Commission* v.

FCC, 513 F.2d 1142 (9th Cir.), cert. denied, 423 U.S. 836 (1975)).

In 1979, the FCC ended Western Union's monopoly of domestic message telegraph service by giving Graphnet authority to pick up, carry, and deliver telegrams within the United States and to interconnect with the IRCs (*Graphnet Systems Inc.*, 71 FCC2d 471 (1979)).

In addition, in order to achieve what the FCC considers beneficial increased competition, it has expanded the authority of AT&T, COMSAT, Western Union, and the IRCs to enhance the opportunities for competition.

COMSAT was permitted to provide television service directly to end users, rather than only to carriers in 1978 (*Authorized User*, 70 FCC2d 2127 (1978)).

AT&T was permitted to transmit data over its domestic and international telephone lines in the Dataphone decision (*AT&T*, 75 FCC2d 682 (1980)); and the IRCs were permitted to handle voice-only traffic on their Datel lines in the Datel decision (*WUI*, 76 FCC2d 166 (1980)). The carriers could only permit these uses, however; they could not apply separate charges or add facilities to provide these services.

COMSAT was authorized to provide its full range of services to end users on the same terms and conditions as the services were provided to carriers in 1982 (*Authorized User*, 90 FCC2d 1394 (1982)).

Also in 1982, AT&T was permitted to provide record services and the IRCs were permitted to provide voice services (*Overseas Communications Services*, 92 FCC2d 641 (1982). In 1979, the FCC had tried to sanction Western Union's provision of international service by interconnection with the foreign administrations in Canada and Mexico (*Western Union Telegraph Co.*, 75 FCC2d 461 (1979)), but the FCC's interpretation of Section 222 of the Communications Act as not barring such a service was overthrown by the Second Circuit (*ITT Worldcom* v. *FCC*, 621 F.2d 1201 (2d Cir. 1980)). Section 222 was finally amended by Congress in the Record Carrier Competition Act of 1981 to permit Western Union to provide international service.

This act also required all the record carriers to interconnect with one another so that users of traditional services would be able to access any carrier from any terminal, regardless of which carrier had supplied the terminal.

The IRCs were also authorized by the FCC to expand the number of cities from which they could provide their international services (*International Record Carriers*, 76 FCC2d 115 (1980)), and in 1982 were authorized to provide wholly domestic nonvoice service between their operating cities (*RCA Globcom*, 88 FCC2d 905 (1982)).

The third approach the FCC has taken to change the traditional market is to remove restrictions and regulatory requirements.

When Graphnet was permitted to compete with Western Union, the FCC reduced Western Union's regulatory requirements, eliminating Speed of Service Studies and application for authorization of agency closings and hour changes (*Regulation of Domestic Public Message Service*, 75 FCC2d 345 (1980)).

In 1980, the FCC required the record carriers to "unbundle" their rates so that terminals, access, and usage would be stand-alone, cost-justified services (*Customer Use of Telex Service*, 76 FCC2d 61 (1980)), and a year later ordered the carriers to detariff their terminal equipment (*IRCs Detariffing of Telex Equip.*, 86 FCC2d 411 (1981)).

In 1980, the FCC also divided common carrier service into basic or enhanced and held that regulation of enhanced services was not required (*Second Computer Inquiry*, 77 FCC2d 384 (1980)). Basic service was defined as the offering of transmission capacity for the movement of information. Enhanced service was defined as basic service with computer processing applications added (protocol and code conversion); providing different, restructured, or additional information; or the customer interacting with stored information. AT&T was also allowed to provide enhanced services but only through a separate subsidiary.

Carriers were required to remove resale and shared use restrictions from their tariffed domestic services in 1980 (*Resale and Shared Use*, 83 FCC2d 167 (1980)). The commission suggested the same requirement be applied to the international carriers in a Notice of Proposed Rulemaking issued in 1980 (*International Telecommunications Competition*, 77 FCC2d 831, (1980)), but strong negative reaction from foreign administrations has resulted in no further action being taken in this proceeding.

In 1980, the FCC also divided the domestic carriers into dominant (AT&T and the independent telephone companies, Western Union, domestic satellite carriers and resellers, and miscellaneous common carriers relaying video signals and associated audio), and nondominant (specialized and resale carriers) (*Competitive Carrier Rulemaking*, 85 FCC2d 1 (1980)). The regulation of the nondominant carriers was reduced so that they do not have to file cost justifications of their tariffs, their

Section 214 authorizations permit them to operate nationwide and they need report additional circuits only on a semiannual basis. Service can be discontinued 30 days after notice to customers.

This deregulation was carried even further in 1982 when resale carriers were completely deregulated (*Common Carrier Services*, 91 FCC2d 59 (1982)). They are no longer required to file tariffs or Section 214 applications for entry or exit. If a reseller acquires its own facilities, it becomes a nondominant carrier subject to reduced reporting requirements.

The FCC has proposed pushing deregulation even further by deregulating all domestic telecommunications services except MTS, WATS and private line services offered by AT&T and the independent telephone companies, and telex and TWX service offered by Western Union, in a Notice of proposed Rulemaking (*Deregulation of Telecommunications Services*, 84 FCC2d 445 (1981)).

Another deregulatory move made by the FCC was to declare the sale of domestic satellite transponders a noncommon carrier activity (*Domestic Fixed Satellite Transponder Sales*, 90 FCC2d 1238 (1982)).

To summarize these changes, as the record industry now stands, the domestic market has been opened up to resale, specialized, and value-added carriers operating with leased facilities or their own facilities, or a combination of the two. Domestic resellers and enhanced service carriers are not regulated. Basic service carriers are fully regulated if they are dominant carriers, and less stringently regulated if they are nondominant carriers.

Internationally, resale and shared use is still not permitted under any tariffs of the IRCs, or under AT&T's tariffs for private line service, and all the carriers remain fully regulated. The FCC applied the basic–enhanced dichotomy of *Computer II* to the international carriers, but has not yet required detariffing of enhanced services and is now reconsidering that decision.

CURRENT LEGAL PROBLEMS

Several of the FCC's actions in attempting to restructure the telecommunications industry are now under review in the courts or being reconsidered by the FCC.

The FCC's attempts to expand the international operating authority of COMSAT and AT&T to allow them to compete with the IRCs is now in the courts. The U.S. Court of Appeals has stayed the effectiveness of COMSAT's service to end users, and the issue of AT&T providing international record service is both before the U.S. Court of Appeals and before the FCC on reconsideration. As noted above, the FCC is also reconsidering its application of the basic–enhanced dichotomy of *Computer II* to the international carriers.

The FCC and the courts will also now have to grapple with case-by-case decisions on which services are basic, which enhanced, and problems which may arise from the deregulation of enhanced and resale carriers, such as quality of service, foreign ownership, access to facilities, etc., as well as trying to apply these concepts to the international market. But the mechanisms exist to deal with these legal issues.

While current legal issues with respect to new or different facilities may not have been dealt with before, they are not qualitatively different from issues long dealt with and resolved by the FCC, the courts, and Congress.

However, it remains to be seen whether the traditional mechanism for problem solving will be effective in dealing with such developing problems as increasing transborder data flow; the need to protect personal privacy and national privacy; the need to protect national "proprietary" technological information; and dependency on foreign computer technology and data sources.

While the problems such as transborder data flow and the new international Integrated Services Digital Network (ISDN) are being addressed by the CCITT, the incipient problem of entry by many new U.S. and European carriers, combined with the thrust for deregulation will severely tax the ability of nations to cooperate within the ITU. Dialogue is possible with one foreign administration speaking for each foreign country, and only AT&T and the five traditional IRCs plus Western Union representing the interests of the United States. If resale or unregulated carriers enter the market in large numbers, they may have no need or no desire to deal with the ITU.

This potential loss of control over international telecommunications is one reason the foreign administrations have been so hostile to the idea of resale and shared use of private line circuits, but changes are already starting. As noted above, foreign administrations allow access by their subscribers to TYMNET and Telenet via the IRCs, and Australia's digital data network interconnects with TYMNET and Telenet. SBS has reached an interconnection agreement with the United

Kingdom. ITT Worldcom has recently entered into a agreement with Data Communications Corporation of (South) Korea, an independent government-sanctioned company in South Korea, to provide data transfer services between South Korea and 17 other countries. Ten European countries have cooperated to develop Euronet as an international data network and the ISDN is being developed.

It is possible that the change to many carriers from a few carriers can be accommodated within the framework of existing institutions and existing laws, just as the radical change from the AT&T and affiliate telephone monopoly to competition for telephone service is being dealt with within the existing U.S. legal and regulatory framework. In fact, if one looks at the history of the record industry, what the FCC is now proposing is actually a *return* to the pre-1934 situation, where multiple nonregulated U.S. carriers were providing record services. It is also possible that if this free market comes about, one day it may again be suggested that problems of wasteful duplication of facilities, noncompensatory rates, interconnection, meeting foreign competition, and the need for reliable service, should be addressed by federal regulation, or perhaps by Congressionally sanctioned mergers resulting in monopolies.

CONCLUSION

Technical problems with telecommunications have been dealt with by the nations of the world since the 1830s. Current technological changes and entry by new carriers may prove to be not so radical a change after all, when looked at in the perspective of 150 years of domestic and international telecommunications.

It remains to be seen, however, if existing laws, legal concepts, and institutions can successfully deal with the conflicting concepts of free entry to the market by any carrier, high quality universal international telecommunications service, and the need to balance insuring the free transfer of data while at the same time insuring national security and privacy. The United States has as yet not found a way to effectively deal with such emerging problems as unauthorized access to computers, foreign monitoring of international U.S. business communications traffic, or pirating of cable television signals transmitted by satellite, for example.

The next 10 years may therefore see the growth of a new body of law in this country and, perhaps, the need for some government-to-government, treaty-type approach to set the ground rules for what telecommunications carriers can and cannot do, if the ITU voluntary cooperation approach proves unworkable.

NOTES

1. The history of the record industry is taken from two sources: W. Bolter, *International Communications Industry Policy, A Study of Competition, New Entry, and the TAT-4 'Voice-Record Dichotomy,'* in OVERSEAS COMMUNICATIONS SERVICES (FCC Docket No. CC 80-632); and D. Intartaglia, The U.S. International Record Carrier: Past, Present, and Future, (Feb. 1972) (unpublished thesis, Pace College Graduate School of Business Administration).

2. Information on the ITU is taken from *General Information & Directory of Carriers and Companies,* 1 WORLD TELECOMMUNICATIONS DIRECTORY (Telecom) (1980) (a looseleaf service).

3. Information on individual carriers and transmission facilities is taken from DATA WORLD (Auerbach) (1982) (a looseleaf service).

CHAPTER 6

INTERNATIONAL RADIO BROADCASTING

Sovereignty Versus Free FLow

WILLIAM H. READ

Dial across the shortwave broadcast bands, and a fact of international life quickly becomes apparent: the airways are filled with foreign radio stations.[1]

In all parts of the world the Voice of America (VOA), British Broadcasting Corporation (BBC), Deutsche Welle, and Radio Moscow can be heard. But there are plenty of others, too. Egypt is a major regional broadcaster in Europe as well as in the Middle East; the Australian Broadcasting Company beams signals throughout Southeast Asia; Cuba targets all its neighbors. From Albania to Switzerland, there is hardly a country in the world without an international radio broadcasting facility.

Nearly all these facilities are government owned, operated, and not-for-profit. But there are exceptions. Private "religious broadcasters" operate in Asia, Africa, and Latin America. Several small Western European countries have found "for profit" international broadcasting to be quite profitable, as is "spillover" broadcasting by border stations in some parts of the world.[2] All these stations are subject to national government control, as well as international rules.[3]

This chapter, written from the author's experience as an executive with the Voice of America, examines three legal aspects of international broadcasting:

1. Establishment of broadcast facilities
2. Regulation of broadcast content
3. Electronic interference, or jamming

BROADCAST FACILITIES

Except where noted, the chapter deals with radio, not television broadcasting. While there are significant situations of crossborder telecasting, the propagation of television signals from terrestrial transmitters generally is of shorter distance than shortwave or high power AM radio transmitters.[4] International television, prior to satellites, did not have the same potential as international radio for communicating with audiences at great distances. Direct broadcast satellites may alter this situation. Such systems are not expected to be operational until the mid-1980s.[5]

International audiences for broadcasting by foreign stations are chiefly composed of three groups: expatriots, the politically curious, and entertainment seekers.[6]

EXPATRIOTS. Communicating with expatriots gave impetus to the inauguration of a number of "overseas" services, particularly during the colonial period. Even today, the BBC External Service, as part of its mission, is

WILLIAM H. READ ● Mr. Read is a partner in Anderson, Benjamin & Read. Prior thereto, he was communications counsel, Bureau of Programs, United States Information Agency, Washington, D.C.

responsible for providing information about their ethnic origins to citizens of the United Kingdom who are traveling or residing abroad. In a similar vein, the overseas service of the Australian Broadcasting Company went on the air to bring radio from home to Australian military personnel stationed abroad or at sea.[7]

Besides expatriots and military personnel, there are today sizeable numbers of foreigners traveling or living abroad, and they often rely on shortwave broadcasts. The families of individuals employed by multinational corporations, for instance, are frequent listeners. So, too, are foreign students.

THE POLITICALLY CURIOUS. The greatest audience, by far, for foreign broadcasts consists of the "politically curious" of the world, especially those whose appetites for information are not satisfied by the local media. In Eastern Europe, the U.S.S.R., and the Peoples' Republic of China, the number of persons who listen to foreign broadcasts ranges in the tens of millions. Because governments there practice internal information control, there is great demand for the services of foreign radio stations. In the Third World, even in democracies like India, the amount of information provided by local media often does not fully satisfy everyone. So, there too, the demand is strong for information transmitted from abroad.[8]

ENTERTAINMENT SEEKERS. A third type of listener is the "entertainment seeker." Radio Luxembourg has long catered to the trans-European youth audience. And even VOA's jazz disc jockey, Willis Conover, once was as popular in Western Europe as he continues to be in Eastern Europe.[9]

Transmission Facilities

To reach these audiences, international radio stations use either shortwave or medium wave transmitters depending on the distance to be covered and the availability of frequencies. Shortwave, or high frequency broadcasting, is more common than medium wave, or AM-dial broadcasting, for international service. Of its 101 transmitters, VOA, for example, has only eight medium wave operating on the AM-dial. Generally, however, broadcasters prefer medium wave because AM-dial receivers are far more numerous than shortwave receivers. But the transmission range of shortwave is greater and this allows for more coverage.

To illustrate, VOA operates two megawatt medium wave transmitters in East Asia—one in Thailand, the

other in the Philippines. Together they cover most of Southeast Asia. With shortwave, an even larger coverage area can be reached using a quarter as much power. The reason is that shortwave frequencies propagate over longer distances than do medium wave frequencies.[10]

When distances are relatively short, medium wave is preferred over shortwave. In the early 1960s, VOA inaugurated medium wave service from the Florida keys to nearby Cuba. In recent years, the Castro government has been beaming medium wave signals into North America, with programs that include those of Radio Moscow. The Reagan administration has initiated a second AM-dial service to Cuba, known as Radio Marti. As a consequence, a "radio war" has begun to brew between the two countries and the stakes are high because the preferred medium of both sides, AM radio, is a fully assigned frequency band in the U.S.[11]

Whether a solution can be found to the "radio war" in the Caribbean is, at this writing, an open question. But the conflict does serve as a fresh reminder that there is a need for mutually agreeable rules for the conduct of international broadcasting.

Access to Broadcast Facilities

For every broadcast organization, international as well as domestic, there is a fundamental question: how to get access to the airways? For the United States, and a number of other countries as well, the question has a dimension beyond use of the electromagnetic spectrum. To reach most parts of the world by radio, the U.S. must operate some of its transmitters from foreign countries. The three other global broadcasters (U.S.S.R., U.K., West Germany) do this too.

All four, for instance, operate transmission facilities in the Caribbean. BBC and Deutsche Welle have a joint shortwave site in Antigua; VOA has an AM facility on the same island, and Radio Moscow operates from an AM facility in Cuba.

To operate a transmitter site in a foreign country requires a negotiated agreement with the host country. This can be difficult, because of differing views in the world over the role, as well as control, of the media. State sovereignty and free flow of information are seldom fully compatible principles. The U.S. itself, under the 1934 Communications Act, does not permit foreign ownership of transmitters operating in the United States.[12] But negotiated arrangements are possible. VOA has transmitters in 10 foreign countries (U.K., West Germany, Greece, Morocco, Liberia, Botswana, Sri

Lanka, Thailand, the Philippines, and Antigua). By comparison, Radio Free Europe and its sister station, Radio Liberty, have transmitters in Spain, Portugal, and West Germany.

Each operating agreement with a foreign country is, of course, different, although some features tend to be common. Most common are demands by host countries for assistance with their own broadcast efforts. This takes a number of forms, e.g., shared transmitter time, provision of equipment to local broadcast organizations, training of local broadcast personnel. Such assistance often constitutes the major cost of doing business in a host country. Successful negotiations often depend upon the flexibility and generosity of the foreign broadcaster.

Foreign broadcasters will not negotiate on program content. They insist on control of what goes over the transmitter operating within their boundaries. Thus, the range of countries willing to host foreign broadcasters is quite limited.

Another nonnegotiable demand of the foreign station is that the host country secure necessary frequencies.[13] By international agreement, frequencies are registered with the International Telecommunications Union (ITU) by the country from which the station operates. Thus, VOA transmitters in the United Kingdom operate on frequencies the British government has registered with the ITU in Geneva.

The system works fairly well between countries with mutual political interests, but can dissolve quickly when interests diverge. The VOA station in Okinawa went off the air under terms of the Okinawa Reversion Agreement. When Japan regained sovereignty over the Pacific Islands from the U.S., it became politically expedient to shut down the VOA station. Political change is a risk any organization assumes when doing business overseas. The VOA station in South Vietnam is presumably a part of Radio Hanoi's network today.

Political stability has been the chief concern of those who operate transmitter facilities in foreign countries. Today, however, the foremost concern is access to the electromagnetic spectrum. As demands for spectrum proliferate—fed by the emergence of new communications technologies—the broadcast bands have become saturated, and the shortwave bands have become congested through crowding and cochannel use. There is simply not enough spectrum available to accommodate all potential users. As a consequence, the 1979 World Administrative Radio Conference[14] did not deal adequately with spectrum matters for international broadcasting.

A special conference on these questions, scheduled for 1984–1986, could prove to be most contentious. Third World countries claim that there exists a gross imbalance in the sharing of frequencies. They claim that the industrial countries occupy 70 percent of the spectrum, while the "have not" countries occupy only 30 percent. This, they contend, is inequitable since, on a per capita basis, the statistics should be just the opposite.

A second area of growing concern to international broadcasters is the use of communications satellites. Like their domestic counterparts in the U.S., foreign broadcasters have begun to interconnect their transmission facilities by satellite circuit. Unlike the U.S. regulatory system, which is becoming more flexible and economically efficient, regulatory practices abroad remain rigid. The price of circuits, therefore, remains artificially high, and on-site satellite receiving stations which could provide greater signal reliability remain unauthorized,[15] much to the economic detriment of the broadcast user.

Moreover, controversy persists over the potential use of satellites for direct-to-home broadcasting on an international basis.[16] A dozen years of often heated debate in the United Nations' Committee on the Peaceful Uses of Outer Space has inhibited the development of Direct Broadcast Satellite (DBS) technology. Meanwhile, DBS technology appears to be more and more promising and this is bound to attract the interest of international as well as domestic broadcast organizations. Japan, the United States, and several Western European countries have authorized DBS for television.

What is noteworthy in the DBS debate at the U.N. is the call by Communist and Third World countries for international regulation of program content. This would be achieved by mandating that there be "prior consent" by receiving countries to the foreign transmission of a DBS signal. The thrust of the debate so far indicates that the proposed "prior consent" rules would apply only to television, not radio, which is not now subject to such regulation.[17]

"Prior consent" greatly expands the law of international broadcasting. It makes explicit what has been implicit—that is, that there exists an international right to establish an international broadcast facility. This legal right, however, is restricted, requiring the "prior consent" of a foreign government before it can be exercised. For the U.S., this presents a conflict with constitutional law, and for the world it marks the beginning of a new legal regime, one that goes beyond the present ITU system of frequency registration on a "first come, first serve" basis.

REGULATION OF CONTENT

Article 19 of the United Nations Declaration on Human Rights[18] can be read to preclude any regulation—international or domestic—of program material broadcast from one country to the next. But the practice is somewhat different than the principle.

Just as the U.S. Congress and Federal Communications Commission (FCC) have prescribed for private broadcasters what kinds of material they should program,[19] the U.S. Congress has, by law, instructed the Voice of America to adhere to a set of principles which include the responsibility to present news that is accurate, objective, and comprehensive.[20] To Radio Free Europe and Radio Liberty, two U.S. government-funded stations, Congress has said they should not operate in a manner inconsistent with U.S. foreign policy interests,[21] nor may they broadcast domestically.

All broadcast organizations operate under some degree of government regulation that includes rules concerning content. This perceived need to regulate content extends, in some instances, to the content of foreign broadcasts received by domestic listeners within the sovereign territory. There have been international protests, for instance, by the U.S.S.R. and Poland over alleged interference by Western radios into the internal affairs of Poland. Such protests are to be expected given the recent political developments in that troubled country.

The most effective restriction on foreign broadcast stations is censorship. While overt censorship is declining, more sophisticated forms are rising as governments try to limit broadcast journalists from collecting news and information. The simplest form of control is to bar sources of information, starting with visa applications that never get processed. International broadcast journalism suffers and listeners are denied information of public interest.

Control of communications is fundamental to the operation of the Soviet state,[22] and this gives rise to both media monopoly and Moscow's asserted right to impose censorship. Even during the height of détente, no VOA newsperson could get more than a temporary visa to visit the U.S.S.R. The Soviet view on information control

has become more influential in UNESCO. There the Western media have been on the defensive in protecting the principles of a free press.[23]

In sum, there is no special status for international broadcast journalists and their organizations. Internationally, the Western private and public media find themselves in much of the same position on issues about content regulation.

THE CASE OF JAMMING

The practice of electronic jamming of radio signals is nearly as old as international broadcasting itself. As early as 1934, the Austrian government interfered with what it considered to be hostile radio programming from Nazi Germany. As pre-World War II tensions rose in Europe, the practice spread. In his book on propaganda and international broadcasting, Julian Hale reports that "both before and after the outbreak of war [World War II], the Axis powers were the most active as far as jamming was concerned."[24]

Nazi Germany had an extensive "Broadcast Defense" system, while Italy and Japan conducted smaller, more erratic operations. France and the U.S.S.R. also jammed to keep unwanted German broadcasts out of their countrymen's ears.

When World War II ended, the practice of jamming did not. In 1946, Spain and the U.S.S.R. began jamming broadcasts beamed by each country to the other. Then, with the beginning of the Cold War, Western broadcasts were jammed by the U.S.S.R. Other Eastern European countries soon joined in this effort.

In the post-World War II period, there have been two times of relative "radio peace." Soviet jamming of the Voice of America stopped unexpectedly on June 19, 1963, only to resume six years later on August 21, 1969, within hours of the Soviet invasion of Czechoslovakia. With the coming of détente, Soviet jamming of VOA again ceased, this time on September 10, 1973.[25] But on August 20, 1980, the jamming resumed in response to VOA coverage of the Solidarity labor movement in Poland.

Even though VOA broadcasts were at times free from jamming, the same has not been the case for Kol Israel, for Radio Peking, and for Radio Liberty, the sister station of Radio Free Europe. All have been jammed even when the U.S.S.R. stopped interfering with the broadcasts of VOA, as well as with those of the BBC and West Germany's Deutsche Welle.

The effectiveness of jamming is difficult to measure. VOA once estimated that as many as 2000 transmitters were in use, located at several hundred sites in the U.S.S.R. and its satellite countries. In large cities, low-power transmitters are employed to disrupt radio signals traveling by ground wave. An additional means is known as "skywave jamming." This is accomplished by radiating the jamming signal of powerful transmitters into the ionosphere, which supports shortwave broadcasting over long distances.

To the listener, this interference distorts or degrades foreign broadcasts in two ways. Either a buzzing sound is imposed on the same frequency as the foreign station, or a distorted version of regular domestic radio programs is transmitted on the same frequency. Intense jamming can be very effective, virtually destroying the signal of the foreign station. But this is not always the case. There have been times of lesser interference, even "selective" jamming of just news, that amounted to little more than annoyance.

To counter the impact of jamming, VOA takes advantage of the fact that it operates a worldwide network of 101 interconnected transmitters, distributed among 15 stations, located in 11 countries. Some of these transmitters are very powerful, up to a quarter-million watts of power. Thus, "saturation broadcasting" is possible, as are other techniques that rely on favorable propagation conditions.

Jamming is more a political than legal problem, although it is not without its legal implications. In his book on international telecommunications, Delbert Smith notes that there are three justifications cited for jamming: disturbance of airspace, threats to national security, and threats to domestic values.[26]

According to Smith, these theories, of course, clash with those of freedom to communicate:

> The significance of the general arguments suggesting the conditions under which external broadcasts could be jammed is tempered by the existence of international legislation which attempts to establish realistic outside limits on jamming activities and tries to balance the concept of national sovereignty against the arguments for a "free flow of information."[27]

The accommodation of these legal principles has been less than fruitful. For example, the set of international telecommunications conventions negotiated at Montreux in 1965[28] contains two conflicting articles. Article 48 prohibits "harmful interference to the radio services of communications of other members," while Article 33 reserves to members "the right to suspend international telecommunications services for an indefinite time." Arguably, Article 33 does not apply to broadcasting, yet there is at least one authoritative interpretation to the contrary.

A more recent example comes from the Conference on Security and Cooperation in Europe which produced the Helsinki Accords. In the group of issues that became known as "Basket III," there was this specific reference to broadcasting:

> The participating states note the expansion in the dissemination of information broadcast by radio, and express the hope for the continuation of this process, so as to meet the interests of mutual understanding among peoples and the aims set forth by this Conference.[29]

To the West, this 1975 statement commended the decrease in Soviet jamming and implied that all jamming should cease. However, Soviet negotiators skillfully prevented the insertion of specific language to outlaw jamming. Instead the Helsinki Accords adopted an ambiguous formula which left Moscow free to continue jamming.

In recognition of this state of affairs, the United States issued a protocol statement at the end of the 1979 World Administrative Radio Conference declaring "so long as this interference [jamming] exists, it reserves the right with respect to such interference to take necessary and appropriate actions to protect its broadcasting interests."[30]

The statement lays the legal basis for "out of band" broadcasting, although out of band broadcasting is contrary to the spirit of international radio regulation. Nonetheless it provides a practical alternative to combat the effects of jamming.

However, no technical solution to the problem exists. Neither is a legal solution practical since the Helsinki Accords, negotiated at the height of détente, failed to provide a de jure rule.

Jamming is essentially a political problem, the resolution of which lies in the political arena.

NOTES

1. O. JOHANSEN & J. FROST, HOW TO LISTEN TO THE WORLD, WORLD RADIO AND TV HANDBOOK (1982).

2. A number of U.S. "border stations" beam broadcast programs into Canadian markets, a practice

that has led to a contentious trade issue between the two countries. *See* O. GANLEY & G. GANLEY, TO INFORM OR TO CONTROL (New York: McGraw-Hill, 1982). *See also* H.R. 5205 and S. 2051, 97th Cong. 1st Sess. (1982).

3.   Grad & Goldfarb, *Government Regulation of International Telecommunications,* 15 COL. J. OF TRANSNAT. L. 384 (1976).

4.   Shortwave and medium wave radio transmissions propagate their signals both by groundwave and skywave. The latter "bounces" off the ionosphere at night and consequently is able to cover a great distance.

5.   *See generally International Broadcasting: Direct Broadcast Satellites: Hearings Before Subcomm. of the House Comm. on Government Operations* 97th Cong. 1st Sess., (Doc. No. 87–104, Oct. 23, 1981).

6.   VOICE OF AMERICA, VOICE OF AMERICA FACT BOOK, (1981).

7.   BRITISH BROADCASTING CORP., BBC HANDBOOK (London, 1981).

8.   P. DAVISON, INTERNATIONAL POLITICAL COMMUNICATION (New York: Praeger, 1965).

9.   *See supra* note 6.

10.   For a discussion of how to propagage shortwave radio broadcasts from outer space, *see* Phillips & Knight, *Use of the 26 MHz Band for Satellite Broadcasting,* 170 E.B.U. REV.-TECHNICAL PAST, August 1978.

11.   Cuban Interference to United States AM Broadcasting, National Association of Broadcasters Science and Technology Department report (Mar. 1982).

12.   47 U.S.C. 151ff.

13.   Frequencies are registered with the International Frequency Registration Board of the International Telecommunications Union. The operation of the IFBR is described by D. LEIVE, INTERNATIONAL TELECOMMUNICATIONS AND INTERNATIONAL LAW: THE REGULATIONS OF THE RADIO SPECTRUM, (Sijthoff: Leyden, Hague, 1970).

14.   *See* INTERNATIONAL TELECOMMUNICATIONS UNION, U.S. DEPT. OF STATE DOC. 116, REPORT OF THE CHAIRMAN OF THE U.S. DELEGATION TO THE WORLD AD-MINISTRATIVE RADIO CONFERENCE OF THE INTERNATIONAL TELECOMMUNICATIONS UNION (1979) [hereinafter cited as WARC].

15.   *See* ORGANIZATION FOR ECONOMIC COOPERATION AND DEVELOPMENT, MONOPOLY AND COMPETITION IN THE PROVISION OF TELECOMMUNICATIONS SERVICES (Nov. 17, 1982).

16.   K. QUEENEY, DIRECT BROADCAST SATELLITES AND THE UNITED NATIONS (Sijthoff: Leyden, Hague, 1970).

17.   *Id.*

18.   Universal Declaration of Human Rights, G.A. Res. 217A, U.N. Doc. A/810, at 71 (1947).

19.   But note recent efforts to "deregulate" in U.S. broadcasting, e.g., H.R. 4726 (1981) proposal to replace the competitive renewal process for broadcast licenses.

20.   Pub. L. No. 94-350.

21.   Pub. L. No. 93-129.

22.   F. BARGHOON, SOVIET FOREIGN PROPAGANDA (Princeton: Princeton University Press, 1964).

23.   *See UNESCO and Freedom of Information, Hearings Before the Subcomm. on International Organizations of the House Comm. of Foreign Affairs,* 96th Cong., 1st Sess. (Doc. No. 50–080, July 19, 1979) Resolution Demanding a New World Information Order, 20th Sess. UNESCO General Conf., and 33rd Sess. U.N. General Assembly (1979).

24.   J. HALE, RADIO POWER (Philadelphia: Temple University Press, 1975).

25.   *See* D. ABSHIRE, INTERNATIONAL BROADCASTING (Beverly Hills: Sage, 1976).

26.   D. SMITH, INTERNATIONAL TELECOMMUNICATIONS CONTROL (Sijthoff: Leyden, Hague, 1969).

27.   *Id.*

28.   International Telecommunication Convention, 63 Stat. 1399, T.I.A.S. No. 1901 30 U.N.T.S. 316; revisions found at 18 U.S.T. 575, T.I.A.S. No. 6267; 28 U.S.T. 2497, T.I.A.S. No. 8572.

29.   Conference on Security and Cooperation in Europe (Helsinki Accords), Aug. 1, 1975, *reprinted in* 14 INT'L LEGAL MAT. 1292, 1295 (1975).

30.   WARC, *supra* note 14.

CHAPTER 7

THE GLOBAL TELEVISION MARKET

CORYDON B. DUNHAM
BARBARA G. HERING

INTRODUCTION

The international television program market is already economically and socially significant. It also could be on the brink of an expansion rivalling the communications explosion that began in this country some ten years ago. Whether or not the potential for growth will be realized in the near future depends on the equilibrium established between the countervailing forces acting on the market. On the one hand, as new and better technology becomes available, it inevitably creates an upward pressure on demand for programming. On the other hand, strong counterpressures are exerted by national trade barriers which are erected out of concerns for domestic cultural integrity and fears of governments over erosion of their power as well as customary economic objectives. These pressures are strongest when foreign or alien entertainment or news programming is perceived as threatening. Such pressures are often far more hostile to information flow than barriers against the flow of trade and are less likely to be overcome by economic interests which lead to trade exchange. Because of this, reduction in programming barriers will not keep pace with technological or economic change and is apt to be slow, indeed.

National barriers and practical difficulties already hamper the international flow of television programs.

Whether increasing consumer desires for such programming will lead to the reduction of those barriers will depend, of course, on economic conditions. But most significantly, it will depend upon the accommodation of national policy over time to the demands of local audiences and, in turn, upon the demands of these audiences coming together through a ubiquitous technology to form a global audience.

THE INTERNATIONAL MARKET FOR ENTERTAINMENT PROGRAMMING

The present world market does not lend itself to an exact description. There is little data of a reliable nature. We can, however, infer its size in approximate terms from the requirements of private broadcast operations for daily programming.[1] Some industry analysts have estimated that this demand now totals approximately 900 hours a day.[2] A substantial percentage of that total is, of course, devoted to categories other than entertainment, such as information, sports, education, advertising, etc. But the number of total broadcast hours and of entertainment programming hours is augmented by requirements of state broadcast operations which are also buyers of foreign programs.

While this chapter concentrates on the transnational flow of entertainment programming, it is obvious from

CORYDON B. DUNHAM • Mr. Dunham is executive vice president and general counsel, National Broadcasting Company. He is responsible for NBC's Washington office, the NBC Broadcast Standards Department, the NBC Law Department, and the NBC Compliance and Practices Department. BARBARA G. HERING • Ms. Hering is assistant general attorney, National Broadcasting Company, where her responsibilities include legal matters involving freedom of the press, First Amendment rights, and Fairness Doctrine issues.

these figures that other categories of programming—most importantly informational programming—constitute an important part of the flow. Most national barriers discussed below apply equally to nonentertainment and entertainment, greatly heightening the seriousness of their burden.

The United States dollar share of worldwide sales to television outlets alone is estimated to have been $500 million in 1983, up from $485 million in 1981.[3]

U. S. total sales of cassettes and discs, cable and pay-TV are estimated to have been $7 billion in 1982 and are expected to reach $11–12 billion in 1985. Foreign sales, which presently account for one third, are expected to be close to one half of the total of such sales by 1985.[4] Clearly the world market for video products and the related software is large and growing.

Conventional Broadcasting

Figures on world broadcasting systems lend support to this conclusion. Of the 155 countries that constitute the world community, only 28 now allow private broadcasting. These 28 countries have a total of 75 private broadcast operations which are on the air approximately 12 hours daily.[5] Eighteen countries still have no television service whatever.[6] The broadcast systems in the remaining 137 countries are either wholly or partly publicly owned and operated, and tend to buy less foreign programming than privately operated systems.[7]

These figures suggest room for many more outlets, and, in fact, expansion is taking place and will doubtless continue, notwithstanding newer technology. France, for example, which now has three state networks, plans to expand its television services with a fourth network.[8]

The French broadcast system is highly developed compared with most of the 137 countries that have some television service. A few countries, the United States, Canada and the United Kingdom among them, have more sets per 1000 population and more extensive service in every category. By far the vast majority of countries have fewer television sets per 1000 and fewer and less extensive services.[9] In fact, the systems of many of the 137 television broadcasting countries today consist of one or two channels offering a very limited schedule.

The Newer Technologies

The potential for cable, pay television, and satellite broadcasting growth are all considerable.

CABLE.   Only 13 European countries have any kind of cable system. Of these, service is most extensive in Belgium, the Netherlands, and Switzerland where 85 percent, 44 percent, and 35 percent, respectively, of television homes are served. Except in Belgium, all or a substantial portion of the service consists of unsophisticated master antenna systems. In France, for example, there are only 60,000 cable subscribers as compared with some 8 million master antenna subscribers.[10] A very recent European development is international cable, a private enterprise which began operations in spring 1982.[11]

The room for growth is unquestionable. Predictions as the extent, however, vary widely. A London research firm recently forecast that cable revenue from Western European households would grow to nearly $4 billion by the end of the decade. Another study predicts that cable subscribers will double by the end of the decade, achieving some 80% penetration.[12] A 1982 report by the Link Corporation, a U.S. research company, anticipates 55% average penetration by 1987.[13] It projects that French cable subscription will increase to over 2 million by 1987. Whichever report is more on target, foreign development promises to be significant; though much less than that projected for the United States, it will still constitute a major program market.

PAY TELEVISION.   Pay-TV is in an even earlier stage of development. Except for the United States, only six countries (three of which are in Europe—the United Kingdom, Finland, and Switzerland) have pay-TV.[14]

DIRECT BROADCAST SATELLITE.   Direct broadcast satellites (DBS) are also in an early stage of development. Again, the United States is in the vanguard, but development in Europe is proceeding apace on national, regional, and multinational levels.

The European Space Agency (ESA) was originally contemplated as a vehicle through which to carry out unified European development projects. Although conflicts of national views and interests prevented agreement, the agency continues to play a role in the nationalistic approach to European cooperation that was agreed upon by the participating members.[15]

In 1978, ESA launched its second Orbital Test Satellite (OTS) which currently distributes French TV to Tunisia.[16] This satellite is also being used by the newly formed Satellite Television, a private English company, to transmit advertiser-supported programming.[17] Among others, Satellite Television feeds the new European international cable system, the only system that obtains all its programming via satellite. Many other proposals to use this satellite for TV distribution are under consideration.

At least seven European countries are developing or planning to develop national DBS systems. Satellite launches are projected for 1985–86. Other countries that are not currently developing their own DBS are participants in various multinational satellite activities.[18] Somewhat paradoxically it is DBS that most acutely raises the national concerns discussed below.

The net of these figures is that there is room for much growth and that there must be growth if consumer demand is to be met. This will in turn increase demand for software.

Programming, however, is already in short supply in at least some countries. France, for one, was recently forced to reduce air time for its broadcast system because of a shortage of programming.[19]

VIDEOCASSETTE RECORDERS. One consequence of increased demand for programming has been to resort to alternative distribution methods such as videocassette recorders and videodisc players. Video cassette recorders (VCRs), relatively new to broadcast technology, have the same capabilities as older audiocassette recorders-plus-video. That is, they can record program material, play it back, and also play prerecorded material. Exclusive of U.S. and Canada, over 21 million VCRs have been sold, a figure that is expected to reach 80 million by 1990.[20]

Television and VCRs can be complementary, as when a VCR is used to tape a program for subsequent viewing while watching another program broadcast simultaneously with the one being taped. However, VCRs and videodiscs may also be used to supplement television fare by viewers unwilling to await the growth of alternative program delivery systems.

Thus, the rapid growth of VCRs in South Africa has been attributed to the fact that the television service consists of a single government-owned channel on the air about five hours a night. Since television service was introduced in 1976, two million sets have been purchased. South African consumers have also purchased 250,000 VCRs, perhaps the highest ratio of VCRs to television sets of any country, and support several cassette rental businesses. The generally accepted explanation for the unusually high VCR sales is widespread dissatisfaction with the quantity and quality of television fare.[21]

In Europe, where absolute sales (i.e., not relative to TV sets) have been even greater, concern has been voiced that they may crowd out the infant pay-TV and DBS delivery systems.[22] The worldwide international market, exclusive of Canada and the United States, is estimated to have spent over one billion dollars for some 16 million units of prerecorded videocassette software in 1982. The United States and Canada, respectively, spent as estimated $400 million and $41.5 million for 4.5 million and 500,000 units.[23]

CONSTRAINTS ON THE INTERNATIONAL MARKET

The large current demand and the even larger future demand should greatly expand the international market for programming. Various national barriers, however, raise concern about the transnational flow of programming material, most dramatically in the case of DBS.

Existing Barriers

Clearly there already exists a substantial unsatisfied appetite for television programming, the dimensions of which can not be gauged precisely. The reasons for the gap between supply and demand fall into two groups. One group consists of natural barriers arising out of practical and cultural factors. The other, which presents the more serious, more difficult problems, includes legal problems and the socio–economic–political considerations that underlie exclusionary actions by government.

CULTURAL DIFFERENCES. The economics of production in the U.S. dictate that a program must appeal primarily to the home domestic market. Foreign markets, however important, are secondary. A successful U.S. program or series of programs may not excite the same enthusiasm abroad. For example, situation and other comedy programs, a staple of American broadcasting, generally do not travel well. For different reasons, but having the same results, action and adventure programs encounter sales resistance in some foreign markets. Although programs in this category have international consumer appeal, governmental bodies and quasipublic groups tend to disapprove of them as having a pernicious effect on viewers.[24] So, some product is not readily marketable outside its country of origin.

LANGUAGE. There is also the barrier of language. English-language programs have a limited market in French, Spanish, or Italian-speaking countries and vice versa.

One solution is to cast the production with actors and

actresses fluent in the languages of the two principal markets. This obviously limits the available pool of talent from which the producer can draw. It may also adversely affect the quality of the program by discouraging spoken dialogue in favor of silent action, a universal language; this solution eliminates the need for double shooting, but limits the range of emotions and ideas that can be expressed.

A second solution is dubbing. However, it is impossible to achieve perfect synchronization between sound and lip motion. Consequently, in some markets, the United States for one, dubbed products do not find ready acceptance.[25] Also, both dubbing and double shooting add substantially to the cost of programs.

COPYRIGHT.   Still another problem, aggravated by the newer technologies, is how to protect the intellectual property rights of contributors to the creative work product. At the risk of drastically oversimplifying, American copyright owners of property distributed entirely by conventional broadcasting have generally been able to gain adequate legal protection by virtue of the Universal Copyright Convention—to which the United States is a signatory—or the Berne Convention—to which it is not (by means of simultaneous publication in the U.S. and a Berne country).[26] Copyrights are relatively easy to enforce against broadcast stations and networks, which are relatively few in number and, whether public or private, are, by and large, responsible and honest. Legal protection, therefore, was a minor problem when programs were delivered solely by broadcast.

The advent of cable and, more recently, of videocassette recorders and direct broadcast satellites have confused the legal picture. The argument of cable operators is that they merely enhance signals, and that this is not a duplication of programs in derogation of the rights of copyright owners. In this country, the argument of cable operators was upheld, albeit many still think wrongly, by the Supreme Court in its 1968 *Fortnightly* decision.[27] The courts of West Germany confronted by the same issue have reached the same conclusion.[28] Swiss courts reached the contrary conclusion that pickup and delivery by communal cable systems (but not by community antenna systems) is an infringing duplication of copyrighted material.[29]

In the Netherlands, unauthorized carriage by cable operators was so widespread that it had been said a pirate lurked behind every windmill.[30] The Dutch cable operators, like their U.S. counterparts, contended that their activity simply enhanced home reception and did not, therefore, constitute infringement. The issue was resolved in 1981 by the Dutch court which, following Swiss law, held that cable transmission constituted a duplication requiring the consent of the copyright owner.[31]

Whatever the merits of the West German and U.S. legal rulings in the context of early cable systems, factual conditions have greatly changed since they were made. Cable at the outset was offered to and purchased by subscribers, largely as a means of improving reception of broadcasts from television stations servicing their area. Imports of distant signals, although injurious to economic arrangements and expectations of program distributors, were secondary.

This accomodation, burdensome but bearable when cable was in its infancy, should be reconsidered in light of more recent technological advances. Advanced cable systems can have almost any number of channels. Formed into networks, their geographical reach becomes greatly extended, enormously increasing their potential for interfering with economic arrangements of the program market. Additional revenues from pay-TV and other special services give cable systems a new and formidable financial strength. They have become competitors with traditional broadcast stations and networks for license rights to all kinds of programming. Some cable systems also compete for advertising revenues, which have been and are the major if not only support of commercial broadcasting. To the extent they compete successfully—and they do so increasingly—free broadcasting and the nonsubscribing public are deprived of programming previously available.

The VCR copyright situation is at least as confused, and in the long run may prove to be the greater barrier to transnational flow of television programming material. Both international law and the domestic laws of some countries undercut the power of copyright owners to prevent individuals from videorecording copyright material for private use.

One school of thought which has considerable currency holds that the Berne Convention and the Universal Copyright Convention permit member states to provide for exemptions for private use under their domestic copyright laws.[32] In the U.S., an exemption for private use is the practical consequence of the Supreme Court's decision in *Universal City Studios, Inc. v Sony Corp. of America.*[33] The Supreme Court reversed the appellate court which, adopting the West German approach, had held that the copyright owner was entitled to payment not from the users but from the manufacturers of blank tape and recording machines. The Netherlands and, apparently, the United Kingdom, permit home recording for private use without any payment to copyright owners.[34]

Contrariwise, there is probably little reason to doubt that domestic law generally is in accord that commercial use of VCR technology to duplicate copyrighted programs without the permission of the copyright owner infringes the latter's property rights. Nevertheless, the practice is commonplace in some countries, notably South Africa, which has been dubbed a "pirate's paradise." The incentive is a demand for programming far exceeding the legal supply. In consequence, rental-library owners are said to treat license acquisitions as a "dispensable formality."

One obstacle to enforcement of the copyright laws in South Africa has been that local registration is a condition precedent to proceeding against infringers.[36] Many foreign production houses that failed to comply had assumed they were protected by international copyright treaties. Some local counsel are under the same impression and have advised clients that, while they could register locally, they would be equally protected if they did not by reason of the programs' registration in the United States.

CENSORSHIP. Finally, there are government-erected barriers which are intended to diminish the flow of programming across national boundaries. The two chief ones are censorship and quotas. Exporting producers and distributors are generally agreed that most countries practice some degree of censorship. Censorship, however, is not always open or obvious. Where the broadcast system is state owned and operated—which is still the case in the vast majority of countries—censorship can be and sometimes is accomplished without formal laws or rules. Public officials simply reject or excise offensive material.

Countries censor program imports for various reasons. Some are concerned about the cultural impact such programs may have. For example, Chinese officials recently criticized rock music—a Western import—as having a corrupting influence on their young people.[37] This concern is by no means limited to underdeveloped countries.[38] The motion picture *E.T.*, now in theatrical exhibition abroad, will presumably be offered to foreign television outlets in the future. This film has been an outstanding success in the U.S., acclaimed by critics, praised by parents, and greatly enjoyed by them as well

as their children. Nevertheless, it has been declared off-limits to youngsters under 11 years of age in Sweden, under 8 in Finland, and under 12 in Norway.[39]

Differences in political ideologies, which can be reflected in entertainment as well as informational programs, are another cause of censorship activity. Many countries prohibit foreign advertising, some prohibit the appearance of minors in commercials, some have a juvenile dress code, etc.[40] The restrictive advertising policies of some countries, including but by no means limited to China, appear to be rooted in apprehensiveness about stimulating consumerism that their economies could not possibly satisfy.

The deletion of material may be as offensive to the producer as its inclusion is to the broadcast executive or public official of the importing country. Some contracts seek to protect production integrity by providing that programs may not be edited except to comply with Boards of Censorship and then only with the distributor's consent. With respect to television news documentaries in syndication, the practice of some broadcasters is to refer the request to news management which may request that the license be revoked if the proposed edit would impair the integrity of the program.

QUOTAS. Every English-speaking country (other than the United States) imposes quotas on the import of foreign productions.[41] Except in countries such as the U.K., which has very large domestic production, the restrictions curtail imports and the available stock of television programs. If not quite universal, the control is certainly exercised in most other countries having broadcast systems. As with censorship, it may be *de facto* rather than *de jure*.

To start with, only Brazil, Japan, and the United Kingdom produce anything like 80% of their requirements domestically.[42] The price of United States-exported programs is usually below the local costs of production. Often the programs are also more popular. Canada, Japan, Australia, the United Kingdom, and Italy are the top five buyers of United States programming.[43] Third World countries produce relatively little of their own entertainment programming, usually for economic reasons. Thus United States programming can be financially attractive. It is this economic appeal of United States programs that gives weight to the Third World charge that the export of U.S. television programming represents cultural colonialism.

Quotas can be substantial. Canada, probably the single most important market for United States programs, would unquestionably import far more than it does were it not for a requirement that Canadian products constitute 60% of the broadcast schedule.[44] This quota represents primarily the concern that Canada will lose its cultural independence if its television reflects not its own cultural experiences and values, but those of the United States.

France limits foreign films to 50% of the 130 films each station is permitted to broadcast annually.[45] Finland requires that 40 percent of material broadcast be domestically produced.[46]

ECONOMIC RESTRICTIONS.   The generally restrictive policies of national Postal, Telephone and Telegraph Agencies (PTTs) also tend to limit growth.[47] As long as these agencies do not permit market forces and consumer demand to determine investment in broadcast hardware, the market for software, domestic and imported, is prevented from achieving maximum growth. In fact, the current watchword in some foreign countries against purchase of United States hardware is based on the fear of the software it will bring with it.

PROSPECTS FOR INTERNATIONAL SOLUTIONS

Given the international dimensions of the problem, logic would seem to dictate that solutions also be sought on the international level. In fact, however, it is hard to find much basis for optimism in that direction. With the possible exception of copyright, it is doubtful that any positive measures can be or will be adopted on the international level.

Copyright Cooperation

Copyright has a history of international cooperation. The Berne Treaty and Universal Copyright Convention already provide a legal framework conducive to growth of cooperation in this area. The theory underlying the copyright law of this and other countries is that artistic creations—such as programs—are encouraged by giving artists, authors, etc., a protected right to receive financial rewards from their intellectual creativity.

There are, however, some differences from country to country as to the extent of protection. The importance of uniformity has and will continue to increase in direct ratio to the international transmission of programs by the newer technologies such as satellite and videocassettes as well as by conventional broadcasting. Equally

important is the need for improved enforcement, perhaps through an international tribunal. Every effort should be made to obtain international agreement and action on these matters.

Provision of incentives to the creative and performing arts through copyright protection is surely worth pursuing when we contemplate the development of programming for one country that may be then distributed in another. If we believe that there could be a transnational or perhaps global audience, then the incentives of the copyright system could be useful in the development of programs that are designed to meet the needs and interests of those audiences. In fact, it may be uniquely the role of the law profession, on this point, to provide realistic encouragement for the development of new types of programming that will be part of the flow of information and entertainment across national boundaries.

Beyond this, however, the prospects for positive international action seem dim indeed regardless of whether programs are looked upon as communication or trade—both of which they are.

The UNESCO Barrier

Article 19 of the Universal Declaration of Human Rights provides that "everyone has the right to freedom of . . . expression [which] includes the freedom . . . to seek, receive and impart information and ideas through any media and regardless of frontiers." This would seem to mandate free and unobstructed passage of programs over national boundaries.

The United States invoked this provision in a recent debate in a special political committee of the U.N. concerning direct satellite transmissions. Notwithstanding, by a vote of 88 to 15 (11 abstentions) the committee adopted a resolution barring direct satellite transmission across international boundaries unless consented to by the receiving country.[48] The resolution did not deny that the programs transmitted by satellite were vehicles of information and ideas, which are the subject of the Declaration. To the contrary, it is precisely because they are recognized to communicate information and ideas that international organizations have taken stands contrary to Article 19.

For example, UNESCO's New World Information Order (NWIO) asserts a right of national governments to protect their "cultural identity."[49] Those who object to foreign programs and advertising as tending to weaken national cultural integrity have an instrument in UNESCO with which to prevent foreign cultural intrusions.

The Third World and Communist countries that have been the continuing source of pressure for NWIO proposals are seeking to control all transnational flow of programming material, out of as well as into their respective countries. indeed, the reason that the main concern of these countries is informational programming is their ideological belief that the press—print and electronic—should serve the interests of the state.

However, even noncommunist, developed nations that endorse the theory of free press and free communication have barred foreign advertising and to a lesser degree foreign programming. In addition to existing national barriers, UNESCO is encouraging new barriers which will prevent the free flow of programming.

These new barriers will not be subject to economic accommodations in international forums as are some trade barriers.

Trade Barriers

In the field of trade, GATT, the international organization created to facilitate international trade, hosted a meeting in 1900 at which the United States tried to persuade participants to lower or eliminate barriers to trade *inter alia* in agricultural products.[50] The results do not encourage use of that forum to eliminate barriers to program transmissions. The recent inclusion of services with trade as part of GATT's jurisdiction may help data flow, but it is doubtful if it will do much for programming in light of the great cultural concerns.

Moreover, there are other dangers in urging that transmission of programs be treated as trade. Viewed as merely another product in international trade, programs are likely to be more vulnerable to taxation. Taxes are already burdensome in some countries, e.g., Brazil, which has a 45% tax on imports.[51] At some level, taxation is as effective in limiting imports, perhaps more effective, than quotas.

Moreover, such a focus plays into the hands of UNESCO advocates of a New World Information Order. It would weaken the position of the United States and other Western nations that have opposed the proposals as inimical to free speech and free press. This is not to say that industry should not seek government aid to facilitate trade in programming. But on balance, the industry would probably do better to stress at every opportunity the communication aspect of their product.

CURRENT TRENDS

Notwithstanding, there will be continued growth of the global marketplace for video products. The favorable indications include (1) expansion of traditional and advanced technology now in progress or on the planning boards, (2) ownership trends, (3) international business arrangements, and (4) public demand. All four will work against the barriers to the transnational flow of television information and entertainment.

Projected expenditures by France and other countries for expansion of their broadcast systems and cable coverage assure that their rapid growth rate of the recent past will continue at an accelerated pace. The new cable systems with their larger channel capacity must necessarily create substantial additional demand for programming, which most nations will be unable to satisfy by increases in domestic productions.

Because private systems seem likely to be bigger buyers than public systems, it is also promising that ownership, or at least operation, of television services is being increasingly opened up to the private sector. This can be seen in England, where a new private network is in the offing, and in Italy, which recently permitted the establishment of another privately owned broadcast system.

The trend toward private systems is more obvious when one looks at cable. Whereas most broadcast systems continue to be publicly owned and operated, that is not the case in cable. Cable systems, although often built by the state, are predominantly privately operated.

The addition of a private network to the Italian broadcast scene increased demand for foreign product far out of proportion to the increment in broadcast hours. If this relationship holds true, the changing ownership mix augurs well for the market.

A particularly promising avenue is the joint venture. American companies are employing various arrangements and combinations, and numerous co-production deals between nationals of different countries have resulted.[52]

The Canadian quota system provides a strong impetus in this direction. Canada identifies programs which need not be counted toward its quota by a point system. Two points each are given for a Canadian director and writer; one point each for lighting, music, and art directors; one point for leading; and one point for supporting actors. An American producer looking to the Canadian market will therefore use Canadian nationals and locale—10 points' worth anyway—where this would not render the program unsaleable. A series which might otherwise have a quota problem might circumvent it by having Canadian nationals on the project, as, for example, NBC's "Saturday Night Live", whose executive producer, Lorne Michaels, and a number of his staff, were Canadian nationals, NBC's "Shogun" and "Marco Polo" series are also co-productions with nationals of other foreign countries. CBS has agreements with commercial networks in Italy and Australia. ABC and Brazil's major network, TV Globo, are discussing a joint venture.

This form has advantages over and beyond its usefulness in penetrating quota barriers. Production has become increasingly costly. The cost of quality programming may be so great as to be, if not prohibitive, at least an unreasonable risk. Co-producing the program or series spreads the cost and reduces the risk to more reasonable dimensions.

Still another advantage long-recognized by multinational companies is that co-ownership gives foreign nationals a stake in the organization. It is thus in their own self-interest to oppose governmental measures that would discriminate against the venture because of the foreign element. In the long run, this practical cooperation among entrepreneurs in different countries may hold the greatest promise for transnational flow of programming.

CONCLUSIONS

In assessing the future of transnational programming flow, it is probably useful to separate entertainment programming from news and informational programming. It seems unrealistic to expect that there will be a totally free West–East flow of news and information. Efforts to increase the flow North–South are beset not only with economic problems, but by what some observers see as the rights of a new colonialism. Certainly, countries with cultural concerns and, even more, individual governments, are often simply not open to news or information from other countries if it adversely affects their interests.

In addition, the development by UNESCO of its New World Information Order and the dedication of the U.N. administrative apparatus to its adoption and implementation threatens further to reduce the free flow of news

and information, if not superimpose an international rule for news coverage that essentially sees news as a legislative instrument of the state.

Certain forms of entertainment programming more easily cross national borders, even though they often have within them information and new ideas. There is consumer demand for this kind of programming, which could lead to a reduction in barriers, and, *if not* the building of a global audience, then a rapidly increasing multinational audience. Technology can make this audience available.

Here again, however, UNESCO tends to strengthen barriers to the flow of programming because it inherently operates to institutionalize worldwide an attitude that news and entertainment programs are not only proper matters for state control, but, beyond that, should serve interests that state wishes to further.

Certainly, the concern of individual countries about the intrusion of foreign cultures is understandable. So, too, is their concern about the threat of standardization of culture that the new mass media of television seems to carry. Might it not be, however, that comparison of a country's own folkways and values with those reflected in foreign programming would serve to reinforce the local traditions? Individual countries must make the judgment for themselves where to draw the line—where to erect a barrier, or where to take it down.

Ceding that national sovereignty to the U.N. World Information Order and its judgment on acceptable culture is the least promising course for any country's freedom or development. International collective action on a matter of any nation's culture will not provide protection, but only a lessening of freedom and opportunity.

NOTES

1. Statistics throughout this chapter should, therefore, be treated as approximations. The authors gratefully acknowledge the contribution of Wendy Stahl, manager, NBC Corporate Planning, in collecting and analyzing the video data presented herein.

2. *A $3 Billion International Program Market*, VIDEO AGE INT'L, Sept. 1982, at 41

3. RCA data

4. 12 HOME VIDEO & CABLE REP., Dec. 13, 1982, at 1.

5. *A $3 Billion International Program Market*,

supra note 2, at 41.

6. Guyana, one of these, has been planning to introduce television since 1963 and it is still uncertain when telecasting will commence. The obstacles are not only economic, but also the cultural concerns discussed below. *See Guyana Isn't Sure About Television,* INTER-MEDIA, May 1982, at 11.

7. Italy, for example, increased its purchases more than proportionately when it opened to privately owned broadcasting. BROADCASTING, Apr. 19, 1982, at 58. Private TV in 1981 carried 84 percent imported programming as against 16 percent imported programming on the state-owned system. *Networks Trim Italian Private TV* VIDEO AGE INT'L, Sept. 1982, at 48–51.

8. *French TV Under Reforms,* VIDEO AGE INT'L, Oct. 1982, at 18.

9. *See* UNESCO, STATISTICS ON RADIO & TELEVISION, 1960–1976 at 25, table, T, U, V, W (1978).

10. LINK CORP. REPORT, CATV & SATELLITES IN EUROPE 49, fig. 7 (Sept. 1982).

11. *Europe's First Satellite Link Promotes Eurocable Idea,* CABLE AGE June 14, 1982, at 13.

12. Communications & Information Technology Research Ltd., *CIT Research Press Information* (Nov. 9, 1982). Schrage, *European Readers Look to Cable,* Washington Post, Nov. 7, 1982, at K-1.

13. LINK CORP., *supra* note 10.

14. *See A $3 Billion International Program Market, supra* note 2. LINK CORP., *supra* note 10, at 55–57. The other countries having pay TV are the U.S., Canada, and Mexico. ADVERTISING AGE, May 31, 1982.

15. LINK REP., AT 79.

16. *Id.* at 80.

17. *Europe's First Satellite Link Promotes Eurocable Idea, supra* note 11.

18. LINK CORP., *supra* note 10, at 7, 79–92. *See also International Update,* VIDEO AGE INT'L, May 1982, at 8.

19. *A $3 Billion International Program Market, supra* note 2, at 19.

20. RCA data.

21. Botha, *South African TV Monopoly,* VIDEO AGE INT'L, Oct. 1982, at 36.

22. LINK CORP., *supra* note 10, at 31.

23. RCA data.

24. *Guyana Isn't Sure About Television, supra* note 6, at 11–12.

25. Dialectal differences further complicate dubbing, since Castillian Spanish is not acceptable in all countries which constitute the Spanish-speaking market. *See* Brown, *Spanish TV Worldwide,* VIDEO AGE INT'L, May 1982, at 27.

26. NIMMER, LAW OF COPYRIGHT 1, § 4.01[C] (1981).

27. Fortnightly Corp. v. United Artists Television, Inc., 392 U.S. 390 (1968).

28. Ball, *Copyright Squabbles,* CABLEAGE Nov. 30, 1981, at 22.

29. Suisa, Schweizerische Gesellschaft v. Kabeliernsihanlage Rediffusion AG, Fed. Ct., Jan. 20, 1981 (Index C 375/79), noted in J. COPYRIGHT SOC'Y U.S.A. 440. *See also* Ball *supra* note 28.

30. *Foreign Television,* VARIETY, April 21, 1982, at 37.

31. LINK CORP., *supra* note 10, at 47.

32. Glover, *International Laws on Videorecording,* 28 BULL. COPYRIGHT SOC'Y U.S.A. 475, 483, 497.

33. 104 S. Ct. 774 (1984).

34. 659 F.2d 963 (9th Cir. 1981).

35. Botha, *supra* note 21, at 36.

36. *Id.*

37. N.Y. Times, Oct. 28, 1982, § A at 2.

38. Washington Post, Nov. 7, 1982, at K-1.

39. N.Y. Post, Jan. 20, 1983, at 10.

40. The International Chamber of Commerce has adopted guidelines for self-regulation that the European Commission of the European Community had before it at the end of 1982. If approved, these may replace some or all statutory regulation. *See* WORLD WATCH, Nov. 1982, at 39.

41. Hausman, *U.S. Cable Programming,* CABLEAGE, Sept. 6, 1982, at 34.

42. *A $3 Billion International Program Market, supra* note 2.

43. BROADCASTING, *supra* note 7.

44. Hack, *Pay TV Born in Canada,* CABLEAGE, Apr. 19, 1982, at 14. A point system, discussed *infra* p. 26, is used to determine the nationality of a product. HOLLYWOOD REPORTER, Nov. 12, 1982, at 1.

45. *French TV Under Reforms, supra* note 8.

46. Howkins, *Communications in Finland,* INTERMEDIA, July–Sept. 1982, at 55.

47. PTTs are the European counterpart of the FCC in the U.S. and often place a severely restrictive limit on expansion of old technologies and development of new ones. Thus, *CableAge* noted in its November

30, 1981 issue that the Western European PTTs were inhibiting cable adaptation of various teletext services (p. 26). *See also European Leaders Look to Cable,* Washington Post, Nov. 7, 1982, at K1–K2.

48.   Broadcasting, Nov. 29, 1982, at 21.

49.   *See* S. MacBride, Many Voices, One World 159–165 (New York: UNESCO, 1980).

50.   Silk, *Gatt Talks,* N.Y. Times, Dec. 1, 1982, at D-2.

51.   Carrazedo, *Brazil's TV Grows,* Video Age Int'l May 1982, at 23.

52.   *See* U.S. Department of Commerce, Foreign Business Practices 75–86 (Washington: GPO, 1981).

CHAPTER 8

TRANSFER AND DISSEMINATION OF ADVERTISING ACROSS NATIONAL BORDERS

L. ROBERT PRIMOFF

ADVERTISING IS COMMUNICATION

Advertising is the art and practice of persuasion by verbal, auditory, or visual communication, i.e., by providing information. It uses words and/or pictures and/or music. It can be soothing or exasperating, convincing or ineffectual. In short, it is subject to the hazards to which all communication is prone.

Advertising is often aimed at selling a product (Coca-Cola), or services (Chemical Bank), but by no means always. It may, for example, be aimed at persuading the viewer to give blood (Red Cross), join the Navy, practice birth control (India), promote a wage and price control program (France), or beware of starting forest fires (Smokey the Bear).

Advertising is an essential element in our growing global economy. The *MacBride Commission Interim Report* noted that "advertising ... must be counted as one of the more important forces in the present world,"[1] and the Centre on Transnational Corporations reported that it was studying "the involvement and the role of transnational corporations in information media and advertising ... with a focus on the structure of these industries and interrelationships between them,"[2] and that "study of the structure of the transnational communications and advertising industries involves study of the links between the two."[3]

MacBride commissioner Mustapha Masmoudi of Tunisia, a leader of the more radical Third-World view, expressed his opinion in a paper annexed to the *MacBride Commission Interim Report*:

"In the developed countries ... domination [of the information fields] involves the whole of the present transnational communications system, that is the press agencies, radio and television, films, magazines, books and illustrated mass circulation journals, data banks and advertising firms."[4]

Advertising is viewed as so essential a part of the communication structure that many countries seek to regulate, limit, or prohibit ownership of advertising agencies by foreign nationals. For example, the Andean Foreign Investment Code,[5] in seeking to protect essential communications industries, lumps advertising together with transportation, commercial radio and television stations, newspapers and magazines, as enterprises closed to new direct foreign investment, and requires that 80 percent of any such existing investment be divested.

Although enforcement of this restriction has been postponed several times, it is now being implemented in at least two of the Andean Pact signatories: Venezuela and Colombia. Many other countries have similar laws, including Costa Rica, Indonesia, Iran, Kenya, Malaysia, Mexico, Nigeria, Panama, the Philippines, South Korea, Spain, and Thailand.[6]

ORIGIN AND SCOPE OF ADVERTISING

The advertising industry had humble beginnings. It began as a give-away service offered by media placement commission agents. According to Ed Ney (chairman and chief executive officer of Young & Rubicam),

L. ROBERT PRIMOFF ● Mr. Primoff is a partner in the law firm of Primoff & Primoff in New York City, specializing in international law including the communications area.

TABLE 8.1 Percentage of total world advertising expenditures by medium in 1978

	PRINT	TV	RADIO	OTHER
U.S./Canada	38	20	7	35
Western Europe	64	14	3	19
Asia	37	33	6	24
Latin America	29	41	16	14
Australia/New Zealand	50	28	10	12
Mideast/Africa	41	13	8	38
Total (72 countries)	43	21	7	29

"at the end of World War II, worldwide advertising was a cottage industry largely centered under the thatched roofs of Madison Avenue in New York City."[7] It has come a long way. 1980 worldwide advertising expenditures throughout the noncommunist world were estimated at well over $111 billion.[8] By 1985 such revenues are expected to exceed $175 billion, and by 1990 are anticipated at $300 billion.[9]

Table 8.1 shows the percentage of total world advertising expenditures by medium in 1978.[10]

ADVERTISING MATERIAL—PREPARATION AND PROCESS

Advertising is part of the marketing process which includes developing, positioning, manufacturing, advertising, distributing, and merchandising. Most leading agencies either involve themselves in the entire marketing picture, or assign account management personnel who are familiar with marketing techniques and philosophies. The advertising alone—i.e., the preparation and publication of a magazine ad, for example, or the production and airing of a television commercial—is only the tip of the iceberg.

The marketing process, including the advertising segments, performed by the agency and/or the client (advertiser), is today highly complex and involves dozens of disciplines and many different media, including print and television. The steps include (1) research to determine new product opportunities, position the product, ascertain its potential users, and decide on the most persuasive product information; (2) design and production of the products; (3) development of media-mix plans to reach targeted audiences most effectively, and purchase of media time and space; (4) research and

creation of the most effective possible advertising; (5) package design and testing to create pleasing and effective packaging; (6) production inhouse and outside of rough and finished artwork, typography, and photographic materials, and contracting, casting, and production of TV commercials; (7) market positioning to determine price and type of retail outlet and new product introduction plans (price discounts, coupons, free samples, etc.); (8) test marketing of advertising, media selection, packaging and positioning; (9) merchandising (shelf-space negotiating with retail outlets, onsite checking of retail display, etc.); (10) preparation, testing, distribution, and follow-up of point-of-sale materials (e.g., counter displays); (11) approval by client at all stages of plans, artwork, TV storyboards, and other mechanical production; (12) and—at all times—legal checking to ensure compliance with truth-in-advertising laws, broadcast and other industry codes and avoidance of defamation, unfair competition, copyright and trademark infringement, violation of privacy, and product liability risks.

Many of the nonadvertising aspects of marketing, which directly affect the practice of advertising, and particularly research and testing, will be heavily impacted by certain of the new technologies such as two-way television, electronic transmittal of data for processing, and others.

PREPARATION AND PLACEMENT OF INTERNATIONAL ADVERTISING

Advertising agencies in the United States followed their advertising clients overseas.[11] Excluding Canada, the first foreign offices of substance of U.S. agencies were not opened until the mid-1920s.[12] Since then, expansion into international markets has been rapid: The Interpublic Group of Companies, Inc., for example, has offices in over 50 countries. Its 1981 gross revenue (commissions, fees, and publications) was $433,000,000 of which 57% was from its foreign agencies. In 1982 such revenue exceeded $532,000,000 of which 59.4% was from foreign operations. Using traditional conversion figures, this represents "billings" (i.e., the cost of total media purchased for client advertising) of over $3.5 billion. Of the 25 largest advertising agencies in the world (all operating internationally), 21 are American. Of the top 50, 32 are American. 1981 worldwide billings of American agencies exceeded $35 billion of which about $15 billion were spent outside the U.S.[13]

A factor conducive to the recent entry of foreign agencies in overseas markets has been the growth in many countries of restrictions on foreign-made commercials, in the form of heavy taxes and/or prohibition, where a foreign language, foreign actors, or foreign production facilities have been used.

Major advertising strategies for worldwide clients (major multinational advertisers)—especially those with internationally known brand names and trademarks—are generally developed, reviewed, and controlled at the agency's headquarters. Although the advertising is usually planned and executed locally (the local agency office working with the local client office), creative work is often influenced by the parent company's work and staff. Moreover, where major global clients are concerned, creative work, particularly television commercials, is often centrally produced (not necessarily in the United States) for use and placement by local agency affiliates in the various foreign markets. This has the advantage of saving substantial production costs, obtaining higher quality advertising than might be possible in many local agencies, assuring quality control at the parent company level, and unifying a brand image worldwide. Language and other local environmental differences of course require adaptations in the advertising.

For other clients, however, television commercials and print advertisements are normally made by the local agency.[14] Where worldwide brand images are not involved, centralized production is neither required nor justified. Also, local agencies are more familiar with local cultural and other factors, and can better create persuasive advertising consistent with their local customs, tastes, visual preferences, needs, and psychology. However, for the purpose of assuring quality control, it is common for the parent company to hold frequent

seminars and provide other professional training, both at the home office and at other locations, and upgrading for creative, research, media, production, and other staff from the local subsidiaries.

For all clients, the local agency will normally place the advertising (e.g., purchase the space or time) so as to assure receipt of the agency's commissions (media generally grant commissions or discounts—which is the agency's primary source of income—only to agencies that are "accredited" in the local market). Moreover, appropriate media schedules would, in any event, almost certainly have to be prepared by a local agency familiar with the local market and media.

Foreign offices of clients (advertisers) invariably submit their proposed local advertising budget to the parent company for approval, as they submit budgets for all items of expense and income. Once approved, however, the local client subsidiary operates autonomously, dealing with the local agency subsidiary, although proposed advertising and marketing plans are frequently reviewed by the advertiser's home office. International agencies, in turn, regard local subsidiaries as profit centers and (within the parameters of protecting overall worldwide relationships with international clients and adhering to approved budgets and profit forecasts) allow the local agency business and professional autonomy.

WHY ADVERTISING IS IMPORTANT

Before evaluating the impact of the new technologies, it is useful to review the value of advertising.

1. The free flow of commercial information is a key factor to economic and social progress at both the national and international levels. In general, nations which develop a free flow of information can expect to enjoy faster economic progress.[15]
2. The speed with which advertising communicates helps to launch a product quickly, thereby justifying the capital expenditure involved. Often a manufacturer could launch a product by slower means (without advertising), but could not afford the capital outlay over a much longer build-up time.[16]
3. Advertising generates competition, because the latter is only as strong as the public's perception of available alternatives.
4. It creates the volume that lowers prices, for,

although mass production permits economies of scale, mass production requires the prior expectation of mass purchasing so that the manufacturer can gear up.

5. It creates awareness of market value (e.g., air-line travel, automotive, grocery, housing, appliances, etc.). Without it there would be no such awareness.

6. It informs people of goods and services about which they might not otherwise have known, adding enjoyment and depth to their lives.

7. It teaches the possibility of change, dramatizes new possibilities, and encourages people to seek change, to challenge, and to expect and demand something better. It thus presents a picture which poses alternatives to the existing structure by confronting caste and "preordained" status with the possibility of altering status (i.e., social mobility).

8. It establishes the concept that desirable goods, services, and know-how can be acquired, thereby changing expectations of what is possible in terms of material well-being and individual development, and opening up new vistas of economic, social, and political possibilities.

9. It provides and encourages people to exercise free choice—in part personal and in part economic—fundamental to a free society and an element of democracy that adds dimension to living.

10. It promotes desirable social aims such as savings and investment, family planning, etc. It provides consumers with information regarding possible patterns of expenditure and equips them to make choices.[17]

11. It sets many positive examples such as cleanliness, balanced diet, and other forms of health care.

12. It inculcates the habit of saving by creating purchase objectives that require the accumulation of capital, and (e.g., in poorer developing countries) "gets across" the use of money to purchase alternatives and thus brings people into the monetary economy.

13. It teaches the ability to discriminate between products and to question different characteristics they have.

14. Advertising provides the financial support which permits private ownership of mass media, making possible a viable, independent, and free press and broadcast media in many areas of the world;[18] and, because advertising revenues come from multiple sources, it fosters economic health and independence, enabling the media to defy pressure from a single economic interest or from political authorities.[19]

Even in countries where broadcast facilities are government-owned, the independence of broadcast authorities appears to be stronger where substantial advertising revenues exist, not only because there is less need to go hat-in-hand seeking State subsidies, but also because of the greater influence of the private sector.

Only 4 of the 17 countries of Western Europe have some privately owned television facilities (and in one of these, Tele Luxembourg, the French government is a large shareholder) in addition to their publicly owned ones. In all the others, television facilities are owned exclusively by government, either directly or through public authorities. Six West European nations have no commercial radio. France has recently authorized private radio broadcasting but not yet permitted it to air advertising, although that seems inevitable.

Government ownership and operation of broadcast facilities, however, are not incompatible with advertising. Only Denmark, Norway, Sweden, and Belgium bar advertising on television, and Belgium is not only largely served by Tele Luxembourg but will itself soon embark on commercial broadcasting.

Governments everywhere increasingly seek advertising revenues to help defray costs, and this inevitably results in increased service to the public.[20]

In France, for example, the government permits commercials to generate 25% of all television revenue (three networks), which is 50% of the revenue of the two of such networks that accept commercials, with user taxes supplying the balance. In India, allowable advertising time is increasing. Governments of all shades freely use advertising for their own goals.

THE IMPACT OF TECHNOLOGICAL INNOVATION

Advertising and the New Technologies

The future will bring continued proliferation of existing means of mass communication, i.e., existing hardware, as well as such newer techniques as direct broadcasting by satellite (DBS), cable (to distribute both satellite and ground station transmissions), videotext systems, and videodisc magazines.

Such new distribution systems will expedite increased coverage and facilitate penetration.[21] Because of the much larger audiences, the potential increase in advertising power (whether consumer product or political) is vast.

CASSETTES. The audio tape cassette, containing Khomeini's recorded speeches and distributed throughout Iran at minimal cost (easily secreted and smuggled into the country), is broadly credited with the overthrow of the Shah.[22] This was a form of advertising, just as political campaign commercials are in the United States.

The videocassette is having an increasingly potent effect in certain markets, such as the United Kingdom, where it is blamed for a substantial decline in TV audiences.

TELEVISION. Broadcasting, and especially television, is the most obvious area in which to look for change. Of all media it is the most effective, both in persuasion and in cost efficiency.

Television's effectiveness results from the combination of words with image, which reinforces the message and its retention in memory, and is particularly effective where the product and its package can be seen as they will appear on the store shelf. The audience is "captive" (provided the commercial is not long enough to justify turning it off).[23] Selling roles can be played by believable actors and actresses in real-life situations. Above all, television advertising is cost effective: TV time is expensive, but the audience can number in the millions nationally (and, one day, in the billions globally).

Internationally, television has the additional advantage that visual images are not as restricted by language differences. This suggests that, as DBS and other transnational broadcasting develop, commercials will become more pictorial and less verbal,[24] and that both advertising and international product packaging will become more uniform.

In principle, regional, as distinguished from national, advertising campaigns can be envisaged, e.g., the pan-European campaign of Schweppes—"Schwepping"—for use throughout Western Europe. Advertising by satellite will be particularly attractive to companies having international brands. Multinational advertisers would strongly welcome the chance to reach large pan-European audiences and would no doubt centralize part of their overall advertising budgets to pay the costs, i.e., by requiring contributions from local subsidiaries' budgets. This would, to some extent, decrease local advertiser autonomy, and would have a centralizing effect on the agency's product and operations.

The practice is still quite decentralized. For example, of the 50 most heavily advertised brands or services in Britain, 29 are not marketed in any other country; 6 are sold outside the U.K. under different names or packages; and the remaining 15 are marketed throughout Europe under the same brand name but with different packaging or advertising. Not one of the 50 is marketed throughout Europe with the same name, packaging, and advertising.

The reasons include (1) differences in culture, tastes, and language[25] and (2) differences in national laws; advertising acceptable in one country may be unacceptable in another. However, both the European Community (Common Market) and Council of Europe are involved in potential rule-making and a strong move toward enacting some kind of regional advertising code is underway.[26]

SATELLITES. Both low-powered (suitable for cable redistribution) and high-powered (permitting DBS) satellite projects are scheduled for Europe during the next few years. Low-powered systems include Telecom I (France, 1984), Unisat (U.K., 1986), and DFS (Germany, 1986). High-powered operations, most of which are planned for 1986, include both basically government-financed operations—TV SAT (Germany), TDF 1 (France, but Luxembourg will get one channel), ESA L-Sat (essentially U.K./Italy), TEL-X (Sweden), and OLYMPUS 1 (U.K., Italy, Holland)—and two which will depend on advertising revenue for financing—LUX-SAT (Luxembourg) and TEL-SAT (Switzerland). Commercial advertising on the three government operations should not be ruled out. There is considerable pressure to obtain more commercial television time, such as that which satellites can provide. Television time in Germany is 200% overbooked. In Italy time must be bought a year in advance and tie-in purchases of other media are customarily demanded. Except for Luxembourg, the U.K., Spain, and Ireland, long waits are the rule.[27]

Multinational advertisers in Europe are experimenting with transmission on a low-powered satellite channel (whose signal can only be received by a large dish antenna of the sort used by cable companies) for distribution by cable. If this proves successful, it could be more popular than both regular television and DBS, would almost certainly carry advertising, and will (as of now) include top soccer games, British comedies, and such popular U.S. shows as "Starsky & Hutch," "Charlie's Angels," and movies. This could spur advertising. Satellite broadcasting of commercials has already begun. Several of Europe's biggest television advertisers are beaming their commercials off a satellite to a few thousand homes in Norway, Finland, Switzerland, and Malta (Coca-Cola, Kellogg, British Airways). In Norway, although privately owned cable TV does not carry advertising, it is distributing Satellite Television (England) program material-cum-commercials.[28]

However, because of satellite development and implementation costs and difficulties, not to mention the debate over regulation (*See* "Concerns over Transborder Advertising,"), the prospect of widespread DBS is still some time off.[29]

CABLE.   Cable TV, whether or not coupled with DBS, will certainly result in media fragmentation. Already in the U.K., as a result of the new Channel 4 (as well, perhaps, as a result of the widespread use of VCRs and rental cassettes), audiences for individual channels have declined. The expected proliferation of satellite channels and cable television will segment the media market even more. Increased competition will lower the cost of advertising, but will also require of advertisers that they more carefully identify their target audiences. The development of optical fibers for electronic transmission will reduce the costs of CATV infrastructures and speed its expansion. CATV is already widespread in many European countries. According to one source, more than half of the households in Belgium, Denmark, and the Netherlands, and nearly as many in Sweden and Switzerland, are covered.[30]

OTHERS.   Videotex, teletext,[31] electronic mail, and similar techniques permitting narrow audience targeting (like cable television when used to reach particular audiences) make possible limited-interest service to highly selected segments. Such audiences, although smaller and more expensive per person to reach, offer advertisers a higher concentration of potential buyers, and are therefore economically attractive, especially for higher-priced goods and services.

It is tempting to describe as ironical the fact that the technology explosion will create not only the means to reach immeasurably larger mass audiences, but also small, individually segmented and selected special interest groups. It is not irony, however, but additional evidence that the new technologies will multiply the choices available to the planet's inhabitants (Cf. "Why Advertising Is Important," p. 107).

Concerns Over Transborder Advertising

Analogies are sometimes made between DBS and the offshore "pirate" radio stations in Europe, beaming unwanted programs and other materials into countries which would prohibit, regulate, or tax the same on local broadcast media. However, uncontrolled saturation of the consumer with advertising from direct satellite transmission seems unlikely.

First, small dish antennae are relatively expensive, (particularly for Third-World viewers) and their sale and use can be controlled or prevented by local authorities. Large dish antennae, intended for use with DBS weak-signal broadcasting to cable distributors, will no doubt have scrambled transmissions. Concerned receiving countries can control content by licensing or prohibiting unscramblers. Also, they can exercise regulatory power over the cable systems which are earthbound by necessity (Cf. "Developing Rules," p. 114, regarding the question of government's power over "passive" cable distributors).

Second, even if small antennae made possible reception of unauthorized or illegal commercials, the authorities would have physical, retributive, and punitive powers over the makers, distributors, and sellers of the advertised products or services, as well as the local offices of the agency or advertiser.

Within the limits permitted by governments, the new technologies will certainly increase transnational, regional, and perhaps even global programming. Advertising will be a virtual necessity to help pay the higher costs of the newer technologies, bringing into homes (and areas where poorer people may share viewing of communal TV sets) products and services they would not normally see or hear about on local broadcast advertising or programming.

What are those limits? In Europe and other developed areas, advertising on cable will have to comply with national laws for the reasons already mentioned;[32] and DBS will presumably be covered by EEC regulation, multilateral agreement, or uniform legislation. In poorer areas, however, where laws and enforcement are not as developed, it will be difficult to deal with culturally offensive or provocative material. The impact of introducing new ideas, services, and products could be powerful. Consider, for example, how sexual and birth control product advertising might alter customs and religious views in more traditional nations. This concern is certain to intensify Third-World efforts to control DBS in WARC and other fora.

Indirect Effects on Transborder Advertising

The new technologies may affect advertising more strongly in an indirect manner, viz., by altering concepts, tastes, goals, opinions, etc., in the viewing public. People will become worldlier, more sophisticated. Advertising will change to keep up.

Because of the transborder potential for reaching much larger audiences,[33] techniques will be aimed at maximizing the effect of commercials by widening audience appeal and standardizing product and packaging, tending to bring about a certain homogeneity in tastes and style. At the same time, more people will be offered a wider diversity of choice in products and services, occupational and pastime activities, and a greatly increased variety of views and perceptions (political, social, economic, religious, etc.).

Governmental authorities may be hard put to deal with the increased consumer expectations resulting from viewers seeing the products and services advertised. Exposure to the expanded wealth of products and services available will create ever-larger expectations of a better material life, in some cases adding stress to local economies. Exposure to alternative lifestyles may have profound democratizing effects, for it can be argued that the experience of mankind has been that civil unrest has more often been caused by shortages of food and other material goods than by deprivation of political liberties.

With the increased use and coverage afforded by the newer technologies, television advertising will become more effective and gain in share of total advertising expenditure. However, the expected overall expansion of competition should increase the absolute volume of competitive advertising in all media. Advertising permits the mass production that results in economies of scale. With increased and faster penetration of new markets, the manufacture and marketing of new products and services will accelerate, resulting in generally cheaper prices and spurring competition. In theory this should also generate greater total local advertising revenue in all media, strengthening those print and other media

that are supported by advertising, and making possible the emergence of additional media.

Effect on Advertising Practice

New data-transmission techniques will make it possible to transmit (e.g., by satellite) print ad or commercial broadcast material to a local production house. Whether this would be worthwhile is problematical; but countries having restrictions on foreign-made advertising might be hard put to decide where such advertising was made (except, of course, as to actors).

Closed-circuit teleconferences, networked creative and seminar-type sessions, involving regional or larger groups of the agency's overseas affiliates, would greatly accelerate fast and effective development and execution of marketing and creative planning. However, secrecy would have to be assured, and the cost of telecommunications linkage might become disproportionately high. Nonetheless, large international agency groups have, in the past, held annual—or more frequent—international meetings at very great expense.

Greater and more effective use of computers can be expected for developing marketing models to devise advertising and media strategies and market research.[34] Home office (or regional headquarters) processing facilities and expertise, coupled with transborder transmission of local data, would facilitate and speed development of such models. This kind of work is now often accomplished by mailing written or typed data to the computer center, and receiving back printouts by mail. In the future such printouts may be delivered electronically.

LEGAL PROBLEMS

Most nations have laws and regulations controlling advertising. These generally (1) regulate in certain subject areas (e.g., tobacco, liquor, sex, pharmaceuticals, food, and advertising aimed at children), (2) limit duration or prescribe permissible maximum time for commercials (or ban advertising altogether in certain media), (3) require truthfulness, (4) prohibit or regulate comparative advertising, (5) prohibit or limit foreign ownership of local advertising agencies, or (6) ban or tax the use of foreign components in locally disseminated advertisements.[35] Such rules are highly developed in Western countries, which also have more or less rigorously applied broadcasting and other self-policing industry codes,[36] but not in many developing nations.

U.S. Regulatory Structure

Advertising regulation in the United States is both statutory and self-policing. The most important statutory basis is the Federal Trade Commission Act:[37] Section 5, which prohibits "unfair or deceptive acts or practices" in interstate or foreign commerce; and Section 12, which makes it unlawful in the case of food, drug, device, and cosmetic advertising "to disseminate, or cause to be disseminated, any false advertisement." Under Section 5, the Federal Trade Commission can move against deceptive advertising formally by complaint and consent order procedures, or informally. For Section 12 violations, the FTC has special enforcement powers, including access to the injunctive and penal remedies of Sections 13 and 14.[38]

Self-regulation in the United States is as important as statutory control (although there is little doubt that self-policing is encouraged in part by the existence of the latter and the potential for more far-reaching legislation).

Much of the industry self-regulation is accomplished through the mechanism of the National Advertising Division (NAD) of the Council of Better Business Bureaus and the National Advertising Review Board (NARB). Both were established in 1971,[39] and are primarily concerned with truth and accuracy in advertising.[40] The NAD hears cases arising out of its monitoring of print, radio, and television advertising, as well as matters originating out of complaints from competitors, consumers, consumer groups, and associations.[41] It investigates, spells out the issues, gathers and evaluates information, and tries to negotiate settlements.

Failing agreement, either side can obtain review by a five-member NARB panel (chosen from NARB's 30 advertiser members, 10 agency members and 10 public members), consisting of three from the advertiser segment and one each from the agency and public segments. Adverse decisions require that the advertising be stopped or corrected. In the event of refusal by the advertiser (or in the event the advertiser has refused to participate in the proceedings), the appropriate government enforcement agency is notified. Few cases reach the NARB, but its existence is salutary.

Broadcast media self-regulation is extremely effective. For many years until 1982 when it was struck down

by consent decree as a violation of the antitrust laws,[42] the Television Code of the National Association of Broadcasters (NAB), which was subscribed to by most of the nation's commercial television stations, prescribed strict rules regarding (among other things) permissible duration and frequency of commercials and the number of different commercials allowed each hour. The NAB code also detailed substantive rules regarding honesty, claim substantiation, taste, and product exclusions (e.g., hard liquor, etc.).

Although no longer in effect, the code's provisions have been largely incorporated separately by each of the major networks into their own guidelines, as expressly permitted by the consent decree. Such guidelines typically deal with honesty and claim substantiation; prohibition of advertising hard liquor (and limitations on other alcoholic beverage commercials), gambling, astrology, and the like; contraceptives, and abortion clinics; strictures on child-directed advertising; good taste and time-of-day requirements for personal products; caution in over-the-counter medical products; and advertising duration and frequency limitations.

New Problems

The new legal problems which might arise are different for two reasons. First because of the expected penetration of program and advertising materials into areas which have not been heavily saturated until now. This means that new laws will be drawn, enforcement of existing laws will be enhanced, and, no doubt, the rhetoric in international fora will increase.

Second, because of the natural focus of new technologies on transmission of the same message to many countries, movement to uniformity of law and regulation, by way of either model codes or treaties, is gaining momentum. Consumer protection proposals appear in numerous U.N. fora, e.g., ECOSOC (Consumer Protection Guidelines); Commission on Transnational Corporations (Code-of-Conduct exercise); WHO (International Code of Marketing of Breastmilk Substitutes),[43] etc.

On the other hand, despite the fact that nations have virtually unlimited power to ban,[44] restrict, or regulate advertising, the power has not been exercised as broadly or widely as it might. There are a number of reasons for this. Revenue is needed—sometimes desperately needed—to support information transport systems and infrastructures. Moreover, many Third World countries are not really opposed to advertising, but only to advertising by "transnational corporations." In many such countries—in Latin America for example—local product advertising, whether food, pharmaceutical, or otherwise, runs riot. This opposition to TNC advertising is due partly to (a stated) fear of importation of "alien" cultures or "inappropriate" products, partly to a Third-World set against "TNCs", and partly—frankly—to protect local agencies and products from foreign competition.

A look at some common perceptions of the negative aspects of advertising may facilitate an understanding of emerging legal problems and the development of rules to cope with them. The following are some of the major criticisms.

1. Advertising can mislead or defraud consumers.
2. It can produce a "commercial mentality" which extols acquisition and consumption at the expense of other values.
3. Need for advertising revenues produces programs appealing to a wide audience often resulting in low quality and an "anticultural" bias.
4. Advertising can distort local development priorities and bring about a misallocation of economic resources by encouraging people to buy things they do not need and cannot afford, thus diverting financial resources from more important economic goals.
5. Advertising, together with "Western" entertainment and program materials, results in cultural domination and a loss of "cultural sovereignty," taking the form of dependence on imported models which reflect alien life-styles and values, and deform local mores and ways of life.

In response to these allegations, it should be pointed out that there are countless local laws and industry self-regulation codes[45] to police advertising and protect against its abuses, and the number and effectiveness of such laws and codes are growing. The charge that advertising produces a "commercial mentality" simply ignores the natural and common desire of humankind to have things that improve and make life more pleasant. As to taste, it is what it is, and only a dedicated statist would argue that the typical bureaucrat should be unleashed to define acceptable "culture".[46] Even if it were true that advertising is the cause of "low-quality" programming, it is also true that in many areas of the world, advertising revenues supporting privately-owned

media provide the only alternative to government support, control, censorship, and cultural *diktat*. As to distortion of local development priorities, the charge confuses cause and effect—it is the market that should determine resource allocation. The dispute is more over the respective merits of the market economy versus the planned one than the pros and cons of advertising (indeed, socialist governments advertise heavily in aid of their plans). Also, it must be remembered that advertising makes possible economies of scale that reduce greatly the cost to the consumer and thus conserve financial resources.

The final contention, that advertising results in loss of "cultural sovereignty," has been made in forum after forum, usually those dominated by Third-World majorities, and very emphatically in UNESCO, as for example in the *MacBride Report*:

> Therefore, advertising is seen by many as a threat to the cultural identity and self-realization of many developing countries: it brings to many people alien ethical values; . . . it affects and can often deform ways of life and lifestyles.[47]

With regard to advertising, the charge of alien lifestyles and cultural domination by foreigners is largely untrue. In many parts of the world print advertisements and radio and TV commercials are made by nationals and produced locally, by writers, artists, and production people who are nationals and residents of the countries where the advertising is used.

The purpose of advertising is to persuade, and this requires that local audiences be addressed in their own tongue and consistently with their own understanding, culture, history, and traditions. One of the very advantages of having worldwide advertising agency systems is precisely so that advertising can be produced by people who are part of, and thus understand, local cultural imperatives.

This allegation is frequently made by vested power groups that oppose change that challenges existing institutional structures. It is not easy otherwise to explain the vehemence with which the U.N. General Assembly on December 10, 1982 adopted by a vote of 108 to 13 the right of the receiving national to prohibit foreign DBS.

Advertising, by communicating information about alternative lifestyles, teaches the possibility of change and encourages people to demand something better.

Difficult question: Should the people of Iran be informed about alternatives to the Mullahs' point-of-view? They assuredly have that right by any reasonable interpretation of the "free flow" of information standard in the UNESCO charter,[48] and of the Universal Declaration on Human Rights (adopted, among others, by the United States and Iran) which states that everyone has the right to "seek, receive and impart information and ideas through any media and regardless of frontiers" (Article 19) and "to change his religion or belief" (Article 18).[49]

Moreover, species die, wilderness areas disappear, cities spring up where medieval forests grew. Civilization is the history of trade-offs, and the new communications technologies also mean greater cultural exchanges, transfer of public health and medical knowledge, rapid expansion of mass education, and many other benefits. There is nothing picturesque about an aborigine, to an aborigine.

Professor Ithiel de Sola Pool of M.I.T., in a paper delivered to the 43rd Annual Meeting of the U.S. National Commission for UNESCO (December 12–15, 1979), states it succinctly:

> For 200 years or more there has been a myth of the noble savage. He may have been poor, but he was seen as moral, intelligent, and uncorrupted by the false values of civilization. It is a myth.
>
> In the typical underdeveloped country not only are the people poor, but everything else is a problem too. The government is corrupt, class lines are sharp, educational institutions are unsatisfactory, and leadership is inefficient . . . .
>
> Noting that the political leaders of the Third World are often corrupt, incompetent, and unsophisticated is not to be supercilious towards their countries. It is merely to say once more that the countries are underdeveloped: that is what must be cured. It is naive to expect that, given their underdevelopment, the general run of Third-World governments will come out on the farsighted side of the complex issued of free flow: why should we expect unstable regimes to do other than seek to expand their personal political controls?

DEVELOPING RULES

The vision of "Television American-style"—which is so publicly abhorred by European politicians and so adored and deliciously consumed by their populations—has, in the words of one observer, "raised the political temperature and brought opponents of advertising of all political shades out of the woodwork."[50]

There are several ways to deal with the transborder regulation of advertising—particularly satellite transmission whether through cable distribution or DBS—which will certainly result from multicountry dissemination of advertising. Legislation (both national and multilateral) and voluntary codes of self-regulation. A critical consideration in the case of legislation, is whether control is to be exerted at the transmitting or receiving end, or both. Regulation will develop first in Europe, where it already has a start. The principal European bodies involved in the potential rule making are the European Economic Community (EEC) and the Council of Europe.

The Council of Europe Parliamentary Assembly in 1982 adopted by a single vote the Scholten Report ("The Means to Check Abuses of the Freedom of Expression by Commercial Advertising").[51] This document broadly attacks advertising, viewing it as an evil—but a necessary one—and calling for strict regulation against cultural "pollution," prohibition on alcohol and tobacco advertising, restriction on advertising to children, and a convention on DBS. At present, the Council's Committee of Ministers is awaiting the report of its Steering Committee on Media, which favors self-regulation. As of now, the issue is in doubt.

Since the Council has no compulsory powers, it is ultimately the EEC itself, legislatively and through its European Court of Justice, that has the greater potential power to regulate. In 1973 the European Court held in the *Sacchi* case[52] that television broadcasting, including advertising, is within the provisions of Articles 59, 60, and 61 of the Treaty of Rome, dealing with services, and that the EEC Commission has regulatory jurisdiction thereover.

On the other hand, discussions aimed at self-regulation of advertising on satellites are in progress (between the European Broadcasting Union, European Advertising Tripartite, and International Chamber of Commerce). Self-regulation has many partisans, and may ultimately be determinative in resolving the advertising-code debate.

The leading contenders for new-style television broadcasting in Europe are cable distribution (CATV) of satellite transmissions[53] and direct broadcasting satellites (direct to the individual set owner).

CATV in Europe has not overly disturbed governments with a threat of unlawful programming or advertising because it is easy to control it at the point of distribution, i.e., the transmission to CATV subscribers can be cut off (CATV companies are licensed by local authorities). Satellite transmission to CATV distribution facilities is low-powered, requiring the costly large-dish antennae practicable only for CATV operations.

Regulation of program and advertising content will therefore be relatively simple if CATV is used to distribute satellite transmission, although such regulation may run into national laws prohibiting cable operators from interfering with the programs they rebroadcast. (European CATV, unlike its "active" American cousin, is "passive", i.e., it redistributes without change and does not originate material.)

In 1979 the European Court of Justice had before it a case[54] involving application of a Belgian law banning television commercials. The court was asked whether, under the free-flow-of-service provisions of Articles 59 and 60 of the Treaty of Rome, Belgium could validly prohibit cable rebroadcast to Belgian subscribers of foreign commercials accompanying program material picked up by the cable company from regular broadcasts originating in neighboring countries.

The court (1) reaffirmed its ruling in the *Sacchi* case that television broadcasting, including advertising, was covered by Articles 59 and 60 of the treaty and within the EEC Commission's jurisdiction, and (2) ruled that Belgium could validly prohibit cable rebroadcast of commercials originating abroad provided the prohibition applied without distinction as to place of origin, nationality, or domicile of the provider of the service, i.e., Belgium could ban *all* commercials, but could not prohibit those from Luxembourg while permitting ones from France.

A number of things about the decision merit attention. First, by giving Belgium the right to stop the redistribution at the *receiving* end of the transmission, it places real power in the hands of local government which, of course, has no power over the foreign originator.

Second, in its argument, the EEC Commission took an opposite view of the thrust of Article 59, particularly since the same broadcasts and accompanying commercials were being received directly, without the use of cable, by a substantial number of Belgian viewers.[55]

Third, France objected to the court's view on the ground that

> it is better that the retransmission of broadcasts via a cable network should be a "passive" retransmission, in other words, having no effect upon the content of the broadcasts ... including advertisements ...
>
> the French Government sets great store by the obser-

vance of such a principle at the national and European level, as being the only way to avoid, first, partial excisions involving an alteration to programs hitherto freely broadcast or possibly leading to censorship itself, and, secondly, the risk of the practice already observed in other countries whereby unscrupulous distributors retransmit only part of the programs and take advantage of their television audience to replace the parts left out with advertisements or other parts of programs of their own.

Fourth, under Belgian law, cable television distributors were legally prohibited from interfering with rebroadcasts. It is not clear that other countries such as Holland or France—or for that matter even Belgium (which in spite of its ferocious anti-advertising history will itself soon commence commercial broadcasting)—will follow the court rather than the Commission, and turn their cable systems into active ones. Should they not follow the court, commercial television is bound to increase if only to maintain competitive parity within the EEC.

Far more difficult to cope with will be DBS, which may begin as early as the mid-80s, whose stronger signal can be picked up directly by the set owner via cheaper (but still fairly expensive) dish antennae.

Western Europe will lead the way toward multinational regulation. The communication technology is there, the markets are there, and the political organization is in place. Is there time for the Third World to learn from the European experience before the onslaught of DBS? Probably not, which suggests transnational action, at ITU, at WARC, at UNESCO, and at all other fora in which the vast majorities of the developing world exist. Expect much more rhetoric and intensive pressure for multilateral codes and conventions.

The *MacBride Report* recommended, as an issue "requiring further study," that

> studies should be undertaken on the social, economic and cultural effects of advertising to identify problems, and to suggest solutions, at the national and international levels, possibly including study of the practicability of an international advertising code, which could have as its basis the preservation of cultural identity and protection of moral values.[56]

The proposed draft program and budget of UNESCO for 1981–1983 included an item for

> case studies ... to analyse the impact of advertising, particularly on the content of messages and on the

management of national communication media. Special attention will be devoted to the bonds of interdependence linking the advertising industry and certain communication industries, and to the specific financial circumstances of the media."[57]

To date, however, there appears to have been no action on advertising, either under the preceding proposed study or under the recently implemented UNESCO facility, the International Program for the Development of Communication (IPDC).

CONCLUSIONS

How can we agree on rules? Who would enforce them? Perhaps the target country could, by acting against importation and sale of products (where imported) or at local manufacturing sites. (At the 1977 WARC, the Russians actually threatened to shoot down any satellites transmitting into their area.)

However, any move toward international regulation of advertising by multigovernmental bodies will probably be strongly resisted in the U.S. both by the private sector and government. Witness our negative votes on the Law of the Sea treaty and WHO Breastmilk Code. Moreover, although Republican and Democratic administrations characteristically differ in their approaches to regulation, all recent administrations, and all major government departments involved (e.g., the State Department, USIA, and the Department of Commerce), have taken the position—at least for the record—that advertising is information entitled to free flow.

Even more difficult questions remain. Within Europe and the Western community of nations, despite much disagreement, there is substantial accord on such matters as economic opportunity, political freedoms, freedom to communicate and, perhaps above all, self-confidence in democratic government's ability to cope with abuses within the framework of democracy. Civilization is of a cloth. But how, for example, to agree on a definition of "pornography" with Iran?

The U.S. regulatory structure, a dual system of statute and industry self-regulation, suggests itself as the preferred approach. Prohibition of hard-core fraud and deception are properly the concern of government, as exemplified by the Federal Trade Commission Act. In areas of taste, prohibited products, allowable time and frequency of commercials, and similar matters, self-regulation is preferable. Statutory controls, and particularly compul-

sory multinational codes, distort and interrupt free flow. They are inevitably too rigid because of the need to satisfy differing national demands, culture, mores, and concepts. They encourage participating states to harden rules which would—and should—otherwise be interpreted, nation by nation, in a more adaptive manner, consistent with and making allowances for local standards and culture. Among such differences, even in the Common Market whose populations enjoy a relatively similar basic orientation, are notions of what products can be advertised (see note 32), allowable duration and frequency of commercial advertising (see note 27), and even its very acceptability.

To impose a standard concept of acceptability upon all parties is as much an invasion of "cultural sovereignty" as that alleged against advertising (*see* "New Problems," p. 112).

Given the value that advertising has in informing people about goods and services, teaching the possibility of change, providing and encouraging the exercise of free choice, permitting economies of scale that reduce prices, and supporting independent media (*see* "Why Advertising is Important," p. 107), statutory controls—and for the reasons mentioned, especially multinational ones—could impair and even cripple these benefits.

Even within a single country, self-regulation is more efficient because it can react quickly to perceived needs and problems, can be amended promptly and—because the industry itself reviews, enforces and changes rules—is administered by practitioners who understand the problems and the process, rather than by career civil servants or legislative bodies. Self-regulatory structures also typically provide for simple individual consumer complaints, and often offer the means for redress without the need for lawsuits (which for the individual is usually out of the question because of its expense measured against the relatively small size of the claim. *See* note 41).

A more sinister consequence of government (and multigovernment) regulation is the opportunity it provides to gain some degree of control over the media, as well as over messages that may not be viewed as "commercial" by all. This threat is very real, as UNESCO, Third-World, and other periodic attempts to legitimize state control over communication demonstrate. (At the extreme end, if all advertising were banned, no medium could exist without government support and approval.)

Ultimately, the proper way to control unwanted commercials is with the on–off switch or channel-selector knob; and the proper person to do the controlling is the viewer.

Thomas Jefferson said: "Men fight for freedom; then they begin to accumulate laws to take it away." Let us keep such laws to the minimum.

NOTES

1. UNESCO Doc. 20 C/94, 72, at 37. The United States, of course, officially withdrew from UNESCO effective January 1, 1985.

2. Report of the Secretariat, 32 U.N. ESCOR 6, U.N. Doc. E/C.10/40 (1978)

3. Report of the Secretary-General, 32 U.N. ES-COR 16, U.N. Doc. E/C.10/35 (1978)

4. "The New World Information Order," 2nd para., 2.

5. Cartagena Agreement, 1977, XVI I.L.M. 138, 152, art. 43, Decision No. 24 as amended.

6. In some such countries, treaties of friendship and commerce protect U.S. agencies from constraints of this kind.

7. Speech to the I.A.A. General Conference, Sao Paulo (May 24, 1982).

8. S. HOOPER, IAA, WORLD ADVERTISING EXPENDITURES 8 (1981).

9. 1979 ANN. REP. INTERPUBLIC GROUP COMPANIES 13.

10. Transnational Corporations in Advertising (1979), U.N. Sales No. E.79.II.A.2 (1979). 1983 estimated % media shares in the U.S. are Print, 32.9; TV, 21.3; Radio, 6.6; Other, 39.2. ADVERTISING AGE, June 13, 1983.

11. In this connection, over 60% of U.S. multinational advertisers use the same agencies (or agency system) for U.S. and overseas advertising. See Transnational Corporations in Advertising, *supra* note 10, at 19.

12. McCann-Erickson, the largest agency system of The Interpublic Group, opened offices in Canada in 1914, in England and France in 1927, in Germany in 1928, and in Brazil and Argentina in 1934. J. Walter Thompson opened its European offices in 1927.

13. *See* ADVERTISING AGE, Mar. 24, 1982 and Apr. 19, 1982. The figures should be viewed in perspective. Total 1981 global advertising expenditures were perhaps $125 billion, of which almost half ($61.3 billion) was spent in the U.S. Of the balance, U.S. advertising agencies accounted for perhaps $15 billion, and non-U.S. agencies for some of the rest. The world's largest individual *agency* (as distinguished from agency groups such as Interpublic) is Dentsu, a Japanese agency whose 1981 billings were about $3 billion. (Of the top 50 agencies worldwide, 10 are Japanese). Accurate, comparable figures are hard to obtain, but it is clear that much—perhaps more than half—of "advertising expenditures" include sums that are not placed through agencies, such as retail ads in local newspapers, radio and television, direct mail, etc.

14. This assumes a full-service agency. Those agencies which are not full service overseas often do the work at home, or with a U.S. team flown in to the local market on a project basis.

15. International Chamber of Commerce Resolution, 137th Session (May 1980).

16. U.K. Advertising Ass'n, Briefing Document 18 (Sept. 1980) (supplied by the U.K. Advertising Association to the U.K. government delegation to the 21st UNESCO General Conference in Belgrade).

17. Final Report of the International Commission for the Study of Communication Problems (MacBride Report) UNESCO Doc. at 191 (Nov. 30, 1979) [hereinafter cited as MacBride Report].

18. When the first commercial independent television station was authorized in the U.K., the two competing BBC channels lost large audiences to it because of the more popular programs that advertising revenues made it possible to buy. In Italy, where privately-owned local TV stations have only recently been authorized, growth in audience and advertising have been phenomenal; and although legally limited to local broadcasting, de facto networking has been achieved by simultaneous broadcast of pre-recorded materials.

19. MacBride Report, *supra* note 17.

20. *See* I.A.A. INTELLIGENCE SUMMARY, Apr./May 1983, at 33. Broadcast media are state-owned and operated in most of Asia, Africa, and Oceania. North and South America have more of a tradition of private ownership. *See* U.N. GAOR Annex at 19, U.N. Doc. A/33/144. The Malaysian government has proposed a commercial TV entertainment channel for 1985.

21. Transborder penetration, or "overspill" of print and radio material has existed for years, as has even that of television. It is reported, for example, that Israeli viewers prefer to watch the Amman, Jor-

dan channel because of a preference for American-style programming.

22.   State Department Public Affairs Release, Current Policy No. 254 (Dec. 5, 1980).

23.   A study by Statistical Research Inc., reported in the I.A.A. INTELLIGENCE SUMMARY, Oct./Nov. 1982, at 30, indicates that cable subscribers with remote control switches are three times more likely to switch channels to avoid commercials.

24.   Simultaneous broadcast of several dubbed languages together with the TV program would lessen this tendency if the technique were affordable. It is reported that such technology is being tested in Japan, which developed the system. *See* Tempest, 1 J. ADVERTISING 143, 147.

25.   Note, however, that a multilingual television channel—RTL (Radio Tele Luxembourg), having broad transborder penetration—is underway in Luxembourg, broadcasting in German, English, Dutch, and French. This is regarded as a pilot for RTL's forthcoming DBS.

26.   In the case of DBS-to-ground cable distributors, the rules would have to be obeyed because the transmission will probably require decoders controlled by governments.

27.   Aggregate time allowed on all channels (minutes per day):

	Number of chanels accepting advertising	Aggregate Time
Austria	1	20
Belgium	0	0
Denmark	0	0
Finland	2	40
France	2 of 3 (soon to be 3 of 4)	22
Greece	2	20 per hr.
Germany	2	40
Italy	2 (plus several private ones)	64
Ireland	2	37 (avg.)
Luxembourg	1	62
Netherlands	2	30
Norway	0	0
Portugal	2	15
Spain	2	83
Sweden	0	0
Switzerland	3	60
United Kingdom	2	150

28.   ECONOMIST, Jan. 22, 1983, at 64.

29.   The launch vehicle, "Ariane," had "an embarassing habit of plummeting into the sea in a ball of flame." CAMPAIGN EUR. Dec. 1980, at 34.

30.   *Id.*

31.   *Teletext* is one-way transmission by regular TV or CATV stations of encoded data to normal TV sets, either accompanying a program (e.g., closed-captions for the deaf) or standing alone (e.g., listings of consumer products and services whose subject-matter categories can be selected for viewing by key pad attached to the decoder). *Videotex* is a two-way wired link between a central computer data bank and a video terminal (e.g., "Dow Jones News Retrieval Service", "The Source," etc.). The link is usually by telephone line although some cable TV systems can also serve. Because it is two-way, viewers can bank, call for data, purchase, and send and receive electronic mail. Videotex is further along in Europe than in the United States. IBM is testing a videotex system for the United States, using a system format now in use in the United Kingdom ("Prestel").

32.   Nevertheless, countries which participate in the satellite enterprise or cable company may well relax restrictions in order to obtain revenue (at least to permit commercial messages and ease limits on minutes-per-hour frequency, if not to allow proscribed subject matter such as alcohol, tobacco, advertising to children, and pornography). In addition to such restrictions, among others, Ireland and the U.K. prohibit advertising of contraceptives; Ireland, the U.K., and Switzerland bar politics and religion; Austria, Finland, France, Netherlands, and Switzerland bar medical products; Italy prohibits advertising of guns, ammunition, pet foods, and horoscopes. As a matter of interest, the U.S. bars cigarette advertising on electronic media (15 U.S.C. Sec. 1335). 39 U.S.C. § 3001, which prohibited use of the mails, among other things, for contraceptive advertisements to members of the public, has been declared uncon-

stitutional. *See* Bolger v. Youngs Drug Prod. Corp., 526 F. Supp. 823 (D.D.C. 1981), *aff'd,* 103 S. Ct. 2875 (1983).

33.   The "footprints" of the satellites approved for Europe at the 1977 WARC have elliptical paths, not congruent with national borders, thus permitting widely dispersed transmission reception areas.

34.   In particular, "Qube" television, which through use of private, in-home terminals, allows audience response to be communicated instantly to the broadcaster, would greatly facilitate advertising and market research.

35.   Transnational Corporations in Advertising, *supra* note 10, at 36 *et seq.*

36.   *Id.* at 53 *et seq.*

37.   15 U.S.C. §§ 41 *et seq.*

38.   Also important are (1) the mail and wire fraud statutes (18 U.S.C. §§ 1341, 1343) that, among others, criminalize "any scheme or artifice to . . . [obtain] money or property by means of false or fraudulent . . . representations" involving, respectively, use of the mails, and "wire, radio or television communication" in interstate or foreign commerce; (2) local anti-fraud consumer protection laws; and (3) U.S. Postal Service injunctive powers (both administrative and judicially obtainable) to block delivery of mail (and return it to the sender) when the addressee is found to be obtaining money or property through use of the mails by means of false representations. 39 U.S.C. §§ 3005, 3007. A pending bill (S. 450) would give the Postal Service power to issue cease-and-desist orders directly to the offender, with penalties imposable by the Federal Courts for violation.

39.   The sponsors are the American Advertising Federation, American Association of Advertising Agencies (the "4As"), the Association of National Advertisers, and the Council of Better Business Bureaus.

40.   NARB recognizes the importance of taste, morality, and social responsibility in advertising, and has established several "consultative" panels to publish position papers on various subjects. Published papers include *Advertising and Women* and *Identifying Competitors in Advertising.* Moreover, in 1974 NAD set up its Children's Advertising Review Unit (CARU), which has established guidelines for, and reviews, such advertising—frequently in advance—at the request of advertisers.

41.   For the nearly 7 years ending April 30, 1978, NAD received 1380 complaints of which 530 were dismissed for adequate substantiation, 474 had the ads modified or discontinued, 298 were closed administratively (trivial claims, etc.), 13 were referred to the NARB, and the rest were pending. The following comparisons of NAD case origins shows an evolving change:

Source of NAD	1971–1978	1982
NAD monitoring	35.0%	39%
Consumer complaints (direct or from organizations)	27.0%	9%
Competitors	14.5%	39%
Local Better Business Bureaus	19.5%	10%
Other	4.0%	3%

42.   United States v. National Ass'n of Broadcasters, 536 F. Supp. 149 (D.D.C. 1982). The court actually invalidated on motion for summary judgment the NAB Code prohibition on multiple product advertising in a commercial of less than 60 seconds, as a per se violation of Sherman Act § 1, reserving other government charges for trial. NAB then withdrew its code and subsequently signed the consent decree. *See* 1982–83 Trade Cas. (CCH) ¶¶ 65,049, 65,050.

43.   World Health Organization (WHO) Doc. WHA34.22, 5/21/81, I.L.M. 1004 (July 1981).

44.   Not so in the United States, however, where advertising enjoys a substantial measure of 1st Amendment protection as speech, John Donnelly & Sons v. Campbell, 639 F.2d 6 (1st Cir. 1980), *aff'd,* 453 U.S. 916 (1981); Virginia State Bd. of Pharmacy v. Virginia Citizens Consumer Council, Inc., 425 U.S. 748 (1976); Bigelow v. Virginia, 421 U.S. 809 (1975), although it is subject to regulation to prevent deception, National Comm'n on Egg Nutrition v. FTC, 570 F.2d 157 (7th Cir. 1977), *cert. denied,* 439 U.S. 821 (1978); *Virginia State Bd.,* 425 U.S. at 770 *et seq.* and even prior restraint, *Virginia State Bd.,* 425 U.S. at 772, n.24.

45.   Such as the International Chamber of Commerce's Code of Advertising Practice (which dates from 1937, often revised, and has been adopted by over 200 organizations in 30 countries), the gist of which is that all advertising should be legal, decent, honest, and truthful. In March 1982, "Guidelines for

Advertising to Children" were adopted by the ICC for inclusion in the code.

46.   French Culture Minister Jack Lang, who likes to be seen with creative people ("creators") and whose tirades against American "cultural imperialism" have earned him considerable derision even in France, and demotion to junior minister, believes, as a good socialist ought, that cultural tastes can be legislated. Alas, despite his efforts, "Dallas" became the most popular TV show in France, *E.T.* was the greatest commercial success in the history of Paris movie exhibition, and a British popular music record, *in English,* led the French hit parade. *See* N.Y. Times, Jan. 9, 1983, Arts and Leisure section at 1; and ECONOMIST, Feb. 26, 1983, at 48.

47.   MacBride Report, *supra* note 17. Similar comments are found in the Interim MacBride Report, UNESCO Doc. 20 C/94 115, para. 47 (Sept. 25, 1978), and, annexed thereto, Masmoudi, The New World Information Order, at 2, para. 2.

48.   The Preamble to the UNESCO Constitution declares that the party states believe "in the free exchange of ideas and knowledge" and Article I, 2(a) calls for the "free flow of ideas by word and image."

49.   *Cf.* Article 19 of the *International Covenant on Civil and Political Rights,* which grants everyone the right to receive information and ideas, regardless of frontiers and in any media, *subject* to restrictions necessary to protect the national security, public order, or public health, or morals.

50.   Tempest, *supra* note 24, at 144. BME's WORLD BROADCAST NEWS. Dec. 1982, at 30, reports that the French government's attempt to promote cultural and educational programs on TV produced an audience of only 3% to 5%, and that the effort has been reversed: back have come American feature films. Private TV channels in Italy, which limit commercials to 14 minutes per hour of programming, now exceed the government-owned network (RAI) in both advertising revenues and prime-time viewers.

51.   A rival, rejected proposal by Dutch Socialist parliamentarian Stoffeler regarded advertising DBS as a threat to culture and national sovereignty.

52.   *Sacchi,* case No. 155 of 1973.

53.   CATV can be—and is—used to distribute transborder signals received by "overspill" from normal transmissions of neighboring countries.

54.   *Debauve et al.,* case No. 52/79 (Mar. 18, 1980).

55.   There is a tension between First Amendment protection of advertising and the right of government to regulate abuses in the U.S. not unlike that which exists in the EEC between the EEC Commission's dedication to further the free flow of information across Common Market frontiers, and the European Court of Justice's determination to uphold member nations' regulatory rights over advertising.

56.   MACBRIDE REPORT, *supra* note 17, at pt. V, B, 8.

57.   UNESCO Doc. 21 C/5–11.A, para. 4344.

CHAPTER 9

INTEGRATED SERVICES DIGITAL NETWORK

Issues and Options

ANTHONY M. RUTKOWSKI

INTRODUCTION

The term "integrated services digital network" (ISDN) has risen to prominence within the past few years to describe a kind of advanced information services system that is expected to be widely implemented during the next two decades. Electronics technology at every level, from small components to large networks, now appears to be evolving toward a common end. It is the complete interconnection and interoperability of nearly all computer and telecommunication systems through a common network model to provide universal and complete services for capturing, storing, processing, and transporting most information which society desires to retain or communicate.

In this integrated environment, a major role of an ISDN is to provide information transport, i.e., a common "digital pipe" network for conveying information among users and facilities.[1] In addition, an ISDN can potentially encompass any other kind of information service, from telephone to teletext, from picturephone to television, from broadcasting to remote meter reading.[2] The extent to which all these services are provided exclusively through a monolithic national ISDN or multiple inter-connected ISDNs or specialized service vendors will vary among nations depending on their communication policies

Until very recently, these matters were regarded as futuristic, and not deserving significant attention. This changed in November 1980 when the major international body for devising telecommunication arrangements, the International Telecommunication Union's (ITU) Consultative Committee on Telegraph and Telephone (CCITT) Plenary Assembly took three bold initiatives: recognition as a global imperative of the need to devise common world principles, strategies, and standards for ISDN; identification of numerous key issues; and a restructuring of its internal organization based on those issues.[3] The effort was jointly undertaken with the primary international body for information standards, the International Organization for Standardization (ISO), which also initiated extensive restructuring and work on the master information standards model known as "open systems interconnection" or simply OSI.[4]

The action appears to have galvanized the giants of the international telecommunication and information community including most major governments, operators, users, manufacturers, associations, and regional organizations. In the past two years, the number of documents and articles concerning ISDN went from almost none to thousands; and the number of ISDN-related meetings now average several per month.[5] Most importantly, major system operators and manufacturers are apparently committing billions of dollars over the next decade to ISDN implementation.

The magnitude of these developments, combined

The comments are those of the author and not necessarily those of the Federal Communications Commission.

ANTHONY M. RUTKOWSKI • Mr. Rutkowski is a staff advisor for international communications issues and technology assessment at the Federal Communications Commission, Washington D.C.; adjunct professor at New York Law School, New York City; and author of many works in the field of international communication.

with the intimidating nature of network engineering which forms the basis for nearly all the current dialogue, has resulted in very limited discussion of the significant public policy issues raised.[6] This paper portrays current ISDN developments, and discusses some of the significant issues that appear to be emerging.

WHAT IS AN ISDN?

It should be noted at the outset that there is some ambiguity concerning the meaning of the term ISDN. To clarify the matter, this paper subdivides the subject into three levels: ISDN as an abstract conceptual model; as a design model emerging from international forums; and as concrete networks being devised by system operators. At each level, a different kind of issue analysis can be performed. The levels also correspond to different degrees of abstractness and time-frame; i.e., the conceptual level is somewhat abstract and long-term, while the operator networks are concrete and near-term.

The ISDN Conceptual Model

At the conceptual level, ISDN is a network model possessing two outstanding characteristics—it is *universal* and *intelligent*. From the viewpoint of a user, universality means that the user can potentially go anywhere in the world with any compatible electronic terminal and if connected to an ISDN, obtain similar kinds of services through common protocols. From a network perspective, universality means an ability to support virtually any kind of user or other network.

Similarly, ISDN "intelligence" has a different meaning from user and network perspectives. For the user, it implies the ability to engage in an extremely sophisticated dialogue with the network to define the desired information services. It also implies the ability to obtain an extremely diverse range of information services in addition to just transmission of information. From the network perspective, however, intelligence is an aggregate of resources that may be located in diverse locations within the network, within other networks, or entirely outside the network. This last capability is highly significant and likely to vary from nation to nation depending on domestic regulatory policy.

Figures 9.1 and 9.2 depict the ISDN concept from both a facilities and a functional perspective. The distinction is important because the facilities perspective fails to reveal two of the most significant ISDN re-

sources—software and the information imbedded in storage facilities.

From an overall facilities perspective (see Figure 9.1), an ISDN consists of just two major components: nodes and transmission links. Looking much like a gigantic Tinker Toy set, the entire globe will be covered with an architecture constructed of nodes and links. The links are employed to interconnect network nodes and to provide a local interface with user facilities.

A few details are worth mentioning. User facilities can be subdivided into two distinct types: single and multiple. The difference is that a multiple user facility has its own internal node which allows the ISDN capability to be shared. Examples include a private branch exchange (PABX) or a local distribution system (LAN, CATV, etc.). Transmission links in an ISDN are essentially passive, fungible pipes. That is, one can be readily substituted for another with similar characteristics. Some, however, may prove undesirable where rapid two-way (duplex) transmissions are desired and long time delays occur—such as with satellite radiocommunication. The nodes internally consist of switching, processing, and storage components all managed by imbedded software.

This superficial simplicity masks, however, the extreme complexity of local, national, and international architectures. Also omitted are any boundaries which discern ownership or control. Nonetheless, for purposes of issue analysis, it is often possible to return to this basic facilities model of simply interconnected nodes and links. Indeed, this was recently done in one of the few United States administration contributions to the CCITT, to depict a domestic architectural preference.[7]

Although the facilities model is useful, indeed necessary for many applications, it is only the functional perspective which reveals all the ISDN attributes and their interrelationship (see Figure 9.2). Here we see the facility resources (processing, storage, transmission links, and imbedded software in the form of programs and information) whether they be the network's, user's or outside vendor's, being dynamically aggregated by an ISDN.[8] This means that an ISDN will call upon these resources and allow them to operate in concert. If specific resources are not identified by the user, the network would be free to decide for itself which would be utilized. It may also substitute similar resources from microsecond to microsecond to achieve maximum network efficiency. This "dynamic aggregation" process

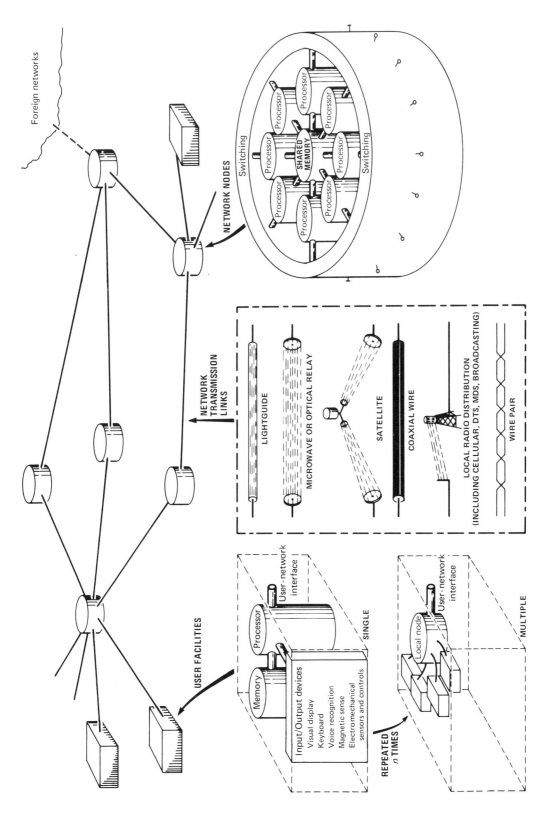

FIGURE 9.1 Basic ISDN Facilities Model

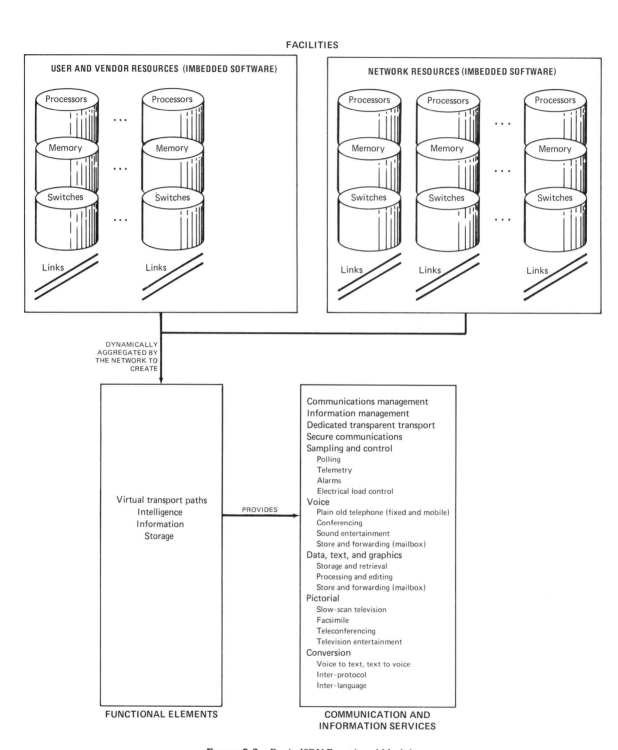

FIGURE 9.2 Basic ISDN Functional Model

creates the ISDN functional elements (virtual transport paths, intelligence, information, and storage) which in turn provide the user with any desired communication or information services.[9] It also allows services to be custom tailored for the user. The user would even have the capability to alter the parameters of the service during the course of its provision by the network.[10] The nature of the services could vary from a simple phone call to the bulk transmission of data, to electronic mail, to high resolution television.[11]

These ISDN developments will also be occurring during a period of remarkable evolution in user terminal capabilities. One can easily envision fifth generation terminals using voice recognition and synthesis capabilities to carry on a plain language dialogue with a human user, and serving as a buffer in dealing with the ISDN intelligence.[12] Already, such terminal capabilities are being marketed by L. M. Ericsson to perform simple telephone calling functions.[13] Such terminals will both enhance the utility of an ISDN and make it easier for users to interact with ISDN intelligence.

It is obvious that at the concept level, ISDN is an idealized mechanism for the provision of all conceivable electronic communication and information. As such it represents a goal toward which all human society will be striving, and ultimately is realizable only in the distant future. However, the exponentially changing technology and related fabrication processes may allow that future to arrive sooner than expected.

These technological and facilities developments will not occur in a vacuum, and can be expected to dramatically transform all aspects of our society. One commentator has characterized ISDN as the future "economic engine."[14] Any attempt to divine the effects, however, is highly speculative, and will not be attempted in this article.

The CCITT/ISO Design Model for ISDN

If ISDN were merely an abstract ideal, it would be relegated to philosophizing in academic environments. However, it is not. Network planners are working hard in dozens of international, regional, national, corporate, and trade association forums to define the precise principles, strategies, and standards to implement ISDNs during the next two decades. The aim is to reach a sufficiently definitive international consensus on these matters during the next two years to allow massive capital commitments.

The international forums for the ISDN dialogue are provided by the ISO and ITU. The former is devising the basic framework of network software, referred to as the "open systems interconnection model" (OSI), and the latter is developing the remainder. At the regional and national levels, numerous additional organizations and committees also provide forums for reaching a consensus on regional and local positions and policies.[15]

The work of the ITU predominently occurs within the context of nearly a dozen CCITT study groups, each possessing an infrastructure of working parties devoted to the examination of specific questions.[16] In addition, each question has its own dedicated rapporteur. Most of the ISDN questions are concentrated in Study Groups VII, XI, and XVIII; although nearly all of them have some ISDN responsibilities.[17] Formal liaisons exist for communicating among the study groups.[18] However, the players are largely the same in all the forums. The ISO has a similar but less extensive structure. There the work is concentrated in Technical Committee 97 and its subordinate subcommittees and working groups.

Within the CCITT, the point of departure is the formal definition of ISDN.[19] Even here, the dialogue is evolving so rapidly that the definition adopted in November 1980 was discarded eight months later in June 1981 in favor of a more generalized approach[20]—one that took special note of the importance of interfaces as a concession to the U.S. regulatory environment.[21] The latest CCITT definition now reads:

> *Integrated services digital network:* An integrated services network that provides digital connections between user–network interfaces in order to provide or support a range of different telecommunication services.[22]

The definition is part of a comprehensive set of ISDN terms prepared at the February 1983 CCITT meeting of ISDN experts.[23]

There now appears to be substantial agreement on this definition, as well as many other facets of the ISDN model. A list of "Principles of ISDN" now exists as a draft recommendation:

> 1. The main feature of an ISDN is the support of voice and nonvoice services in the same network. A key element of service integration for an ISDN is to provide a limited set of multipurpose user–network interface arrangements as well as a limited set of multipurpose ISDN bearer services.

2. ISDNs support a variety of applications including both switched or nonswitched connections. Switched connections in an ISDN include both circuit-switched and packet-switched connections and their concatenations. As far as practicable new services introduced into an ISDN should be arranged to be compatible with 64 kbit/s switched digital connections.

3. An ISDN will contain intelligence for the purpose of providing service features, maintenance and network management functions. This intelligence may not be sufficient for some new services and may have to be supplemented by either additional intelligence within the network, or possibly compatible intelligence in the user terminals.

4. A layered protocol structure should be used for the specification of the access to an ISDN. Access from a user to ISDN resources may vary depending upon the service required and upon the status of implementation of national ISDNs.

5. It is recognized that ISDNs may be implemented in a variety of configurations according to specific national situations.[24]

The CCITT community has sought and largely achieved an international consensus on principles and standards in seven key areas during the 1981–1984 study period:

1. Systematic approach to service types and network features to support them
2. Information types
3. Channel types
4. Access types
5. Reference models for customer access configurations
6. Principles on interfaces
7. Reference models for network structures of the ISDN[25]

The achievement of international agreements on these matters is critical to the creation of ISDNs on a global scale. In order to maximize the global efficiency of interconnected ISDNs, a common model is being devised for all nations.[26] The effort may determine the nature and structure of future information transport systems for the entire world on both domestic and international levels. The arrangements seem to allow considerable implementation flexibility. This is necessary to accommodate the different regulatory environments existing among nations. It may be difficult and

potentially costly, however, for users or networks to significantly deviate from the basic provisions.[27]

The initial product of this mammoth international effort is a sufficient consensus on as many ISDN features in as great a detail as possible. This consensus is then embodied in reports and recommendations of the CCITT.[28]

In February 1982 at Munich, the European Conference of Postal and Telecommunication Administrations (CEPT) countries had reached a preliminary agreement among themselves on certain basic ISDN features, and embodied this in Recommendations I.XXW, I.XXX, and I.XXY.[29] They sought formal approval in June 1982 under a special acceleration procedure.[30] Other nations, principally the United States, felt, however, that such approval was premature and that further work was necessary.[31] The approval was thus not obtained.[32] Since 1982 considerably more work has been done, and there now exists an entire set of "I-series' recommendations, fleshing out the technical standards and operating principles of ISDNs in great detail.[33] Formal approval was obtained at CCITT Study Group Plenary Sessions in 1983 and 1984.[34]

Nascent ISDN Facilities

In most of the major industrialized nations, the principal communication and information system operators are beginning to plan and implement ISDN-like capabilities. It's difficult, however, to obtain details due to the proprietary nature of the work, and the rapidity of these developments. In addition, in the United States, the effects of recent regulatory decisions concerning the provision of information services by AT&T (known as the *Computer II* decision), and that company's divestiture of its local operating companies, has served to compound the confusion.[35]

Nonetheless, occasional details become evident. For example, at a recent seminar on ISDN at the Massachusetts Institute of Technology at Cambridge, the principal AT&T spokesman closed his presentation with the bold comment that "the future of AT&T is ISDN."[36]

AT&T has taken a commanding lead in the United States in shaping ISDN developments. Most general comments have emanated from their spokespersons, and the preponderance of the U.S. written contributions to CCITT forums, and the fact that participation in those forums is by AT&T employees.[37] The following statements are illustrative.

What is the ISDN? It is a public end-to-end digital telecommunications network providing a wide range of user applications.

[The challenge of] network planners is to fulfill the ISDN's potential as much as possible. As usual when vision and reality meet, there is a crucial period of challenge when basic decisions must be made. Now is such a time, a time when standards are being set, large amounts of capital are being committed, and new industry structures are being mandated not just in Washington, D.C., but in other capitals around the world.

The main motivation for the ISDN are the economies and flexibilities which the integrated nature of the network would foster. The economies occur because many of the emerging new services are digital and can be combined with existing services to use an integrated transport capability at a significantly lower overall cost than it would take for each service to use a separate transport capability.

Most people will agree with the general architecture. Where we may have different perspectives is in such issues as: first, the details under this scheme; second, interface specifications; third, how to go about making this happen; fourth, what should motivate the evolution; fifth, how rapidly it will evolve; and sixth, what will be the services driving the evolution process.[38]

Recently the new AT&T unregulated subsidiary, AT&T Information Systems, has introduced NET 1000, a fledgling ISDN.[39] At the same time, they have revealed advanced work on systems incorporating additional ISDN features. A similar situation exists in other industrialized countries, with spokesmen making general statements concerning ISDN in a variety of periodicals and conference symposia, and announcing the implementation of new network capabilities.[40] It is evident that the ISDN race is on. Around the world, billions of dollars are being earmarked for investment during the next decade to bring the ISDN concept and the CCITT/ISO designs into reality.[41]

ISDN ISSUES

The emergence of an ISDN environment raises a panoply of issues. Some are fairly abstract or long-term. Others are concrete and apply to current controversies. It is difficult, however, to separate these matters into neat categories. Often the near-term decisions have substantial long-term consequences. Similarly, today's regulatory policies may have little applicability to an ISDN environment being planned now, but whose effects will not be evident for a decade.

The following discussion of issues attempts to strike a balance by using a generic communication issues framework and applying it to current ISDN developments. The details discussed below may appear to be arcane and inconsequential jargon of interest only to network engineers. While much of the ongoing dialogue does indeed fall into this category, important matters with substantial public interest or economic consequence have been sifted out.

Domestic Regulatory Response

The emergence of an ISDN environment presents each nation with some fundamental decisions regarding methods to be employed for implementing and operating information networks. For the preponderance of countries, who perform these tasks through a government monopoly, there are relatively few procedural problems. Existing decision-making mechanisms are simply used to balance national interest considerations, user demands, and prevailing economics.[42] Even in these countries, however, there may be some important consideration given to the exent a monopoly should assume control over all telecommunication *and information* for the nation. The creation of information is highly dependent on motivated, innovative individuals in a society. If human experience has demonstrated anything, it is that monopolies and bureaucracies are not conducive to promoting motivation and innovation.

In other countries such as the United States where the nation's communication and information services are largely provided by the private sector, an ISDN environment produces substantial procedural dilemmas. Here the means for divining the national interest and regulating the private sector become very complex. The matter is compounded by government processes which are extremely cumbersome and slow, and by the lack of expertise and resources to make satisfactory judgment.[43] The international momentum toward reaching universal ISDN agreements, on the other hand, is fast and strong. Government decisions capable of being developed only after years of comment, reflection, and adjudication may be of little use in such an environment.

The United Stated Congress established a goal in 1934 "to make available, so far as possible, to all the people of the United States a rapid, efficient, Nationwide, and world-wide wire and radio communication service with adequate facilities at reasonable charges."[44] The Federal Communications Commission was established to achieve that goal through regulation or private-sector communication facilities. Rather than devising a concept for a national communications architecture, however, it is contemporary policy to achieve this goal largely through private-sector competition.[45] Although such a policy has many merits, it may nonetheless present considerable additional complexities in the design and implementation of domestic and international ISDN components. Many of the more significant ISDN issues relate to architectural configurations. The inability of government to directly address these matters means it can only indirectly control the results. In addition, the prospect of information being routed through a potentially large number of facilities under independent ownership and management, with no national mechanism for operational coordination and standards setting, looms as a serious problem in assuring satisfactory operation of the national communication system.[46]

The Japanese telecommunications entity, NTT, has recently done some very innovative analysis of ISDN regulatory issues. They have taken the Open Systems Interconnection (OSI) model presently used for devising ISDN design details, and are considering its utility as a regulatory framework.[47] Thus applied, the several bottom layers which deal with basic information transport would be earmarked for government monopoly. The middle layers dealing with virtual networks would be open to some private-sector competition. The highest layer dealing with the actual provision of information services would be almost exclusively provided by the private sector. This kind of highly sophisticated regulatory approach indicates a Japanese desire to blend together the best features of the world's divergent political–economic methodologies. As discussed at the IIC's Washington Symposium on Communications and International Trade in December 1981, transborder data flow issues also appear to be usefully analyzed through the same OSI-model approach.[48] Indeed, it is only through such a structured model that many issues related to "virtual" information services can be meaningfully explored.

External Interfaces

Issues dealing with external interfaces are among the most important in the ISDN repertory. They were recog-

nized as a priority item within the CCITT, and continue to consume most of the energies devoted to reaching ISDN arrangements.[49] AT&T in particular has focused almost exclusively on the subject, and even succeeded in amending the ITU terms of reference for ISDN studies to emphasize user–network interface issues.[50]

This emphasis is certainly technologically appropriate. In classic engineering methodology, it is the interface specifications that establish most of the basic characteristics of the system. In the real world, they are imperative in establishing boundaries for separate ownership and control of different segments of the overall network. This is a particularly significant matter in the United States, where the regulatory environment mandates several such divisions—terminal equipment separated from the local network; local network separated from the long-haul network; and (for dominant networks such as AT&T) "basic" facilities separated from "enhanced" facilities.[51]

Before delving into the intricacies of the user–network interface, it should be mentioned that the question of interfaces presently needs additional study. The threshold question of what interfaces should exist and for whom only began to be substantively explored at the 1982 meeting in Kyoto of ISDN experts. Of particular interest is the network–network interface and the many problems of interworking among diverse networks.[52] The network–network interface becomes even more dicey when the networks are those of different countries or involve an international organization operator such as INTELSAT. This is where issues related to transborder data flow arise and questions relating to encryption, and the extent of foreign interoperability and control, become highly significant. Up to now, however, there has been little dialogue on these subjects.[53]

There may be a need for other kinds of network interfaces. For example, a "network–information services facility" interface may be desirable. This could be important in light of U.S. domestic regulatory developments relating to the *Computer II* basic–enhanced decision, the promotion of competition in providing services, and the AT&T divestiture of local distribution systems. Such interfaces have just begun to be discussed.

Even beyond the United States and its regulatory approaches, many nations might wish the flexibility of allowing some competition in the provision of information and communication services. It seems, however, that the present trend to emphasize only one kind of interface (one basically designed for small-scale users) may predispose the network to exist as a monopoly.

The User–Network Interface

Thousands of pages or material have been generated over the past three years in the attempt to wrestle with the details of the basic user–network interface.[54] Much of this detail does not give rise to significant issues. It simply involves reaching agreement on such fundamentals as the number and size of pins on the universal connector for attaching to an ISDN, and the like.[55] All of this is important, however, because it will substantially determine the manner in which all of us will communicate by electronic means. And, virtually every decision will have some significant effect on costs and the extent of our communication capabilities and options.

There are a broad class of issues that deal with user–network interface alternatives. Here there is an attempt to reach agreement on sufficient details to allow the design of equipment, yet not so much detail and inflexibility as to prevent innovative or alternative approaches. This is no easy task when the technology is changing rapidly, but nonetheless a critical threshold step which must be taken if the ISDN is ever to become a reality.

The first of these choices involves certain assumptions regarding the type of local transmission medium. Virtually all the work to date on the so-called Universal Physical Interface between the user and network has proceeded on an assumption that the transmission link from the network is a standard copper wire pair.[56] This may have the effect, however, of impeding the rapid implementation of alternative media such as radio or optical fibers at this interface.[57] Admittedly, it makes considerable sense to maximize the use of the local transmission medium most pervasive in the world—the telephone pair terminating at homes and offices—but the exclusivity of the focus appears inappropriate.

Another basic choice involves the precise placement of the interface in terms of functions provided by the user terminal and those provided by the network. Because of the differing regulatory environments of countries, this is a particularly difficult matter, and it was necessary to recognize two different kinds of user–network interface functions. In ISDN jargon these are known as the NT1 and NT2 functions.[58] The NT1 interface function is a relatively dumb one, corresponding to layer 1 of the OSI reference model (physical termination). The NT2 function corresponds to levels 2 and 3 (data link & network). It provides intelligent functions such as local subdistribution to a number of users, or code and protocol conversions. A private branch exchange (PABX) is an example of a NT2 function. In some countries such as the United States, considerable controversy exists concerning exactly what will be provided at these interfaces.[59] It is a high-stakes game among network and non-network providers of terminal equipment that is highly intricate, and on which hundreds of millions of dollars in potential market opportunities may ride on the placement of a line.

Of recent and related vintage is the question of whether to allow a "passive bus" to be provided by the network.[60] Such a scheme would allow a small number of users, perhaps up to several score, to share a single user–network link on a random, ad hoc basis. Considerable cost savings could result for certain user classes. However, the need, technical feasibility, and competitive effects have only begun to be analyzed.

Some of the interface alternatives give rise to significant national public interest considerations. These include such matters as the activation/deactivation of terminals by the network for remote sensing, for nonpayment, or in times of emergency when orders of priority of use might need to be established.[61] Interwoven with the last is the provision of emergency power by the network.[62] Although sophisticated terminals clearly require more electrical power than can be easily provided by the network, it seems that some minimal amount of power should be available from the network for plain old telephone service. This is pretty much the situation today in nearly all countries, and allows the general populace to use the phone when local electrical power fails—a particularly important matter in times of emergency. It would seem that most nations would want to mandate a similar capability for an ISDN. The matter becomes more tricky, however, with the use of optical fibers for local service. The answer may lie in recent demonstrations of providing sufficient light energy from the network as to allow the powering of basic telephone service at the terminal end.[63]

Another area which might give rise to public interest considerations is the matter of "hybrid access."[64] Here the question is whether it might not be more economical and appropriate for some large class of users to refrain from taking a leap to a fully digital, high capacity interface. Digital capabilities would simply be "piggy-backed" on top of existing analogue voice telephone service. One side in this debate argues that in the near term, many users would have little use for the full array of ISDN services, particularly in developing countries. The hybrid-access option would allow the partial and selective implementation of some services using largely existing equipment. The other side argues, however, that the costs of providing fully digital service is plummeting, and that the use of an intermediate hybrid arrangment might result in greater long-term costs and delay imple-mentation of standard ISDN features.[65]

In the ISDN dialogue, it is sometimes amazing how the shifting sands of technology can play havoc with the standards making process. One of the best examples involves the basic ISDN channel structure. Fairly early, a consensus was achieved that "standard" service would consist of two "basic" or B channels with 64 kbps duplex capability, and one 16 kbps D channel for a dialogue between the user and network intelligence.[66] The D channel would also be used for low bit-rate data collection and control services such as remote meter reading or electrical load control.[67] The choice of the 64 kbps rate was largely based on the necessity—in the past—to use that rate for reasonably good-quality digital voice communication. Today, technology has advanced to allow the same quality to be provided with only 32 kbps with the possibility of 16 looming in the near future.[68] Because of this, some have begun to question the efficacy of the original channelization scheme.[69] The original plan will probably be kept, because of the need to adopt some kind of a uniform approach. But, the technical rationale has somewhat disappeared.

As different, wider bandwidth transmission links to the user become available, there are plans to offer multiples of the B channel capacities all the way up to 140 Mbit/s.[70] This would encompass, for example, the provision of high-resolution video programs. Although the implementation of this magnitude of digital capa-city to individual users remains largely unstudied, the recent availability of low-cost VLSI digital television packages operating at 6 Mbps may stir the CCITT to action.[71]

There are few profound regulatory issues posed by the above developments. The possible exception may be in the United States where the *Computer II* basic–enhanced dichotomy may need clarification to recog-nize a distinction between basic communication ser-vices and those provided incidental to the user–network dialogue over the D channel.

How Much User Control?

The most far-reaching user–network interface issues concern the user options, i.e., the amount of control a user will have in shaping and controlling the nature of the functional elements and services made available at the interface.[72] There is a fundamental tension here between the desire of the network to enhance network efficiency and market opportunities, and the desire of the user to minimize costs and maximize flexibility. The ISDN will make available an array of options far beyond that offered in today's networks. These choices will include such things as bandwidth (actually bit-rate), error rates, time delay, etc. The list stretches on to include scores of different characteristics.[73] But, what it may or may not include, depending on the current ISDN dialogue or subsequent national regulatory option, is a choice of alternative providers of transmission links, storage and processing facilities, or software and in-formation. These highly important matters involving all sorts of national and international considerations have only circumspectly been addressed, and largely under the veil of technical options.

Perhaps the most contentious of the user-control issues involves the availability of so-called leased lines.[74] These are simply a fixed transmission capacity between two points for which the user pays a flat rate independent of use. In recent years, both communica-tion entrepreneurs and large or specialized users of communication have found it attractive to lease such lines and create their own networks.[75] In some cases this is done to provide high levels of priority and reliability for their communication. In other cases it is done to directly compete with the lessor, attempting to siphon off its business. In the latter case, particularly where the lessor is a government monopoly, the matter has become very contentious.[76] Indeed, several D-Series CCITT Recommendations rather explicitly spell out the circumstances under which this can be done, and additional restrictions find their way into contractual agreements.[77]

The controversial subject of leased lines necessarily arises during the course of ISDN discussions. Some large users of existing leased circuits fear ISDN as a devise to limit the future availability of such circuits.[78]

Although there is now explicit reference to a "non-switched or leased" connection type in the draft ISDN recommendations, reference is also made to "permanent virtual circuits."[79] While the possibility of future restrictions exists, it is probably remote. What seems to be lacking, however, is significant user participation in delineating specific leased circuit attributes that might be adopted as a virtual equivalent.

The lack of user participation at ISDN forums goes beyond leased circuit matters. It is a matter of some concern in all the ensuing discussions. There is little effective representation of user interests.[80] As noted, an intrinsic tension frequently exists between the desires of users versus networks. Countless decisions must be made that balance these divergent interests in some sort of mutually acceptable way. However, there are few if any effective advocates for the user side. There is thus a danger that the resultant arrangements may tip rather decidedly in favor of network interests.

Network Model and Architecture

Considerations related to the network model and architecture are of less interest to the user, and more to network operators and (in those countries where the network operator is not a PTT-type government monopoly) national regulatory authorities. The former have interests in operating an economically efficient network capable of satisfying user demand. The latter, including PTTs, impose a variety of requirements on the network based on public interest and national security determinations. These requirements have the effect of altering the model and architecture.

Preferential Configurations

In most countries, the architecture is simply established by the government authority that owns and operates the nation's telecommunication system. Straightforward engineering decisions based on user demand, cost, and national topography are amended to accommodate public interest considerations such as cross-subsidization for certain segments of the populace, enhancing the reliability of government circuits, promoting the use of domestic facilities, and assuming control over the network during national emergency.[81] Even countries such as the United States, which are departing from a national telecommunication monopoly environment, manipulate the architecture in some significant fashion.[82] There may be less consideration given to cross-subsidizations, but

that is replaced by encouraging competitive, redundant local and long-haul facilities and services through a variety of government regulatory devices.

One of the most recent and important of these devises is the *Computer II* basic–enhanced dichotomy. The effect of this regulatory mandate on the ISDN architecture in the United States is, among other things, to require that AT&T create physically separate nodes, owned and operated by a fully separated subsidiary known as American Bell, for the provision of anything more than information transport.[83] Aside from the regulatory motivation for this result, it may also serve a technologically useful purpose by optimizing transport node facilities for maximum transport efficiency rather than for all sorts of general-purpose information services. Whether this would be sufficient to offset the transmission and protocol penalties incurred as a result of the separation is unclear. Thus, the dichotomy might be worthy of emulation by other nations, although different distinctions between "basic" and "enhanced" information services, or a different connotation of "separation," might be considered.

There are other important examples of preferred architectural configurations. One that remains a source of considerable controversy relates to the transit time of different transmission links. The delays which are intrinsically part of space satellite links are highly undesirable in some applications.[84] This led the CCITT to adopt a preliminary restriction on the use of such links in international ISDN communications. An optimal transit rate, in addition to other attractive features, seems to have spurred an increased commitment to optical fiber links for interexchange transmission in an ISDN environment. Thus, it would appear ISDN architecture is destined to be a largely terrestrial, switched, distributed configuration for most industrialized nations.

There are many situations, however, where a more centralized facility based on space radiocommunication will prove an attractive ISDN configuration. Nations which have difficulty in implementing terrestrial routes are obvious examples.[85] Even for developed countries with compact populations, space facilities should remain an important means of long-haul mobile communication, or effecting multipoint distribution. Similarly, national interests in a reliable network in times of national emergency may dictate particular architectures. Generally, these will be the switched distributed configuration, with satellite backup.[86]

Just as there may be preferences for certain configurations based on national interest considerations, other architectures may be undesirable. Some have begun to worry that the procompetitive fragmentation of both local and long-haul communication facilities in the United States may produce sizable independent private networks and a consequential detriment to the public networks. This phenomenon is also referred to as *network bypass*.[87] The problem is not new. Indeed, in the early days of telephone in the United States the difficulties posed by multiple independent private networks led to AT&T being regarded as a regulated monopoly.[88] However, it is not clear that the problems are as grave, or that they are outweighed by the benefits of competition.

Interface and Interoperability Among Networks

Several interesting and contentious issues arise in conjunction with the interface and interoperation among networks. The former term refers to the points at which networks physically, electrically, and functionally interconnect. Interoperation refers to the ability of one network intelligence to give instructions to that of another (in other words, to direct a foreign network to provide resources or services). From the first international telecommunication conference in 1865 until today, the arrangements for accomplishing these tasks have been the most fundamental part of creating a global communications capability.[89] At the domestic level in the United States, questions relating to interface and interoperability among networks have assumed substantial significance as the nation's communication and information providers have become more fragmented in the quest to promote competition.

These matters will assume such great significance in the ISDN environment because of the tremendous new flexibilities available in terms of interface and interoperability options, and the concomitant ability to skew the availability of particular network resources for competitive advantage. A few examples are illustrative.

At the interface level, a question arises regarding the extent to which encrypted public communications will be allowed to transit among nations. Devices to accomplish encryption are becoming increasingly inexpensive and sophisticated; and users have increasing incentive to use them, if nothing else, to protect a copyright interest.[90]

A more difficult interface question involves international gateways. The ISDN environment and the procompetitive policies being fostered in some countries will tend to promote a proliferation of gateways.[91] Other nations not sharing those views, and desiring to avoid the associated technical and operational complexities, or perhaps preferring a particular gateway because of a cable investment, seem reluctant to see such a proliferation.[92] Even international organization providers of telecommunication service such as INTELSAT, INMARSAT, and INTERSPUTNIK, have obvious substantial interests in the outcome of such arrangements. Looking into the future, the matter could become even more complex if INTELSAT, for example, introduced switching, processing, and storage capabilities on board its satellites, and thus became an ISDN node interposed among national systems. Already, TAT-8, the new transatlantic optical fiber cable in the process of being implemented, gave rise to controversy concerning the manner in which it was to be split and was to appear among European countries.[93]

It is the interoperability issues that will continue to vex network operators around the globe. Indeed, it is these issues to which the ITU's 1988 World Administrative Telegraph and Telephone Conference (WATTC) may be dedicated.[94] These issues are an extension of those posed at the user–network interface. At that interface it was noted that many a key question dealt with the extent of control a user would have over the network resources and services being provided. For example, could alternative providers of those resources and services be specified? Could a user specify particular transmission paths? Could dedicated or leased circuits be specified and assembled by the user—even to compete with services offered by the network? Could levels of priority or reliability be requested and assured? And so on.[95] Here the same questions arise in conjunction with how either that user's requests or similar ones originating from a network will be carried out by another network.

These matters can become complex and highly contentious. Take, for example, the situation where the networks are those of different countries, and one of them restricts for economic or policy reasons the availability of certain user options. To what extent can the more restrictive national network now allow foreign users or networks to obtain resources or services unavailable to its citizens? If it does institute two operational standards, what is to prevent a citizen from establishing a circuit to a foreign network and requesting of that foreign network the services and resources unavailable from his native country network?

This area of exterritorial activities of citizens and foreign entities through information networks is virtually bereft of guidelines or international law.[96] The default condition may be to impose the policies manifested by the most restrictive nation. This is not a welcome result for those who value freedom of inquiry and freedom of communication among nations and people.

Another important interoperability question concerns the basis for making resource-utilization decisions when they are not specified or allowed to be specified by a user or foreign network. The problem applies not only to the international transit facilities, but also to situations like the U.S. competitive network configuration. If, for example, a user in the U.K. desires to communicate with someone in San Francisco, and that user either does not specify the routing or is not allowed to do so, the U.K. telecommunication authority must make a decision regarding the choice of gateway to the United States, then someone must make further choices regarding the choice of long-haul path from the gateway location to San Francisco, and then choose a local path within San Francisco to reach the ultimate addressee. This is not an entirely new matter. However, both the extreme interoperability flexibilities of ISDN and the competitive fragmentation of information transport resources in countries such as the United States pose very significant problems that must be satisfactorily addressed in devising the standards and operating principles for ISDN.

A third interesting and significant interoperability issue relates to the matters of addressing and terminal portability.[97] Concerns over privacy become entwined. Basicly, the matter devolves to the meaning of a terminal address. Does that address connote a real person, or a location? Although existing communication network schemes generally use the latter, the technology now exists to adopt the former. For example, if someone's telephone number is dialed, that person as an individual is not being dialed, but rather a fixed network terminal where that person is expected to be. It is now possible, however, to permanently associate a numerical identity with a person, and have the network communicate directly with that person irrespective of location—so-called terminal portability.

There are many benefits to such portability. The network can be made highly efficient in communicating with a mobile population. It is very attractive for billing purposes. It allows each of us to communicate with another without the necessity of forwarding others or being forwarded every time we leave a fixed location. Indeed, this is the attractiveness of mobile telephones now coming into extensive use through cellular radio systems.[98] It also means, however, that a highly efficient electronic system will potentially be aware of everyone's geographical location and movements through time. Lest any paranoid readers be left with ominous impressions, the obvious answer to inhibiting such tracking is simply to leave one's terminal at home or to turn it off. The price paid, however, is the inability to communicate.

The above interoperability issues are not exhaustive. One of a more technical nature relates to the synchronization of networks.[99] The entire network must adhere to a synchronization agreement if errors in transmission and processing are to be minimized. If a centralized timing reference is utilized, it should be available to all ISDN participants in a nondiscriminatory fashion.[100] A continuous, close-operating environment among all providers of transport service is important in a network which embraces nearly everyone.

There are issues involving the management role of intelligence within the among networks. The responsibilities of the intelligence would include control of all resources available to the network in response to general or specific directions by customers. It is not clear how these responsibilities are to be shared. There are significant national security considerations associated with such control in times of emergency. Depending on the nature of the emergency, different management criteria may apply.

There are also significant legal issues, not the least of which is the matter of liability. Information might potentially transit dozens of different, independently owned and operated functional elements. In many if not most instances the user might be unaware of whose facilities were being utilized. In our emerging information societies, great costs might be associated with the loss, delay, or distortion of information. The law must eventually provide answers in the apportionment of liability.

Rate Regulation

In one way or another, ISDN users will pay for the information services made available. In some cases this will be done through direct arrangements between user and provider. In others it will be done on the basis of national or international tariffs. Irrespective of the mechanism, the problem of assessing costs must be resolved, presumably in a manner which reflects costs incurred in providing the services.[101]

These problems are as old as communication networks. The difference in the ISDN environment lies in the extreme flexibilities and options associated with each provision of service. The relevant factors include transmission quality, transport distance, routing complexity, short- and long-term information quantities, degree of dissemination, burstiness, priority, bit-rates, or social/political/economic characteristics of the sender or recipient of the information. This area may present special problems for the United States due to the tendency of other nations to devise tariffs for international transport based on criteria unrelated to transport alone, or to establish tariffs for nontransport information services.

Trade

Because the essence of ISDN involves global standardization and interoperability, significant foreign trade issues arise with respect to equipment and the provision of transborder information services. A major concern in this area involves the extent of departure of any one nation from the rest of the world in devising different domestic standards, and impact of that action on foreign trade. For example, a governmental regulatory decision designed to further domestic competition may result in domestic equipment which is at a competitive disadvantage internationally. Although less likely, the ability of foreign users of national information services to efficiently access those services could similarly be made less attractive by domestic ISDN regulatory decisions. In the ISDN environment, considerable interdependence will exist between domestic and international effects.

The provision of transborder information services raises many new issues of a political/economic nature. A foreign entity will have the potential technical capability not only to gather and furnish information, but also to provide a considerable range of information services within any given nation. Concerns relating to foreign competition and alien activities are already scuttling the old platitudes such as "free flow," and leading to a thorough scrutiny from national security and foreign trade perspectives. For example, a London-based group recently noted the increasing U.S. restrictions on Soviet-bloc user access to publicly available data bases.[102] Similarly, the United States Congress is now contemplating placing this entire area in a foreign trade framework.[103]

Spectrum Management

An ancillary issue to central ISDN questions is the matter of allocating and allotting radio frequency bands and channels. In the integrated transport environment implied by the ISDN model, most means of radiocommunication would be operating in concert under the direction of network intelligence to provide internodal or termination services.[104] The plethora of existing, content-oriented radio "services" such as broadcasting, maritime mobile, aeronautical mobile, land mobile, fixed, etc., can be expected to largely devolve into two: internodal and termination. The government's traditional methods for deciding among competing services and applicants for frequency bands and channels will be significantly impacted. Some new basic scheme will probably become necessary for managing the public's radio resource.

CONCLUSION

In summary, ISDN represents the implementation of new technology to provide a universal, intelligent information network. Beginning in early 1981 and continuing over the next two decades, massive efforts involving manufacturers, users, national administrations, and international organizations will take place to establish for the ISDN the principles, strategies, and standards that will provide a stable foundation for the commitment of the substantial capital required.

These developments present a broad range of technical and national policy questions. The answers will explicitly and profoundly shape the nature of future domestic and global communication.

NOTES

1. In the integrated information environment, the term "information transport," as a species of generic information services, seems more appropriate and is increasingly being used as a replacement for the term "telecommunication." *See* Report on the Meeting of the Group of Experts on ISDN Matters of

Study Group XVIII (Kyoto, Feb. 14–25, 1982), Period 1981–1984, CCITT Doc. No. COM XVIII–No. R15 [hereinafter cited as Kyoto Report] (Temp. Doc. 65 at 29 in the absence of the final printed version of this report at the time of this analysis, citation will be made to the temporary documents that comprise the report). *See also* Report on the Meeting of the Group of Experts on ISDN Matters of Study Group XVIII (Munich, Feb. 17–25, 1982), Period 1981–1984, CCITT Doc. No. COM XVIII–No. R8 (Mar. 1982) at 51–54 [hereinafter cited as Munich Report].

The term "digital pipe" appears to have been coined by Irwin Dorros, assistant vice-president for network planning of AT&T. *See* I. Dorros, Keynote Address to the IEEE Communications Society, Integrated Services Digital Networks Symposium (ISDN '81), Innisbrook, Florida (Jan. 7, 1981) (subsequently published as Dorros, *Challenge and Opportunity of the 1980s; the ISDN,* 200 TELEPHONY, Jan. 26, 1981, at 43, as amended 200 TELEPHONY, Feb. 23, 1981, at 28).

2. *See* Munich Report, *supra* note 1, at 53–54.

3. *See* Proposals for the Organisation of CCITT Work on the ISDN and New Services, CCITT VIIth Plen. Ass'y Doc. AP VII-109 (Aug. 1980); Working Methods of the CCITT, CCITT VIIth Plen. Ass'y Temp. Doc. No. 60-E/PLEN (Nov. 1980); Final Report to the VIIth Plenary Assembly (Part IV), CCITT VIIth Plen. Ass'y Doc. AP VII-No. 103 (Sept. 1980); Questions Allocated to Study Group XVIII for the Period 1981–1984, CCITT Doc. No. COM XVIII–No. 1 (Feb. 1981) [hereinafter cited as Questions].

The ITU is an international organization located in Geneva, Switzerland, which serves as an umbrella for the nations of the world to gather and fashion international arrangements for telecommunication and information systems. It consists of numerous bodies, one of which is the CCITT. Participants in the CCITT's work include not only representatives from member states—largely the Post, Telegraph and Telephone ministries (PTTs)—but also delegates representing Recognized Private Operating Agencies (RPOAs) such as AT&T and Scientific and Industrial Organizations (SIOs) such as IBM. Together they fashion the CCITT Recommendations that consist of hundreds of principles, standards, and tariffs for operating the world's telecommunication and information systems. *See* Chap. 10 in G. CODDING & A. RUTKOWSKI, THE INTERNATIONAL TELECOMMUNICATION UNION IN A CHANGING WORLD (1982).

4. *See* International Organization for Standardization, Data Processing—Open Systems Interconnection—Basic Reference Model, Geneva Doc. No. ISO/TC97/SC16 N719 (Aug. 1981).

5. *See* OFFICE OF SCIENCE AND TECHNOLOGY, FEDERAL COMMUNICATIONS COMMISSION, BIBLIOGRAPHY OF DOCUMENTS ON THE INTEGRATED SERVICES DIGITAL NETWORK (ISDN), BULL. NO. 57 (Aug. 1982) [hereinafter cited as BIBLIOGRAPHY].

6. *See, e.g.,* Rutkowski & Marcus, *The Integrated Services Digital Network: Developments and Regulatory Issues,* 12 COMPUTER COM. REV., July & Oct. 1982, at 68; ABA Sect. of Science & Technology, American Bar Association Policies for the Integrated Communications Environment of the Future, (Aug. 7, 1981) (panel transcript, New Orleans); R. Eward, Integrated Services Digital Networks: Impacts & Industry Strategy (Martech Strategies, Indialantic, Fla.); Structural Issues in Global Communications 23–36 (The Tobin Foundation, Washington, D.C.).

7. *See* Philosophy and Concept of ISDN, CCITT Doc. No. COM XVIII–No. 130 (Sept. 1981).

8. *See* Draft Rec. I.310, ISDN Functional Model, Kyoto Report, *supra* note 1, Temp. Doc. 65 at 27.

9. *See* Draft Rec. I.2XX, Services Supported by an ISDN, Kyoto Report, *supra* note 1, Temp. Doc. 64 at 6, 53–57.

10. *Id.* Temp. Doc. 63 at 6. The utilization of a separate signaling channel (referred to as the "D channel") inherently allows user-network dialogue during the course of providing any service. *See id.* 1, Temp. Doc. 63 at 1–7.

11. *Id.* 1, Temp. Doc. 64 at 20. Type U3 information encompasses bit rates up to 140 Mbit/s, well within that necessary to encompass high resolution television. *Id.* at 21.

12. The term "fifth-generation computer" implies the existence of information systems possessing sufficient intelligence to learn from a dialogue with a human or other machine or sensory device. *See* Preliminary Report on Study and Research on Fifth-Generation Computers, Japan Information Processing Development Center (Fall 1981).

13. *See* L. M. Ericsson Introduces Phone With Voice-Activated Dial, Worldwide Report, Telecommunications Policy, Research and Development [hereinafter cited as Worldwide Report, No. 245, Joint

Publications Research Service (JPRS) 82,083 at 106 (Oct. 26, 1982); More Details Revealed on Experimental Voice-Activated Phone, Worldwide Report, *supra,* No. 248, JPRS 82,267 at 36 (Nov. 18, 1982).

14. Kenedi, *Plotting a Strategy for the Emerging ISDN,* 200 TELEPHONY, June 22, 1981, at 22.

15. In addition to the ISO and the CCITT, the CCIR (Consultative Committee on Radio), and the International Federation of Information Processing also provide international forums. On the regional level, the European Computer Manufacturers Association (ECMA) and the European Conference of Post and Telecommunication Administrations (CEPT) provide forums. At the U.S. domestic level, the U.S. Organization for CCITT (a Dept. of State public advisory committee), the Institute of Electrical and Electronic Engineers (IEEE), the Federal Telecommunication Standards Committee, the American National Standards Institute, and the Electronic Industries Association also provide forums.

16. *See, e.g.,* Questions, *supra* note 3.

17. *See* Study of ISDN, Report by Committee A on Working Methods of the CCITT, Annex E, CCITT Yellow Book at 128 (1981).

18. The persons conducting such liaison are referred to as rapporteurs for the other study groups. These representatives may convey ad hoc questions and answers between groups, or introduce relevant documents from the represented group.

19. *See* para. 9012, Vocabulary of Pulse Code Modulation (PCM) and Digital Transmission Terms, Rec. G.702, CCITT Yellow Book (1980) (ref. Final Report to the VIIth Plenary Assembly (Part III), VIIth Plen. Ass'y Doc. AP VII-No. 102-E at 24 (July 1980); para. 2 et seq., Minutes of the Seventh Plenary Meeting, VIIth Plenary Ass'y Temp. Doc. No. 83-E/ PLEN (Nov. 24, 1980)).

20. *See* Report of the Meeting of Working Party XVIII/1 (ISDN), Period 1981–1984, CCITT Doc. COM XVIII–No. R3 at 5 (July 1981).

21. *See* Definition of Integrated Services Digital Networks (ISDN), CCITT Doc. COM XVIII–No. 31 (Apr. 1981) (contribution of AT&T).

22. *See* Draft Rec. I.112, Vocabulary of ISDN Terms, Kyoto Report, *supra* note 1, Temp. Doc. 51 at 4.

23. *Id.* at 1–7.

24. *See* Kyoto Report, *supra* Temp. Doc. 56 at 9.

25. *See* Report of the Meeting of Working Party XVIII/1, *supra* note 20, at 4.

26. "The CCITT [considers] the need for a common basis for the future studies necessary for the evolution towards an ISDN . . .," Rec. G.705, CCITT Yellow Book, Fascicle III.3 at 65; "[M]any countries wish to adopt a common strategy for . . . Integrated Services Digital Networks," Questions, *supra* note 3, at 7.

27. Nonconforming networks would at best be required to fashion special interfaces, or at worst be precluded from interconnecting with an ISDN, depending on the nature of the deviation. A user would incur a similar penalty.

28. *See* G. CODDING & A. RUTKOWSKI, *supra* note 3; Organization and Work of the CCITT, Series A Recommendations, CCITT Yellow Book at 233–49.

29. *See* Munich Report, *supra,* note 1 at 34–37, 13–20, and 21–25, respectively.

30. *See* Comments on the Results of the ISDN Experts Meeting, Munich, Feb. 17–25, 1982, CCITT Doc. No. COM XVIII–No. 101 (Apr. 1982).

31. *See* Summary Minutes of U.S. CCITT ISDN Working Party for the Apr. 14, 1982 Meeting, Department of State, Office of Communications Policy.

32. *See* Report on the Geneva Meeting (June 10– 22, 1982), CCITT Doc. No. COM XVIII–No. R9 at 4 (June 1982).

33. *See* Draft Rec. I.110, General Structure of the I-Series Recommendations, Kyoto Report, *supra* note 1, Temp. Doc. 56 at 3–7.

34. *See* NCS Technical Information Bulletin 83- 1, at 1–10.

35. *See* Final Decision, Docket No. 20,828, FCC 80–189,77 F.C.C.2d 384 (1980); Memorandum Opinion and Order, Docket No. 20,828, FCC 80–628, 84 F.C.C.2d 50 (1980); Memorandum Opinion and Order on Further Reconsideration, Docket No. 20,828, FCC 81–481, 88 F.C.C.2d 512 (1981), *aff'd sub nom.* CCIA v. FCC, 693 F.2d 198 (D.C. Cir. 1982) cert. den. sub. nom. Louisiani P.S.C. v. FCC, 461 U.S. 938 (1983). [the above decision materials are hereinafter cited as Computer II]. *See also* Modification of Final Judgment (entered on Aug. 24, 1982), in United States v. American Tel. & Tel. Co., Civ. Nos. 74-1698, 82-0192; 532 F. Supp. 131, 47 Fed. Reg. 40,392 (D.D.C. 1982); Bell Operating Companies, 95 F.C.C.2d117. *aff'd* sub nom Maryland v. U.S., 460 U.S. 1001 (1983).

36. *See* Minutes of the Seminar on Integrated Services Digital Networks, MIT Research Program on Communications Policy, Cambridge, Mass. (Oct. 7, 1982).

37. *See, e.g.,* Summary Minutes of U.S. CCITT ISDN Working Party for the Mar. 10, 1983 Meeting, Department of State, Office of Communications Policy; List of Participants, Munich Report, *supra* note 1, at 113.

38. Dorros, *Challenge and Opportunity of the 1980s, supra* note 1.

39. *See* American Bell, An Introduction to AIS/Net 1 Service; Hindin, *What American Bell Offers,* 55 ELECTRONICS, June 30, 1982, at 88.

40. An extensive bibliography of many of these materials was published by the Federal Communications Commission. *See* BIBLIOGRAPHY, *supra* note 5, at 25–28.

41. *See, e.g.,* Haag, *Telecommunication War: Ericsson Goes Its Own Way,* STOCKHOLM VECKANS AFFARER, Feb. 3, 1983, at 40, as reproduced in Worldwide Report, *supra* note 13, No. FOUO 5/83, JPRS L/11,204 at 6 (Mar. 21, 1983); *View of Ministry of Posts and Telecommunications* (noting 20-year plan for investment of 20 trillion yen in INS), TOKYO SENTAKU, May 1982, at 72, *as reproduced in Worldwide Report, supra* note 13, No. FOUO 16/82, JPRS L/10,697 at 16 (July 29, 1982); Krajnc, *One Hundred Twenty-Five Million for the World Center,* PARIS ZERO UN INFORMATIQUE HEBDO, Dec. 20, 1982, at 7, *as reproduced in* Worldwide Report, *supra* No. 261, JPRS 82,869 at 48 (Feb. 16, 1983).

42. *See* Ch. III, Economic and Technical Aspects of the Choice of Switching Systems, CCITT (Geneva 1981).

43. See LEGISLATIVE AND REGULATORY ACTIONS NEEDED TO DEAL WITH A CHANGING DOMESTIC TELECOMMUNICATIONS INDUSTRY REPRT TO CONGRESS U.S. GENERAL ACCOUNTING OFFICE REP. NO CED-81-136 (SEPT. 1981).

44. Sec. 1 Communication act of 1934, as amended, 47 U.S.C. sec.

45. See, e.g., Carterphone, 13 F.C.C.2d 420 (1968; Second Report and Order in Domestic Communications Satelite Facilities, 35 F.C.C.2d 844 (1972); Specialized Common Carrier Services 29 F.C.C.2d 870 (1971), aff'd sub nom. Washing Utilities Transportation Comm'n v.FCC,513 E.2d 1142 (9th Cir.) cert. denied, 423 U.S. 836 (1975): MCI Telecommunica-tions Cor/v. FCC, 188 U.S. App. D.C. 327, 580 F.2d (1978 Cert. denied, 439 U.S. 980 (1978); Resale and Shared Use of Common Carrier Services, 60 F.C.C.2d 261 (1976), Resale and Shared Use, 83 F.C.C.2d 187 (1980); Authorized User Modification, 90 F.C.C.2d 1394 (1982), Authorized Entities and Users, 4 F.C.C.2d 421 (1966); Competitive Carrier, 91 F.C.C.2d 59 (1982); Computer II, supra note 35.

46. The Commission's pro-competitive regulatory policies now allow a user to obtain information services by using alternative local, inter-exchange, and enhanced service facilities. See n. 46 references, supra. Formerly, the national network was governed by AT&T specification. See Bell System Practices, American Telephone and Telegraph Co. The Commission currently has no regulations to govern the manner in which the new telecommunication network configurations should operate. SeeRules and Regulations of the FCC. pts. 63,64,68, 47 C.F.R.

47. See unofficial conceptual material given the author by representative of Nippon Telephone & Telegraph Public Corp.

48. See Rutkowski, Emerging International Information Transport Barriers, Proceeding of the International Institute of Communications, Symposium on Communications and International Trade, Washington, D.C. (Dec. 10, 1981)

49. See Report of the Geneva Meeting (June 22–July 1, 1981), CCITT Doc. COM XVIII–No. R2 (July 1981).

50. See Definition of Intergrated Services Digital Networks (ISDN), supra note 21.

51. See Computer II, supra, especially Final Decision, 77 384, 418-21, and Memorandum Opinion and Order, 84 50, 53-54.

52 See Munich Report, supra note 1, at 99-100.

53. Id.

54. See BIBIOGRAPHY, supra note 50.

55. See Draft Rec. 1.431, ISDN User-Network Inerfaces: Layer 1 Recommendations, Kyoto Report. *supra* note 1, Temp. Doc. 55 at 34-49.

56. Id.

57. See ISDN Interoperability with Alternative Local Transport Network Technologies, draft CCITT Study Group XVIII contribution submitted to the U.S. CCITT ISDN Working Party meeting of Aug. 26, 1982.

58 See Draft Rec. 1411, ISDN User-Network Interfaces-Reference Configurations, Munich Report

supra note 1, at 13 *as amended by* Kyolo Report *supra* note 1, Temp. Doc. 49

59. See Minutes of FCC Intra-Agency Committee on ISDN Regulatory Issues, Attachment 1 (Mar. 1, 1982) (notes of IBM representatives presented to the Committee).

60. See Summary Report of the joint Meeting of U.S. CCITT Study Group D and the ISDN Working Party, Feb. 3, 1983, U.S. Natinal Committee Doc. No. 276.

61. See Considerations for Activation and Deactivation of Network Termination Equipment, AT&T Draft Study Group XVIII document submitted to U.S. Organization for CCITT (Jan. 1983).

62. See The Non-Provision of Exchange Originated Power to T1 or NT2, AT&T Draft Study Group XVIII document submitted to U.S. Organization for CCITT (Jan. 1983).

63. See *Laser Powers Phone Via One Optical Fiber,* ELECTRONICS, July 14, 1982, at 92.

64. See Munich Report *supra* note 1, at 25; Hybrid Arrangements for Subscriber Access to the Local Exchanges AT&T Munich Report *supra, Doc. No. CM.*

65. See Author's personal snotes from meeting of U.S. Organization for CCITT, ISDN Working Party Technical Working Group meeting at Washington(Jan. 18-21, 1983).

66. See Munich Report *supra* note 1, at 12.

67. Id. at 22.

68. See *supra* note 65.

69. Id.

70. See Kyoto Report, *supra* note 1, Temp. Doc. 64 at 20.

71. See *Digital TV VLSI Goes Into Mass Production,* 56 ELECTRONICS, Apr. 7, 1983, at 86.

72. See Draft Rec. 1.2XX supra note 9.

73. Id.

74. Id, Temp. Doc. 64 at 13.

75. Id.

76. See Sanger, *Waging a Trade War Over Data* N.Y. Times, Mar. 13, 1983, at F26.

77. See General Principles for the lease of Intercontinental Private Leased Telecommunication Circuits, CCITT Yellow Book Rec. D.1 (1980).

78. See *supra* note 59.

79. Draft Rec. 1.3XX, Network Connection Types, Kyoto Report *supra* note 1, Temp. Doc. 65 at 16.

80. See Committee for Information Computer

and Communications Policy, Special Session on the International Implications of Changing Market Structures in Telecommunications of Changing Market Structures in Telecommunication Services, OECD Doc. ICCP (83)1 at 11-12 (Jan. 1983).

81. See, e.g., Economic and Technical Aspects of the Choice of Telephone Switching Systems, CCITT GAS6 Handbook (1981); Proceedings of teh Second CCITT Interdisciplinary Colloquium on Teleinformatics, Montreal (1980).

82. See, e.g., Session on National Security, Proceedings of the Symposium on [Internatl.] Telecommunications and Information Policy, George Washington Univ., Washington, D.C. (1983); Stine, Relationship of ISDN to Future DCS Architectures, ISDN Symposium, Mitre Corp., McLean, Vag (1982).

83. See *supra* note 51.

84. See Rutkowski, *The Role of Satellite Radiocommunication in ISDN* 17 TELECOMMUNICATIONS, June 1983.

85. Id.

86. See Stine, supra note 82; Ross, *Military/Government Digital Switching Systems* 21 IEEE COMMUNICATIONS, May 1983, at 18.

87. See Attachment 1, Third Report and Order,FCC 82–579, (Dec. 22, 1982).

88. See Herring & Gross, TELECOMMUNICATIONS 189-91 (1936).

89. See G. CUDDING & A. RUTKOWSKI, *supra* note 3, chs. 1, 10 (1982).

90. See Pool & Solomon, *Intellectual Property and Transborder Data Flows* 16 STAN. INT'L L. 113 (S1981); Solomon, *New Technology Impacts on Copyright,* OECD Doc. DSTVIC/81.15 (May 1981).

91. See Competition and Deregulation in International Telecommunications, An Analysis of Fifteen FCC Actions and Their Combined Effects (Mar Tech Strategies Indialantic, Fla., 1981).

92. See Letter from Hans Wurtzen, Chairman of NORDTEL, to various U.S. common carriers, (June 30, 1982).

93. See Italian Interest in TAT8 Transatlantic Fiber Optic Cable Landing in Sicily. U.S. Dept. of State Telegram Rome 28598 (Dec. 23, 1982).

94. See World Administrative Telegraph and Telephone Conference, Res. No. PLA/1, Final Acts of the Plenipotentiary Conference, Nairobi (1983).

95. See Framework for Describing ISDN Services,

AT&T draft submission to U.S. Organization for CCITT, Working Group on ISDN (Jan. 1983).

96. See, e.,g., Chandler & Smiddy, Contract and Tort Liability in Transnational Data Transfer, Science and Technology Section, ABA Project on International Data Networks (1983); Bing, Forsberg, & Nygaard. Legal Issues Related to Transborder Data Flows, OEC. ED Doc. DSTVICCP/81.9 (1981).

97. See Draft Rec. 1.320, ISDN Numbering and Addressing Principles, Kyoto Report, *Supra* note 1, Temp. Doc. 65 at 47.

98. See, e.g., Williams, *Capacity Dynamics in Cellular Mobile Telephone Systems* 17 TELECOMMUNICATIONS, Feb. 1983, at 32.

99. See Report of Working Party, XVIII/4 (Switching and Signalling), Doc. COM.XVIII–R12 (June 1982); Abate & Cooper, *Switched Digital Network Synchronization*, 199 TELEPHONE, Nov. 10, 1980, at 33.

Abate & Cooper, *Switched Digital Network Synchronization*, 199 TELEPHONE, Nov. 10, 1980, at 33.

100. Abate & Cooper, *supra* note 99

101. Such matters have begun to be addressed in the context of CCITT Study Group III, Question 21, entitled Tariff Guidelines for Integrated Services Digital Networks. See CCITT Doc., COM III/No. 1 (Dec–1980).

102. See *Freezing Technical Data Flows Called Dangerous* 5 TRANSNAT'L DATA REP, July-Aug. 1982, at 232.

103. See, e.g., H.R. 5158, 5205, S 898, S.2058, S.2094, S.999 98th Cong.;   104. See ISDN Interoperability with Alternative Local Transport Network Technologies, supra note 57.

104. See ISDN Interoperability with Alternative Local Transport Network Technologies, supra note 57.

Part II

GLOBAL INFORMATION USERS AND INFORMATION TRANSFER SYSTEMS

CHAPTER 10

COMPUTER SERVICES INDUSTRY NETWORKS

STEPHEN H. BEACH
HERBERT E. MARKS

INTRODUCTION

Computer services firms offer data processing services to their customers through data networks that span most of the globe. Typically, the customer's information (data) is processed at the computer services firm's computer center in the United States or Europe. The customer, whether nearby or on a different continent, sends information to, and receives information from, the computer center by way of transmission facilities provided by a telecommunications common carrier or a governmental authority performing such functions. Outside of the United States, telecommunications transmission services are generally provided by governmental authorities.

Thus, it is possible for a customer with a data processing requirement to input data at an office in one country, have such data transit several countries on its way to a computer center in another country, and, after processing in that country, have such data transit several countries before it is "retrieved" at a terminal in the customer's same office or at an office in an entirely different country. For example, financial data of a multinational corporation may be derived from input from various countries, stored in a computer in a different country, and then made available to corporate offices throughout the world. In traveling between the input/output terminal and the computer, the data may traverse several countries.[1]

The growth of the computer services industry and its importance to world trade have expanded dramatically in recent years. Corporations throughout the world have become increasingly reliant upon remote computing services for their information and data processing needs. The actual and potential size of the market for computer services can be measured in a number of ways. However, because of the variety of services potentially involved and because there is not one authoritative reporting mechanism, all data must be viewed as an approximation.

In 1981, computer services revenues in the United States exceeded $22 billion. Processing services contributed over $11 billion in revenues. And, remote computing services contributed over $5 billion of that amount.[2] Computer services companies that were primarily U.S.-based received almost $3 billion in revenue from foreign operations in 1981; of this, about $1.1 billion was for processing services alone.[3] Remote computing services are estimated to have generated 1981 revenues of about $2.1 billion in Western Europe, $700 million in Japan, and about $400 million in Canada.[4]

The U.S. computer services industry is important to the U.S. economy and its balance of trade, not only because it is a growth industry, but also because the operations of many other businesses are dependent upon it.[5] Although U.S. companies have, historically, provided remote access data processing services in foreign countries, there has been little exporting to the U.S. This, however, has changed.[6]

Even where U.S. companies are significant net exporters of computer services, the importing country still

STEPHEN H. BEACH • Mr. Beach, formerly vice president and associate general counsel of Control Data Corporation, is counsel to Rogers, Hoge & Hills in White Plains, New York. HERBERT E. MARKS • Mr. Marks is a partner in the law firm of Squire, Sanders & Dempsey in Washington, D.C. The firm is special counsel to the Association of Data Processing Service Organizations, Inc. (ADAPSO).

benefits. These companies often provide ready access to valuable computer services and data bases not available in the importing country. Where a domestic data processing capability is still evolving, local users benefit from the availability of a wide variety of services. Finally, U.S. companies also help to improve the training of local personnel and improve the use of technology.

In order to establish data networks for providing data processing services to their customers, computer services firms must open offices in countries where customers are to be serviced, contract for telecommunications transmission services from the local (usually governmental) provider, import products for use in providing services, and generally conduct business in that country. Thus, in many respects, the problems encountered by U.S. computer services firms in establishing and operating international data networks for the purpose of providing data processing services are not that different from the problems that are, or could be, experienced by other operators or users of such networks. Computer services firms, however, may attract more than the usual number of problems because foreign governments regard computer services as a special "target" in developing their domestic industry.[7] This chapter is a recitation of the types of problems encountered to date. In the Appendix, there is a more detailed description of the problems encountered by one computer services firm. Some of the problems described in this paper may be legal problems with a special character because they involve international transactions and operations. Others are problems related to trade barriers.

CORPORATE ESTABLISHMENT

The attempts of computer services firms to establish operations in a foreign country are often met with long delays, burdensome restrictions, or flat denials.[8]

Some countries have foreign investment laws which preclude or limit U.S. ownership of businesses in their nations.[9] Mexico does not permit U.S. computer services firms to have controlling ownership in a Mexican subsidiary.[10] Canada has a foreign investment review act which governs foreign investments in Canadian businesses. Since October 1975, the Foreign Investment Review Agency has approved only two of six proposed new foreign investments in computer services.[11] One American company was, for an extended period, denied entry into French markets because the competition that such a company would provide to domestic companies

was deemed not to be in France's national interest.[12]

Other countries have established elaborate formal procedures which delay the applications of U.S. companies to incorporate, acquire, or establish branch operations abroad.[13] U.S. applicants have been forced to make agreements with foreign governments stipulating to such items as employment levels, research and development investments, and capital expenditures.[14]

For example, in Japan, two American companies were subjected to detailed inspections of their equipment centers and had to comply with oppressive terms before securing Japan's approval to do business there.[15]

TELECOMMUNICATIONS REGULATIONS

Even after securing approval to begin operations in a foreign country, computer services firms are often subject to a variety of local telecommunications regulations. These often surface in tariffs that increase the costs of doing business and, ultimately, the costs of service to the consumer.

Foreign countries have required computer services firms to use public data communications networks. This increases costs and creates technical restraints which decrease efficiency.[16]

Computer services firms have been required to terminate international private lines in a single computer in a foreign country or perform substantial data processing there. This type of regulation severely restricts information flows and the provision of data processing services in the host countries.[17]

Several countries are trying to replace full period leased channel service, that is, service for which a flat fee is charged regardless of the amount of use, with usage-sensitive service, in which fees vary with the volume of use. Others are attempting to price offerings on a value-of-service, rather than cost-related, basis.[18] All of these rate structures would ultimately result in increased costs for computer services companies and consumers.

Some foreign-government controlled communications monopolies have required American computer services firms to do all of their procurement from domestic firms.[19] Once again, this increases the costs of doing business for U.S. firms.

As a condition of providing private line service, Japan's international telecommunications carrier at one time required U.S. computer services firms to terminate leased lines in specified computers or computer centers in the U.S. and thus offer only a limited number of their services in Japan. This condition limited the competition provided by U.S. companies and increased their costs.[20] After years of dispute, the condition was modified so as to allow private lines to terminate at multiple points within the United States, as long as some processing of the information being transmitted was performed at each location.

DATA PROTECTION LAWS

Many foreign countries have enacted data protection laws that are ostensibly aimed at protecting the personal privacy of individual citizens. These laws generally apply only to collections on natural persons compiled by electronic means. Most such laws are omnibus in nature and are not limited in application to particular data collections, such as credit information.[21] Many laws require a data processor to obtain a license or register with a government body before the collection of data can be undertaken. This enables the government agency to generate a master list of all data collections.[22] Many foreign government agencies have also considered the imposition of restrictions on the transfer of data outside the host country as a condition to licensing or registration. Such restrictions may impede the flow of data and limit the services that data processors can offer.[23] Some countries do not differentiate between natural persons and legal persons, such as corporations. Such laws expand the scope of information subject to regulation and thus potentially further limit export.[24]

In addition to national laws, there have also been multilateral efforts to achieve a coordinated approach to privacy protection. The OECD has developed guidelines that are intended to reconcile the regulatory approaches of various countries, so as to permit the free flow of information.[25] The U.S. is among the countries that have actively endorsed the guidelines, which define minimum standards for privacy protection. These standards include limitations on the collection of personal data and on its disclosure without consent or legal authority; requirements that the data collected be accurate, relevant, and protected from unauthorized access, and that the subject have the right to see and correct it; and, finally, disclosure of the purposes for which the data will be used and the policies and practices regarding its collection. The Council of Europe has enacted a convention that would attempt to protect an individual's right to privacy in signatory countries by regulating the maintenance, automatic processing, and transborder flow of personal data.[26] Contracting parties may expand coverage to include data on legal persons. This convention went into effect when ratified by five member countries. The convention is intended to diminish the obstacles to transborder flow of personal data among signatory countries, but it permits a party to restrict data transfers destined for countries that do not have privacy protection legislation equivalent to the legislation in the signatory nation. It is likely that the U.S. will not ratify this convention because privacy protection in the U.S., though extensive, is derived from a variety of sources, including case law, and is not embodied in an all-encompassing statute as required by the convention.[27] Although it is too early to determine whether signatory countries will, in fact, limit regulation in a manner that will adversely affect U.S. competitors, U.S. firms are apprehensive that such restrictions will be imposed.[28]

Recently, there has been a movement in some foreign countries to impose restrictions that are not related to privacy concerns. Agencies in some countries are considering imposing taxes, duties, and other restrictions on the domestic use of imported information.[29]

U.S. GOVERNMENT POLICY

The foregoing sections dealt with actions by foreign countries that affect the ability of U.S. computer services firms to maintain international data networks. Actions by our own government also directly affect this capability. There are at least three areas in which the U.S. government is presently adopting or is considering adopting policies which will have a significant impact on international telecommunication facilities and information transfer. These areas include the Federal Communications Commission (FCC) decisions relating to whether enhancement services offered internationally will be deemed unregulated, proposals to restructure the U.S. government's organizational mechanisms for establishing relevant international policies, and legislative considerations of how to respond to foreign trade barriers.

FCC Decisions

The provision of international and foreign telecommunications is regulated in the United States by the FCC. Because international telecommunications service is provided in partnership by two or more countries, no one country can unilaterally alter the terms and conditions pursuant to which such service is made available. The Commission, however, has recently taken actions which will have a significant impact on international data networks.

In August 1982, the Commission stated that its Computer Rules, 47 C.F.R. Sec. 64.702, apply to international telecommunications.[30] This action means that international enhanced services will no longer be regulated.

Under international conventions, however, some of the services which the FCC would classify as unregulated enhanced services are considered telecommunications and thus fully subject to regulation. The action of the FCC in deregulating such services could lead to retaliation, or to renewed attacks on certain uses of telecommunications facilities that some foreign authorities fear are an infringement of their regulatory scheme. This latter fear is part of the justification for attacks on private line services. The Commission's action will also cause certain U.S. carriers to lose their status as such under U.S. law. As a result they may be less able to secure operating agreements with foreign authorities. To make the matter more complex, the Commission has authorized Communications Satellite Corporation (COMSAT) to make its international satellite services available to noncarrier users, and the COMSAT tariff does not bar resale.[31] While the services of U.S. carriers may now be in jeopardy, the decision aids entry of non-U.S. organizations in U.S. markets by deregulating the U.S. market.

The potential effect of the Commission's August 1982 order on international competition is highlighted by recent events. A wholly-owned subsidiary of a non- U.S. company that provides international communications services has recently applied for a Data Network Identification Code from the FCC.[32] As a result of the FCC's 1982 order, it could enter the international market completely free from regulation if it chose to provide enhanced services and, along with its parent, could offer complete end-to-end international service on a totally unregulated basis. This kind of entry by unregulated foreign organizations could in time divert substantial international traffic from regulated American international record carriers.[33]

A separate problem raised by the deregulation of international enhanced services was recently highlighted by the proposals of the Nordic and Benelux PTTs to have packet-switched services between the United States and their countries provided on what appeared to be a sole or limited source basis.[34] Under *Computer II*,[35] however, these packet-switching services would likely be considered enhanced and therefore not subject to regulation by the FCC. If a carrier such as Western Union were considered an unregulated entity, the commission's ability to encourage competition would be more limited. If the foreign PTT were willing to do business with an unregulated service provider, the commission would arguably have been without authority to stop sole source procurement by foreign PTTs remains a distinct lar situation was resolved through informal negotiations between representatives of the United States and the Nordic and Benelux administrations,[36] further sole source procurement by foreign PTTs remains a distinct possibility.

Government Organization

The United States has no central authority responsible for the development and implementation of international telecommunications policies. Responsibility is currently divided among the FCC, the Department of State, the Department of Commerce, and the Office of the U.S. Trade Representative.[37] No effective mechanism exists to respond promptly in a coordinated manner to international disputes that require immediate attention. The current multiplicity of governmental entities responsible for international telecommunications and information policy in the United States stands in marked contrast to the situation that prevails in most foreign nations. Many countries have adopted comprehensive telecommunications policies and have made pronouncements confirming the value of computer services in promoting their domestic and international interests.[38]

The United States will never "coordinate" telecommunications policy to the extent that it is done in other countries. The U.S. government does not plan the economy, and regulation is generally more limited than in other countries. It is essential, however, that when the U.S. government does set policy in international telecommunications or information matters, it be able to do so promptly, efficiently, and with effective coordination among the various affected U.S. government agencies.

A number of recent legislative proposals have sought to improve the implementation of U.S. telecommunications policy by providing a mechanism for coordinating the efforts of various federal agencies. The Senate Committee on Commerce, Science and Transportation reported S. 2469 (97th Congress), a bill that would create an International Telecommunications and Information Task Force, the purpose of which would be to develop a consistent and comprehensive approach toward the development and implementation of United States international telecommunications policy within the federal government and with the private sector. The House of Representatives has also addressed this issue and proposed a similar solution. H.R. 1957 (97th Congress) would have established a cabinet-level interagency committee to provide a coordinating mechanism for the development and implementation of international communications policy. Neither bill was enacted during the 97th Congress, but similar legislation has already been introduced in the 98th Congress. S. 999, introduced into the Senate on April 7, 1983, would establish a task force similar to that contemplated by S. 2469. In addition, it would create an office of the special representative for telecommunications and information in the executive office of the president, which would be responsible for coordination of international telecommunications and information policies within the executive branch. The special trade representative for telecommunications and information would be chairman of the task force and would be the chief representative of the U.S. at international telecommunications and information conferences.

The Commerce Department's National Telecommunications and Information Administration has also advanced several proposals for restructuring government organization in this area.[39] In a recent report, NTIA presents a number of options, but seems to favor consolidation of authority in a centralized location within the executive branch. The centralized authority would have the power to mediate differences among agencies and would be charged with coordinating and finally determining international telecommunications policy. The report also suggests that a restructuring that would increase executive branch control over the FCC might be appropriate.[40]

Trade Issues

As initially introduced, S. 2469 would have authorized the FCC to establish rules implementing a policy of equitable market access, pursuant to which foreign suppliers of telecommunications and information services would have access to U.S. markets only if American companies had comparable equitable access to markets in the country of the foreign supplier. Restrictions on foreign suppliers could only be imposed after consultation with the task force. This provision was deleted from the bill prior to its passage by the Senate. The concept of equal trade access was also reflected in a general trade bill introduced in the 97th Congress, the Reciprocal Trade and Investment Act of 1982. This bill, S. 2094, would have required the president to implement a policy of reciprocity of market access with regard to all types of goods and services, not just communications or information services.

Reciprocity legislation was not enacted by the 97th Congress because of the view of many legislators and the president that the world would benefit more from free trade and the free flow of information than from reciprocity. Under this view, free trade practices should be curtailed only under special circumstances and reciprocity should be used only in the most judicious manner.

CONCLUSION

Computer services are viewed as important areas of domestic and foreign trade both in the U.S. and in foreign countries. Foreign access to data banks in the U.S. and elsewhere has made up-to-date technology and extensive information available to many countries. Yet many foreign countries have expressed concern that the computer services provided within their country are often not domestically controlled. These countries believe that such foreign-controlled services interfere with the development of local data processing and communications industries. Other countries have national sovereignty concerns, and fear that foreign data processing services threaten national security, contribute to a loss of domestic cultural identity, and lead to the dominance of multinational corporations. Finally, there are concerns that the host country of the data bank will provide insufficient privacy protection, or permit the data to the misused.[41] These concerns have led many foreign countries to create certain restrictions on the transborder transfer of data.[42]

Computer services firms have encountered legal barriers in their efforts to do business overseas, and adverse conditions have been placed on their use of telecommunications services. The legal problems encountered in the operation of international data networks by computer services firms are not necessarily unique. But, because computer services are targeted for domestic expansion by certain foreign countries, and because computer services firms process the data of others, they are more vulnerable to restrictive trade practices, and have a very great stake in the successful resolution of these problems.

It is difficult to formulate a comprehensive approach to the legal problems encountered by computer services firms, because the legal barriers affecting the operation of international data networks are so diverse. A more effective route may be to adopt a multifaceted approach that will address each legal issue in the manner best tailored to resolve the problem. The most promising framework for a reasonable resolution of the data protection barriers motivated by privacy concerns is voluntary adherence to the OECD Guidelines referenced above. These guidelines promote privacy protection in a manner compatible with diverse legal traditions, yet they seek to advance the free flow of information across national boundaries and the removal of unjustified obstacles to transborder data flow. With respect to other barriers, there is a need for continued bilateral and multilateral discussions that should lead to an elimination of barriers and restraints.

All nations benefit from the unfettered operation of international data networks, either as users or providers of those services. As a user, the country receives modern processing technology and access to valuable data bases. As a provider, a country benefits from open market principles of free trade. Effective bilateral and multilateral negotiation of outstanding legal problems appears to offer the best prospect for ensuring the successful development of international data networks in a manner that benefits both exporter and recipient nations.

APPENDIX

PROBLEMS ENCOUNTERED BY ONE COMPUTER SERVICES FIRM

There is set forth below an enumeration of some of the problems encountered by the Control Data Corporation in doing business outside of the United States in the field of remote data processing, also known as information processing, employing communications lines and networks.

MEXICO

Control Data has attempted to obtain authorization to install private leased line services in Mexico for use in the marketing of remote access data processing services. The Mexican government refuses to allow the marketing of remote access data processing services in Mexico by foreign corporations and still prohibits the use of private line services for this purpose. There is no satisfactory solution to this problem in Mexico. A foreign corporation that wishes to market remote access data processing services in Mexico is free to make arrangements with a wholly-owned Mexican company to market and maintain the services within that country. The foreign corporation is allowed to install leased lines to deliver the service to the Mexican border and connect with a network of the Mexican company.

GERMANY

In 1980 the German telecommunications administration passed some regulations which would prohibit the installation of private lines running from another country into Germany unless such circuits were either "hard-wired" to a single terminal device or were terminated in a computer system in Germany where actual computing took place before the processed data was passed into the German public telecommunications network. Control Data entered into direct negotiations with the German telecommunications authorities explaining that Control Data did process work for German customers on systems that were located outside of Germany. They were told that Control Data processed work at its Frankfurt processing center for customers who were located in other countries and that work was processed for German multinational companies needing access to files located outside of Germany. Finally, we suggested that the new regulations would force Control Data to move processing then being done in Frankfurt to other centers outside of Germany. The German authorities, after due consideration and a series of meetings, agreed to allow Control Data to carry on its then method of processing for a period of seven years. Their rationale was that the concentration of equipment installed by Control Data in Germany had a remaining useful life of seven years. Today the German telecommunications authorities are taking a second look at their new regulations as they are encountering a number of other problems with them.

JAPAN

In 1976, Control Data attempted to install a private leased circuit between Tokyo, Japan and the United

States for the purpose of marketing a variety of remote access data processing services in Japan. After a considerable period of time and protracted negotiations, a circuit was installed in the fall of 1977. However, there was a condition on the installation that the circuit had to be terminated in the United States at a single computer mainframe located at Control Data's center in Cleveland, Ohio. Only services that were processed on this single system could be marketed in Japan. This restricted Control Data to utilization of only about 10% of its leased line capacity, and only about 10% of its total line of marketable services. Control Data sought the help of the Department of State, the Japanese-American Trade Facilitation Committee of the Department of Commerce, and the National Telecommunications and Information Administration of the Department of Commerce. Little practical help to resolve this problem resulted from those contracts. Control Data then filed formal and informal petitions with the office of the special trade representative under the Trade Reorganization Act. Through its trade organization, ADAPSO, formal complaints were filed with the Federal Communications Commission. In addition, numerous negotiations were held between Control Data and authorities of the Ministry of Posts and Telecommunications of Japan and KDD, the international common carrier of Japan. Many meetings were held in Tokyo, New York, Washington, and at CCITT meetings in Geneva, Switzerland. The problem was considered for solution through legislation during hearings before the Committee on Government Operations of the United States House of Representatives. Finally, in May 1981, after years of negotiations, the Ministry of Posts and Telecommunications of Japan modified its regulations to allow Control Data to use its private leased line to process data services applications for Japanese customers on systems located at Control Data processing centers within the United States other than that at Cleveland, Ohio, including Rockville, Maryland; Sunnyvale, California; Arden Hills, Minnesota; Minneapolis, Minnesota; etc. This now permits Control Data to market its full line of remote access data processing services in Japan.

SPAIN

In 1978 Control Data attempted to arrange with the Spanish telecommunications authorities for the installation of leased private line service between Madrid, Spain and Brussels, Belgium. The purpose was to market a timesharing offering of Control Data known as CALL/370. The Spanish authorities advised that if Control Data wished to secure leased lines for the delivery of CALL/370 timesharing services, it would be necessary to install

the circuits from Madrid directly to the location where the processing was to be done. In this case it was to be done in Cleveland, Ohio, and therefore they demanded that we install a circuit directly from Madrid, Spain to Cleveland, Ohio. Their demand did not take into account that we had a switching point in Brussels, Belgium which would enable us to go from Madrid to Brussels and then to Cleveland, Ohio via our Control Data network.

Control Data determined that the potential volume of CALL/370 business in Spain did not justify the installation of a direct circuit to Cleveland and accordingly dropped plans for the marketing of the service in Spain. Later, various Control Data multinational customers began to take terminals into Spain and place long-distance calls to nearby French cities that were on the Control Data network, thereby allowing them to access the system through Brussels. After two years of consideration, the Spanish telecommunications authorities realized that they would obtain more revenue through leased circuits from Madrid to Brussels and decided to allow Control Data to install such circuits.

NOTES

1. For example, American Express Company routinely transfers financial data relating to its principal businesses (insurance payment systems, asset management, international banking, and securities) from computers in its offices overseas to computers in the U.S. via international telecommunication lines. *See* 129 CONG. REC. E717:120 (daily ed. Mar. 2, 1983) (statement of Rep. Wirth) [hereinafter cited as Wirth statement].

2. ASSOCIATION OF DATA PROCESSING SERVICE ORGANIZATIONS, INC., SIXTEENTH ANNUAL SURVEY OF THE COMPUTER SERVICES INDUSTRY-6, 9 [hereinafter cited as ADAPSO SURVEY].

3. *Id.* at 24.

4. ADAPSO estimate (Mar. 13, 1983).

5. Statement of Malcolm Baldrige, Secretary of Commerce, before the Subcomm. on Telecommunications, Consumer Protection, and Finance of the House Committee on Energy and Commerce (Mar. 23, 1983).

6. During the period 1960–1977, exports of information services generally (not broken down by remote computer services) rose 12 percent for U.S. firms, but the same exports rose 25 percent for Japan, 19 percent for Germany, and 16 percent for Canada. *See* Ergas, "International Trade in Information Goods

and Services, (a) The Role of Information Goods in International Trade," in OECD, *Information Activities, Electronics and Telecommunications Technologies* II (1981): 90.

7. S. Nora & A. Minc, Report of the Computerization of Society Cambridge, Mass.: MIT Press, 1980.

8. Such denials are often in contravention of various international treaties and agreements. See, e.g., note 10 and accompanying text.

9. *Hearings on H. R. 1957 Before the Subcomm. on Government Information and Individual Rights of the House Comm. on Government Operations*, 97th Cong., 2d Sess. 3 (1981) (Statement of Richard L. Crandall) [hereinafter cited as Crandall Statement]: H. R. Rep No. 1535, 96th Cong., 2d Sess. 18 (1980) [hereinafter cited as H. R. 1535]. *See also* Office of the U.S. Trade Representative, *Trade Barriers to Telecommunications, Data and Information Services,* V Transnat'l Data Rep on Information Pol. & Reg. June 1982, at 181, 183 [hereinafter cited as U.S. Trade Representative Report].

10. Control Data Corporation, a data processing company with foreign operations, experienced many difficulties in its attempts to establish operations in various countries. A more detailed explanation of its problems is contained in the Appendix to this paper.

11. Crandall Statement, *supra* note 9, at 3.

12. This denial was in violation of a treaty of friendship and trade. Crandall Statement, *supra* note 9; *International Data Flow: Hearings Before the Subcomm. on Government Information and Individual Rights of the House Comm. on Government Operations*, 96th Cong., 2d Sess. 21 (1980) (statement of Philip C. Onstad) [hereinafter cited as *Subcomm. Hearings.*].

13. Crandall Statement, *supra* note 9, at 4; Markoski, *Telecommunications Regulations as Barriers to the Transborder Flow of Information*, 14 Cornell Int'l L.J. 287, 311–12 (1980).

14. Crandall Statement, *supra* note 9, at 4; H.R. 1535, *supra* note 9, at 13; National Telecommunications and Information Administration, Long-Range Goals in International Telecommunications and Information, An Outline for United States Policy 175 (Feb. 1983) [hereinafter cited as NTIA Report].

15. Crandall Statement, *supra* note 9, at 4; Mar-

koski, *supra* note 13, at 311–12; *Subcomm. Hearings, supra* note 12, at 21–23.

16. Crandall Statement, *supra* note 9 at 5; H.R. 1535, *supra* note 9, at 13; NTIA Report, *supra* note 14, at 174; U.S. Trade Representative Report, *supra* note 9, at 179.

17. Crandall Statement, *supra* note 9, at 5; Markoski, *supra* note 13, at 317–19; U.S. Trade Representative Report, *supra* note 9, at 179–81; *Subcomm. Hearings, supra* note 12, at 21. See, e.g., Telegram from American Embassy, Bonn, West Germany, to U.S. Secretary of State (Apr. 15, 1980). Control Data Corporation suffered from these kinds of restrictions in their operations in Germany.

18. *Subcomm. Hearings, supra* note 12, at 19; Markoski, *supra* note 13, at 297–304; H.R. 1535, *supra* note 9, at 14. NTIA Report, *supra* note 14, at 145–46. The report notes that if private leased service availability is curtailed by foreign administrations, international telecommunications costs of the Department of Defense, a major user of these lines, could increase by 300–700 percent.

19. Crandall Statement, *supra* note 9, at 6; NTIA Report, *supra* note 14, at 163.

20. *See* Petition to Deny Applications of ITT World Communications, Inc., RCA Global Communications, Inc., Western Union International, Inc. and Association of Data Processing Service Organizations, Inc., File Nos. I-T-C-2664-11, I-T-C-2657-8, I-T-C-2678-1 (filed Apr. 11, 1979); Application for Review of the Association of Data Processing Service Organizations, Inc., File Nos. I-T-C--2678-1, I-T-C-2657-8, I-T-C-2664-11 (filed Jan. 14, 1980). When first confronted by these restrictions, the FCC's Common Carrier Bureau declined to consider their foreign trade implications. *See* ITT World Communications, Inc., Memorandum Opinion, Order, Authorization and Certificate, Mimeo No. 24434 (released Dec. 14, 1979). Commission review was sought of this decision. When the foreign authorities eventually relaxed, but did not eliminate, the restrictions of U.S. companies the application for review was withdrawn.

21. Marks, *A Perspective on Information Policy, Privacy and Transborder Data Flow Restrictions*, Bigelow CLS § 7–5, art. 2, at 4 (1979). H.R. 1535, *supra* note 9, at 19; *Subcomm. Hearings, supra* note 12, at

20,704 (letter submitted by Jerome L. Dreyer); Allen Transborder Data Flow Debate: An Overview of the Issues 10–14 (Nov. 20, 1979). This group drafted a set of nonbinding guidelines for privacy laws. H.R. 1535, *supra* note 9, at 3.

22.   Marks, *supra* note 21, at 4.

23.   *Id.* at 5; H.R. 1535, *supra* note 9, at 15–16.

24.   H.R. 1535, *supra* note 9, at 15–16; NTIA Report, *supra* note 14, at 196.

25.   Guidelines on the Protection of Privacy and Transborder flows of Personal Data, OECD (1981).

26.   Convention for the Protection of Individuals with Regard to Automatic Processing of Personal Data, Council of Europe (1981).

27.   NTIA Report, *supra* note 14, at 196.

28.   *See Pact Would Restrict Data Flow in Europe,* COMPUTERWORLD, Feb. 28, 1983, at 7; *Data Flow: The U.S. Takes on Europe,* IV TDR-TRANSNAT'L DATA REP. ON INFORMATION POL. & REG., JULY/AUG. 1981, AT 7.

29.   *See Data Could Spark a Trade War,* BUS. WK., Nov. 29, 1982, at 100; NTIA Report, *supra* note 14, at 198–200; U.S. Trade Representative Report, *supra* note 9, at 183.

30.   *See* GTE Telenet Communications, FCC 82–377 (released Aug. 25, 1982).

31.   *See* Communications Satellite Corp., FCC 83–41 (released Feb. 2, 1983); *see also* Letter from Chief of Common Carrier Bureau to Communications Satellite Corp. (Dec. 29, 1982). This decision is currently stayed pending appeal.

32.   Letter from Counsel for PACNET Communications to Chief of Conference Staff, Common Carrier Bureau (June 15, 1982). Pacnet Communications Inc. is a subsidiary of Cable and Wireless Ltd., an international carrier for several major foreign trading countries.

33.   A full discussion of the potential for anti-competitive conduct inherent in this situation is presented in the NTIA Report, *supra* note 14, at 151.

34.   *See* FCC WK., July 26, 1982; NTIA Report *supra* note 14, at 147. Nortel, the Nordic PPT, includes the Administrations of Denmark, Finland, Iceland, Norway, and Sweden.

35.   Amendment of Section 64.702 of the Commission's Rules and Regulations (Second Computer Inquiry), 77 F.C.C.2d 384, *on reconsideration,* 84 F.C.C.2d, 50 (1980), *on further reconsideration,* 88 F.C.C.2d (1981), *aff'd sub nom.* Computer and Communications Indus. Ass'n v. FCC, 693 F.2d 198 (D.C. Cir. 1982), *petitions for cert. filed,* No. 83-1331, 51 U.S.L.W. 3614 (U.S. filed Feb. 9, 1983), No. 83-1352, 51 U.S.L.W. 3615 (U.S. filed Feb. 10, 1983).

36.   NTIA Report, *supra* note 14, at 147.

37.   *Id.* at 71–77 describes the functions of these various agencies.

38.   Markoski, *supra* note 13, at 293–95; *Subcomm. Hearings, supra* note 12, at 19–20, 62 (statement of Warren Burton), 706 (letter from Jerome Dreyer); H.R. 1535, *supra* note 9, at 9.

39.   NTIA Report, *supra* note 14, at 85–94.

40.   *Id.* at 83–85.

41.   U.S. Trade Representative Report, *supra* note 9, at 180–81; *Implications for Host, Particularly Developing, Countries,* V TDR-INTERNAT'L DATA REP. ON INFORMATION POL. & REG., Oct./Nov. 1982, at 349–55; NTIA Report, *supra* note 14, at 7–9; S. NORA & A. MINC, REPORT OF THE COMPUTERIZATION OF SOCIETY I (1978); Papers Presented at Transnational Data Regulation Online Conference, Brussels (Feb. 7–9, 1978); Gliss, *Uniform International Data Transfer Policies Needed,* V TDR-TRANSNAT'L DATA REP. ON INFORMATION POL. & REG., Sept. 1982, at 303–07.

42.   U.S. Trade Representative Report, *supra* note 9, at 179–85.

CHAPTER 11

GLOBAL MANAGEMENT SYSTEMS FOR MULTINATIONAL CORPORATIONS

JOSEPH H. McCANN, JR.

INTRODUCTION

Multinational corporations are very dependent upon international information flow. For example, IBM does business in over 120 countries and is, therefore, very dependent upon a free flow of information in order to maintain its worldwide operations.

This information flow is divided into many different areas of its business. Some information is confined to technical engineering, design, and manufacturing information. It is also used to inform IBM customers about technical changes and improvements to hardware and software on which, in turn, their operations may depend. Other parts of the information flow concern the matching of available engineering, manufacturing, and market support resources with customer requirements. IBM has laboratories in the United States, Canada, the United Kingdom, Germany, France, Sweden, The Netherlands, Switzerland, Austria, Japan, and scientific centers in many other countries of the world. It has major manufacturing facilities throughout North and South America, Europe, Asia, Africa, and Australia. All of these facilities must communicate with certain other areas of the business which may, or may not, be located within the same national borders as the originator of the message.

IBM products are designed, developed, and manufactured on a worldwide basis. That is, almost no single country designs, develops, or manufactures the total product line. This requires a constant stream of information flow between laboratories, sales offices, ordering and scheduling departments, manufacturing plants, and warehousing areas. Not only must the various components of a system, shipped from two or more separate countries, arrive at a customer location at the same time, each unit must work with each other. Because an individual customer order can have a substantially different number of features, types of computer programs, memory sizes, numbers of display terminals, tapes and disc-type storage units, the requirement for uninhibited flow of information cannot be overemphasized. This strategy of worldwide integration of products optimizes the ability of IBM to balance payment flows between countries. It also provides for scientists and engineers in many countries to participate in the design and manufacture of computers. This results in building a technology base in several nations, but at the expense of dependence upon a transborder information flow of great magnitude, and in real time. This is so, because rapid response of communication between countries is so essential that there is no time for government intervention or control procedures. Permission must be a prior blanket approval for the uninterrupted flow of data. There is no way to envision a requirement to license each transmission.

This recitation has not included any recognition of the requirements for financial, statistical, transportation, personnel, and the other masses of information necessary to run the daily affairs of this enterprise, all of which are essential components in efficient management.

JOSEPH H. McCANN, JR. • Mr. McCann is corporate counsel for IBM World Trade Americas/Far East Corporation, North Tarrytown, New York.

IBM COMMUNICATIONS NETWORKS

In order to satisfy this demand for the free flow of information, IBM has three separate, but interrelated, communication systems. The first system is identified as the Corporate Consolidated Data Network. This is described as an interactive system. It lends itself to individual inquiries and responses. There are an estimated 15,000 separate terminals around the world that can use this system. There are almost 50 major applications usable within, and by, this system.

The second system is the Integrated Bulk Transfer System. This is a system of 200–300 computers transmitting large batches of statistical, etc., information back and forth over high-speed data lines.

The third system is the V-Net. This is both a user inquiry interactive system and a bulk transfer system. It originated as a laboratory-to-laboratory, engineer-to-engineer communication system. This is probably the largest civilian data network in the world. It interconnects over 500 computer centers across the world. As a peer-to-peer network, there is no central host control of its traffic, no single point at which its use can be regulated except that IBM has established protocols for its use since it is a wholly internal network. Without V-Net, IBM could not allow the scientists and engineers of two dozen nations to participate in the evolution and applications of our technology.

These three systems each have dedicated applications and purposes, but they can also interrelate. They are in an evolutionary process and are growing and changing as technology changes and improves. They use satellite and cable to communicate. Some messages are confined to leased lines, other messages can be transmitted by open PTT, or commercial communication facilities.

LEGAL IMPLICATIONS OF NETWORK APPLICATIONS

The operation of three worldwide networks is not without some complications. Not only must IBM conform to the U.S. laws on exportation of technical data, it is also subject to the laws of the countries in which it sells, leases, manufactures, and maintains its products. IBM has been impacted by the regulations of local country PTT rules, regulations, and rates. It has experienced some difficulties, mostly minor, in several countries. IBM is presently negotiating with one country in South America on transborder data flow. It has been IBM's experience that openness and candor can solve most difficulties. IBM subsidiaries are staffed by nationals of the countries where they are located. When a question arises from any government, it is answered in the language, and by a national, of that country. In this kind of situation, misunderstandings and confrontations are less likely to occur.

IBM, in order to minimize the impact upon its operations of possible changes in the present international telecommunications environment, has examined the situation in OECD countries. This factual examination has led to the following conclusions.

Use of Information Products

USE OF DATA BANKS IN FOREIGN COUNTRIES. Excluding privacy legislation, there are no legal or administrative restrictions preventing access to data banks in OECD countries. It would appear that unrestricted access will continue for nonprivacy-related information. However, if protective legislation increases in countries concerned about nurturing their own data processing services, then restrictions could develop that would prevent access to the use of data banks in other countries.

CUSTOMS DUTIES ON INFORMATION PRODUCTS. Customs duties are in effect now only on products of the mass media, but information content studies are currently underway. There are two critical issues involved in any change in the present system of applying duties beyond the value of the medium used. First, the mere transmission of data from France to Italy, via Switzerland, would mean an entry and exit tax merely for transiting Switzerland. This hardly seems to make any kind of economic sense. Second, in order for a government to classify the value of content of the data being transmitted, the owner would be exposed to disclosing proprietary data or perhaps secret design information. This could create horrendous problems for the information provider as well as the government employees to whom the information is disclosed. Therefore, any change in present practices should be discouraged. It would be very difficult to administer such duties. However, the feasibility of evaluating data based upon the value of the information, which would place the burden on the sender and/or receiver to identify and classify the information, is under study currently.

REQUIREMENTS TO STORE CRITICAL INFORMATION LOCALLY. There are few such requirements in effect presently (e.g., in Canada, Sweden, Brazil). However, such requirements do provoke higher costs; vulnerability studies are being carried out by some OECD countries, notably Sweden.

RESTRICTIONS ON THE TRANSFER OF NATIONAL SECURITY INFORMATION. Transborder transfer of information designated secret is difficult to control. However, most nations do attempt to establish effective local controls prohibiting the export of such information.

In some cases the definition of information pertinent to national security has been broadened to include quasi-secret information (e.g., banking, transportation, energy). This threatens to restrict the transfer of business information considered vital by the companies involved in international business transactions.

For instance, IBM transfers confidential financial data and technical information in an encrypted mode. Some governments, e.g., France, and to some extent, Chile, require that encryption keys be made available to government security services.

There is concern in high technology industries concerning future government reactions to possible export of technical data via internal enterprise data networks. IBM is very careful to comply with U.S. export licensing requirements, but other countries may become apprehensive of such loss. There have been discussions in conferences of the National Security Community over the potential exposures in international data networks. If there is some future overreaction to this matter that impedes such use of data networks, it could be a crippling blow to many types of international industries.

APPLICATION OF PRIVACY LEGISLATION TO THE INTERNATIONAL TRANSFER OF BUSINESS INFORMATION. Present national legislation and the OECD guidelines for transborder flows of personal data appear to present no problem generally with most enterprises. However, application of the guidelines to the international transfer of business information could present serious problems, depending on the implementation.

OECD is monitoring government attitude and business acceptance of its guidelines for transborder flows of personal data, as well as their possible application to nonpersonal data. In some countries application could take place by extension of privacy legislation to legal persons (e.g., Austria, Denmark, Luxembourg, and Norway).

Use of Telecommunications Facilities

ACCESS TO PRIVATE LEASED LINES. Use of private leased lines is restricted for data communications among unrelated companies with exceptions being made for CITTA (Airline Network) which applies standard rates and SWIFT network (500 banks) for which PTTs apply additional surcharges based on volume. The definition of "unrelated companies" varies by PTT and in some cases the PTT's definition can be quite restrictive.

The trend to interconnect several private data networks to gain economies of efficiency is just emerging, and may eventually become a competitive necessity.

PRESSURES TO USE PUBLIC SWITCHED NETWORKS. Presently access to public switched networks is unrestricted. However, many PTTs are trying to force everyone to use the public data networks they provide. This may be a desirable goal, but the present technology used in public data networks is not optimum for the varied business uses currently available.

The prognosis is that access to public data networks will not only continue to be unrestricted, but will be encouraged through the establishment of tariffs or regulations which favor access through the public data networks.

RESTRICTIONS ON FOREIGN ATTACHMENTS. Homologation procedures vary by country and the criteria used generally goes well beyond that required to prevent harm to the network. In many cases the homologation process can preclude or delay availability of products or product features to users.

Tariff Differentials

HIGHER RATES FOR INTERNATIONAL VERSUS NATIONAL COMMUNICATIONS. Rates for Paris/Frankfurt are about twice the rate than for Paris/Grenoble (same distance of 450 kms); PTTs claim that it is more costly to maintain international lines.

International rates could go down if savings realized through introduction of new technologies, e.g., satellites and fibres, are passed on to users. International competition through choice of alternative routes could lead to decrease of some of the higher tariffs.

DISPARITY IN NATIONAL RATES (BETWEEN SWITCHED AND LEASED LINES). Large differences in the rates between countries in Europe are a result of different government views concerning the role of communications in the economy. Also, higher leased lines rates are often used to encourage users to use public switched services. Differences in rates will continue. Some convergence is likely under the pressure of users to relate charges to the cost of services but some PTTs will continue to use service rates as a means to encourage usage of their preferred service.

Standards: Procedures, Interfaces, Etc.

The work of the CCITT in the development of international telecommunications standards has broadened to involve aspects of the information system area. Currently there are no serious problems with CCITT international standards except in countries where national regulations supplement the CCITT standards, as in Germany. National requirements supplementing CCITT international standards will tend to disappear because of continuing international understanding which could be achieved through the work of CCITT.

CONCLUSIONS

On the whole, IBM believes that international enterprises will not be operationally impacted in the near term. It is believed that countries will react as their self-interests dictate. Undue regulation can be a two-edged sword. A regulation intended to control the flow of commercial information may also impede the flow of information about science, technology, medicine, and the arts. Most nations do not deliberately pass laws and regulations that deprive their citizens and industries of the benefits available from the international flow of information in such fields. Most countries understand that they benefit more from the free flow of data than they are injured by it.

CHAPTER 12

HUMAN RESOURCES INFORMATION SYSTEMS (HURIS)

F. W. DIETMAR SCHAEFER

INTRODUCTION

Personnel practices, in any business organization, are and should be an important policy objective. Of necessity, they become more complex if the company involved is an international or multinational business organization with subsidiaries and affiliates in both the United States and foreign countries. Multinational business organizations for years have benefited from relying, for purposes of discovering and developing management talents, on international personnel or human resources pools available to them through their foreign subsidiaries and affiliates. Standard means of "tapping" such pools usually involve (1) temporarily transferring to the parent company in the U.S. talented and promising personnel from the staffs of the American parent company's foreign subsidiaries for purposes of training and development, (2) horizontal transfers of foreign affiliate executives to line and staff positions with other foreign affiliates, not only for purposes of gathering experience but also to make available to one foreign affiliate the expertise of executives from other foreign affiliates, and (3) promoting executives on the staffs of foreign subsidiaries or affiliates to management positions on the staff of the parent company in the United States, after such foreign executives have demonstrated their abilities abroad and during temporary assignments to this country.

Clearly, when promotions to executive positions on the staff of a U.S. parent company are involved, prior international experience has been given and will continue to be given significant weight.

Thus, restrictive national legislation and practices which purport to limit the gathering and maintenance of relevant data on U.S. and foreign personnel ultimately qualified to be transferred and promoted across national boundaries (1) virtually restrict foreign executives to work and career development in their own or home countries, thereby (2) limiting not only essential transborder data flow but also free movement of personnel across national boundaries and optimum use of international personnel pools within multinational organizations.

Graduates of foreign universities who seek careers in the business environment see in promotability across national boundaries a strong incentive to apply for positions with foreign subsidiaries of U.S.-based multinational business organizations. Therefore, any restrictive national legislation and practices inhibiting the free flow of relevant personnel data (and the transfer of personnel) across national boundaries is bound to become a disincentive to the seeking of career opportunities with foreign affiliates of U.S.-based multinational business organizations—with the United States ultimately being deprived of the valuable contributions which such persons otherwise would make to research, development, and management of international business.

The purpose of this chapter is to demonstrate that while reasonable regulation of the format of personnel records that multinational business organizations main-

---

F. W. DIETMAR SCHAEFER ● Mr. Schaefer is counsel to the Mobil Oil Corporation in New York.

tain and exchange is probably necessary, such regulation can be adequately accomplished by enlightened self-regulation on the part of multinational business organizations. Such regulation need not and should not become the subject of narrow, national legislation, fraught with the "domestic politics" of the national jurisdictions involved, and it certainly should not escalate to the level of international treaties which, either ignorant of or with varying degrees of disregard for the facts of international business life and practices, would purport to regulate a complex subject that enlightened multinational business organizations, being cognizant of both the public interest and their own internal situations and needs, can demonstrably best regulate themselves.

It is hoped that the type of enlightened self-regulation discussed in this chapter, although it relates to one large company only, can and will contribute toward persuading governmental policymakers that national legislation and international treaties purporting to regulate individual and corporate privacy of personnel records, when such "privacy" involves the relationship between international and national employer-corporations and their employees, are neither necessary nor desirable because of the complexity of the subject, the impossibility of developing "uniform international standards," and the demonstrated ability of self-regulation shown by individual, progressive, international business organizations.

U.S.-PROPOSED LEGISLATION

In January 1975, Congressman Goldwater, son of Senator Barry Goldwater, introduced in the House of Representatives for himself and then-Congressman Koch, now the Mayor of New York City, a bill entitled the "Comprehensive Right to Privacy Act."[1] The purpose of the bill was to assure safeguards for personal privacy from "recordkeeping organizations," both private and public, by adherence to a number of principles of information practice. The controlling principles were that there should be a prescribed procedure for an individual to know the existence of information stored about him or her; the purpose for which it has been recorded; particulars about its use and dissemination; and a right to examine, correct, erase, or amend inaccurate, obsolete, or irrelevant information.

Insofar as transborder data flow was concerned, any organization maintaining an information system including personal information would have been enjoined from transferring personal information beyond the jurisdiction of the United States without specific authorization from the data subject or pursuant to a treaty or executive agreement guaranteeing that any foreign government or organization receiving personal information would comply with the applicable provisions of the Comprehensive Right to Privacy Act with respect to such personal information.

The bill would have established a "federal privacy board" charged with administering and enforcing the act. Substantial criminal penalties in the form of fines or imprisonment or both were provided for willful violations of the act by any individual or organization. In addition, the bill, if enacted into law, would have provided for severe liability for "unfair personal information practices" and injunctions for compliance.

Unlike the Federal Privacy Act of 1974,[2] the bill applied to records maintained by private business organizations, such as Mobil Oil Corporation, its subsidiaries and affiliates.

INDUSTRY RESPONSE

Congressmen Goldwater and Koch were quite candid in admitting that they did not know what impact the bill would likely have on the business community in general or on complex international business organizations operating transnationally. With equal candor, they requested analyses of the predictably onerous burdens that the various sections of the proposed act would have imposed on private companies. The business community's response was virtually unanimous; while no one questioned the desirability of establishing safeguards for personal privacy within recordkeeping organizations by adherence to fair principles of information practice, the need and desirability of establishing such safeguards by means of national legislation was severely questioned and the desirability of establishing such safeguards by means of self-regulation was strongly advocated. Mobil Oil Corporation and IBM were among the leading public advocates of this view.

It is interesting to note that, within Mobil Oil Corporation, the impetus for such self-regulation emanated from the Computer Systems and Management Sciences Department. In so doing, the department pointed to comparable legislation then pending in certain European countries and subsequently enacted between 1977 and 1978 in the Federal Republic of Germany and in France.

EUROPEAN LEGISLATION

German Data Protection Law

The German Federal Data Protection Law,[3] for instance, defined the "rights of the party concerned" as the rights to (1) information about the stored data concerning his or her person; (2) correction of stored data concerning his or her person if they are incorrect; (3) "blocking" (i.e., blocking of dissemination) of the stored data on his or her person if neither the correctness nor the incorrectness of the same can be established; and (4) deletion of the stored data concerning his or her person if their storage is not lawful *ab initio* or after the conditions for their storage that had originally been met no longer existed.[4]

The German Data Protection Law was expressly made applicable to "natural persons and legal entities, corporations and personal associations of private law insofar as they process protected personal data as a resource for the fulfillment of their business purposes and objectives."[5]

There was little doubt that the German act, unlike the Federal Privacy Act of 1974, went beyond protecting individuals against dossiers maintained on them by government agencies but also aimed at protecting, for instance, employees of Mobil's German subsidiaries from irresponsible or arbitrary personnel recordkeeping practices.

French Data Protection Act

Under the French act,[6] data subjects may demand that inaccurate, incomplete, ambiguous, or obsolete data, or data that has been illegally gathered, used, communicated, or stored, be corrected, completed, clarified, updated, or destroyed. Data subjects are entitled to receive, without charge, a copy of information modified under the provisions of the act.

The following "transborder provision" contained in the French act is noteworthy:

> Upon proposal or pursuant to opinion of the National Commission on Data Processing and Liberties, the transmission between French territory and foreign countries, under whatever form, of (personal) data that has been the subject of data processing ... may be submitted for an authorization in advance or regulated according to modalities stipulated by a decree of the Conseil d'Etat, in order to guarantee compliance with the principles laid down by the present law.

MOBIL MANAGEMENT GUIDELINES

Thus, the combination of a proposed "Comprehensive Right to Privacy Act" and comparable national legislation in European countries, where the principal affiliates of Mobil Oil Corporation are operating, stimulated an internal response by all interested departments of the company. The company was prepared to demonstrate to the legislative arms of domestic and foreign governments how the privacy rights in employee–employer records could be assured without creating onerous internal and external recordkeeping and reporting requirements and without subjecting the entire system of employee–employer records to the full panoply of expensive and time-consuming litigation, administrative processes, and judicial review.

The result of the company's efforts was a management guide, issued under the humble title *Employee -Employer Records*, consisting of 23 pages and two schedules totaling seven additional pages. It took approximately two years to obtain the consent of all interested and affected company divisions and departments on the policies and procedures contained in this guide. This is no reflection on the speed with which the company moves, but rather a vivid demonstration of the obstacles which were encountered and the compromises which had to be made to incorporate, to the extent possible, the varying positions.

The purpose of the guide is to provide guidelines for establishing, maintaining, and controlling employee–employer records in a manner which complies with applicable laws and regulations, and protects the interests and respects the privacy of both the employer-corporation and its employees.

The guidelines were designed for use by Mobil Oil Corporation and its subsidiaries operating in the United States. Subsidiaries of Mobil Oil Corporation operating outside the United States were requested to establish guidelines that are similar to and compatible with the guidelines in the parent company's management guide. However, any guidelines established by subsidiaries outside the United States were required to conform to the laws and customary practices in each subsidiary's operating area.

The relationship between an employee and his or her employer is described in the management guide as a voluntary one which is initiated and maintained through an exchange of essential information by the parties involved. When an individual applies for a job, the employer-corporation needs information about the person's job-related skills, education, and prior work experience to make the employment decision. During employment, the employer-corporation needs to correct and maintain information related to the employee's work and progress. Information is also recorded concerning the employee's participation in various employer-corporation benefit plans and programs. Other information is required by government agencies. According to the guide, "only information required by the employee–employer relationship should be collected and each item of information should be maintained only as long as required."[7]

Before defining an employee's right to privacy, termed employee-confidential information, and the employer's right to privacy, denoted as company-confidential information, the guide classifies the sources of employee–employer information as follows:

1. Employee-supplied information, e.g., biographical data such as education and work experience prior to employment, elections and decisions by the employee with respect to benefit plans, and tax withholding;
2. Employer-generated information, e.g., appraisals of an employee's performance, career development plans, and pay and work history;
3. Information obtained from other sources, e.g., employment reference reports and medical information.

The privacy of employee–employer information is defined as follows:

The nature of the employee–employer relationship is such that it is in the interests of the employee and the Company that employee–employer records are maintained in a manner which satisfies each of the parties that they are accurate, timely, protected against unwarranted use, and complete as necessary, to assure that they are not the cause of unfairness in employment-related decisions made on the basis of them.

The company expressly recognizes the employee's right to privacy by creating an information category denoted as "employee-confidential information." In so doing, the company acknowledges that employees have the right

To be free from unreasonable invasions of personal privacy;

To expect that personal information obtained by the employer-corporation about them will be used for purposes consistent with those for which it was given or solicited;

To expect that employer-corporation custodians of employee information will take precautions to see that the information is reasonably safeguarded, used only on a "need to know" basis internally within the employer-corporation, or by any service bureau engaged by the employer-corporation to process employee information, and not otherwise released to sources outside of the employer-corporation without the consent of employees;

To examine information about themselves in employer-corporation files except for records which are deemed to be 'Company Confidential';

To request correction of inaccurate information about themselves in employer-corporation files, or submit statements to be added to the files when a record involving a business judgment or opinion is disputed by an employee and the difference of opinion is not resolved.

Records which an employee has a right to examine and correct are deemed to be 'Employee-Confidential.' Included are: all records stored in the Personnel File, the Payroll File, the Benefits File, the Medical File, and any Employee-Confidential Employee Relations or Department Administrative File. Excluded are all records classified as Company-Confidential.

However, the guide further states that an employee must recognize that the employer-corporation also has a right to privacy and thus has the responsibility and the right

To exercise its management prerogative to protect the interests of its shareholders, employees, customers, and the public at large;

To make and carry out private business plans to achieve the objectives of the organization;

To protect the confidentiality of any staffing plans, forecasts of potential, or placement summaries, and any other personnel plans related to overall business plans;

To protect the confidentiality of any job-related information about employees obtained, with the authorization of employees under a commitment of confidentiality, from sources other than the employee or the supervisor, e.g., reference reports;

To protect the confidentiality of any private communication to, from or between management representatives not communicated to the employee concerning the employee's performance or behavior on the job in "special" or "problem" cases, i.e., cases involving:

> actual or potential complaints related to EEO,[8] unfair labor practice charges, grievance and arbitration under labor agreements or complaint procedures in nonunion facilities, disputes over alleged "promises" or "commitments" made to employees by Managers, Benefits Advisors, or Employee Relations Adivsors, or problem situations expected to lead to discharge or resignation.

In short, information related to employer-corporation business plans, staffing plans or compensation plans; and information obtained under a commitment of confidentiality; and private communications concerning "special" or "problem" cases, not communicated to the employee, are deemed to be "Company-Confidential" and not subject to inquiry or access by the employee.

The key to privacy of employer–employee records, as previously described, is the recognition that an unlimited right of employee privacy with respect to records collected and maintained on the employee would be open to abuse as much as an unlimited right of employer privacy with respect to records accumulated by the employer on its employees. Consequently, the company carefully established categories covering an employee's privacy rights, i.e., employee-confidential information, and those covering the employer's privacy rights, i.e., company-confidential information. In so doing, the company was aware that such categories did not possess the force of law and might well fall by the wayside in the event of litigation initiated by an employee against the employer-corporation or vice versa. It was also recognized at the time these information categories were established that subsequently enacted statutes might establish different criteria of privacy. For instance, it was recognized that a statute might well determine information to be "employee-confidential" that the guide currently denotes as "company-confidential." In order to provide for such eventualities, the guide expressly recognizes that privacy laws in about a dozen states in the U.S., for instance, allow employees of a company, either past or present, access to certain records maintained, regardless of whether a company's

policy would seek to forbid such access. Employee relations units, therefore, are directed by the guide to consult assigned counsel when past or present employees want to see and read records maintained by the company that are kept as company-confidential in separate and confidential company files. Inasmuch as the guide was based *ab initio* on notions of privacy that had carefully balanced an employee's and the employer's privacy rights, the company has thus far had no adverse experiences in implementing the policies and procedures set forth in the guide.

Special provisions were also made in the guide for outside inquiries about employees in response to which only so-called directory information is disclosed unless the express prior written authorization of the employee is obtained for the disclosure of further or additional information. An explicit exception is made for the disclosure of information required by federal, state, or municipal statues, ordinances, or regulations and in response to administrative summonses or judicial orders, including search warrants or subpoenas. However, the company responds to such processes only after prior notification to the employee (wherever and whenever practicable) thus affording the employee an opportunity to take such personal opposing action as, under applicable laws, may be available in the then-prevailing circumstances.

THE HUMAN RESOURCES INFORMATION SYSTEM

Fortunately, the management guide on employee–employer records was in place and operative before Mobil Oil Corporation's Human Resources Information System (HURIS) had been developed and became operative.

HURIS is a computerized system that collects, organizes, updates, and retrieves personal and payroll data for all domestic employees of Mobil Oil Corporation and most of its domestic subsidiaries operating in the United States. However, HURIS also maintains personal and payroll data on selected foreign nationals employed by certain of Mobil's foreign subsidiaries who, for career development purposes, are working in the United States on temporary assignments to Mobil Oil Corporation and its domestic subsidiaries.

Implementation of the total HURIS System, consisting of personnel, payroll data, and benefit plans information, was completed by the end of 1983, culminating a

6-year effort to absorb and process massive amounts of employee data. Employee personnel records are standardized for over 70,000 U.S.-based employees of 40 separate corporate entities that constitute the Mobil group of companies in the United States. Most of these corporate entities had their own separate payroll and personnel data systems before electing to synchronize their systems with that of HURIS.

As in any computerized system that deals with highly sensitive data, security and confidentiality are of paramount importance. Access to the system is strictly controlled. Authorized personnel must enter their identification number, password and several other pieces of information in the proper sequence before they can activate their terminals. HURIS can precisely limit the types of data any given individual can see. For instance, HURIS can limit a person's ability to call up data to just "directory information," such as an employee's home address or telephone number and whom to contact in the event the employee encounters an emergency.

Essentially, HURIS aims at consolidating information on employee's pay, special skills or training, job history, company benefits, and personal items such as education, in a single data processing operation. HURIS provides all employees on a regular basis with a printout of key personal information contained in the system to make sure that it is accurate and up-to-date.

As indicated previously, in addition to information on domestic employees of Mobil Oil Corporation and its domestic subsidiaries, HURIS maintains information on selected foreign nationals who are employees of some of Mobil's foreign subsidiaries. These selected foreign nationals are deemed to have a high potential for promotability to positions on the staff of the parent company and are usually assigned to attend courses in the United States and to training assignments on the staffs of the various departments of Mobil Oil Corporation and its domestic subsidiaries.

Personal data on such selected foreign nationals must be obtained, at least in part, from Mobil's foreign subsidiaries. The foreign affiliates involved and the data so furnished must comply with the applicable foreign data protection and other foreign privacy laws, particularly insofar as these laws may seek to impose restrictions on transborder data flows of this kind.

It has been Mobil's experience that its policy on privacy of employee–employer records[9] has neither prevented nor unreasonably restricted the necessary transborder flow of such personal data. The primary reason for this favorable experience is unquestionably the strictness in adherence to Mobil Oil Corporation's policy and procedures on privacy of employee–employer records, all of which aim at collecting, maintaining, and updating only those data that are demonstrably job-related and necessary to protect both the employee's and the employer's interests in the privacy of these records. In other words, the soundness of Mobil's policy on the subject has been proven, at least thus far, by (1) the Mobil organization's ability to implement it, (2) its compatibility with thus-far-existing domestic and foreign data-protection and other privacy laws, (3) its contributions toward voluntary self-regulation by business organizations in the United States, and (5) its contributions to averting the negotiation of binding international treaties on this subject, as will be shown hereafter.

Certainly, a system such as HURIS has the potential for invasion of an employee's privacy, not only by the company but also by government and its agencies. This potential has been curbed by not loading the data base with information that contravenes Mobil Oil Corporation's policy on privacy of employee–employer records. Given central coordination and control of and by HURIS, it has not been difficult, at least thus far, to adapt this system and its operations to specific requirements of federal and state legislation and foreign data protection laws insofar as these laws purport to regulate the collection, maintenance, and dissemination of personal data on selected employees of Mobil's foreign subsidiaries. Given also the absence of abuses in the creation and maintenance of the HURIS system, there have been no demands for legislative action against such private systems either in the United States or abroad.

OECD GUIDELINES AND U.S. RESPONSE

Rather, international concern has aimed in the opposite direction, as exemplified by the OECD *Guidelines Governing the Protection of Privacy and Transborder Flows of Personal Data*.[10] One of the essential recommendations was that "member countries endeavor to remove or avoid creating, in the name of privacy protection, unjustified obstacles to transborder flows of personal data."

In letters dated December 22, 1980 and July 20, 1981, over the signature of Mr. Malcolm Baldrige, secretary of commerce of the United States, to the chief executive officers of major American corporations, the U.S. government took action to implement the OECD Guidelines and the OECD council's recommendations to member countries.

The December 22, 1980 letter pointed out that

> The absence of widespread and well publicized support for the Guidelines within the U.S. private sector would substantially increase the prospects for the imposition of conditions, limitations, and administrative difficulties in the exchange of personal data between your U.S. and non-U.S. [affiliates] and would encourage foreign insistence on a binding treaty approach. Such developments would be neither in the U.S. national interest, nor in the commercial interests of U.S. multinationals.

The July 20, 1981 letter stated:

> Privacy concerns have prompted recent passage of new laws, both here and abroad. These laws could adversely affect the flow of data. The United States is firmly committed to safeguarding privacy and other individual rights. We believe that this can best be achieved within existing law by relying on voluntary private initiative.

The letter urged executives of firms with a stake in assuring the international free flow of information to endorse publicly the OECD Guidelines and our national policy of relying on voluntary private-sector compliance to safeguard privacy.

In a letter dated October 2, 1981 to the secretary of commerce which responded to the secretary's previous communications concerning the OECD Guidelines, Mr. Rawleigh Warner, Jr., chairman of the board and chief executive officer of Mobil Corporation (the parent holding company of Mobil Oil Corporation), Container Corporation of America, and Montgomery Ward & Co., Incorporated, the three major operating companies within the Mobil organization, stated that

> Mobil's policies and procedures for the acquisition, maintenance and use of data concerning individuals are consistent with the principles set forth in Part II of the OECD Guidelines. We believe the Guidelines strike a balance between the necessity for preserving individual privacy and the vital need to ensure the continued free flow of information between nations. Consequently, we are pleased to support the principles set forth in the Guidelines.
>
> In taking this opportunity to express our support of

the Guidelines, we also concur with your statement that safeguarding privacy can best be achieved within existing laws by relying on private initiative.

It should be emphasized that while the OECD Guidelines are voluntary between governments, they nevertheless represent a significant commitment of the member states, including most Western European states and Japan. In participating in the negotiation of the OECD Guidelines, the United States was careful to assure that private-sector initiative in this area would be given weight in assessing a country's privacy policy.

CONCLUSIONS

Mobil, by adopting a voluntary policy of self-regulation on the privacy of employee–employer records, and doing so as a major national and international business organization, sought to render unnecessary any (1) legislated, mandatory government action, and (2) binding international treaty machinery to administer government-mandated administration of privacy principles on the international level. Mobil is proud to have made a significant contribution to the efforts of the U.S. government to forestall mandatory national and international legal restrictions that would affect adversely the management of personnel within companies which operate on a global basis employing nationals of many different countries.

NOTES

1. H.R. 1984, 94th Cong., 1st Sess. (Jan. 23, 1975), Mr. Goldwater for himself and Mr. Koch. Referred to the Committee on the Judiciary. The bill was designed to protect the constitutional right of privacy of individuals concerning whom identifiable information had been recorded by enacting principles of information practice in furtherance of Articles I, III, IV, V, IX, X, and the Fourteenth Amendment of the *United States Constitution.*

2. Pub. L. 93-579, 88 Stat. 1987, *as amended by* Pub. L. 94-183, 89 Stat. 1057, 5 U.S.C.A. 552a (Dec. 31, 1975).

3. German Federal Republic, Law for the Protection of Personal Data Against Misuse in Data Processing (Jan. 27, 1977) [hereinafter cited as Federal Data Protection Law—BDSG].

4. *Id.* at § 4.

5. *Id.* at § 22(1).

6.   Republic of France, Law No. 78–17 of January 6, 1978 Concerning Data Processing Files and Liberties, regulated "nominative automatic data processing," i.e., the collection, registration, addition to, storage and destruction of personal data, defined as "information identifiable with specific natural persons," in both the public and private sectors. *See also* International Convention on the Protection of Individuals vis-a-vis Automatic Records, Council of Europe, Draft Resolution (Jan. 1978).

7.   MOBIL CORP., MOBIL MANAGEMENT GUIDE NO. 03-0102 EMPLOYEE–EMPLOYER RECORDS (effective Oct. 15, 1980).

8.   Equal Employment Opportunity, Exec. Order No. 11246, (Sept. 24, 1965); Federal Civil Rights Act of 1964, tit. VII, 42 U.S.C.A. § 2000e–2(a), 29 C.F.R. § § 1606.1, 1606.5.

9.   Mobil's policy on privacy of employee–employer records was initially intended as self-regulation in the United States only but was also made available to the personnel or employee relations departments of foreign subsidiaries for information and guidance purposes.

10.   Council for Economic Development and Cooperation, Guidelines Governing the Protection of Privacy and Transborder Flows of Personal Data (adopted by the council at its 523rd meeting on Sept. 23, 1980).

CHAPTER 13

ENERGY INFORMATION FLOWS

JOHN CAS CZELEN

INTRODUCTION

The energy sector of world industrial activity encompasses organizations involved in the production and distribution of various natural resources including petroleum, natural gas, coal, nuclear fuels, electricity, and other marginal sources. There are thousands of entities involved, ranging in size from individuals who monitor shipping schedules for insurance and pricing purposes and spot-market trading, to multinational conglomerates that manage multi-resource flows, to nations whose nationalized petroleum companies are their greatest income source. Thus, an overview of information flows and practices must be constrained by several key criteria.

First, only United States-based corporate activities will be addressed because they exemplify the broadest needs. Second, only petroleum-oriented operations will be addressed. Although other energy flows do include international aspects, e.g., coal exports, their international activities are not as central to overall corporate functions as in the petroleum industry. Third, major petroleum corporations are substantially horizontally integrated. An understanding of their petroleum operations will generally suffice for their other resource operations since their petroleum operations usually include their most extensive and sophisticated international information flows. Fourth, only specific petroleum production activities will be addressed. The information flows associated with other sectors, e.g., credit, insurance, etc., will substantially cover those non-energy-specific operations that are undertaken by petroleum concerns.

The material for this chapter is derived from the personal and professional background of the author coupled with the results of a limited survey conducted in 1981–1982. Based upon prior contacts developed through the author's participation in statistical surveys undertaken by a United States government agency, several major petroleum corporations were requested to participate. Therefore, the group selected varied randomly in size and capability. Although the results are not necessarily statistically precise, they are generally representative. The corporations were contacted through either their general counsel or their telecommunications branch. The study purposes were explained, project materials provided, and telephone interviews conducted based on the outline in Table 13.1. Additional materials have been collected that are not presented in this chapter, but they are provided through other aspects of the effort producing this book.

OVERVIEW OF PETROLEUM OPERATIONS

The major functions of petroleum production can be characterized by the flow diagram in Figure 13.1, which illustrates the technical activities required in the life-cycle of petroleum. Most petroleum organizations, and other energy-related concerns, are typically structured into subdivisions along similar functional lines. For example, there would be a subsidiary for exploration, another for transportation, and so forth. Further subdivi-

---

JOHN CAS CZELEN ● Mr. Czelen is an attorney experienced in bridging legal analysis and systems design, and the executive director of SYSTEMS, INC., a tax-exempt non-profit organization providing advanced software and systems development for government and service organizations.

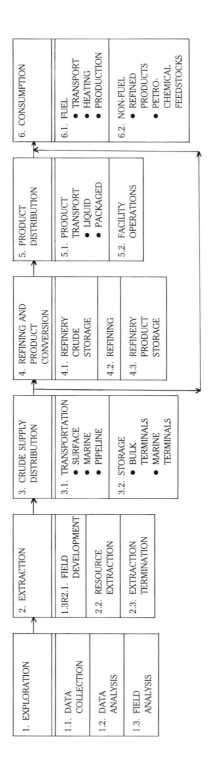

Figure 13.1 Petroleum Life-Cycle Functions

TABLE 13.1   Interview Outline

1. Project overview/objectives
2. Corporate structure and functions
3. Networks (flows, hardware, software, uses, content, etc.)
4. Data (flows, functional objectives, sources, content, destination and use, modes, logic, etc.)
5. Transactions (intra- and inter-corporate)
6. Countries/borders
7. Budgets
8. Services (in-house, DP firms, Intelsat, Telenet, Cybernet, Nimbus, Landsat, etc.)
9. Benefits
10. Problems (legal, organizational, hardware/software, political, privacy, etc.)
11. Related technical information
12. Other contacts

sions can be found for more specific functional and geographic bounds. Within the continental United States, geographical units typically include Eastern and Western divisions, and a Central division is sometimes found. Similarly, there may be European, Mideastern, Southern Pacific, and similar continental and nation-based units. Most information flows occur primarily within the functional areas with concomitant reporting and transaction flows between these functional areas and between themselves and corporate headquarters.

Exploration activities are directed toward the location of resources and are based on substantial data collection and analysis with associated field activities including test drilling. Extraction covers medium- to long-term field functions, including initialization of field operations and withdrawal of natural resources, preparation of resources for transportation to conversion centers, and termination and maintenance functions implemented when resource extraction is no longer cost-effective. Crude supply distribution includes the shipping and storage of bulk volumes of crude oil (and natural gas) by surface and land transportation, frequently across national boundaries. Refining and product conversion includes those processes whereby crude oil is modified by distillation and similar related processes into either end products (e.g., gasoline) or intermediate petrochemicals required for specialized products. Product distribution provides for the shipment of both consumer-directed petroleum-based products such as gasoline, typically within national boundaries, and the shipment of petrochemicals, which may be international. Consumption is the final stage wherein the product is utilized and thus destroyed, or combined into an end product. It thus loses its separate identity. Local

distribution activities may occur within the consumption stage and are typically intranational.

Exploration

Although petroleum explorers nurture their self-description of "wildcatters," the gamble of the petroleum search is lessened by substantial research and data collection. Geology and related earth-sciences assume a high profile within all exploration activities, and cartography and surveying support field definition. Data collection activities range from library research by individuals, to field survey terms of six or more people, to acoustical engineering and geophysical analysis involving fleets of air and water vehicles. Four major data collection activities can generally be identified: (1) library analysis and research, based on sources including United States Geological Survey data and other geologic services, seismographic surveys, exploratory well cores and logs, associated maps and photographs (especially LANDSAT products), and magnetic and airborne remote sensing; (2) topographic mapping, based on field surveying, satellite and aerial photography, and topographic plotting; (3) geophysical investigations, including gravimetry, magnetometry, electric resistivity, and acoustical methodologies; and (4) exploratory leasing and drilling.

All of these activities are based upon international data flows. Data are collected across many national boundaries and frequently in international waters. These data are usually transmitted to the United States and other locations where geologic interpretation occurs. All media are utilized, as can be understood from the range of types of data collected. For example, core samples need to be physically transported by air, photographs must be placed in hand, and digital data, such as gravimetric signals, must be delivered by tape, physically delivered by air if they are analog graphs, or condensed and results transmitted. All data eventually are filtered analytically and concentrated into corporate decision making to result in exploratory well-drilling. Data transmission should be expected to increase, especially as large-array data processors, where massive amounts of numerical data can be utilized, make geological modeling more feasible.

Of course, in addition to actual geologic data, exploratory leasing and drilling are based upon economic and political factors. These information flows are at least as complex as the geologic information flows. These flows and similar contextual information required in the other portions of petroleum production will not be described in this chapter. Other chapters supply descriptions of portions of these flows and the remainder must be addressed in following works.

In addition to primary field definition data, other responsibilities may call for additional data collection. For example, environmental impact studies are sometimes required, especially in more developed countries. These studies usually focus on the recognition of geological hazards, surface or subsurface in nature, which can adversely affect further exploratory work by causing oil spills or similar surface pollution. Additionally, cultural and sociological data are sometimes being required for adequate impact analysis.

As mentioned earlier, the result of exploration activities is the ability to make decisions whether to lease or otherwise secure the right to drill wells for additional exploration or production. Leasing agreements and related financial transactions thus occur, with their associated data flows, and later information flows are established, such as lease payments based upon production. Although well drilling does occur in exploration, exploratory drilling data aspects will be discussed in detail in the next section.

Extraction

Extraction can be characterized by three general activities: (1) field development, which includes drilling and site production preparation, (2) resource extraction operations, and (3) extraction termination, either temporary or permanent.

Field development efforts are logistically complex and entail negotiation of rights and fees for development and preparation of the site, including designing, ordering, and installation of drilling systems and support facilities. Because of the magnitude of costs involved, joint ventures are typical. Major information flows occur in planning and execution, e.g., contracting for basic services such as site-leveling if onshore, or construction and towing of drilling platforms if offshore. The full panoply of transmission services, from public mail transmission to broad-bandwidth satellite carriers, can be used in design, contracting, and service preparation. Much of this communication is international.

One primary production requirement is direct communications between an offshore drilling platform and onshore and central corporate offices. Regularized exploratory and operational data must be produced and communicated to corporate planning. For example, weekly drilling reports containing depth, stratigraphic aspects, and potential volume and rates are typically required. After regular production is established, weekly and even daily production, storage, and transported volumes are required. Ongoing data transmissions cover a wide range of subjects, such as installation of equipment, production schedules and results, personnel times, wages and related expenditures, borehole analysis including electric logging, material ordering and delivery, production inventories and deliveries, workovers (overhauls of equipment), and resource transportation deliveries. Field resource data are significant, including measures of crude characteristics such as specific gravity (API gravity), basic sediment and water (BS&W), and sulfur content.

Where newer offshore technology is utilized for exploration or production, the establishment of communications typically might proceed in the following manner. An application would be filed with the "post office" or similar government communications entity requesting transmission privileges from the offshore facility to an onshore linkage point. A microwave radio transmission frequency would be assigned to the offshore facility. From this facility, microwave transmission would be directed to the local onshore office, usually owned and operated by the petroleum production company, who would then act as a link to other data channels such as a ground-based microwave common carrier or a private leased-line satellite. The data would then be integrated into the decision making network of the exploration organization. In more recent circumstances offshore facilities communicate directly over satellite leased-lines without a separate ground facility onshore. Naturally, additional communications services, such as mail drop-off and delivery services and limited personal telephone calls, are provided to employees working on the offshore platform.

Crude Supply Distribution

Crude supply distribution is accomplished by a wide combination of methods: tank trucks, railroads, barges, tankers, or pipelines. The most common methods are tankers and pipelines, both inherently international. Importantly, storage is a necessary element of the transportation function to smooth and sort delivery flows and "bubbles" according to geographic demand and availability. Thus, terminal facilities/tank farms are commonly found at ports of entry for imported crude oil and at various points along crude oil transmission pipelines.

On a worldwide basis, there are over 3000 ocean-going tankers over 10,000 deadweight tons and the information flows associated are of similar magnitude. Usually, tanker voyage-planning occurs in conjunction with overall strategic planning for crude streams from specific resource areas to planned refining centers. Thus, major routes can be established. However, the flows of crude oil can dramatically shift as do the sources themselves.

On a single-voyage basis, planning usually begins prior to a discharge of crude oil. While the ship is on the high seas, the tanker's master receives voyage orders directing the ship where to go next to load the crude oil, the amount to be loaded, the temperature at which the crude will be loaded, and the discharge point. The voyage orders may also contain information on the amount of fuel the ship should carry on the voyage, the specific cargo tanks to be loaded, and the amount of ballasting, it any. In addition, some shipping firms may also include tentative orders for the following voyage as well as for schedule and manpower planning. Of course, certain ships are operated in long-term repeating runs.

In combination with voyage-planning information, which is usually communicated by a combination of transatlantic cable, microwave, and common-carrier satellite transmission, other data flows must be recognized, including contracts and agreements between shippers, sellers, and receivers, and associated financial and insurance parties. Cargo and tanker inspections are also a prime activity, with reports created at loading, importation, and discharge, for all parties to the transaction and government agencies as well.

Pipelines are operated typically by independent pipeline companies on a monthly schedule. Around the 24th or 25th of each month, the pipeline scheduler checks with each of the oil companies using the pipeline, to obtain estimates of their shipping needs for the following month. Such information can be collected in a series of informal and formal communications, by media including telephone, telex, and mail. These communications cover aspects of delivery including scheduling of receipts and deliveries, costs, blending, storage, and related options. When schedules are complete, paper copies are distributed by mail or by telex to all shippers. Naturally, based on operating factors such as changing market conditions or breakdowns, revisions of schedules are moderately frequent. Additionally, long-term standard shipping schedules are integrated with the short-term schedules.

Pipeline operations are highly automated with equipment such as remote solenoid valve controls and measurement devices. Substantial operations data and records are created at end terminals and along the entire length of the pipeline. For example, pump stations that maintain pipeline pressure monitor all variables and communicate with operating centers. Maintenance operations, such as cleaning, are scheduled, based on reported data, and inspections are made when warning signals are detected.

Crude (or product) deliveries at shipping interfaces are carefully monitored since prices are determined by the volume and characteristics of the crude oil (which is not totally fungible). Refineries must receive crude oil batches with optimized physical characteristics. Thus, metering and testing is important and pipeline and facility "run tickets," in paper form, usually are produced. This data will make its way to multiple destinations, frequently in digital form, to interested parties including central pipeline operations, refinery operations, shippers, and crude source and refinery companies' central dispatching, planning, and accounting facilities.

Storage facilities such as tank farms are the hubs of information as well as hubs of transportation. Their data flows parallel their crude flows, and consist of scheduling, crude characteristics, and costs. These flows may issue between shippers, receivers, and the storage facilities' central offices. Accuracy of measurement and reporting are of crucial concern, especially regarding times of custody transfer. Crude characteristics must be carefully monitored and reported.

Refining/Product Conversion

Refining and similar operations have become highly organized and automated and the data created is similarly extensive. Data similar to that created in transportation activities is likewise created here, including volumes received, characteristics, scheduling, and so forth.

Although refineries operate within a narrow range of crude types that can be accepted (typically based on sulfur content), in order to optimize production and profit, modifications can be made in the product slate (types and volumes of different products) depending upon market conditions that apply to the parent company and the specific characteristics of the available crude supply. Thus, operations are continuously monitored and operating parameters are directed to the refinery by corporate headquarters.

Within the actual operations, both manual and automated processes are found. Frequently, manual control is found, augmented by automated sensors and recording devices, computer modeling, and parameter controls. Usually, computers are utilized for process control for product slate optimization, and integrated process controls monitor chromatographic results, product outputs, overhead, and residuals or by-products, and select parameters. Besides the feedback loops within a plant's gates, similar data is transmitted, typically by paper, but electronically when additional haste is required, for overall process optimization to attain corporate marketing objectives, for research, for overall business strategic planning, and for regulatory purposes. Importantly, many refinery and chemical plants operate in conjunction with other plants across multiple national boundaries, matching crude acceptance, output needs, and so forth. Thus, process control-based data for optimization and business is extensive and international as well.

Product Distribution

The marketing of petroleum products, including the process of transport from conversion plants to consumers, varies with the product type, the distance to market, and the size of the consumer. The distribution network is best typified by the marketing of gasoline, which accounts for nearly one-half of the yield of refined products from a barrel of crude oil. The handling of products differs from the handling of crude oil in one

essential element. In every phase of transportation and storage, different products must be kept segregated from each other to a degree far greater than required for different grades of crude oil. Contamination must be reduced wherever possible to insure purity. Each storage tank and transportation vehicle must be used for a single product and if contamination occurs, the higher grade product is usually then merged with the lower grades. Thus, scheduling of deliveries becomes a major consideration in product transportation and distribution. Otherwise, the functions, equipment, and information types and flows are quite similar to crude distribution.

However, because crude is distributed internationally and the conversion processes and plants were established near distribution, most products, especially major bulk commodities such as gasoline, are distributed on an intranational basis. Thus, a substantial portion of the associated information flow is not international.

Consumption

As with product distribution, consumption is also primarily intranational in scope. Facilities for consumer goods production are located where feasible as close to consumers as possible, depending upon factors of cost of production, transportation, taxation, and so forth. Thus, any international aspects of information flow would be based upon corporate structure with production and sale in multiple countries.

In terms of actual consumption in a multinational sense, transportation industries are worth observing, insofar as they may include the transport of fuel necessary for vehicle use. However, the data flows here are limited and primarily related to billings for fuel loading and consumption in a foreign facility or jurisdiction.

One major group of petroleum refinery products is not in the form for direct consumption when arriving at its destination after leaving the refinery—industrial feedstocks called petrochemicals, the production-oriented intermediate chemicals derived from the petroleum industry. Literally millions of products are manufactured from these chemicals. Petrochemical production in the United States is still appreciably greater than that of the whole of Western Europe, the next largest in size, although major developments are being undertaken world-wide. Chemical plants are similar to refineries in operation and are becoming increasingly automated in process controls, management optimization, and reporting. Although most plants are located where possible near refineries and consumption, many individual facilities in multiple nations are owned and operated by multinational corporations with associated transnational general management and data flows. For example, many U.S.-owned facilities are located in the Caribbean area. Industries especially noteworthy are plastics, synthetic textiles and rubbers, sulfur and sulfuric acid, basic carbon atom combinations (methane, ethane, etc.), and agricultural fertilizers. In many instances, where there are innovations in petrochemical production there will be exports with associated data flows. Major flows, therefore, exist between economically advanced nations that produce petrochemical-based products and the rest of the world.

RELATED DATA CENTERS

Most governments monitor the major aspects of energy production. For example, within the United States, resource and production data are collected or used by the Customs Service (imports), Departments of State (international flows and reserves), Interior (reserves), Energy (production, end-use, and conservation), Commerce (infrastructure), Census (general statistics), Intelligence (all), and others. Although much of this data is related to U.S.-based operations and/or companies, much data is based on matters outside U.S. territory (e.g., crude oil in transit), and significant data is collected on non-U.S.-based organizations.

In the international sphere, in addition to other nations or business-oriented consortiums, the International Energy Agency collects similar data on crude oil production and prices and is concerned with crude oil sharing agreements between member nations (including the United States, EEC nations, and Japan). Reports are provided to member nations, and to the public and other nations.

Additionally, a substantial number of firms and periodicals monitor resources, prices, contracts, discoveries and similar significant events. For example, *Platt's Oilgram*, a weekly publication, is distributed worldwide and contains coverage of many significant oil industry events (plant construction, political trends, prices, and so forth) and its information on the European spot market is relied upon extensively for pricing and production decisions.

Industry organizations also monitor selected market and production variables and collect data from member companies and distribute publications and reports to members and others. The American Petroleum Institute (API) collects data on international aspects of all phases of the petroleum industry. Other similar organizations include the National Petroleum Council, American Gas Association, Edison Electric Institute, National Oil Jobbers Council, and the National Coal Association. Frequently, these organizations are themselves major sources of government information.

OVERVIEW OF INFORMATION PROCESSING

The data processing and telecommunications operations of larger petroleum organizations typically include state-of-the-art hardware and software; even the relatively smaller firms, who in the world market are nonetheless substantial organizations, effectively utilize current technology. Although most firms may "grandfather" many manual and paper processes, because of the massive costs and profits associated with the production and distribution of petroleum and related products, the costs of information technology are usually justifiable, saving manpower costs and increasing the likelihood of intelligent analysis. For example, the objectives of improvement of refinery operations and chemical synthesis have been a stimulus to advanced linear programming and chemical graphic presentation. Similarly, remote-sensing satellite images are a key source of geologic data. Moreover, because of the size and complexity of the organizations and the international aspects of their trade, these companies rely on telecommunications functions wherever possible.

Much of the field work information associated with energy flows remains unautomated because paper documentation is required for the interfaces with the myriad number of less automated concerns. Paper remains less expensive for many functions and is still mandatory for audit requirements. However, internal management and financial, analytical, and process-control activities have automated at least as quickly as, and usually more quickly than, other industrial sectors. Additionally, based upon diversification strategies, major energy companies have acquired smaller organizations that are in the information technology sector, such as microcomputer manufacturers and software developers. Thus, energy companies, in one role or another, will be using or developing the latest aspects of telecommunications techniques.

However, because of the world-ranging nature of petroleum operations and the continuous changing of production patterns, overall transnational data flows are typically in a state of flux and not organized into very formal or fixed private networks. They are essentially ad hoc systems of mid-term life utilizing commercial common carriers' leased lines. While mid- and long-term leased lines may be utilized for a series of communications of extended frequency or repetition, such as between the United States and European headquarters, the typical mode of line use is long-distance dial-up. Where dedicated leased lines are utilized, typically combination alternate voice and data circuits are used, with voice transmission occurring during normal business hours and the switch to a data transmission mode occurring during evening and off hours, except for high priority data.

Telecommunications and computing centers are found in the United States and Europe in major urban areas. Management and accounting information centers have traditionally been located apart from operating areas which are usually remote or rural, widely distributed, and frequently changing. Major centers of management and analytical operations are located in Houston, Dallas, Chicago, New York, and other urban areas in the United States, and in Frankfort, London, Cairo, and other major European and Mideastern cities. Communications between operations and management centers are based mostly upon telephone and mail, although all other modes of information transfer, such as telex, are significant. Where data is being transmitted for on-line processing, cable is frequently used, rather than satellites, because the satellite link signal propagation delay is too great for computer cost efficiency. However, there appears to be a shortage of suitable transatlantic cable and satellite transmission is used in spite of increased processing costs.

Many international corporations with United States-based management centers may have a second major operation in London, or a European center such as Frankfort, as a center of a star communications pattern, with branches in other major European and Mideastern cities and countries such as Brussels, Geneva, and Japan. Communications between U.S. and foreign locations is typically based upon mail, telex, and telephone, and major data transmission occurs over dial-up common carrier lines. Significant amounts of data transmission are encrypted.

In sum, energy-sector companies' international information and communications needs are crucial to their operations. Activities are fundamentally worldwide in nature and speed of transmission directly augments competitive capacity and business advantage. All modes of current business telecommunications usage are found and the major companies are innovators in both development and applications. Although much of the energy production field work relies upon paper documentation, the increasingly automated processes involving ever-growing large volume deliveries provide a solid basis for accelerating conversion to extensive digital transmission.

ENERGY INFORMATION FLOW ISSUES

The issues arising from global energy information operations principally relate to the requirements of energy firms for information services. Additionally, because of the close relationship of energy operations and national security, governmental concerns are also important. These issues can be grouped under the following general topics: (1) corporate service requirements; (2) government and corporate relations; (3) intergovernmental relations.

These issues do have implications that transcend these topics, especially for commercial energy activities that are directly government-owned and operated. Increasingly, many energy organizations are entering into joint ventures with governments in order to adequately finance the immense ventures that are technologically suitable. Since government participation is frequently found in energy enterprises in both the United States and elsewhere, a complete consideration of issues should attempt to discern the implications for government operations. However, based upon the same assumptions stated in the beginning of this chapter, issues will be addressed mainly from the point of view of individual organizations that are either completely private or purely governmental.

Corporate Service Requirements

Petroleum energy flows are fundamentally global in nature since most developed areas have already substantially depleted their larger hydrocarbon reserves and current exploration and extraction occur in less-developed countries. Resources therefore flow from the source to the consuming industrialized and developed nations, and the associated information flows are intrinsically international. Moreover, these resource and information flows can rapidly shift as new resource flows come on-stream or political change affects the capacity to produce and ship in a specific nation. Energy organizations thus require the capability to flexibly respond to these changing requirements and have a concomitant demand for flexible communications. Additionally, most phases of energy activities are information intensive and rely heavily on information flow to support centralized decisionmaking. Thus, a high priority is placed on the adequacy and responsiveness of information and communication services.

As described earlier, the technical capabilities of most energy firms rival those found anywhere. Moreover, since advanced communications capabilities usually are cost justified because of the large scale of operations, significant financial resources are available and committed. The result is that most firms have confidence in their own information and communications capabilities and would most prefer to operate without government assistance or interference. As is typical of most business operations, they at least would prefer to do business with other private service organizations. Government communications operations are generally viewed as a necessary evil to be avoided where possible in favor of in-house capabilities or private services whose aim is to provide competitive rates and services.

The disfavor for governmental information service-providers manifests itself in specific attitudes and responses. For example, when a new communications line is to be installed for a new site, the primary objective is to establish accurate secure communications. However, frequently a practical challenge to the energy operation would be to determine how government-imposed technical barriers and limits could be overcome. If the government requires specific hardware to be used or limits the location of data processing activities, other strategies need to be devised. Additional barriers might be faced, such as currency restrictions, licensing limits, taxes, and tariffs, depending upon the relationship of the export of the natural resource to the overall economic profile of the nation in question.

A common optimistic assumption exists that many typical governmentally-imposed technological barriers can be avoided when operations are introduced in less-developed countries. Since these countries frequently have not developed the communications infrastructure that results in protective or regulatory standards, barriers to the introduction of advanced technology can be leapfrogged. However, this optimism is offset by the reality of increasing nationalization of communications

or, at best, direct government intervention and control of private services.

Finally, it cannot be overstressed that the communications in question relate to resource flows of considerable size with related significant value. Since the economic implications are so great, security is of paramount concern. Either resource or purely financial data must be accorded strict protection from both other competitors and government as well.

Government and Corporate Relations

Information and communications support access by U.S. energy corporations to world markets where their relative competitive advantage makes them successful. A world market exists and inherently international worldwide information is necessary to be competitive. If it is assumed that this corporate success is in the national interest, how can the extensive information needs of energy-related firms be met while protecting the needs of the U.S. government?

Government interests are far from clear and policy must reconcile vast conflicts. The results of wide energy commodity price swings are profound. Stable prices are sought by official encouragement of an orderly market. An orderly market requires information services regarding production, delivery, price, and related business transactions. However, competition and nonmonopolistic market structures are official government goals. Most governments limit and control potentially monopolistic activities, especially trading of information regarding market activities. What is the proper balance between information sharing and distribution by private enterprise, and conflicting government antitrust policies?

Additionally, what is the proper government role regarding the collection, use, and distribution of market data collected by government from private energy firms? Government frequently collects broad ranges of data, sometimes collecting data down to the level of specific business transactions, recording the parties, commodities, and prices. At a threshold level, there is a strong historical basis for government data collection at national borders where import or export occurs. Customs agencies collect basic data on energy commodity volumes, qualities, ownership, value, and so forth. Although there is similar data collection on each side of a border, the burden has not historically been seen as overly severe. However, additional data is being collected about operations that are external to national boundaries, where the firm is U.S-based. For example, data is collected (or attempts to collect it are made) regarding foreign ownership, value, and production. What are the limits that should be imposed upon government beyond which further data collection is too invasive? Likewise, what is a suitable minimum for extraterritorial data that a nationally-based firm should submit? While there is an interest by all parties that government should be able to respond in emergencies and an understanding that government needs certain basic information in order to function in the interest of the firm and society, the level of suitable data collection is always in dispute.

Next, this market data, which has national security implications and is of proprietary value to the reporting firm, has similar value to competitors. Thus, government is under an obligation to limit disclosure. How should government use this data? Although high standards for accuracy and completeness are promised, political values can shift interpretations. Similarly problematic, the use of data in modeling and forecasting activities often exceeds the abilities of the prognosticator and the recipient, and can bias social and political decisionmaking. For example, several intelligence agency reports regarding likely petroleum production and consumption of the Soviet Union have proved to be highly inaccurate. Similarly, the predictions made by the U.S. Departments of Energy and the Interior regarding likely U.S. domestic gasoline and electricity consumption have been significantly inaccurate. Thus, the question poses itself—how ambitious should government be regarding interpretation of data, especially where the models are also ambitious and the resulting effects can significantly affect market operations and investment and more fundamental economic and social relationships.

Finally, which information services should government continue to offer and which should be assumed by private firms? For example, satellite weather data has been collected and disseminated by the U.S. National Oceanagraphic and Atmospheric Administration (NOAA). After recent recommendations by the current administration to sell the satellite network to a private firm, further analysis of government's role has occurred. Others have suggested that a similar approach be taken to LANDSAT satellites and data, and that the geographic

data collection mechanism that is so crucial to petroleum exploration be placed in the hands of private enterprise.

Intergovernmental Relations

Since energy is seen as the "lifeblood" of a modern industrial state, information concerning energy and resources is directly related to national security. Moreover, the business and financial implications are enormous and directly and significantly affect national and regional economies. The United States presently possesses an unmatched capability to gather information worldwide. This data collection is frequently seen as a tool of economic expansionism and control. The implicit truth in this assertion is easily grasped with the knowledge that agreements for exploration and resource access will be more favorable to the individual or organization that knows more likely locations of resources.

Can any nation continue to maintain information collection supremacy? Can the disparities of data collection abilities be addressed, especially where data collection is government sponsored, such as the U.S. Geological Survey (USGS)? Can any nation politically justify unequal access and distribution of data, especially where nations assert their property and national security rights to economic information regarding their own territorial assets? In fact, many less-developed countries advantageously have had access to LANDSAT data in support of their current agricultural programs, resulting in new levels of production. Nonetheless, although benefits are received, access by mere permission is intrinsically limited and is perceived as a vulnerability.

Presently, the U.S. is in a position where many of its data collection mechanisms cannot be easily constrained and where other nations do not have the ability similarly to gather data. Although the capabilities of other nations will increase, it is likely that new techniques for data collection will become useful. As potential resources expand with increased extraction technology and new information technology becomes practical, any nation wanting to be competitive or to control its own resources will require continuous access to or development of information technology.

CHAPTER 14

EVOLVING COMPUTER NETWORKS IN AMERICAN HIGHER EDUCATION

JOHN W. McCREDIE

WILLIAM P. TIMLAKE

INTRODUCTION

Heterogeneous computer networks are growing in an uncontrolled, almost chaotic, manner to support the expanding needs of scholars and administrators in American higher education. This growth will continue for the foreseeable future. Unplanned and rapidly changing, the networking area is often confusing to both novice and veteran users. There are too many "standards" and the range of options is expanding. Exciting prototypes, as well as production systems, exist and more are sure to appear soon.

Networking activities are moving in many different directions. Recent testimony before congressional committees called for governmental actions to encourage the formation of computer networks that would link all scientific disciplines and make supercomputers easily assessible to researchers.[1] The National Science Foundation is supporting the development of CSNET, a network for the computer science research community, with grants and contracts totalling about $5 million. Other academic networks are springing up with almost no formal planning and/or budget because a particular technology exists and individuals want to use it to communicate (e.g., BITNET—"**B**ecause **I**t's **T**ime"). Individuals on campuses throughout the country are evaluating dozens of local area networking options, and many managers are concerned about gateways that will connect their network with others.

This chapter describes several of the traditions and pressures in the academic environment that account for the early and continuing involvement of higher education with computer networking. Brief descriptions of several established academic networks illustrate the wide range of applications currently available. It is interesting to note, and contrary to the authors' expectations, that currently little international academic computer net-working involving Americans seems to take place.* Finally, several policy issues of particular significance in academic networks will be discussed.

DESCRIPTION OF THE NETWORKING ENVIRONMENT IN AMERICAN HIGHER EDUCATION

Definition

Computer networking, like many other technical concepts, is difficult to define well because it means many

*Since the article was submitted for publication, a significant amount of network activity has happened in Europe. In fact, there are several European networks linking European universities and research centers with links to similar American institutions. Similar efforts are underway in the Far East.

JOHN W. McCREDIE ● Dr. McCredie is Director of University Research Programs, Digital Equipment Corp., and former president of EDUCOM, a non-profit consortium of approximately 450 participating colleges and universities. EDUCOM's primary mission is to transfer successful applications of information technology among its members. WILLIAM P. TIMLAKE ● Mr. Timlake is Director of Technical Assessment for the Information Systems and Storage Group of IBM.

different things to many people. For the purposes of this paper we shall concentrate on networks having the following features:

- a system of interconnected, autonomous computers, terminals and communications facilities
- at least national in scope with significant academic usage
- availability of special software to manage resources in the network
- lists of host computers and users with their associated network addresses

The term "network" is often used to refer to both a collection of computers and communication hardware (physical network) *and* the groups of individuals connected by telecommunication links (logical network). A particular computer may be part of several different physical networks at the same time. More often, an individual will belong to more than one networking group, possibly on different physical networks. For example, a colleague of the authors has on his business card six different network addresses, in addition to a postal address.

Most higher-education networks are based on the diverse needs of many individuals rather than on one underlying large system required to support the "business" of the institution. Such academic networks stand in sharp contrast to the high transaction rates and tight control structures of many commercial networks designed to support an organization's needs for reservation, order entry, and/or electronic fund transfer facilities.

Several important kinds of academic networks are beyond the scope of this paper (e.g., local area networks connecting computer systems on a campus, and regional networks serving a specific geographical area, such as a state). However, the question of how such local and regional networks connect to national and international networks is of great concern to the academic community.

Networks and the Academic Environment

Several underlying features of American higher education help to explain the kinds of computer networks evolving to support the many needs of the broad academic community.

Scholars tend to identify with their own disciplines rather than with their departments or their colleges/universities. Often only a small group of individuals share common research interests within a department, and these people want to communicate with peers located throughout the country, or the world. For example, the natural affinity of widely dispersed researchers in the same discipline leads to efforts to establish networks such as COGNET, a proposed distributed computer network for the field of cognitive science. The COGNET proposal summarizes the reasons for creating such networks.

> We want a network, because it will provide . . . research tools for the community at a reasonable cost and in a reasonable time. The network will be a service facility for all interested in cognition regardless of their field, their location, or their resources. It will provide a communication system that will help those in this emerging field talk to each other despite the fact that they are in different departments and at different universities. It will provide one way to train scholars about research involving cognitive simulation, and other advanced programs and systems, through access to specialized software. Most important, it will provide these capabilities in a way that can grow with the field and be shaped by the field in a manner of its own devising.[2]

This quote summarizes four of the most important general reasons for establishing discipline-based computer networks: *accessibility* to a service facility; *communication*; access to *specialized resources*; and *control* by the discipline.

There is a strong tradition of free and open interchange of information within the academic community. The information explosion and the breakdown of traditional channels for publishing and distributing timely research information have created what some call "invisible colleges." Informal working papers, preprints, drafts, and even raw data, flow among members of invisible colleges. Since much of this information is often computer-based, networks are natural communication channels. Computer networks offer the potential for greater participation in, and easier entry to, "invisible colleges."

A significant amount of academic activity goes on outside of the traditional workday and away from a traditional office setting. Computer networks can support this kind of workstyle very well. It is often easier to contact an individual through a computer network than by telephone because participants do not have to be available simultaneously to use computer-based communication systems.

Many educators are interested in developing new technologies to reach learners who are not necessarily located on campus. The growth of the home computer industry and the availability of networks create new opportunities for dealing with distant learners that are just beginning to be explored in the United States.

The widespread and growing availability of microcomputers, communicating wordprocessors, departmental minicomputers, local campus networks, and national networking organizations (both commercial and nonprofit) are combining to make networking more economical, and much more convenient, than it was a few years ago. When asked what are the three most important factors to the growth of computer networking, a network manager recently replied "convenience, convenience, and convenience."

Computer-based networks, if well designed, are able to support the many needs and traditions of academia. Several different types of networks currently exist, and the number is growing. There are no political forces to inhibit or to consolidate this growth; there are no national governing bodies that could impose an unwanted standardization. Of course, if one technology emerged that was clearly superior to, and more economical than, all others, it would be widely adopted for new applications. However, successful older networks would continue to exist for a long time.

Typical Academic Applications

The previous section described several features of American higher education consistent with the characteristics of emerging computer networks. In order to understand how computer networking is evolving in the academic community, it is useful to examine both the broad categories of applications most common today and those that are growing quickly.

Many important applications belong to the broad class of *resource sharing*. To replicate unique hardware, software, and data resources on every campus is prohibitively expensive. Consider, for example, the costs of operating the largest available supercomputers on many different campuses to satisfy the computational requirements of relatively few researchers. It is more economical to satisfy most common computing needs locally, and to access remote resources for important, but not heavily used applications. The same argument can be made for sharing unique software and data resources.

Several successful networking applications in higher education have been justified using resource-sharing arguments, but the actual number of such cases is fewer than was predicted several years ago. For example, a 1966 summer study of information networks conducted by EDUCOM reported:

> Thus, a network could facilitate making the resources of one institution available to others. Universities could share library materials, data banks, computing facilities.[3]

The rapidly declining costs of hardware and the almost universal desire for local, even individual, control of information-processing facilities, are two of the strongest pressures for localized computing capabilities. The *relative* lack of importance of academic resource sharing contrasts with many networks in the private sector where resource sharing is of paramount importance—for example the strong motivation to share airline reservation information among many companies and passengers.

If resource sharing, although vital to some applications, is not the primary driving force in much of academic networking, what is? *Communication* among people is the obvious answer. Most academics must communicate with others to accomplish their goals. Since they are often separated from peers by large distances, and since the nature of their work is often collaborative and asynchronous, faculty, students, and administrators who have tried computer communication networks have, by and large, found them to be useful. Traditional communication channels (annual meetings, mail, telephone, etc.) do not have the needed capacity, or more importantly, the appropriate response time.

Many items are routinely sent electronically by people with access to computer networks—short mail-type messages, reports, drafts of papers, data, programs, preliminary ideas, requests for comments and help, etc. Computer-based communication in networks has always been valuable, but often its importance was not freely admitted because it was not the primary reason for a network. Interpersonal communications are growing rapidly in all networks known to the authors. Once many independent system components are in place, communication applications among previously disjoint elements are often important enough to justify networking.

The widespread use of computer networks for communicating is causing new forms of communication services to be developed. Electronic bulletin boards and sophisticated conferencing systems are two examples popular in higher education.

SIX ILLUSTRATIVE NETWORKS

ARPANET

In the late 1960s, the Advanced Research Project Agency of the U.S. Department of Defense established a basic research effort in computer networks. ARPA (now DARPA; **D**efense) made several grants to computer science departments to help develop the field of computer networking. This research led to the implementation of a small prototype network in 1969 that has grown to approximately 100 nodes (and almost 200 computers) distributed throughout the U.S. and several other countries.* These nodes are connected mostly by leased telephone lines and, in a few cases, by leased satellite channels.

Many of the important concepts, such as packet switching, commonly used in several operational networks, were developed by these research projects. The results of these developments had immediate positive impacts on the computer science community, and ARPANET became very popular within colleges and universities. In a technical sense, ARPANET is the real father of modern academic networking in the United States.

The host computers were those involved in research projects supported by DARPA. Thus the early ARPANET served two primary purposes—it connected an important group of computer scientists who were working on problems of interest to the entire group, and it served as a pioneering research vehicle for development work on networking. A. Newell and R. Sproull report that

> [ARPANET] hosts still represent the full spectrum of university and industrial research groups in computer science, but also now include numerous military organizations with diverse operational missions. The network is essentially saturated.... The traffic consists largely

of mail messages and files, the latter containing programs, data, or text. There is substantial remote access, and several organizations use the net to do all their computing remotely. The use of the ARPANET has become intergral to the operation of many of the organizations connected to it.[4]

A problem of ARPANET in higher education has been its strict policy of limited access. Since it serves both research and operational Defense Department roles, ARPANET has not been able to expand to satisfy the needs of academic computer scientists who are not part of the DARPA community. ARPANET has obviously been unable to expand to accommodate faculty in other disciplines.

CSNET

Because of ARPANET restrictions on membership, the University of Wisconsin at Madison, on behalf of 15 other participating institutions, submitted a networking proposal to the National Science Foundation. In January 1981, NSF approved funding of approximately $5 million for a computer science research network (CSNET). CSNET is a community effort to provide open network services throughout the United States to computer scientists. There is cooperation between the Department of Defense and NSF to allow message communication between CSNET users and ARPANET sites. Presently 19 CSNET members also participate in ARPANET.

At the end of 1982 there were about 70 participating sites in the first phases of CSNET. An NSF program solicitation for an organization to manage, operate, and develop CSNET, describes the network as follows:

> The Computer Science Research Network (CSNET) is a project of the National Science Foundation that is intended to provide network services and access for all qualified computer science researchers. It is a logical network utilizing the services of several physical networks.... Over the long term, CSNET must meet the network needs of the computer science research community sufficiently well to generate its own financial support.[5]

CSNET is growing rapidly among computer science departments. There are three major kinds of services the network will eventually offer, although only the first was operational at the end of 1982:

- network mail including an addressing (directory) facility

---

*The networking technology is spreading so rapidly that it is very difficult to give an accurate count of the number of nodes or institutions involved. The most up-to-date (April 1985) count is: ARPANET, 1155 nodes (includes Defense Department sites); BITNET, 357 nodes at 114 sites; CSNET, 104 nodes; EARN (European), 156 nodes at 119 sites; MAILNET, 23 nodes; NETNORTH (Canadian), 40 nodes at 20 sites; and USENET, 1150 nodes.

- file transfer from one CSNET host to another
- remote log-in (the ability to use a remote host as if it were local)

EDUNET

In 1979, EDUCOM, a nonprofit consortium of more than 450 participating colleges and universities, announced the operational phase of EDUNET, a computer network that was founded to meet the *general* networking needs of higher education. The design of EDUNET came from the work of The Planning Council on Computing in Education and Research, which was composed of about 20 universities. The Council met for several years to study the types of networking arrangements that could best lead to a self-sustaining organization capable of providing viable academic network services. The Planning Council grew from ideas developed at three seminars conducted in late 1972 and early 1973 by EDUCOM with the support of the National Science Foundation.

EDUNET's primary focus has been to make it easy for people located throughout the world to interact directly with sophisticated computer resources supported by 18 host institutions.

EDUNET has evolved into an international computing network for higher education, research organizations, and not-for-profit companies. To promote the sharing of computerized resources, EDUNET provides access to specialized programs, services, and databases of 17 leading university computer centers in the United States. In addition, the University of Stockholm, Sweden recently became the 18th, and the first international, supplier.

Typical services include electronic mail and conferencing, access to unique computer hardware (e.g., the CRAY-1 supercomputer at the University of Minnesota), database management, modeling, and hundreds of programs in topical subject areas. EDUNET services are used by administrators, faculty, and students in more than 150 participating institutions. Services can be accessed through terminals, microcomputers, and word processors with communications capabilities. Local access is available in 250 U.S. cities and 30 foreign countries through public data communication companies such as TELENET and TYMNET.

Electronic mail and computer-based conferencing are the fastest-growing services provided by EDUNET suppliers. A new EDUCOM activity is MAILNET, a project to transfer the electronic messaging facilities developed by the CSNET project beyond the computer science research community to all of higher education. MAILNET will link together local campus-based electronic mail systems to support transmission of messages and documents between persons on different campuses—all of whom use their own local electronic mail systems. Virtually any campus electronic mail system may connect to MAILNET regardless of the type of computer or operating system used.

BITNET

BITNET (in mid-1984) is a network of about 175 computers located at approximately 60 universities. The first link was established between The City University of New York and Yale in May 1981. The network is based on a software product developed and used internally by IBM to support a multinational internal corporate network (VNET) of approximately 1400 nodes. The software provides store-and-forward message capabilities. The only special networking hardware required is a modem and a leased telephone line to the nearest BITNET host.

In the past, BITNET software was available only on IBM computers, but recently communication protocols were developed at Pennsylvania State University to enable several types of computers made by Digital Equipment Corporation to be part of BITNET. Ira Fuchs, one of the organizers of BITNET, describes it in the following way:

> The primary purpose of BITNET is to facilitate communications among universities by lowering the threshold of effort normally associated with other means of exchange. BITNET was designed using simple, inexpensive software and cost-effective telecommunications facilities. Thus an institution can connect to BITNET easily, with negligible programming effort and cost, providing speedy and simple access for faculty and staff. BITNET users share information via electronic mail, specifically in the form of interactive messages, text files, and computer programs.[6]

Each site pays for the cost of the telephone link to the next BITNET site. The administrative, technical, and operational costs of running the network are shared by each participating organization. BITNET will soon extend into Canada and Europe.

USENET

USENET, an informal network of approximately 600 computer systems running the UNIX Operating System (UNIX is a trademark of Bell Laboratories) is similar in many ways to BITNET. Several years ago students extended a communications package that is part of the UNIX system to include a news facility. This facility is really an electronic bulletin board to which sites may subscribe for various services ranging from news about data communications and microcomputers to wine tasting and jokes. An extensive electronic mail facility is a part of USENET. Systems can enter and leave USENET very easily since there is really no central administrative structure. One drawback of the informality of this network is that users must know, and specify, valid routings through the network to reach users at other sites.

Library Networks

There are several important library networks supporting activities in higher education that are very different from those described in the preceding paragraphs. The largest of these networks is OCLC (Online Computer Library Center) which was established in 1971 to provide cataloging support to libraries in Ohio. The organization has now grown into an international network serving all types of libraries. Several regional networks collaborated with OCLC to spread its services throughout the United States and into Canada and the United Kingdom. Two other major bibliographic systems have emerged in the United States—WLN (the Washington Library Network) and RLIN (the Research Libraries Information Network).

It is beyond the scope of this paper to explore these networks in any depth, but they must be discussed briefly because of their uniqueness and importance. These networks have emerged not along discipline lines like CSNET or COGNET, nor because a technology was available like BITNET or UNENET, but because of functional specialization and the need for resource sharing on a grand scale. Large bibliographic information retrieval systems face many of the problems of other networks, and in addition, they have specialized technical and legal concerns. For example, there are very complex legal, political, and economic implications concerning the sharing and exchange of bibliographic data among operating libraries. Who owns the data and how may it be distributed? Many of the organizational and technical developments in this field are such that precedents and ground rules do not yet exist.

Several companies provide abstracting and indexing services that are widely used in higher education as well as in other market areas. These services are usually provided through campus libraries with trained staff members serving as the interface to the information retrieval networks.

LEGAL AND POLICY ISSUES

From these brief selected descriptions it is clear that university networks in the United States are growing both in type and size, that efforts to categorize them are difficult, and that efforts to control them would be impossible. Because they are heterogeneous, campus telecommunications facilities are difficult to manage. In addition, to reach the academic community on a broad basis one must have access to and use of many different networks, a tedious procedure at best. Obviously the networking picture in American higher education is confusing now and growing more so each year.

In this section we will discuss several issues that have legal implications. As non-lawyers, we cannot address these issues from a legal perspective. However, we will mention them and give our view of the technical challenges associated with each.

Security

As the number of users gaining access to a computer system through a network increases, the probability of a security breach becomes higher. Since this probability is very small, the fear of exposure should not overshadow the benefits of networking. But network users should be aware that other individuals are using the system outside of their department, university, or country. Computer systems can be penetrated, so users must take appropriate precautions.

For academic systems it is useful to divide data that should receive special protection into two classes. First, there is data owned by the university whose loss would be financially injurious or embarrassing to the university. Examples include test answers, grades, salaries, purchase agreements, proposed changes in administrative policies, etc. Commercial enterprises face a similar exposure. For either the commercial or the educational institution, the remedies could include standalone systems, data encryption, secure operating systems (completely secure operating systems are beyond the state of the art), or network nonparticipation.

Because of the nature of university work, a second class of data should be considered. An example is data that represents ideas prior to publication. The loss of attribution of a tenured professor's new theorem in an abstruse branch of mathematics could be a loss of fame, perhaps significant to history and to pride, but not to commerce. How then can a value be placed on the loss? What recourse could one take? This example was chosen to avoid commercial overtones, but the theft of an idea whose publication could lead to a tenured position might have clear financial implications. Perhaps a clearer example of financial loss would be the loss of a patent because confidential information is widely circulated over a network too much in advance of filing a patent application.

Faculty members often serve as consultants to government or private industry. Confidential data may be created or used by the faculty member during the course of this consultancy. In the event of the loss of such data from a system owned by the university, what recourse would the government or private industry have against the consultant or the university? How can the faculty member assure protection of the data as the contract obligates him to do? If the network were international and if the research were in cryptography, who could insure that the Munitions Act would not be violated?

Privacy issues have not been mentioned. The law covering such matters might be vastly different from the law protecting other types of data discussed in this section. However, from the computer scientist's point of view, there is no difference in the protection mechanisms involved.

Junk Mail and Unmonitored Bulletin Boards

Normally junk mail is no more than an inconvenience, costing only a few seconds a day to throw material away. For networks, the issue of unwanted correspondence is more serious. First, it is easier to create junk mail in a network. A few key strokes—far easier than stuffing envelopes—are all that is required. Since the effort is relatively easy, the volume is potentially higher. Furthermore, there is the potential that the recipient must unwillingly expend his own resources to receive junk mail. This expenditure could come in a variety of ways including the loss of the communications channel availability, or local storage availability being filled by unwanted material. How can one protect oneself? Since in many instances of academic networking, the user does not pay directly for either the communications or

systems cost, there is no brake to hold back junk mail. Are unlisted electronic addresses sufficient?

Libel and Defamation

It is interesting to note that the ease mentioned above with which a file can be transmitted to many others raises questions of libel. If a libelous electronic note that is retransmitted widely results in denial of tenure, might there not be possible legal action?

Unmonitored bulletin boards provide an opportunity for mischief ranging from undergraduate pranks to calls for insurrection. While the authors have no knowledge of such misuses, the potential is real. Would the courts draw a parallel between electronic and physical bulletin boards in a labor relations dispute? What controls should be put in place to avoid the misuse and allow the obvious benefits?

Copyright/Licensing Issues

Most software and hardware vendors have licenses limiting the use of a product to a particular user, or for a particular purpose (e.g., instructional use only). The advent of computer networks and local area networks make a university's ability to enforce these vendors' policies exceedingly difficult. A pirated piece of software can easily be sent to many network users without laborious copying of the program. Perhaps new technologies will obviate these difficulties, but the approach is not clear at this point.

Network Control and Funding

The ultimate evolution of approaches to funding of academic networks is not yet clear. Some networks are supported by granting agencies, others by participation fees covering various levels of use, others by incremental charges for each use, and still others by a combination of these methods.

One might think that in a network of peer institutions, one node or one institution would dominate the amount of traffic generated and consequently create the need to balance equitably the charges for network use. In the BITNET example, the fundamental assumption is that such a node does not and will not exist. There are no charges for individual messages. Organizations pay for a communications channel to one other node in the network (the charge depends on the length of this connection), and they do not pay any marginal charges based on usage of the network.

A balanced usage pattern is not an unreasonable assumption for some types of networks—particularly store-and-forward message systems with a well-designed topology. For example, there is at least one large industrial network which validates this assumption. For that company, the traditional accounting practice would dictate that division A would charge division B for any excess utilization of A's resources by B. However, repeated test cases have shown that the cost of the differences between resource utilization were not sufficiently high to warrant the computer time required to calculate charges. The authors believe that this balance of usage is one of the reasons for BITNET's success.

Many networks are based on different pricing assumptions. For example, EDUNET performs a rebilling function for its participants. A significant amount of EDUNET's traffic is for remote use of computer-based applications that are much more costly than message forwarding. A few EDUNET hosts account for a large portion of the network activity. In this case a "balance of trade" does not exist, and hosts charge for usage on a monthly basis.

Control of what traffic is allowed on the network might seem to be the natural province of the university administration, subject to the usual practices of academic freedom. However, for a heavily used network with peer nodes in multiple countries, it is beyond the state of the art to exercise any substantial direct control. One can issue guidelines, have awareness meetings, etc., but direct monitoring is simply not feasible. To the authors of this chapter it is not clear whether technical impossibility of control is sufficient legal protection for the academic administration.

Incentives for the Growth of Networks

The authors believe that computing systems are cost justified on other than networking requirements, and that once a computer is justified, networking is a natural, straightforward, and relatively inexpensive next step that is often taken. Therefore an obvious incentive to more networking is to increase the availability of computers within the higher education community.

A good way to increase the availability of computing capabilities in higher education is to increase tax benefits for the student or faculty member who buys a system

or for the individual or corporation donating a system to a university. Such tax laws already exist, but their liberalization could significantly increase the penetration of university networks and the concomitant benefits. At the same time a reduction in the cost of data transmission would be beneficial. Perhaps educational discounts for data communication facilities and tax benefits for the donation of bandwidth should become part of our tax laws.

These initiatives could have the benefit of increasing networking in less well endowed institutions. Most of the major institutions in the United States have several computers and a wide variety of networking facilities. In fact, some institutions have stated their intent to make a microcomputer a condition for entrance. At a cost (not necessarily the price) of approximately $60,000 for four years of education, a computer for another $5,000 is not that significant. Consequently, the liberalization of tax benefits would have their most significant impact on the less well endowed institution. This would clearly benefit the United States in the same sense that the Land Grant Act and the GI Bill have encouraged a broad and deep penetration of educational opportunities.

Another approach is for state education departments to decide to develop well-planned and integrated regional facilities. For example:

> The Center for Learning Technologies of the New York State Education Department, is investigating the possibility of developing a comprehensive computer-assisted communication system (NYSNET). Its primary purpose will be to insure that all people in the education community of the State have access to the most advanced communication capabilities that modern technology can provide at an acceptable cost.[7]

FUTURE TRENDS IN ACADEMIC NETWORKING

The limited number of nonUnited States nodes participating in American educational networks is a mystery to the authors (except for obvious policies in CSNET and ARPANET). With a few exceptions, there are no heavily used academic computer links from the United States to other countries. There are several interesting networking activities in the European higher education community. Are there policies in place in other countries that limit access? Is it the expense of telecommunications links, or is it just that the evolution of American academic networking has not reached the stage where international links are of great importance? It seems obvious that academic networking connections between the U.S. and other countries will grow in importance as the technology evolves.

Since there are no political forces to limit the number of different academic networks, the authors believe they will continue to grow in size and to proliferate in variety. This growth will be compounded by the constantly decreasing cost of computer hardware. This proliferation has obvious associated costs and disadvantages. However, the newness of this field and the dynamic growth of new ideas are such that it is premature to try to restrict the growth with artificial means. Gateways among networks offer the only reasonable technical and organizational approach to the problems inherent in this proliferation.

NOTES

1. K. Wilson, The State of U.S. Science-1982, (Feb. 23, 1983) (prepared statement submitted to the Committee on Science and Technology, U.S. House of representatives).

2. COGNET Planning Committee & Departments of Psychology & Computer Science, Proposal for COGNET—A Computer Network for Cognitive Science (Carnegie-Mellon University: March 1981).

3. G. Brown, J. Miller, & T. Keenan, EDUNET: Report of the Summer Study on Information Networks 323 (New York: Wiley, 1967).

4. Newell & Sproull, *Computer Networks: Prospects for Scientists,* 215 Science, Feb. 12, 1982, at 847.

5. National Science Foundation, Mathematical and Computer Sciences Division, program solicitation (Nov. 5, 1982).

6. Fuchs, *BITNET—Because It's Time,* 3 I.B.M. Perspectives on Computing, Mar. 1983, at 17.

7. New York State Network for Education Telecommunications (NYSNET), Request for Information (Albany, N.Y.: State Education Department, Mar. 31, 1983).

CHAPTER 15

INTERNATIONAL PUBLIC SERVICE DATA SYSTEMS

WILSON P. DIZARD, JR.

Other papers in this volume have focused on problems involving commercial network services. This is realistic since such services represent the largest single segment of electronic data traffic worldwide. It is also important because the U.S. private sector is the major international purveyor of such information services.

There would be a gap in this volume, however, if another facet of international information flow is not included. This is the area of noncommercial information networking, involving what might be generally classified as public service data.

The subject tends to be ignored because, for the present, the amount of such networking is small compared to commercial operations. The largest single source of public networking is the United Nations and its agencies. Together they operate over 300 data bases, most of them international in scope.[1] The United States government also operates international public networks. One of these is the National Library of Medicine's MEDLARS/MEDLINE system. At the present time, the system has direct links with a number of foreign countries, as well as cooperative data-transfer arrangements with the World Health Organization and the Pan American Health Organization.

Moreover, public service networking is growing, with the expectation that it will expand considerably in the coming years for a variety of reasons. Here we will take a look at its role, with particular attention to the U.N. systems, for the purpose of evaluating their relationship to overall American policy and practices in international information transport.

The future of these public service networks cannot be examined in isolation, however. They are part of a larger body of international information issues which tend, however, to be treated separately by U.S. policymakers. There have been good reasons for this reluctance to link issues. Primarily they involve a feeling that aggregating international information issues would work against American interests, particularly in encouraging trends toward more international controls over information resources.

Nevertheless, the time has come to look at these information-transport issues in a more cohesive, integrative manner. Specifically, they need to be evaluated in terms of their role in overall information resources management in the international arena.

It is a subject that makes Americans uncomfortable. As noted above, it raises fears of curbs on information flow, a reaction justified by the tone of the debate on information in international forums during the past decade. The issue has tended to settle into a confrontation between those few countries, lead by the United States, that advocate lowering barriers to global information flow, as against the majority that support greater restrictions, based on political, economic, and ideological claims. The issues are encapsulated in a massive UNESCO-sponsored study on information policy produced by an international commission in 1979 under the

WILSON P. DIZARD, JR. ● Mr. Dizard is a vice-president of Kalba Bowen Associates, a communications and information policy and management consulting firm in Cambridge, Massachusetts, and a senior associate, Center for Strategic and International Studies at Georgetown University, in Washington, D.C.

leadership of former Irish foreign minister Sean McBride. The McBride study is an attempt to establish a consensus between free-flow advocates and those calling for more restrictive approaches. The attempt is only partially successful, given the sharp ideological differences between the two sides.[2]

The ideological issue cannot, of course, be easily dismissed. Important principles are involved, with long-term effects on the shape and purposes of the international information system. There may be temporary truces and limited agreements in the debate, but the basic differences will be around for a long time. The United States, in particular, has an obligation to continue to uphold free-flow principles.

Having said this, there is a case for setting aside, to the extent possible, these ideological aspects in order to examine some of the more pragmatic developments in the international information pattern. While ideologues argue, this pattern is expanding swiftly. A worldwide communications network is being built; the amount of data moving through the networks increases in quantum leaps. Practical decisions on keeping the system efficient are needed constantly. One example is the current effect to develop international rules for technical standards in the proposed new Integrated Digital Services Network (ISDN), a system for permitting a high degree of interchangeability of traffic between hitherto incompatible networks throughout the world.

These and other subjects are falling, slowly but surely, under the rubric of what can be called global information resources management. Whatever our hesitations, the world is moving toward an international pattern of more, not less, rules and regulations in this area.

The United States has an important role in helping shape these new global information resource patterns. There will be increasing efforts by other countries to promote restrictive institutional controls in this area. An early manifestation of this has been UNESCO's attempts to establish itself as the international channel for both ideological and operational responsibility in this area. Another example is the attempt to expand the ITU's mandate to include information matters—a proposal put forward by the Japanese at the organization's 1982 plenipotentiary conference in Nairobi.

The United States, as noted, has good reasons to resist these attempts to consolidate information issues in any international organization. Our interests are best served by keeping the subject diffused throughout the international system. Any organizational concentration would clearly work against us, given the restrictionist predelictions of the majority of countries which would be involved in any such venture.

This argues for more, not less, attention to the development of a more cohesive U.S. strategy, one that would continue to try to limit the trend toward international restrictions, while at the same time clarifying the more positive aspects of our overall approach to global information resource management problems. As noted above, this would cover the full range of communications and information issues such as the radio spectrum and the international standard-setting needs of ISDN and related technologies.

Here we will take a look at the division between commercial and publicly-supported data bases and networking arrangements as an example of the opportunities and pitfalls involved in integrating American policy in this area.

This is an issue that is relatively clear-cut in our domestic policies. Public policy historically favors commercial operation of information systems. Public-sector operations are limited specifically to certain areas where government involvement appears justified. The domestic information industry has served a watchdog function, monitoring ways in which it can supplant government information activities. The Reagan administration, in particular, has attempted to reduce government data-base operations where it feels industry can perform a similar service more efficiently.

This domestic policy takes on different dimensions in the international arena. Whatever preferences the United States may have favoring commercial data-base and networking operations run up against an opposite trend abroad favoring publicly-controlled data resources. This is true overseas at two levels—nationally and internationally.

Nationally, there is a presumption in most countries favoring public control of data resources, together with a predeliction for limiting reliance on foreign data bases as much as possible. The trend is by no means limited to Communist and Third World countries, with their ideological preference for information controls. It is also strong in Europe, where governments see dependence on foreign (i.e., American) data bases as not only undesirable from an overall national security standpoint but also as inhibiting the development of domestic data and networking capabilities. It is a point made forcefully in an influential French government policy study of information policy, the so-called *Nora-Minc Report* published in 1978.[3]

Reducing the conflicts involved in this kind of data sovereignty issue is an important part of any U.S. approaches to shaping a viable international information resources management environment. It is a subject that deserves continuing study within this context. As noted earlier, public service data resources are, for the present, a relatively small part of the overall international pattern. There are, however, strong indications that this will be a growing sector as pressures increase for limiting commercial operations in favor of resources operated by public entities. Given this possible shift, the United States needs to know where its policy interests lie in this area.

To get a perspective on the subject, we will look at the largest single example of international public-sector data resources and networking—the information systems operated by the United Nations and its agencies. As the country that supplies a quarter of the U.N.'s annual budget, the United States is a major financial contributor to these systems. It is also a major supplier, and user, of information from the systems. The U.N. is a useful test case in relating U.S. policy toward a more comprehensive view of issues involved in global information resources management.

The United Nations sponsors a wide range of international data resources. The *Directory of U.N. Information Systems* lists over 300 systems, operated by more than 35 agencies. Many of these systems are small and obscure. The "World Fish Catch Database" is not one that concerns most of us, but the "World Weather Watch" affects us to the point of influencing how we dress each day.

The United Nations inherited a number of its information activities from the League of Nations and other international organizations which were in existence in 1945, the year the U.N. was founded. However, most of its information systems are new, set up in response to postwar needs, and specifically the requirements of the major powers. The effectiveness of its individual information resources can usually be measured by their relevance to the interests of these large powers. Thus the International Atomic Energy Authority's Nuclear Information System (INIS) has been very successful, primarily because it serves U.S. and Soviet interests to have a central data base under U.N. auspices on nuclear technology.

The major U.N. information services are in three categories. The first consists of bibliographic information services like INIS, which collect, store, and distribute a wide range of materials on specific subjects. The storage and distribution modes may involve on-line computers, magnetic tape, microfiche, or traditional print. The Food and Agricultural Organization's AGRIS system provides data on food-productivity research, a subject where information transfer can have long-term consequences for the health and welfare of everyone. The complexity of maintaining a global information base is well illustrated in AGRIS; it deals with over 500 agricultural documentation services in 50 countries, containing materials in 22 languages.

Another area of U.N. information activity involves monitoring services like the "World Weather Watch." A particularly important monitoring service is the World Health Organization's epidemiological service, a worldwide telex network that tracks diseases through notifications under international health regulations.

A third major activity is record keeping and dissemination, such as the Patent Information Network, run by the World Intellectual Property Organization (WIPO) with its 7.6 million citations, and the ITU international Frequency Registration Board, with a data bank of over 1.25 million notifications of radio frequency registrations. A major record-keeping effort is conducted by the U.N. Statistical Office, particularly in the economic area. The office's commodity trade file has over 90 million transaction records, with about 15 million updated annually.

The U.N. has also sponsored useful projects for encouraging common standards for improving international data flow. Technical committees of the ITU have been particularly active in developing technical compatability standards, such as the current ISDN project. At another level, a UNESCO project known as UNISIST has been the catalyst over the past decade for promoting cooperative networking of science and technology information. One of the barriers to such cooperation is the lack of agreed-upon terminology in transferring information from one S & T information system to another. This problem has spawned a UNISIST project to sort out this special linguistic difficulty, with its own data base in Vienna.[4]

UNISIST's goal is a coordinated S & T network interconnecting many national, regional, and international grids. The project has been active in encouraging the development of new data bases such as the DEVSIS system for economic development information and POPINS for population studies information. These new data bases have particular problems because they are intended primarily to serve developing countries, many of which do not have the information infrastructure to process and distribute complex data. Getting the right mix of usable data to these countries has been difficult to accomplish.

The U.N.'s information-resources systems leave much to be desired. They suffer from the organization's heavy-handed bureaucracy, and particularly its tendency to sacrifice managerial and technical competence to the political need to keep its variegated member-state constituents happy. Information resource activities tend to be underfunded, primarily because they do not have strong political support within the organization. The U.N. has not been able to take advantage of many of the newer communications and information technologies (satellites, for instance) because of funding problems.[5]

There is also the question of the integrity of some U.N. data. This is generally not a problem with technical data bases where everyone has an interest in straightforward information. It is, however, an ongoing concern in the more general areas of social science data. There have been disturbing examples of tampering with research data, particularly in the economic area, where the U.N. has a staff of 3000 specialists and an annual budget of $300 million. Attempts to alter or suppress data which do not conform to the U.N.'s officially-endorsed New International Economic Order concept have been documented.[6]

The U.N. information systems work best when they deal with relatively objective areas of science and technology, an important but partial component of international information flow. The systems are weakest in providing useful data in politically sensitive areas such as disarmament, arms control, and human rights. In theory, at least, the U.N.'s supranational status should allow it a constructive, useful monitoring role in these areas. In fact, it is not able to play this role given the conflicting interests of the major powers and, more recently, the Third World.

In summary, the large, growing United Nations data resource system is a mixed bag in terms of U.S. interests. It does some things very well and others less so.

Nevertheless, there are good reasons to support the overall system, with some caveats. One of these is to insure that U.N. data bases do not compete with other public or private systems that can do similar information tasks more effectively. Another is to assure that these systems are kept reasonably free of the information-restrictionist philosophy that has taken hold in the more political parts of the U.N. organization.

It might be useful to debate the value of individual parts of the U.N. data resources system. The point of this chapter, however, is to suggest that these activities are part of a larger subject—the management of global information resources—in which the United States has strategic interests. We need to rethink our national reluctance to look at our overall information policies in this light. Whether or not we like it, a new kind of international information policy pattern is developing. It contains elements that clearly affect U.S. interests at the political, economic, and ideological levels.

Despite these negative factors, there are also opportunities for influencing the evolving pattern in positive ways. It will happen, however, only if we are prepared to look at the overall pattern, and not simply at its disconnected parts. Such an undertaking will take time, primarily because we do not have the organizational structure at the federal government level to handle this kind of coordinated approach. Moving toward such a coordinated policy can, however, be an important step in strengthening our effectiveness to handle the new global information resources management challenge.

The U.N. data resources system described above is a relatively small part of the overall pattern. However, as suggested earlier, it is an interesting test case. As an issue, it has been handled by U.S. policymakers largely in isolation from other information issues, to the point of being virtually ignored. Yet it is relevant to the prospects of a more integrated American approach in dealing with the trend towards more restrictive international information policies and practices.

If we were to look at U.N. data resources within such a framework, we could better identify policy options that are now hidden in the tangle of uncoordinated information issues. These options could involve either supporting the present U.N. data resources pattern basically in its present form, or proposing that it be cut back, or that it be expanded.

Given a coherent policy framework, the third option might prove to be attractive, with political and economic benefits at a relatively low cost. U.N. data systems could, for instance, be an important element in helping correct the imbalance in world information flow, particularly between the industrialized North and the developing South. Stronger support for U.N. activities in this area could be part of our strategy for keeping the information-flow debate focus on ending the imbalance without recourse to political and economic actions aimed at restricting information traffic internationally.

Any upgrading of U.N. data systems would involve two related areas. The first is the question of whether additional data bases should be added to the system. There are a number of perennial candidates for an expansion of the organization's data resources, involving such areas as health information, environmental monitoring, and remote sensing from space.

The other area is the question of improving the capabilities of the present U.N. data programs, making them more available to member-states. With some exceptions, the U.N.'s communications capabilities are chronically weak. Successive secretary-generals have complained that they cannot provide needed communications services, particularly in Third World areas, because of the organization's poor communications resources. An American-supported program for upgrading the U.N.'s worldwide networking capabilities, including on-line data transmission, could have important effects in defusing the current arguments about Northern dominance of global data resources.

One practical example involves the U.S. government's MEDLARS/MEDLINE medical research information network. Currently the system operates primarily within North America, with extensions to Europe and Japan. An improved U.N. communications capability, operated through the World Health Organization, could make this valuable data base available in Third World areas now denied access.

There are policy advantages and disadvantages in each of the prospects suggested above. The important point, however, is that we will not be able to judge them accurately until we have a more comprehensive strategy for measuring our overall interests in the fast-developing area of global information resource management. We need such a strategy if only to be better able to counter the forces which are pressing for greater restrictions on information flow. However, there are also more positive reasons. These involve our own potential ability to propose constructive policies and actions based on the premise of an open global communication system. In the long run, this is where the political and economic advantage lies for the United States.

NOTES

1. UNITED NATIONS, DIRECTORY OF UNITED NATIONS INFORMATION SYSTEMS Vol. i, at 465 (Geneva: Intergovernmental Board for Information Systems, June 1980).

2. For a useful overview of United Nations policies on information flow, see Questions Relating to Information, 35 GAOR (Agenda Item 59) (Dec. 1980).

3. S. NORA & A. MINC, THE COMPUTERIZATION OF SOCIETY (Cambridge, Mass.: MIT Press, 1980).

4. A summary of UNISIST accomplishments and future plans is given in Final Report of the Intergovernmental Conference on Scientific and Technological Information for Development of UNISIST II, UNESCO Doc. (1979).

5. The opportunities and difficulties in this area are described in Miller & Wild, *A Strategy for International Information Systems*, 69 SPECIAL LIBRARIES, Nov. 1978, at 435–42.

6. Examples can be found in *A Third World Bias at the U.N.*, BUS. WK., July 20, 1981, at 156–161.

CHAPTER 16

INTERNATIONAL ACCESS TO MEDICAL DATA BASES

RICHARD JAY SOLOMON
with the collaboration of
ITHIEL DE SOLA POOL

HISTORY OF *MEDLARS* AND INTERNATIONAL DATABASE ACCESS

The National Library of Medicine has pioneered in developing computerized scientific information services. The history of computerized bibliographic aids and that of the NLM's efforts to use machine processing for indexing, cataloging, and retrieval are almost synonymous. NLM began using computers to prepare citations for the *Index Medicus* in the late 1950s aided by a grant from the Council on Library Resources. This experimentation led to MEDLARS (Medical Literature Analysis and Retrieval System) with funds provided by the National Heart Institute.

MEDLARS became operational in 1964 after three years of design effort. Retrieval of citations from *Index Medicus* tapes using MEDLARS began for the medical research community in 1967. Using a computer process called "batch search," the tapes would be scanned after a researcher had selected index terms from a special thesaurus. These terms would be keypunched and submitted to a computer, which would match them against an index of what was on the tapes; the citations would then be read by the computer from the tapes and printed on a high-speed device for mailing to the researcher. Compared with today's "online" systems, where a user connected directly to the computer gets information only a few seconds after typing in thesaurus terms, turnaround times for the batch processes during the 1960s were measured in weeks.

Access to machine-based MEDLARS by foreign users was originally by distribution of tapes to European centers which had quid pro quo agreements with NLM. This began immediately after the tapes became available in the mid-1960s. We discuss these agreements further in section 3 on restraint of trade issues.

Online Access to MEDLARS MEDLINE

Research and development on computers that would permit continuous online access by sharing resources between users—called "timesharing"—began development at the same time as work on MEDLARS, in the mid-1960s. Initially, high costs and poor performance of both data communications and data terminals contributed to the slow acceptance of remote online systems.

One of the first scientific databases to be offered in an online fashion was based on MEDLARS. NLM began a

RICHARD JAY SOLOMON ● Mr. Solomon is a research associate of the MIT Research Program on Communications Policy, Center for International Studies, Massachusetts Institute of Technology, Cambridge, Massachusetts. He is editor and publisher of *International Networks*, a newsletter on world communications technology and policy. ITHIEL DE SOLA POOL ● Professor Pool was the director of the MIT Research Program on Communications Policy, Center for International Studies, Massachusetts Institute of Technology, Cambridge, Massachusetts, and the Arthur and Ruth Sloan Professor of Political Science at MIT. He died in March 1984.

timesharing experiment in 1970 for bibliographic retrieval using an abridged database of articles from the most important English language journals in clinical medicine. The service, called AIM–TWX, was initially offered on Western Union's TWX (now Telex-II) teletypewriter network, with alternate access via ordinary direct distance dial (DDD) telephone lines. It is significant that many users opted to access the NLM timesharing machine directly via DDD primarily because communication costs could be lowered using telephone WATS and tie lines. Overseas users had the option of using Telex connections to TWX since U.S. as well as foreign telephone tariffs generally forbade international data access at that time.

Users of the experimental system report that the "AIM" part of AIM–TWX was quite satisfactory, but the communications offered by TWX left much to be desired. To remedy this, NLM experimented with new systems, including Tymnet which had evolved from Tymshare's dedicated data access network. One of Tymshare's first nondedicated customers was NLM's MEDLINE network, which began one year after the experiment with AIM–TWX. MEDLINE customers could dial Tymshare ports in a number of cities, or have direct connections from dedicated terminals to the Tymshare network, and then access NLM computers for an online search. Service was also offered to defense and other government researchers via a connection to the ARPANET, an experimental packet network of computers operated by the Department of Defense.

In 1972, MEDLINE offered citations from over 1,000 journals for the current year and the previous three years. It was essentially the MEDLARS database for those years offered online instead of via a time-consuming batch search process.

Development of Modern Data Communications

To keep things in perspective in this rapidly changing field, it should be emphasized that distinctions between online and batch processes are blurring because of distributed small but powerful computers linked together by high-speed data networks that we discuss below. MEDLARS and other databases still offer a batch service for older citations where the user submits requests via the online system, and citations are searched and printed overnight in a so-called background job.

In a classic case of market-push, the development of timesharing systems spurred the FCC to open up the industry to competition in intercity data networks and

data terminal devices. One result was the growth of specialized communications common carriers, such as TELENET and TYMNET, designed and tariffed especially for online data access to timesharing systems. Another was the proliferation of inexpensive computer terminals and improved interconnection devices. And most important is the offering in the U.S. of several thousand online databases, accessible to the general public at quite low telecommunications costs. These systems and networks were several years ahead of similar efforts to provide database access in Western Europe, and the ease of interconnection of computer terminals (and even of computers) is still far better in the U.S. than elsewhere. We discuss comparative access and costs between U.S. and European databases in later sections of this chapter.

Had inexpensive data communications links and devices not been introduced, the MEDLARS system would most likely still be the same today as it was a decade ago. However, cheap telecommunication is not always a boon, for electrons and microwaves respect no borders and tend to change traditional ways of doing things just as they bring other benefits of instantaneous communications. For example, the MEDLARS contracts with foreign computer centers do not specify that users external to their borders cannot access these links; some contracts even state that this is permissible. Restrictions on access are set by the nations themselves, usually through the telecommunications tariffs, or by general agreement among the user community. However due to open access to telecommunications links across European borders, backed by agreement among the European nations themselves, enforcement of such tariff restrictions is a pure fiction. Enforcement by NLM or its vendors has only been through password controls, which is extremely dificult to monitor. We discuss this further in later sections.

In many countries, inducements are offered to process data locally. It should not be surprising that a nationally-subsidized medical community could be encouraged by another government agency to do its bibliographic searching on domestic machines. In some cases MEDLARS services are offered at rates lower than those offered by NLM itself—even free in some countries. Despite subsidies, in general these institutional goals to localize data processing are often in conflict with the goals of the database user. The user prefers convenience in accessing systems, the opportunity to access competing services to maximize retrieval possibilities, and to minimize total costs. The telephone carriers, some of whom also dominate timesharing or data processing in their countries, want to maximize revenue and are not interested in competitive services.

Other subtle restrictions on the use of the NLM database overseas are designed to prevent data from being processed outside of a nation's borders. These rules are somewhat indirect, and rarely overtly stated in terms of computer processing. One rule concerns transmission lines used for data which are tariffed at a higher price than if used for voice, so a user may not send data over an ordinary telephone line. The other rule is that the device that attaches a digital computer terminal or computer to the analog telephone line (called a "modem" for modulator–demodulator) must be obtained from the telephone administration. Where the telephone administration is a powerful government agency, such as in West Germany, enforcement of such rules severely restricts the attaching of terminals and computers to the telephone system.

Technology is forcing a shift in these regulations, albeit much more slowly than in the U.S.

CURRENT INTERNATIONAL ACCESS TO BIOMEDICAL DATABASES

The ability to access MEDLARS in Europe via means other than national database centers has changed primarily because of two basic trends: (1) the growth of specialized data telecommunications networks, and (2) changes in the nature of database computing. The telecommunications changes are relevant to the current situation; while the computing changes are imminent, they will be discussed in later sections on future scenarios for scientific database systems.

During the past few years, the European telephone administrations have instituted several different types of networks optimized for the connection of terminals to timesharing computers. Most important to the users of database computers, such as those which offer MEDLARS, cost of service for access is not based on distance. Instead charges are normally related to the connection time and the amount (measured in bits) of data transmitted, plus a connection charge. As a result, a user often can access a distant timesharing system as easily, and at the same telecommunications cost, as a nearby machine.

These European systems are similar to the "packet nets" in the U.S., but the state-monopoly Post, Telegraph

and Telephone administrations (PTTs) have chosen not to pass all the savings on to the end user. On packet systems, data is only transmitted between terminals and computers when a key is pressed or a letter is received, instead of maintaining a continuous connection between two points, as on an ordinary telephone or telex circuit. This data traffic travels in relatively small packets and is switched or routed via a complex network of computers that also may process the data as well as transmit it. Though this technique shows distinct economies in line utilization, since most traffic on timesharing systems tends to be in small "bursts," traffic from traditional telex systems represent a threat to the PTTs' revenue base.

Technically, a worldwide system of packet data networks could equalize charges to virtually any point on the globe, since packet networks have the additional advantage of combining the distance-insensitive characteristics of satellite technology with computer switching. But, in practice, other factors have intervened, so that artificial pricing barriers to uniform-cost data transmission exist between Europe and North America.

European Data Networks

In the U.S., thousands of databases are being offered on hundreds of timesharing systems and via thousands of networks. These databases range from specialized systems such as NLM's MEDLINE to general services for consumers who have home computers or terminals. Similar services, plus specialized language databases, are now available in Europe, though some require direct access to the U.S. A few such services are being offered directly from Europe for U.S. consumption. These are mostly newswires and commodity services.

Most of the European PTTs have also established some national network for data communications and, in addition, have joined in a continent-wide consortium to provide data services, called Euronet. As a result of this dynamic environment in telecommunications carriage and end-user equipment, database timesharing systems have been able to proliferate in Europe as well as the U.S., though access is much more difficult and charges tend to be an order of magnitude higher than here.

To overcome some of the problems of access to U.S. databases, some American firms offer the full MEDLARS database via timesharing systems on Euronet. Due to PTT tariff barriers, there is a tradeoff between transatlantic data links and European data processing in favor of the latter for certain services. BRS has licensed Datastar in Geneva to offer MEDLARS using the proprietary BRS search system, and Lockheed similarly will mount MEDLARS tapes on a computer in London connected to Euronet. Separate copies of NLM's tapes are purchased for these European machines, since the NLM contracts prevent copying of the tapes (except for normal time-sharing computer operations at a single site). Later in this chapter we discuss other options that would be possible if the PTTs had a more liberal tariff policy under the concept of distributed data processing.

Though Euronet restricts its network host-computers to machines physically located in Europe, major European cities are also connected to the U.S. packet carriers, Tymnet and Telenet. MEDLARS may be accessed via these carriers from most developed nations either directly on NLM's computer in Bethesda, Maryland or on the computers of several private U.S. vendors who lease MEDLARS tapes. However, international charges on these services, plus high PTT access charges for the U.S. carriers, and other inconveniences, mediate against their use. Often it is cheaper to dial U.S. timesharing machines directly via international DDD, or to use international private lines, than to use the U.S. packet carriers. Most PTTs forbid this, but control is difficult. It is now permitted in the telephone tariffs of the United Kingdom and Japan.

The private U.S. vendors offer more extensive search services through superior software for searching, or a more comprehensive online coverage of MEDLARS, than those services an overseas user can get domestically from national centers. The private vendors keep more of MEDLARS online than NLM or most national timesharing centers do, so MEDLARS users have an incentive to use them. This is the only way they can compete with national MEDLARS centers in Europe, despite disincentives in the form of higher online charges and end-user problems with access. Other U.S. services such as *Chemical Abstracts* follow similar competitive patterns, though these services have less of an obligation to the national foreign database centers than NLM has.

RESTRAINT OF TRADE ISSUES

The National Library of Medicine has come under inceasing criticism in recent years by database vendors for practicing what appears to be restraint of trade in offering MEDLARS to end users. The basis behind these criticisms are primarily a set of agreements made with foreign medical research organizations to share input to

the MEDLARS database in exchange for some exclusivity in offering NLM database to their own nationals. These are called *quid pro quo* arrangements.

The Quid Pro Quo Arrangements

International access to the machine-searchable MED-LARS began as soon as the initial bibliographic tapes were available in 1964. Sweden and the United Kingdom began experimental testing of batch searching, and bilateral agreements, the initial quid pro quo arrangements, were drawn up then to share input data. These followed the general pattern that there be

> no transfer of monies between the participating country and NLM. NLM makes available the MEDLARS system, either through tapes or [when this became possible] on-line access to the NLM computer, technical documentation and training. The participating country must meet technical criteria involving personnel, equipment, and fiscal resources and have a user community large enough to justify an extensive computerized service activity. The participating country then provides and/or funds the indexing of journals for input to the MEDLARS database in return for access to the system. This concept is consistent with a policy ... that Federal information systems would be made available in return for some form of contribution.[1]

This policy has been modified several times. In March 1979, in response to pressure from the MEDLARS vendors, NLM sent this message to their contractees in the U.S.:

> The licensee is authorized to provide information services and products resulting from the use of these [MEDLARS] tapes to the U.S., its territories, or possessions, and to countries outside the U.S. *for which NLM does not have bilateral agreements.* [emphasis added]

This was the first time NLM recognized a private vendor offering MEDLARS outside of the U.S. without violating an assumed quid pro quo agreement. In effect, it made it possible for foreign users of MEDLARS to connect to other sources if they were willing to take the risks, and make the effort, of establishing such connections since transnational telecommunications links were readily available, though at some cost.

The next major step in a modification of the original agreements was a change in rate structure. In August 1981, again in response to vendor pressures, NLM stated:

This letter modifies any contract on an interim basis pending a change which our Board of Regents recommends on basic terms, procedures and fees. We expect to modify our arrangements to be more consistent with other tape generators and licensors where the total fee will be a combination of a basic fee plus a usage fee. We shall advise you as soon as the determination has been made as to the price structure. We plan to implement this change by January 1, 1982.

The fees were set at $4.00 per hour for each online user, and an offline or batch process fee of $0.01 per citation printed for a user. There was a minimum charge of $20,000 per year, which included tape copies of the entire MEDLARS updated backfile. For a user of a commercial service, these fees would be added on to the vendor's own costs and revenue requirements. Only services performed by an online database vendor are covered by this pricing schedule; novel, evolving technology could not fit this pattern, since usage might not be necessarily measured temporally or by batch printing increments.

There are several important points about these arrangements:

1. *The flow of medical information, like most information, is not a one-way flow.* This is a basic consideration in any policy adopted by the U.S. government in respect to information, particularly technical information. A rough examination of the MEDLARS citations in recent years would show that the percentage originating in the U.S. has remained relatively stable at about one-third of the total biomedical serial literature. In addition, more than one-half of the medical research in the U.S. is supported by NLM's parent National Institute of Health, giving NLM a certain responsibility in disseminating the results of that work.

2. *Furthermore, NLM's quid pro quo exchange agreements are quite important in the future since the costs of publishing overseas have continued to remain below those in the U.S. and the probabilities of using electronic methods for dissemination of research results may reduce the U.S. percentage.* With a large percentage of medical journals being published overseas, NLM has organized a valuable cooperative international system, mostly among governments or quasi-governmental organizations, which benefits U.S.

citizens as much if not more than foreign nationals.

3. *Most of the foreign organizations are governmental or quasi-governmental, reflecting the nature of their medical-care systems.* Bilateral agreements between governments are a more natural mechanism, though successful arrangements between private and public organizations across national boundaries can be demonstrated. Rarely, however, will the latter agreements be completely devoid of some governmental involvement.

Foreign MEDLARS Centers

In 1966, the U.S. approached the Organization for Economic Cooperation and Development (OECD) with an offer to set up a MEDLARS center in Europe as an operational batch-process information system. With the cost of international communications still at a high level then, any thought of direct access to a U.S. center would have been foolish. After three years of discussion, no decision could be made at OECD, and the pattern of national development of MEDLARS centers was underway by 1969.

NLM often found that more than one national center wanted to establish a MEDLARS database. Not wishing to interfere in foreign politics, they permitted the choice to be made by the country itself "after meeting certain criteria established by the NLM."[2] This is a nice way of saying that NLM did not want to get involved in messy affairs that were not relevant to their mission, but by acquiescing in restriction of access to only one center per country, NLM essentially created the environment for later accusations of restraint of trade.

One alternative to the national centers would have been to simply permit any and all to make copies of the tapes at a reasonable fee, but then the establishment of the valuable quid pro quo would have been quite difficult. Even more important, the operation of a computerized database, particularly maintenance, input of citations, and use of the thesaurus and index, required skills that NLM had to disseminate along with the tapes. This was particularly relevant in the early days, since very few computer centers had experience with databases and index programs the size of MEDLARS.

Not knowing that the database being created might have valuable commercial applications someday, and needing the citations from foreign medical journals—

including translation services and indexing help—NLM had no choice but to work within a system of bilateral agreements with other national centers. It was difficult enough in the late 1960s to convince skeptics that computerized database systems were cost-effective. It was harder still to imagine a future where multiple versions and competitive products might exist for something as esoteric as a scientific database, and in which private entrepreneurs would be using such databases for their business purposes.

As the network of quid pro quo agreements grew, many countries chose to maintain their own databases. But, as satellite communications drove downward the cost of transatlantic links, others linked directly to NLM computers. However, in general, foreign centers required their national users to link through dedicated lines or locally-based terminal computer interfaces. Canada, having a fully integrated telephone network with the U.S., chose initially to allow users to link directly to NLM when online service became available, but eventually made MEDLARS services available via a Canadian governmental center with telecommunications to NLM.

Had events in the late 1960s moved differently at OECD—and at the European telephone and telegraph administrations—we may have seen totally different patterns for MEDLARS access. By 1970 it was clear that transatlantic satellites and specialized terrestrial data networks were becoming an important force in data communications. With only one center in Europe, and one in the U.S., national centers would not have developed and the issues of restrictions might have taken a different course today. In fact, the incipient changes in technology, which tend to track anything related to computers, might have been much easier to introduce in 1981 if OECD could have collected its thoughts in 1966. This has obvious implications for the decisions we may be making in the next few years about the next generation of U.S.-sponsored public database systems.

OTHER MAJOR INTERNATIONAL ISSUES

Though the European systems have lagged behind the U.S., in recent years both European data networks and databases have made great strides. However, unlike the U.S., where minimum network restrictions are placed on the user accessing timesharing systems, either via direct dial telephone, packet carriers, or private circuits, European telephone administrations still have several layers of subtle barriers that prevent maximum efficiency

from the user standpoint. Why have restrictions? They do nothing for the scientific research community. But these rules evolved for other reasons: (1) data access over telephone lines or private circuits threatened the very lucrative Telex message traffic of the postal and telegraph administrations; and (2) when timesharing began a decade ago it appeared to be a new industry worth encouraging locally, and a potentially lucrative source of revenue for the PTT or some governmental agency. Again, technology is changing these assumptions, but first we must describe how the restrictive rules operate in practice.

Restrictions by the European telecommunications carriers take the following forms:

- forbidding the connection of computers not in Europe to Euronet via transatlantic or other networks
- network access barriers such as modem restrictions mentioned above, or the need for special passwords just to use the network, or initial high connection tariffs unlike the open access found on U.S. networks
- requirements for certain types of processing to be done on national machines if international connections are to be made

MEDLARS in Europe

As a result of these restrictions, European access to scientific databases such as MEDLARS still tends to be via national timesharing centers, or via the EURONET packet system to other timesharing systems in Europe MEDLARS and other biomedical databases are currently available directly in any European city via EURONET, as well as telephone, Telex, and in a few cases, on videotex, from several different sources. Though restrictions are still maintained by checking passwords that are linked to billing addresses, if one has a valid password, a link is not prevented by the network.

It is not NLM's mandate to be concerned about overseas user access to MEDLARS, and there is little that they could do about it if they wanted to. Transnational data barriers are in the province of other U.S. agencies that deal directly with communications and international issues. (In the U.S., NLM has a good track record of working to modernize access to MEDLARS as the telecommunications technologies have become available.)

As noted earlier, some American firms offer the full MEDLARS database via timesharing systems on Euronet.

But there would be other technological options if the European telecommunication administrations' restrictions were to be lifted. For example, it might be cost-efficient to have a high-speed link from U.S. timesharing systems to either a data concentrator in Europe, or to provide service directly to users via a packet network connection between U.S. and European systems. If for no other reason, the labor input required to mount tapes and to maintain the search software would not have to be duplicated if such data processing were centralized. Of course, economics may dictate centralizing the processing in Europe, or Hong Kong, as readily as the U.S. Another option would be to maintain the physical database in one location but decentralize search strategy processing.

Data could remain in one location with the index being distributed, which is the private vendor's creation. Software for large machine-readable databases make use of sophisicated look-up tables to minimize search and retrieval time. Much of the creative database skills and investment is in the design and creation of these index tables. But is not necessary to maintain both the index and the actual data in the same place. It is beyond our scope to explain optimum choices in this regard since this is highly technical. There is no one solution for such distributed database architecture, but as long as the European PTTs hold onto these restrictions to timesharing access, these concepts will remain academic.

The concepts of distributed data processing have been alien to the services historically offered by timesharing vendors and the PTT networks, yet these very restrictions may force NLM to reevaluate their own contracts regarding distributed database uses. While no one has challenged NLM on whether such access would be permitted, it is neither explicitly allowed nor disallowed. (NLM would have the final say if it frowned on the practice by cancelling a contract and refusing to update the MEDLARS database in the future.) It may be to NLM's advantage to encourage vendors to use distributed processing, or to market MEDLARS via videodiscs or even some other technologies in order to maximize both income and utilization in the face of communications-carrier barriers.

National Restrictions

NLM has attempted in the past to assuage the domestic policies of other nations in respect to medical database dissemination through contractual provisions of exclu-

sivity while maintaining a pattern of broad access for U.S. users. Not only is that policy contradictory, but it has only been enforceable through gentlemen's agreements to honor national boundaries in respect to database access. No one has the slightest idea of whether this policy has been followed by the users, since it is trivial to violate it. All one has to do is disguise the nationality of the ultimate reader of the data. Control is by restricting access by passwords—the passwords being linked to a billing address.

Protests against the grant of exclusive purchase to a single national center, by other potential foreign customers for the NLM data, has led to a change in policy. New contracts will not contain a national exclusivity clause. However, new contradictions and unenforceable requirements have now been introduced in regard to Communist countries. The standard contract has recently been extended to prevent resale of databases (from either U.S. vendors or foreign centers) to the Soviet Union or the People's Republic of China without NLM permission, but resale to other Communist nations is not prevented.

This approach by NLM is ineffective, for all a potential user in those nations would have to do is establish a cover billing address in an authorized nation and access the MEDLARS databases through any number of public networks. In fact, this is a common pattern for information transfer to Soviet-bloc nations. Such rules are almost as unenforceable as would be one that told book buyers that they may not resell a book at second hand to a Communist buyer.

In other fields NLM has realized the unenforceability of resale restrictions provisions in their contracts concerning where a resale can take place. Yet the various European telecommunications administrations still use tariff policies to maintain the fiction of transborder control of data flows, even though this may violate the Treaty of Rome. In addition, the Florence Agreement, signed before remote databases were feasible, may also apply here.[3] This agreement, signed by most of the world's nations, prohibits the charging of customs duties on books, magazines, and newspapers for educational, scientific, and cultural purposes, and on educational materials, scientific instruments, and materials for exhibitions.

Furthermore, European centers still refuse (when they know who the buyer is) to permit U.S. residents from accessing, or purchasing copies, of databases that have originated in the U.S., if the prices charged in

Europe are lower than those charged by U.S. vendors, or U.S. government agencies.

However, the mere fact that pricing remains competitive (taking communications costs into account) for the average user indicates that these restrictions are not likely to be enforced seriously. Indeed, insofar as such transborder access to low-cost data bases is prohibited, it is the foreign user, not just the American, who suffers. For the user, wherever located, the desirable arrangement is to use low-cost telecommunications to access MEDLARS or any database where it is cheapest. Of course, detection of such use would be a violation of telecommunications privacy, so the telephone administration would have no easy way of monitoring such technical tariff violations.

International Copyright in the Computer Age

The use of copyright to protect various forms of property or artistic rights is not an abstract application of property law. Traditionally it has been linked to the technologies of creation, reproduction, and distribution of literary, artistic, or commercial works. The radical changes in information-processing technology that will affect international database access become even more confusing in the sphere of copyright law, especially when applied to United States government-owned materials such as MEDLARS.

The detailed changes brought about by the computer are beyond the scope of this chapter.[4] It should be sufficient to note here that there is a radical difference in concepts of copyright based on the printing press, or on similar devices which slowly impress exact copies of an artistic or literary creation, and property rights based on the use of computation-based techniques to store and replicate information. For the printing technologies, copying is the penultimate step before distribution or storage, while the use of computers to perform parallel functions requires "copying" at *every* step in the process, from creation of the work to its final application. In the coming decades the most useful information will be machine-readable. Thus automation of reproduction will alter the essence of "copying," as well as "authorship" and the meaning of "original work." Even today, magnetic and optical methods, and computerized techniques of data manipulation, make it possible to automatically reproduce and save virtually anything humans can see.

Attempts to enforce rules that were designed for a different age may make the existing copyright conventions and laws ineffective and, perhaps, counterproductive. For example, with modern electronic technologies, pirate editions of the MEDLARS database could be produced by Third World or Soviet-bloc nations for distribution on some mass storage device, perhaps by scanning the printed database with a laser character reader and placing the resultant data on a videodisc. Justification for such activity could be made on the basis that public-health-related materials should have as low a price as possible, and copyright enforcement is unfair to poorer nations.

Distribution of the pirated database would be open to all comers. More important, quality control by the original producer would be lacking. Essentially, the pirate would have accomplished an income shift from the MEDLARS producer to the pirate. Without the cost of production of the original data, the pirate would have lower overhead. But this form of cream-skimming simply increases the costs to the legitimate database subscriber. Electronic publishing contains many variations of this theme, with other less-invidious schemes for capturing and replicating information.

Contradictions in the U.S. Copyright Law

These problems are exacerbated by the realization that the recent revision of the U.S. copyright and patent law neither came to grips with the underlying problem of the computer and related technologies, nor confronted the issue of the copyrightability of government publications.

We will discuss below the future implications of copyright for access to the MEDLARS database. However, the more mundane current copyright problems deal with gaps in the law protecting the U.S. government's investment in MEDLARS. An additional issue is the difficulty of defining for machine-readable and machine-manipulated databases which property rights are entitled to protection. But, it must be recognized that technology is moving quite rapidly in these areas. Consequently legal solutions may quickly become obsolete unless technological evolution is taken into account.

In general, the U.S. government is prohibited by section 105, title 17 of the *U.S. Code* from maintaining a copyright against its citizenry. This prohibition has the effect of preventing the government from relying on copyright protection in international markets for technical reports done by contractors or research centers funded by federal funds. The Conference Committee on General Revision of the Copyright Law stated in its 1976 report that

> widespread copying of NTIS [National Technical Information Service of the Department of Commerce] publications is especially prevalent in foreign nations. In Japan it is reported that NTIS reproductions are sold having a value of $3,000,000 annually. A United Kingdom copier sells nearly twice as many copies of NTIS publications as NTIS does directly to the U.K. The U.S.S.R. buys a substantial volume of NTIS publications from European copiers for further copying in the U.S.S.R. The lack of copyright protection in NTIS publications also results in widespread foreign use of U.S. tax-funded research and development without any return to the U.S.[5]

One solution would be to permit the U.S. government to copyright its publications with a compulsory license permitting copying within the U.S.A. This would make it easier to defend U.S. copyright privileges outside of the U.S. without denying U.S. taxpayers the right to materials already paid for. However, the current practice of placing a copyright notice in printed versions of *Index Medicus* and of placing copyright notices in the code of MEDLARS computer tapes offers questionable protection.

Furthermore, the NLM contract provisions regarding replication of the database have made analogies to printing in the mounting of computer tapes. The vendors will deny that they copy the tapes for any purpose when they mount them on their machines, but this is a contradiction in terms as any programmer knows. *There is no way to read a tape without copying it in some fashion*. Yet, despite this fact, BRS, for example, purchases a second set of tapes for their European center in Geneva. This would be unnecessary if BRS operated a distributed system with a link between the U.S. and Switzerland, but their interpretation of the NLM contract assumes that such an operation would be prohibited, and it is not even considered, despite potential customer savings and other efficiencies.

As database retrieval methods move toward distributed processing in the next few years, the issue of copyright will be raised in a new form: e.g., what of a vendor who may want to sell low-cost copies of the database on videodiscs?

FUTURE TRENDS FOR DATABASE ACCESS

Most of the practices used for selling and distributing databases today grew out of book publishing. Indeed, most present databases, such as MEDLINE, can be bought either in bound books or as computer tapes.

Where a bibliographic tape is for sale at the price of making a copy, it is preferred because searches are more rapid by machine. However, in many cases, including that of MEDLARS, pricing practices for the tape assume a large number of users for a small number of tapes; access was assumed via a time-shared machine, and relatively high level leasing charges were set. This may be contrasted with the book publishing pricing policy which is usually to sell as many copies as possible.

The MEDLARS pricing policy may have distorted the actual demand by charging a relatively high cost—especially for serendipitous research. There is no indication that charging for use of information by the hour is either the most effective way to recover costs, or the most effective method of disseminating the data. Had the technology been available a decade ago to follow the book-publishing model for pricing, a different pattern of usage than reliance on centralized computer processing may have evolved. We will discuss a mode similar to publishing by using videodiscs later in this section.

Centralized access to the MEDLARS tapes made sense during the batch-processing computer systems of the 1960s, and perhaps during the 1970s phase of timesharing; both techniques were improvements in scanning data bases whose basic content was not different from that of a set of reference books, albeit much faster to use. In the future, a new pattern may yet evolve for "publishing," using inexpensive computer-based mass storage devices such as videodiscs, updated, perhaps via telecommunications links, and with processing on decentralized computers.

But the current techniques of distributed data processing violate many of the rules that may have seemed common sense in the print age. For example, the first stock market information systems put on tape exactly the same summary tables that are printed in newspapers. Today, transaction systems that are used to complete stock sales and do billing for them can be tapped "on the fly" to provide data about the changing prices and volume of sales. The development, creation, distribution, and income transfers for computerized databases increasingly require a completely different infrastructure in order to work, whether as private, public, or mixed enterprises.

Although the pattern of publishing based upon printing is quite inappropriate for computer-communications, the hybrid system that has evolved appears to be counterproductive. Attempts to fit the new technologies into the procrustean bed of publishing practices regarding copyright, royalties, and division of publishing and retailing, raise the danger of stifling many advantages of the computer by making it merely imitate a fast printing process.

Characteristics of Computerized Databases

Computerized databases have unique characteristics, especially when used by scientists to aid their research activities. These characteristics are a function of the use, users, and structure of the database, all of which have made computerization of this information desirable in the first place. Machine input, vocabulary structure, timeliness, and comprehensiveness, all lend themselves to the computer. But the very process of developing machine-based bibliographic storage and retrieval technologies for scientific use, coupled with the exponential growth of such literature, is transforming search-and-access processes.

With the raw information being created with the help of computers, being documented with computerized word processors, being "published" with the aid of computers, and being disseminated via computer-based telecommunications, search-and-retrieval techniques will inevitably become just one step in the total computerized information process. Computers are used more and more in all aspects of technology and research, and biomedical uses are in the forefront of this. More than citation and abstracting services need to be supplied in online databases; researchers need computer programs, raw data from significant experiments to be validated by peer groups, and other similar types of information.

It would be futile to expect the processes related to information transfer in this field to remain any more static than it would be to expect biomedical technology to remain static. This is illustrated in the necessity of workers in the area of genetic engineering to access raw data on genetic code—one of the fastest growing areas of biotechnology, and perhaps one of the most lucrative.[6]

Biomedical Information

Biomedical information has another characteristic: by its very definition, it is information that concerns the total human community. More than any other science, medicine cannot be easily segregated into simple public and private spheres. Also, as science gets more and more complex and interdisciplinary, it is more difficult to separate disciplines. Genetic engineering, for example, affects not only medicine but agriculture, energy, chemical production, and other fields. Some of this can be considered for the public good, like public health and agriculture, and some of it is for private gain.

There is undoubtedly a role both for private enterprise and for the government in medical information; there always has been. Countries differ in the balance of which parts of medical care are public functions and which are private. Bilateral agreements for information transfer with foreign countries must take this into account. Furthermore, there is no simple rule of thumb for separating information provision between public and private vendors. Some governments will subsidize access to medical information on the grounds of the social benefit of reducing possible sources of contamination, others will expect to recover part or all of the costs. The result is that the price of medical information will differ greatly from country to country. In an age when foreign data bases are no further away than the nearest telephone, a problem is created for those who are subsidizing information access for the benefit of their own people, not for the whole world.

The apparently easy answer is for all to charge "true cost." But cost recovery for information is not the simple matter of average pricing that it is for a nondifferentiated physical product.

Future Trends

There are several trends underway today that will change the way researchers access databases within the next few years. They cannot be ignored, for unlike the first generation of medical-information retrieval, the pioneers are outside of the biomedical field and the evolution of the technology will go on no matter what resolution is made of current problems with access to MEDLARS. Many of the problems that private vendors have with NLM's policies reflect tensions being created by these changes. Six major trends are summarized here; detailed discussion is beyond the scope of this chapter.

WIDESPREAD USE OF MICROCOMPUTERS. We are now in the age of desktop microcomputers, which have the power of the large computers of about a decade ago. Within the next two years, desktop machines with the ability to make sophisticated searches of the entire MEDLARS database will be for sale in computer stores. Many, if not most, of MEDLARS's users in the developed nations will have such machines as general-purpose office-research tools just as they now have typewriters, calculators, and lab equipment.

The key to matching indexes to a citation or abstract database lies more in the size of a computer's core memory and the amount of external data it can access rapidly than in its speed of operation. About one million characters (one megabyte) of core and 10 megabytes of disk storage would be adequate for a stand-alone desktop machine for database retrieval. Such machines are now on the market costing about $8,000 to $10,000. Their price should drop by half or more in the next few years. These are also precisely the type of machines that many scientists would use for general number crunching, and they may make central processing on time-sharing systems obsolescent.

TIMESHARING, AS A MODEL FOR DATABASE ACCESS, IS EXPECTED TO BE RADICALLY ALTERED AS DISTRIBUTED COMPUTING BECOMES MORE WIDESPREAD. In the 1970s, databases were placed on large central computers to which many terminals had simultaneous access. That was called "timesharing." MEDLARS and most of today's electronic databases reflect that technology, which is undergoing transformation. The coming crop of 32-bit micro-computers attached to mass local storage devices, and using sophisticated database software, represents a several-orders-of-magnitude advance in computing, while commensurate improvements in long-distance data communications and thus in timesharing during the next few years may be only one or two orders of magnitude beyond that of today.

With a microcomputer, a user would only have to slide in the database mass storage device—perhaps a videodisk or removable hard magnetic disk—to access most of the database without waiting for a timesharing connection or paying time charges. The latest information, always a tiny percentage of the total database, could still come via telecommunications lines, but not necessarily at that instant. Each evening, for instance, a microcomputer could be programmed to call in for the latest citations, articles, or specialized data. The amount

should be able to easily fit on the disk drives that hold some 5 to 40 million characters of data. These hard disks are now available for desktop machines at costs ranging from $2,500 to $6,000.

Any user will tell how constrained one can feel when trying to browse through an online database and the meter is ticking; in fact, browsing and experimenting with searches is the antithesis of current database networks, but would be encouraged by distributed processing on a user's own machine. Many other features would be possible such as generating a private profile of interests, reuse of material often needed, retransmission of important information to colleagues, reformatting information to one's own needs or tastes.

COMPUTING COSTS TEND TO DROP FASTER THAN COMMUNICATIONS COSTS. This relationship has been true for the past thirty years and all indicators show that this trend will continue for the near future. While these technologies are linked—the cost of telecommunications drops because of computer-related and electronics advances—the decline of both do not follow uniform parallel lines. While the cost of computing has been dropping regularly and in half every two to three years, universal telecommunications advances tend to come in somewhat unpredictable spurts (for reasons that are beyond the scope of this chapter) and on the average at a slower rate.

As a result, the "time windows" are different for the introduction of computing and communications products. It appears that computing devices for local database processing will enter the market about two to three years before the advanced telecommunications systems. The database products now available are the microcomputers already mentioned, and laser videodisks capable of storing all of MEDLARS on one or two disks.

Laser disks that can store digital data are being manufactured commercially today for about $5.00 in small lot quantities. The master disk costs about $2,000 not including the cost of the original mastertape. (Problems of data itegrity and software for search and access on such disks are still to be resolved.)

If MEDLARS had 5,000 customers worldwide, each paying $500 per year for a complete updated database to date (assuming two disks) then the cost of producing 10,000 disks would come to $50,000 + $2,000 + distribution. The revenue of $2,450,000 annually surely would cover distribution and a great deal of the cost of production of the database. Another $500 per year could be charged for updating via floppy diskettes or some other system, and the user would still be saving a great deal of money, not to mention the added revenue to NLM or a private vendor providing the service. These figures are only meant as an illustration of the economics of the new medium of videodisk plus microcomputers for database access; the normal scientific marketing algorithms for pricing such a service might come out with more appropriate fees.

THE FUTURE TELECOMMUNICATIONS NETWORKS WILL MIX DATA, VOICE AND OTHER TRAFFIC, MAKING IT SIMPLE TO CONNECT DISTRIBUTED MACHINES, BUT ALSO CONFUSING NATIONAL BOUNDARIES AND PROPERTY RIGHTS BASED ON PRINT, VERSUS WHAT IS INFORMATION AND WHAT IS COMMUNICATIONS. Even Euronet is expected to disappear as new technology is introduced that will merge telephone, telex, and data systems into "Integrated Services Digital Networks" (ISDNs). With the ISDN, virtually all local telephone connections will be able to handle voice as well as high-speed data; the data links will connect directly to a packet-like network permitting instantaneous connections, the ability to transfer hundreds of pages per minute between computers or desktop workstations and, most likely, distance-insensitive pricing for data. Most major cities, however, will offer some sort of ISDN service by the end of the decade both in Europe and the U.S., if replacement projections for older telephone equipment continues at the current rate. The design and application of integrated data and voice communications circuits is quite complex and beyond the scope of this chapter.[7]

Scientific information has always been a valuable commodity, but the speed and processing power of computers and telecommunications have changed the locus of this resource. The United States has always maintained that the free flow of information tends toward the greatest good. The logistics and economics of information both support the inevitability of a free flow and destroy some of the national protections which made the U.S. and other countries less vulnerable to that flow. Differences in language, distance, and cost of transport protected separate markets for printed matter in the past, even in the absence of governmental controls. Now that free flow is becoming increasingly instantaneous, cheap, and therefore inevitable in free societies, U.S. information distributors may find themselves at a disadvantage in dealing with information from less free countries. Other nations may make the dissemination of foreign information harder in their countries, but disseminate their own information abroad.

The ease with which information can be remotely accessed by telecommunications, and the economies of scale in the collection and dissemination of such information does not necessarily mean that U.S. citizens will always have the ready access to necessary technical information that they tend to enjoy today. The criticisms that other nations have made about U.S. dominance of computer technology inhibiting developments elsewhere could just as readily be turned around in specific fields to our detriment; if a national resource such as NLM finds itself constrained from exploiting new technologies, it may not be the U.S. private sector which takes up the slack, but foreign firms or even hostile governments.

COPYRIGHT QUESTIONS IN THE COMPUTERIZED INFORMATION AGE ARE EXTREMELY COMPLEX. International property rights are also complicated since property rights are defined differently in different jurisdictions. Though U.S. copyright law forbids NLM from claiming copyright protection domestically, NLM places a copyright notice in its printed material claiming protection internationally and claims contractural rights both domestically and internationally, preventing computer centers from replicating its tapes.

Furthermore, applying property concepts derived for the printed press to computer-based scientific information necessary for worldwide health and biomedical research creates a need to reconcile some mutually exclusive goals. Do we want to minimize U.S. government expenditures in regard to medical information at the risk of encouraging the development of more highly subsidized, competitive foreign biomedical databases that may create a negative balance of trade in information? Do we want to restrict access by foreigners to government-originated publicly available information? Is it strategically effective to try to use this resource to trade for similar rights to foreign databases? Do we want the originators of the literature to share in the proceeds from abstracting or retrieval or do we want to encourage the widest dissemination of information at the risk of discouraging future information providers? (Abstractors or bibliographers in the print media have never had to pay royalties to the authors of the material described.) How do we fix property rights if a computer does the abstracting? What rights do the authors of the abstracting program have? Countries are likely to answer these questions differently—once more making costs in different countries very different.

MACHINE RETRIEVAL OF BIOMEDICAL INFORMATION HAS ONLY SCRATCHED THE SURFACE WITH ONLINE LITERATURE CITATIONS AND ABSTRACTS; THE TECHNOLOGY IS EVOLVING TO PERMIT RETRIEVAL OF FULL TEXT OF ARTICLES, RAW DATA AND, EVENTUALLY, AUTOMATED SEARCH. Precedents established for the rather primitive technologies of today can hamper further developments in the future; the converse could be also true. Imaginative solutions to the technologies of today can hamper further developments in the future; the converse could be also true. Imaginative solutions to the domestic public–private mix of MEDLARS database vending may encourage new techniques and industries to develop in the U.S. rather than elsewhere. Several complex issues come to bear here: (1) the ability to enforce a form of international copyright on U.S. government-generated data; (2) the property rights of the originator and "publisher" of the cited material, and (3) the comparative economics of database development and input outside and inside of the U.S.

CONCLUSIONS

Solutions to these problems are not going to be simple. Transnational as well as cross-industry agreements will be necessary to protect information property rights. In some cases there will be conflict between societal goals, particularly where information important to policy and technological decision-making is involved. It is going to take a great deal of skill in anticipating technology as well as anticipating application to design laws that will withstand decades of change.

NOTES

1. Corning, *International Biomedical Communications,* 6 HEALTH COM. & INFORMATICS 228–29 (1980).

2. *Id.* at 229.

3. The Agreement on the Importation of Educational, Scientific, and Cultural Material (The Florence Agreement), July 1950. An international agreement concerning custom duties.

4. Pool & Solomon, *International Property and Transborder Data Flows,* 16 STAN. J. INTERNAT'L L., Summer 1980; Policy Implications of Data Networks in the OECD Area OECD, (1980) POOL, TECHNOLOGIES OF FREEDOM (Cambridge, Mass.: Harvard University Press, 1983). *See also* INTERNAT'L NETWORKS, Feb. 1984.

5. HOUSE CONFERENCE COMM. ON GENERAL REVISION OF THE COPYRIGHT LAW, CONFERENCE REPORT, H.R. REP. NO. 1733, 94th Cong., 2nd Sess. 69–70 (Sept. 29, 1976).

6. *See* Gingeras & Roberts, *Steps Toward Computer Analysis of Nucleotide Sequences* 19 SCIENCE, Sept. 1980, at 1322–1328. The authors make a plea for their fellow workers to send tapes of code sequences and analytic computer programs to a central depository. Apparently everyone working in this field has access to a relatively large computer for data analysis, and the demand to supply a timely genetic code updating service may be awaiting an on-line database entrepreneur.

7. In the U.S., such networks should begin to emerge within the next 3–4 years, at first in industrial suburban and some rural areas. A useful introduction to the ISDN from the European viewpoint can be found in a special issue of *Electrical Communication,* vol. 56, no. 1, 1981, published by International Telephone and Telegraph Corp., Harlow, England. *See also* Rutkowski, *infra* chap. 9 (on ISDN).

CHAPTER 17

WORLDWIDE COMPUTERIZATION OF THE LAW

BETTY W. TAYLOR

In the three decades since 1946 when ENIAC, the first computer, was dedicated, the application of computer technology to storage, retrieval, and manipulation of information has completely altered the concept of acquiring and utilizing information for the benefit of human-kind. Automated techniques applied to the literature of the law are revolutionizing access to the world's legal information. While legal groups in some countries are more active than others, the interest in and stimulus for creating legal databases exists worldwide.

Early American efforts began in the late 1950s. One of the first began at the University of Pittsburgh Health Law Center under the direction of John Horty, who designed a system for searching health law information in the Pennsylvania statutes. The first public demonstration of John Horty's information storage and retrieval system, applying computer capability to legal research, was sponsored by the American Bar Association at its annual meeting in 1960.[1]

During the 1960s European and American programs created interest on the international level and sufficient progress was rumored to arouse curiosity in the legal world.

INTERNATIONAL PROPOSALS

The World Peace Through Law Conference in July 1967 provided a logical vehicle for bringing together those throughout the world who were involved in or who were contemplating the development of computerized systems for law. A World Peace Through Law Center committee of European Experts on the Computerization of Law prepared a proposal for the "Computerization of Law Internationally." A World Exhibit of Computers and Law, part of the Geneva World Conference, attracted live demonstrations of research in progress in Flemish, French, and Italian, as well as English.

The challenge in the proposed plan stated

> It is technically feasible to store the "law of the world" on one or more computers for instant retrieval worldwide. This project explores the potential of world peace by stitching the world community together via computerized law. The information explosion would be converted into a law explosion which would bring into being a law system for the world so useful and credible as to eliminate today's reliance upon force as the ultimate factor in international relations.[2]

Twenty-two projects in progress were identified: 11 in the United States, and others in Belgium, Geneva, The Hague, Great Britain, France, Israel, Sweden, Poland, the U.S.S.R. and the United Nations. Other projects in various stages of experimentation surfaced at the meeting.

Unfortunately, the ambitious proposal to automate the world's law proved impractical, but that was not a deterrent to the continued development of databases on a national or institutional level. Indeed, some of those early identified projects have continued to expand. Others have faded into obscurity.

BETTY W. TAYLOR • Ms. Taylor is director of the Legal Information Center at the University of Florida School of Law in Gainesville, Florida. She is a member of the Task Force on the Use of Computers in Education at the University of Florida, and a member of the Graduate Study Committee at the College of Law.

A few years later (1973) another ambitious proposal for the Western hemisphere was drafted. The Inter-American Bar Association announced at its 18th Conference held in Rio de Janerio "A Proposal to Undertake a Study of the Feasibility of Establishing a Pan American Legal Information Center with Help of Electronics." While this meeting was not nearly as large as the World Peace Through Law Conference, still the interest in computers was surprisingly keen, considering the fact that many delegates represented developing countries where no law was, as yet, in automated format, and few computers even existed.

The promulgators proposed to automate the law in the nations of the Americas, ultimately leading to a Pan American Legal Information Center. The advantages of expanding American and Canadian automated systems were sought for other nations of the hemisphere. Again, the benefits from computerization of the law were proclaimed:

> To automate the law will forward social justice and economic progress, for its purpose is not only to determine the feasiblity of computer application to the law, but more importantly, to decide how best computerized law can serve the people of Brazil and all the Americas, improving their Well Being, Physical Health, Material Standard of Living, Security of the Person; in other words, enhance Social Justice. It will be a significant contribution of the Legal Profession to Human Welfare in the Americas.[3]

The proposal never got off the ground. For one thing, it was rather obviously a proposal to promote the Brazilian system—the only one in the Pan American Union in Portuguese and, therefore, not universally acclaimed. For another, financial support was almost entirely dependent upon outside sources. Experience in other networking systems indicates that self-supporting networks fare much better than those heavily reliant upon outside support funds.

Even though another lofty proposal faded into oblivion, the Brazilians were undaunted. PROSADEN continued to expand and a new database, SIJUR, including use of C.O.M. (computer output on microfiche) emerged.

INTERNATIONAL NETWORKING

These far-reaching proposals indicate that international networking is more easily developed at local levels and cannot be mandated by some superstructure governance at the top. Attempts at organizing into networks at the international organizational level raised numerous questions; Who pays the costs? Who pays the benefits? How are contributors compensated? Who sets standards? Why should an advanced country expend funds to change its system merely for uniformity when it sees no immediate need for another country's database? Do the benefits in international networking among countries in different languages justify the costs?

Such questions are not unique to international networking schemes. The same issues were hotly debated in the United States in 1977 and 1978 at the local levels in the pre-White House Conferences on Libraries and Information Services. The debate continued on to the White House Conference itself in 1979 and is still a live issue with the Library of Congress. That library, filling the role of the national library of this country, is vitally interested in the concept of a national network and the appropriate structure for building one, since it could be heavily involved in the implementation of such a program. The questions are no more easily resolved in this country when dealing only with one language than they were on the international level dealing with multilingual problems. Regardless of the jurisdictional level, proprietary interests, territorial rights, priorities in use, advanced operational systems, governance, and funding, all play a role in determining whether or not cooperation can exist among entities for sharing information worldwide. To date the issues have not been resolved.

That is not to say that nothing is happening to bring the world closer together informationally. Since the World Peace Through Law Conference in 1967, much has happened to promote the orderly development of national and local computerized law databases in the United States and abroad. Hardware costs have dropped dramatically; communications systems have improved substantially; software, while remaining fairly constant in cost, has improved in quality and quantity. Purchasers of equipment and users of databases have increased in numbers, making the development of more systems economically viable. Predictions indicate that in the future law offices will have word processors or microcomputers with adequate communications capabilities to access databases worldwide. Personal computers in the home with the same features will be as common as automobiles and television sets. Lawyers in their electronic cottages will be linked with other members of the global village by way of convenient communications devices.

Often after one acquires and installs computer equipment, and masters the technology, a search begins for expanded uses to justify the system and maximize its capabilities. The logical progression is to turn to local and national databases for access. Only recently has the concept of an individual's accessing information beyond national boundaries emerged as a viable opportunity for the legal profession. The ultimate goal of tapping the world's resources to retrieve information from a microcomputer in one's office or home is not yet a reality. To accomplish this millennium requires further technological advances.

Several database suppliers are gradually expanding their coverage beyond national borders through cooperative agreements with existing networks abroad. These activities can be justified on the existence of increasing numbers of interactive terminals in law offices, courts, and libraries. Serving the international market are Mead Data Central, Inc., (producers of the LEXIS database), the Commission of European Communities (a governmental entity inputting law databases into CIRCE), and West Publishing Company (producers of WESTLAW, now cooperating with EUROLEX). They exemplify organizations that are developing databases, setting standards, and defining international protocols. Two are dealing with multiple languages, all involve private and public databases and international communication. Although LEXIS originally required dedicated terminals, most legal databases are now available from multipurpose terminals, e.g., EURONET DIANE is able to communicate with CIRCE, and WESTLAW multipurpose terminals will access EUROLEX.

AMERICAN DATABASES EXPANDED INTERNATIONALLY

LEXIS is well-known to the American legal profession. Its extensive state and federal case databases have been augmented by libraries in tax law, tax treaties, labor law, bankruptcy, Supreme Court briefs, the *Federal Register*, and the newspaper library known as NEXIS. Services also include expanded litigation-support and private-library files. Now AUTOCITE, SHEPARD'S CITATIONS, and the Matthew Bender library of treatises are available. But for the purposes of this chapter, the most important files that are being added to the databases consist of the English and French legal materials.

Five English libraries and the European Communities Library are now accessible. ENGLISH GENERAL consists of general case law as reported in *Law Reports*, *All England Reports*, *Weekly Law Reports*, *Lloyd's Reports*, beginning in 1945, as well as unreported cases beginning in 1980. It also contains statutes and statutory instruments, *Property and Compensation Reports* (1949+), *Criminal Appeals Reports* (1945+), and *Criminal Appeals Reports—Sentencing* (1945+), and specialized case reports in the following libraries:

1. *Tax*: A library of cases, statutes, statutory instruments, and double-taxation agreements, these are cases reported in *Reports of Tax Cases* (1875–1972), and in *Simon's Tax Cases* (1972 to date), *Value Added Tax Tribunal Reports* (1973+), and unreported cases (1980+).

2. *Industrial relations* (roughly the same as labor and restrictive-practices law in the United States): This is a library of cases, statutes, and statutory instruments. The cases are those reported in *Industrial Tribunal Reports* (1966–1978), *Industrial Case Reports* (1972 to date), *Industrial Relations Law Reports* (1973+), *All England Reports* (1945 to date), unreported cases (1980+), and *Reports of Restrictive Practices Cases* (1959–1973).

3. *Intellectual property*: statutes, *Statutory Instruments*, cases in *Reports of Patent Design and Trademark Cases* (1945+), *Unreported cases* (1980+).

4. *Local Government*: *Statutory Instruments*, cases in *Local Government Reports* (1945+), *Ryde's Rating Cases* (1956+), and *Unreported Cases* (1980+).

5. *European Communities*: Cases in *European Communities Reports* (1954+).

The last comprehensive compilation of *English Statutes in Force* was published in 1968–1970. No comprehensive compilation of statutory instruments has ever been published. LEXIS will offer the only means of conducting a search through the entire body of English statues and statutory instruments.

In late 1981 French, English, and American lawyers began to search the law in French cases. This service is being provided under an agreement with Hachette, France's largest publisher. Hachette will provide the legal materials, market the service, and instruct users in France. The LEXIS retrieval system will be adapted for use by French lawyers. Computer support comes from the Mead Data Central MDC facility in Ohio, and MDC provides database creation and storage, the communications network, and the dedicated terminals.

While the French legal materials are, of course, in French, it is possible for American and English lawyers to search that library file. Instructions for use of the French libraries are identical to LEXIS.

The LEXIS libraries of French law that are available to subscribers include

1. *Public Law*, containing general and fiscal cases decided by the Conseil D'Etat, beginning October 1964; cases decided by the Conseil Constitutionnel, beginning in 1958; and cases decided by the Tribunal des Conflits, beginning January 1964.
2. *Private Law*, containing civil, criminal, labor, and commercial cases decided by the Cour de Cassation, beginning in 1959.
3. *Statutes and regulations*, contained in the *Journal Officiel*, beginning in 1955.

LEXIS subscribers will also have access to Lockheed's DIALOG system through the LEXIS terminals. DIALOG is an online storage and retrieval system offering access to more than 120 databases with more than 40 million references. DIALOG is available through a telephone and a computer terminal to more than 60 countries. LEXIS is not available through DIALOG because of the special terminal requirement.

Database originators can build their databases inhouse and then contract with Lockheed to offer their databases online in the DIALOG system. Royalties on database use are computed and paid in accordance with the contract terms.

A wide variety of databases is available to assist the legal researcher. Using DIALOG, a researcher can locate expert witnesses and obtain information on their backgrounds; search the medical and technical literature for factual information to support personal and product liability litigation; find information on companies, industries, and government regulations; trace legislative histories and follow current legislation through Congress; and keep up to date with state, national, and international developments in criminal justice.

Specialized business and technical databases frequently contain information on legal and regulatory matters pertaining to industry.

Databases of particular interest to legal researchers include *Legal Resource Index*; NCJRS (National Criminal Justice Reference Service); CIS (Congressional Information Service, Inc.); *Federal Index* (Capitol Services, Inc.); FRANCIS (French Retrieval Automated Network for Current Information in Social and Human Sciences).

West Publishing Company has entered into an agreement providing for the availability of EUROLEX to its WESTLAW users and to extend its WESTLAW database to EUROLEX users abroad. *Shepard's Citations* is a library offered to WESTLAW users.

EUROPEAN DATABASE DEVELOPMENT

The Commission of the European Communities is the policy-formulating arm of the European Communities (European Common Market, or E.E.C.). As such, it is responsible for the collection, translation, and dissemination of the official documents of the organization. Early in its organizational life, a policy was formulated to store and retrieve pertinent information for the benefit of the E.E.C. community. The legal service of the commission began investigating online information retrieval in 1967. A database comprising the legal documentation of the European communities came into operation in 1971. For the first three years it could be operated only in batch-processing mode, but in 1973 interactive searching became possible. The system was first known as CELEX but in 1977 it was merged with ECDOC to become CIRCE, a full-text, multilingual legal-information retrieval system. It is expected to be publicly available through EURONET DIANE.

Between 1977 and 1979 the Commission of the European Communities financed a Technical Study in Legal Information in Europe (project leader, N. H. Nunn-Price), which was intended to investigate the needs of the European legal profession for such services, to assess to what extent these were being met by existing services, and to study problems and make proposals for their solution.

> The Study consisted of a survey of users' needs and a technical investiagion. This exercise might well have proved a turning point in European developments in computers and law; unfortunately, the survey of users was probably methodologically unsound, and the "Eurosoftware" envisaged by the Study Team has received less than enthusiastic reception. At a Symposium held in Strasbourg in June 1979, where the Technical Study was introduced to the public by the Study Team, Italian delegates saw no reason for adapting their own large, expanding systems to another, not yet developed.

It remains to be seen what, if anything, will emerge from the technical study.[5]

Other informational databases are produced by the commission for online use. These include Agricultural Research Projects (AGREP), scientific and technical research conducted or sponsored by the E.E.C. (EURO ABSTRACTS), and Environmental Research Projects (ENREP).

As long as the E.E.C. organization continues to flourish, the database development, no doubt, will also continue to flourish. A high priority of the commission is the rapid dissemination of documents critical to the membership. This proved to be a challenging task at the beginning, primarily because of the language barriers. When the system first became operational in 1971, French was the only language entered into the database. Now, documents are entered in six languages: French, English, German, Dutch, Italian, and Danish. Colin Tapper recently stated that 70 percent of the headquarters staff is devoted to translation activities.[6] As new members are admitted, particularly those introducing another language, the impact reverberates throughout the whole system.

Once an interactive system was devised, a system for interacting became essential. The long-range solution, an international communications network, gave birth to EURONET (European Online Information Network) DIANE (Direct Information Access Network for Europe). EURONET DIANE was conceived, sponsored, and designed by the Commission of the European Communities as an international packet-switching network that would support major online systems to serve the information requirements of the European community. It is operated through the cooperation of the Post, Telegraph, and Telephone authorities (known as PTTs) of the nine European Community members. Utilizing a common command language, EURONET DIANE permits online access to over 170 databases held on the computers of more than 20 hosts. The databases cover a wide spectrum of scientific, technical, legal, social, and economic knowledge. Additional services under development include referral and user guidance, document delivery, European Community databases, a multilingual terminology data bank, and a user's forum. To further improve EURONET DIANE, the commission encourages the coordination of sales conditions between host members, and sponsors the development of common services and facilities to overcome language and distance barriers.

The points of entry in all nine European Community countries provide rapid, low-cost data transmission using packet-switching technology. Tariffs for the network are based upon volume and time. Switching exchanges are located in Frankfurt, London, Paris, and Rome, with additional remote-access points at Amsterdam, Brussels, Copenhagen, Dublin, Luxembourg, and Zurich. Access to the network is provided through direct access circuits, the public telephone network, and public data networks. Search fees are established by the individual hosts for the databases and by the PTTs for the network.[7]

The Commission of the European Communities itself is one of the host service units of EURONET DIANE for its databases. As such it is known as ECHO (European Commission Host Organization).[8]

Similar network systems are installed in countries throughout Europe serving the local networking activities internally. Most connect with EURONET DIANE or hope to in the near future. Some of these networks are TRANSPAC (France), SCANNET (Nordic countries), and IPSS (Great Britain and North America). The American networking systems known as TYMNET and TELENET transmit internationally.

As these networking systems develop and the demand for access increases, pressures will be created for interconnections and soon each network will have the capability of tying into the others providing access to databases worldwide.

Availability of legal information in computer databases raises the question, is there a need for worldwide legal information, especially if the information is in multiple languages. Colin Tapper, speaking at the American Association of Law Libraries convention in June 1981, believes that it would be far better for a lawyer to have access to a good lawyer in another country than to the legal materials of that country. However, where there is a link in the law between or among countries, as with common law nations, access to the information may prove beneficial as persuasive authority or in providing arguments of legal principles. In spite of the arguments that can be made pro and con, law databases are proliferating throughout the world.[9]

Whatever the philosophical attitudes are in the emerging databases and networking systems, they are evolving side by side. Those creators of databases on national and local levels may soon be dependent upon the advancing technology to unite them under an umbrella of networking systems as the only feasible method for marketing the databases. In the near future satellite data communications may provide the linkage necessary to join the networks.

An examination of events in several countries may shed some light upon the prospects for the international scene. England is a latecomer to actual automation of the law even though there has been keen interest in computers and the law for some time. Colin Tapper conducted a demonstration at the World Peace Through Law Conference in Geneva in 1967. Information on the special Law Commission Project in which statute law was being automated was presented, but little has been heard of the work since.

Because of the interest in automation, The Society for Computers and Law was formed in December 1973, for the purpose of bringing together lawyers and computer experts in the United Kingdom so that they might study problems of common interest in the context of furthering the sound development, administration, and knowledge of the law.

Principal objects of the society are

1. To promote the study of, and research into, the use of computers as an aid to legal research and legal practice, and to disseminate the results thereof to the public and the legal profession;
2. To promote the use and development of computer systems applied to law, for the benefit of the public and of the legal profession;
3. To promote the establishment of legal information retrieval systems based on computer technology; and
4. To monitor the specification and performance of legal retrieval systems on behalf of the public and the legal profession.[10]

In June 1978, a committee was formed for the purpose of studying the whole area of computer-assisted legal information retrieval, to project the potential for the successful establishment of a national system in the United Kingdom. The report published in February 1979, entitled *The National Law Library*, has been extremely well received and indeed is often referred to as the definitive report on the subject. A charitable trust for the National Law Library was recommended to encourage cooperation between legal publishing houses while ensuring that the system will be of the greatest possible benefit to the legal profession as a whole, keeping in mind that the majority of those who will access the

system will be practicing solicitors in small firms of one or two partners. The society seeks to ensure that lawyers appreciate the potential of computer technology, and that computer experts understand the daily practical needs of the lawyer.[11]

Because of the encouragement that the *Report* gives to the potential of automation of the law in England, database developers have commenced creation of two systems that are now accessible online. EUROLEX was launched in January 1980 by the European Law Centre, Limited, a wholly-owned subsidiary of the publishers, International Thomson Organisation. It contains a combination of European law, United Kingdom law, and industrial and intellectual property law. The other system is INFOLEX, developed by two English practitioners, offering case and statute law updating services. It became operational in 1978 through PRESTEL. LAWTEL is a new database being added to PRESTEL. Additionally, the American-based LEXIS is now operating in England.[12] PRESTEL is a

three-way partnership between the Post Office, the TV set manufacturers and approximately 150 so-called PRESTEL Information Providers. The Post Office's role is that of designer, owner, and operator of the computer and communications hardware and software, and common carrier of the information. The TV industry's role is as manufacturers of the special view-data TV sets required.

The most important ingredients in this unique and at times understandably difficult three-way partnership, are the independent and distinct commercial or public firms or corporations, individually responsible for creating and maintaining the information content of their own particular areas of the whole PRESTEL database. The information providers acquire frames on the system for inputting their data. Currently about 250,000 frames are committed which will offer access to a wide range of residential, business, public and government information subjects. It should be noted in passing that in general the TV terminals used for PRESTEL are in all other respects completely normal sets, capable of receiving BBC and ITV broadcasts.[13]

Italy is the leader among the European countries in converting its legal literature into machine-readable form. The impetus for development of the databases stems from the governmental support of the work. The database users bear the cost of the hardware and the telephone line charges but access to the computer databases is free of cost. Enhancement of the databases by addition of periodical literature and bibliographic information continues at a rapid pace. The Italian databases are now connected with EURONET DIANE and can be accessed by all subscribers to that network. The Italian materials constitute the largest segment in the network at the present time.

The French have been involved in numerous local projects for a number of years as well. At one time 10 different databases were in various stages of development. Entry of a French database in LEXIS with dedicated terminals adapted to the language has brought about a new concept in accessing legal information.

Other countries, too, have automated activities in progress.

LEGAL IMPLICATIONS FOR LEGAL INFORMATION RETRIEVAL SERVICES

Widespread acceptance of accessing legal information in computerized databases as supplementary to or in lieu of traditional methods of searching legal literature is transforming the procedure by which the legal profession seeks solutions to legal problems. Increased user reliance upon the accuracy and stability of database services is accompanying the transition from experimental and developmental stages to the fully operational legal information retrieval services. As expectations of users rise and possibly exceed the ability of suppliers to guarantee those expectations, issues on legal liabilities are forming.

In this country the legal database suppliers most heavily relied upon by the legal community are private developers who limit liability to users by contract entered into for the services. These systems require direct user contact with the databases and the output is unaccompanied by advice or commentary. A detailed statement of database contents appears on the screen as part of the sign-on process so there can be no confusion about completeness of the databases. A training session is required for new users and detailed manuals with frequent updates are supplied to subscribers. While there are several governmental legal databases in use, these are not accessible to the public at large.

In Europe development of computerized legal databases has occurred primarily under the auspices of governments. Most have begun as information centers.

While the legal documents were input in machine-readable form, lawyers could telephone for information, specify the desired result either in bibliographic, abstract, or legal opinion form, and the time period for the response. Searches of the databases and traditional sources were conducted. An entirely different set of legal issues arises out of this environment as the legal information centers convert to computerized databases accessible directly by lawyers at terminals or indirectly through intermediate users. In addition, the implications from regulations or guidelines imposed by the European Communities may further complicate the process.

The ease with which legal information can be transmitted across domestic, national, and international boundaries raises legal questions both internally and externally. Now that information can be accessed by individuals, computers, and networks at short and long distances around the world through the technology of satellites, coaxial cables, and microwave systems, national concerns for protection of nationals at home and abroad are being addressed as the impact of international exchange of information is recognized. When information is contained within national boundaries, governments seem to be satisfied that they can maintain control and regulate the activities. However, when information escapes through the communications devices and becomes absorbed in the international flow, governments become concerned about the loss of control over the information flow. They also question whether this may have an adverse affect upon their nationals.

A primary concern of the Council of Europe in its goal of European cooperation is the protection of individual rights. In sponsoring a symposium on the protection of users of legal data processing systems, the council anticipated that the results could be applied to the larger problem of access and protection of individuals in using other types of data banks as well. Representatives from 18 countries heard experts describe the issues they anticipate as a result of the increase of database use, numbers, and linkage. The availability of EURONET DIANE as a conveyor of data may have played a role in urging consideration of protection of users and assessing the responsibility and liability of database suppliers.

Expectations of the suppliers and users may differ widely. As the contrast between manual and automated legal information retrieval becomes evident, users soon realize that an entirely new approach to research must be learned, combining the traditional with the technological. On the other hand, the suppliers are expected to assume new responsibilities for user reliance upon information in databases that is quite different from the liability of books publishers, for example.

In order for an online system to be successful, the expectations of the user must be justified in terms of benefits weighed against costs as well as anticipated success of using the traditional resources. The user expects the database to be accurate, comprehensive, and current. What is the responsibility of the user who alleges the loss of a "big" case because of failure of the system to turn up the case on point? Who determines if the supplier has failed to meet this test? What is the liability of a supplier if it is determined that its quality, coverage, and timeliness are substandard? What is the measure of damages?[14]

The quality of the database content concerns every database supplier, for "garbage in—garbage out" can destroy the perceived integrity of the system. To avoid liability for errors in the database, some suppliers have set up elaborate editing and proofreading procedures. Double inputting and matching data for discrepancies is a way database accuracy is addressed by one supplier.

Lack of comprehensiveness and timeliness of a database would be difficult arguments to make against a supplier who furnished information about contents of titles, volumes, and dates in the sign-on process, and whose contents were entered in accordance with literature advertising the system. Some suppliers select contents to insert in the databases and these groups are concerned about litigation challenging their judgmental decisions in the selection process.

Because costs for developing, testing, and maintaining databases are high, commercial suppliers usually are anxious to offer data as soon as the database is large enough to justify subscription costs to recoup the financial investment. Governmental suppliers may not be under similar pressures. Assessing database user fees and the impact upon different types of users may bring charges of discrimination by the infrequent user or the small law firm. Some government suppliers have discussed offering databases free of use-charge, but most discard that idea because of opportunity for abuse of the system by indiscriminate users who do not have to account for computer time. Different suppliers have different pricing systems. Some charge on the basis of expenses and costs, others on the nature of users, and still others on the frequency and time of use. A sliding

scale of amount and time of use seems to have received user acceptance, although the trend seems to be toward a flat-rate charge per unit of time the system is used. If a database is offered as a public service, ordinarily developmental costs are not assessed and no charges over expense are calculated in the rates. In the private sector where profits are an element in the rate charged, a board of use-representatives will help to alleviate the allegations of overcharging and profit-taking.

Challenges by users that they failed to retrieve information in response to their inquiries and sustained damages as a result can be met in part by increased user education and training.[15] Enhancements in the user interface with the computer by simplifying the language, with many queries now in the natural language, and more computer-assisted instruction woven into the search-formulation process will improve the output. It is unlikely that a user would prevail in a suit of this nature because of the difficulty in proving system failure as opposed to human failure. But improvements in performance of the system will improve user success. Aids like special command keys, facility in switching databases, termination dialogue, clear and helpful error messages, corrections explanations, help features, and other messages will assist the user in searching the system effectively. User training sessions, system documentation and user manuals, and a clearly stated information policy will provide the users with backup as security for understanding the system's operation.

Copyright of primary legal authority is troublesome to database suppliers in some countries. Fortunately, in this country primary law is not copyrighted although as the database suppliers venture beyond primary law, the copyright problem does present obstacles. In England, for example, some primary law is copyrighted but the problem is not considered insurmountable. While authors' rights to protection for unique works are recognized, the database suppliers are concerned that strict application of copyright laws creates with authors a monopoly which "could restrict the development of legal retrieval systems." ... "Translating the text into machine-readable form is the exclusive right of the copyright owner" ... and "the act of storing a text in a computer is infringement of copyright if done without authority, express or implied, of the copyright owner ..." This raises a "conflict of interest between authors and the public." ... "Compulsory licensing of primary law" is a suggestion that might resolve this dilemma.[16]

Criminal liability, while a possible factor in operating

an information service, is considered academic for all practical purposes.

> There would have to be a deliberate breach of professional secrecy or an offence against privacy due to the storage and dissemination in unlawful circumstances of nominal data connected with legal proceedings, for example.[17]

Mr. Lucien Mehl addressed the symposium directly on the question of civil liability of legal data-processing centers from first-hand knowledge of their operation as president of the Centre d'informatique Juridique (CEDIJ) in Paris. He outlined the liabilities, as follows:[18]

First, supplier that enters into a contract with a user is required to "fulfill his contractual obligations and upon any failure to do so will incur liability."

The user has a remedy in damages and may also enforce the right to service, refuse to pay for the service rendered, and/or cancel the contract. In the event of a dispute about the contract, the liability will be determined by law. Even if the contract provides that the supplier will incur no liability, the supplier may be liable if the user can prove gross negligence on the supplier's part that resulted in the damages. Naturally, the supplier wants to limit liability but if there are penalty clauses in the contract, the supplier may be liable for minor failures. The user may be at a disadvantage under contractual arrangements with suppliers as he must sign if he wants the service.

Second, legislative changes may alter the liabilities of legal data processing centers. If special rules are adopted concerning liability of information centers, these may affect the extent of their liability.

Liability may arise if the user is unable to obtain the result expected or if the supplier does not perform all the operations promised in the contract to which the user has a claim of right. Ordinarily in breach of contract there is an obligation to make good the whole of the damage sustained, but it is unlikely that "a centre could be held liable for making good the whole of the damage resulting, for a business firm, say, from incomplete, inaccurate or belated information supplied by that centre." Under the law "the loss complained of must be certain, material and direct before it can be required to be made good, the court will order payment of compensation only for loss that was foreseeable and not for actual loss, which may be much greater." If the user was involved in a large business deal, for example, he may have an obligation to verify the accuracy of the informa-

tion to mitigate the liability of the supplier. The court may examine the relationship between the cost of the search and the amount involved in the business transaction to reach this result.

A supplier is under an obligation to furnish adequate information to a direct-access user about the operation of the system, the terminal, and the search process. A supplier may incur liability for "delay in delivery of information, abnormal waiting at the terminal or interruption of the service." Suppliers in this country are addressing this problem by restricting certain classes of noncritical users from use of terminals in peak periods. Liability of suppliers may result from contractual relationships with other suppliers of hardware, software, computer storage, or telecommunications facilities.

Liability of information centers that accept inquiries, perform search functions, produce results, advice, commentaries, and even legal opinions is quite different from the liability of offering online search capabilities directly to users who perform their own access functions at terminals. The actions of the user in this case play a major role in the liability of the supplier. The adequacy of the information supplied to the user about the database contents and operation of the system is critical to issues of satisfactory search results.

> In the event of a dispute, in order to escape liability the centre will have to show that the information sought is actually included in the corpus and that the failure of the enquiry is attributable to the user who did not put the question properly or failed to use the system's resources to the full.[19]

Differentiation of users in the legal community may be important to determine liability; for example, a delay in retrieval of legal information may be critical to the judge or lawyer but not to the professor or student. The level of user expertise may be another controlling factor in the issue of liability.[20]

Other relationships may affect the liability of legal information suppliers, e.g., relationships with hardware vendors based or assumed product reliability, those with software suppliers based on assumed adequacy of programming, and those with public carriers. Factors such as product liability, telecommunications regulations, pricing policies, unfair competition rules, protection of computer software, administrative regulations, freedom of information, and secrecy of information, may all have a bearing at some point on the liability of information suppliers.

Mr. Seipel, representing the University of Stockholm, suggests that

> The application of these legal norms to computers and automatic data processing is still uncertain but it is not unlikely that it will tend to be in the favour of the users. Finally, data processing insurances are a part of the framework of contracting. Since the trend is in the direction of broad EDP policies, and increasing number of risks—programme failures, errors and omissions of the data processor, criminal acts directed against computer systems—will not have to be carried by each user alone.[21]

Mr. Vittorio Novelli, representing the Italian legal data processing system, Italgiure, emphasized that this is a governmental database developed by the state, and that the center was concerned about "the liability assumed by the State when it furnishes data which—especially in cases of errors of omission—might damage persons who rely on such data."[22] Its liability derives from administrative law rather than contract law.

Concerning incomplete data, he advocates "comprehensive legal data" to satisfy the need for legal information. When the goals are achieved, the liability for incomplete data will be circumvented.

Erroneous data entry does occur but facilitation of error correction is constantly in progress. It can never be accused of "gross negligence."

Difficulties of access to legal information is experienced by the lay public but that access will be delayed until the government and legal community are accommodated. Public libraries, public and private organizations, and individuals eventually will be provided access.

As to liability of Italgiure, he considers the type of service

> as a documentation service with the resulting obligation to provide the means of research rather than the results. In practical terms, it must be looked on as a vast computer library consulted by the user on the one hand and the computer itself on the other.[23]

He states that it probably would be "difficult to base a claim on liability for non-performance of a contract or of most non-contractual obligations." Given are the following reasons:

1. The difficulty of establishing the causes of an unsuccessful search (owing, for instance to the user's lack of expertise).

2. The systems—all systems—are constantly evolving and limits to capacity are still met with, although there are many means of eliminating them.

3. Delays and omissions depend largely on the organisations supplying the data and there can be no question of involving them in the relationship between the computer centre and its users, even for the purpose of obtaining compensation, for this would complicate the problem enormously.

4. Functional breakdowns are caused chiefly by circumstances beyond human control (breakdown of hardware and transmission network).[24]

The whole area of transborder data flow involving the free flow of information in conflict with the legal rights of individuals is the topic of other chapters in this volume.[25] The Council of the Organisation for Economic Cooperation and Development (OECD) has adopted a set of guidelines governing the protection of privacy and transborder flows of personal data.

CONCLUSION

Fifteen years after Charles Rhyne's vision of automation of the world's laws in one database housed in a computer in Geneva, we live in the present reality of the still-developing machine-readable databases of legal information. The difference between the vision and reality lies in the means of storage and the transmission but not in the concept. While the reality has not come about as rapidly as Rhyne had hoped, progress is noted in most countries of the world.

Within this decade pertinent legal information, at least in the industrialized nations, will be accessible to all who desire to conduct a law search. The cost probably will be reasonable and the access will be from hardware in the office or home.

The legal aspects of developing and maintaining legal information databases are not insurmountable. They may be resolved through time by the expansion of databases, implementation of common command languages, greater experience in using automated systems, and the adoption of international uniform laws, treaties, or conventions. Even with the simplification of computer access, users still must be protected from the negative consequences of using databases, and this is a task yet to be undertaken.

Protection of legal rights of privacy, patents, copyright, etc., will be of prime importance as information flows freely throughout the world. International groups are addressing these concerns and it behooves the American Bar Association to join in the common goal of defining the rights and liabilities of users and suppliers while at the same time assuring access to legal information in databases throughout the world.

NOTES

1. 2 M.U.L.L., June 1960, at 90.

2. World Peace Through Law Center, registration materials, Geneva World Conference (July 9–14, 1967).

3. Inter-American Bar Association, conference materials, 18th Conference, Rio de Janerio (Aug. 1973). Summary of conference proceedings in Portuguese published in 247 REVISTA FORENSE 355 (1974).

4. Jeffries, *Celex*, 11 LAW LIB., Dec. 1980, at 60.

5. Bull, *Technical Developments in Legal Information Retrieval: A Guide for BIALL Members*, 11 LAW LIBR. Aug. 1980, at 34. Study reviewed in 1 SOC. SCI. INFORMATION STUD., Oct. 1980.

6. Tapper, *International Law Databases*, in LEGAL INFORMATION FOR THE 1980s: MEETING THE NEEDS OF THE LEGAL PROFESSION 221 (B. Taylor ed., Littleton, Colo.: Fred B. Rothman for the American Association of Law Libraries, 1982).

7. A. KRUZAS & J. SCHMITTROTH, JR., ENCYCLOPEDIA OF INFORMATION SYSTEMS AND SERVICES 92 (4th ed., Detroit: Gale Research Co., 1981).

8. *Id.*

9. Tapper, *supra* note 6.

10. Woods, *Society for Computers and Law*, 5 POLY. L. REV., Spring 1980, at 35.

11. *Id.*

12. *Id.*

13. Castell, *The Infolex, 'National Law Library'*,

10 LAW LIBR., August 1979, at 24.

14. Leliard, Cost of Systems—Charges Payable by Users, in *The Protection of Users of Legal Data Processing Systems, Proceedings of the Fifth Symposium on Legal Data Processing, Vienna, May 7–9, 1979*, Council of Europe, 39–46.

15. Svoboda, The User Interface, in *The Protection of Users of Legal Data Processing Systems, Proceedings of the Fifth Symposium on Legal Data Processing, Vienna, May 7–9, 1979*, Council of Europe, 49–68.

16. Niblett, Copyright Aspects of Legal Databases, in *The Protection of Users of Legal Data Processing Systems, Processings of the Fifth Symposium on Legal Data Processing, Vienna, May 7–9, 1979*, Council of Europe, 71–86.

17. Mehl, The Civil Liability of Legal Data Processing Centres, in *The Protection of Users of Legal Data Processing Systems, Proceedings of the Fifth Symposium on Legal Data Processing, Vienna, May 7–9, 1979*, Council of Europe, 91.

18. *Id.* at 89–102.

19. *Id.* at 100.

20. Seipel, Relations between Hardware and Software Providers and Users, in *The Protection of Users of Legal Data Processing Systems, Proceedings of the Fifth Symposium on Legal Data Processing, Vienna, May 7–9, 1979*, Council of Europe, 105–116.

21. *Id.* at 115.

22. Novelli, The Protection of Users of the Italgiure Legal Data Processing System, in *The Protection of Users of Legal Data Processing Systems, Proceedings of the Fifth Symposium on Legal Data Processing, Vienna, May 7–9, 1979*, Council of Europe, 131–139.

23. *Id.* at 137.

24. *Id.* at 138.

25. See other chapters in this volume.

Chapter 18

INTERNATIONAL DIPLOMATIC TELECOMMUNICATIONS

THOMAS J. RAMSEY

INTRODUCTION

An examination of issues associated with "global networks" would be incomplete without a discussion of the relatively arcane world of international diplomatic telecommunications. The legal literature rarely treats governmental communications systems despite the enormity and complexity of such systems.[1] The United States government in the conduct of foreign and military affairs comprises the largest single user of telecommunications networks in the world.

Government officials responsible for global communications have been mission oriented—preoccupied with operational issues, i.e., the planning, construction, and maintenance of systems; but there is a growing interest within this community in the broad and complex policy and legal issues.

Officials charged with the conduct of foreign affairs, not only in the United States but around the world, are becoming more and more dependent upon new telecommunications systems to properly discharge their responsibilities. The purpose of this chapter is to introduce the reader to some of the issues they face.

A GLOBAL TELECOMMUNICATIONS MISSION

In order to conduct its foreign affairs and provide for its national security the United States government maintains many of the most extensive and complex telecommunication and information systems in existence today. These global systems range from the more basic, e.g., stand-alone word processing equipment, to the most advanced, e.g., high-speed enhanced telecommunications networks forming part of our national security C^3 matrix.[2] Agencies charged with developing and maintaining such systems include the Department of State (DOS), the Department of Defense (DOD), the National Aeronautics and Space Administration (NASA), and the Federal Aviation Administration (FAA).

Role of Department of State

The secretary of state, as principal adviser to the president on foreign policy matters, directs the department in the formulation and implementation of foreign policy, including representation of the United States in relations and negotiations with other countries, the United Nations, and other international organizations. Inherent in this mission is the continuing need to report and communicate with posts abroad.[3] The reporting function, which is essential in the formulation and implementation of U.S. foreign policy, accounts for the greatest volume of record communications. DOS also provides telecommunications services abroad to approximately 50 agencies including Agency for International Development, United States Information Agency, Department of Justice, Department of Labor, Department of Commerce, and Department of Agriculture.

THOMAS J. RAMSEY • Mr. Ramsey is Deputy Director of the Bureau of International Communications and Information Policy, U.S. Department of State; Chairman of the International Telecommunications Law Committee in the ABA Sciences and Technology Section; and author of several law journal articles in the field of international law.

Communications in support of foreign affairs are not new. From their inception, effective communications have been recognized by Congress as a necessary tool in the accomplishment of the foreign affairs mission. The first "congressional" action in the field of foreign relations was assumed by the First Continental Congress.[4] The Continental Congress exercised its control over foreign relations sometimes directly but often through committees. One such committee, known first as the Committee of Secret Correspondence,[5] entered into communications with various persons in Europe for the purpose of ascertaining sentiment toward the colonies and obtaining any other information that might be useful.

Such responsibilities were subsequently transferred to the new "Executive Department," on July 27, 1789.[6] The secretary for the Department of Foreign Affairs was to

> Perform and execute such duties as shall from time to time be enjoined on or intrusted to him by the President . . . relative to correspondences, commissions or instructions to or with public ministers or consuls, from the United States, or to negotiations with public ministers from foreign states or provinces, . . . or other matters respecting foreign affairs, as the President . . . shall assign to the department, and . . . that the principal officer shall conduct the business of the said department in such manner as the President . . . shall . . . order or instruct.[7]

The DOS is responsible for providing those methods of communications which are deemed necessary to accomplish its mission. Implicit in the secretary's duty to communicate with the representatives of foreign governments, international organizations, and representatives of the United States,[8] is the mandate that it be done effectively, utilizing the most appropriate and efficient channels.

The Department of State's Office of Communications has been designated the responsible entity for providing worldwide telecommunications support to the secretary of state.[9] The mission of the office is similar to other government entities responsible for developing, programming, and maintaining other national security systems. Deputy assistant secretary of state for communications (retired), Stuart E. Branch, commenting on C[3] systems within the department of state, has noted:

The Department of State utilization of such systems derives from its primary mission, i.e., advising the President in the formulation and execution of foreign policy. In this regard, the primary business of the Department of State is the exchange of information. Such exchange is the keystone of diplomacy. It is essential in peacetime, times of escalating crisis and during and after conflict. C[3] systems provide the mechanisms for this exchange. They are the means, according to one authority, which allow an organization to probe its environment, plan, act and react, in order to avoid threats and to exploit opportunities, as well as provide the means for it to mobilize, deploy and integrate its energies and resources. From this perspective, the Department of State sees the continued maintenance of its command, control and communications systems as essential for achieving its global responsibility and as such constitutes the touchstone of the Office of Communications' primary mission, i.e., the provision of fast, secure and reliable telecommunications for the foreign affairs community.[10]

The department provides these services utilizing the Diplomatic Telecommunications Service (DTS). The Department's overall system is particularly complex given the varied nature of the services provided and the broad geographical area the network must cover; to wit, the DTS network includes approximately 260 posts in over 150 countries. The transmission media available to the DTS include commercially leased circuits, U.S. military circuits, U.S.-controlled high frequency (HF) radio, and U.S.-owned satellite circuits. The commercially leased circuits (leased lines) follow many paths, e.g., oceanic cable, land lines, microwave (radio), and satellite.

From a technical point of view the government communicator is not unlike his counterpart in the private sector. New technologies have created increased service demands from the government's international user community. Interest is increasing in real-time distributed information systems. Government managers, when designing global telecommunications/information networks, must consider the same design parameters as private sector managers: availability of economical high-speed transmission facilities, location of electronic switching facilities with advanced multiplexing equipment, and maintenance of the associated peripherial hardware and software at each terminal point.

Government communicators, like their private sector counterparts, share the challenges of an expanding and complex national telecommunications agenda. The agenda is not static and continues to be defined by the availability of new high-technology products, services, and user requirements; deregulatory policies of the Federal Communications Commission, the Courts, and the Congress; and a series of executive branch initiatives relating to national security/emergency preparedness.[11]

OFFICIAL COMMUNICATIONS

Government and private telecommunications managers share global responsibilities and similar technical and policy concerns. However, from an international law perspective, the DOS communicator enjoys certain privileges not available to private users, i.e., the privilege to transmit and receive *official communications*. Article 27 of the Vienna Convention on Diplomatic Relations, 1961, in relevant part, reads:

> The receiving State shall permit and protect free communication on the part of the mission for all official purposes. In communicating with the Government and the other missions and consulates of the sending States, wherever situated, the missions may employ all appropriate means, including diplomatic couriers and messages in code or cipher. However, the mission may install and use a wireless transmitter only with the consent of the receiving State....
>
> The official correspondence of the mission shall be inviolable. Official correspondence means all correspondence relating to the mission and its functions.[12]

Article 27 of the Vienna Convention conforms to the generally accepted principle that there should be full freedom of communications between diplomatic missions and the government of the sending state, including the right to use the diplomatic pouch.[13] The privilege has been interpreted to include communications by post, telegraph, and pouch.[14] The underlying basis for the privilege is that the uninterrupted flow of the communications between the mission and the sending state is essential to the effective performance of the diplomatic function. The corollary rule to the privilege is that the communication must be official. If a sending state violates the rule, the host state is within its right to prevent future violations by restricting the use of the host state's communications facilities or insisting that such violations be discontinued.[15]

While the freedom to communicate between a sending state and its missions is well established, there are certain restrictions, e.g., a "wireless" transmitter may be used only with the consent of the host government.[16]

In the United States the Federal Communications Commission has jurisdiction under the Communications Act of 1934, as amended, over all foreign communications by wire or radio. However, the president may authorize a foreign government to construct and operate a low-power radio station in the fixed service at or near the site of the embassy or legation of such foreign government for transmission of its messages.[17] Authority may be granted only if it is determined that such installation is consistent with and in the interest of national security, and reciprocal privileges by the relevant foreign government are granted to the United States to construct and operate radio stations within territories subject to its jurisdiction.[18]

The reciprocity provision was promulgated by Congress to assure that the U.S. government could construct and maintain its own communications systems in countries where the local communication systems were inadequate *and* where permission to operate U.S. government-owned systems was contingent upon reciprocal rights for the foreign government to operate in Washington. While the act speaks of low-power radio in the fixed service, it has been interpreted to permit operation of satellite ground stations on embassy premises.

EMERGING ISSUES

The rules and practices associated with the transmission of diplomatic communications evolved when low-speed teletype and the diplomatic pouch were the primary means of conveying official correspondence. Interesting new issues, however, may arise as government communicators around the world rely more and more on the merging technologies of telecommunications, computers, and automated data processing (ADP) to meet their needs. Initiatives to develop and maintain the new advanced systems for the diplomatic community may encounter problems in certain countries or regions of the world where regulatory authorities are promulgating laws, rules, or policies that restrict the flow of information, e.g., privacy protection laws, restrictive tariffing of long-haul voice grade circuits, stringent terminal equipment accessing standards, and procedures regarding the processing of data outside of national boundaries.[19] Thus far the national or international fora responsible for this evolving body of law and policy have not directly addressed such issues as whether or not such regulatory regimes impact upon the recognized privileges associated with diplomatic communications. Unanswered questions include:

- To what extent do the evolving data-protection laws apply to the transmission of diplomatic correspondence? For example, would diplomatic missions be required to register with locally controlled data protection boards? Would national privacy protection authorities attempt to monitor diplomatic transmissions?
- Should the distributed information networks of diplomatic communications systems be subject to the emerging national laws relating to the processing of data outside the territory of the host/regulating state?
- Could a foreign government levy a transborder data tax on diplomatic correspondence as it might on private information providers?
- To what extent may a host government regulate the type and installation of terminal equipment for a diplomatic mission? Where does the local communications network terminate (e.g., at the point where the local "hardwire" reaches the mission, or to and through the PABX)?
- Should foreign missions be immune from increasingly restrictive telecommunications tariffs, i.e., those which might effectively eliminate the availability of flat-rate leasing of international high-speed circuits?
- To what extent should a host government impose its local telecommunications rules regarding domestic or international switching to the diplomatic traffic of a sending state, e.g., should a foreign mission have the privilege to freely distribute an official message received from the sending state to consulates located in or outside the territory of the host country?
- If national laws and policies erect barriers to the free flow of diplomatic correspondence, do they conflict with those articles of the Vienna Convention on Diplomatic Immunity and the Vienna Convention on Consular Relations noted earlier?

Foreign initiatives may not present the only potential "problems." U.S. law or practice may also need revision to provide the necessary flexibility to foreign missions located in the United States to communicate freely and flexibly with their states of origin.

CONCLUSION

While the DOS has successfully established and currently maintains rapid, secure, and reliable worldwide communications systems, the question remains open whether laws and regulations restricting the free flow of nondiplomatic private information will affect diplomatic interchange. To the extent they are deemed to do so, the U.S. may need to negotiate bilateral or multilateral agreements, introduce reciprocity mechanisms, or take other steps to ensure the flow of diplomatic communications to and from its overseas missions.[20]

NOTES

1. *See generally* Whiteman, 7 DIG. INT'L L. 174–254; Lyons, *Personal Immunities of Diplomatic Agents*, BRIT. Y.B. INT'L L. (1954).

2. C³ is a term often employed by government communicators and refers to systems associated with "Command, Control and Communications"; for further readings on the subject of C³ see *generally* Signal, the journal of the Armed Forces Communications and Electronics Association.

3. See Vienna Convention of Diplomatic Relations, Apr. 18, 1961, 500 U.N.T.S. 95, 3(1)(d): "The functions of a diplomatic mission consist *inter alia* in: . . . (d) ascertaining by all lawful means conditions and developments in the receiving State, and reporting *thereon* to the government of the sending State" (emphasis added). The Vienna Convention on Consular Relations, Apr. 24, 1963, 500 U.N.T.S. 95, has a similar provision. Article 5 provides that "consular functions consist in: . . . (c) ascertaining by lawful means conditions and developments in the commercial, economic, cultural and scientific life of the receiving State, *reporting thereon* to the government of the sending State and giving information to persons interested (emphasis added).

4. E. BURNETT, THE CONTINENTAL CONGRESS 118 (New York: Macmillan, 1941).

5. *Id.*

6. Immediately before the adoption of the Constitution the following language was adopted by resolution: "He [the Secretary] shall use means to obtain from the ministers and agents of the said United States in foreign countries, and abstract of their present state, their commerce, finances, naval and military strength, and the characters of sovereigns and ministers and every other political information when may be useful to the United States." 1st Cong. 1st Sess., chap. 4, nt. (a) (1789).

7. *Id.* at chap. IV, § 1; 22 U.S.C. § 2656.

8. In most U.S. missions the U.S. government community is made up of representatives from various federal agencies. In addition to the Foreign Service, representatives come from AID, USICA, DOD, DOC, DOA, etc. The persons charged with the responsibility for directing, coordinating, and supervising all U.S. government employees (except persons under military command) at posts abroad are the chiefs of mission. 22 U.S.C. § 3927. Section 207 of the Foreign Service Act of 1980 (22 U.S.C. § 3927) also mandates then that U.S. chiefs of mission keep fully and currently informed with respect to all activities of the U.S. Government in foreign countries (22 U.S.C. § 3927(a)(2)). Inherent to such responsibilities is the requirement that chiefs of mission report back to the President. It is the Secretary of State's responsibility to see to it that the communications capabilities exist to report back.

9. The Office of Communications is directed by a deputy assistant secretary of state for communications. The Department of State Appropriations Act each year provides funds for communications. Certain of the secretary's communications responsibilities have been recognized in various executive orders: Exec. Order No. 12,472, Assignment of National Security and Emergency Preparedness Telecommunications Functions (Apr. 3, 1984); Exec. Order No. 12,046, Transfer of Telecommunications Functions (July 20, 1979); Exec. Order No. 11,556, Assigning Telecommunications Functions (Sept. 4, 1970); Exec. Order No. 11,490, Assigning Emergency Preparedness Functions to Federal Departments Agencies (Fall 1969); and Exec. Order No. 11,087, Assigning Emergency Preparedness Functions to the Secretary of State (Feb. 26, 1963).

10. *See* Branch, SIGNAL, May 1983, at 17. The mission and systems to which Mr. Branch refers include developing and implementing policies, plans, and procedures to provide dependable, responsible and secure communications for the conduct of U.S. foreign policy. Communications services include record, voice (HF, VHF/UHF radio and telephone), secure voice, high-speed electronic distribution, electronic file management for classified information, and facsimile; providing other government agencies (with overseas presence) with mail and pouch services as well as a variety of telecommunications services, including telegraphic and high-speed data transmission voice; and providing special communications services in support of domestic and overseas security programs.

11. The "national level agenda" affects all government communicators. Actions of note from a Department of State perspective would include the FCC's decision in *Computer Inquiry II* and GTE Telenet Communications Corp., 91 F.C.C.2d 232 (1982), *appeal pending sub nom.* GTE Telenet Communications Corp. v. FCC, No. 82-2007 (D.C. Cir. filed Dec. 7, 1982), which, in essence, applies *Computer Inquiry II* rules to international services; International Carriers Scope of Operations, 76 F.C.C.2d 115 (1980), *aff'd sub nom.* Western Union Tel. Co. v. FCC, 665 F.2d 1126 (D.C. Cir. 1982), where the FCC permitted the IRCs to expand their operations to 21 additional cities and each of the several INTELSAT earth stations. From a U.S. Government international-user perspective, the decision may result in better and more diverse circuitry (e.g., increased alternate routing) at less cost; Western Union Telegraph Co., 91 F.C.C.2d 1051 (1982). Here the FCC authorized the Western Union Company to provide international record communications services; International Communications Policies Governing Designation of Recognized Private Operating Agencies, Grants of IRUs in International Facilities and Assignment of DATA Network Identification Codes, FCC 83-516 (released Dec. 22, 1983), an inquiry currently underway at the FCC that is examining certain policies relating to international telecommunications; and United States v. AT&T, 552 F. Supp. 131 (D.D.C. 1983), *aff'd sub nom.* Maryland v. United States, 103 S. Ct. 1240 (1983); United States v. Western Elec. Co., 569 F. Supp. 1057 (D.D.C.), *aff'd sub nom* California v. United States,

104 S. Ct. 542 (1983). The decree, resolving the Department of Justice's longstanding antitrust suit, eliminates line of business restrictions that were imposed on AT&T from an earlier 1956 consent decree. From a national security perspective the implications of the decree are far reaching and still under review. In the legislative arena items on the "agenda" include repeated attempts to rewrite the Communications Act of 1934, e.g., S. 898/H.R. 5158 (domestic) and S. 2469 (international), during the 97th Congress; S. 1660/H.R. 4102 (domestic) and S. 999 (international) during the 98th Congress. Recent legislation that affects government communications/information managers includes Paperwork Reduction Act of 1980, Pub. L. No. 96-511, 94 Stat. 2812 (codified at 44 U.S.C. §§ 3501–3520). Other examples include executive branch initiatives that relate to national security telecommunications policy. Such initiatives, however, are generally classified and cannot be discussed in this chapter.

12.   500 U.N.T.S. 95, *supra* note 3, at 108–110. An analog to Article 27 is found in Article 35 to the Vienna Convention on Consular Relations, T.I.A.S. No. 6820. Other relevant privileges found in the Vienna Convention on Diplomatic Relations include those described in Articles 24 and 25. Article 24 provides *inter alia*, that "the archives and comments of the mission shall be inviolable at any time and wherever they may be." Article 24 would, therefore, apply to databases that contain information identified as archival. *See also* Article 25, which requires that the "receiving State shall accord full facilities, for the performance of the functions of the mission." Thus, a receiving state shall impose no barriers to the normal functioning of an embassy, e.g., access to the local telecommunications systems. Article 25 in this instance could be read in conjunction with Article 27.

13.   Whiteman, *supra* note 1, at 176–80, cites numerous examples of how this generally accepted principle has been interpreted: Whiteman notes: "In considerable part, article 27 of the 1961 Convention was derived from draft article 25 of the International Law Commission's 1958 draft. The Commission's comment on draft article 25 read in part: (2) This article deals with another generally recognized freedom, which is essential for the performance of the mission's functions, namely free communication. Under paragraph 1, this freedom is to be accorded

for all official purposes, whether for communications with the Government of the sending State, with the officials and authorities of that Government or the nationals of the sending State, with missions and consulates of other Governments or with international organizations. (The term "official communications" is used interchangeably with "diplomatic communications" throughout this chapter.) Paragraph 1 of this article sets out the general principle, and states specifically that, in communicating with its government and other missions and consultates of that government wherever situated, the mission may employ all appropriate means, including diplomatic couriers and messages in code or cipher.' "

14.   *See* Lyons, *supra* note 1, at 299. Lyons has noted,

> It is perhaps not too much to say that the privilege of freedom of communications is one of the most vital of those required by and accorded to envoys. It enables them to send home reports of what they have done, said, and observed. The privilege consists of the transmission without delay of the envoy's communications and the immunity of those communications from any form of censorship. The communications may be sent by post or telegraph—and in the latter case it is essential that the envoy be free to use code if he so desires, any local regulation to the contrary notwithstanding. The communications may also be sent in the diplomatic bag by courier; and the courier must enjoy a degree of freedom of movement similar to that of the ambassador, and it attaches to his messenger because it is necessary for the interest or convenience of the ambassador that his messages pass freely and without delay.

15.   This interpretation was taken from a Department of State circular airgram sent to all diplomatic and consular posts by Secretary of State Rusk. His advice related to the question of whether a post can properly use its communications facilities (i.e., those which pass official papers and correspondence) to pass press dispatches for dissemination by newspapers in the United States. Secretary Rusk noted that

> The receiving state shall permit and protect free communications on the part of the mission for all official purposes . . . The official correspondence means all correspondence relating to the mission and its functions.

The basis for the rule is that the uninterrupted flow of the communications between the mission and the sending state is essential to the effective performance of the diplomatic function. The rule is obviously valid only for official communications. Other messages enjoy no protection. The host government is perfectly within its right to censor them or to insist on their discontinuance. Moreover abuse of the privilege may lead to the imposition by the host government of a variety of other restrictions on our use of communications facilities which, of course, would seriously impair our operations.

Secretary of State Rusk to all diplomatic and consular posts, circular airgram (May 18, 1966) (Ms. Department of State, file CR-7-6).

16.   500 U.N.T.S. 95 *supra* note 1, at art. 27. Whiteman, *supra* note 1 at 182, notes that the chairman of the United States delegation to the 1961 Vienna Conference commented on this provision in his report on the conference as follows:

Although there was little objection in principle to the mission's use of a transmitter, there was sharp division whether its use should be subject to the consent of the receiving State. The Commission [ILC] had provided that the mission might communicate 'by all appropriate means,' but did not mention transmitters. Six delegations proposed amending this to require that use of a transmitter by a mission should be subject to the laws of the receiving State and in accordance with local law and international regulations.The United Kingdom, however, advocated retention of the Commission's text, without amendment, contending that the words 'by all appropriate means' included use of a wireless transmitter. It also expressed the view that international telecommunications conventions and regulations had no application to a diplomatic mission and that the receiving State's right to object to the mission's use of a transmitter should be limited to cases of abuse. The Soviet Union agreed that the Commission had intended the words 'by all appropriate means' to include transmitters, but suggested that the use of a transmitter might be made subject to prior notification to the receiving State and to compliance with

technical provisions of international regulations. By a vote of 41 to 20, with 9 abstentions, the 6-power amendment revised to provide that a mission may install and use a transmitter only with the consent of the receiving State, and after obtaining authorization in accordance with the laws of the receiving State and international regulations. The United States voted against the 6-power amendment Consultations led, however, to the deletion of the additional requirement that the sending State obtain authorization in accordance with the laws of the receiving State and international regulations. These words were particularly objectionable as their meaning was uncertain and it was feared that they might be construed as requiring the mission to obtain the consent both of the receiving State and of local authorities.

(U.N. Conference on Diplomatic Intercourse and Immunities, Mar. 2–Apr. 14, 1961 (report of the delegation of the United States with related documents).

17.   47 U.S.C. § 305(d)

18.   By Exec. Order No. 12,046 (July 20, 1979), the President's authority to grant such permission to a foreign country was delegated to the National Telecommunications and Information Administration. NTIA, however, may only consider and grant such authority pursuant to a request to do so by the Secretary of State.

19.   See Teleinformatics issue, 14/2 CORNELL INT'L L. J. (1981), which includes articles by John Eger, Joseph Markowski, Thomas J. Ramsey, and Jane Bortnick, dealing with the laws, regulations, policies, and programs being developed by foreign governments and multilateral organizations.

20.   The newly enacted Foreign Missions Act of 1982 authorizes the Secretary of State to issue instructions which, when implemented, could place on a foreign mission located in the United States the same degree of regulation or restriction as imposed by that foreign mission's government on U.S. missions. *See* Pub. L. No. 97-241, 22 U.S.C. tit. II §§ 4301 *et seq.* (enacted Aug. 24, 1982, effective Oct. 1, 1982). *See also* H.R. REP. No. 693, 97th Cong., 2nd Sess. 39 *et seq.* (Aug. 3, 1982) (on Department of State Authorization Act).

PART III

EMERGING LEGAL AND POLICY ISSUES IN GLOBAL INFORMATION FLOW

CHAPTER 19

INTELLECTUAL PROPERTY ISSUES

NICHOLAS P. MILLER
CAROL S. BLUMENTHAL

INTRODUCTION

The combination of new technology, aggressive competition, and quickly changing business relationships has created substantial gaps in certain areas of the law of property. The question of who owns what has become far more complex. One area that is especially susceptible to this phenomenon is property rights in electronically stored information. This chapter will review the major legal disputes that have arisen, and will continue to arise, in the context of electronic databases. It will suggest how the traditional regimes of intellectual property law might apply and then will propose a framework for international discussion of the issues that remain unsolved.

PROBLEMS WITH PROPRIETARY RIGHTS IN ELECTRONIC DATABASES

Increased worldwide access to information is changing the way international business is conducted. As the demand for quick and accurate information increases, so too do the business opportunities of those who compile, analyze, process, and distribute information. These compilers, analysts, processors, and distributors, not surprisingly, want legal protection for their investments in equipment, time, and creative effort.

Therefore, a significant question for them is, who has what legal rights to use information? For example, the question arises when an original copyrighted work, like a news story based on information in the public domain, is fed into several databases, each owned by a different person. The databases connect to telecommunications distribution networks, which contract with researchers and other users who want access to the information contained in the databases and who in turn contract with secondary or tertiary users. While the owner of a database may, as a practical matter, be able to limit access to the file to specified users, these users can easily transfer the information to other users or shift it from one database to another.

The problem of unauthorized use of information will increase in the next several years. The trend is away from "hard copy" text. Soon, most information will be retained in pure electronic form on cassette, floppy disk, or bubble memory devices for later transfer to "hard copy" form. In fact, most information stored electronically may never be transferred to hard copy but will simply be used, modified, and amplified in electronic form. The author will have little control over this process. Indeed, it may be difficult to determine who the author is in a distributed network environment.

For example, an airplane manufacturer may spend considerable resources and engineering time designing

NICHOLAS P. MILLER ● Mr. Miller is an attorney with the firm of Miller & Young in Washington, D.C., representing a wide range of communications clients. He was a private consultant to the Carter administration on issues of national communications policy. CAROL S. BLUMENTHAL ● Ms. Blumenthal is a partner in the Washington law firm of Blumenthal & Shanley. Her general commercial practice includes an emphasis on copyright law, especially as it pertains to computer databases and software protection.

a new aircraft wing without ever putting pen to paper. The work is created at video terminals and retained in a database. During the design period the staff may make hundreds of modifications, all electronically. The specifications of this "final" wing may then be tested in a computer simulation of a wind tunnel. Based on these test results the specifications for a modified "final" wing are stored in the data bank. The company may never manufacture this design. It may instead use the "wing" as a base line to measure other wing design performances. The data and specifications, constantly updated with experience, contain valuable ideas which are constantly modified as the host computer absorbs more engineering data. But the wing design, and the ideas it embodies, may never be "expressed" in traditional printed or actual form. Thus, when the aircraft company allows a subcontractor access to the database it is unclear exactly how much protection the wing design will receive.

To complicate the situation, modern communications technology allows information transfers across national borders with very little delay and no physical conveyance to mark the transfer. These information transfers are difficult to place under the legal control of a single nation.[1] Nevertheless, many countries attempt to control the type and quantity of information crossing their borders. Except for the United States, few nations acknowledge the importance of free access to information. For example, Eastern European countries recently united against a free-access policy in discussions before the Legal Subcommittee of the United Nations Committee on the Peaceful Uses of Outer Space.[2] Also, some Western European privacy statutes already allow government authorities to substantially restrict the transfer of information abroad.[3] This lack of international consensus will make it far more difficult to implement an ordered policy on the problems of international information transfers.

PROTECTION OF INTELLECTUAL PROPERTY

The legal solutions to the problems surrounding proprietary rights in computer stored and manipulated information fall within the ambit of "intellectual property law." Of the different intellectual property law regimes—patents, trade secrets, unfair competition, and copyright—an analysis of how each might apply to computer database information shows that one of the regimes—copyright—has been, and can be, adapted to

resolve many of the growing tensions over proprietary rights in international transfers of computer database information.

Historical Perspectives

Today's intellectual property statutes are based on the natural rights concept that an individual should enjoy the fruits of his own labor.[4] Accordingly, natural law theorists believed that an inventor should be protected against unauthorized manufacturing of his invention, an author against unauthorized copying of his book, and a painter against unauthorized copying of his painting.[5] This natural rights concept of an author's right to his intellectual property was formally embodied in the first British copyright act in 1709.[6] This act, the Statute of Queen Anne, protected against unauthorized copying of printed works.

Current Copyright Law on Databases

The Statute of Queen Anne and all later copyright statutes protected only the *tangible expression* of ideas or information—say, in a book—but *not the ideas or information themselves*. This limitation is significant. Before computers it had not created substantial difficulties. Most copyrighted materials were works of literature or the like whose primary value was derived from the expression of the information and ideas. Films, books, and catalogs all contained valuable ideas whose usefulness was directly related to possession of their physical expression. However, with the advent of computers and electronic databases much valuable information exists which is never expressed in a permanent fixed form. Since the law has traditionally not granted copyright protection to pure information, an extension of copyright principles was required to remove electronic databases from legal limbo.

TANGIBILITY.   A threshold question in any discussion of current database law relates to the age-old problem of tangibility. For copyright protection to exist a work must be fixed in some "tangible medium of expression."[7] At one time it was thought that databases that existed solely in electronic form might not meet this requirement. However, the Copyright Act of 1976, in Sec. 102(a), changed the law to reflect modern technologies. Under the new law

copyright protection subsists, in accordance with this title, in original works of authorship fixed in any tangible medium of expression, now known or later developed, from which they can be perceived, reproduced, or otherwise communicated, either directly or with the aid of a machine or device.[8]

The addition of "can be perceived ... with the aid of a machine or device" was designed to bring electronically stored work within the reach of copyright.[9] The language was proposed by the Database Committee of the National Commission on New Technological Uses of Copyrighted Works and was subsequently adopted by Congress.[10]

Although the recent changes in copyright law recognize electronic formats as "tangible," the question of tangibility is still bothersome because of the difficulties of proving infringement in electronically stored works. In the past, information used frequently, repeatedly, or by many people, usually has been printed. The usefulness of information has been directly related to the number of copies made of the work, i.e., the number of times it was expressed in tangible form. A single copy of a book could serve as the communication medium and memory device to only one user at a time. The ideas in the book were hard to replicate by word of mouth or other intangible forms of expression. And the ideas quickly faded unless they were preserved in written form. Therefore, the tangible property—the book—although conceptually separable from the ideas in the book became in fact commercially inseparable from the intangible value—the information. Today, the value of information is no longer dependent on or even tied to tangible, fixed expression of the information. Information need not be printed. It can be transferred from user to user, or machine to machine, through modern technological means that are totally beyond the control, or the knowledge, of any third party.

When this happens, notions about property transfers become clouded. For instance, if someone buys a book, enjoys it, and wants to share it with someone else, he generally must give up his own copy; both tangible and intangible property are transferred. It is easy to see that a property transfer has taken place. In contrast, if someone buys computerized information, enjoys it, and wants to share it with someone else, he generally need not give up his own "copy." It is more difficult to see that a property transfer has taken place. Technology makes it vastly more difficult to prove that an infringement has occurred, even if the proper legal remedies exist.

COPYRIGHT AND COMPILATIONS.   Copyright laws protect an author's rights in his own expression even when that expression makes use of nonoriginal information. For example, copyright protects compilations of preexisting material such as anthologies or telephone books.[11] Such compilations are protected because of the time and energy the author or editor spends in collecting and organizing the material. The protection of such compilations is significant, although not as great as the protection of original works.[12]

Some databases are conceptually quite similar to compilations such as telephone books. Both consist of previously available pieces of information (often noncopyrightable in themselves) brought together in a single place. Indeed, an electronic database is simply a technologically new form of a type of work long eligible for copyright protection. In order to preserve the compiler's incentive while, at the same time, keeping individual facts in the public domain, the courts have sought some approach that would simultaneously justify and limit the property interest recognized in compilations of facts. The approach most frequently employed protects the compiler's arrangement of data.[13] The individual bits of information stay in the public domain, but a court is free to find infringements of arrangement if large parts of a work are copied. However, this approach provides little or no protection to those types of work, such as electronic databases, where the information is stored with no inherent order. Computer databases contain randomly stored information which can be retrieved by a computer program in a wide variety of ways. There is no "organization" to protect.

There exists a minority view, disfavored by some commentators,[14] which a few courts have used to directly protect the labor invested in compiling information.[15] In *Leon* v. *Pacific Telephone & Telegraph Co.*[16] the plaintiff had compiled an alphabetical telephone directory. The defendant copied names and telephone numbers from the plaintiff's directory, and instead of arranging them in alphabetical order, arranged them in numerical order by telephone number. Although the defendant's use of the material in no way infringed on the organization of the plaintiff's directory, the court found the defendant's use to be an infringement.

Some of the recent cases which follow *Leon* have explicitly stated that the compiler's labor is what should be protected.[17] In *National Business Lists* v. *Dun and Bradstreet, Inc.*[18] the court, in determining that copyrights were infringed, said,

Compilations such as D&B's have value because the

compiler has collected data which otherwise would not be available. The compiler's contribution to knowledge normally is the collection of the information, not its arrangement. If his protection is limited solely to the form of expression, the economic incentives underlying the copyright laws are largely swept away.[19]

This view was echoed in *Dow Jones & Company, Inc.* v. *Board of Trade of the City of Chicago*,[20] where the Court held that the plaintiff's indexes were copyrightable "due to the effort and judgment exercised in their composition."[21] These decisions, which protect a compiler's industry in collecting information, prevent any unauthorized use (except "fair use")[22] of the compiled information. In effect, they circumvent the prohibition on copyrighting facts and make full copyright protection available to collections of information. Since electronic databases are nothing more than electronically stored collections, they can receive full copyright protection under these opinions.

However, these recent decisions have not eliminated the traditional doctrine that only protects organization. In *Triangle Publications* v. *Sports Eye, Inc.*[23] the court denied the plaintiff an injunction against the use of its horse racing information, holding that the copyright only extended to "the method or form for expressing the data."[24] Moreover, some courts have attempted to cut back on the protection afforded compiled information by using the "fair use doctrine."[25] These decisions reflect the courts' confusion in applying copyright protection to databases. Copyright, at least in theory, can be extended to solve the questions presented by unadorned collections of information such as databases. Yet the courts' decisions to date show that such an extension will be opposed.

Other Intellectual Property Regimes

In addition to copyright there are three other legal regimes—patents, trade secrets and unfair competition—that conceivably could be used to protect databases. However, for various reasons which will be discussed below, none of them will be as effective as copyright.

PATENT LAW. Patent law applies to mechanical devices, "processes," and "compositions of matter."[26] It accomplishes two goals: promoting invention by protecting inventors and, at the same time, promoting the spread of information about innovative industrial techniques by protecting inventors only if they disclose detailed information about their inventions.

To obtain a patent, an invention must meet a threshold standard: it must be a "process, machine, [or] manufacture or composition of matter." Then it must meet three further standards: novelty, utility, and nonobviousness.[27] There has been a controversy about how these standards apply to computer software. The Patent and Trademark Office (PTO) had consistently opposed the protection of software, granting only a handful of claims. For example, the PTO has rejected patent claims for the algorithms—the iterative computational routines comprising the core of programs—because the PTO believed their quasi-mathematical character did not meet the threshold requirement. There are, however, indications that after a recent Supreme Court decision[28] the policy of denying patent protection to computer software will be changed.[29] This protection, unfortunately, will only apply to software imbedded into the hardware itself.

Even so, while computer programs may be the subject of patent protection, the information contained in a database retrievable through a patentable program still probably will not be patentable. Since it is not a "new or useful process, machine, manufacture or composition of matter, or any new and useful improvement thereof,"[30] it does not meet the threshold requirement.

TRADE SECRETS. The Restatement of Torts states that "a trade secret may consist of any formula, patent, device or compilation of information which is used in one's business and which gives him an advantage over competitors that do not know or use it."[31] This broad statement includes anything that can be patented or copyrighted and other forms of property whose protection has been in doubt, such as microorganisms and computer programs.

There are, however, two significant drawbacks to using trade secret laws to protect proprietary rights in data bank information. First, information, once published, is no longer a trade secret. Therefore, a data bank that makes information available to many customers cannot invoke trade secrets protection.[32] Second, data banks often gather publicly available information and put it in a useful, quickly accessible form. Because the information is publicly available, it probably has no trade secrecy protection at all.[33]

However, even if it is assumed that the information

has trade secrets protection, the owner can protect against divulging a secret only through a licensing contract with an information user. If one user breaks the contract by giving the information to another user, the owner has a remedy only against the first user who breached the contract, not against the second user.[34]

Finally, in contrast to the federal statutory theories of protection under patent and copyright statutes, the length of common law trade secret protection is often unclear.[35]

UNFAIR COMPETITION. The doctrine of "unfair competition" is intended to prevent the misappropriation of the fruits of one's labor by another.[36] Like trade secrets, unfair competition is based on common law concepts. No national standard of the elements of unfair competition exists. Internationally the uncertainty becomes even greater. Different countries have substantially different approaches to unfair competition law, and it is unclear how comity principles apply to unfair competition.[37] Uncertainty about the limits of unfair competition law makes its legal protection of little value for commercial data base proprietors.

INTERNATIONAL COPYRIGHT PROTECTION

Before the nineteenth century, copyright protection was not an important international issue. This was because the potential international market was small; it consisted only of a small number of literate aristocrats who spoke each others' national language.[38]

This changed in the nineteenth century. Literacy spread, support for freedom of expression increased,[39] and commerce and communication between nations thrived. As a result, some nations became concerned with protecting their literary works abroad. One of them, France, began dismantling barriers to international copyright protection. In 1852, it unilaterally extended copyright protection to all works, regardless of the place of publication or the nationality of the author.[40] Other countries later reciprocated.[41] Thus began the framework for an international copyright regime. In 1886, after several international conferences, the original framework was completed at the Berne Convention.[42]

The Berne Convention remains the framework of today's elaborate international copyright structure. Several other international conventions, whose membership and intentions often overlap Berne's, also exist.[43]

The most important of these conventions is the Universal Copyright Convention (U.C.C.).[44]

These international agreements, like domestic copyright laws, originally were developed to protect written works and have been adapted to protect some modern art forms such as films. But the status of computer information databases under international agreements is even more unclear than it is under the United States' domestic copyright laws because it is difficult to synthesize different nations' forms of copyright protection into a single international standard. For example, most nations' copyright laws protect traditional forms of expression, like books, but vary about how they protect new forms of expression. Some treat the production of radio or television broadcasts as "authorship" and protect it fully.[45] Others do not treat such production as authorship and protect it, if at all, under the theory of "neighboring rights."[46]

An even more important problem with the international copyright conventions is the tension between developed and developing nations as businesses demand greater international copyright protection for databases.[47] The developed nations have the technological know-how and manufacturing capability to establish efficient, modern computer information services. The developed nations want to encourage the establishment of such services by clarifying property rights to the information provided by these services.

However, this clarification of property rights indirectly reduces access to the information these services provide. At the same time, in order to accelerate their development, developing nations want increased access to the information. However, they cannot afford to buy the information itself or to build the computer information services necessary to provide similar information. Therefore, the less-developed countries proclaim that the information itself should belong to everyone. In short, tension is growing between developed and developing nations, the former seeking greater protection for information, the latter seeking greater access to it.[48]

Despite these problems, the Berne Convention has attempted to keep up with technological advances.[49] The most recent attempt came during the 1970s when the World Intellectual Property Organization (WIPO), a special United Nations agency that administers the Convention,[50] studied the legal protection of computer programs. In 1977, it issued a model law, for the protection of computer software,[51] that incorporates both copyright and patent concepts. But the model law, although useful, does not promise true international protection for computer databases. It falls short in two respects. First, it pertains to only computer programs, not computer databases. Second, so far not a single nation has adopted it.

A MODEL FOR INTERNATIONAL DISCUSSION

Introduction

This chapter has drawn four conclusions: technological breakthroughs require the adaptation of existing intellectual property law doctrines to protect databases; copyright is the existing intellectual property law doctrine that can best be so adapted; copyright law should be adapted on international rather than merely national scale; and there are several significant problems that will beset the world as it adapts international copyright law to databases. This chapter will now describe the process of adapting international copyright law to databases. More specifically, it will describe the issues that must be addressed; then it will describe how the discussion of these issues can begin.

Designing an Appropriate Legal Regime

ISSUES. Several issues quickly become apparent during a discussion of a model law to protect database information—the problems of proof of infringement, the definition of "fair use," and the definition of authorship. An understanding of the disagreements over these issues will facilitate the crafting of the compromises needed to resolve them.

In many cases, even though a work is clearly protected by copyright, it is extremely difficult to prove that infringement has occurred. For instance, if an author were to write an original story and a second author, unaware of the first author's work, happened to write a story identical to the first's, both stories would be eligible for copyright protection. Of course, this seldom occurs. What does occur is that a second author, inspired by the first's work, invents a similar set of characters, setting, and plot, but writes a different and new work. Both works are eligible for copyright protection.

When applied to databases, this may be the correct result. Information gathered in databases often is in the public domain. A law protecting database proprietors should protect only unauthorized taking of the collected and formatted database information. If a second person takes the same information from the public domain and creates his own data base, he should be allowed to do so, and under current U.S. law he may.[52]

The real problem is proving what eventually happened. When a database can be randomly "accessed," it will be difficult to tell whether a suspected infringer actually gathered his information from a copyrighted database rather than from the public domain. The solution to this problem of proof should be the same for computer databases as for printed works. Although it theoretically is possible for two authors to independently create identical stories, it seldom occurs. If the second author can be shown to have read the preexisting story, he probably will be declared an infringer. Similarly, if a second database author can be shown to have used a data base containing the same information that he later calls his own, he should be declared an infringer, and once again, under current U.S. law he will be.[53]

Regarding fair use, the unauthorized copying of material or its arrangement now constitutes copyright infringement.[54] But a database is seldom reproduced in raw form. Instead, only selected useful pieces of information are extracted and used in new combinations. Further, a computer can modify information in an almost infinite number of ways. The modification itself might be an entirely new copyrightable work that in no way infringes the source material.[55]

This situation parallels a long-standing controversy under copyright law about what constitutes a fair use and what protection it receives.[56] In electronic publishing, the issue may be posed as follows: if a database user exercises skill, imagination, time, and ingenuity selecting portions of a database and creating an entry into his own computer system—has he created a new work subject to copyright protection? A user can, and in many instances does, reformat, reorder, select, and consolidate database information. Often, a step process is used in database searches. In such a case the initial "copy" may itself be narrowed, reordered, and consolidated into a new copy with the whole process repeating itself many times. Each time, the resulting copy is somewhat different but is based on the same contents of the initial copy. In such a case, copyright doctrines rooted in the print medium are not easily transferred.

There already is disagreement about what constitutes authorship. In some countries, the term "author" refers only to a natural person.[57] In other countries, it may also refer to a legal entity.[58] The increased use of computers will exacerbate this disagreement. Computer technology is automating the creation of a broad range of musical compositions, visual arts, architectural designs, poetry, translations, dictionaries, and sound recordings. These works are created in a way that bears little resemblance to ordinary collaborative works. This creates difficult questions. For example, who is the "author" of a computer-generated musical score?

There are two schools of thought on the question. The first holds that works created through fully automated processes are outside copyright protection because of the uncertainty of human authorship in the specific work.[59] The second holds that such works are inside copyright protection because the process of creation is controlled by a computer program that reflects human expression.

HOW TO BEGIN. To begin a fruitful discussion of international protection of database information two steps must be taken.

The first step is on a national level. Most of the issues described in this chapter arise regarding national as well as international protection of database information. Therefore, just as international protection of printed works sprang from national protection of them, international protection of database information will spring from national protection of it. More specifically, the most important task is for the United States to develop doctrines that strike the proper balance between creator and user rights. This balance then can be synthesized with that struck by other nations and the synthesis eventually adapted and applied internationally.

For the United States to move in this direction, Congress, not the courts or the Copyright Office, must act. This is for several reasons. First, only a comprehensive federal law will result in clear and complete protection. As was noted previously, only a few cases have interpreted copyright law in a fashion that will sufficiently protect electronic databases. Moreover, one leading commentator has suggested that protecting collections of information does not "render the finder an author" and "distorts basic copyright principles."[60] If a comprehensive law is not enacted, the slow and time-consuming process of "judicial legislation" will take years to reach an answer, and then the answer may well be economically or politically unacceptable. Current and potential database owners will, as a result, be

unable to exploit the market fully because investment uncertainty will prevent them from taking the necessary risks. Finally, only the passage of a comprehensive federal law will send the worldwide signal necessary to encourage international discussions. Just as France's unilateral action encouraged the development of international copyright protection, America's unilateral action could encourage its expansion and refinement. Copyright law has shown that it can be adapted to resolve many of the problems surrounding electronic databases, but it is up to the Congress to make the policy decisions needed to fully implement a coherent scheme.

The second step is to draft a model code that covers database information. Initial work along this line has begun under the auspices of the Organization for Economic Cooperation and Development (OECD). That agency commissioned a report by a Norwegian, Jon Bing, to outline the full range of legal concerns raised by international data flows, of which intellectual property is only a small part.[61] At the moment, it is unclear just where these discussions will go.

Since 80% of the worldwide development and manufacture of computer services takes place in the United States, exporters here are concerned that an international agreement on uses of computer data and software would inevitably restrict the United States' commercial opportunities. Therefore, although the U.S. State Department's position in regard to the OECD discussions has not been fully formulated, the United States may move slowly towards an international regime (favored by Bing and generally by Europeans) until it has developed its own legislation. For the moment some uncertainty in regard to the regulation and protection of data in international trade must be anticipated.

CONCLUSION

The most appropriate course for current international discussion is to focus on broad principles of agreement such as general recognition that property rights exist in computer databases and that access to, and use of, information stored in computers is subject to the consent of the proprietor. The time is not right for establishing an international legal regime to govern information transfer because of the rapid development and change in computer design and software sophistication, and the still-developing pattern of computer networking. Rather,

as has historically been the pattern, international negotiations should follow closely the development of
domestic national policies in this area. Once national
laws are in place, their success or failure can be judged
over time and models can be found upon which to
develop an international regime.

Such an approach, however, does not solve the
problems currently being faced by businesses involved
in the exchange of information across national boundaries. While organizations such as the World Intellectual
Property Organization (WIPO) and UNESCO observe and
evaluate national laws, problems occur daily in terms of
unauthorized use of computer-stored information. Few
nations have any legislation prohibiting theft of computer information. Such laws must be adopted. Until an
international agreement is reached on the comity of
laws, the questions involved in differing domestic regimes governing theft of information, enforceability of
contracts, and private contracts on use of computer
information, should include choice of law clauses enforceable in national courts.

The ability of information providers to develop information resources will be inhibited by erecting nationalistic barriers against information trade. Cognizant of
this fact, national legislatures must develop legal protections for information bank proprietors. Copyright law
provides a beginning. Among intellectual property regimes, copyright statutes are the most easily adapted to
the protection of database information. In addition,
because of multilateral recognition of copyright principles under multilateral conventions, if nations enact
statutes protecting rights in information within the
framework of existing copyright laws, some international cooperation will be automatic.[62]

Finally, the United States should take the lead in
creating a statutory model for the world. Copyright
protection in the United States has developed with a
concern for balancing public and private interests.
Indeed, such a concern is expressed in the constitutional provision establishing copyright protection under U.S.
law.[63] Further, the United States already leads the world
in computer hardware and software development and
computer networking. By amending U.S. copyright law
to specifically accommodate computer database information and usage, the United States could establish an
effective domestic regime, provide a model for other
countries, and potentially shape future international
discussions.

NOTES

1. For an overview of issues involved in trans-
border data flows, see AMERICAN FEDERATION OF IN-
FORMATION PROCESSING SOCIETIES, INC., TRANSBORDER
DATA FLOWS (1974); Fishman, *Introduction to Trans-
border Data Flows,* Stan. J. Int'l L (1980); Gotlieb,
Dalfen & Katz, *Transborder Transfer of Information
by Communications and Computer Systems,* 68 AM.
J. INT'L L. 227 (1974).

2. Fishman, *supra* note 1, at 41.

3. *Id.* at 18.

4. Pool & Soloman, *Intellectual Property and
Transborder Data Flows,* 16 STAN. J. INT'L L. 113, 116
n.3 (1980). *See also* E. PLOMAN & L. HAMILTON, COPYRIGHT
13 (1980) [hereinafter cited as PLOMAN].

5. PLOMAN, *supra* note 4. *See also* Peyton, *The
Creation of Information: Property Rights and Subsidies,* in ISSUES IN INFORMATION POLICIES 76 (J. Yurow
ed. 1981).

6. Statute of Queen Anne, 1709, 8 Ann., ch. 21
(repealed 1824).

7. 17 U.S.C. § 102(a) (1976).

8. *Id.*

9. Keplinger, *Computer Intellectual Property
Claims: Computer Software and Data Base Protection,*
WASH. U.L.Q. 466 (1977).

10. *Id.* at 465, *see also* NATIONAL COMMISSION ON
NEW TECHNOLOGICAL USES OF COPYRIGHTED WORKS
(CONTU), FINAL REPORT (Washington: GPO, 1978)
[hereinafter cited as CONTU].

11. *See, e.g.,* 17 U.S.C. § 103 (1976).

12. Dow Jones & Co. v. Chicago Board of Trade,
546 F. Supp. 113, 120 (S.D.N.Y. 1982).

13. Denicola, *Copyright in Collections of Facts:
A Theory for the Protection of Non-fiction Literary
Works,* 18 COLUM. L. REV. 527 (1981).

14. M. NIMMER, NIMMER ON COPYRIGHT § 3.04, at
3–16 (1978).

15. Denicola, *supra* note 13, at 524–32.

16. 91 F.2d 484 (9th Cir. 1937).

17. *See* Northwest Bell Tele. Co. v. Bedco of
Minnesota, Inc., 501 F. Supp. 299 (D. Minn. 1980)
(telephone directory); Central Tel. Co. v. Johnson
Publishing Co., 526 F. Supp. 838 (D. Colo. 1981)
(telephone directory); Triangle Publications Inc. v.
New England Newspaper Publishing Co., 46 F. Supp.
198 (D. Mass. 1942) (horseracing charts.)

18. 552 F. Supp. 89 (N.D. III. 1982) (National Business Lists ("NBL") brought a monopolization claim against Dun & Bradstreet, Inc. ("D&B") and D&B counterclaimed for copyright infringement. The jury held for D&B on both claims and the court rejected NBL's posttrial motions. The case arose from D&B's publication of various credit reference books. NBL took the information from these books and compiled a series of mailing lists.)

19. *Id.* at 92.

20. 546 F. Supp. 113 (S.D.N.Y. 1982) (The plaintiff filed an infringement action to keep the defendant from issuing a rulebook containing a copy of the plaintiff's stock market indexes. The court said plaintiff's indexes were copyrightable but refused to grant a preliminary injunction against the defendent because the plaintiff was unable to prove any link between the defendant's copying and the alleged harm.)

21. *Id.* at 116.

22. 17 U.S.C. § 107 (1976). The "fair use" doctrine allows a copyrighted document to be used for purposes such as teaching, criticism, research, etc. without the copyright being infringed.

23. 415 F. Supp. 682 (E.D. Penn. 1976).

24. *Id.* at 685–86.

25. In New York Times Co. v. Roxbury Data Interface, Inc., 434 F. Supp. 217 (D.N.J. 1977) the court held that the defendant's copying of entries from the New York Times index for its own index was not an infringement. The court was unwilling to decide whether protection under a copyright extended only to arrangement and instead decided that defendant's copying was "fair use" since the potential effect of the taking was "slight." (Note: Defendant's index contained citations to New York Times Index, not to New York Times newspaper, so it would not serve as a substitute.)

26. R. CHOATE & W. FRANCIS, PATENT LAW 83 (1981). The Patent Act of 1836 was amended to provide for design patents in 1842.

27. 35 U.S.C. §§ 101, 102, 103 (1976).

28. Diamond v. Diehr, 450 U.S. 1975 (1981).

29. Following the *Diamond* case, the PTO has recently begun issuing patents for computer programs.

30. 35 U.S.C. § 101 (1976).

31. RESTATEMENT (FOURTH) OF TORTS § 757 comment b (1939). The U.S. Supreme Court has recognized this definition as "widely relied upon." *See* Kewanee Oil Co. v. Bicron Corp., 416 U.S. 470, 474–75 (1974). Twenty-five states and all federal jurisdictions have approved of all or part of this definition. *See* R. MILGRIM, TRADE SECRETS § 2.01 (1978).

32. The Supreme Court has held "that when an article is unprotected by a patent, state law may not forbid others to copy it because every article not covered by a valid patent is in the public domain. Congress in the patent laws decided that where no patent existed, free competition shall prevail; . . . and that the States may not 'under some other law, such as that forbidding unfair competition, give protection of a kind that clashes with the objectives of the federal patent laws'." Kewanee Oil v. Bicron Corp., 416 U.S. 470, 495 (1974) (Douglas J., dissenting) (quoting Compco Corp. v. Day-Bright Lighting Inc., 376 U.S. 234, 231 (1964)). Further, "matters of public knowledge or of general knowledge in [the] industry cannot be appropriated by one as his secret." Sperry Rand Corp. v. Pentronix, 311 F. Supp. 910, 193 (E.D. Pa. 1970). But, "it is not necessary that a trade secret be absolutely secret; qualified secrecy is sufficient." E.W. Bliss Co. v. Struthers-Dunn, Inc., 291 F. Supp. 390, 400 (S.D. Iowa 1968). *See also* Digital Dev. Corp. v. International Memory Sys., 185 U.S.P.Q. 136, 141 (S.D. Cal. 1973); Data Gen. Corp. v. Digital Computer Controls, Inc., 297 A.2d 433, 438 (Del. Ch. 1972).

33. *Digital Computer,* 297 A.2d at 438.

34. An interesting question with no uniform answer to date is whether a party destroying a trade secret by improper disclosure to the public is free to use the matter formerly subject to trade secret protection, since once the secret is disclosed, no further protection is afforded. For a discussion of this issue see E. KINTNER & J. LAHR, AN INTELLECTUAL PROPERTY LAW PRIMER, 221–223 (1975).

35. *Id.* at 222.

36. *See* International News Serv. v. Associated Press, 248 U.S. 215 (1918). Generally unfair competition law proscribes (a) false advertising and (b) representing another's work as one's own.

37. *See* E. KINTNER & J. LAHR. *supra* note 34, at 223.

38. PLOMAN, *supra* note 4, at 18–21.

39. *Id.* at 18–21.

40. French Copyright Law of 1852, Recueil General de Lois et des Arvets 2ᵉ Serie—AN 1852, 416–417.

41. PLOMAN, *supra* note 4, at 20.

42. Berne Copyright Convention of September 9, 1886. English text printed in the Second Schedule to the Order in Council of the United Kingdom, June 24, 1912 issued under the Copyright Act (U.K.), 1911, 1 & 2 Geo. 5, ch. 46 STAT. R. & O., 1912, No. 913). Ten states were parties to the original Convention concerning the Creation of an International Union for the Protection of Literary and Artistic Works.

43. Most notably the Universal Copyright Convention, September 6, 1952 of which there were forty original parties, UNESCO Copyright Bulletin, 1952, Vol. V, Nos. 3–4. For an English text *see* UNESCO *Records of the Intergovernmental Copyright Conference, Geneva, 18 Aug.–6 Sept., 1952. Paris, 1955.*

Montevideo Copyright Convention, Jan. 11, 1889. The official Spanish text is with the Ministry of Foreign Affairs in Uruguay. The Convention consists of twelve signatories, all of which are South American and European countries. (The Convention does not have much modern applicability. It was replaced for South American nations by the Buenos Aires Convention in 1910 and the Washington Convention in 1946. Relations among European signatories are not governed by the Rome or Brussels Conventions of the Berne Union. Both these conventions are later in date than the Montevideo Convention);

Mexico City Convention, Jan. 27, 1902. This Convention originally consisted of seven signatories. "Law and Treaty Series," No. 17 Pan American Union (Washington, D.C. 1944) (Applied between the Dominican Republic and El Salvador, El Salvador and the U.S.);

Rio de Janeiro Copyright Convention, Aug. 23, 1906, "Law and Treaty Series," No. 19 Pan American Union (Washington D.C. 1946), 19 signatories, nine ratifications (Remains in effect between El Salvador and South American parties);

Buenos Aires Convention, Aug. 11, 1910, "Law and Treaty Series," No. 22 Pan-American Union (Washington, D.C. 1948), 21 signatories, 18 ratifications (Still applicable among South American nations and in U.S.-South American copyright relations);

Caracas Copyright Agreement, July 17, 1911. Official text was deposited with Ministry of Foreign Relations of Venezuela, and consisted of five South American signatories and four ratifications;

Havana Copyright Convention, Feb. 18, 1928, "Law & Treaty Series," No. 34 Pan American Union (Washington, D.C. 1950), 20 signatories, only five ratifications (Some applicability between Panama and other Central American nations);

European Regional Agreement on Exchange of Television Films, Dec. 15, 1958, European Treaty Series, No. 27, 15 parties ratified or acceded;

Rome Convention—protects performers and producers of Phonograms and Broadcasters, Oct. 26, 1961, UNESCO Copyright Bulletin, Vol. XIV at 173—82, 23 parties;

European Agreement on Protection of TV Broadcasts, June 22, 1960, European Treaty Series, No. 34, nine parties;

Phonogram Convention—Convention for the Protection of Producers of Phonograms Against Unauthorized Duplication of their Phonograms, Oct. 29, 1971, 32 parties:

Convention Relating to the Distribution of Programme-carrying Signals Transmitted by Satellite, May 21, 1974, five parties.

44. Originally signed in 1952, the Universal Copyright Convention was revised in Paris in 1971. As of October 31, 1979, 73 States have acceded to the Universal Copyright Convention.

45. PLOMAN, *supra* note 4, at 32.

46. *Id.* at 32–33. (*E.g.* France "neighboring rights.")

47. *See* 17 U.S.C. § 117 (1976).

48. Fishman, *supra* note 1.

49. The United States is not a party to the Berne Convention, which has undergone seven modifications. Approximately 88 countries have ratified or acceded to one version or another of the Berne Convention.

50. WIPO is a specialized agency of the United Nations that promotes the protection of intellectual property throughout the world and is charged with ensuring administrative cooperation and coordina-

tion among the intellectual property unions, the two principal ones being the Paris Union of countries signatory to the Paris Convention of Industrial Property of 1883 and the Berne Union of countries signatory to the Berne Convention of 1886. Overall administration of the U.C.C., however, is provided by another United Nations agency, UNESCO, which provides the Secretariat of the Intergovernmental Copyright Committee, which is the governing body of the U.C.C.

51. MODEL PROVISIONS ON THE PROTECTION OF COMPUTER SOFTWARE 814 (E) (World Intellectual Property Organization, International Bureau 1978).

52. *Central Tel. Co.* 526 F. Supp. at 843.

53. *Id.* at 844.

54. *See, e.g.,* 17 U.S.C. § 103(b) (1976).

55. *See generally* Risset, "Copyright Problems Arising from the Use of Computers to Create Works," 15 (1979) 232.

56. M. NIMMER, *supra* note 14, at 3–15. *See also Copyright Protection of Directories,* 76 HARV. L. REV. 1569 (1963).

57. PLOMAN, *supra* note 4, at 111, 114. Authors must be natural persons under most European laws, hence copyright in collaborative works such as motion pictures is vested in either several significant contributors (writer, director, composer), as in France, or in one person around whose conception the work is made, as in West Germany, where copyright in a film is usually held by the producer. The continental position has been adopted in the Berne Convention which is based on the concept of authors' rights. Under this view an author has both an economic and "moral" or personal relationship with his creation; hence an author must be a physical person in order to enjoy a "moral" right.

58. Under the law of countries following the Anglo-American tradition of copyright, a legal entity such as a corporation or partnership may own a copyright. *See, e.g.,* 17 U.S.C. § 201(b) (1976) dealing with works made for hire. *See also* PLOMAN *supra* note 4, at 92.

59. CONTU, *supra* note 10, at 109. The U.S. Commision to Study New Technological Uses of Computers concluded on the point: "there is no reasonable basis for considering that a computer in any way contributes authorship to a work produced through its use."

60. M. Nimmer, *supra* note 14, at 3–16.

61. Bing, Forsberg and Nygaard, Legal Issues Related to Transborder Data Flows, Preliminary Study for Expert Group on Transborder Data Flows, OECD (1981).

62. Since the operative principle of both Berne and the U.C.C. is "national sovereignty," equal treatment should result in regard to aliens and nationals within a country. There will still exist a problem, however, in regard to international standardization.

63. U.S. CONST. art. I, § 8.

CHAPTER 20

DATA PROTECTION

JANE H. YUROW

INTRODUCTION

Increasingly, personal information is collected, maintained, and transmitted electronically. Governments seek to protect the right of individuals to control the way in which information about them is used. Usually, their focus is on the large, impersonal institutions, both public and private, that have arisen in modern, technologically advanced societies.

Many advanced, industrialized democracies have enacted data protection or privacy laws. The purpose of these laws is laudable—to avoid adverse consequences of misuse or abuse of personal data. However, their effect, particularly when applied to international data transfers, could be to limit the availability of information vital to commerce, or to government or corporate decision making.

Data protection laws and international agreements apply to records of individuals, which are held by a variety of institutional recordkeepers—corporations, hospitals, research organizations, and the government, for example—usually in electronic data systems. A few countries have extended the application of these laws to a limited class of corporate, nonpersonal records. They have done so by analogizing corporations to individuals and, consequently, calling them "legal" persons.

Although the transborder data flow provisions of most national laws apply to government as well as private-sector records, and to a range of records maintained by private-sector recordkeepers, the bulk of data affected by these provisions is related in some way to the international business dealings of U.S. firms. These firms include information services companies that receive foreign data for processing or storage in this country, multinational corporations whose internal information flows are transmitted internationally, and firms such as banks and airlines that regularly transmit transactional information over international electronic networks.

DATA PROTECTION AND DEMOCRACY

Data protection laws and agreements arise in and among economically and technologically advanced democracies where the regular relationships among nations are premised on sharing roughly equivalent political and economic values. The value protected here is the right of individuals (and sometimes organizations) to control the way in which information about them is used by the large, impersonal institutions that have arisen in technologically advanced societies.

Data protection laws impinge on another deeply held value that advanced democracies share—that information of all kinds should be widely available to citizens and institutions. Privacy protection laws authorize restrictions on international communications, commerce, research, or investment, which limit the unimpeded flow of information across borders. Thus, the reliance of

JANE H. YUROW ● Ms. Yurow is director of Jane Yurow Associates, Bethesda, Maryland, consultants in telecommunications and information policy. Formerly, she was director, Organization for Economic Cooperation & Development (OECD) Privacy Guidelines Project, and senior policy analyst at the National Telecommunications and Information Administration, U.S. Department of Commerce (NTIA).

democracies on unimpeded information flows, in addition to enhancing the effectiveness of their political systems, has encouraged economic growth. This is particularly true since the advent of electronic information technologies which can process and transmit great quantities of information at high speeds. But the capabilities of electronic technologies for enhancing information flow have heightened the concern of many societies for protection of data in these systems from misuse and have given rise to demands for data protection laws.

DATA PROTECTION LAWS AND AGREEMENTS

At this time, ten European countries have passed data protection legislation containing provisions authorizing restrictions on transborder flows of personal data. These are Austria, Denmark, France, Germany, Ireland, Norway, Sweden, Iceland, Luxembourg, and the United Kingdom. Israel also has such a data protection law. Several more countries are on the verge of passing these laws. The United States, Canada, and Australia also have data protection laws, although their scope and focus are somewhat different. Significantly, these laws do not include provisions limiting international transfers of personal data.

Although the laws differ among countries, they all contain certain basic categories of provisions. These are

- limitations on the collection of personal data;
- requirements that what is obtained be relevant, accurate, complete, and up-to-date;
- specification of purpose for which the data will be used;
- limitations on disclosure without the subject's consent or by authority of law;
- safeguards against unauthorized access;
- openness about developments, practices, and policies with respect to personal data;
- establishment of the right of subjects to see information about themselves and to challenge, correct, or amend it.

European Law

Generally, the European data protection laws are comprehensive in scope, addressing personal data in virtually all automated, and some manual, record systems. In each country there is a data protection administration—a centralized, national bureaucracy that licenses or registers all automated databases containing personal

information. The administration has authority to inspect the records of institutions, and to process or initiate complaints against agencies or organizations that do not comply with the data protection law.

The transborder data flow provisions in European laws authorize the national data protection agency to restrict flows of personal data destined for countries that do not have similar sorts of laws. In addition, two international agreements, referred to later, include provisions limiting transborder data flow.

U.S. industry is particularly vulnerable to the possibility of restrictions on the international flow of personal data. Many European countries view U.S. data protection laws as less comprehensive and effective than either European national laws or the international data protection agreements. The United States' position is that while our data protection laws are somewhat different in concept from other laws and agreements, they provide a broad range of protection to personal records mantained in both the public and private sectors.

U.S. Law

United States privacy law, for the most part, is state law. It focuses on recordkeeping in specific sectors of the economy—banking, health care, insurance, government employment. It provides record subjects with direct remedies against illegal abuses rather than placing this power in a centralized bureaucracy. A brief review of the significant sources of U.S. privacy law is important to an understanding of the current U.S. position that protections available respect the rights of individual record subjects adequately.

THE CONSTITUTION.   The Fourth Amendment to the U.S. Constitution protects letters and documents in a person's home or carried on one's body from search or seizure by police without a warrant. The Fifth Amendment protects individuals from testifying against themselves in court. The First Amendment places limits on the government's use of information about a person's beliefs or affiliations. The equal protection clause of the Fourteenth Amendment limits government use of information about a person, such as race or national origin, to penalize him or her.

FEDERAL LAW.   The Privacy Act[1] is the only comprehensive federal privacy protection legislation, although many states have similar laws governing public records. This statute establishes a regime of fair information practices for all personal records maintained by both federal civilian and military agencies, with limited exceptions for criminal investigations in progress and national security data. This includes access and correction rights, and certain limits on collection all of data.

Federal sectoral legislation includes the Family Educational Rights and Privacy Act[2] which provides students in federally funded schools with access to their records and protects the confidentiality of these records against disclosure to third parties. The Tax Reform Act of 1976,[3] and the Right to Financial Privacy Act,[4] limit government access to personal records to specified, exceptional circumstances.

Several federal statutes regulate private-sector record-keeping relationships when the institutions involved do business in interstate commerce. For example, the Fair Credit Reporting Act[5] restricts the activities of companies that investigate applicants for credit, insurance, or employment.[6] It requires "consumer reporting agencies" to institute certain fair information practices respecting subjects of data collection, including informed consent of subjects to collection, limited rights of access to data, and protections against unauthorized disclosures. The purpose of the act is to assure that financial and other personal data used by institutions for making business-related decisions are accurate and complete, relevant to the intended use, and respecting of the confidentiality of the data subject.

STATE LAW.   Most data protection legislation is at the state level. State constitutional provisions frequently recognize a right to privacy.[7] State laws regulating many aspects of the financial services and insurance industries frequently contain fair information practices provisions. Several states have enacted the Insurance Information and Privacy Protection Model Act,[8] prepared in 1979 by the National Association of Insurance Commissioners. Although personnel records are generally unprotected by law, a few states do have laws requiring employers to grant employees access to records. There are numerous statutes limiting use of information about an employee's race, sex, age, or medical condition, in making decisions. In addition to the comprehensive acts covering government-maintained records in general, there is a voluminous body of state law protecting criminal justice records from disclosure to third parties.

COMMON LAW.   The confidentiality of information is protected at common law in a number of contexts, although the protection is more limited than the data protection laws. Banks are required to keep transactional information confidential. Physicians, attorneys, and, sometimes, clergymen have a privilege against compul-

sory disclosure of information in a legal proceeding. The law of defamation is complex, but does limit the scope and encourage the accuracy of information disclosed by private-sector recordkeepers.

VOLUNTARY COMPLIANCE.   In addition to a wide variety of legal protections, the United States has a tradition of self-regulation that has been fairly effective in establishing data protection codes or policies. The medical and legal professions, for example, address confidentiality in their codes of ethics, as do the hospital administrators. Increasingly, large corporate employers are recognizing that internal personnel privacy policies are an aspect of corporate responsibility.

International Agreements

Because of U.S. concern about the impact of European data protection laws, the federal government has participated in drafting an international agreement to harmonize national data protection laws. The U.S. is a signatory to the Organization for European Cooperation and Development (OECD) Guidelines Governing the Protection of Privacy and Transborder Flows of Personal Data.[9] This voluntary agreement was adopted in October 1980, and has been approved by 23 of the 24 OECD countries. The United States, in turn, is implementing the agreement solely through the voluntary decisions of U.S. multinational corporations to develop internal data protection policies.

A second agreement, the Council of Europe Convention for the Protection of Individuals with Regard to Automatic Processing of Personal Data[10], is binding on those countries that have ratified it. It requires comprehensive national data protection laws as a prerequisite to ratification. To date, five countries have ratified. Others are expected to follow suit. The United Kingdom has passed national legislation so that it can ratify. The United States, with no comprehensive national privacy legislation, is ineligible to ratify. This agreement has provisions authorizing countries party to it to restrict transborder data flows to nonsignatory countries. It puts signatory countries in a position to discriminate against U.S. industry by restricting its critical data flows.

SIGNIFICANT ISSUES

The emergence of national data protection laws with restrictions on international data flows raises a number of questions. This chapter addresses three of these: How do different national approaches to privacy protection affect the formulation of data protection policies? To what extent do data protection laws serve to fulfill national economic or social objectives unrelated to privacy? Does the rationale developed to protect personal data justify the extension of similar coverage to corporate nonpersonal records?

Different Views of Privacy Protection

Democratic countries generally protect both personal privacy and unimpeded flows of information. But decisions as to what information should and should not flow internationally are generally made on the basis of what each society considers to be best for its own citizens. One country is not likely to respect another country's desire for openness at the expense of its own citizens' right to privacy, or vice versa.

HOW COUNTRIES RESPOND TO DATA PROTECTION LAWS OF OTHER COUNTRIES.   One country may pass a data protection law because its legislature decides that personal data is inadequately protected by its government and private-sector institutions. It solves the problem to its own satisfaction, usually by establishing centralized administrative mechanisms with broad powers respecting the rules under which government and private organizations may establish and maintain automated record systems. But, the problem may occur again for some of its citizens if personal data passes to another country, say through a financial network or an intracorporate data system of a multinational corporation. The receiving country may not protect data in the manner in which the sending country does, although it may offer what it considers adequate protection. The sending country, not wanting this result, may pass a law authorizing it to refuse to let personal data flow to the receiving country.

The sending country does not have authority to require the receiving country to handle the data in a way that would satisfy the sending country's law, so it simply doesn't allow the receiving country to have access to the data at all. This is obviously disruptive of the financial transactions involved or of the ability of multinational corporations to rely on the availability of information that may be vital to decisions about its customers, suppliers, or employees.

The receiving country has several nonexclusive options: to pass similar or equivalent legislation; to make no public policy decision while recognizing that each affected organization or corporation is free to make its own arrangements with the sending country to ameliorate the impact of its law; or to enter into international agreements that establish a standard of performance by each country agreeable to all signatory countries. An additional option is to retaliate on a case-by-case basis against a country that restricts data flows, by in turn restricting that country's flows, or by some related form of reciprocity. This option, although threatened by the United States with regard to telecommunications services, has not yet been considered in the context of data protection.

Countries, like the United Kingdom, whose encounters with another countries' data protection laws are frequent, are likely to choose the first option and bolster it with the third. Countries like Turkey and Greece, whose institutions have only occasional brushes with another country's privacy law, are likely to take the second option.

The United States, whose economic and political interests are pervasive worldwide, has chosen a combination of the second and third options—noninterference and an obligation to encourage a minimal standard of data protection. The United States has traditionally combined its strong bias towards openness with a belief that openness is generally best achieved through limiting government's authority to direct the way in which both private and public institutions handle information. Thus, although U.S. law offers extensive examples of privacy protection, these laws generally place the principal mechanisms for their enforcement in the affected individuals rather than in government agencies. With respect to international data flows, the tendency in this country, consistent with more general limits on government, is to allow industry to use its economic power to resolve on a country-by-country basis whatever differences exist over data protection policies. At the same time, the government has negotiated an agreement in an international forum on a minimum standard of data protection.

NATIONAL APPROACHES TO DATA PROTECTION.   The way a country approaches data protection is directly influenced by its approach to social problems in general. This helps to explain the difficulty in achieving uniformity among nations in the legal regimes each develops to protect personal records. Frequently, mistrust that countries express about the effectiveness of other countries' data protection laws reflects pervasive misunderstanding about their political and legal systems.

Differences in national data protection laws reflect different views of the relative importance of individual privacy or open information flows, the role of government in society, and response to historical experience. The last two concerns are interwoven with the first. While there are subtle differences among the provisions of various European data protection laws, there is a chasm between these laws and U.S. laws. However, despite technical and philosophical differences, all these countries share similar objectives.

The United States   Historically, the United States political system has shunned long-range government planning to resolve economic and social problems. Until recently, the United States economy has been one of abundance, built on principles of limited government interference with the activities of private individuals and organizations. We do not anticipate problems. We address problems as a result of identifiable abuses. This has definitely been the case with data protection legislation. Congress passed the Fair Credit Reporting Act in response to identified misuse by credit companies of recorded personal data. In other areas of law, a similar rationale motivated the passage of the Occupational Safety and Health Act (OSHA), Employee Retirement Income Security Act (ERISA), and even the Social Security Act.

The prevailing environment in the United States fosters deregulation of many aspects of private-sector operations. The pattern of administrative supervision set by European data protection laws is unlikely to be repeated in the United States, and central data administrations will not be created. Indeed, the likelihood of even minimal government supervision of corporate record keeping about individuals is slim.

In addition to the absence of planning and the aversion to regulation, the U.S. legal system, despite its revolutionary origin, is evolutionary. It eschews radical new solutions to problems and tends to view apparently novel problems as conceptual extensions of concerns that U.S. law has addressed over time in different guises. The Anglo-Saxon common law tradition continues to provide a fundamental rationale for the growth of the U.S. legal system.

Privacy law is influenced by this phenomenon. Although the effects of technology have given impetus to the need for data protection legislation, privacy as a legal concept is as old as the republic, and is embodied in the Fourth and Fifth Amendments to the Constitution. For legislators, then, it is logical that establishment of a new legal regime is not an appropriate solution. They prefer to use traditional mechanisms to protect against privacy invasions made possible by electronic technol-

ogy. Thus, although U.S. law offers many examples of privacy protection, it generally empowers the affected individuals, rather than government agencies, to redress any grievances through private law suits. This follows the pattern of contract and tort law. It is equivalent to the redress provided against violations by government of the traditional privacy protections of the Fourth and Fifth Amendments.

The U.S. citizens' mistrust of a powerful central government is another pervasive theme that influences U.S. policy and law generally. This fear of government actions against citizens is the very basis for the Fourth and Fifth Amendments. In other areas, the law frequently limits government interference with business practices to situations of demonstrated abuse. The Constitution itself limits government power over individual actions. In data protection, U.S. concern focuses on the potential for the government to misuse recorded information about individuals. Both federal and state data protection laws emphasize the protection of government records.

Historically, this attitude of mistrust of government interference with individuals and organizations has been accompanied by officially sanctioned encouragement of openness. This has occurred both among individuals and from the government to the citizen. The First Amendment limits government interference with private transfer of information, both at the sender's and the receiver's ends. Laws like the Freedom of Information Act and the Government in the Sunshine Act[11] require the government to conduct much of its business before the public view.

Europe   European data protection laws reflect a civil law approach to problem solving. The United Kingdom, a common law country, is caught between its legal traditions and its pragmatism. Although earlier legislative proposals included common law procedures and remedies, the recent data protection law is very much on the continental mode.[12] This attempt at harmonization is motivated by Britain's close economic relationship to the Continent. Britain needs to trade with those countries without fear of restrictions on data flows. It needs a data protection law to ratify the Council of Europe Convention. Ratification assures free flow of personal data to Britain from the Continent. But the provisions of this law do not sit easily with British legal tradition.

The civil law systems frequently solve social and economic problems by anticipating abuses. Often they design comprehensive governmental structures to prevent or limit the effects of these abuses. Traditionally,

European countries have engaged in economic and social planning as a preventive approach to solving problems and setting national priorities. Also, Europeans accept a greater governmental role in the operations and decisions of business and in the general economy than Americans do. There is more cooperation between business, government, and society in general in Europe than in the United States. This may in part be the result of the greater range of political ideologies that must be satisfied with the decisions made by any government in power. The data protection laws follow this pattern of preventive legislation.

Data protection laws have been enacted, in part, to deal with the problems that potentially could arise from abuse of computerized records. For the Europeans, the application of these laws to international data flows follows logically. Computers have the capacity to enhance the volume and speed of information dissemination worldwide. Consequently, the inclusion of domestic and international records under the same regulatory umbrella makes perfect sense from the viewpoint of the social planner. A comment of Jan Freese, the director general of the Swedish Data Inspection Board, sums up the European attitude: "I am not sure we can afford computerization of society to develop like a 'happening.' To me it is important to solve problems and I prefer to do so before they occur."[13]

SOCIETAL EXPERIENCE AND FEAR OF COMPUTERIZATION. The overriding concern in all countries behind passage of privacy protection laws has been fear of the impact of computerization on society. For example, representatives in the European Parliament have pressed such laws as a means "to the equality of all individuals in a modern computerized society."[14]

Two kinds of fear lie behind the pressure for data protection laws. The first is that computerization might expose individuals' private lives to the view of impersonal institutions. These institutions could use the information to make adverse economic and social decisions about individuals. This embodies a fear of the impact of technology on bureaucracy. The second fear is that computerized personal record systems might facilitate a future authoritarian government in conducting purges of dissenters, as Hitler did in the 1930s and 1940s. This reflects a perception of technology as a tool of tyranny. Both of these concerns are behind European data protection legislation. The first is expressed most vocally in Scandinavia, and the second in France and Germany.

In the United States, the increasing use of computer technology by large institutions in the early 1970s gave rise to the call for privacy laws. But because U.S. citizens also have a long tradition of skepticism about government intrusion into their affairs, the legislative solutions have been different than those developed in Europe. For example, Congress has been reluctant to create national data banks containing personal information on large numbers of citizens. In Europe, many governments routinely maintain such data banks.

MUTUAL MISTRUST. The different experiences and attitudes toward government and toward computerization have resulted in different laws and policies on both sides of the Atlantic. Often these are not adequately understood by countries on either side. On the one hand, some Europeans do not view U.S. efforts at establishing data protection laws as adequate to insure the protection of data about Europeans that is transmitted to the United States. They then surmise that the United States does not share their concern about the impact of computerization on individual rights. On the other hand, a prevalent U.S. perspective is that data protection laws are a stalking horse for economic protectionism, and that the Europeans don't care about giving their citizens adequate access to information.

Both Europe and the United States may be mistaking differences in national emphasis on the relative importance of privacy protection and free information flows, for a more profound lack of regard for democratic values. Also, there is not enough mutual understanding of different attitudes toward government and toward historical experience. Clarification of fundamental misunderstandings is essential to resolving the transborder data flow dilemma.

Data Flow Regulation and National Economic and Political Goals

Although the impact of personal data protection laws is sometimes similar to economic protectionist policies, it is difficult to prove that their intent is protectionist. For one thing, this thesis denies that other democracies share with the United States the value of privacy protection. It essentially accuses them of the same lack of concern of which they accuse us. Also, it ignores the reality that when governments, both democratic and authoritarian, wish to place economic, cultural, or national security restrictions on transborder data flows, they do so by clearly identifiable regulation in these areas. International flows of personal information are generally considered to be a miniscule pecentage of total data flow and so, from an economic vantage point, do not seem worth regulating.

ECONOMIC CONCERNS. Many countries have articulated a fear that their indigenous information industries will not be able to compete effectively, either domestically or internationally, with countries having a lead in developing and marketing electronic information technologies and services. These countries also fear the use of electronic technologies to enhance the competitive position of the multinational corporations. U.S. industry, as the leader in marketing electronic products and services, stands to suffer serious economic consequences when other countries pass laws taxing software or databases or requiring domestic processing of data. The effect, and sometimes the purpose, of these laws is to restrict data flows or to regulate the manner in which data can be transmitted across national borders.

There are some interesting, current examples of laws that protect domestic industry by restricting international information flows. The Brazilian government has passed a law requiring the registration of all software entering Brazil,[15] not so it can acquire legal protection, but so that the software can be distributed to Brazilian firms for use in enhancing domestic research, product development, or education. The Federal Republic of Germany has regulations, the precise application of which remains unclear, requiring that, where PTT lines are used to communicate data internationally, the data must be processed in Germany.[16] Germany also has a stringent data protection law, but has chosen to regulate data processing directly.

The Canadian Bank Act[17] prohibits banks from processing, storing, and maintaining banking data, much of which is personal in nature, outside of Canada. U.S. industry analysts complain that this is an economic sanction on U.S. banks doing business in Canada. The Canadian position is that the purpose of the law is to strengthen the authority in its own Banking Commission over activities of banks. This would not be possible if data were maintained outside of Canada. Whatever the purpose of the law, privacy protection is now being used as a shield for accomplishing other national objectives. Canada has a federal privacy law that applies only to federal records and has no transborder data flow provisions.

CULTURAL CONCERNS. Canada has an openly stated policy on foreign influence of its mass media, which stems from a desire to preserve its culture.[18] This policy will limit flows of U.S. television programming into Canada. It is, however, not necessarily a pretext for trade protectionism or any other objective of the Canadian government.

NATIONAL SECURITY CONCERNS. The United States, because of its increasing concern for national security, is becoming protective of certain types of information, while at the same time championing the importance of unimpeded flows of information. Technology transfer, including sharing of consultants, teachers, and training materials, is undergoing greater scrutiny in the Commerce Department's Export Control Administration (ECA) than in the past. The Defense Department is becoming increasingly concerned about transfer of "know-how," particularly to unfriendly countries. The ECA is interpreting broadly federal law, which limits technology transfer on national security grounds. It is limiting the export of categories of U.S. scientific and technical knowledge heretofore freely exchanged with other nations.[19] Although the declared intent is to keep this information from Eastern-bloc countries, the effect at times is to deny access to it by U.S. trading partners. These countries complain that such restrictions create barriers to competition with U.S. industry.

Tension is developing in the United States between policies favoring unimpeded flow of information and policies opting in some circumstances for increased protection of information in the name of national security. This protection has the effect of economic protectionism and parallels the pull in other industrialized democracies between protecting indigenous industries through restricting information flows while supporting the basic value of open access to information. Despite the foreign view of current policies on technology transfer, the United States government expresses sincere concern about national security and shuns suggestions that its policies in this area reflect nefarious hidden agendas.

PRIVACY IS A DISCRETE CONCERN. As national security and economic and cultural policies are discrete, identifiable concerns which often lead to restriction of transborder data flow, privacy is also a discrete concern. To many Europeans, it is difficult to separate the need for data protection from economic and cultural issues. They view their interest in privacy protection as part of a continuum of concerns. These all need to be addressed to ensure that their societies continue to have unique identity and economic viability in the face of widespread reliance on electronic information technologies. These countries are legislating on many fronts simultaneously to accomplish societal objectives that take into account a variety of social, economic, and political factors.

Policies to deal with privacy are probably not intended to address other goals. No democracy can function effectively by merely paying lip service to the fundamental importance of unimpeded information flow. But the need to balance the right to information and the right to privacy, which exists in all democratic societies, is separable from economic, national security, or other interests of these countries and deserves consideration on its own merits.

Legal Persons Data

Four countries—Austria, Denmark, Luxembourg, and Norway—have extended their data protection laws to include firms or "legal" persons. There is some support for this viewpoint in the European Convention on Human Rights,[20] which allows nongovernmental organizations to allege violations of human rights against the government, including the right to privacy. The principal impact of this provision on corporations is that it requires them to give other corporations access to their records if the records contain information about the other corporations.

Both in Europe and in the United States, there are strong objections to applying data privacy concepts to commercial activities, for two reasons: it is more difficult to document abuse of recorded information on businesses than on individuals, and the moral arguments relevant to physical persons generally do not fit the business context.[21]

RATIONALE. The rationale for covering firms is that, because misuse of data could injure a corporation in much the same way as it could an individual, the corporation should be similarly protected.[22] The legal-persons provisions apply to transborder data flows. Thus, in terms of records affected, the consequences to multinational firms of widespread adoption of legal-persons legislation could be infinitely more burdensome than personal-privacy provisions.

Countries whose privacy laws extend to legal persons have many small, closely held companies that may be like individuals in their need for confidentiality around certain transactions—credit, banking, or insurance, for example. One analyst, M. E. Hogrebe, reports that firms in those countries generally accept this legislation, but assume that strategic company files will be exempt from

the law on a case-by-case basis through arrangements with the data authorities.[23]

The actual implementation of these laws has been described as "very cautious and pragmatic."[24] The director of the Danish Data Inspectorate reportedly has stated that "companies have been given rights to confidentiality and security in several laws and should not be barred from protection in privacy statutes."[25]

PROBLEMS. The analogy of certain business data to personal data may provide a rationale for protecting small businesses against misuse of limited categories of information. But if protection is extended to data about large firms—for example, multinational corporations—the kinship of legal persons to individuals breaks down. This is particularly so because none of the national laws clearly defines the categories of corporate data protected. Company data, of which personal data are generally small subsets, cover an almost infinite variety of possible data categories.

The need to protect the confidentiality of credit ratings is probably not very significant to large firms. These organizations are likely to be more concerned about the potential for access to their records by competing corporations under the record-subject access and the record-lising provisions of data protection laws.[26] Under the access provisions, an organization has a right to review data about it maintained in records of another organization. The listing provision requires organizations to list the categories of records they maintain on other organizations. This may permit data-subject firms access to information of the sort usually protected as proprietary information.

U.S. firms express concern about the ability of the federal government to protect from obligatory disclosure under The Freedom of Information Act the proprietary information it collects. Hogrebe disputes this effect of the access provisions, indicating that to date companies have not taken advantage of them.[27] Emerging European legislation promoting public access to government information tends to identify this contradiction and to make express provisions in law to protect proprietary information.[28] Thus, the sensitivity of large corporations in both the United States and Europe about accessibility of corporate data may be exacerbated rather than diminished by extending the reach of privacy laws to corporate records.

In Europe, private-sector firms of all sizes have identified problems with applying the privacy law to legal persons. It enables the government to intervene so as to limit business freedom. It also enables the government to oversee data systems and possibly to jeopardize the security of that data. Finally, it provides government with a means of leverage against individual companies to achieve economic or political gains unrelated to its data-processing authority.[29] U.S. companies, traditionally even more wary of government involvement in their affairs, share these concerns.

IMPLICATIONS OF APPLICATION TO LEGAL PERSONS. In both European and U.S. law, organizations and associations, including corporations, are recognized as legal entities with certain obligations and restrictions. These entities are not generally considered to be entitled to the humanitarian rights of individuals. The countries whose privacy laws cover legal persons have made an exception for the principles embodied in these laws.

Firms may not be entitled to rights equivalent to individuals, including a right to privacy protection. But, under concepts of equity and fairness, they may still be entitled to protection for information about them maintained in the files of others. This is particularly plausible where lack of protection causes adverse economic effects.

The European Community's *Study of Data Security and Confidentiality* suggests that the protection of firms as data subjects be recognized under commercial law principles rather than by analogy to privacy protection.[30] This concept would necessarily recognize the right of trade secrecy, and build in certain rights for subjects of nonphysical data. The study proposes a "right of awareness" of the general structure of both public and private files in which a firm is a data subject. In addition, the report recommends a dual obligation of "right to know" and "right to dispute," rather than a correction right, since it is often difficult to locate and correct specific files on firms. The concept proposed is one of fair and responsible relationships between commercial agents.[31]

In the view of U.S. firms, the actual implementation of any data protection law affecting confidential business records, even one based on commercial principles, would require close scrutiny. As with personal records, the mechanisms for enforcement are suspect when they involve considerable governmental authority. Fair commercial practices, embodied in the Uniform Commercial Code and widely accepted by U.S. businesses, generally apply to contractual relationships and to warranties.

Data protection as an aspect of fair business practices introduces an unfamiliar element, outside of the evolutionary tradition of U.S. law.

HARMONIZATION. Many European governments consider the solution to differences in national laws to lie in harmonization of these laws through treaty provisions. The Council of Europe's convention on data protection, although essentially intended to protect personal records transmitted internationally, recognizes the right of countries with legal-persons laws to apply the convention to nonpersonal records, as an extension of privacy principles.[32] A number of the countries likely to ratify this convention in the near future have legal-persons provisions in their laws. An additional mechanism could be provided through the European Parliament. The European Community Study proposes that the community consider legal-persons data to be protected in international commercial law by assimilation into the Treaty of Rome principle regarding fair competition.[33]

Under a harmonization scheme, all countries ratifying a treaty would agree to abide by similar rules for protection of international information flows. Nonsignatory countries would be subject both to the national laws of each country in which they maintain data, and to any treaty provisions setting out terms for transmission of data from or among these countries. The firms of a country that is not a signatory to a harmonization treaty would be vulnerable to restrictions on data flow that their government did not participate in formulating. The impact of these restrictions could be very costly for these companies. The United States, for example, is not a signatory to either the Council of Europe Convention or to the Treaty of Rome. Consequently, U.S. firms transmitting data from or among countries ratifying these treaties could face restrictions on international flows of such data, without significant recourse.

INTERNATIONAL IMPLICATIONS. The provisions of the several national laws extending privacy protection to legal persons vary considerably. According to Hogrebe, countries could have bilateral negotiations concerning the impact of the law on transborder data flows between those two countries.[34] This could result in the data protection law being used as a political tool. The inclusion of transborder data flows within these laws creates virtually insuperable compliance problems for firms doing business internationally, and major enforcement problems for data authorities. It also increases significantly the potential for legalized access to a company's records, and disperses this access geographically.

THE UNITED STATES AND THE DATA PROTECTION CHALLENGE

Until now, data protection laws rarely have been applied to the records that U.S. firms transmit internationally. U.S. firms operating in countries with privacy laws increasingly recognize that they are obligated to comply with these laws for records maintained within those countries. But the inconvenience of satisfying several sets of national criteria has not yet led U.S. industry in great numbers to support international harmonization treaties. Nor has the potential for restrictive application of national data protection laws and international agreements, like the OECD Guidelines and the Council of Europe Convention, encouraged firms to pressure Congress to pass either comprehensive or sectoral data protection laws.

Although many European countries have adopted increasingly restrictive policies to protect domestic telecommunications and data processing industries, privacy laws have not been a significant vehicle for carrying out these policies. The number of countries with data protection laws is likely to grow. This may or may not result in greater regulation of transborder flows of personal data.

A few countries may enact legal-persons laws, but this trend probably will not be as strong as that toward personal privacy protection. The appropriate scope of legal-persons laws is unclear, and its benefits to record subjects have not been adequately documented. International agreement on harmonizing legal-persons language will be difficult to achieve.

CONCLUSION

The dire prediction of the early 1980s was that data protection laws would seriously hamper the ability of U.S. firms to compete in Europe. Data processing firms would be kept from offering low-cost services to European customers. Multinationals, unable to transmit corporate records across national boundaries, would suffer serious financial loss. This potential still exists, but the prediction has not yet become reality. At this time, U.S. corporations seem to be focusing their concerns about international competition on other types of national policies, such as laws requiring domestic data processing or restricting the use of national telecommunications facilities.

NOTES

1. 5 U.S.C. § 552a.
2. 20 U.S.C. § 1232g, *as amended by* Pub. L. No. 96-26, 93 Stat. 342.
3. 26 U.S.C. § 7609.
4. 12 U.S.C. § 3401, *et seq.*
5. 15 U.S.C. § 1681, *et seq.*
6. *See also* Equal Credit Opportunity Act, 15 U.S.C. §§ 1691–1691f, which protects against ethnic or racial discrimination in lending money; Fair Credit Billing Act, 15 U.S.C. §§ 1666–1666j and Electronic Funds Transfer Act, 15 U.S.C. §§ 1693–1693r, which establish rights to procedural fairness.
7. *See, e.g.,* Cal. Const. art. 1, § 1.
8. Copies of the model law may be obtained from the National Association of Insurance Commissioners, 633 W. Wisconsin Ave, Suite 1015, Milwaukee, Wisconsin 53203.
9. OECD, Paris, France, adopted September 24, 1980.
10. Council of Europe, Strasbourg, France, adopted September 18, 1980.
11. 5 U.S.C. §§ 552, 552b.
12. Data Protection Act 1984, ch. 35, July 12, 1984.
13. OECD "Preserving the Open Flow of Information Across Borders," in *Transborder Data Flow and the Protection of Privacy* (Paris, 1979).
14. Van Aarssen, Denmark, Debates of the European Parliament (Sept. 24, 1979).
15. Normative Act 22/82, For Registration of all Computer Software (effective Dec. 7, 1982).
16. *See, e.g.,* 17th Order for Amending the Telecommunications Regulations, adopted Sept. 4, 1981 by the Administrative Council of the Deutsche Bundespost, Bundesgesetzblatt Teil I [BGBl] 97, (Sept. 26, 1981).
17. Banks & Banking Law Revision (Bank Act) §§ 157, 174.
18. Ministry of Communications, Broadcasting Strategy for Canada (1983).
19. Commodity Control List, 15 C.F.R. § 399 (1982).
20. Council of Europe, 1954, (signed at Rome, Nov. 4, 1950, 5 Europ. T.S., 257 U.N.T.S. 103.

21.   Bancilhon, Chamoux, Grissonnauche, & Joinet, *The Physical Person/Non-Physical Person Problem,* in Study on Data Security and Confidentiality
§3, at 3–12 (Commission of the European Community
(E.C.C.), Jan. 1980) [Hereinafter cited as Bancilhon].

22.   *See* M. Hogrebe, Guidelines Governing the
Protection of Privacy and Transborder Flows of Personal Data, OECD D511/ICCP 81.25 (Sept. 1, 1981).

23.   *Id.* at 23.

24.   *Id.* at 24.

25.   III Transnat'l Data Rep., Nov. 1980, at 10.

26.   Bancilhon, *supra* note 21, at 3–4.

27.   Hogrebe, *supra* note 22, at 44.

28.   Bancilhon, *supra* note 21, at 3–7.

29.   *Id.* at 3–11.

30.   *Id.* at 3–36, 3–43.

31.   *Id.*

32.   *Council of Europe Convention, art. 3, sec.
2(b).*

33.   Bancilhon, *supra* note 21, at 3–43, 3–44.

34.   M. Hogrebe, *supra* note 22, at 32.

CHAPTER 21

NEGOTIATING CONTRACTS FOR TRANSNATIONAL SERVICES

SUSAN H. NYCUM

In his enlightening ditty "New Math," Tom Lehrer teaches that "base eight is the same as base ten, with two fingers missing." By analogy, international computer contract law is the same as domestic computer contract law with several fingers added.

The first part of this chapter describes key domestic computer contract issues and the second part discusses certain added "fingers" of international issues. The third part of the chapter provides a checklist of considerations for a U.S. concern doing computer related business abroad.

KEY U.S. DOMESTIC COMPUTER LAW ISSUES

The basic domestic computer contract, whether for hardware, software, systems, or services, has certain important common components. We will examine each of these in turn.

Description of the Item to Be Provided

The computer products and services to be provided under a contract are rarely completely standard items that are easily recognizable by someone not a party to the transaction. It is necessary to define the subject of the transaction with a high degree of detail lest the matter look like gibberish to an outsider—including a contracts administrator or a judge. Frequently this is

done by an exhibit that more fully defines the terms thereafter referred to in the agreement as the "software," the "system," or the "hardware."

It is recommended that these definitions serve as a starting point for setting out in the contract exactly and completely what the business arrangement is between the parties. Computer agreements are frequently complex transactions that have evolved over time into their final form. A well-drawn contract serves the good business purpose of a plan or blueprint of the activity to be performed. From a legal standpoint it serves as a memorandum of what was promised and hence is useful if and when disputes arise.

Applicability of the Uniform Commercial Code to the Transaction

A second domestic legal issue is whether or not the item is governed by article 2 of the Uniform Commercial Code (UCC), which governs the sale of goods. Clearly hardware is included,[1] but what about software and systems and services? Does the UCC apply to leases and licenses as well as to sales?

The later question has been addressed by courts who have applied the UCC to some ostensibly nonsales transactions.[2]

Similarly the UCC has been applied to transactions in which goods and services have been combined.[3] To

SUSAN H. NYCUM ● Ms. Nycum is a partner in charge of the high technology group of the national law firm of Gaston Snow & Ely Bartlett and is resident in its California office in Palo Alto where she specializes in the legal aspects of computers. She is also co-principal investigator of the SRI International Studies of Computer Abuse for the National Science Foundation and the Department of Justice.

date, data on the applicability of the UCC to pure software licenses is scant, principally because parties usually contract on the assumption that the UCC would be applicable and have agreed on terms and conditions that achieve UCC-required results. Additionally, as a practical matter, UCC principles appeal to business people so that concepts of limitation of warranties, remedies, and damages are common to most computer agreements.

The Price to Be Paid

Some transactions are for simple dollar amounts payable entirely upon execution of the agreement or delivery of the product or service. But many transactions contain quantity discounts in which the quantity measurement may be complicated. Still others are royalty based with degrees of complexity in the calculations of the royalty. Still others have lease credits toward a purchase with opportunity for upgrade. In these more complex contracts the questions regarding price can become quite confusing.

Particularly in a software license, the fee based on royalty can be tricky. The Bell Laboratories' Unix System is licensed for a fee based on the number of users. Some new systems do not lend themselves to a reliable "head count" so licensees are concerned about inadvertent miscounting. Some other vendor software is licensed to run on a single designated Central Processing Unit (CPU), yet in the "nonstop" environment of Tandem and Stratus computers, a CPU designation is not applicable. And, in the personal computer market the vendor repair policy may mean total replacement of the machine. This will result in a different CPU in the possession of the customer than that identified to the software license contract.

In the software royalty arrangement whereby an "author" is compensated on the basis of the amount of distribution, the question of the royalty base is critical. Some distribution contracts count simply the numbers of product distributed and pay the author a fixed dollar amount per unit. Others have formulas for arriving at the net or gross sales price and exclude or adjust for, inter alia, returns, review copies, discounts, upgrades, enhancements, and taxes. These transactions look more like traditional book publishers agreements and have many of the same payment terms. These terms include the designation of the schedule for payments of royalties earned during a set period and provision for audit of the

transactions on which the royalties are paid. Certain other contracts for software to the mass market provide not for the transfer of complete items, but rather are for transfer of a master version of the software and the accompanying documentation to the distributor who then manufactures the finished product for distribution. This later course may have tax and duty implications in international transactions. These will be discussed in the section on international aspects of computer contract law.

Taxes

Tax consequences are a substantial consideration of any U.S. transaction. Many transactions are structured for the purpose of achieving the advantages of depreciation and investment tax credit (ITC) at the federal level and for the purpose of avoiding or minimizing state and local property and sales and use taxes.

The legal issue most relevant to the tax analysis is that of tangibility versus intangibility. At the federal level tangibles, i.e., hardware, can qualify for the favorable ITC and depreciation treatment. The Internal Revenue Service categorizes software as intangible property unless it is bundled with the hardware; then it is treated as part of the hardware for purposes of ITC and depreciation deductions.[4] One case gives some support for the view that software is tangible property.[5]

Recently, the IRS proposed removing most software development from the list of activities that qualify for the incremental research credit under section 44F of the Internal Revenue Code and the section 174 research and development deduction. Testimony at hearings and individual written responses convincingly stated the long-range negative implications to the industry and to the country from such a change, and the proposal is now being revised.

At the state level, jurisdictions differ as to the applicability of sales and use taxes to software. Some states consider it intangible, others classify certain types of software, e.g., custom software and maintenance, as intangible or a service, and packaged software as a tangible "thing."[6]

The application of personal property taxes to software has generally not been addressed by the courts, but when so addressed software has generally been held not to be subject to tax at all.

Finally, with respect to property tax, the California taxing authorities have interpreted real property tax provisions to include the value of computers located on the taxpayer's premises on the basis that these are "fixtures" and thus part of the building that is part of the real estate!

Ownership of Proprietary Rights

Proprietary rights in computer products are protected in the United States by patent, copyright, trade secret, and trademark laws.

Commercially available hardware is frequently patented or, if new and experimental, may be considered a trade secret by its owner. The hardware component known as the semiconductor chip is apparently not protected by patent or by copyright or effectively protected by trade secret. A bill entitled The Semiconductor Chip Protection Act of 1983 is pending in Congress to provide a special form of protection for the chip. (The chip itself is not to be confused with the program embodied in the chip.)

Software is protectible by copyright, pursuant to the Copyright Act of 1976 as amended, and by trade secret.[7]

Trademarks and service marks for computer products and services abound and are registerable on the Principal Register of the Patent and Trademark Office in international classes 42 and 9.

The copyright law is explicit on the issue of copyright protection for software.[8] U.S. courts have generally interpreted the law to include software in object form and embodied on a chip (ROM, RAM, PROM, EPROM).[9]

In the patent arena, a two-stage test known familiarly as the Freeman Two-Step has evolved for finding software patentable by the Patent Office.[10] Step one, does the claim recite an algorithm? If so, step two, does the claim in its entirety wholly preempt the algorithm? A negative answer to either question will clear the hurdle of rejection for software as nonpatentable subject matter. This of course does not eliminate the need for the invention to pass the other applicable tests of novelty, nonobviousness, etc.

Contracts for computer products and services should recite the ownership interests in the items. In the software and services contract, that issue is key. For the most part software is licensed and the trade secret or copyright (or both) interests are specified as residing in the owner-developer with a nonexclusive or exclusive right to use or to sublicense in the vendee. For the purpose of analysis and drafting one must distinguish between a transfer of the source code (human-readable) and the object code (machine-readable). If the object code is transferred, copyright may be relied on and publication presumed from the transaction. In this event, the items should bear the copyright notice.[11] Any copies that the licensee is permitted to make should also be required to contain the notice. Because of the ease of disassembly (a form of reverse engineering) many contracts prohibit reverse engineering by the licensee.

In the mass market where copies are sold to consumers over the counter in retail establishments, software owners have attempted to bind the customer to a license for the intellectual property contained in the copy in one of two ways. The first way is to require the buyer to execute and return a registration card that entitles the user to any service provided by the licensor and the opportunity to receive news of updates and corrections. The card serves as a log of legitimate sales (and hence a check on the dealer records and a way of separately tracing piracy) and also serves as a customer execution form for the license included with the product. The second way is to place the license agreement inside a sealed package containing the software so that it is clearly readable through the wrapping and to state prominently on the outside of the package that the opening of the package constitutes acceptance of the product and the terms of the license. No reported cases are available so the efficacy of each of these methods of binding a consumer is in doubt. Traditional contract law favors the second method because of case law that holds a consumer bound by the warranty restrictions on a product by the act of purchase of the goods. Traditional contract law may disfavor the first approach because until the purchaser executes the card, no meeting of the minds has been evidenced and no agreement to abide by the license may exist. This indicates a likelihood that those products for which a card is not returned would not be subject to the license but protected only by copyright (which may well be enough in many cases). Experience with the rate of consumer return of the cards is that few cards are returned of those distributed.

When the source code is licensed, the agreement will usually be for a higher price because of the higher intrinsic value of the source code. Because source code is human-readable, owners generally wish to keep it secret. Hence the product often is treated as a trade secret or as both a trade secret and an unpublished copyrighted work. Increasingly courts are upholding this approach as applying two complementary but non-identical forms of protection. Thus the state trade secret protection is generally not held to be preempted by section 301 of the Copyright Act of 1976.[12]

In some source code licenses, the licensee is granted the right to modify the source code, sometimes to include it in new works which it then in turn markets to third parties. A number of copyright issues can arise as to the ownership of the modified work. Among the more troublesome results may be that the product is a joint work as defined by the Copyright Act and that absent an allocation of interests between the parties they will each own an undivided half of the whole product. This is hardly ever what the owner of the original work intends and indeed if he has licensed multiple customers in the same way—as would be common in an OEM (or wholesale) environment—the result could be a jungle of conflicting rights.

In a services contract, including custom tailoring of a hardware or a software product to meet a customer's needs, ownership interests in the resulting product are stated in the agreement. Sometimes "user groups" of customers of a similar base product contribute to the vendor or each other changes they have made to the basic vendor product. These exchanges pose difficult problems for ownership interests, particularly trade-secret protection, and should be addressed in the proprietary rights section of the services agreement.

When employees or consultants perform work for a company which purports to own the product they work on (and may so represent and warrant in its license agreements), another area of proprietary rights issues arise. The work-for-hire rules of trade secret law and the Copyright Act vest ownership of the intellectual property in the employer without the necessity of written agreements. However, written agreements are necessary from consultants and other nonemployees who produce copyrightable works, in order to vest the copyright of the work in their clients. The rapid movement of computer professionals from company to company within the industry has made the employer, employee, and consultant area a prolific source of litigation when proper contracting procedures are not followed.

Warranties and Limitations Thereof

If the contract is for goods, the panoply of provisions in the UCC regarding warranties is applicable.[13]

Most contracts for computer equipment and software

recite an express warranty that the product will work in accordance with some specification and usually a covenant to repair or replace the product if it is defective. They then disclaim any and all other warranties including the implied warranties of fitness for a particular purpose and merchantability. This is permitted in the U.S. in nonconsumer agreements pursuant to section 2-316 of the UCC.[14]

As these articles point out, the climate in the warranty area is becoming more favorable to the customer and lawyers are counseling their clients and drafting agreements accordingly. In some foreign jurisdictions, as is discussed under international aspects of computer law, the legal environment is even more customer-oriented.

Although vendors have been customarily taking only limited voluntary responsibility that the product will work, they are much more receptive to giving warranties of title and accompanying indemnities for infringement of third party proprietary rights. These warranties are generally that the vendor owns or has the right to transfer the software and hardware. As stated earlier, when vendors have the contractual right to modify the software licensed to them for sublicensing, difficult questions may arise as to the ownership of the product *including the underlying work*.

The indemnity given may be for patent infringement, copyright infringement, and/or trade secret misappropriation. It may be for "any action or claim" or only as to "damages finally awarded after all appeals have been taken" and it may require that the vendor manage the case or merely notify the vendor that a claim has been made. Because claims of software piracy are increasingly made and pursued, these warranties and indemnities have great value in software, systems, and services agreements.

Remedies and Limitations Thereof

Most computer agreements reflect both parties' desire for a noninfringing product that works. Thus, the remedies of repair or replace and make noninfringing (by rework or license from the true owner) are the preferred choice both of the customer and the supplier. However, sometimes the product cannot be fixed or reprogrammed.

When the item cannot be repaired or replaced and that course is the exclusive remedy provided under the contract, then if the contract is governed by the UCC, the remedy is deemed to fail of its essential purpose and the full range of other remedies under the UCC is available to the customer.[15] As a hedge against this situation, the parties usually contract for a "backup" remedy of a refund of some or all of the purchase price or a sum certain in damages. This safety net will forestall the contracted for remedy failing of its essential purpose.

In the infringement case, many vendors successfully contract to terminate the agreement if the product cannot be made noninfringing or cannot be licensed for use from the true owner. Increasingly, however, customers are negotiating agreements containing covenants obligating the vendor to pay some or all of the customer's costs to obtain a product that is noninfringing.

Limitation of Liability

Computer contracts generally reflect the prevailing view that the consequential damages in this new technology could well put a supplier out of business and as such the vendor could not charge enough to compensate him for assuming that risk in the agreement. Hence, agreements typically exclude consequential damages "even if the vendor has been appraised of the possibility of same...." Such limitations are permitted by section 2-719(3) of the UCC and have been upheld by the courts when the loss is commercial and the limitation is not unconscionable.

Dispute Resolution

Dispute resolution in the United States is undergoing change. Though most disputes are still resolved by litigation, arbitration and mediation in various forms are gaining popularity.

Some litigation is heard in state courts, while disputes involving patent and copyright infringement are heard exclusively in federal court. By virtue of diversity of citizenship between the parties, other matters can be heard in federal court. Remedies available in litigation include money damages, specific performance, and injunctive relief. In addition, in copyright disputes, the copyright law sanctions the impounding of the alleged infringing material and upon a finding of infringement, the destruction of the infringing materials.

Arbitration is governed by state law except for international matters, maritime matters, and transactions and contracts evidencing a transaction involving interstate commerce. These are governed by the Federal Arbitration Act, 9 USC et. seq. The state arbitration process is regulated by the laws of the particular state, and if the

parties choose to involve them, the rules of the American Arbitration Association or the rules the parties agree to themselves. Though the arbitration provision in an agreement was earlier thought by most draftsmen to be boilerplate, more and more parties are using the procedure and insisting on carefully crafted clauses which, inter alia, permit discovery, limit the arbitrators to those persons skilled in computer technology or computer law, and require arbitrators to report the basis of their findings and to reconsider the finding on the motion of a party.

Dispute resolution in the computer area can be difficult. Computer-related disputes are often complex, both as to legal issues and factual determinations including understanding the technology. Often the matter is a case of "first impression" where traditional legal principles are being applied to new applications. This requires sophistication and imagination on the part of counsel and the trier of fact. In a number of instances courts have held on both sides of the same issues on similar fact patterns.

Choice of Law Provisions in Domestic Contract

Modern choice of law rules utilize an analysis of the facts and policies involved in a contract dispute. For example, the "most significant relationship" rule applies the law of the state with the strongest relationship to the contract dispute. Thus, courts consider the place of negotiation, making, and performance of the contract, the location of the subject matter of the contract, and the parties' domicile, place of incorporation, place of business, and nationality. The "center of gravity" approach chooses the law of the state in which most of the relevant facts occurred. The "government interest" analysis compares the interest of the states involved in the contract dispute, and applies the law of the state with the greatest interest.

A common feature of high-technology cases has been the use of contractual choice of law provisions by the parties. These contractual stipulations usually have been honored by the courts. In *Bruffey Contracting Co., Inc.* v. *Burroughs Corp.*,[16] the district court noted that Maryland courts will honor contractual choice of law provisions. Therefore, the court applied Michigan law to the computer dispute, in conformity with the parties' contractual agreement. In a similar computer contract dispute, *Samuel Black Co.* v. *Burroughs Corp.*,[17] the district court applied Michigan law in compliance with the choice of law provisions of the contract. The court did require that the relevant transaction had a reasonable relation to Michigan, and found such a relationship because Michigan is Burroughs' state of incorporation and principal place of business.[18] In both of these cases, it should be noted, the choice of law provision appeared to meet Burroughs' needs more than the other party's wishes. However, in neither case did the court challenge the choice of law provision as an ineffective provision of an adhesion contract.

In *Triangle Underwriters, Inc.* v. *Honeywell*,[19] the court noted that the New York choice of law analysis would result in the application of New York law, while the parties had agreed by contract that Massachusetts law would apply. The court did not resolve this conflict, for there was no practical difference between the relevant New York and Massachusetts law.[20]

In the two *Burroughs* cases,[21] the courts relied on state statutes as a basis for enforcing choice of forum clauses. Courts will also enforce contractual choice of forum clauses absent a relevant state statute. The landmark case of *The Breman* v. *Zapata Offshore Co.*[22] held that forum clauses are prima facie valid.[23] *The Bremen* involved international choice of laws, but also has been applied to domestic choice of laws. A forum clause will be specifically enforced unless the party opposing its application can "clearly show that enforcement would be unreasonable and unjust, or that the clause was invalid for such reasons as fraud or overreaching."[24] "A contractual choice-of-forum clause should be held unenforceable if enforcement would contravene a strong public policy of the forum in which suit is brought, whether declared by statue or by judicial decision."[25] According to the *Bremen* court, a forum clause also might be unenforceable if the chosen forum were "*seriously* inconvenient" for the trial of the action, especially if the remoteness of the forum suggested that the agreement was an adhesive one.[26] In general, however, forum clauses will be enforced.

INTERNATIONAL ASPECTS OF COMPUTER CONTRACT LAW

The international aspects of computer contract law will be discussed in this chapter from the standpoint of the U.S. product vendor or service provider doing business abroad.

Certain considerations affecting the vendor in an international transaction are new concerns (the added "fingers") not discussed in the first part of this chapter, such as U.S. export control provisions, foreign currency control and payment restrictions, import duties, and data control laws. Other concerns apply to the items discussed previously in this chapter, but may differ from the domestic treatment, such as limitations of remedy and warranty. Others, such as description of the transaction and choice of law, are similar. In this part the new concerns will be first discussed, followed next by the concerns that vary from domestic concerns, and lastly by the concerns that are similar.

Export Control Regulations

Controlled commodities and technical data are governed by the Export Administration Act of 1979, as amended,[27] and the Export Administration Regulations promulgated pursuant thereto.[28] The commodity control list includes computers and media; technical data includes software. There are two kinds of licenses for controlled commodities—a general license and a validated license.[29] The regulations also specify the declarations and notices that must be designated on the parcel or filed with the carrier and customs or post office at the place of export.

Technical data can be exported under a general license (GTDA) used for data already generally available to the public, and data for teaching, research, and patent applications. Much software is exported pursuant to a GTDA license for technical data. This license requires the exporter to obtain assurances from importers that they will not re-export the item or its "direct products" to a country on the restricted list. These must be either in the license agreement or side letter prior to shipment. Penalties for knowing and for willful violation are very severe.[30] Query as to what constitutes "knowing"—if less than actual knowledge is enough, it argues for close diligence on the part of the exporter as to the intentions of any purchaser or distributor.

Customs and Import Duties

These vary country by country and should be checked frequently for change. It is also important to know on a country by country basis how the item is categorized. For example, in Canada application software in machine-readable form is assigned no value for customs evaluation; the measurement used is the value of the storage media only.[31] Mexico imposes import quotas on manufacturers and computer suppliers, a 30% custom tariff on microcomputers, and a 15% on micros and macros.[32] The EEC countries have a common customs tariff.[33]

Exchange Control Laws

Exchange control laws deal with controls on foreign payments and usually arise in countries that have balance-of-payment problems. The laws prohibit making any payments abroad without proper authorization. The laws will vary from country to country and may classify types of transactions differently. Some transactions will qualify as liberal transactions wherein payments can be made freely and others will be controlled transactions. These controlled transactions again fall into categories. One category is the general authorization where approval is obtained through registration of the underlying agreement. Another category is that in which authorization is specifically required for each payment. In addition to the controls, legislation may set up multiple exchange rates with favorable rates for preferred transactions. Exchange controls can vary frequently within a country and are increasingly being imposed by countries that have traditionally not employed them in the past. It is therefore wise to check before entering into computer products and services agreements including software distribution contracts, where payment will be made abroad.

Data Protection Laws

To date the countries of Austria, Canada, Denmark, Federal Republic of Germany, France, Iceland, Luxembourg, New Zealand, Norway, Sweden, Switzerland, and the U.S. have some form of data protection law. These laws were ostensibly enacted to protect the rights of individuals whose personal data is contained in automated data banks, but in many of the European countries the laws are oriented rather more to issues of sovereignty and support of local industry development than to privacy concerns. The laws vary from country to country and in some countries apply to company data as well as personal information (e.g., Austria, Luxembourg, Denmark, Norway). In some countries the legislation has set up a data protection board or individual to administer the requirements which may include advance approval before a transborder data transfer can be made. Indeed a requirement may be that the secured country have similar protections as the host country.

Other countries require only notice or registration of the database. Two multinational bodies have adopted data-protection resolutions, the Council of Europe (COE)—the U.S. is not a member—and the Organization of Economic and Cultural Development (OECD)—the U.S. is a member. The COE agreement has treaty effect on its signatories, but to date only Sweden has endorsed the treaty. The OECD has no treaty effect but serves as a set of guidelines for its members.

Protection of Poprietary Rights

The status of protection of proprietary rights outside the United States varies widely from country to country and can change within countries fairly rapidly. In many respects computer products and the intellectual property contained therein are treated the same as in other industrial property. Thus, patent and copyright concerns are substantially similar to those in other industries. However, the area of protection of proprietary rights in software has raised some unique considerations.

Increasingly, nation-states are by court decision (e.g., Federal Republic of Germany, France, Australia, and Japan) or by legislation (e.g., Hungary, United States) extending copyright protection to computer programs in source or human-readable form. The protection of proprietary rights in object form in some countries is unclear, e.g., United Kingdom, Canada. Patent protection for software as such is not generally available in foreign countries, but the German Federal Patent Court held such an invention patentable as early as 1973,[34] and some countries have said that an otherwise patentable invention is not rendered unpatentable because a computer program is a part of the invention.

In June 1983 the World Intellectual Property Organization held a meeting of a Committee of Experts to consider a draft international treaty on software and chip protection. The 30 participating countries chose overwhelmingly not to endorse such a treaty at this time, and noted that national developments were proceeding so as potentially to obviate the necessity for such a treaty.[35] As litigation occurs in various countries and the decisions are published, further information will be available.

Some countries that are not members of any of the copyright conventions and/or do not have a patent system, nevertheless recognize the protection of technology by contractual commitment or by relationships of trust and confidentiality. Most countries recognize some form of trade secret protection arising out of the agreement or the relationship between the parties. In Canada by statute, copyright and trade secret protection may exist simultaneously in the same work.[36] However, even those countries that do recognize contractual provisions for retention of trade secrets may have national laws that create serious problems in technology transfers. For example, in Brazil, all technology licensed to a Brazilian licensee becomes the property of the licensee in five years.

Taxes

International transactions involving the provision of computer goods and services raise a variety of tax issues both at home and abroad.

Since domestic corporations are taxable by the IRS on their worldwide income, many exporters of computer products distribute their goods and services abroad through the use of controlled foreign corporations. If this strategy can be successfully implemented, U.S. taxes can be deferred on the foreign corporation's profits until they are repatriated to the United States. The Internal Revenue Code contains two sets of rules (the foreign personal holding company and "subpart F" provisions) which are designed to prevent abuse of this deferral opportunity.[37] These are among the most complicated provisions of the Internal Revenue Code, and need to be carefully studied by anyone contemplating the use of a controlled foreign corporation to implement their export strategy.

A second tax deferral vehicle for U.S. exporters is the Domestic International Sales Corporation (DISC). A DISC is a specially-formed domestic corporation whose export profits are partially tax deferred. The European Community has argued for a number of years that the DISC rules constitute an illegal export subsidy because, in substance, they allow for an indefinite deferral of direct taxes on export income earned in the United States. The United States has recently advised the European Community that it will shortly replace the DISC rules with another export subsidy vehicle that is compatible with the General Agreement on Tariffs and Trade. This vehicle is expected to be of benefit to computer manufacturers.

International transactions involving computer equipment may also expose the U.S. computer vendor to foreign tax issues. For example, in some South American countries, passing title to a computer in the buyer's home country may cause the seller to become subject to that country's taxes. Similarly, local withholding taxes may be imposed on user rents, royalties, and interest payments that are bound for the United States.

Extensive service and other activities in a foreign country may cause a U.S. vendor to have a "permanent establishment" in the country and become subject to local tax on its business profits associated therewith.

The strategies for dealing with these problems vary from case to case. For example, withholding taxes can often be passed along to the local user of computer goods and services through a carefully drafted contract clause. There are also increasing efforts to expressly cover certain transactions involving computer software in tax treaties. Other tax issues may be resolved through a proper structuring of the transaction in light of specific tax legislation.

Dispute Resolution

Dispute resolution abroad has been evolving in much the same way as in the United States. Business people and lawyers are attempting to find ways to decrease the costs and time of litigation. As in the U.S. the shortage of judges qualified to understand the technology has added to the desire to choose alternatives to litigation. Two principal alternatives have emerged internationally; one is international arbitration, the other is conciliation. UNCITRAL has promulgated rules for both of these which have been endorsed by the U.N. General Assembly. In both areas the enforceability (of the decision of the arbitrators or of the settlement) is a key concern. UNCITRAL is working toward a model law on international commercial arbitration.[38] In the meantime, there are several bilateral treaties and six multilateral treaties presently in force.[39]

Choice of Law

As in domestic contracts, the parties' choice of law provisions will often be honored by the foreign country unless there are clear local public policy reasons against the choice or there is no relation of the choice to the matter or the parties. As is true domestically, some provisions for arbitration will be disallowed when such issues are not arbitrable in the foreign country. Because of the disparity of legal systems in which one may be doing business, choice of law provisions are key concerns in the contract and require close attention.[40]

Terminology

A major difficulty in computer contracting is that the terms of art in the technology do not have a commonly accepted meaning within the industry. It is even more difficult to translate these generally "coined" terms from language to language, and translation nuances may lead to disasters in product delivery. For example, consider the possibility of confusion over the word *software*. Within the U.S. software may mean a computer program or it may mean a computer program plus documentation and other materials. In any case it does not mean a specific program and as such must be more particularly defined. When literally translated into languages other than English, the term may prove even more confusing in understanding the transaction. (In the U.S., the garment business has recently capitalized on this tendency to confusion by using the term software to advertise leisure clothes to be worn for at-home uses of computers!)

A SUGGESTED CHECKLIST OF CONSIDERATIONS FOR THE U.S. COMPUTER VENDOR DOING BUSINESS ABROAD

At the 1982 MCLE conference, Jane Devlin, Esq., then Cullinet marketing representative for Latin American and the Far East, began her speech with a long sentence in Mandarin Chinese. This she said was a famous saying by Confucius that freely translated means "When doing business abroad always hire local country counsel." Amen and hear, hear! At the outset both pride and concern for the client's purse may argue against this course, but the changing nature of foreign governmental treatment of outsiders and the changing nature of the technology will probably affect the legal and regulatory environments abroad. Thus, pride and the client's purse will make the association of the best available local counsel a conservative decision.

The true multinational that is interested in setting up its own presence in a foreign country has a host of legal concerns that are beyond the scope of this chapter. Recent experience indicates that a number of countries are wooing business, e.g., Belgium and India, with tax and other incentives for locally controlled installations and personnel. Firms interested in establishing abroad should consult not only with local counsel but with

other U.S. firms to learn of their experience and particularly problems encountered.

Many computer-related companies, however, have an interest only in distributing abroad. Some of these companies are unsophisticated and assume that either they can use their U.S. agreements as is, or draw up one universal foreign agreement. In company with many lawyers, the author has had the duty of convincing the client that each new country it chooses to distribute to or within means a review of other prior agreements and preparation of special documents for use in the new country. The tendency of the uninitiated client is to assume that if U.S. export-control restrictions are met, there are no more "wrinkles" to doing business abroad.

The most dramatic way of getting the client's attention is to tell it about Brazil's and Mexico's license laws that effectively put its technology in the hands of the licensee or into the public domain within 5 years in Brazil and 10 years in Mexico. Such statements lead naturally to the first item on the checklist that follows:

1. The reasonableness of doing business in the target country. If there is a chance of nationalization of the technology (or the local business) it may be wiser not to do business there at all. The dream of huge short-term profit may fade with fear of loss of the company's investment.

2. Although patent and copyright laws are evolving favorably abroad, the protection of proprietary rights in software is still best handled at this time by contractual restrictions between the owner and the customer. Safer yet is to distribute only the object form of the program so that what is transferred is not the bare secret. When dealing with a U.S. arm of a foreign company, attention should be given to warranties of and indemnities for proprietary protection by the U.S. subsidiary when the parent company's country has no intellectual property law, e.g., many Mideastern countries.

3. The manner of delivery from the U.S. into the host country may pose tax problems in some countries with respect to software. It will be necessary to know whether it is better from a duty and tax standpoint to deliver the finished unit or a master copy which is duplicated in the host country.

4. Host country approvals are often necessary for doing business. These may be general to all business (e.g., Japan, which requires approvals from MITI), or for doing specific kinds of business, such as data protection

board registration for information processors (e.g., Sweden), or for approval-of-technology licenses (e.g., Mexico, Spain, and the Andean Pact Countries). In the case of teleconferencing systems, service bureaus, and time sharing companies, issues related to the PTTs such as use of leased lines will have to be resolved.

5. Payment ideally should be made in U.S. dollars payable at a given time at one's U.S. address, net of currency controls and restrictions, and foreign tax and other assessments. Each of these criteria must be examined to see that there are no hidden problems with enforcement of the payments provisions. Counsel should be comfortable with payment mechanisms from each country to which the company sells. When contracting with a U.S. arm of a foreign country, care should be given that currency problems are not included as a *force majeure* provision.

6. Warranty disclaimers and limitations of liability that are taken for granted under UCC provisions in U.S. law may not be enforceable against buyers in foreign countries. The EEC countries do not permit such limitations to the extent currently enforceable in the U.S. Other consumer laws or public policy issues should be studied in each country. The difference may be compensated for by a higher price for the acceptance of the risk or, as in the case of transfer of ownership of the technology in Mexico and Brazil, it may kill the deal.

7. In the case of the sale, lease, or license of a product that requires maintenance it may be better to have U.S. technicians provide service or have the item returned to the U.S. Although more cumbersome, the confidentiality of company trade-secrets is more easily preserved in this way rather than via contracts with a local company to provide service. Economies of scale for parts inventory, and concentration of expertise, may also be achieved from U.S. locations. However, in the 1981 OECD meeting on national vulnerability, some European delegates charged that such dependence on U.S.-based service would be a national vulnerability in the event of an interruption in normal communications or transportation.

8. Because of the changes in methods of dispute resolution internationally as well as domestically, and because of the changes currently being made to the rules of some of the international dispute-resolution bodies, it is imperative that the issues of choice of law, choice of forum, and manner of resolution be carefully selected and the applicable contract clauses crafted with great care. Indeed, it is wise to review existing agreements to alert the parties to changes that may affect the prior contractual provisions.

9. If the product is to be distributed by a third party a number of questions arise as to the distribution agreement.[41] One should consider the restrictions on exclusive territories, such as the difference between selling into or inside countries. The export-control laws may place the burden on the U.S. company for compliance with their terms. This argues for a warranty and an indemnity by the distributor or distributee against his tranferring the product or the technology into restricted areas. Some countries require that distribution agreements be exclusive. This may be a trap for the unwary company that grants such a license only to find that the licensee had no intention to work the license, and thus effectively foreclosed the company's opportunity to do business in the host country.

The distributor agreement must address the question of proprietary rights of the U.S. vendor. The International Copyright Convention permits the work copyrighted in a country party to a convention to be accorded the same protection in a host country as the work would receive had it been created by a national of that country. For full protection, the Universal Copyright Convention requires that the © symbol be used on the copies of the published work and the Buenos Aires Convention requires placement of the phrase "All Rights Reserved." Distributorship agreements should require that the distributor place appropriate legends on distributed copyrighted works, e.g., manuals, computer programs.

Agreements should spell out the rights to use the vendor's trademarks in the foreign country. It is important to remember that unlike copyright protection, in some countries the first person to use a trademark has the right to use it in that country.

As in the direct-sale contract, provision must be made for payment received from sales of the distributed materials. This can be best effected by an irrevocable letter of credit payable at the licensor's local bank.

The need to specify in detail the duties of the distributor is important not only because of business reasons, but because so doing establishes performance criteria by which the distributor can be measured, and if necessary terminated. A number of countries have cancellation or termination regulations that make it difficult and costly to terminate the distributor. Under certain circumstances some countries do not even recognize the efficacy of a provision of not renewing a renewable contract.[42]

CONCLUSION

The world is shrinking. International transfers are limited only by the speed of light and people's ingenuity in providing new computer and communications applications. By the close of this century all U.S. business but the local independent shopkeepers will take part in some international transactions, and even the local merchant may accept credit cards or debit cards that "clear" through international networks. The numbers of technical legal and policy issues that will need to be faced and resolved as societies move closer together are awesome. Some of the basic questions to be explored include the identification of the rights and liabilities of parties with respect to information. First, it is important to come to terms with the legal characteristics of information. In the author's view, information carries with it a bundle of rights that can be asserted by its owners or possessors and infringed or invaded in various ways by users and other third parties.

These rights include both in personam rights and rights in rem. Thus far U.S. courts have recognized the rights in rem.[43] That case involved a carnival act that consisted of a performer being shot from a cannon. The act was 30 seconds in duration and was filmed and shown in its entirety on a television news program. The performer alleged an invasion of his privacy but the court found for him on the basis of the property value of the loss of fees paid by people who saw the act.

It is not yet clear what laws apply to information as such and apart from the media on which it resides. Nor is it clear what value should be placed on such information under civil and criminal law.

In personam rights include privacy rights in information. Here again the issues of what constitutes an invasion of privacy and how to value the injury are unresolved.

Rights in data or information (the two may be different) may extend beyond individuals or private persons to nations. Information consisting of growing patterns of crops or of demographic data that can be viewed by users of satellite photographs may constitute a national resource. This information may have commercial property value but it also may have national defense value or other value associated with the sovereignty of a nation state.

Because the technology makes possible many such information uses and appropriations, issues such as these will confront organizations and their legal advisors almost immediately. Their resolution will demand our best efforts. The computer and communication legal issues that those of us who practice in this area must address will demand our best efforts.

NOTES

1. U.C.C. § 2-102.
2. *See, e.g.,* Citicorp Leasing, Inc. v. Allied Institutional Distrib., Inc. 454 F. Supp. 511 (W. D. Okla. 1977).
3. *See* Triangle Underwriters, Inc. v. Honeywell, Inc. 457 F. Supp. 765, 769 (E.D.N.Y.), *modified on other grounds,* 604 F.2d 737 (2d Cir. 1979).
4. Rev. Rul. 71-177, 1971-1 C.B. 5.
5. *See* Texas Instruments v. United States, 551 F.2d 599 (Ca-5 1977).
6. *See, e.g.,* N.Y. TAX LAW § 1105(c)(3) and CAL. REV. & TAX CODE § 6010.9 and regulations promulgated thereunder.
7. *See, e.g.,* Data General Corp. v. Digital Controls Corp., 297 A.2d 437 (Del. 1972), and in the proper instance by patent, see Diamond v. Diehr, 450 U.S. 175 (1981).
8. *See* § 117 enacted in 1980.
9. *See, e.g.,* GCA Corp. v. Chance, COPYRIGHT L. REP. (CCH) § 25,464 (N.D. Cal. Aug. 31, 1982); Apple Computer v. Formula Int'l C.V. 82-5015-H (C.D. Cal. Apr. 11, 1983); Apple Computer v. Franklin Computer Corp.
10. *In re* Freeman, 573 F.2d 1237, 197 M.S.P.Q. 464 (C.C.P.A. 1978).
11. *See* U.S. Copyright Office regulations for the form and location of the notice in programs and note that a C in parenthesis is not acceptable as an alternative to the C in a circle.
12. *See, e.g.,* Management Science Am., Inc. v. Cyborg Sys., Inc., 6 921 (N.D. Ill. 1978) Computer L. Serv. Rep. (Callaghan) Technician Medical Information Sys. Corp. v. Green Bay Packaging, Inc., 211 U.S.P.Q. 343 (E.D. Wis. 1980), *aff'd,* 687 F.2d 1032 (7th Cir. 1982). *But see* Videotronics, Inc. v. Bend Elec. 26 196 PAT. TRADEMARK & COPYRIGHT J. (BNA) June 30, 1983 (D.C. Nev.).
13. For a more complete discussion of these issues, see Marcellino, Nycum, Sherry, *Warranties, Limitation of Remedies and Limition of Actions,* 3 ANN. COMPUTER L. INST. (1983) (ALI-ABA).
14. For a discussion of consumer warranties, see

Franklin, *Retail Marketing*, 1982 New Eng. Computer L. Conf. (MCLE-NELI).

15. U.C.C. § 2-719(2).

16. 522 F. Supp. 769 (D. Md. 1981), *aff'd*, 681 F.2d 812 (4th Cir. 1982).

17. Samuel Black Co. v. Burroughs Corp., No. 78-3077-F, slip op. (D. Mass. Dec. 18, 1981).

18. *Id.* at 7, 8.

19. 457 F. Supp. 765 (E.D.N.Y. 1978), *modified*, 604 F.2d 737 (2d Cir. 1979).

20. *Id.* at 768.

21. See the two *Burroughs cases, supra* notes 16 and 17.

22. 407 U.S. 1 (1972).

23. *Id.* at 10.

24. *Id.* at 15.

25. *Id.*

26. *Id.* at 16 (emphasis in original).

27. Pub. L. No. 96-72, 93 Stat. 503, 50 U.S.C.A. app. §§ 2401–2420.

28. 15 C.F.R. pts. 370–99.

29. Export Administration Act of 1979, §§ 379.4–379.5.

30. *See* 50 U.S.C.A. app. § 2410.

31. Revenue Canada, Customs & Excise, Memorandum No. D-13-11-2, Value for Duty of Computer Application Software and Computer Data Which Are Contained on Physical Media (July 1, 1982).

32. Mexican Bureau of Industries, Development Program for the Manufacturing of Electronic Computer Systems, Their Main Modules and Peripheral Equipment, 2-VIII, Mexico, Fed. Dist. (1981).

33. Community Regulation 803/68 (OJL148 6/28/68).

34. 4 Computer L. Serv. Rep. (Callaghan) 574 (1973).

35. World Intellectual Property Organization Doc. LPCS/II/6 (June 28, 1983).

36. Copyright Act (Canada), Can. Rev. Stat. 1970 C.C.-30, § 45.

37. *See* I.R.C. §§ 551-58, 951-64.

38. Stein & Wotman, *Commercial Arbitration in the 1980s: A Comparison of the Major Arbitral Systems and Rules*, 38 Bus. Law. 1686 (1983).

39. *See, e.g.,* Brussels Convention of 1968, 21 O.J. Eur. Comm. (No. L 304) 36 (1978); European Convention on International Arbitration, 484 U.N.T.S. 349.

40. For a full discussion of these and related issues, see Smiddy, *infra* chap. 23.

41. *The Termination of Agency and Distributorship Agreements: A Comparative Survey*, Nw. J. Int'l L. & Bus. (1981).

42. *See, e.g., Belgium, id.* at 473.

43. *See, e.g.,* Zacchini v. Scripps–Howard Broadcasting Co., 433 U.S. 562 (1977).

CHAPTER 22

CRIMINAL LIABILITY

National and International Strategies Against International Computer Crime

JAY BLOOMBECKER

INTRODUCTION

Computer crime is the serpent in the informatics Eden.[1] Like the serpent, it forces those who contemplate the future of international information networks to confront questions of good and evil. The intentional and adversary nature of crime brings with it problems quite different from those presented by the other major threats to international information networks: employee errors and omissions, and acts of God like fire, flood, and earthquake.[2]

Rational criminals will attack a system where (1) it is least protected; (2) they can gain the most; or (3) they can cause the victim the most damage.

The topics covered in this chapter provide all the motivation some criminals might need to conclude that international information networks are excellent targets for material gain or dramatic disruption.

The more computers are used to manage the affairs of individuals, businesses, groups, and nations, and the more the management is dispersed through the use of international communications facilities, the greater the risk to all computer users and usees.[3] Thus (with one critical qualification) every application of computers or international communication is likely to increase the motivation of would-be criminals in direct proportion to the potential increase in access to valued assets resulting from the application, and the increase in the value of those assets.

The qualification that offers hope to those who maintain a faith in a computer-and-communication-based future is the first factor determining whether the would-be criminal will act—the level of protection against such action. In the ideal world of risk analysis, any crime can be prevented simply by arranging the system concerned so that the potential reward, discounted by the likelihood of "failure," is not worth the effort to attempt to get it by criminal means.

It would be neater, and lead to more coherent paragraphs, if I could use the word detection instead of the word "failure." Unfortunately, detection does not necessarily equate with failure, where the computer criminal is concerned. Consider this case. An embezzler was detected. He was allowed to leave his job with the victim company, with a letter of recommendation. So armed, he went to work for another company and stole from them, committing another computer crime.[4]

"Failure" is a subjective term, depending on the consequences of the sanction applied when someone is detected and processed through the criminal justice system or sanctioned in some other manner. It may involve prosecution, imprisonment, or loss of job.

The application of any of these sanctions may not, however, be adequate to deter the would-be computer

JAY BLOOMBECKER ● Mr. BloomBecker is director of the National Center for Computer Crime Data and editor of the *Computer Crime Law Reporter*. He is on the editorial board of *Computers and Security, Computer Fraud and Security Bulletin, Computer Law Strategist,* and the *Computer Law Reporter*.

criminal. Before the inherent and factual errors in the statement brought it into disfavor, computer crime consultants would point to the figure than only one in 22,000 computer criminals ever goes to prison.[5] This belief, whether true or not, would increase the motivation of computer criminals. "Crime pays," an author wrote in a book on white collar crime.[6] To the extent would-be criminals believe that crime involving computers and communications facilities pays, it can be reasonably expected that this is a type of crime they will attempt.

In view of this analysis, we can articulate the basic question to be discussed in this chapter, and break it down into a number of subquestions.

QUESTIONS PRESENTED IN THIS CHAPTER

The question concerning us most on a global level is this: How should the international criminal/legal system be structured to best prevent excessive damage to—or through—international information networks? Three significant subquestions can help sharpen this question.

1. What do "international information networks" encompass—or who may encounter the problems of international computer crime?

2. What is the international criminal legal system? Computer crime laws, both on national and international levels, are significant components of the international legal system, as it pertains to computer crime. This chapter sets out a framework to analyze these laws, summarizes the thought inside and outside the United States concerning computer crime, and then takes the analysis one step further, describing in brief the various groups currently involved in pursuing national and international approaches to the question of computer crime.

3. What structures should be considered—what can law do in the area of preventing computer crime? In this chapter I suggest the theoretical underpinnings for a redefinition of computer crime, offer examples of the sorts of procedural and systemic changes that could also facilitate computer crime prevention, and speculate on changes likely to occur in the near future concerning computer crime.

SCOPE OF ISSUES

Who Encounters the Problem?

NATIONS. Informatics use is found in those areas most critical to national economic, political, and

perhaps even cultural security. As might well be expected in a cost-conscious world economy, much of the use of informatics has been to solve the most pressing problems faced by those governments and businesses that have paid for them. Consequently, it is not surprising that one finds considerable dependence on computing and communications in areas vital to the political and economic strengths of the governmental and business computer users.

A gauge of the dependence of one government on computers is offered by the United States. A 1979 report estimated that over 14,500 computers were operated by the United States federal government, and many more by state and local governments.[7] The applications included finance, economic planning, record-keeping on individuals, defense, intelligence, daily scheduling, and numerous ministerial duties. "Automated decision-making," where computers perform various management operations without checking for authorization or errors by human personnel, was also noted as a significant factor.

The realization that government computers need protection is explicit in the proposed Federal Computer Systems Protection Act of 1979. In the findings section of the bill, the following language appears: "The opportunities for computer-related crimes in federal programs, in financial institutions, and in other entities which operate in interstate commerce . . . are great".[8]

In Sweden, a group called the Committee on the Vulnerability of Computer Systems (SARK) issued a report which has become a classic. Called *The Vulnerability of Computerized Society*,[9] this report details a number of concerns arising from the extensive use of computers in Sweden, and the dependent position into which these computers put Sweden vis à vis the rest of the world. The report summary gives a flavor of SARK's concern:

> The growing international data flow involves security and vulnerability problems of other dimensions than those existing under purely national conditions. If data processing is done on a computer in another country or on another continent, and if input and output data are to pass through several countries, the misappropriation risks of various kinds increase. Protection against events abroad is naturally more difficult than to build up a domestic system of protection.[10]

The fears of the Swedes are hardly unique. The *Clyne Report*[11] demonstrates a similarly strong concern on the part of its Canadian authors. It concludes: "Of all the technologies that are developing so rapidly today, that of informatics (computer communications) poses possibly the most dangerous threat to Canadian sovereignty in both its cultural and commercial aspects."[12]

Authors have expressed fears that growing informatics use will increase their nation's vulnerability to computer and communication suppliers. "National sovereignty" is the phrase used to express these fears. In the now classic study, *The Computerization of Society*,[13] Simon Nora and Alain Minc say this:

> The development of network systems renews the old problem of relations between the state and the communications media.... The multiplicity of agents it puts into contact, its ability to aid information exchanges, and its role as an instrument of power explain its importance. Without control, computerization would then be subject to influence of communications administrators.[14]

Adopting a social and political interpretation of the old "the medium is the message" theme, these authors warn that unless the nations of the world take power to determine the future of data processing standards and protocols, they will be abandoning the future of their language and their culture. Nora and Minc argue that as computer science and technology develop, national culture will be influenced by developments in programming languages, computer-aided instruction programs, business forms, and procedures. They argue that these developments should not be totally outside of national control.[15]

Agree or disagree with the specifics of their conclusions, one is hard pressed to deny their basic premise. Computers will cause dramatic changes in every country where they are used, and it is not surprising if a country chooses to attempt to influence those changes as much as possible. Many issues are less far-reaching, but not less significant.

The 1978 Intergovernmental Bureau for Informatics (IBI) Intergovernmental Conference on Strategies and Policies for Informatics (SPIN) conference[16] demonstrated beyond doubt that Third World nations are concerned with the potential effects of computers and communications on their sovereignty. It has been predicted that many less-developed countries and developed countries will soon follow the lead of Brazil. That country established a Special Secretariat for Informatics to coordinate, plan, and finance national

informatics policy.[17] In short, as never before, the nations of the world are realizing the staggering implications in the concept that "knowledge is power."[18]

Even the most superficial listing of current computer applications demonstrates the extent to which modern nations depend on computers. Computers are central to military,[19] financial,[20] transportation,[21] and communication systems[22] in much of the developed world. Analogously, communications are central to the functioning of most of these far-flung and complex systems.

BUSINESSES. The multinational corporation is a fact of life. Its effect on national economies is demonstrable and significant; without computers and communications its current structure would be impossible. It is for this reason that data networks have already become characterized as "the infrastructure of international business and government operations."[23]

Hewlett-Packard illustrates the complexity of a modern multinational. It makes approximately 4,000 different products at 40 divisions around the world and has offices in 65 countries. It uses 130 high-speed communications systems in 94 locations, transmitting some 12 million words daily to corporate headquarters in Palo Alto.[24] It is estimated that the total output of multinational corporations is expected to be 16 to 20 percent of the world's output by 1985.[25]

THE USEES. As suggested in note 3 above, a complete consideration of the participants in the arena of international information networks includes those people and groups to whom data in computers relates, and about whom data is transferred over international networks. In addition, there are people and groups whose various rights may be considerably altered depending on the actions of computers.

The Context: Problems in Computer Security

Oddly, for all the dialogue about the importance of transnational data flows, until recently fears have focused almost exclusively on the acts of governments, mainly that of the United States, and computer and communications businesses, mainly IBM, but not the computer criminal. Yet if one looks at the security implications of the international development of computers, it is hard to escape the conclusion that computers provide an attractive target to many types of international criminal.

There are numerous ways in which international computer use is accompanied by inadequate security.

The most obvious aspect of the computer security problem is simply the fact that with each new computer installed, and each new terminal added to a network, the exposure to computer crime increases. Nanus has noted that "the larger and more distributed a computer network becomes, and the more people with access to it, the more vulnerable the system becomes to criminal activity."[27]

International use of computers and communications, growing as fast as it has, has created an economic "frontier" atmosphere. The competition for sales of hardware, software, and services is beginning to heat up, as the long-term economic consequences of the shift from an industrial to an information economy become clearer. Analysts see various foreign efforts to erode the dominance of the United States in the computer industry. Brazil is trying to set up its own minicomputer industry.[28] Japan, according to one author, delays the effectuation of agreements that would allow American data processors greater business in Japan.[28] French,[30] Canadian,[31] and English[32] government projects have been designed to foster competition in the communications industry.

Any readers doubting the relevance of this paragraph's discussion to the question of computer crime are invited to consider the issues raised by the Japanese government and representatives of Hitachi and Mitsubishi after "Operation Pengem" resulted in the arrest of employees of the two companies, and the charge that IBM was using the Department of Justice to fight the economic fight with its Japanese competitors.

Justice is often rough at the frontier. When the potential profits are high and it's not always easy to tell exactly what is going on from a technical point of view, the situation is rife for crime. Where computer communications are concerned, the main source of potential crime problems is the gap between the technical capability of the systems we set up, and the ability of our support systems to keep pace. It may take us 5 years to develop a data encryption standard, but 50 years to educate all those people who might need to use it. The following sections discuss the most significant problems with the support system needed for growing worldwide computerization.

PERSONNEL SHORTAGES. Since computer crime often results from the intentional actions of individual employees of computer and communication facility owners, personnel security is a key problem. Before a

Japanese bank employee absconded to the Philippines with stolen funds, a Japanese bank official explained his own comfort in predicting a low incidence of computer crime in his bank, or any other major Japanese bank: "If someone committed a computer crime against our bank, not only would we fire him, but he would be unable to find work with any other bank."[33] In contrast, a computer criminal in the United States told a panel in which this author took part that he is frequently asked to commit other computer crimes, and has had no difficulty finding work.[34]

Few underdeveloped countries have enough people to fill the jobs in the computing and communications areas that are available. A *Computerworld* story in 1979 spoke of a tripling of the personnel needed to staff Mexico's data processing installations.[35] When Moises Sorkin Alvarez, head of the Informatics Career Program at the Instituto Politecnico Nacional, was interviewed by *Computerworld*, he noted that his program could produce only 60 graduates per year. He went on to say that the government was aware of the shortage and was working to develop a national informatics training class.[36]

Mexico is hardly unique. The Peace Corps sent computer programmers to Columbia, where one reported that "their equipment is just as modern but they are two to three years behind in technique."[37] In 1980 it was reported that Algeria was one of the few developing countries with a coherent national plan for education in computing.[38]

The problem is not only one of underdevelopment. Saudi Arabia must offer exotic travel opportunities, generous benefit packages, and high salaries to lure programmers and analysts.[39] These shortages make it hard to turn down competent people, even if their past has clouds of criminal behavior.

In addition to the general shortage of computer personnel, the lack of computer security personnel is in some ways far more severe. No profession has yet arisen to address the many dimensions of the computer security problem. This author's conversations with computer experts in various countries throughout the world indicate that few people in security, law enforcement, accounting, data management, or allied fields have the necessary expertise.

It would be inaccurate to assume that these problems are limited to the Third World. Anyone looking through the want ads in a major metropolitan area's Sunday paper can quickly see the high premium put on computer expertise. Industry magazines are constantly referring to the high mobility of the programmer, and suggesting that few workers in the field have as much loyalty to their companies as they do to their machines.

INADEQUATE ACCESS TO TECHNOLOGY. The experience of the Peace Corps in Columbia is apparently typical. George Sadowsky, a technical advisor with the United Nations Statistical Office, has pointed out that some countries' professionals have never heard of the computing industry's major trade associations, publications, or conferences.[40] They also may be quite ignorant about available products. Given the seemingly worldwide disinclination of manufacturers to discuss either computer vulnerability or computer security at any length, it would seem that this technology gap is likely to be particularly critical in terms of handicapping those computer users who would like to safeguard their machines and communication networks.

PART SHORTAGES. Competition and rapid developments in computers and communications lead to part shortages, and with them, growing demand. Buying state-of-the-art equipment may mean chancing insecurity if it turns out to have been improperly debugged. Old equipment may no longer be easily repaired, maintaining initial security requirements. To get the system working one may have to give up some security. Part shortages can themselves be a motive for crime. Integrated circuit chips are already a hot item, as security directors and law enforcement officials in Silicon Valley in California readily attest.[41] There is an active "gray" market for integrated circuit components. Espionage and violations of technology transfer laws also demonstrate the active worldwide interest in access to the latest technology.

INADEQUATE TECHNOLOGY. Some developments in computing are implemented before adequate technology is available. A recent pair of articles discussed the cryptographic equipment and processes available to protect satellite data, and concluded that they were inadequate to meet the needs of the satellite system.[42] In addition, the implementation of telecommunication links presents technical problems. Professor Rein Turn points out that the technical characteristics and quality of telecommunications links in various countries that may participate in transnational data flows are different. Consequently, he concludes, "the extent to which these

systems are vulnerable to security problems varies greatly."[43]

LEGAL PROBLEMS. The belief in the "sovereign right" of each country to regulate its telecommunications[44] has tended to carry with it the right to monitor communications. It has been suggested that this right has to include the right to possess the keys to any encryption system.

GROWING TECHNOLOGICAL CAPACITY FOR CRIMINAL USE. In addition to difficulties in getting information to computer users who need to keep computing secure, we have difficulty in keeping technological information away from those who would use it to compromise computer systems. In England, France, and the United States, groups have used their computer expertise to facilitate unlawful access to computer systems.[45] Jan Freese, director-general of the Swedish Data Inspection Board, reported that there appears to be a growth of tampering with microwave communications and growing ease in disturbing satellite messages.[46]

ABSENCE OF CONTRARY SIGNS. There is certainly nothing in the logic of economic development which guarantees that rapid change will produce less security rather than more. We have marshaled those facts which lead to the conclusion that there are considerable security vulnerabilities that were not present before the rapid growth of international informatics use. We find no countervailing facts to report. The impression, apparently shared by those with whom we have discussed the topic, in England, France, Taiwan, Japan, Israel, and South Africa, is that there are few developments that are cause for celebration or hope.

The Frequency of Such Encounters

No statements of statistical significance can be made about the frequency of crimes involving computers or communication facilities. Donn Parker, doubtless the leading source of information about computer crime, is quite clear in his assessment of the state of the statistical art where computer crime is concerned: "There is no valid method of collecting data that are representative of all computer abuse."[46A]

Computer crime has been studied in a number of countries including Australia, England, Japan, and the United States. None of the studies views itself as an adequate indication of what is happening in the population studied, let alone the country of its venue, or the universe of international information networks.

(As a result, the statistical critique of Stanford Research Institute's database remains more persuasive to this author than any of its targets.)[47]

OUTLINE OF APPLICABLE LAWS AND POLICIES

We can distinguish three sorts of problems observed by students of computer crime, and infer that the same sorts of problems will be significant concerns for students of informatics crime. We can call the problems definitional, procedural, and systemic. Consequently, the goal of protecting computers and communication facilities can be achieved, in part, through the use of three related legislative strategies.

Definitional Strategies

Law can be used to proscribe any or all behavior that presents unacceptable interference with the various rights that we choose to recognize as arising from the use of computers or communication facilities. Those arguing for the establishment of new computer crime laws often argue that the definitions used are inadequate to cover the new modalities of crime by computer. A few cases have demonstrated the difficulties predicted by these arguments. These cases involve difficulties in the definition of theft of services, theft of time, theft of communication facility services, and malicious destruction of computer information. These cases are summarized below.

Procedural Strategies

Changes in the laws governing criminal and trial procedures can be made to increase the likelihood of successful prosecution and meaningful sentencing of those whose behavior is proscribed. It is common to hear arguments that the criminal justice systems of the various nations do not adequately deter white collar crime in general, or informatics crime in particular. Some of the procedural weaknesses that have also been noted are short sentences, the low likelihood that a crime will be filed by a prosecutor if there are any technical or economic difficulties in filing such a case, possibilities of destruction of evidence by an inexperienced officer unfamiliar with informatics media, search and seizure problems, and difficulties in producing admissible evidence.

Systemic Strategies

A third area of problems is the entire system of business practices, responses to informatics criminality, and representations about informatics. This category we call "systemic problems."

It has been noted by many studying the phenomenon that few cases of informatics crime are reported to authorities, and there is a considerable body of behavior and opinion that holds that costs of involvement in the criminal justice system where informatics crime is involved are often far too high to make such action cost effective.

For example, Robert Courtney has characterized two classes of computer-related crimes: one class often reported because hard to ignore, and another seldom reported. He claims that between 10 to 12 percent of all cases are reported to law enforcement authorities.[47A]

A comment in *Washington and Lee Law Review*[47B] suggests that the solution to computer crime lies not in defining certain acts as criminal, but in getting more reporting of the crimes and in causing the use of more technology capable of preventing and detecting misuse of informatics systems. Laws can mandate changes in the use of computers and communications facilities that will increase the likelihood that proscribed behavior will be detected by computer users and reported to law enforcement authorities.

(There is no intent to suggest that all criminals are rational, that the criminal justice system will ever work so well that it will deter all criminals, or that other sanctions or approaches to the problem of crime might not be effective. A good argument can be made, we would suggest, that the metal detectors at airports are far more important to the prevention of hijacking than any changes in the criminal justice system relating to that topic, though there have been numerous changes of the latter sort. This chapter is written from the perspective of what can be achieved through the vehicle of criminal law.)

National and International Strategies

The problem of computer crime exists for each country that has computers within its jurisdiction. The problem of international informatics crime exists, in like manner, for each country in which one or more computers is accessible from outside the country's own boundaries.

Thus, virtually every country on the globe can ask

whether its own laws could be used to increase the level of protection accorded to computers within it. In addition, groups of two or more countries can profitably examine the possibilities of crime involving computers and communication facilities not all located in the same country, asking how definitional, procedural, and systemic strategies could be used to increase the level of protection against such crimes.

Against this background of possible legislative strategies, we turn to the strategies suggested by students of computer crime and implemented in various American and foreign laws.

American Definitions of Computer Crime

Starting with Donn Parker's work in 1968,[47C] research in computer crime in the United States has been the most extensive, a situation paralleling the amount of computer use within and without the United States. Thus, it is appropriate to begin the consideration of computer crime with Donn Parker's approach or, more properly, approaches. Recognizing the variety of purposes served by the different characterizations of activities associated with computers, Parker has offered several related definitions, as Table 22.1 illustrates.

Parker suggests that the effort to develop exact definitions of computer abuse and crime "is not particularly productive." His ideal definition, proposed 11 years ago, remains a base point for current discussions. We summarize that formulation thus:

1. *Computer as subject of attack.* This category includes theft of computers and computer components, unauthorized use of computer services, and vandalism against the system.
2. *Computer as environment of the attack.* This category includes theft or unauthorized use of programs, and alteration of programs or data.
3. *Computer as tool of the attack.* This category refers to cases where computer applications are used in the perpetration of an illegal act.
4. *Computer as symbol.* This category refers to cases in which the computer intimidates or otherwise influences people because of their unreasonable reaction to it.[47D]

Kling, a professor of computer science, criticizes Parker's approach, describing the Stanford Research Institute database on computer crime as "a peculiarly biased collection" of cases. "Business crimes are typically excluded from attention, though this is perhaps the most important category for a variety of consumer frauds."[48]

Consequently, Kling defines computer abuse broadly as "an incident associated with computer technology," Parker's definition adding, however, the following gloss:

"Computer systems must be a critical handmaiden to the loss or the abuse. The fact that a computer is 'associated with' a long-distance extortion because the dialing is automated should not influence our laws," he contends.[49] Kling goes on to define "association" as "being instrumental and essential in fostering the loss, or by being the object of the loss."[50] A second kind of association between computer technology and an abuse can occur when computerized products or services are

TABLE 22.1 Definitions of Computer Crime and Abuse

PURPOSE	DEFINITION
Security controls and practices	A *computer abuse* is any intentional, malicious act involving a computer as object, subject, tool, or symbol where a victim suffered or could have suffered a loss and a perpetrator made or could have made a gain.
Investigation and prosecution	A *computer crime* is any illegal act for which knowledge of computer technology is essential for its perpetration, investigation, or prosecution.
Legal	A *computer crime* is any act as specified in a computer crime law in the applicable jurisdiction of the law.
Other	A *computer crime* is any crime in which a computer is necessary for its perpetration. A *computer crime* is a crime where a person "may use the computer either directly or as a vehicle for deliberate misrepresentation or deception, usually to cover up the embezzlement or theft of money, goods, services or information."

(Krauss and MacGahan, *Computer Fraud and Countermeasures*, Prentice-Hall, 1979.)

deceptively represented or contracted for, in Kling's definition of computer abuse.

The logic of Kling's position is clear:

> To the extent that computer-related abuses and crimes are business or occupational activities, strategies for abatement will have to be altered. That means that programs to minimize computer abuse would emphasize matters other than the detection and prosecution of clever computer manipulators. They would attempt to inhibit contractual abuses of computer systems by providing some protection for whistle blowers.

American Computer Crime Legislation

THE RIBICOFF BILL. Though unsuccessful in two sessions of Congress, the Federal Computer Systems Protection Act has become the model followed by most American states that have passed computer crime laws. The text of the Ribicoff bill is followed, in substance, in 14 states as well as in a proposed bill in Canada. (See Exhibit 1.)[50A]

It contains a provision forbidding fraudulent or deceitful actions in the nature of theft and involving the use of computer systems, and another prohibiting trespassory-type offenses to computer systems. Each solves a number of legal problems that had been raised from time to time.

The theft provision, coupled with the bill's definition section, gives recognition to a number of types of assets which were not always explicitly covered by other theft statutes. Typically, theft statutes failed to accord protection to intangible items of value, required an intention to permanently deprive, and had limited definitions of services, seldom including computer time.

The trespassory provisions dealing with alteration of programs are aimed at a variety of wrongs that might have presented problems under preexisting laws. The key questions have been damage, and whether proof of a requisite amount of damage was required before there could be jurisdiction. The question of damage turned on whether intangible changes in the structure of storage media could be considered damage within the traditional damage to property statutes. California, for example, defines malicious mischief as damage to real or personal property, a definition which does not immediately translate to electronic impulses.

The question of amount of damage is significant in the many jurisdictions where major trespasses are felonies, and the rest misdemeanors. It was suggested that given the value of computer resources, a misdemeanor sentence was not appropriate deterrence to someone who might choose to destroy them.

(We note in passing that this question of sentencing is one of the many procedural questions that are addressed in the computer crime legislation introduced in various jurisdictions. The Ribicoff bill, providing for punishments of up to five years or fines of up to $50,000 or twice the amount stolen, was explicitly designed to indicate federal commitment to get tough on computer criminals.)[51]

The Ribicoff bill leaves open a number of significant questions from the perspective of this study. It has a narrow definition of "computer system,"[52] arguably precluding the use of the computer crime laws where the system involved is a combination of manual and computer systems.[53] The bill does not deal explicitly with the theft of computers or computer components,[54] the theft of trade secrets outside computer databases,[55] violations of copyright,[56] or computerized obscenity,[57] all of which have been issues of considerable liveliness of late.

The bill is typical of the point of view Kling describes, focusing on individual challenges to computers rather than possible illegitimate uses of computers or business crimes involving computers. It does not deal with any changes in the procedures for computer crime investigation and prosecution, and it does not attempt to enforce any systemic changes.[58] It is noted that the suggestion of enforced reporting of computer crimes, though believed by all to be a valuable assistance to the effort to contain computer crime, was not made part of the bill for fear that it would arouse too much opposition from computer users' business interests.[59]

It is perhaps notable that one of the reasons the Ribicoff bill did not pass was its perceived conflict with state authority over computer crimes.[60] A lengthy list of priorities was added to S. 240, the second version of the Ribicoff bill (see Exhibit 2), to allay the fears of state prosecutors and others that the federal jurisdiction under the computer crime laws would preclude effective prosecution at a state level.

THE FLORIDA MODEL. A year before the introduction of the Ribicoff bill, then-state Senator William Nelson introduced the first computer crime bill in the United States into the Florida legislature (see Exhibit 3). This bill[61] is quite similar to the Ribicoff bill in its definition of terms and in its declaration of legislative findings, but defines the substantive offenses comprising computer crime in a slightly different way. The bill breaks down computer crime into three categories: offenses against intellectual property; offenses against computer equipment or supplies; and offenses against computer users.

The offenses against intellectual property are defined to include modification, destruction, or taking of that property.[62] Where the purpose of the action is fraud or theft, the punishments are increased in severity.[63]

The offenses against equipment are defined to include willful, knowing, and unauthorized modification of equipment or supplies, used or intended to be used in a computer system or computer network.[64]

The offenses against supplies are defined to include modification, destruction, or taking of those supplies. Modification is a high misdemeanor unless it is done for the purpose of theft or fraud.[65] In this case it is a low felony. (Throughout this section of analysis high means more punishment than low.)

Taking or destruction of equipment or supplies are punished more severely, with greater punishment if the damage to a computer is between $200 and $1000,[66] and more if the damage is greater than $1000 or results in an interruption or impairment of governmental operation or public communication, transportation, or supply of water, gas, or other public service.[67]

Offenses against computer users are defined to be willful denial of access to a computer or to computer services.[68] Again, where the purpose of the act is fraud or theft, the punishment is upgraded.[69]

This law differs from the Ribicoff bill in its structure, its extent, and its use of enhancements. Where the Ribicoff bill defined two classes of prohibited acts, this bill begins with three classes of protected interests. For each protected interest, the bill proceeds to list those acts which compromise the interest, and to define the degree of punishment with which each act is to be dealt. It covers theft of trade secrets explicitly.

Like the Ribicoff bill, this bill is not directed to protection of the interests of the consumer to any appreciable degree, nor to the prevention of computer abuse involving businesses. However, the language of offenses against computer users, if "usees" were defined as users, might serve to be such a vehicle. It is argued that inaccurate or damaging computer products, bills, or credit ratings, for example, if knowingly produced, are denials of service, to wit a service which is accurate and secure, and that those responsible for such actions would be guilty of an offense to computer users.

As an additional aspect worth note, this bill further strengthens the criminal justice system in Florida by providing that it is cumulative to any other legislation defining certain acts as criminal, except where such cumulation violates other provisions of the Florida law.[70]

OTHER STATE LAWS. The states that have passed computer crime laws have varied very little from the patterns of the Ribicoff and Florida bills. Two notable exceptions are Virginia,[71] which made no change in its substantive law, instead redefining property for the purpose of its theft, false pretenses, and embezzlement provisions (see Exhibit 4), and Alaska. Ohio has a bill much like Virginia's.[72] Alaska defines defrauding a computer as a crime.[73]

California has two interesting additions to the types of computer crime laws mentioned herein. Section 502 (d) of that state's penal code prohibits alteration of credit data.[74] This provision resulted from the case of an individual whose credit data was used by another individual to get credit. The second fellow shared the first's name, but not his creditworthiness. The victim was unable to get prosecutors in San Diego, Los Angeles, or Sacramento to prosecute the case.

In San Diego, prosecutors reasoned that the only suspect was the person who received the credit information. Since California lacked a statute like that in Virginia applying to receiving stolen property, the prosecutor's office was unable to establish that "property" had been received as the state law defined the term.[75] The Los Angeles and Sacramento offices were hampered by the distance between the alleged victim and the "scene of the crime." Neither office concluded that a full investigation of the case was warranted, given the relatively small total loss to the victim, and the logistical problems presented by the distances involved.[76]

This case is significant for two reasons. First, it demonstrates a scenario in which the motive for the computer user to report a crime or to actively pursue its prosecution might well be absent. The computer user has no motive of direct profit, or recovery of considerable lost funds, to foster reporting the crime or trying to prevent it. Clearly it is not good for business for a computer user's computer to be compromised. But it is not bad for business unless the potential users of the computer system become aware of the crime.

On the contrary, as Kuitenbrouwer points out, there is a motive for the user to maintain silence, as silence is far less costly when the user is not itself victimized.[77] The risk, particularly in the long run, that the user will be found out and lose too much credibility to remain in business, does not seem a significant deterrent. Then again, with the exception of a few cases, there have been too few cases reported to tell what sort of profiles the users would actually have.

Another provision in California law demonstrates a systemic provision designed to deal with informatics theft. The penal code section used to protect against theft of vehicles and other items of property with identification markings on them was amended recently to include as a crime the alteration of markings on computer components.

While the bulk of the state computer crime laws are addressed to substantive issues, particularly the definition of those actions which are prohibited, almost all contain significant procedural provisions concerning punishment. A few contain other procedural or systemic provisions. A multiplier provision in several punishment sections provides for fines of two times the amount taken in a computer crime in one proposed bill, and two-and-one-half times the amount involved in another state's law. A few states specifically provide that their statutes do not preclude other prosecutions for the actions involved. In addition to Florida, mentioned above, California so provides. Other procedural issues include provisions that the computer crime bill will neither enlarge nor diminish the rights of parties in civil litigation (Illinois and Minnesota), provision for a special statute of limitations, and statutes specifically defining jurisdiction or venue (Delaware and Georgia).

Georgia declares a duty of every business, partnership, college, university, person, state, county, or local government agency, or other business entity, to report any violation of the computer crime law where there is reasonable ground to believe it has been violated. The provision also provides immunity from any civil liability for such reports. There does not appear to be any sanction for the violation of this duty.

The same provision was considered by the New York group, which rather cryptically remarked: "We question the need for this extraordinary immunity provision."[79]

Computer Crime Definitions from Other Countries

The phenomenon of computer crime has been explored in a number of countries other than the United States. Most of the commentators have been considerably influenced by Donn Parker, as will be seen, but there are significant threads of difference in the fabric of conversation about computer crime in Europe, threads that support a more expanded definition of informatics crime than the American model itself might support.

VON ZUR MUHLEN. If we look at a comparison between Rainer A.H. von zur Muhlen's definition of computer crime and that of Donn Parker, as expressed in Kuitenbrouwer,[80] we can see slight differences between the two (see Table 22.2).

Solarz summarizes von zur Muhlen's definitions of *computerkriminalitat* (computer crime) thus: "Every criminal action directed at computers or for which computers are used as instruments." He includes those cases in which the actions are not punishable, but owing to their nature and character should be criminalized.[81]

SIEBER. Sieber defines the same term differently. He would not include theft of an empty magnetic tape as computer crime, whereas von zur Muhlen would. Unfortunately, the rationale for this distinction is not clear. Further limiting the definition of *computerkriminalitat*, Sieber would exclude all but property crimes related to computer systems. Thus according to his definition, "*computerkriminalitat*" embraces property crimes in which computer data have been intentionally altered (computer manipulation), destroyed (computer sabotage), improperly appropriated and utilized (computer

TABLE 22.2   Comparison of Computer Crime Definitions

VON ZUR MUHLEN	*PARKER*
Manipulation of data and/or programs	Direct financial fraud or theft
Theft of computer time	Unauthorized use or sale of services
Sabotage	Vandalism
Economic espionage	Information or property theft

espionage), or used together with data processing equipment (theft of time).[82]

ENGLISH AUDIT INSPECTORATE. The Local Government Audit Inspectorate, responsible for the statutory external audit of some local authorities in England and Wales, performed a survey in order to identify those aspects of computing that could be shown to pose the greatest risks of fraud involving computers. After discussing the difficulties involved in defining computer fraud, the report defines it as "any fraudulent behavior connected with computerization by which someone intends to gain dishonest advantage."[83] Clearly, the purpose of this report is limited to possible crimes against the "clients" of the audit department, an interest common to many of those who have defined computer crime.

SOLARZ. Solarz, studying computer crime for the National Swedish Council for Crime Prevention,[84] does an exhaustive analysis of computer crime, winding up close to Parker. He concludes that "computer crime describes the new criminological phenomenon which is a side product of the development of computer technology." He goes on to say that the term embraces "several juridical classifications of crime which have a common denominator—the computer, and its system—which may function as object, subject, instrument, or symbol for a crime."[85]

However, more than Parker, Solarz recognizes that the crime need not be economic:

> Owing to the spread of computer technology through all possible spheres of life, computer crime can take place at any point in the society and may also comprise other types of crime than those covered by the difficultly definable concept of economic crime.[86]

CANADIAN. A Canadian report[87] dealing with computer crime lists four problem areas in the Canadian definition of computer crimes requiring legislative assistance. These are (1) unauthorized appropriation of computer software, (2) unauthorized appropriation or use of computer data or information, (3) unauthorized appropriation of computer services, and (4) unauthorized manipulation or destruction of computer data or information.

In addition, the report suggests two other areas in which legislation could assist the operation of the criminal justice system: territorial jurisdiction and the issuance of search warrants.

GERMANY. Notes from the INTERPOL 1979 Symposium on International Fraud indicate the definition used in the German computer fraud statute:[88]

Section 263 (a) Computer Fraud
(1) Anybody who, with a view to procuring himself or a third person any unlawful property advantage, causes prejudice to the property of another by influencing the results of a property-related data processing activity through the use of false data or the distortion, or suppression, of true data, or by affecting the program flow, shall be sentenced to imprisonment not exceeding five years or to a fine.

AUSTRALIA. The Computer Abuse Research Bureau defines computer crime thus:

1. Unauthorized manipulation of computer input and/or output;
2. Unauthorized access to the system, through terminals;
3. Unauthorized modification or use of application programs;
4. Trespass on data processing installation, theft of equipment, files, or output;
5. Sabotage of computer installation equipment;
6. Unauthorized data interception.[88A]

FORUMS FOR RESOLUTION

Only recently has there been significant effort to deal with the problem of international computer crime. The International Police Organization (INTERPOL) began its concern with computer crime in 1979, when samples of the German computer crime law were introduced at a seminar on international fraud. Subsequently, Stein Schjolberg did a study of international computer crime under the auspices of INTERPOL,[89] using the facilities of Stanford Research Institute. The results of his study are now available, and include a proposed model computer crime law. Schjolberg's work continues with a study now being performed for the OECD. As in his INTERPOL research, Schjolberg is circulating a questionnaire to ascertain the views of the member nations about incidence of computer crime and appropriate reactions thereto.

The Intergovernmental Bureau for Informatics (IBI) has designated informatics penal law as one of the areas of concern in its consideration of an informatics legal order. BloomBecker, Sarzana, and Vilarño have prepared papers on informatics penal law,[89A] and IBI appears likely to continue its studies with further work.

The approaches of the various groups have thus been limited primarily to fact-finding and the proposal of model laws to deal with the problem of computer crime. It would seem that there are many areas for international cooperation yet to be explored.

RECOMMENDED APPROACH—A PROPOSED CLASSIFICATION SYSTEM FOR INFORMATICS CRIMES

In view of the remarks made above, it is suggested that the definition of crimes constituting informatics crime is but the first of four steps to adequately use the apparatus of the criminal law in an optimal fashion to protect the values emerging from the development of informatics. Without exhaustively discussing the other possible strategies, a few definitional, procedural, systemic, and international strategies designed to reduce the threat presented by informatics crime are summarized below.

Definitional Strategies

Much of the dialogue about what computer crime is, has been conditioned by the considerable resistance of computer manufacturers and users to the concept of computer crime.[90] Fearing that association of the word *computer* with the word *crime* will decrease the confidence with which people view the output of computers,[91] or that the association will result in more caution before computers are purchased,[92] individuals from these groups have argued vigorously against use of the term.[93]

Thus much of the conversation about how to define computer crime or, by inference, informatics crime, is based on the attempt to limit computer crime to "real" computer crimes, or those which are effectuated through changes of programming. However pleasant that limitation may be to computer manufacturers and users, it has little in the way of intellectual support, at least in the literature of computer crime.

Computer crime cannot be defined without an awareness of the context in which the definition is intended to serve. Since this chapter attempts a global approach to the problem of informatics crime, one not bounded by the approaches so far described in the literature, it seems appropriate to begin with a new set of premises.

Why do we want to define informatics crime? I suggest that the goal of laws dealing with informatics crime cannot reasonably be maintained to be the elimination of such crimes. A more realistic goal is to allow society to have the same level of protection against these crimes, now and in the near future, as it has against the large variety of crimes now dealt with by the varied penal codes and other such laws reflecting various nations' commitments to protect other socially defined assets, both tangible and intangible.

Thus, the process for definition of informatics crime should begin with an analysis of the social changes resulting from the growth of informatics, and proceed to a list of the assets resulting from those changes that seem to present the greatest need for protection through the criminal law.

We thus start from the premise that informatics use results in the creation of numerous assets, things of value, which were either not present before the introduction of informatics, or were not of significant enough economic (or other) value to require protection. An example of the first kind of asset is computer time. Clearly the criminal law was perfectly adequate to protect the social interest in preventing this kind of theft in the 1930s. There were no laws, but there were also no computers.

An example of the second kind of asset is computer components. In the early days of computing, computer components were vacuum tubes, not so valuable in themselves to warrant much effort to steal them, and consequently not worth much effort to protect them. The multimillion dollar thefts of components in the last few years reflect both the fact that technological advances have dramatically changed the value of the assets inside computers, and the more significant fact for the would-be protector of informatics facilities, that criminals are quite aware of the value of these components and have developed institutions to steal, transship, and even falsify the origin of these components.[94]

As we have seen above in our study of the changes resulting from informatics developments, changes in degree often become significant enough to be considered changes in kind. Another way of looking at the problem is a simpler economic view. The value of assets to society determines the value of assets it will devote to their safeguarding. (One hastens to add that the relationship is hardly a straight-line correspondence. Social definition of value works one way in the marketplace, another in the legislature, and a third way in the mind of every individual who makes choices about which economic decisions to make and which laws to follow.)

If the goal of society is to protect those assets that result from informatics growth, the process would seem threefold:

1. List the assets under consideration
2. List the laws that protect them
3. Conclude which assets are not adequately protected by the laws.

This division of the universe of informatics crime is certainly not the first. We analyze other views of the problem below. Suffice it to say we believe that this list is more in consonance with the crimes that have been reported in the last few years, and that the studies on which many of the earlier conclusions and analyses are based were hampered not only by undue solicitude for the interests of computer manufacturers and others who feared sullying the computer's good name, but also because they were completed before the criminals of the late 1970s and early 1980s began to demonstrate their evaluation of the variety of crime to which the informatics society is most prone.

We disregard the conclusions of criminals only if we choose not to benefit from their often well-informed risk analyses. Given the notable lack of success on the part of those who practice risk analysis in coming up with adequate raw data to perform reliable statistical work, and the theoretical shortcomings of their work, the criminals' views are even more valuable.[95]

At the core of this argument is a simple truth. The bundle of rights and responsibilities that comes with the ownership, use, or operation of a computer is a vast, complex, and novel bundle. We might hark back to the whalers of yore who were constantly finding new uses for parts of the whale that were previously thrown out.[96] Many criminals succeed by finding uses for parts of the computer system that were unanticipated by those who set up the security for the computer system—or those whose indecision led to the default decision not to set up security. Consider, just for color, the embarrassment of the Washington D.C. bank whose customers' account information blew across a number of suburban lawns when printouts that had been discarded somehow escaped the shredder and got caught in a sizable windstorm.

The categories that follow are an expansion of the four types of computer crime Parker and von zur Muhlen describe. Each category is treated as an asset and is followed by an illustrative list of the different actions that have been reported to compromise this asset. The observations and categories are based on the study of computer crime cases from around the world. It should be remembered that this is a preliminary categorization. This list would benefit from intense exposure to and study by attorneys and others concerned with the legal issues involved in informatics. In addition to adding instances of crime that are not adequately covered by our categories, they can do the invaluable job of indicating the extent to which their national laws and procedures provide adequate protection for these assets.

What is a computer system? Unless we answer this question, it is impossible to list those of its components that are assets.

A FACILITY. The most obvious asset in a computer system is the physical asset—the facility that is, or contains, the computer system. Given the vast variety of computer systems, the variety of facilities is equally vast. For the purpose of this definition, "facility" means a physical location at which computing is performed. The values of the facility include security, continuity, and image. That is, the owner or user of a computer facility values the ideas that computer operations can be carried out without interference from those intending to stop or hamper those operations, that the operations will be sufficiently continuous to allow planning by those who depend on the operations, and that the owner of the system will be able to point to the facility as proof of the efficiency of its computer operation.

Here, as throughout the following pages in this section, I will list attempts to interfere with the value of the asset I have just described. The following are threats to the facility:

Destruction of Facility The most dramatic threat to a computer facility is its destruction, by fire, bombs, or other means. Bombing has been a tactic used by numerous terrorists to achieve political goals. Bombing computer centers is a tactic used by numerous groups in Italy,[97] and by a lesser number in the rest of Western Europe.[98]

Disablement of Facility Physical occupation of a facility, while differing from destruction in the permanence of its effects, has the same short-term effect. Not only does operation stop, but the security and image factors clearly suffer. Computer facilities have been occupied by strikers protecting the implementation of computer systems[99] and by students protesting American involvement in the Vietnam war.[100]

Taking of Parts of Facility   In addition to the other values of the computer facility it is also a capital asset, often representing a considerable investment on the part of the owner. Parts of the facility may be taken without impairment of the processing of data, and thus with no direct interruption of service, only a diminution of the value of the assets purchased or otherwise acquired for the computer facility.[101]

Exploitation of Facility Location   If we consider the automated teller locations that allow remote access to banking computers as part of the computer facility, we find an interesting exploitation of such facilities by the confidence men in New York who fast-talked thousands of customers of one bank into allowing them access to their debit cards, and managed to spy the personal identification numbers each customer had to enter to make their own transactions. The bank—currently paying a $500,000 amount to those customers who were defrauded by the criminal scheme—certainly experienced a diminution of its assets as a result of this exploitation of its facility.[102]

COMPUTER SERVICES AS ASSET.   The most obvious asset resulting from adoption of informatics is computer services, the general term describing the total output of computer systems including communication, production of reports, maintenance of and access to data files, control of processes, facilitation of research, experimentation, and as many other applications as the ingenuity of humankind is capable of. With the exception of some home-computer buyers or the occasional dupe of an overzealous sales pitch, most people who buy computers buy them because they want to produce certain types of output that will be useful in business or government. Where those services cannot be produced, the value of the asset to the owner is diminished.

Destruction of Facility/Occupation of Facility   In addition to the harms listed above, these acts also result in the temporary or permanent disruption of computer-system services.

Disablement of Programming   Central to the delivery of services is reliability. The computer is used because we believe that it will produce reports with greater accuracy, in less time, and at less cost than the

manual systems that were used previously. Where reports or other services cannot be produced because the programming is not adequate for the task, the value of the computer system is diminished.[103] An employee seeking revenge if he should ever be fired from his position as a system programmer can program a logic-bomb into a system. Activated only if he is no longer on the payroll, the logic-bomb will cause certain files to be destroyed.[104]

Destruction or Taking of System Components   Less severe than destroying entire facilities, the act of destroying components is no less common. On the contrary, instances of irrational assaults on computers have been reported almost as long as there have been computers. Computers have been attacked with guns, screwdrivers, hatchets, and other hard objects that have been at hand.[105] Some of these attacks cause no interference to service, just the loss of the value of the asset that is disabled. Others require reduction or suspension of services until the components in question can be fixed or replaced.

An interesting philosophical question with practical implications is whether changing the organization of information is the same as destruction of an asset. Consider the case of the fired librarian who changed all the labels on the tapes under her control.[106] No "damage" was done, in the traditional sense, but considerable time had to be spent before the tapes were usable again. In any case, if we have the freedom to define informatics crime in whatever way suits our evaluation of the social values resulting from informatics, it would certainly be wise to explicitly recognize the value that comes with ordering of information, and to specifically provide, in any proposed legislation, the recognition that ordering of information is an asset that we do not want to see unprotected.

Theft of Programming   The growing importance of programming is universally perceived (witness testimony at SPIN conference).[107] Without programs, the most high-priced computer is merely a pretty display item, unable to do any work. Programs can be removed from the memory of the computer. They can be taken out of the computer facility if they reside on media outside the computer and have to be read into the computer before they are used. Thus in the absence of these programs, service can be interrupted. An example of this sort of crime is the English case in which an individual stole a valuable program and ransomed it, arguing that without this program the operation of the ransomee's computer would be impossible.[108]

False Advertising by Computer Vendor   Given the importance of service, it seems appropriate to include under this category the act of misrepresenting the services a computer can perform. Although arguably not the subject of criminal laws,[109] this category of act diminishes the services a computer owner or user will be able to provide, by causing the buyer to purchase or otherwise acquire a system that will not meet the desires of the buyer.

EXCLUSIVE USE OF THE SYSTEM.   Traditional property law defines the right to exclusive use as one of the chief characteristics of property.[110] This definition finds itself sharply in contrast to the business practices of most computer users, and in general fails to describe the leeway that most business owners of property allow their employees when it comes to the use of company property. It is clear that the insurance company owns the electric typewriters on which its secretaries may type personal letters during their lunch breaks. No one suggests that the typists commit crimes in this act. It is clear that the flower shop owns the trucks with which it delivers flowers. No one suggests that the delivery boy can drive to a city several hundred miles away with the same impunity as the secretary who types the letter. What is the difference? Which analogy better serves the case of computer time? This question is logical only after we agree that the owner of the computer has a right to exclusive use of the computer system, except, of course, to the extent that the owner transfers that right.

Time Theft   The problem of delimiting the rights that computer owners seek to protect is difficult because there is not yet enough experience to set up reasonable and widely accepted dividing lines between acceptable and unacceptable uses of computer time without permission.[111] Some of the hardest cases of application of the American computer crime laws deal with this situation.

NONCOMMERCIAL TIME THEFT.   Though not represented in the literature, a distinction between commercial and noncommercial time theft seems an appropriate one. As is sometimes done in dealing with other cases of employee use of employer resources (see theft of services laws), it is easy to rule out computer uses that are not intended to result in any commercial transactions.

Thus the programmer who prints a "Snoopy" calendar, producing the beagle made famous by American cartoonist Charles Schultz and referred to in the hearings on the American computer crime bill,[112] is in a class separate from the two programmers in New York who ran a business of selling computer services that were all performed on their employer's computer.[113]

As a rule, the direct cost to the computer owner may be none, or negligible, in noncommercial uses of computer time. The cost will depend on volume of use, interference with other jobs, and auxiliary questions such as other support facilities used (e.g., lights, air conditioning, and electricity to run the machine at a time when the machine would not ordinarily be running.)

We must be careful to note the changed environment where computers are concerned, and the consequent change in conditions defining computer use. Programmers trying to make extra money through freelance work are quite common in these times.[114] The runaway success of various software-based products like "Visicalc," "PacMan," and dBase II all make the market for programmers' efforts look quite attractive. It is hard to tell what is commercial and what is just hobby use. The difference may only be the employee's decision to sell the results of what was, up until that moment, a hobby. It certainly cannot be assumed that noncommercial use is not substantial, as even a hobbyist's ambitions can know no bounds.

COMMERCIAL USE OF COMPUTER TIME.   In the case referred to above,[115] a system manager and his assistant used the capacity of a New York engineering school to service two clients, a mail order firm and a magazine with an extensive mailing list. According to one of the investigators, the school was required to purchase additional peripheral devices and computer capacity in order to do the school's data processing, as it was burdened with the extra load of the unauthorized processing.

USE OF COMPUTER SPACE.   A computer system includes storage space on the various computer media in the system. At any time, the central processing unit of the computer will have certain information in it; disks, drums, memory sections, etc., will all have information that can be manipulated by the computer. In certain circumstances, use of this space is trivial. A personal computer system in which each employee maintains all files on diskettes presents no issues of use of computer space. Not so, however, a system with limited file capacity, and in which unauthorized files cause reductions in the speed at which the other files can be processed.[116]

OUTSIDER USE OF COMPUTER TIME. Recognizing that different expectations and legal restrictions apply to employees and others, it is well to add nonemployee use of computer time to the list as a different threat. From a technical point of view, this kind of theft is far more difficult to counter, as it represents greater sophistication than time theft by employees. Where the employee usually has access to the computer for some purpose, the nonemployee seldom does. In the case of unauthorized access to a computer by an outsider, either there were no access restrictions, or the restrictions proved inadequate.

In a celebrated case in New York,[117] students at a private high school were able to use computers in Canada and in the United States without any authorization. They used the passwords they discovered by illegal means to gain access to TELENET, a timesharing system used by a number of corporations in the United States and Canada. Once they had access to the different corporate computer systems, they were able to outwit the security systems the companies used to prevent and detect unauthorized access.

For obvious reasons, university computer systems have been subject to more than their share of attempted unauthorized accesses, some with the explicit approval of teachers who believe that the act of gaining access is more useful as a learning experience than it is immoral.[118]

The point to be made is that the right to exclusive use is a concept that eliminates the need to prove loss resulted from violation of that right. As Don Ingram noted, in every trespass there is the interference with an intangible amount of another's property rights. We allow for a finding of guilt by proof of the act, without requiring a specification of how much of the right was violated.[119] In like manner, if we accept the concept that computer owners have the right to exclusive use of their computers, we must also accept the need to protect them against trespass.

INFORMATION. Though the other problems are legion and real, no problem typifies the dilemma of informatics law as well as that of defining the property and other rights in information that come into being as a result of informatics. To start, we must note that different forms of information are valued, created, stored, secured, and viewed legally, in different ways. Consider these types of information in computer systems:

- Programs
- Data files
- Plans for new product introduction
- Manufacturing details for a new product
- Client files
- Trade secrets
- Private files

Each represents an investment on the part of its owner, usually in the form of an ongoing business function for which an accurate accounting cannot or has not been done. The following cases demonstrate the threats to these different forms of information.

Program Theft through the Mainframe   In northern California, an employee of a timesharing service used the password of a client of that service to get access to the program used by a competing timesharing service.[120]

Internal Program Theft   Far more common than the case summarized above is the case in which an employee with access to programs used by his or her employer leaves the company with those programs, usually intending to set up a company in competition with the former employer.[121]

Personal Computer Programs   The growth of piracy of computer programs for microcomputers has given rise to legislative suggestions that American copyright laws be expanded to punish those who copy programs without authorization and sell the same.[122]

Data Files   Mailing lists on the computer can be the greatest asset for a magazine or other organization with a successful history of direct mail advertising. Thefts have demonstrated the value of such lists to *Reader's Digest* in Denmark[123] and American Express in the United States.[124]

Plans   The litigation concerning Hitachi, Mitsubishi, and IBM includes the charge that books describing the business plans of IBM were stolen from that company.[125] Do we want to include these materials within the ambit of information we want to protect under an informatics crime law? Will we want to give any more protection to IBM's business plans than we want to give to a noncomputer company like General Motors? This sort of question needs to be asked at every step of our analytic process.

Private Files As discussed above,[126] private files are among the kinds of information that are of value to the computer user or owner. Depending on one's theory of privacy in the context of computers, the owner of the computer may be the bailee of certain property rights in the subjects' records,[127] the owner of some property rights in the records itself,[128] both of the above, or neither. In any case, most jurisdictions now enforce privacy rights concerning information in computers. If we view these rights or responsibilities as inherent to any degree in the computer owner, then they must go into our calculation of assets requiring protection.

RELIABLE EFFECTIVE PROCESSING OF DATA. The most common form of informatics crime resulting in economic losses involves exploiting the expectation that computer processing is accurate and effective. Accuracy is usually a function of good system design and implementation. Effectiveness requires that the right goals be articulated initially, and the system designed to implement those goals. Thus, where unintended consequences are not noticed, there is often considerable leeway for crime.

Change of Application Programming The application or task on which the computer is working is a key area. Programs are depended on to produce a payroll that pays each employee the right amount, and only the money to which he or she is entitled. If a programmer can add a small loop into a program that causes the computer to double his or her salary whenever it is being printed, this is an interference with the owner's expectation that the computer will accurately calculate his or her employees' salaries.[129]

Change of Input Data It is usually far easier to compromise a computer system by altering the data to be input into the computer, than it is to change the internal functioning of the machine.[130] There is more access possible and there are more people who might be compromised (since the average business system has more than one input device). Statistically, this is the sort of abuse that occurs most frequently in the cases encountered.[131]

Change of File Data A simple example is the case in California where an employee of the Department of Motor Vehicles was convicted of offering to change the information in the department's vehicle owner files to indicate that the person buying her services was the real owner of the car that person actually intended to steal.[132]

COMPUTER INTEGRITY. One of the assets of the computer is the expectation people have that a computer will produce a correct answer, no matter how difficult the problem. It is questionable that this asset will survive the century, as practical understanding of computers replaces "gee whiz" television accounts. In the meantime, there are a number of frauds taking advantage of the expectation that the computer will produce the right result. From the point of view of the computer industry, it is probably important to put some effort into preventing the misuse of computers, by communicating the powers and limitations of computing. The following are examples of the sorts of infringements of this right that have been reported.

Use of Computers to Mislead Consumers Companies offered "computer dating" (the use of computers to match compatible members of the opposite sex). In the simple cases, no computer was used. In the more complex cases, a computer was used, but it was nearly impossible to demonstrate that the computer was at all useful in producing the result advertised.[133] With the advent of personal computing as a major economic event, it may be expected that the number of fraudulent representations of what computers can do will increase in proportion to the gullibility of the people who attempt to buy computers.[134]

Use to Mislead Other Businesses The over-2-billion Equity Funding fraud was based on the premise, long proven accurate, that businesses would not question assets represented by computer systems. In this case, Equity Funding was able to grow to shocking size by reinsurance of nonexistent insurance policies existing only on the company's records, many of which were computerized.[135]

Use to Mislead One's Own Business A small company had its one employee serving as both its only accountant and its entire data processing department. The employee stole from the company by falsifying its accounts so that the company appeared less efficient. He increased losses from inventory shrinkage, bad debt losses, and the like. As a result, the company suffered gradual and persistent drainage of its assets.[136]

Recently the J. Walter Thompson company found that the billings in one of its departments had been inflated by $23 million.[137]

Use to Facilitate Crime It is certainly possible for a company to program its computers to cheat every customer by miscalculating the interest charge so as to benefit the company, or to mislead those who receive computerized billings.[138]

Stanley Mark Rifkin demonstrated the usefulness of the international wire transfer system by demonstrating the ease with which he could gain access to the system and cause the transfer of $10.2 million to Switzerland.[139]

Use to Mislead Investors Two cases recently surfaced in which confidence men promised to produce staggering returns for investors. Each scheme was based on the lie that a computer was being used to manipulate investments when in fact none was in use.[140]

Misuse of Computer Data Information in the computer can be used unfairly, in order to reach decisions that are illogical or contrary to other values recognized in a jurisdiction. The former case is demonstrated by the allegation in certain American jurisdictions of redlining,[141] or the use of economic data to increase insurance premiums for poor areas of a city. An example of the latter is use of evidence of certain prior criminal convictions that a jurisdiction has declared to be too remote, or too prejudicial, to be used in a criminal trial.[142]

Procedural Strategies: Problems in Investigation and at Trial

In addition to redefining the substantive act involved in computer crime, we can take steps to improve the procedures of individual jurisdictions in the criminal justice systems to facilitate the investigation and prosecution of computer crime. This section focuses solely on problems within a single jurisdiction, unlike a subsequent section on strategies for the international criminal justice system. The two are closely related, since the international criminal justice system depends on national (and subnational) legal systems.

ADMISSIBILITY OF EVIDENCE IN INFORMATICS CASES. The admissibility of computerized evidence has been discussed extensively in common law jurisdictions,[143] and in other jurisdictions as well. The theoretical problems that face the proponent of evidence generated by a computer are staggering. To establish the reliability of a computer system that produces a document would entail establishing that the system was adequately secured against intentional abuse or negligent harm. As we have seen in our discussion of computer security, such proof will not be found readily in the documentation of many systems.

USE OF EXPERTS AND MASTERS. As the complexity of factual issues in computer crimes grows, some experts

predict the growing need for masters and other finders of fact to determine difficult technical questions.[144] In the *Wells Fargo* case,[145] for example, considerable argument revolved around the accounting practices used to represent the finances of the defendants. Examples of such procedures are not lacking in the area of fraud.

EVALUATION OF COMPUTER MEDIA. It is often remarked by investigators that the lack of standard valuation for computer goods gives rise to considerable difficulties in trial. Cases with which we are familiar have involved accusations that allegedly stolen programming was not proven to be worth the jurisdictional minimum required for a felony.

In one interesting case of time theft, the defendants were accused of stealing time from their employer to do their own work. In response to the theft charge they argued that the employer bought time on a monthly basis, and paid no more whether the company used the purchased time or not. The argument pointed up the usefulness of the California computer crime law, since that statute makes it clear that theft of services is forbidden without proof of any minimum value of the services.[146]

Analogously, a case of theft of a program was challenged on the basis that the item stolen was to be valued at the value of the tape, and not the value of the information on the tape.[147] Where there is evidence of purchase and sale of a program, this sort of argument seldom succeeds.

This list is in no way exhaustive. Further thought might well be directed to the questions of venue and jurisdiction posed by the Georgia, Delaware, and proposed Canadian computer crime laws,[148] and the questions of preemption of more general laws (addressed by the California and Florida laws).[149]

We pass laws to criminalize activity concerning informatics because as a society we conclude that certain assets have a value that our laws do not adequately protect. We attempt to deter the calculating criminal from types of criminality we find particularly disagreeable, by increasing the punishments attached to those acts. If burglary of a home were made far more serious than burglary of an automobile, burglars would tend to burglarize fewer homes and more automobiles.

In this sense, it is important to consider the capacity of informatics to provide assistance in the commission of a crime. Are there certain informatics-assisted crimes that society will want to keep people from committing?

What about assault by means of turning off the computer that controls critical function-monitoring for a hundred critical patients in a large government-run hospital?[150] In this obviously extreme and hypothetical instance, it is clear that the use of informatics allows direct physical harm to be inflicted on a great number of people. The capacity for physical harm is a frequent reason for enhancing punishment. A typical example of such enhancement is the punishment for armed robbery in many jurisdictions.

It is not clear how many, if any, instances of computer abuse would fit into this category. Burglary tools are made illegal in some jurisdictions because they are used primarily for the commission of a crime.[151] Should certain programs, say "Locksmith,"[152] be made illegal for the same reason?

Systemic Strategies

As suggested above, legislation directed to increasing the likelihood that an informatics crime will result in an unacceptable cost to most potential criminals can focus on any aspect of the criminal justice system, including development of standards for minimum computer-security levels, licensing users of computers that can be used to the disadvantage of the computer usee, mandating or rewarding the reporting of computer crime, and strengthening requirements for corporate reporting of details of computer use. All of these efforts are addressed to the system of computer use in our society, hence the term "systemic strategies." The use of criminal sanctions to effect such social policy goals is of course not uniformly accepted as appropriate or wise.

Perhaps the strongest argument for such an expanded definition of informatics crime comes from Kuitenbrouwer. He argues that in order to assure the enforcement of citizens' rights to privacy, criminal provisions concerning the improper use of data banks are desirable.[153]

His position is supported by an interesting development in European privacy legislation. Provisions of recent Italian[154] and British[155] data-protection bills make criminal certain behavior on the part of data bank managers and personnel. Hondius[156] quotes similar legislation from Germany[157] and Austria.[158] The implication seems clear. In these jurisdictions, informatics crime has been defined to include strengthening of the system of protections against violation of the rights of usees of computerized information.

The underlying rationale for Kuitenbrouwer's position is summed up in the following quotation:

> Automation has a tendency to get out of hand. No important computer project is installed on time, within the estimate, and with the same staff it started with. No longer does a project reach its original goals. Naturally, the computer community does appreciate the risks of its business. It is completely unrealistic, however, to expect that the people who set up and run a computer project will examine their own performance really critically. Computer projects are often crash projects. The predominant concern is to keep moving. Troublesome questions must take second place.[159]

An American law review article[160] offers interesting contrast and comparison. In "A Suggested Legislative Approach to the Problem of Computer Crime" the author stresses the need for detection and prevention, if the problem of computer crime is to be addressed:

> If computer crime is serious enough to warrant legislative attention, the drafters of the FCSPA (Federal Computer System Protection Act) have only partially addressed the problem. Although prosecutors of computer crimes have had to rely on tangentially related criminal statutes, virtually no criminal prosecution has failed for lack of statutory sanction. A district attorney, however, cannot prosecute an undiscovered or unreported computer crime. Furthermore, any preventive or deterrent effect of clearly applicable strict penalties exists only to the extent that the courts are able to apply the penalties to detected illegal acts. Thus the solution to the problem of rising computer crime should couple measures directed toward detection and prevention with the creation of direct legal sanctions.[161]

The author goes on to suggest that increased reporting should be fostered, adding that funding of law enforcement projects on computer crime would facilitate the investigation and prosecution of reported incidents.[162]

Considering the users of computers, the manufacturers of computers, and the outside auditors for the computer users, he concludes that it is unlikely that the law can be used to motivate any of these groups to change their behavior:

> Reluctance on the part of computer users to adopt voluntary security measures to prevent computer crime does not suggest that involuntary requirements are a

workable alternative. The original hearings on the FCSPA indicated that licensing of individual computer systems is an unacceptable method of insuring compliance with minimum security procedures. Standard procedures that are applicable to the myriad of possible computer users would be virtually impossible to develop. Once developed, government attempts to require the user to maintain and enforce the security procedures would result in a regulatory quagmire. In short, the government's attempts to stimulate crime prevention and detection in users of computers may be limited to efforts to increase public awareness of the computer's potential for crime.[163]

The author further points out that suggestions for a mandatory reporting provision in the Federal Computer Systems Protection Act were rejected for reasons ranging from fear of creating distrust within the affected business entity to doubts about the effectiveness of a reporting requirement.[164]

Strategies for the International Criminal Justice System

For simplicity, the preceding discussion has focused only on the problems faced by a country attempting to fashion an internal strategy against informatics crime. When consideration is extended to the problems of international informatics crime, the possibilities for further legislation are numerous.

AGREEMENTS AS TO CRIME DEFINITIONS. As with national legislation, the first area that can be approached is the substantive definition of informatics crime. Such a definition, I would suggest, can occur only after each country that is party to such definition determines its own interest in protecting the different assets resulting from developments in informatics.

Once the internal values are established, there can be agreement on which problems require harmonized definitions. The following types of crimes appear to pose the greatest problems on an international level:

- Terrorism
- Wire-transfer theft
- Theft of high-technology equipment, components, and information
- Data havens
- Opportunism based on weaknesses in international law[165]

PROCEDURAL STRATEGIES. As with national informatics strategies, international informatics strategy can focus on a procedural level as well as a substantive one.

Extradition In this context, consideration must be given to the requirements for extradition of informatics criminals, since they are far more mobile than their predecessors.

Mutual Assistance in Criminal Matters In the same way, the various agreements issuing from the Council of Europe[166] in response to the increased movement of peoples within the European community indicate other areas for possible cooperation in connection with informatics problems.

Discovery and Investigation Procedures The mobility of information as a result of informatics and telecommunications has resulted in the possibility that a crime can be committed virtually from anywhere to anywhere. The consequences of this ability are significant to the investigator trying to gather evidence of an informatics crime in an environment where rules concerning discovery are different from the rules under which the investigator is used to working. In the investigation of the case against Stanley Mark Rifkin,[167] the defendant was believed to have transferred $10.2 million to Switzerland for the purchase of diamonds from Russalmaz, the Russian diamond-trading firm. Agents of the United States government had to arrange special procedures because they were not allowed to investigate the case directly, as they would have if it had occurred on American soil.

Conflict of Laws The ability of teleinformatics to connect virtually any two informatics systems promises problems for the forseeable future in the area of conflict of laws. Traditional questions about the extraterritorial application of the criminal law will be confounded with questions of almost medieval quality when attempts are made to apply locus of action to the nearly instantaneous movement of electronic impulses across great distances in complex and not always readily ascertainable patterns.

SYSTEMIC STRATEGIES. In the international context, it is not clear that so complete a rejection of systemic goals is possible, as is suggested in the American context.[168] European privacy concerns have been recognized by American computer users voluntarily subscribing to the OECD privacy guidelines. Perhaps the interests or protecting data or other components of international information networks will lead to similar efforts toward uniformity where systemic strategies are involved. In the prognosis that follows, I suggest several systemic strategies.

PROGNOSIS—PRACTICAL AND THEORETICAL

The efforts described in the preceding section seem likely to keep the dialogue about appropriate computer crime legislation alive for the foreseeable future. Within the groups concerned, it is likely that model legislation will emerge, and given the cooperative nature of each group, it is likely that further steps toward cooperation will be taken as well. The experience of the United States Congress in unsuccessful attempts to pass computer crime legislation in the early 1980s suggests that the relative lack of interest on the part of manufacturers and users may keep legislation concerning computer crime a low priority item both in the United States and abroad. At the same time, the fact that 36 states have passed computer crime legislation suggests that within more limited jurisdictions the interest has been significant.

The approach taken here, suggesting that procedural and systemic changes are needed, derives more support from European efforts than from those within the United States. Whether the generally greater concern for privacy demonstrated in certain European quarters will manifest in additional computer crime legislation is a significant question, one posed most sharply by the Kuitenbrouwer article to which this chapter refers with such consistency and obvious admiration.

The history of international definition of crimes as international crimes suggests that unless computer crime becomes as significant a problem as hijacking, or terrorism in general, that computer crime will not become an international crime. Whether agreements can be reached to facilitate the prosecution of computer crime is a different question, however, and it would seem that this question is more a function of whether diplomatic priorities of those nations involved in negotiation over criminal cooperation will put computer crime sufficiently high to get action.

Against this rather measured analysis of a still-nascent field, I would add the comment that what one author said about terrorism applies to the whole of international computer crime. "A determined response to international terrorism is not a matter of choice—it is a question of survival."

It would seem that the following trends are likely to emerge in the years ahead as significant contributions to the development of an international law dealing with the problems of computer crime:

Emergence of a Uniform Definition of Computer Crime

The first stages of this uniformity are suggested by the number of states that have adopted the Ribicoff bill definitions virtually unchanged. The efforts on national and local levels to develop model bills, and the usefulness of such model and uniform legislation for purposes of international cooperation, would suggest that this is an obvious and important area for further development.

A Redefinition of Property

As suggested above, probably the single most difficult area in the prosecution of computer crime and other crime involving communications facilities is a redefinition of property to include intangible items and other related questions. Within the framework of a uniform computer crime bill, one would anticipate a major role for such redefinition.

Facilitation of Law Enforcement Efforts

With the strong interest of INTERPOL in the area of computer crime, and the obvious logic of strengthening law enforcement in order to prevent such crime, one can anticipate considerable effort both to provide training opportunities for law enforcement officers throughout the world, and to facilitate the exchange of information between those agencies and other individual interested parties.

Closer Interaction with Laws Protecting Privacy

The irony of one set of standards to punish computer crime and another to protect personal privacy involving computer use is likely to change. One can see the connection between these two areas in papers such as Kuitenbrouwer's, which point to the incidence of computer crime as proof positive of the need for stronger protections for individual privacy.

Standardization of Security Precautions

Closely allied to the preceding point is the observation that many privacy regulations include certain restrictions on data-processing procedures, in order to maintain adequate levels of security. The intense work in the United States to develop security standards, and the logic behind developing such standards for inherently dangerous activities such as certain types of information processing, suggests that this is an area in which much foment and ultimate cooperation can be anticipated in the foreseeable future. One may well anticipate the growth of voluntary standards and debate over whether or not laws should be used to make certain standards mandatory. The use of regulatory law, administrative misdemeanors, and other punishments for individuals failing to maintain their data centers at appropriate levels seems an appropriate inference to be drawn from current activities and discussion in the field.

CONCLUSION

Nothing threatens the continued growth of computers and communications as much as the possibility that they might be subverted. Criminals (or oppressive governments, or oppressive businesses) can turn computer systems and communications against the society that gives rise to them. Thus, the need for computer crime prevention rises in direct proportion to the amount of international information network use.

Nowhere can we turn without being struck by the breadth and magnitude of this rapidly growing global network. The book now in your hands does nothing if not document that fact. As Parker points out, computer crime reflects the failure of society to develop supportive and protective systems equally rapidly. Protection requires more than laws. But laws can bring consensus and consensus can bring action. Both, I submit, are needed if we are to adequately protect the fruits of the informatics revolution from becoming the spoils of informatics crime.

EXHIBIT 1

95th Congress
1st Session S. 1766

IN THE SENATE OF THE UNITED STATES

June 27 (legislative day, May 18), 1977

Mr. Ribicoff (for himself, Mr. Domenici, Mr. Griffin, Mr. Heinz, Mr. Jackson, Mr. Kennedy, Mr. Metcalf, Mr. Percy, and Mr. Thurmond) introduced the following bill: which was read twice and referred to the Committee on the Judiciary

---

A BILL

To amend title 18, United States Code, to make a crime the use, for fraudulent or other illegal purposes, of any computer owned or operated by the United States, certain financial institutions, and entities affecting interstate commerce.

Be it enacted by the Senate and House of Representatives of the United States of America in Congress assembled, That this Act may be cited as the "Federal Computer Systems Protection Act of 1977".

Sec. 2. The Congress finds that—

(1) computer related crime is a growing problem in the Government and in the private sector;

(2) such crime occurs at great cost to the public since losses for each incident of computer crime tend to be far greater than the losses associated with each incident of other white collar crime;

(3) the opportunities for computer related crimes in Federal programs, in financial institutions, and in other entities which operate in interstate commerce through the introduction of fraudulent records into a computer system, unauthorized use of computer facilities, alteration or destruction of computerized information files, and stealing of financial instruments, data, or other assets, are great;

(4) computer related crime directed at institutions operating in interstate commerce has a direct effect on interstate commerce; and

(5) the prosecution of persons engaged in computer related crime is difficult under current Federal criminal statutes.

Sec. 3. (a) Chapter 47 of title 18, United States Code, is amended by adding at the end thereof the following new section:

"Sec. 1028. Computer fraud

"(a) Whoever directly or indirectly accesses or causes to be accessed any computer, computer system, computer network, or any part thereof which, in whole or in part, operates in interstate commerce or is owned by, under contract to, or operated for, on behalf of, or in conjunction with, any financial institution, the United States Government, or any branch, department, or agency thereof, or any entity operating in or affecting interstate commerce, for the purpose of (1) devising or executing any scheme or artifice to defraud, or (2) obtaining money, property, or services by means of false or fraudulent pretenses, representations, or promises, shall be fined not more than $50,000, or imprisoned not more than fifteen years, or both.

"(b) Whoever, intentionally and without authorization, directly or indirectly accesses, alters, damages, or destroys any computer, computer system, or computer network described in subsection (a), or any computer software, program, or data contained in such computer, computer system, or computer network, shall be fined not more than $50,000, or imprisoned not more than fifteen years, or both.

"(c) For purposes of this section, the term—

"(1) 'access' means to approach, instruct, communicate with, store data in, retrieve data from, or otherwise make use of any resources of, a computer, computer system, or computer network;

"(2) 'computer' means an electronic device which performs logical, arithmetic, and memory functions by the manipulations of electronic or magnetic impulses, and includes all input, output, processing, storage, software, or communication facilities which are connected or related to such a device in a system or network;

"(3) 'computer system' means a set of related, connected or unconnected, computer equipment, devices, and software;

"(4) 'computer network' means the interconnection of communication lines with a computer through remote terminals, or a complex consisting of two or more interconnected computers;

"(5) 'property' includes, but is not limited to, financial instruments, information, including electronically produced data, and computer software and programs in either machine or human readable form, and any other tangible or intangible item of value;

"(6) 'services' includes, but is not limited to, computer time, data processing, and storage functions;

"(7) 'financial instrument' means any check, draft, money order, certificate of deposit, letter of credit, bill of exchange, credit card, or marketable security;

"(8) 'computer program' means a series of instructions or statements, in a form acceptable to a computer, which permits the functioning of a computer system in a manner designed to provide appropriate products from such computer system;

"(9) 'computer software' means a set of computer programs, procedures, and associated documentation concerned with the operation of a computer system;

"(10) 'financial institution' means—

"(A) a bank with deposits insured by the Federal Deposit Insurance Corporation;

"(B) a member of the Federal Reserve including any Federal Reserve bank;

"(C) an institution with accounts insured by the Federal Savings and Loan Insurance Corporation;

"(D) a credit union with accounts insured by the National Credit Union Administration;

"(E) a member of the Federal home loan bank systems and any home loan bank;

"(F) a member or business insured by the Securities Investor Protection Corporation; and

"(G) a broker-dealer registered with the Securities and Exchange Commission pursuant to section 15 of the Securities and Exchange Act of 1934.".

(c) The table of sections of chapter 47 of title 18, United States Code, is amended by adding at the end thereof the following:

"1028. Computer fraud.".

EXHIBIT 2

96th Congress
1st Session S. 240

To amend title 18, United States Code, to make a crime the use, for fraudulent or other illegal purposes, of any computer owned or operated by the United States, certain financial institutions, and entities affecting interstate commerce.

IN THE SENATE OF THE UNITED STATES

January 25 (legislative day, January 15), 1979

Mr. Ribicoff (for himself, Mr. Percy, Mr. Kennedy, Mr. Inouye, Mr. Jackson, Mr. Matsunaga, Mr. Moynihan, Mr. Williams, Mr. Zorinsky, Mr. Domenici, Mr. Stevens, Mr. Chiles, and Mr. Nunn) introduced the following bill; which was read twice and referred to the Committee on the Judiciary

A BILL

To amend title 18, United States Code, to make a crime the use, for fraudulent or other illegal purposes, of any computer owned or operated by the United States, certain financial institutions, and entities affecting interstate commerce.

Be it enacted by the Senate and House of Representatives of the United States of America in Congress assembled, That this Act may be cited as the "Federal Computer Systems Protection Act of 1979".

Sec. 2. The Congress finds that—

(1)   computer-related crime is a growing problem in the Government and in the private sector;

(2)   such crime occurs at great cost to the public since losses for each incident of computer crime tend to be far greater than the losses associated with each incident of other white collar crime;

(3)   the opportunities for computer-related crimes in Federal programs, in financial institutions, and in other entities which operate in interstate commerce through the introduction of fraudulent records into a computer system, unauthorized use of computer facilities, alteration or destruction of computerized information files, and stealing of financial instruments, data, or other assets, are great;

(4)   computer-related crime directed at institutions operating in interstate commerce has a direct effect on interstate commerce; and

(5)   the prosecution of persons engaged in computer-related crime is difficult under current Federal criminal statutes.

Sec. 3. (a) Chapter 47 of title 18, United States Code, is amended by adding at the end thereof the following new section:

"Sec. 1028. Computer fraud and abuse

"(a)   Whoever knowingly and willfully, directly or indirectly accesses, causes to be accessed or attempts to access any computer, computer system, computer network, or any part thereof which, in whole or in part, operates in interstate commerce or is owned by, under contract to, or in conjunction with, any financial institution, the United States Government or any branch, department, or agency thereof, or any entity operating in or effecting interstate commerce, for the purpose of—
    "(1)   devising or executing any scheme or artifice to defraud, or
    "(2)   obtaining money, property, or services, for themselves or another, by means of false or fraudulent pretenses, representations or promises, shall be fined a sum not more than two and one-half times the amount of the fraud or theft, or imprisoned not more than fifteen years, or both.

"(b)   Whoever intentionally and without authorization, directly or indirectly accesses, alters, damages, destroys, or attempts to damage or destroy any computer, computer system, or computer network described in subsection (a), or any computer software, program or data contained in such computer, computer system or computer network, shall be fined not more than $50,000 or imprisoned not more than fifteen years, or both.

"(c)   For purposes of this section, the term—
    "(1)   'access' means to approach, instruct, communicate with, store data in, retrieve data from, or otherwise make use of any resources of, a computer, computer system, or computer network;
    "(2)   'computer' means an electronic device which performs logical, arithmetic, and memory functions by the manipulations of electronic or magnetic impulses, and includes all input, output, processing, storage, software, or communication facilities which are connected or related to such a device in a system or network;
    "(3)   'computer system' means a set of related, connected or unconnected, computer equipment, devices, and software;
    "(4)   'computer network' means the interconnection of communication systems with a computer through remote terminals, or a complex consisting of two or more interconnected computers;
    "(5)   'property' includes, but is not limited to, financial instruments, information, including electronically processed or produced data, and computer software and programs in either machine or human readable form, and any other tangible or intangible item of value;
    "(6)   'services' includes, but is not limited to, computer time, data processing, and storage functions;
    "(7)   'financial instrument' means any check, draft, money order, certificate of deposit, letter of credit, bill of exchange, credit card, or marketable security, or any electronic data processing representation thereof;
    "(8)   'computer program' means an instruction or statement or a series of instructions or statements, in a form acceptable to a computer, which permits the functioning of a computer system in a manner designed to provide appropriate products from such computer system;
    "(9)   'computer software' means a set of computer programs, procedures, and associated documentation concerned with the operation of a computer system;
    "(10)   'financial institution' means—
        "(A)   a bank with deposits insured by the Federal Deposit Insurance Corporation;
        "(B)   a member of the Federal Reserve including any Federal Reserve bank;
        "(C)   an institution with accounts insured by the Federal Savings and Loan Insurance Corporation;
        "(D)   a credit union with accounts insured by the National Credit Union Administration;
        "(E)   a member of the Federal home loan bank systems and any home loan bank;
        "(F)   a member or business insured by the Securities Investor Protection Corporation; and

"(G)   a broker-dealer registered with the Securities and Exchange Commission pursuant to section 15 of the Securities and Exchange Act of 1934."

(c)   The table of sections of chapter 47 of title 18, United States Code, is amended by adding at the end thereof the following:

"1028. Computer fraud and abuse.".

EXHIBIT 3

Fla. Stat. Ann. Secs. 815.01–815.07 (West Supp.).

815.01   Short title

The provisions of this act shall be known and may be cited as the "Florida Computer Crimes Act."

815.02   Legislative Intent

The Legislature finds and declares that:

(1)   Computer-related crime is a growing problem in government as well as in the private sector.

(2)   Computer-related crime occurs at great cost to the public since losses for each incident of computer crime tend to be far greater than the losses associated with each incident of other white collar crime.

(3)   The opportunities for computer-related crimes in financial institutions, government programs, government records, and other business enterprises through the introduction of fraudulent records into a computer system, the unauthorized use of computer facilities, the alteration or destruction of computerized information or files, and the stealing of financial instruments, data, and other assets are great.

(4)   While various forms of computer crime might possibly be the subject of criminal charges based on other provisions of law, it is appropriate and desirable that a supplemental and additional statute be provided which proscribes various forms of computer abuse.

815.03   Definitions

As used in this chapter, unless the context clearly indicates otherwise:

(1)   "Intellectual property" means data, including programs.

(2)   "Computer" means an internally programmed, automatic device that performs data processing.

(4)   "Computer software" means a set of computer programs, procedures, and associated documentation concerned with the operation of a computer system.

(5)   "Computer system" means a set of related, connected or unconnected, computer equipment, devices, or computer software.

(6)   "Computer network" means a set of related, remotely connected devices and communication facilities including more than one computer system with capability to transmit data among them through communication facilities.

(7)   "Computer system services" means providing a computer system or computer network to perform useful work.

(8)   "Property" means anything of value as defined in s. 812.011 and includes, but is not limited to, financial instruments, information, including electronically produced data and computer software and programs in either machine-readable or human-readable form, and any other tangible or intangible item of value.

(9)   "Financial instrument" means any check, draft, money order, certificate of deposit, letter of credit, bill of exchange, credit card, or marketable security.

(10)   "Access" means to approach, instruct, communicate with, store data in, retrieve data from, or otherwise make use of any resources of a computer, computer system, or computer network.

815.04   Offenses against intellectual property

(1)   Whoever willfully, knowingly, and without authorization modifies data, programs, or supporting documentation residing or existing internal or external to a computer, computer system, or computer network commits an offense against intellectual property.

(2)   Whoever willfully, knowingly, and without authorization destroys data, programs, or supporting documentation residing or existing internal or external to a computer, computer system, or computer network commits an offense against intellectual property.

(3)   Whoever willfully, knowingly, and without authorization discloses or takes data, programs, or supporting documentation which is a trade secret as defined in sec. 812.081 or is confidential as provided by law residing or existing internal or external to a computer, computer system, or computer network commits an offense against intellectual property.

(4)(a)   Except as otherwise provided in this subsection, an offense against intellectual property is a felony of the third degree, punishable as provided in sec. 775.082, sec. 775.083, or sec. 775.084.

(b)   If the offense is committed for the purpose of devising or executing any scheme or artifice to defraud or to obtain any property, then the offender is guilty of a felony of the second degree, punishable as provided in sec. 775.082, sec. 775.083, or sec. 775.084.

815.05   Offenses against computer equipment or supplies

(1)(a)   Whoever willfully, knowingly, and without authorization modifies equipment or supplies used or intended to be used in a computer, computer system, or computer network commits an offense against computer equipment or supplies.

(b)1.   Except as provided in this paragraph, an offense against computer equipment or supplies as provided in paragraph (a) is a misdemeanor of the first degree, punishable as provided in sec. 775.082, sec. 775.083, or sec. 775.084.

2.   If the offense is committed for the purpose of devising or executing any scheme or artifice to defraud or to obtain any property, then the offender is guilty of a felony of the third degree, punishable as provided in sec. 775.082, sec. 775.083, or sec. 775.084.

(2)(a)   Whoever willfully, knowingly, and without authorization destroys, takes, injures, or damages equipment or supplies used or intended to be used in a computer, computer system, or computer network; or whoever willfully, knowingly, and without authorization destroys, injures, or damages any computer, computer system, or computer network commits an offense against computer equipment or supplies.

(b)1.   Except as provided in this paragraph, an offense against computer equipment or supplies as provided in paragraph (a) is a misdemeanor of the first degree, punishable as provided in sec. 775.082, sec. 775.083, or sec. 775.084.

2.   If the damage to such computer equipment or supplies or to the computer, computer system, or computer network is greater than $200 but less than $1,000, then the offender is guilty of a felony of the third degree, punishable as provided in sec. 775.082, sec. 775.083, or sec. 775.084.

3.   If the damage to such computer equipment or supplies or to the computer, computer system, or computer network is $1,000 or greater, or if there is an interruption or impairment of governmental operation or public communication, transportation, or supply of water, gas, or other public service, then the offender is guilty of a felony of the second degree, punishable as provided in sec. 775.082, sec. 775.083, or sec. 775.084

815.06   Offenses against computer users

(1)   Whoever willfully, knowingly, and without authorization accesses or causes to be accessed any computer, computer system, or computer network; or whoever willfully, knowingly, and without authorization denies or causes the denial of computer system services to an authorized user of such computer system services, which, in whole or part, is owned by, under contract to, or operated for, on behalf of, or in conjunction with another commits an offense against computer users.

(2)(a)   Except as provided in this subsection, an offense against computer users is a felony of the third degree, punishable as provided in sec. 775.082, sec. 775.083, or sec. 775.084.

(b)   If the offense is committed for the purposes of devising or executing any scheme or artifice to defraud or to obtain any property, then the offender is guilty of a felony of the second degree, punishable as provided in sec. 775.082, sec. 775.083, or sec. 775.084.

815.07   This chapter not exclusive

The provisions of this chapter shall not be construed to preclude the applicability of any other provision of the criminal law of this state which presently applies or may in the future apply to any transaction which violates this chapter, unless such provision is inconsistent with the terms of this chapter.

EXHIBIT 4

Code of Virginia (1979 Supp.)

Sec. 18.2-98.1.   Computer time, services, etc., subject of larceny.

Computer time or services or data processing services or information or data stored in connection therewith is hereby defined to be property which may be the subject of larceny under sec. 18.2-95 or 18.2-96, or embezzlement under sec. 18.2-111, or false pretenses under sec. 18.2-178.

NOTES

1. For the purposes of this chapter, *informatics* refers to the use of computers and communications facilities to process information. *Informatics crime* is used as synonymous with computer crime, in its most general meaning. Given the contention that defining computer crime is an important and yet-uncompleted project of those concerned with the topic, it should not be surprising if the term has different meanings when used by different authors. The section on applicable laws and policies attempts to articulate a number of these definitions, and the section entitled "Recommended Approach: A Proposed Classification System for Informatics Crimes," suggests the author's favored definition. A much more detailed examination of communications crime remains to be completed, but it is believed that the principles articulated herein will be of assistance in that enterprise.

2. D. Parker, Computer Security Managment 12–13 (Reston, Va.: Reston, 1981).

3. Adrian Norman, in his book Computer Insecurity (New York: Atheneum, 1984) defines "usees" thus: "Whereas the user of a computer system in some way controls its operation, the usee is affected by the system without having an effective say in its operation." The political overtones of this definition make it both extremely useful and somewhat limited. Its usefulness comes from the importance of acknowledging the fact that the operation of computers does impact individuals and groups who normally have no control over the operation of the system. At the same time, one would think that a more appropriate definition would not be limited by the political power of the usees. For instance, if a community college district uses a computer to calcuate student attendance records, it would seem clear that the students are the usees. If a progressive administration accorded those students the right to review the procedures used in the implementation of the computer programs, it would appear that Norman would no longer call those students usees. This would seem an unfortunate limitation of his definition.

4. T. Whiteside, Computer Capers, 72–74 (New York: Thomas Crowell, 1978).

5. Becker, *Computer Crime: Career of the Future?*, Computer Careers Mag., Oct. 1980.

6. T. Plate, Crime Pays, New York: Simon & Schuster, 1975).

7. Transborder Data Flows 157 (R. Turn ed. 1979) (report of the AFIPS Panel on Transborder Data Flow) [hereinafter cited as AFIPS report].

8. Federal Computer System Protection Act (FCSPA), S. 240, 96th Cong., 2d Sess. (1980) 2 Computer/Law J., nos 2, 3 *passim* (1980) (a symposium on computer crime, available from the Center for Computer Law, Los Angeles) [hereinafter cited as Computer/Law J.].

9. Committee on the Vulnerability of Computer Systems (SARK), Vulnerability of the Computerized Society (1976) (English summary on file at National Center for Computer Crime Data) [hereinafter cited as SARK report].

10. *Id.* at 12.

11. Consultative Committee on the Implications of Telecommunications for Canadian Society, Canadian Department of Communications, Clyne Report (1979).

12. Discussed in Fishman, *Introduction to Transborder Data Flows*, 16 Stan. J. Int'l L. 64 (1980).

13. S. Nora & A. Minc, The Computerization of Society (Cambridge, Mass.: MIT Press, 1980) (English translation).

14. *Id.* at 73–74.

15. Not everyone agrees. Reviewing the Nora and Minc study, de Sola Pool comments: "I must admit I find it hard to see what alienation follows from using *Chemical Abstracts* that were produced abroad." 22 Tech. & Culture 352 (1981).

16. *See* Fishman, *supra* note 12, at 24.

17. *Id.*

18. Eger, *Emerging Restrictions on Transborder Data Flows: Privacy Protections or Non-Tariff Trade Barriers?*, 10 L. & Pol. Int'l Bus. 1055, 1065–66 (1978) (Quoting Louis Joinet, French Magistrate of Justice, before the OECD Symposium on Transborder Data Flows and the Protection of Privacy, Vienna, Sept. 1977) "Information is power, and economic information is economic power. Information has an economic value and the ability to store and process certain types of data may well give one country political and technological advantage over other countries. This in turn may lead to a loss of national sovereignty through supranational data flows."

19. See statement of Richard Gutman, before Subcommittee on Research and Development, Committee on Armed Services, U.S. House of Representatives, on Problems Associated with the World

Wide Military Command and Control System (Apr. 23, 1979) (on file at the National Center for Computer Crime Data) [hereinafter cited as Gutman Statement]. *See also* SARK report *supra* note 9, at 7.

20. BANK FOR INTERNATIONAL SETTLEMENTS, SECURITY AND RELIABILITY IN ELECTRONIC SYSTEMS FOR PAYMENTS 3–4, (1978) *passim*; OECD, II THE USAGE OF INTERNATIONAL DATA NETWORKS IN EUROPE 199–208 (Paris, 1979) (discusses SWIFT) [hereinafter cited as OECD II]; Berenyi, *SWIFT International Bank Network to Expand,* COMPUTERWORLD, Jan. 22, 1979; COMPUTER LAW J., *supra* note 8, at 43–44; Eaton & Rosenblatt, *$8 Billion Transferred in 40 Minutes,* Los Angeles Times, Jan. 21, 1981, § 1, at 5; Parker, The Potential Effects of Electronic Funds Transfer Systems on National Security (available from SRI International, 333 Ravenswood Ave., Menlo Park, CA 94025) [hereinafter cited as Parker, Potential Effects].

21. OECD II, *supra* note 20, at 209–18 (discusses SITA, the airline reservation system used worldwide); AFIPS report, *supra* note 7, at 44.

22. Whittaker, "Satellite Business Systems (SBS): A Concept for the 80s," in T. Oka, *Data Network Developments and Policies in Japan,* in OECD, III POLICY IMPLICATIONS OF DATA NETWORK DEVELOPMENTS IN THE OECD AREA 35–39 (Paris, 1980) (proceedings of a special session of the Working Party on Information, Computer, and Communications Policy of the OECD, Paris, 1978) [hereinafter cited as OECD III].

23. Schickich, *Transborder Data Flow,* 11 L & COMPUTER TECH. 63 (1978) (estimates a 20–25 percent worldwide growth rate for telecommunications).

24. AFIPS report, *supra* note 7, at 50.

25. *Id.* at 56.

26. *See* A. NORMAN, *supra* note 3.

27. Nanus, *Business, Government, and the Multinational Computer,* 13 COLUM. J. WORLD BUS., Spring 1978, at 19–26.

28. Szuprowicz, *Brazil Protecting Its Domestic Minicomputers,* COMPUTERWORLD, Mar. 27, 1978, at 79; Pantages, *Cracking Brazil Nuts,* DATAMATION, Feb. 1979.

29. Eger, *supra* note 18, at 1062–63; Blumenthal, *Anti-U.S. Moves Overseas High on Adapso's List of Issues,* COMPUTERWORLD, Nov. 13, 1978, at 87.

30. S. NORA & A. MINC, *supra* note 13, at 39–44; *The French Invasion,* OUTPUT, Mar. 1981, at 14; Malik, *Europe Moving to Protect Faltering DP Industry,* COMPUTERWORLD, Jan. 14, 1980, at 12; Brenner, *Eu-*

ronet and Its Effects on the U.S. Information Market, J. AM. SOC'Y INFORMATION SCI. Jan. 1979, at 5–8.

31. Ganley, *Loosening the Telecom Link,* DATAMATION, Sept. 1980, at 149–52.

32. Reid, *Prestel, The British Post Office Viewdata Service,* in OECD III, *supra* note 22.

33. Personal conversation with Mr. Sumio Ishizaki, general manager, Kanda Branch, Fuji Bank, Tokyo, Japan.

34. Remarks of "Val Smith" (the pseudonym given him in D. PARKER, CRIME BY COMPUTER, 71–79 (New York: Scribners, 1976),) at *Computer Decisions Seminar,* Mar. 7, 1981; *see* COMPUTER DECISIONS, June 1981, at 104–128.

35. French, *Mexico on Brink of Severe DP Staff Shortage,* COMPUTERWORLD, Apr. 2, 1979.

36. *Id.*

37. Dooley, *Peace Corps Aide Notes Columbian DP Experience,* COMPUTERWORLD, Sept. 6, 1976, at 7.

38. *DP in Developing Nations, A Long Road Ahead,* COMPUTERWORLD, Mar. 31, 1980, at 32.

39. Shoor, *Travel, Rewards, Austere Life Anticipated by Saudi-bound DPer,* COMPUTERWORLD, June 9, 1980, at 12.

40. Beeler, *Third World's DP Infancy Attributed to Isolation,* COMPUTERWORLD, June 18, 1979, at 14.

41. Personal conversations with Lieutenant Robert McDiarmid, Organized Crime and Criminal Information Section, Santa Clara County Sheriff's Office, and William Bankert, Intel Security Department.

42. Kim & Woods, *Satellite Data Needs Special Security* (pts. 1 & 2), COMPUTERWORLD, Dec. 17, 1979, at 22, Dec. 24, 1979, at 35–36.

43. Turn, *Privacy Protection and Security in Transnational Data Processing Systems,* 16 STAN. J. INT'L L. 82 (1980).

44. *Id.*; Nelson & Reisman, *Transborder Data Barriers May Restrict Encryption,* COMPUTERWORLD, Mar. 23 & 24, 1980, at 41; Nelson & Reisman, *Packet Nets Need New Encryption Tools,* COMPUTERWORLD, Mar. 24, 1980, at 35, 40; Wermdalen, *A Manufacturer's Experience* in OECD III, *supra* note 22, at 73.

45. BloomBecker, *Playpens and Cookie Jars: An Invitation to Computer Crime,* COMPUTERWORLD, May 4, 1981, In-Depth, 20–22.

46. Freese, *Pro (Transborder Data Flow: Should it be Regulated?),* COMPUTERWORLD, Oct. 30, 1978, at 64.

46A. D. PARKER, FIGHTING COMPUTER CRIME 23 (New

York: Scribner's, 1983) [hereinafter cited as PARKER, FIGHTING].

47. Taber, *A Survey of Computer Crime Studies,* 1 COMPUTER/LAW J., no. 2, at 275–328 (1980); Taber, *On Computer Crime,* 1 COMPUTER/LAW J., no. 3, at 517, 537 (1979).

47A. Courtney, *The Democratization of White Collar Crime,* 1 COMPUTER SECURITY J., no. 1, at 40–41 (1981).

47B. Couch, *A Suggested Legislative Approach to the Problem of Computer Crime,* 38 WASH. & LEE L. REV. 1173–94 (1981).

47C. D. PARKER, CRIME BY COMPUTER 23–40 (New York: Scribner's, 1976) [hereinafter cited as PARKER, CRIME].

47D. *Id.* at 12–21.

48. Kling, *Computer Abuse and Computer Crime as Organizaional Activities,* 2 COMPUTER/LAW J., no. 2, at 42, 403–428, *passim* (1980).

49. *Id.* at 408.

50. *Id.*

50A. Since this article was submitted, the U.S. Congress has passed a computer crime bill that has much of the language of the Ribicoff bill, but is limited in application to governmental computers, financial information, and national security information. The text of 18 U.S.C. § 1030 can be found in COMPUTER CRIME L. REP. (1984).

51. S. 240, 96th Cong., 1st Sess. (1979); COMPUTER/LAW J., *supra* note 8 (Sokolik, *Computer Crime—The Need for Deterrent Legislation,* 353–85; Volgyes, *The Investigation, Prosecution, and Prevention of Computer Crime: A State of the Art Review,* 385–403; *but see* Taber, *A Survey of Computer Crime Studies,* 275–328; Kling, *Computer Abuse and Computer Crime as Organizational Activities,* 403–28); STAFF OF SENATE COMM. ON GOVERNMENTAL OPERATIONS, 94TH CONG., 2ND SESS., REPORT OF PROBLEMS ASSOCIATED WITH COMPUTER TECHNOLOGY IN FEDERAL PROGRAMS AND PRIVATE INDUSTRY, COMPUTER ABUSE (Comm. Print 1976) (includes General Accounting Office's report, Computer-Related Crimes in Federal Programs, 73–94); STAFF OF SENATE COMM. ON GOVERNMENTAL OPERATIONS, 95TH CONG., 1ST SESS., STAFF STUDY OF COMPUTER SECURITY IN FEDERAL PROGRAMS (Comm. Print 1977); *Hearings on S. 1766 Before the Subcomm. on Criminal Laws and Procedures of the Senate Comm. on the Judiciary,* 95th Cong., 2d Sess. (1978); AM. CRIM. L. REV. 370–86 (1980); BUREAU OF JUSTICE STATISTICS, U.S. DEPART-MENT OF JUSTICE, COMPUTER CRIME ELECTRONIC FUND TRANSFER SYSTEMS AND CRIME (1982).

52. 2 COMPUTER/LAW J., no. 3, at 723 (1980).

53. BloomBecker, *Lessons from Wells Fargo,* 1 COMPUTER CRIME DIG., no. 3, at 8–9, (1982).

54. Simpson, *Electronics Underworld,* COMPUTERWORLD, Aug. 31, 1981, at 1, 6, 7, 9, Sept. 7, 1981, at 1, 8–10; Sept. 14, 1981, at 1, 8; Sept. 21, 1981, at 1, 8; Nov. 23, 1981, at 1, 8, 9.

55. *Compare* FLA. STAT. ANN. § 815.04(3) (West).

56. E.g., COMPUTER CRIME DIG., no. 2 (1983) (re H.R. 6420).

57. One of the more recent issues to surface in a related field is the question of the appropriateness of certain computer games. Feminists, Native Americans, and others have protested certain computer games as being demeaning to women, Native Americans, or others. At present, their efforts have been limited to attempts to get local jurisdictions to ban the use of such games, and the issue has not yet been litigated in court. Notably, First Amendment attorneys who have previously specialized in the defense of writings charged with obscenity have been hired by the purveyors of these games.

58. Couch, *A Suggested Legislative Approach to the Problem of Computer Crime,* 38 WASH. & LEE L. REV. 1181 (1981).

59. *Id.* at 1184.

60. *U.S. Doesn't Need Federal Laws to Curb Computer Crimes,* 1 COMPUTER CRIME DIG., no. 3, at 10 (1982).

61. FLA. STAT. ANN. §§ 815.01–815.07 (West).

62. *Id.* at § 815.04.

63. *Id.* at § 815.04 (4)(b).

64. *Id.* at 815.05.

65. *Id.*

66. *Id.* at § 815.05(2).

67. *Id.* at § 815.05(3).

68. *Id.* at § 815.07.

69. *Id.*

70. *Id.*

71. VA. CODE §§ 18.2–98.1 (1979) (repealed 1984).

72. OHIO REV. CODE ANN. §§ 2901.01, 2913.01.

73. ALASKA NEW CRIM. CODE § 11.46.985.

74. CAL. PENAL CODE § 502(d).

75. Conversation with William Holman, deputy district attorney in San Diego (notes on file at National Center for Computer Crime Data).

76. Conversation with George Cox, victim in case

(notes on file at National Center for Computer Crime Data).

77. F. KUITENBROUWER, COMPUTER CRIME, SOME MARGINAL NOTES ON RECENT LITERATURE REGARDING A NEW PHENOMENON (1975) (translation produced by the United States National Criminal Justice Reference Service, Rockville, Md. Original title is "Komputerkriminaliteit, Enige Kanttekeningen bij Recente Literatur over een Nieuw Verschijnsel").

78. CAL. PENAL CODE § 537(e).

79. *Limited Computer Crime Law Proposed for New York,* 1 COMPUTER CRIME DIG., March 1983, at 1–2.

80. *See* F. KUITENBROUWER, *supra* note 77.

81. A. SOLARZ, COMPUTER TECHNOLOGY AND COMPUTER CRIME (Stockholm: National Swedish Council for Crime Prevention, 1981).

82. *Id.* at 25.

83. LOCAL GOVERNMENT AUDIT INSPECTORATE, U.K. DEPARTMENT OF THE ENVIRONMENT, COMPUTER FRAUD SURVEY (1981).

84. *See* Solarz, *supra* note 81.

85. *Id.* at 41.

86. *Id.* at 41.

87. D. Schofield, Some Practical Perspectives on Computer Crime and the Present Law in Canada (a presentation to the Computer Crime Investigative Techniques Course, Canadian Police College, Ottawa, Ontario. On file at the National Center for Computer Crime Data, JFK Library, CSULA, 5151 State University Drive, Los Angeles, Calif. 90032).

88. Notes from 3rd INTERPOL Symposium on International Fraud, St. Cloud, France (Nov. 12, 1979) (on file at National Center for Computer Crime Data).

88A. K. FITZGERALD, THE COMPUTER ABUSE PROFILE IN AUSTRALIA (Victoria, Australia: Computer Abuse Research Bureau, 1982).

89. S. Schjolberg, Computers and Penal Legislation (1983) (available from Norwegian Center for Computers and Law University of Oslo, Niels Juels gt. 16 Oslo 2 Norway).

89A. Intergovernment Bureau for Informatics, Informatics Criminal Law (1983) (three studies by Sarzana, Vilarno, & BloomBecker).

90. Watkins, *Computer Crime: Separating the Myth from the Reality,* CA MAGAZINE, Jan. 1983.

The author takes full responsibility for drawing this inference from a number of disparate and inconclusive sources. My view gains some support from the comment of Donn Parker:

No manufacturer wants its product associated with crime, let alone facilitating criminal activities. One is reminded of the National Rifleman's Association slogan: 'Guns don't kill people. Only people kill people.' It is a slogan that can be adapted for computers or any powerful product, even though we would not equate computers with guns. IBM wouldn't provide security in its products if there weren't a good reason for it. (PARKER, FIGHTING, *supra* note 46A, at 120–24.)

Parker's remarks were directed to a two-page advertisement that showed a police line-up consisting of four men and a computer terminal. The ad was headlined "The Computer Didn't Do It."

The author's perspective is further spelled out in 1 COMPUTER CRIME DIG., no. 1, at 6–8 (1982). Finally, the remarks of representatives of both IBM and Honeywell at the 1982 World Future Society Conference indicated both companies' preference for the term "computer-related" crime over the term "computer crimes." Time (and perhaps crime) will tell whether the author's observation is paranoid or perceptive.

91. The author was told by a vice president at the Security Pacific Bank that the bank thought it important not to call Stanley Mark Rifkin's theft of $10.2 million a computer crime because it did not want to unfairly impugn the accuracy of the bank's computers.

92. See Kling, *supra* note 48, *passim.*

93. See Taber, *supra* note 47.

94. E.g. United States v. McVey, No. CR83-188 (C.D. Cal. filed Mar. 1983).

95. L. Becker, Risk Assessment Management in an Information Handling Environment (1979) (available from National Criminal Justice Reference Service, No. 62935); D. PARKER, COMPUTER SECURITY MANAGEMENT, at 144–45 (Reston, Va.: Reston, 1982) (The application of analytical methods to computer security is in its infancy. Much experimentation, experience with different methods, and stronger consensus on the best methods are needed."

96. H. MELVILLE, MOBY DICK *passim* (New York: Macmillan, 1962).

97. *See* PARKER, FIGHTING, *supra* note 46A, at 125–29, 279.

98. Interview with Charles Wood of SRI International; Parker, Potential Effects, *supra* note 20, at 7; Lloyd, *DP: An Easy Target*, DATAMATION, June 1980, at 99–100; Mickolus, *Chronology of Transnational Terrorist Attacks on American Business People*, in POLITICAL TERRORISM AND BUSINESS app. B, 297–318 (Y. Alexander & R. Kilmarx eds. New York: Praeger, 1979).

99. Tennant, *Computer Fraud—Industrial Aspects The Most Dangerous*, CHARTERED ACCT. AUSTL. April 1979, at 11.

100. J. CARROLL, COMPUTER SECURITY 17 (Los Angeles: Security World, 1977).

101. *Id.* at 18.

102. *New York State Challenges Adequacy of Citibank's Automated Teller Machine Security*, 1 COMPUTER CRIME DIG., no. 2, at 1–3 (1983).

103. Kling, *supra* note 48, at 414–415.

104. PARKER, FIGHTING, *supra* note 46A, at 96–97.

105. J. CARROLL, *supra* note 100, at 16–17.

106. *Id.* at 30.

107. Intergovernmental Bureau for Informatics, Intergovernmental Conference on Strategies and Policies for Informatics, Aug. 28–Sept. 6, 1978, Torrerolinos, Spain.

108. Tennant, *supra* note 99, at 11; J. CARROLL, *supra* note 100, at 19. Fictitious version appears in F. HUBER, APPLE CRUNCH (New York: Seaview, 1981).

109. Kling, *supra* note 48, at 414.

110. M. GEMIGNANI, LAW AND THE COMPUTER 103–32 (New York: Seaview, 1981).

111. D. PARKER, ETHICAL CONFLICTS IN COMPUTER SCIENCE AND TECHNOLOGY 25–27 (Arlington, Va.: AFIPS Press, 1979).

112. COMPUTER/LAW J., *supra* note 8, at 68.

113. People v. Rosenblum; Moulton, *Strategy for Dealing with Computer Fraud and Abuse: A Case Study*, 1 COMPUTER SECURITY J., Winter 1982, at 31–40.

114. *The Case of the Daytime Moonlighters*, 1 COMPUTER CRIME DIG., no. 5, at 1–3 (1983) [hereinafter cited as *Moonlighters*].

115. *See supra* note 113.

116. Consider the following hypothetical (provided by Richard Solomon of M.I.T.): The user of an electronic mail service is charged rent for the computer space taken up by other peoples' messages directed to him. Can the service charging him rent increase its profit by directing more messages to his space?

117. Friedman, *The Dalton Gang's Computer Caper*, NEW YORK MAGAZINE, Dec. 8, 1980, at 69–74; PARKER, FIGHTING, *supra* note 46A, at 114–147.

118. PARKER, FIGHTING, *supra* note 46A, at 135.

119. Ingraham, *On Charging Computer Crime*, 2 COMPUTER/LAW J., no. 2, at 429 (1980).

120. Comer, *Chip Design Theft*, COMPUTER FRAUD & SECURITY BULL., July, 1981, at 3.

121. Search warrant concerning Western Business Corporation (on file at National Center for Computer Crime Data).

122. *See* 1 COMPUTER CRIME DIG., no. 2, at 5 (1983).

123. Notes on file at National Center for Computer Crime Data.

124. *See* J. CARROLL, *supra* note 100, at 20.

125. *Pengem and the Problems of Prosecuting International Crime*, 1 COMPUTER CRIME DIG., no. 1, at 1–4 (1982).

126. *See* NORMAN, *supra* note 3.

127. Grenier, Marion & Winkler, Liability for Breaches of Computer Data Security 459, NCJRS No. 19113 (1974) (presentation at 2d International Conference on Communications, Stockholm, Aug. 12–14, 1974).

128. *Id.*

129. L. KRAUSS & A. MACGAHAN, COMPUTER FRAUD AND COUNTERMEASURES 276–90 (Englewood Cliffs, N.J.: Prentice Hall, 1979).

130. *See* CARROLL, J. *supra* note 100, at 23.

131. *See* PARKER, FIGHTING, *supra* note 46A, at 71.

132. P. v. Pearson, California Department of Motor Vehicles File No. C830573 (on file at National Center for Computer Crime Data).

133. PARKER, CRIME, *supra* note 47C, at 41–58; *but see* PARKER FIGHTING, *supra* note 46A.

134. Scannell, *Personal computer Scene Misrepresented by Vendors*, COMPUTERWORLD, June 9, 1980, at 8.

135. *See* Report of the Trustee of Equity Funding Corporation of America in Proceedings for the Reorganization of a Corporation, No. 73-046 (C.D. Cal. 1973).

136. PARKER, CRIME, *supra* note 47C, at 71–79.

137. *Log Fake Revenues on Ad Agency's CPU*, MIS WEEK, Mar. 3, 1982, at 4.

138. Kling, *supra* note 48, at 414–19. The author has seen another case in which funds erronenously remitted to a public utility were used by an employee to offset thefts he was making from the utility's funds. Since the funds erroneously remitted were poorly accounted for, the utility was unaware of the fraud until the perpetrator's car was stolen and on recovery, evidence of the crime was uncovered by the police.

139. BloomBecker, *Rifkin: A Documentary History*, 2 COMPUTER/LAW J., no. 3 at 471 (1980) [hereinafter cited as BloomBecker, *Rifkin*].

140. *See* PARKER, FIGHTING, *supra* note 46A.

141. *C.f.* Kling, *supra* note 48, at 413.

142. Menard v. Mitchell, 328 F. Supp. 718(1971).

143. A. KELMAN & R. SIZER, THE COMPUTER IN COURT 453 (Hampshire, England: Gower, 1983).

144. Lewis, *White Collar Crime, The Emerging Threat,* 33 AUSTL. POLICE J., July 1979, at 131–38; Penrose, *Preventing Computer Crime—Australia,* 49 CHARTERED ACCT. AUSTL., Apr. 1979, at 10, 11, 13–15, 17–21.

145. 1 COMPUTER CRIME DIG., no. 3; BloomBecker, *Lessons From Wells Fargo,* COMPUTERWORLD, July 5, 1982, In-Depth, 19–30.

146. *See Moonlighters, supra* note 114.

147. Case on file at National Center for Computer Crime Data.

148. 1 COMPUTER CRIME DIG. Sept. 1982, at 6–9; 1 COMPUTER CRIME DIG., Oct. 1982, at 6–9.

149. 1 COMPUTER CRIME DIG., Sept. 1982, at 8–9.

150. A fictitious example is provided in N. HAR- TLEY, QUICKSILVER, 185–219 (New York: Atheneum, 1979); another in L. CHARBONNEAU, INTRUDER *passim* (Garden City, N.J.: Doubleday, 1979).

151. *See, e.g.,* CAL. PENAL CODE §§ 466 (burglary tools), 466.3 (vending machine theft tools), 466.5 (automobile master key posession).

152. "Locksmith" is a program used to copy computer programs protected by software. It allows the user to defeat those protections.

153. KUITENBROUWER, *supra* note 77, at 8.

154. Italian Data Protection Bill, arts 22–31, Transnational Data Reporting Service Doc. No. (ITL 01.REF) (Jan. 15, 1983).

155. U.K. Data Protection Bill, cls. 15, 16, Transnational Data Reporting Service Doc. No. (UK 01.REF) (Jan. 17, 1983).

156. F. HONDIUS, EMERGING DATA PROTECTION IN EUROPE 239 (Amsterdam: North-Holland, 1975).

157. *Id.* at 238–39.

158. *Id.*

159. KUITENBROUWER, *supra* note 77, at 9.

160. Couch, *supra* note 58.

161. *Id.* at 1179–80.

162. *Id.* at 1180.

163. *Id.* at 1184.

164. *Id.*

165. BloomBecker, *International Computer Crime,* 1 COMPUTERS & SECURITY 45–49 (1981).

166. *See* BASSOUNI, INTERNATIONAL CRIMINAL LAW 3 (Germantown, Md.: Sijthoff Noordhoff, 1980).

167. BloomBecker, *Rifkin, supra* note 139.

168. *See supra* notes 153–156.

CHAPTER 23

CHOOSING THE LAW AND FORUM FOR THE LITIGATION OF DISPUTES

LINDA O. SMIDDY

INTRODUCTION

Questions of jurisdictional competence over contract and tort claims arising in the context of transborder data flow are particularly complex because of the nature and numbers of the participants and because of the variety of contexts in which the transborder flow of information may occur. Participants may include nation-states, states that are part of a federal system of government, legal entities operating either privately or as heavily regulated government agents, and private individuals. Considerations of territory and nationality play important roles as well.

As the following hypotheticals suggest, it is not difficult to imagine the many contexts in which complicated jurisdictional questions may arise. For example, Microbuild, a U.S. corporation, has entered into a contract with France to construct and operate a series of microwave transmitters along France's northern boundary. The transmission devices are part of a joint information-exchange project entered into by France and Germany. Luxembourg has complained that it is harmed by the use of the devices to transmit data between France and Germany. The transmitters emit radioactivity harmful to Luxembourg's citizens. They also interfere with transmission activities occurring within Luxembourg's borders. In addition, Luxembourg regards the transmission of unwanted information within its borders as a danger to its national security. The complained-of activities, however, occur entirely within France's borders and are lawful under France's jurisprudence.

In this context, the questions for our consideration might include what prescriptive and enforcement rights does Luxembourg have against France; what enforcement rights do Luxembourg's citizens have against France or Microbuild; what enforcement rights does Microbuild have vis-à-vis its contract with France; and in what forums could the disputes be litigated?

Other situations raise equally difficult questions. For instance, a Canadian organization, either public or private, accesses, via satellite, remote databases located in Texas. The information within the databases is wholly owned and provided by the Canadian organization, whereas physical control of that data resides within Texas. An individual located in Louisiana has improperly accessed the databases and has stolen, altered, or destroyed the information therein. This example, like the preceding one, raises questions of which state has jurisdictional competence to apply its law to the events just described, and what forum is available for dispute resolution.

A third hypothetical might involve a plaintiff who is a U.S. national and the wife of a Lufthansa pilot killed in a crash somewhere in the Himalayas. The alleged cause of the crash was a garbled transmission from a weather data processing firm that is located in the United Kingdom and maintains its database in Jamaica. The data were relayed to the aircraft via an anti-Clarke

LINDA SMIDDY ● Linda O. Smiddy formerly associated with the firm of Cravath, Swaine & Moore, holds an L.L.M. from Yale University Law School; is a member of the Connecticut, Illinois and Vermont State Bar Associations; and is now associated with Cummings and Lockwood of Stamford, Connecticut, where she concentrates on computer law.

orbiting satellite run by a consortium of nations including Sri Lanka, India, Nepal, Afghanistan, Pakistan, and the oil emirates. It is not clear whether the erroneous weather data were garbled because of transponder interruptions, an error in the computer program controlling the database, or a "brown out" of the electric generator in the CPU in Jamaica. In this hypothetical, the central questions are who can be sued, where may the suit be brought, and what law applies?

APPLICABLE LAW

Conflicts between States

In an international law context, the term "jurisdiction" embraces three aspects of the legal process. First, it refers to a state's competence to prescribe or apply its law to persons, things, or events, without any mediation by others. Jurisdiction also includes a state's enforcement competence, its ability to compel or induce compliance with its lawmaking authority. Finally, the term encompasses a state's adjudicative competence, its power to subject persons or things to the process of its tribunals.[1] The three powers are not always coterminous; in some circumstances a state having prescriptive competence may lack enforcement competence. Nevertheless, one may reasonably conclude that the power to prescribe is a necessary antecedent to the power to enforce, and that the adjudicative power will draw its strength from the enforcement power.[2] The unlawful exercise of jurisdiction by a state is recognized as a breach of international law.[3] However, a state's lawful exercise of its jurisdictional competence need not be recognized by other states so long as their refusal to give it effect is not arbitrary.[4]

According to the Restatement of Foreign Relations Law of the United States, a state may exercise prescriptive jurisdiction over the following:

1. (a)   conduct, a substantial part of which takes place within its territory;
   (b)   the status of persons or interests in things present within its territory;
   (c)   conduct outside its territory which has or is intended to have substantial effect within its territory;
2. the conduct, status, interests or relations of its nationals outside its territory; or

3. certain conduct outside its territory by persons not its national which is directed against the security of the state or certain state interests.[5]

For the purpose of this chapter, the two most important bases of prescriptive competence are those of territoriality and nationality (nos. 1 and 2 in the preceding list). Together these two jurisdictional bases determine which nation-states may regulate data-flow activities occurring both within and beyond their boundaries, and which states may bring claims in an international forum either on their own behalf or on behalf of an individual or a corporation deemed to be a national. Each will be discussed in turn.

THE TERRITORIAL PRINCIPLE OF JURISDICTION.   The territorial principle of jurisdiction recognizes the right of a state to exercise its authority as a state over events, persons, and things within its borders.[6] The doctrine of territoriality, however, embraces two principles with conflicting implications. As a sovereign, a state should be permitted to conduct within its borders any activity which is not per se illegal. Sovereignty, however, also implies that the state should be free from unwanted interferences or harm caused by acts occurring outside its borders.[7] The territorial principle has been expanded to include allocation to the affected state of jurisdictional competence over conduct occurring outside its borders, if the conduct is generally recognized as a crime or a tort or its effect within the territory is substantial.[8] As subsequent discussion suggests, this expansion of the territorial principle of jurisdiction has important implications for the regulation of transborder data flow.

The issue of jurisdiction over extraterritorial acts having effects within a state's territory has arisen in two contexts: (1) the affected state's competence to participate in the actor state's decision to perform the conduct in question; (2) the affected state's competence to impose liability and assess damages for harm caused by the actor state's act.

The well-known *Lake Lanoux Arbitration* (France V. Spain)[9] is relevant to the discussion of the affected state's competence to participate in the decision-making process of the actor state. A dispute between France and Spain arose when France began a development project for Lake Lanoux, whose waters fed the Carol River which flowed from France into Spain. Although the proposed project altered the source of the waters flowing into the

Carol River, it did not change the volume of water flowing into Spain. Spain was not apparently injured by the alteration.

Rejecting Spain's argument that it should be afforded a right to participate in the decision to change the river, the panel upheld France's right to make a unilateral decision regarding activities carried on entirely within its borders. Yet the panel did not permit France to behave autistically. Instead, its interpretation of the treaty imposed upon the actor state, France, an obligation to include within its decision-making process consideration of the interests of those affected by its activities. The actor state also had an obligation to develop a solution that reasonably took into account those adverse interests. Once a decision was made, the affected state could bring a claim based on any injuries that resulted.

A similar principle was expressed in Article 30 of the United Nations Charter of Economic Rights and Duties.[10] Although international law does not permit an affected state to participate in or exercise veto power over the decision-making process of the actor state, it may impose on the actor state an obligation to be cognizant of outside interests when determining its course of action.

The implications of this trend with respect to transborder data flow are clear. For example, in the first hypothetical presented at the beginning of this chapter, France and Germany would have an obligation to consider Luxembourg's interests in developing their joint information-exchange plan, even though the complained-of activities were to be conducted entirely outside of Luxembourg's territory. France and Germany, however, would retain the right to exercise their sovereignty within their borders without direct interference by Luxembourg. Although the hypothetical presents a situation in which Luxembourg viewed the activities of France and Germany as harmful, harm is not a prerequisite to the lawful exercise of prescriptive competence based on the territorial principle. It is enough if the contemplated activity has substantial extraterritorial effect.

The expanded principle of territoriality does, however, permit an affected state to impose liability and assess damages for harm caused by the extraterritorial act. The principle thus provides a jurisdictional basis for tort claims among nation-states.

The Multilateral Treaty on Principles Governing the Activities of States in the Exploration and Use of Outer Space, Including the Moon and Other Celestial Bodies,[11] requires that its signatories bear international responsibility for activities occurring in outer space.[12] It further provides that each state that directs the launching of an object into outer space or from whose territory or facility an object is launched "is internationally liable for damage to another State Party to the Treaty or to its natural or juridical persons by such object."[13] Thus liability may be imposed against a state whose acts harmed another even though the acts occurred entirely within the first state's territory.[14] A similar result may be found in an exchange of notes between the Mayor of Ciudad Juarez, Mexico, and the United States Secretary of State.[15] Mexico protested pollution of its air and of the Rio Grande River by companies located in the United States. The United States apparently accepted responsibility for the situation and implicitly conceded Mexico's right to bring the claim.

One final international arbitration should be included in this discussion of jurisdiction over civil claims based on activities with extraterritorial effects. It is the *Trail Smelter Arbitration* (U.S. v. Canada),[16] which, like the preceding case, involved the question of transborder pollution. The *Trail Smelter Arbitration* dealt with the question of jurisdiction both to claim liability and to assess damages. The dispute arose during the late 1920s, when sulphur fumes emitted from a Canadian smelter plant polluted the air and damaged crops in the state of Washington. The panel found that damage had occurred but it awarded compensation only for injuries for which pecuniary loss could be proved. The tribunal also concluded that

> under the principles of international law, as well as the law of the United States, no state has the right to use or permit uses of its territory in such a manner as to cause injury by fumes in or to the territory of another in the properties or persons therein, when the case is of serious consequence and the injury is established by clear and convincing evidence.[17]

As the preceding discussion demonstrates, the principle of territoriality provides one basis for the exercise of jurisdiction by a nation-state. It includes a state's competence to exercise jurisdiction not only over persons, things, and events within its geographic borders, but also over events occurring outside its borders, the effects of which are felt within. Emerging international law suggests that jurisdictional competence extends to claims of both liability and damage awards. In addition, developing law requires nation-states undertaking activities that either are potentially harmful or have a substantial effect on other members of the international community to give meaningful consideration to outside interests in making their final determinations.

The expansion of the principle of territoriality has important implications for situations involving transborder data flow. First, activities conducted within one state's territory or between consenting states are subject to review by other states affected by the activities. Their interests must be considered in the decision-making process. In this instance the trend of the law may be particularly suited to the transborder data flow context in which a state's territorial limits have little real meaning and in which considerations of the interests of the global community as a whole become increasingly important. The expanding principle of territoriality is, however, also problematical in the transborder data flow context. It may become a powerful aid to those nation-states who would seek to limit the broad dissemination of information by others. Claims of liability and damages, perhaps based on alleged harm to the nation-state's national security, could function as a veto over the lawful activities of other states exercised within their own territories. Nevertheless, the expanded approach is to be preferred, as it is more likely to avoid autistic resolutions of issues that affect large segments of the international community.

THE NATIONALITY PRINCIPLE OF JURISDICTION. As the Restatement of Foreign Relations Law provides, a state may exercise prescriptive competence over the "conduct, status, interests or relations of its nationals outside its territory."[18] Consequently, persons living in a state other than the one of nationality may be subject to the prescriptive claims of both the state of residence and the state of nationality. States also may extend their protection against injury to their nationals, whether they are found at home or abroad. Thus, an important aspect of the question of nationality is the circumstances under which a state will represent its national's interests in an international tribunal.

Nationality may be ascribed to individuals in three ways: (1) by applying the *ura sole* (law of the land) principle to those born within a nation-state's territory; (2) by applying the principle of *ura sanguinis* to those whose parents or grandparents were nationals and who maintained their nationality; and (3) within the United States, by passing a private bill. In order for a country to have standing to bring suit on behalf of one of its nationals, the citizen must have been a national continuously from the time of the injury or transaction in question to the time of the suit.[19]

Under international law, the nationality of a corporation is usually determined by the place of incorporation. The Restatement (Second) of Foreign Relations Law of the United States specifies that "a corporation or other private legal entity has the nationality of the state which creates it."[20] The structure of a multinational enterprise, however, complicates the question of nationality. Although the multinational organization, like the domestic corporation, is created by national rather than by international law, "it is not a single entity, but rather a structure made up of many corporations each incorporated under the laws of some nation and tied together by links of stock ownership and other contractual arrangements."[21] Thus the issue of access to an international forum may be one of great importance.

The case concerning the *Barcelona Traction, Light and Power Company, Ltd.* (Belgium v. Spain)[22] is relevant to this discussion. Although Barcelona Traction was formed to develop power in Spain, it was incorporated in Canada as a holding company for Spanish and Canadian subsidiaries. Many of the company's shareholders were Belgian nationals. When Spain forced the company into bankruptcy and seized its assets, the Canadian government, acting on the company's behalf, attempted to negotiate a settlement with Spain. Canada's efforts proved to be fruitless and after several years it ceased to pursue a diplomatic resolution of the problem. At that time, Belgium sought to bring a claim against Spain on behalf of the shareholders. The court concluded that only the country of the nationality of the corporation could bring a suit on the corporation's behalf. Because the place of incorporation, not the nationality of the shareholders, determined nationality, Canada, not Belgium, had standing to bring the claim.

A separate opinion by Judge Jessup, however, took a different view. He proposed that the place of incorporation alone not be conclusive on the question of nationality, but that a determination should be made whether the state of incorporation had sufficient links to the corporation for it to be considered a national of that country. The significance of his approach is that a company's nationality would be based on more substantial links than the fact of registration. If sufficient links were present, a nation would be justified in acting on the corporation's behalf.

The United States has taken a third approach to the question.[23] It considers the nationality of the stockholders in determining whether it may treat the corporation as a national. Thus the nationality of the owners of a corporation or another legal entity may both subject it to United States jurisdiction and entitle it to United States protection.

The multiplicity of approaches to determining the nationality of a corporation has important consequences for the corporation engaged in transborder data flow, whether its role is that of the owner of the information or the transferor of the information or both. This is particularly true for the transnational corporation, which may have several places of incorporation and stockholders located all over the world. It may find itself in the unwelcome position of being subjected to the regulations of many different nation-states with widely varying policies regarding the transborder dissemination of information. On the other hand, the same corporation may be unable to secure representation by a nation-state in an international forum because its states of incorporation are not states with substantial interest in the corporation's activities.

A flexible approach to the question of corporate nationality seems to be preferable in the transborder data flow context. Subjection to conflicting regulations is already a reality for the transactional corporation. Formal rules of corporate nationality, such as those found in the *Barcelona Traction* case, are not likely to alleviate the complexities of international regulation and may result in further harm by denying the real parties in interest access to an international tribunal.

Claims between an Individual and a State or between Individuals

CHOICE OF LAW.

Contracts The multinational character of contracts arising in a transborder data flow context invariably produces tensions between the needs of the contracting parties and those of the associated nation-states. To the parties to the contract, certainty in the law is of paramount importance. Nation-states, however, must also be able to effect their policies free from the threat of incurring liability and from interference by other sovereign entities acting on behalf of their nationals. The following doctrines in international law have developed in response to these tensions.

THE INTERNATIONAL MINIMUM STANDARD. In any contractual situation, the parties may specify in their agreement what law will apply to the subject and execution of the contract and what forum will be used to resolve disputes. This is equally true for contracts between individuals and for contracts in which one of the parties is a foreign state. When one of the contracting parties is a state, however, the question of specifying what law will govern the contract becomes particularly problematical. The difficulties arise from the fact that the state is at once a lawmaker and a contracting party. Acting in its governmental role, it may enact or change laws affecting the terms and execution of the contract. Consequently, tensions emerge between the need for stability and predictability in the law of the contract and the equally pressing need for the governmental party to preserve its ability to enact laws for the public good without incurring excessive liabilities. In this context, the government is both a contracting party and a sovereign acting in the public interest.[24] Thus, even though applicable law is specified in the contract, if the local law of the host country is to be applied, it may be changed by the unilateral act of one of the contracting parties.

Although not the basic law of a contract, international law may, in some contexts, operate as a secondary restraint on the application of local law by the governmental party to the contract.[25] Thus international law may function as a check on actions that could otherwise unjustly be effected through the application of local law or through the execution of certain governmental acts. An example of the use of international law to limit otherwise lawful sovereign actions may be found in the case of *Texas Overseas Co. v. Libya, Award on the Merits.*[26] Libya and several oil companies entered into a concession agreement in which Libya agreed not to take any action that would jeopardize the rights granted under the concession. The agreement also contained a stabilization clause which, for the purposes of the contract, "froze" Libyan petroleum legislation as of the date of the contract. Subsequently, Libya nationalized the oil companies. The arbitrator concluded that international law could be applied to limit the effect of the nationalization of assets covered by an international contract to which the sovereign had been a party and which contained a stabilization clause. Thus, principles of international law were used to protect the contracting party from the governmental party's breach of the contract through the exercise of its governmental function.

THE CALVO CLAUSE. The Calvo Doctrine developed in response to diplomatic and military intervention in host countries on behalf of foreigners doing business in those countries. Its policy is to require foreigners doing business in a country to consent to be treated like the host country's nationals. In return, the foreigners are entitled to nondiscriminatory treatment by the host country. The Calvo Clause is a provision appearing in contracts, legislation, or state constitutions which is designed to make the doctrine explicit. A classic statement of the Calvo Clause may be found in the *United States of America (North American Dredging Co. of Texas) v. United Mexican States*:[27]

> The contractor and all persons, who as employees or in any other capacity, may be engaged in the execution of the work under this contract either directly or indirectly, shall be considered as Mexicans in all matters, within the Republic of Mexico, concerning the execution of such work and the fulfillment of this contract.... They are consequently deprived of any rights as aliens, and under no conditions shall the intervention of foreign diplomatic agents be permitted, in any matter related to this contract.

The Restatement (Second) of the Foreign Relations Law of the United States approves the principles of the Calvo Clause if (1) economic interests are involved; (2) the alien does in fact receive national treatment; and (3) the national courts provide a bona fide remedy satisfying the requirements for procedural justice.[28]

Similarly, Article 22 (5) of the Draft Convention of Professors Sohn and Baxter (Reporters) on the International Responsibility of States for Injuries to Aliens would enforce a Calvo Clause for injuries to economic interests that arise from the contract, if the governmental entity has complied with the agreement.[29]

THE LAW OF THE CONTRACT. Neither of the two doctrines discussed in the preceding sections seem well suited to the transborder data flow context. Both aggravate rather than alleviate the tensions they were developed to redress. The use of an international minimum standard, although perhaps providing a private party with some protection vis-a-vis a sovereign party to the contract, may only add to the uncertainties of the

contracting situation. It is unclear what legal standard would be applied in a transborder data flow context. Although it is true that few areas of international law have clearly defined contours, we cannot overlook the fact that transborder data flow is today still an emerging area of both law and technology. Current international standards may be ill suited to the resolution of disputes arising in this context.

The use of the Calvo Clause to ward off the threat of foreign intervention may be equally inappropriate. Transborder data flow, by its very nature, is transnational in concept and execution. The Calvo Clause was developed for a world in which the business of the foreign entity would be carried on within the territorial boundaries of the host state. In contrast, transborder data flow contexts involve participants from many nation-states conducting their business not only in the territories of multiple nation-states, but in air space and outer space as well.

Perhaps a better approach would be to develop a law of the contract for transnational data flow agreements. In other words, the contract itself would set out the legal structure used to resolve disputes. The goal of such an approach would be to establish the autonomy of the contract by insulating it from the law of any state. Such an approach is, in fact, not only possible, but plausible. It has been used by international organizations such as the International Bank for Reconstruction and Development.[30] It would alleviate some of the uncertainty inherent in applying an international minimum standard; it would avoid the autistic approach of the Calvo Clause; and it would encourage the development of a body of international law that is well suited to the context in which it arises.

Torts When a dispute arises from a tortious act, ordinarily the forum resolves the question of which law to apply through the application of its choice of law principles. This approach would be followed in cases involving a state as well as in suits between private parties. In the United States, the trend has been away from formalistic choice of law rules to interest-weighing analysis such as that found in the case of *Lauritzen v. Larsen*.[31]

Larsen, a Danish seaman, while temporarily in New York, joined the crew of a ship of Danish flag and registry and owned by a Danish citizen. The ship's articles, signed by Larsen, provided that the rights of the crew would be governed by Danish law and by the employer's contract with the Danish Seamen's Union, of which

Larsen was a member. In the course of his employment, Larsen was negligently injured while in Havana Harbor. The seaman subsequently sued his employer, under the Jones Act, in the Southern District of New York. He sought to avoid the damage limitation imposed by Danish law. In answer to the question of whether Danish or United States law applied, the court held that the events were governed by Danish law. In reaching its conclusion, the court used an interest-analysis test to review the several factors applicable to a tort claim, particularly a maritime tort: (1) the place of the wrongful act; (2) the law of the flag; (3) the allegiance of domicile of the injured; (4) the allegiance of the defendant; (5) the place of contract; (6) the inaccessibility of a foreign forum; and (7) the law of the forum.

The approach of the Larsen court is appropriate to tort claims arising in a transborder data flow context for at least two reasons. First, a formal rule, such as that of applying the law of the place where the tort occurred, may be totally unsuitable to an international data flow transaction. To reiterate the hypothetical presented at the beginning of the chapter, a Canadian company or governmental agency may access remote databases located in Texas. The information contained in these databases, however, may be owned by the Canadian organization and perhaps regulated by Canadian law. If someone seated at a terminal in Louisiana gained unauthorized access to the databases and either stole or destroyed the information therein, the question of where the tort occurred would be problematical indeed.

Second, an interest-analysis approach is consistent with emerging international law providing for shared jurisdictional competence over events occurring within one state's borders but having extraterritorial effects. In the transborder data flow context, the concept of events occurring solely or even primarily within national boundaries may have little real meaning. One example of this can be found among the hypotheticals given at the beginning of this chapter. The case involved an air crash in the Himalayas caused by a garbled satellite transmission from a British weather data processing firm accessing a database in Jamaica. Thus, a weighing of state interests to determine jurisdictional competence may prove to be a satisfactory approach in situations where formal rules are inapplicable.

LIMITATIONS ON ACTIONS AGAINST A STATE

Sovereign Immunity The doctrine of sovereign immunity is based on the principle that courts of one jurisdiction will not question the acts of foreign sovereigns. During the nineteenth century, the prevailing view in this country and others as well was that the immunity of a sovereign state should be unrestricted. But pressure on the rigidity of this rule built up as states engaged in commercial activities and individuals doing business with the states were increasingly unable to enforce contracts made with foreign sovereigns. As the twentieth century matured, the restrictive theory of sovereign immunity began to replace the older classical theory, which was unsuited to the contemporary commercial world. Under the restrictive theory, as is shown by the two examples that follow, immunity applies only to the sovereign's governmental acts and not to its private or commercial acts.

The Foreign Sovereign Immunities Act[32] represents an attempt by Congress to enlarge the competence of the federal courts regarding suits involving foreign sovereigns. The act gives federal district courts jurisdiction to hear claims in which a foreign state is not entitled to immunity. As defined in the act, the term "foreign state" includes, in addition to the sovereign, the political subdivisions and agencies or instrumentalities of the foreign state. The act etablishes the general rule that a foreign state will be immune from the jurisdiction of the United States courts unless specified exceptions apply. The most important of these are (1) the foreign state has waived immunity; (2) the action is based on certain specified types of commercial activity; and (3) property rights taken in violation of international law are at issue.

A sovereign may waive immunity either explicitly or by implication. A waiver of immunity by treaty or in a contract would of course be explicit. Several types of actions constitute implicit waiver. For example, in *Victory Transport Inc. v. Comisaria General*,[33] the Court of Appeals for the Second Circuit held that a charter contract between a United States company and the Spanish Ministry of Commerce containing an agreement to arbitrate disputes in the United States constituted a waiver of sovereign immunity within the meaning of the act. Waiver may also be accomplished if the defendant sovereign or its agent appears in a United States court and does not make a timely objection to the court's jurisdiction.

The jurisdictional reach of the Foreign Sovereign Immunities Act has recently been restricted by the decision *Carey v. National Oil Corp. & Libya.*[34] The act provides that sovereign immunity will not apply to "an act outside the territory of the United States in connection with a commercial activity of the foreign state elsewhere [where] that act causes a direct effect in the United States." The Court of Appeals for the Second Circuit interpreted the direct-effects test in light of the standard established in *International Shoe Co. v. Washington.*[35] Due process requires the defendant to have certain minimum contacts with the forum state. An act that merely affected the United States would not satisfy the requirement.

The European Convention on State Immunity and Additional Protocol[36] contains exceptions to immunity for certain kinds of commercial, contractual, and tortious activities. For tortious conduct, immunity may be waived only if the tortious activity occurred in the forum state and the author of the injury was present in that territory at the time the tortious conduct occurred.

The trend toward a restricted doctrine of sovereign immunity is an important one for participants in transborder data flow, especially for private parties contracting with sovereign entities. The doctrine seems to provide some assurances that nation-states will no longer be able to use their sovereign status as a shield against liability for torts or for breach of contractual obligations. Yet, in light of the fact that data transmission facilities are often state owned or state controlled to an extent that they become quasi-governmental entities, it may be difficult to distinguish governmental from commercial activities. If the law is unable to provide satisfactory guidelines for making these important distinctions, the restrictive doctrine of sovereign immunity may, in fact, provide little additional protection.

The Act of State Doctrine   The policy of the Act of State Doctrine is that "the courts of one country will not sit in judgment on the acts of the government of another done within its own territory."[37] In the context of transborder data flow, the Act of State Doctrine may come into play if the defendant is a government entity or an entity that is so heavily regulated or controlled by the government that a persuasive argument may be made that the defendant's activities are actually those of its government. The doctrine may be pled as a defense to a claim against a government or against a nongovernmental entity claiming title through a state action. It may also be raised *sua sponte* by the court itself. In either case, the doctrine is applied at the court's discretion. It raises the question of whether a United States court should hear a case containing a substantial foreign element. Its application requires a balanced consideration by the court of both the potential for interference of

the judicial decision with the acts of a foreign government and the need to give the plaintiff a day in court.

The trend of the judicial decisions of the United States Supreme Court has been toward avoiding disputes involving the acts of foreign sovereigns, leaving resolution of such issues to the executive branch of the government. Courts have chosen this course even when the executive branch would have preferred that the courts adjudicate cases of this type. In *Banco Nacional de Cuba v. Sabbatino,*[38] Justice Harlan, speaking for the Court, refused to review acts of a government transpiring within its own territory, even if the act violated international law, unless the circumstances were controlled by a treaty or agreement establishing controlling legal principles.

In response to this decision, Congress passed the Foreign Assistance Act,[39] which provides that United States courts may not use the Act of State Doctrine to avoid reaching the merits of a claim against a sovereign state for taking property in violation of international law. The act does not apply to cases in which the president determines that the foreign-policy interests of the United States require the application of the Act of State Doctrine and files with the court a suggestion to that effect.

Subsequent developments have left the contours of the Act of State Doctrine somewhat ill defined. The Supreme Court has been reluctant to assume the role directed by Congress in the Foreign Assistance Act.[40] Nevertheless, the Act of State Doctrine has important implications in the context of transborder data flow. Because it is applied at the discretion of the Court, it may be used to limit the application of the restrictive doctrine of sovereign immunity. Although the executive and legislative branches of our government have attempted to restrict the application of the Act of State Doctrine and to direct United States courts to proceed to the merits of cases involving foreign sovereigns, the courts have apparently been unwilling to assume the proffered role. Thus, the use of the Act of State Doctrine potentially limits the access to foreign sovereigns provided for in the restrictive doctrine of sovereign immunity.

United States Constitutional Doctrines   An interdependent relationship exists between international and domestic law. Each may limit or prohibit what would otherwise be the lawful exercise of jurisdiction under the regime of the other. Thus international law may restrict domestic prescriptive competence. Similarly, in the United States, due process considerations of fairness and requirements of minimum contacts may limit jurisdictional competence authorized by international law. As McDougal and Reisman have stated

> There is a curious intersimulation and interlimitation between international and constitutional principles regarding "jurisdiction" or the allocation of competence to prescribe and apply. First, the international legal process restrains the exercise of national jurisdiction.... Second, national constitutional law and procedural rules may sometime serve to prevent a national court from exercising fully a competence that international law would allow it. Some of the principles expressed in *International Shoe* [and] *Shaffer v. Heitner* ... effectively limited U.S. courts from exercising competences international law had properly accorded [them].[41]

United States domestic law may therefore limit the jurisdictional reach that would otherwise be available to participants in transborder data flow under international law or under other United States domestic law. As we have seen, the Court of Appeals for the Second Circuit has already interpreted the Foreign Sovereign Immunities Act to include the minimum contacts standard of *International Shoe*. Consequently, despite the expansive provisions of the act, United States courts may not hear a case involving a foreign activity having an effect in the United States, unless minimum contact requirements are met.

Similarly, domestic jurisdictional requirements may limit the applicability of choice of forum clauses contained in contracts arising in a transborder data flow context. The contracting parties may agree to litigate disputes in a particular country. If, however, the defendant has no other links with that country, it may be problematical whether the choice of forum clause alone will constitute sufficient consent to that court's jurisdiction. Conversely, a nation-state that was not selected as the forum and that otherwise would have jurisdiction over the dispute may not agree to the "ouster" attempted by the choice of forum clause in the contract.[42]

Forums for Resolution

Disputes arising in a transborder data flow context, whether between private parties or between a private party and a government, may be initially adjudicated in domestic courts or be submitted to arbitration. If a conflict remains unresolved, it may be elevated to a controversy between two governments. Other disputes

will arise initially on an intergovernmental level with little or no participation by private parties.[43] The types of forums suitable for the allocation and exercise of jurisdictional competence and resolution of disputes are almost unlimited, as the previously cited cases, treaties, and resolutions indicate. State courts (both domestic and foreign), international tribunals, quasi-governmental bodies, treaties—all are within the realm of possibilities.

When a dispute arises between sovereign states, international tribunals will be unable to obtain jurisdiction unless the parties agree. Consent of the sovereign is also often required for a domestic tribunal to obtain jurisdiction when the dispute is between a sovereign and a private party.

Although private contracting parties would seem to have a broad range of forums to select from, their choices may be more limited than appearances suggest. First, there is the problem, previously discussed, of whether choice of forum clauses will be honored both by the forums that were not selected, as well as by those that were. Furthermore, even if a court accepts jurisdiction on the basis of the choice of forum clause, it may subsequently refuse to hear the case for other reasons, such as *forum non conveniens* considerations. And finally, the transborder data flow context may introduce further complications. Disputes involving transborder data flow may, of course, involve broad policy questions concerning widespread dissemination of information. They will also involve matters that are factually and technically complex and call for an understanding of the communications industry and its technology. The number of forums suited to dealing with cases of this factual complexity may be limited indeed.

For the foregoing reasons, it may be preferable to establish a separate tribunal for hearing disputes involving transborder data flow. This approach would have several advantages. The panel could consist of experts in the field who understand both the technology and the industry in question. The process itself may be less expensive and less time-consuming than adjudication in domestic courts. In addition, parties may have a greater opportunity to fashion procedures and outcomes that are suited to their circumstances.

Recommended Approaches

An appropriate approach to questions of jurisdictional competence regarding tort and contract issues arising in a transborder data flow context seems to be one based on the principles suggested by the *Lake Lanoux* arbitration discussed previously. The case can be said to stand for the proposition that, although one state whose activities affect another has the right to make unilateral decisions regarding activities carried on within its borders, it has an obligation not to make the decision without considering the interests of those adversely affected by its activities.

A similar approach is reflected in the recommendations of the OECD Council on Principles Concerning Transfrontier Pollution.[44] The OECD advocates the principle of equal right of hearing.[45] It affords persons who either have been damaged by transfrontier pollution or are exposed to a significant risk of transfrontier pollution the right to participate in all administrative and judicial proceedings within the country of origin for the purpose of preventing or abating pollution or obtaining compensation for the damage caused. Under its provisions, persons from jurisdictions other than the polluting state must seek their remedies within the polluting state.

These OECD recommendations go considerably beyond the principles of the *Lake Lanoux* decision in that they permit individuals and other states to participate in the decision-making process. The principles also advocate equitable balancing of the rights and obligations of countries concerned with transborder pollution. The principles envision meaningful consultation and the harmonizing of pollution policies among countries. The OECD proposes that an international commission be established and that coordinated pollution policies be incorporated into bilateral and/or multilateral treaties.

Both the *Lake Lanoux* decision and the OECD principles implicitly recognize the need for exchange of ideas and coordinate planning with respect of the use of shared resources. Also implicit is the recognition of the need for a shared jurisdictional competence. Although a state may unilaterally make decisions about activities within its borders, those damaged by its activities may bring a claim against the actor state.

The foregoing discussion has focused on the need for shared competence when the activities in question are perceived as harmful by the affected state. As the Restatement of Foreign Relations Law of the United States demonstrates, however, shared prescriptive competence is not limited to situations in which one state's activities are dangerous to another. Shared prescriptive competence is also appropriate to situations in which one state's activities have substantial effects on another.

Exchange of ideas, cooperative planning, and shared jurisdictional competence are also appropriate to situations involving transborder data flow. The physical transmission of data involves the use of shared resources of air space and outer space. More important, perhaps, is that the information itself becomes a resource which, when shared, potentially benefits participants in the information exchange. International financial transactions, airline reservation systems, and the collection and exchange of weather data are just some of the types of transborder data flow that yield positive benefits for those involved.

It must be recognized, however, that the collection and transmission of data has its negative side as well. Questions of privacy become paramount as do the concerns of some nation-states that the transmitted information will become an unwelcome intrusion into the affected state's territory and a threat to its control over its bases of power, such as its people and/or national security. The development of meaningful consultation and shared jurisdictional competence would, it is hoped, produce a regime that takes into consideration the interests of both those countries that are the source of international transmission data and information and those that are the recipients.

The strength of this approach is, of course, its recognition that, in today's world, individual states must consider needs other than their own. Because of the high volume of transborder flow of goods and information, limiting prescriptive competence to territorial boundaries is not only unrealistic but also potentially destabilizing in the international arena. Autistic decisions impede progress toward harmonizing disparate political, economic, and social concerns. Nevertheless, one must also recognize that requiring states to consider interests other than their own raises the spectre that nation-states with adverse interests may attempt to exercise veto power over activities occurring entirely within their neighbors' boundaries. Neighboring states not only could interfere to an unacceptable extent with the decisions of other states, their veto power could be used to entrench the status quo.

Prognosis

There seems to be an emerging approach to jurisdictional competence that involves contextual rather than formalistic analysis. States no longer, if they ever did, have unlimited and unchallenged jurisdictional competence over their own territory. While performing their lawmaking roles within their own geographical boundaries, states are called upon to be cognizant of the effects of their decisions on other members of the international community. The principles suggested by the OECD and the *Lake Lanoux* arbitration suggest that affected states have at least limited access to the actor state's decision-making processes. Further, states have increasing jurisdictional competence over extraterritorial events affecting them. As the Outer Space Treaty, the Rocket Agreement, and the *Trail Smelter Arbitration* suggest with respect to potentially harmful activities, lawmaking and law-applying competence extend to both the question of liability and the question of damage assessment.

The implications for transborder information flow are that the interests of both transmitting and receiving states must be reconciled. Affected states may seek to enforce upon the transmitting state an affirmative duty not to engage in acts within its own territory that are harmful to the receiving or third-party states. In addition, states may seek to exercise their jurisdictional competence over events occurring outside their borders that affect them.

Jurisdiction based on nationality is still unclear, particularly with respect to the nationality of corporations. The majority opinion in the *Barcelona Traction* case used a formalistic approach in applying the principle that the place of registry determines corporate nationality. Judge Jessup advocated, as more appropriate, a consideration of significant links between the corporation and the state of its creation. United States law also has not been constrained by the place-of-registry rule. Exercise of both prescriptive and protective competence with regard to corporations is based on the nationality of the corporation's owners as well as the nationality of the corporation itself.

The lack of clarity of the law in this area may have significant consequences for corporations, particularly transnational corporations. Like nationals of all types, they may be subject to prescriptive competence of both the states of nationality and the states of residence. Transnational corporations thus may be subject to conflicting regulations expressing irreconcilable policies. Furthermore, at times, transnational corporations may be unable to obtain the protection of a nation-state and access to an international forum. The place of registry may be important to the company for tax purposes but not be the situs of significant events related to the conduct of the company's business. If the state of registry fails to act on the company's behalf, the company may find itself without judicial redress.

The choice of law to be applied is also still unsettled. Because a few countries dominate data and information-transmission technology, importing states may be required to contract with alien companies for the provision of needed transmission technology. Although contracting parties may specify the law to be applied, almost any specification of law in an international context will be tentative and subject to change, particularly when one of the contracting parties is a state or state representative. Contracting individuals can attempt to avoid the effects of changes in local law by including an arbitration or a stabilization clause within the contract. Such clauses, however, are not necessarily effective in contracts with governmental entities. Aliens contracting with a state may attempt to limit the application of local law by specifying that international law or the law of the contract applies. If a dispute arises as a result of a public action by the contracting state, the aggrieved party may attempt to limit the effects of the state's action by arguing that the contract is governed by an international minimum standard. The difficulty of this approach is that there may not be a relevant standard applicable either directly or by analogy to issues arising in the context of contracts governing transborder data flow.

The contracting state, on the other hand, may seek to protect itself from being subject to the intervention of a foreign state in the name of the protection of the private contracting party. One available method of protection is to include within the contract a Calvo Clause to secure for the contracting state a jurisdictional competence over the private contracting party. However, the application of the Calvo Clause has on occasion been limited by a construction that transforms it into nothing more than an exhaustion of remedies requirement for access to an international tribunal.

Choice of law in connection with an international tort may be equally problematical. Within the United States, courts have tended to apply an interest-balancing rather than formalistic approach to the decision of which law to apply. This approach, though less certain than a formalistic rule, is preferable, as it includes an analysis of the context in which the tort arose.

An individual seeking to sue a foreign state under either a contract or tort theory must confront the issue of sovereign immunity. The United States Foreign Sovereign Immunity Act and its foreign counterparts generally accept the theory of restrictive sovereign immunity. States or their agents engaged in certain types of commercial activities or committing specified torts are subject to suit in national courts.

On first impression, the restrictive doctrine of sovereign immunity may seem to afford important protections to private parties contracting with or affected by the action of a state. But in the context of transborder information flow, it may be difficult to distinguish governmental from commercial activity, particularly in light of the fact that data transmission facilities are often state-owned or state-regulated industries. Contracts related to the provision of these facilities may be realistically viewed as a complex mixture of both commercial and governmental activities. Furthermore, within the United States, the jurisdictional sweep potentially available under the restrictive theory of sovereign immunity may be limited by the application of the Act of State Doctrine and constitutional due process principles.

NOTES

1. M. McDougal & R. Reisman, International Law in Contemporary Perspective 1273 (1981); Restatement of Foreign Relations Law of the United States § 401 (Tent. Draft No. 2, 1981).

2. Restatement (Second) of Foreign Relations Law of the United States § 7 (1965).

3. *Id.* at 8.

4. *Id.* at 9.

5. Restatement of Foreign Relations Law of the United States § 402 (Tent. Draft No. 2, 1981). Its predecessor, Restatement (Second) § 10, listed the following as jurisdictional bases: "(a) territory . . ., (b) nationality, (c) protection of certain state interests not covered under (a) and (b) . . . and (d) protection of certain universal interests."

6. Restatement (Second) of Foreign Relations Law of the United States § 17.

7. Handl, *An International Legal Perspective on the Conduct of Abnormally Dangerous Activities in Frontier Areas: The Case of Nuclear Power Plant Siting*, 7 Ecol. L.Q. 1, 4 (1978).

8. Restatement (Second) of Foreign Relations Law of the United States § 18 (1965) states:

A state has jurisdiction to prescribe a rule of law attaching legal consequences to conduct that occurs outside its territory and causes an effect within its territory if either

(a) the conduct and its effect are generally recognized as constituent elements of a crime or tort under the law of states that have reasonably developed legal systems or,

(b) (i) the conduct and its effect are constituent elements of activity to which the rule applies; (ii) the effect within the territory is substantial; (iii) it occurs as a direct and foreseeable result of the conduct outside the territory; and (iv) the rule is not inconsistent with the principles of justice generally recognized by states that have reasonably developed legal systems.

9. Int'l L. Rep. 101 (1957).

10. Charter of Economic Rights and Duties of States, U.N. Doc. A/RES/3281 (XXIX) (adopted Dec. 12, 1974); 14 Int. Legal Mat. 251 (1975).

11. 18 U.S.T. 2410 (1967).

12. *Id.* at art. VI.

13. *Id.* at art. VII.

14. *See also* Agreement Concerning Rocket Launches, 1975 Canada-United States, 26 2605 U.S.T.

15. Whiteman, 6 Dig. Int'l Law 256–59 (1968).

16. R. Int'l Arb. Awards 1905, 1967 (1941).

17. *Id.* at 1965.

18. Restatement of Foreign Relations Law of the United States § 401 (Tent. Draft No. 2, 1981); *see* 15 U.S.C. § 78dd-2 (Supp. 1980); *see, e.g.,* DeBeers Consolidated Mines Ltd. v. Howe, (1906); A.C. 455, Decision of Dec. 18, 1963, Federal Finance Court (Federal Republic of Germany), 1963 79 Entscheidungen des Bundesfinanzhofs 57.

19. Nottebohm Case (Second Phase) (Liecht. v. Guat.), 1955 I.C.J. 4, 16; Flegenheimer Case (U.S. v. Italy), 14 R. Int'l Arb. Awards 327 (1958), Decision of the Italian—United States Conciliation Commission, Sept. 20, 1958).

20. Restatement (Second) of Foreign Relations Law § 27 (1965).

21. H. Steiner & D. Vagts, Transnational Legal Problems 1177 (1979).

22. I.C.J. Rep. 4 (1970).

23. Foreign Assets Control Regulation, 31 C.F.R. § 500.329 (1959); Restatement (Second) of Foreign Relations Law of the United States § 172 (1965); H. Stei-

NER & D. VAGTS, TRANSNATIONAL LEGAL PROBLEMS 239 (1979).

24. H. STEINER & D. VAGTS, *supra* note 23, at 508 (1976).

25. *Id.* at 515.

26. Arbitral Award, Jan. 19, 1977.

27. United States (North American Dredging Co.) v. United Mexican States United States—Mexican Claims Commission, 1926 (1926–27), 4 R. Int'l Arb. Awards 26.

28. RESTATEMENT (SECOND) OF FOREIGN RELATIONS LAW OF THE UNITED STATES § 202 (1965).

29. 55 AM. J. INT'L L. 548 (1961).

30. H. STEINER & D. VAGTS, *supra* note 23, at 505 (1976).

31. 345 U.S. 571 (1953).

32. 28 U.S.C. §§ 1330, 1602 *et seq*.

33. 336 F.2d 354, *cert. denied,* 381 U.S. 934 (1965).

34. 592 F.2d 673 (2d Cir. 1979).

35. 326 U.S. 310, 316 (1945).

36. Council of Europe, May 1972, Europ. T.S. No. 74.

37. Underhill v. Hernandez, 168 U.S. 250, 252 (1897).

38. 376 U.S. 398 (1961).

39. 22 U.S.C. § 2370(e)(2).

40. First National City Bank v. Banco Nacional de Cuba, 406 U.S. 759 (1972); Alfred Dunhill London, Inc. v. Republic of China, 425 U.S. 682 (1976).

41. M. McDOUGAL & R. REISMAN, *supra* note 1, at 1434 (1981).

42. H. STEINER & D. VAGTS, *supra* note 23, at 192 (1976).

43. *See, e.g., id.* at 809–25.

44. Organization for Economic Cooperation and Development, *Council Recommendation on Principles Concerning Transfrontier Pollution*, 14 INT'L LEGAL MAT. 242 (1975), 15 INT'L LEGAL MAT. 1218 (1976), 16 INT'L LEGAL MAT. 977 (1977).

45. *Id.* at 14 INT'L LEGAL MAT. 249 (1975), 15 INT'L LEGAL MAT. 1219–20 (1976), 16 INT'L LEGAL MAT. 908–81 (1977).

CHAPTER 24

APPLYING TRADITIONAL TRADE PRINCIPLES TO THE INTERNATIONAL FLOW OF INFORMATION

ROBERT E. HERZSTEIN

TWO CULTURES: INTERNATIONAL COMMUNICATIONS AND INTERNATIONAL TRADE

The rules and institutions that shape international communications bear little relation to those that were developed to govern the international market for goods. We have two cultures in which lawyers, officials, and businessmen in one evolved field have little understanding of the basic assumptions that guide those in the other field. These two cultures—the communications experts and the trade experts—must develop common concepts for structuring and regulating international information flows. This paper explores ways in which the experience of the Western trading nations under the Trade Agreements Program might provide guidance in the effort to avoid unnecessary barriers to trade in telecommunications and computer services.[1]

The government officials, businessmen, and lawyers concerned with international communications have largely been those who were affiliated with common carriers, government-owned telephone systems, and communications regulatory authorities such as the Federal Communications Commission. Recently, however, an entirely new group—trade policy officials, trade negotiators, trade lawyers, manufacturers, importers and exporters, shippers, financiers, and insurers—has become interested in the organization and economics of international communications. This new group is finding that, as a result of modern business patterns and developing technologies in telecommunications and data processing, international trade and finance are heavily dependent upon the transmission, storage, and processing of information throughout the global marketplace. Indeed, in businesses such as banking, consumer credit, investments, transportation, and insurance, a substantial part of the activity consists of the transmission and manipulation of information. Conventional manufacturing businesses also depend increasingly on the expansion of international information flows.[2]

In this chapter I outline the principles and techniques developed in the trade liberalization process,

The author is very grateful for the able assistance of Messrs. Robert Thorpe and Bijan Amini in the preparation of this paper. The paper is based on a speech in which the author was requested to make an initial exploration of the extent to which the Trade Agreements Program provides lessons for those concerned with the recent problems of information flows. The paper is intended to be suggestive rather than definitive. In future work the concepts suggested here can be applied—and tested—by using them to analyze the problems encountered in international competition by businesses in individual areas of telecommunications and information processing.

ROBERT E. HERZSTEIN ● Mr. Herzstein is a senior partner in the law firm of Arnold & Porter in Washington, D.C. He was previously the Under Secretary for International Trade, U.S. Department of Commerce.

and the problems that have not been mastered. I then examine activities involved in international data flows to see whether the trade liberalization experience can provide guidance in reducing information flow barriers. I conclude that those concerned with international information flows have much to learn from the successful features of the Trade Agreements Program and from its shortcomings.

SYNOPSIS OF RELEVANT FEATURES OF THE TRADE AGREEMENTS PROGRAM

The trade liberalization process, which started in the mid-1930s under Cordell Hull's Reciprocal Trade Agreements Program and then accelerated with the adoption of the General Agreement on Tariffs and Trade (GATT) in 1948,[3] did not involve the design and implementation of a model world economic system. Rather, it was a process of gradually peeling away layers of national economic barriers that had been erected over many years. The most obvious impediments to trade at that time were high tariffs and quotas, and these were the focus of initial liberalization efforts.[4]

It is not accidental that these efforts to liberalize international trade relationships began during the Great Depression and came to fruition just after World War II. Both catastrophes increased the desire of Western nations for closer economic ties and an ordered system of global trade. This history also explains the orientation of the GATT toward the trade practices of developed Western nations operating under essentially free market or "mixed" economies.

The Trade Agreements Program has not been as successful in formulating a coherent regime of trade relations among developing nations, and it has had very little effect on trade with Eastern bloc countries. Thus, to the extent that the lessons of the trade liberalization process can be applied to resolving problems in the international flow of information, it follows that these lessons will likely be more instructive for ordering relationships among developed Western nations.

It is also important to recognize that agreements for multilateral reductions in trade barriers did not spring instantly into being simply because someone thought their reduction would be desirable. Every agreement, every concession, and every achievement was the result of difficult international negotiations, planned and conducted over lengthy periods. Each negotiator represented national concerns and national interests, and

was, in some measure, accountable to those interests and concerns. But success was achieved because the participants reached the point where the benefits of each nation's "autonomy," "sovereignty," and economic self-sufficiency were clearly outweighed by the benefits each nation would gain from a common undertaking that achieved a freer global marketplace.[5] And as will be seen, the process of accommodation included an escape clause for use by a nation when the shared objective of open trade simply could not override its national interests in particular cases.

This process of dismantling existing barriers has gone through two phases, distinguished by the types of obstacles that were faced. We are now entering a third phase, in which nations are trying to cope with obstacles to an effective global marketplace entirely different from those previously confronted.

The First Phase of GATT

ELIMINATING ECONOMIC RESTRAINTS.   The first phase of the trade liberalization process focused on eliminating national barriers that operated exclusively to impede or distort trade. We can refer to these barriers as economic restraints. They were an obvious starting place for trade liberalization.

Tariffs   For over three decades, the trade-liberalizing efforts of the GATT nations focused primarily upon reducing tariffs. The most conspicuous success of the Trade Agreements Program has been the virtual elimination of tariffs as a significant trade barrier for many products.

Quantitative Restrictions   Quotas, or quantitative restrictions, are prohibited by Article XI of GATT. Despite their recent resurgence, quotas on imports of manufactured goods have, with few exceptions, been largely eliminated by the industrialized nations.[6]

Discrimination Against Products Based on their Origin   Discriminatory treatment of imports is prohibited by various GATT rules. The most-favoured-nation requirement of Article I obligates a nation to treat imports from all GATT countries equally when collecting import duties. Similar language in the National Treatment provisions of Article III requires that a GATT member neither tax nor regulate imported products less favorably than products made within its borders. Articles XI and XIII prohibit the discriminatory application of quotas. As a result of these provisions, goods originating in a GATT country should be treated (once any applicable duties are paid) the same as those from any other country in any of the GATT nations.[7]

Discrimination in Government Purchasing In most, if not all, countries the government is the largest single purchaser of goods. Discrimination by a government purchasing agency in favor of domestic suppliers, or among foreign suppliers, creates a serious additional obstacle to international competition. An effort to reduce these barriers was iitiated by the GATT Agreement on Government Procurement, established in 1979 as part of the Tokyo Round of negotiations.[8] This agreement commits each subscribing nation to certain practices designed to promote fair competition in government procurement between domestic and imported products.[9]

Government Subsidies When a government subsidizes its industries and thereby enables them to compete more effectively in world markets, the impact is similar to that of import tariffs or quotas, since the subsidies discriminate for or against products on the basis of where the products are made. Subsidies were recently addressed, although only partially, in the GATT Code on Subsidies and Countervailing Duties.[10] The code goes beyond the GATT in prohibiting "export subsidies"—i.e., government benefits that would lower export prices below domestic prices. it also attempts to regulate other government benefits to industry that lower the price of a product both in its home country and abroad. Although the code does not prohibit these "domestic subsidies," it does allow other countries to take offsetting or retaliatory action when products benefiting from such subsidies cause injury to one of their industries. The code has been rather effective in discouraging export subsidies, but problems in defining "domestic subsidies" have been considerable.[11] With the current recessionary environment, the use of controversial subsidies has greatly increased—with the result that much world trade is influenced more by competitive subsidization than by normal market forces.[12]

All of the trade barriers and subsidies discussed thus far are designed to divert industry from one location to another, and to preserve jobs and investment within national boundaries. They tend to balkanize the free global market that the GATT sought to promote. A good deal of progress has been made in developing legal tools that can serve to reduce or eliminate these trade distortions.

ESTABLISHING SAFEGUARDS. As part of the first phase in which the trade barriers described above were significantly reduced, various safeguards for vital national interests were created. These safeguards were intended to give political leaders and governments the confidence to go forward with the dismantling of protective barriers at their borders and thereby subject their national industries to the rigors of international competition. The safeguards included the following provisions:

- A provision in the GATT allowing a nation to restrict imports when absolutely essential for its national security.[13] This safeguard has been invoked very cautiously and infrequently, since each nation realizes that its own excessive use of this excuse for limiting imports will set a precedent that other nations could use against its exports.
- A provision for emergency action—the so-called escape clause—which allows a country to limit imports temporarily when a large and rapid increase in imports threatens a sudden disruption of a domestic industry or its workers. This import protection can only be temporary and is designed to allow time for the domestic industry to adjust to the increased import competition.[14]
- A provision allowing import restrictions when a country is encountering a balance-of-payments emergency.[15]

Apart from the national security clause, no provision exists for indefinitely protecting an industry that a nation views as important. The basic commitment of the Western countries has been to move toward a global economic system rather than a set of separate national ones.

CREATING A DISPUTE-RESOLUTION PROCESS. One final element of the progress made in the first phase of the Trade Agreements Program was the establishment of dispute resolution processes within the GATT.[16] More modern processes were also established in several of the Tokyo-Round codes singed in 1979.

In general, the GATT articles and codes call for member states to consult each other on any dispute which has arisen. If consultation fails to resolve the issue, it is taken up by a committee established to administer the article or code under which the issue has arisen or by a panel set up to investigate the complaint. Ultimately, if the above steps fail to bring about a resolution of a dispute, the matter is brought before all the member states for consideration.[17] The dispute resolution process has not worked as well as some expected in establishing a "rule of law" role for the GATT. It is likely that proposals for improving this process will be considered in the next trade negotiating round.

The Second Phase of GATT: Eliminating Technical Barriers to Trade

The second phase of the trade liberalization process focused on the internal regulations of many countries. Unlike the economic barriers discussed above, these regulations were not designed to discriminate against trade. They were simply designed to achieve internal regulatory purposes. But in many cases they had the effect of discriminating against imports. One might call these technical, rather than economic, restraints. They include health and safety regulations, technical product standards, and inspection procedures and certification requirements.[18]

One of the most significant aspects of the Tokyo-round agreements was the achievement of an Agreement on Technical Barriers to Trade (Standards Code), which will probably eventually result in a good deal of progress toward eliminating the discriminatory impact of national regulatory systems. The code places member nations under an obligation to avoid product standards, testing requirements, and certification systems that interfere with international trade.[19]

With great difficulty, the GATT has, since World War II, gone through the two phases in which economic and then technical restraints were reduced. Substantial advances have been made in both stages, though much remains to be done.

The Third Phase of GATT: Coping with National Industrial Policies

We are now encountering a third phase. We find that, having achieved many of the benefits from reducing the barriers described above, enterprises trying to operate in the global market are still somewhat distressed at the imbalance of competitive opportunity. This imbalance results, in large part, from the different roles that governments play in different economic systems, affecting both the structure and the behavior of companies and industries. This third phase, which policymakers are only now beginning to cope with, is best summed up in the phrase "industrial policy"—national government intervention to foster or stimulate a key or "targeted" industry to build the industry's competitiveness.[20]

This new phase—the third layer of the onion as one tries to peel away obstacles—raises a tremendous challenge to U.S. domestic and international economic policymakers. The challenge is best summed up by the following question: Do we want to say to U.S. workers, managers, and investors ten years from now in, for example, the computer industry—"Sorry, you didn't make it; the Japanese were better"—when one of the factors in Japan's success was its ability to mobilize and equip its industry in a way that the U.S. government could not or would not do?

American companies, American workers, and the American public can accept losing out in a competitive struggle to superior skill, zeal, or industry on the part of a foreign competitor, or to the greater willingness of a foreign competitor to risk its capital, or to a simple natural geographic advantage (e.g., proximity to resources) that a foreign competitor might possess. But losing is difficult to accept when, for example, the foreign competitor had exclusive access to sources of low-cost, long-term capital, enjoyed a sustaining relationship in its research and development with its government, or enjoyed support from its suppliers or distributors not available to the American company.

Coping with foreign industrial policies is very difficult for American policymakers because few of them believe the U.S. government should imitate the practice of Japan or other interventionist governments. The American political system has not been structured to place in high office persons whom the business community and the labor community regard as competent to make basic economic decisions affecting industrial structure and performance. Nonetheless, the fact is that we are discovering that competition in the modern world is not just competition between enterprises; it is also, to some extent, competition between societies. And we must evaluate just what role our government plays in seeing that all the resources of our society are brought to bear in helping the American economy compete in the global market that we have created by reducing trade barriers.[21]

The above description is a broad outline of the types of problems, and methods of coping with them, that have been encountered in the trade liberalization process. As noted, the Trade Agreements Program was established to create a free international marketplace in goods. The participants in that program have not concerned themselves thus far with the problems that are only now beginning to be encountered in services, including information and information processing services. The preceding overview, however, provides a starting point for evaluating the potential for applying the lessons learned in the trade liberalization process to the problems that are emerging in the international information business.

APPLYING THE EXPERIENCE OF THE TRADE-AGREEMENTS PROGRAM TO TRADE PROBLEMS IN INTERNATIONAL INFORMATION FLOWS

Service Industries and the GATT

The GATT rules were not drafted to apply to services.[22] Thus, the GATT rules are not much help to a company that seeks to sell services, such as data processing, or to enter a foreign country with a subsidiary to sell its services in that country. The failure to extend the reach of the GATT to the service industries simply represents an oversight on the part of those who framed the GATT—explainable by the fact that when the GATT was drafted services comprised a negligible portion of international trade.[23] Nor do the GATT rules apply to investment.[24]

The Current Environment for Teleinformatics

Companies engaged in the telecommunications and information processing business (teleinformatics) do not, for the most part, confront long-established industries ensconced behind national systems of tariffs and quotas, as existed when the Trade Agreements Program was initiated. *So basically there is less need, in the case of the international data industry, to go through the process of negotiating away accumulated economic barriers than there was during the early decades of the GATT.*

We can, if we wish, leap directly to a global market system unimpeded by national economic barriers. The current environment in which teleinformatics businesses operate is analogous to a developing country installing its first long-distance telecommunications system—today, no need exists to install cables for the long-distance telephone lines; the developing country can go directly to the new technologies of microwave, laser, and satellite systems, avoiding the heavy investment involved in the old system. Similarly, we can establish a global teleinformatics market without erecting, and then painfully dismantling, separate national markets.

However, to avoid repeating the mistakes of history, we must keep in mind the restraints faced in the initial stages of the Trade Agreements Program.

The Three Phases of GATT Applied to the Problems of International Information Flows

If we examine each of the three sets of obstacles—the explicit economic barriers, the technical barriers, and the disparities in competitive opportunity created by national industrial policies—we can begin to outline what might become the fundamental elements of a U.S. trade policy for teleinformatics.

PHASE I: ECONOMIC RESTRAINTS AND INTERNATIONAL INFORMATION FLOWS.

As noted above, nations can, in effect, probably skip the process of eliminating economic restraints since these restraints do not appear to be generally prevalent in the area of international data flows. This does not mean that we can avoid being sensitive to the existence of such restraints. Certain steps will be necessary to avoid the emergence of these restraints in the teleinformatics industry.

Committing to the Free Flow of Information First, a commitment must be made to reject economic protectionism. This commitment would recognize the value of uninhibited flows to the extent that the information exchanged is an economic activity, or bears on and facilitates other economic activities, such as banking, insurance, and multinational business generally. This does not mean the subordination of all other values—such as privacy, national security, or the need to avoid sudden and severe dislocations of workers. It does mean that protectionist measures, such as tariffs and quotas, should be avoided as a means of obtaining a competitive advantage. And it does mean a commitment to the market process, reserving for national regulation only those activities and decisions clearly vital to important national interests of a noneconomic nature.

The proliferation of telecommunication and related services indicates that, if government-imposed barriers can be avoided, the information industries will be widely dispersed geographically. Unlike steel or autos, which require heavy investment in one place, the information industries are basically footloose. The LEGIS database is supplied in Korea, where Koreans with a knowledge of English write legislative digests and beam them into a New York computer bank. Satellite Data Corporation of New York offers customers the word processing and data entry services of a facility in Barbados. After receiving information via satellite at the Barbados plant, local workers type the data or other written material into a computer that transmits the final product back to the

United States at a total cost 20 to 50 percent less than that charged by its landlocked competitors. In the small town where I vacation in Maine, there is little economic activity after summer vacationers depart. Yet, two women have started a computer programming business that they can operate as effectively on the remote northeast coast as they could in New York or San Francisco.

The information industries are making other service industries footloose also. In India and Pakistan, engineers feed their designs through data links to engineering companies in Houston or Los Angeles. Global computer links are enabling banking, investment, insurance, and other traditional service industries to operate in diverse locations, using local workers to bring sophisticated services to their local markets.

Indeed, the information industries may not conform to traditional patterns of centralization or concentration. The attraction of utilizing resources and serving markets in dozens of different countries may render obsolete nationalistic efforts such as Brazil's, which has attempted to concentrate all the elements of a new information industry within its borders.[25]

There are vast opportunities and incentives for international cooperation that would create a highly efficient global information industry, utilizing the best and the cheapest resources throughout the world. If countries avoid explicit economic barriers, they may become less fearful of the consequences of new telecommunication processes as the benefits, for everyone, of this global activity become more apparent.

Applying the Techniques of the Trade Agreements Program If the Western nations can avoid economic protectionism and commit to the development of a global market in teleinformatics, the following practical concepts and mechanisms, derived from the experience of the first phase of the Trade Agreements Program, might prove useful.

PROHIBITING TARIFFS. Customs duties on transfers of information across borders should be avoided. Some countries, for example, are considering tariffs on data carried over their facilities between other countries. To facilitate taxation, some countries have implemented regulations requiring disclosure of data transmissions. Japan's postal and telecommunication authorities and all of those in Western Europe have required disclosure of all codes used to transmit data to and from their countries. France has offered to sell Brazil an electronic

"customs house." This international telephone exchange, already installed in France, is intended to accommodate computer networks, while automatic monitoring features that are built into it facilitate the collection of tariffs. Users of private leased international communication lines could be charged on the basis of volume or information content rather than the present fixed rates based on the cost of services. Some countries have suggested denying access to private leased lines, which are priced at flat rates, to force users to transmit over public lines priced at higher rates according to usage. Charges of these kinds would have the same effect as customs duties, since they burden foreign-based services with costs not charged to local services.[26]

To inflict such barriers on this new industry would be to step back in history and forget about the 35-year struggle to reduce tariffs on industrial products. Customs duties on information flows would amount to sheer economic protectionism and would burden user industries as well. They would also hinder scientific and cultural exchanges, for which commitments to a free exchange of information have already been made.[27]

ESTABLISHING SAFEGUARDS. Where important national interests are likely to be undercut by foreign competition in one country's market, the Trade Agreements Program teaches us that safeguards may be erected, subject to limitations and disciplines designed to insure that the safeguards do not undermine the global market. The principles upon which such safeguards are based include the following:

• Restrictions should be imposed only according to agreed international criteria, similar to those in the escape clause, the balance-of-payments emergency, and the national security provisions of the GATT. The need to justify such restrictions exerts considerable inhibition on their indiscriminate use. Each country knows that it may be creating a precedent upon which others may rely to its detriment.

• Restrictions should be "transparent." Each participating government should be required to make available to others full information concerning any restrictions or distortions it imposes on the international flow of information. Transparency of any national measures that impede the global market is vital to maintaining the spirit of cooperation and the confidence necessary for a global market system.

- Any import restrictions must be limited in scope to what the criteria justify.

- Import restrictions should be phased out over a reasonable period of years, so that movement toward an open market is resumed and domestic industries do not rely for their growth upon continued protection.

- The country imposing restraints should compensate countries that have lost trade opportunities by creating other opportunities or providing other reciprocal trade benefits.

ACCEPTING LIMITATIONS ON NATIONAL SOVEREIGNTY. Generalized concerns about "sovereignty," as expressed in some official statements on national data policies, are too vague to justify national barriers to information flows.[28] The Trade Agreements Program has brought substantial benefits to the participating countries only because the countries accepted the limitations on their sovereignty required by the international trade rules. As a technical matter, each nation still has the "right" to restrict trade as it wishes at its borders, but none of the GATT members asserts that right as nations once did. The growing economic interdependence in recent decades has dramatized the significant benefits of the global market system that each nation risks losing if it asserts its full "independence" from its trading partners. Thus, trade policy officials seldom espouse policies comparable to those recently expressed by information policy officials, calling for "economic independence" and "control over the economic destiny" of a nation. These abstractions are no longer acceptable as statements of national goals in trade, and progress toward a global information market will be impeded so long as objectives are expressed in these terms.

PROHIBITING SUBSIDIES. There should be a clear prohibition on export subsidies. These amount to a discrimination against foreign competition in favor of domestic industry, just as import tariffs do.

Export subsidies on communication and data processing services will no doubt arise as a result of the "informatique"[29] plans and the prospective moves of state-owned telecommunication monopolies into the services business.[30] Export subsidies have been an important factor in the telecommunications and computer equipment business.[31]

Domestic subsidies that give a domestic industry an advantage in its own market over foreign companies seeking to compete there should also be avoided if we are to achieve the potential for an internationalized marketplace. The European Community has organized its own subsidized telecommunications service (EURONET), which serves European computer services at one-quarter or less of the price that non-European computer services must pay local PTTs for similar access to communication systems. This subsidy does not promote exports, but it excludes imports of computer services and balkanizes the market.

DEFINING A BROAD MARKETPLACE. In establishing marketplace disciplines for the information industries, care must be taken not to overlook any area of exchange in which some of the decisions can usefully be made by market forces. We would not want to repeat the mistake made by the drafters of the GATT when they overlooked the services area. Thus, efforts to devise rules and disciplines governing international data flows should extend not just to the data processing business, but to the mass media as well.

- *Newspapers, books, and magazines:* The Economist and The Wall Street Journal are read all over the world. Several years ago a group of individuals met in Boston with the idea of putting out a global paper. Today, with a full-time staff of only seven, *WorldPaper* is a monthly supplement subscribed to by 15 newspapers on four continents and in Japan.[32]

- *Entertainment television:*[33] "Dallas" is seen in 85 foreign countries. It has been the number-three television program in Germany and Canada. It has been number two in the United Kingdom, with other American programs ranking number one and number three.[34]

- *Sports television:* The World Cup soccer match was seen by 1.3 billion people worldwide. Americans are acquiring a taste for soccer while the Japanese pack stadiums to see American college football games.

The economics are extremely favorable for mass distribution of news and entertainment publications and programming, since the marginal cost of additional readers or viewers is very low, most costs having been incurred in the initial production.

AVOIDING THE GROWTH OF INDUSTRIES ENSCONCED BEHIND NONMARKET PROTECTIONS. Care should also be taken to limit the proliferation of organizations that are exempt from market forces.

We are seeing a natural process in which national post, telephone, and telegraph systems (PTTs), which have had monopolies over certain communications channels, seek to extend their monopolies to the new economic opportunities created by modern telecommunications and data processing technology.

They seek to control the equipment manufacturing for data communications.[35] They are also seeking to extend their service monopolies to new kinds of information flows and related activities—such as data processing and storage. And they appear to be charging for communications channels needed for high-speed business-data communications, over which they continue to maintain monopoly control, on principles other than cost recovery, using the excess revenues to subsidize other communication services and equipment-development activities.

When industries within a nation enjoy a large market share as a result of protection from foreign competition, it becomes difficult to revert to free market forces.[36] If the national PTTs develop commanding market positions in data processing, equipment manufacturing, and other new areas of business, we will face a world in which these economic activities are pursued mostly by large state-owned monopolies, and it will be difficult to achieve an efficient global marketplace.

PHASE II: TECHNICAL RESTRAINTS AND INTERNATIONAL INFORMATION FLOWS.

General Technical Restraints Government regulations of a technical nature currently appear to be the most significant and widespread impediments to the development of a global communications market. Although not necessarily aimed at imports, such restraints operate to discriminate against imports. Some of the more traditional primary restraints can be identified as follows: government regulations that prevent domestic operations from employing foreign personnel even though domestic expertise is lacking; local taxation rules that in practice apply higher rates to foreign-based operations; intellectual-property laws that often place limitations on technology transfers to and from the country or discourage transfer to a country by failing to provide adequate patent and copyright protections; and government-licensing and product-standardization requirements that are in practice applied discriminatorily to foreign-based operations and often impose excessive obligations and costly delays.

Examples abound of countries that have already imposed technical restraints that interfere with information flows, such as requiring that computer hardware and software used by a domestic processor of information be purchased domestically even though less expensive and more appropriate equipment can be purchased

elsewhere more cheaply; requiring that data be processed and stored locally, even though the capacity already exists elsewhere; and refusing PTT interconnections for foreign-owned enterprises, and, even where interconnection is permitted, imposed inconsistent product standards that impede the efficient transmittal and delivery of information.[37]

In 1982, the Commerce Department filed a complaint with the Japanese government on behalf of Tymshare, Inc., a computer programming service, charging that Japan's public international carrier, KDD, had placed unnecessary restrictions on Tymshare's Japanese operations.[38] The local restrictions on customer access to Tymshare's computer networks were arbitrary and economically burdensome, and according to the complaint "served no other purpose than to create an artificial barrier to trade in services." Contol Data Corporation experienced a similar problem when it was required by the Japanese to limit the number of computer bases in the United States to which it could link its Japanese customers, thereby effectively limiting the number and types of services it could offer in Japan. Only after the United States government filed a formal protest and entered into negotiations with the Japanese government were these restrictions lifted.

West Germany in 1982 imposed a requirement that private international leased lines could only be connected to the German public networks if the company seeking the connection carried out some of its computer processing activities locally. In response to the U.S. trade representative's assertions that this performance requirement was protectionist, the German minister of posts and telecommunications wrote accusing the U.S. trade representative of "distorting" and "sometimes completely misrepresenting" German laws.[39] In Canada, all banks are required to maintain and perform domestically at least the initial processing of data on Canadian citizens.

These technical requirements by some governments for data flows and processing can distort competitive conditions and prevent economies of scale even more than economic barriers such as tariffs and subsidies.[40]

Many of these technical restraints are of a sort that have been encountered before in manufactured-products trade, and have been at least partially alleviated in the GATT system. The guiding principles can be found in the new Agreement on Technical Barriers to Trade (Standards Code), perhaps the most novel and far-reaching of all the GATT Agreements. The Standards

Code places each nation under an obligation to avoid product standards, testing requirements, and certification systems that (1) are intended to create obstacles to international trade, (2) in fact discriminate against imported products, or (3) create "unnecessary obstacles to international trade."[41] Probably the most fundamental obligation in the code, and one which can have the most far-reaching effects, is the requirement that nations use international standards as a basis for their own technical regulations and standards.[42] The code requires national governments to ensure that their own measures comply with the code,[43] and to use "such reasonable methods as may be available to them" to avoid inconsistent technical standards established by state and local governments and by private organizations.[44] To achieve compliance with the code, existing technical standards must be published, and open procedures must be used in formulating new standards. When a nation proposes a technical standard that will be applied to imported products, the code requires that other code members be notified and given an opportunity to comment on the proposed standard. A dispute resolution procedure is also provided.

It appears likely that much progress could be made in liberating data flows from parochial national boundaries if the principles of the GATT Standards Code were followed in establishing and implementing rules on data interconnects and equipment usage.

Data Privacy Laws In recent years, largely in response to the growth of international information flows, several countries in Europe have enacted laws to protect individual privacy rights by regulating the storage and processing of electronic data. Although considerable variation exists among the European data privacy laws,[45] most do not define the scope of the right to privacy they purport to protect.[46] They impose obligations on data users, confer rights on data subjects, and provide for a supervision and enforcement mechanism, often in the government. Typically, they are enforced through licensing or registration of data users.

There is little evidence that data privacy regulations have been designed or intended as protectionist measures. They do express a legitimate concern for important noneconomic values.[47] It is encouraging to find that normally the "data commissioners" are not part of the economic ministries of their countries. In fact, most data protection agencies or commissions work closely, or are linked through an appeals process, with the justice ministries of their countries.[48]

The internal dynamics of such regulations do, however, have a way of favoring domestic industry—much as product safety standards for industrial products can favor national manufacturers, because the standards are often drawn up by local industry on terms comfortable and convenient for the industry.[49]

These data privacy laws are in effect technical and safety regulations similar to other regulations that affect trade in industrial products. Reconciling the laws with an open international market does not present a conceptual problem; the problem is one of legal engineering— i.e., seeing that the rules and the compliance programs serve the proper purpose of privacy protection without having an adverse impact on foreign competitors in data processing or communications.[50] The data protection laws can be dealt with through international disciplines in much the same way that health and safety regulations and product standards are dealt with by the Standards Code.

The OECD Recommended Guidelines Governing the Protection of Privacy and Transborder Flows of Personal Data (OECD code)[51] represent a sound set of principles for starting to guide and regulate national privacy protection policies, without impairing the operation of international market forces. The guidelines govern the transborder flow of personal data. They set forth basic principles of data protection, which recognize the right of individuals to know the existence and purpose of data maintained about them; the right of access to data about themselves; the right to challenge the accuracy and request additions or changes to the data; the right to prevent dissemination of that data; and the right of restitution for harms suffered as a consequence of any unwarranted dissemination of, or errors contained in, the data.

The OECD code also includes a general commitment to the "uninterrupted and secure" flow of data across borders.[52] It admonishes countries against using data protection as an excuse for achieving "obstacles to transborder flows of personal data that would exceed requirements for such protection."[53]

Media Laws The various media can in large part also be treated as commercial activities—lines of commerce. Considerable economic benefits can be achieved if the media can operate in an open international marketplace. When noneconomic interests of a political or cultural nature must be protected from what a national government, through legitimate processes, has determined are harmful foreign media, regulations should be adopted in accordance with the international disciplines described previously.[54]

When a nation decides to restrict media access for ostensibly cultural reasons, it is a sensitive matter for other nations to challenge the legitimacy of its objectives. However, if principles similar to those in the Standards Code or the OECD data-privacy code were applied to media access restraints, a nation imposing such restraints would at least be committed to avoiding restraints that intentionally discriminate, or have the effect of discriminating, against foreign media products. And the nation imposing restrictions would be called upon under its international obligations to use transparent procedures in formulating and enforcing its regulations, so that discriminatory restrictions would be easier to detect.

As noted, free-speech values are also impaired by national restrictions on media. Those values, too, have a measure of international consensus[55] and can serve to inhibit restraints motivated by economic or political objectives.

As a sequel to the OECD data-privacy code, it might be useful now to begin work on an international code that sets standards for achieving maximum flows and minimizing intervention by national governments in the international trade that takes place in the form of mass media (broadcasting, publications, etc.). Such standards might be only advisory, but would be useful as a framework upon which some later, and more authoritative, agreement could be built.

PHASE III: INDUSTRY POLICY AND THE INTERNATIONAL FLOW OF INFORMATION. If we avoid Phase I economic barriers and deal with Phase II technical barriers through international codes, we are still confronted with the problem of national industrial policies—comprehensive programs aimed at the development and support of national telecommunication and data processing industries. At this point we encounter a genuine void in the existing trade law and a lack of established concepts for use in negotiating proper limits on government interventions. Apart from the rules previously discussed, neither the GATT nor any other agreement restricts nations in their efforts to organize and equip their industries for more effective global competition.

Public statements by government officials in a number of significant countries have made it quite clear that national control of information sources and flows is a high priority.[56] Some countries have already implemented programs that are designed to achieve national control, such as directing large-scale government purchases to a selected supplier in order to build efficiency and economies of scale; sponsoring and funding research-and-development programs and, to a certain extent, using some of the discriminatory economic and technical restraints discussed above.[57] If left unchecked, these programs fostering closed national systems of information processing and dissemination will undoubtedly increase.

How do we cope with these nationalistic policies? The following are a few possible elements that might stimulate thinking about possible guidelines:

First, the Western trading nations could seek to dispel myths and apocalyptic fears about the effects on national destinies of developments in the teleinformatics industry. These fears could perhaps be dispelled through a careful collaborative economic study—prepared under impeccable auspices (such as the OECD)—of the likely future course of development of the teleinformatics industry. Answers should be sought to questions such as these: Will the teleinformatics industry geographically concentrate or proliferate? What will be the role of multinational corporations? How important will the nationality of a corporation be? Will the industry be too concentrated in a few hands? These are questions of economic structure that call for a classic type of antitrust analysis, carried out on the scale of the international, rather than the U.S., market.

Second, the Western trading nations could also begin to develop internationally-approved guidelines for government industrial policies. The guidelines would suggest that governments solve their problems by concentrating on macroeconomic policies instead of industry-specific programs. For example, the GATT Code on Subsidies and Countervailing Duties prohibits only subsidies to a specific enterprise or industry, or group of enterprises or industries. All governments operate programs of benefit to all industries, such as public education, internal transportation facilities, and tax incentives for investment. Such macroeconomic policies are not restricted by the GATT subsidies code.[58]

In addition, the international guidelines would suggest that any industry-specific program pursued by a government should adhere to the following practices:

• Avoid erecting market-access obstacles. The

program should be open, and not just benefit firms that are organized or owned domestically.

- Focus on improving the general pool of national resources, e.g., education and technology, which would facilitate expansion of the domestic telecommunication and data processing industry without being targeted exclusively on that industry.

- Set as its objective the increase of international welfare, rather than simply seeking competitive advantage for the individual country.

- Provide mechanisms for any industry-specific programs to phase out automatically, so as to avoid the perpetuation of an inefficient national industry that is dependent for its existence and growth on the indefinite continuation of a national industrial policy.

Third, the Western nations could also seek to harmonize national laws and programs affecting the telecommunications and information processing industries, in order to achieve optimal conditions for enterprises to compete globally without advantages or disadvantages resulting from national boundaries. In other words, we should seek to promote competition among enterprises rather than among nations. An example of this approach is the Agreement on Trade in Civil Aircraft, negotiated during the Tokyo round. The agreement provides for government purchasers of civil aircraft to select suppliers on the basis of commercial and technological factors, rather than on the national origin of the products, and to refrain from requiring or exerting pressure on airlines, aircraft manufacturers, or other entities engaged in the purchase or production of civil aircraft, to procure their supplies from a particular source.

Finally, the trading nations could expand and refine the mechanisms by which one country may offset, for its industries, advantages granted by another country to its telecommunications or information processing industries. Countervailing duties are sanctioned by the GATT to allow a country to defend its industry against injury caused by subsidized exports from a foreign nation. The GATT also allows one nation to retaliate against another, when subsidized exports by the second nation are depriving the first of markets it previously enjoyed in a third country. To the extent a nation's industrial policies confer unfair advantages on its industry and deprive others of competitive opportunities, similar offsetting or retaliatory techniques might provide a useful discipline.

CONCLUSION

Since its inception after World War II, the Trade Agreements Program has progressed through two difficult stages of development—reduction of economic, and then technical, barriers to international trade in goods. Regrettably, the program has not yet been applied to trade in services, including telecommunications and data processing. However, the principles learned in the GATT experience can in many respects provide for cooperative efforts to reduce trade barriers in these industries.

Economic barriers to trade in the telecommunications and information processing industries are not yet so fully developed or established; thus, a strong commitment to the uninhibited flow of information across national boundaries could help prevent their emergence or entrenchment.

Technical barriers, on the other hand, appear to be prevalent in this industry. The principles underlying the GATT Standards Code can be usually applied to reduce these barriers.

International trade in both goods and services, including telecommunications and data processing services, can be seriously distorted by national industrial policies. Such policies, aimed at developing key industries through government-coordinated programs, can interfere with the benefits and mechanisms of the free marketplace. These industrial policies have not been tackled in the GATT or anywhere else. To discourage them before they become widespread and entrenched, it would be useful to define a set of norms governing the industry-specific programs of national governments. These norms would be designed to promote an efficient international marketplace for these services, in which (1) competition is conducted among enterprises, not among nations; (2) the role of national governments is limited as much as possible to macroeconomic programs; and (3) industry-specific programs are temporary, nondiscriminatory, and designed to enhance rather than impede the global market system.

NOTES

1. The Trade Agreements Program is a cooperative effort to reduce obstacles to trade among most of the countries of the non-Communist world. The foundation of the program is a system of rules, subscribed to by the participating governments, that significantly limit the actions that may be taken by national governments to obstruct the flow of manufactured products across their borders. These rules, as well as the rudimentary institution that attempts to help them work and also sponsors successive negotiating meetings, are known as the General Agreement on Tariffs and Trade (GATT).

2. International business today depends upon elaborate data support systems. Three major international computer telecommunication networks have supported the financial and air transportation industries for a number of years. Eurex S.A. and the Society for Worldwide Interbank Financial Telecommunication (SWIFT) integrate the international financial community while the Société Internationale pour la Télécommunication Aéronautique (SITA), established in 1959, is essential to the effecient operation of the international air transport system. These networks illustrate the importance of unimpeded international information flows to international trade in services. *See,* e.g., the Report of the National Telecommunications and Information Administration (NTIA), *reprinted by* SENATE COMM. ON COMMERCE, SCIENCE AND TRANSPORTATION, 98TH CONG., 1st SESS. (Comm. Print 1983). The report sets forth recommendations for establishing a long-range strategy to promote and protect U.S. economic interests in the field of telecommunications and information flows.

3. The GATT was originally drafted between 1946 and 1947. It was first applied by a Protocol of Provisional Application made effective on January 1, 1948. There were 22 original signatories to the GATT. As of January 1983, 119 countries participated in the GATT, although only 88 of them were signatories to the document. Of the remaining 31, one acceded provisionally while 30 continued to maintain a de facto application of the GATT pending final decisions as to their future commercial policy.

4. The GATT has fallen far short of achieving the almost mythical goal of "free" or completely unfettered trade. It is simply an institution established to pursue the common goal of reducing barriers to international trade. Although significant progress has been made in certain areas, most obviously in reducing tariffs, reductions in other modes of protecting domestic industries have advanced slowly and, in some cases, not at all. Building a free global marketplace is an evolving process that continues to this day.

5. There are perhaps two primary economic inducements for a country with trade barriers already in place to participate in an international regime of reduced barriers. First, there is the promise of long-term economic benefits that result from such a liberalized trading regime. The phenomenal growth of the world economy during the past several decades attests to the benefits to be achieved from the liberal trade approach. Of course, there are those who argue that free trade is not necessarily beneficial to certain countries, particularly among the developing nations. *See,* e.g., U.N. Center on Transnational Corporations (UNCTC), Transnational Corporations and Transborder Data Flows: An Overview, U.N. Doc. E/C.10/87 (1981). A second inducement is the desire to avoid the short-term risk of provoking retaliation from existing and potential trading partners for national barriers that already exist or are being contemplated. *See,* e.g., § 301 of the Trade Act of 1974, as amended, 19 U.S.C. § 2411, which empowers the President to take retaliatory actions against the products and services of countries that have unjustifiably, unreasonably, or discriminatorily burdened or restricted U.S. commerce.

6. Certain exceptions to the general prohibition in Article XI of the GATT still remain, particularly with respect to agricultural goods. A balance-of-payments exception is also provided for in Article XII, as well as related provisions in Articles XIII, XIV, XV and XVIII. Quotas on steel shipments to the U.S. were negotiated by the United States with a number of supplier nations in 1984–85. These were justified by United States officials on the ground that they were needed to eliminate the effects of unfair practices in the supplier countries, and therefore were not in conflict with the quota prohibition in the GATT.

7. Difficulties are still encountered over the definition of "originating in," particularly for products that contain components from several countries, some of which are not members of GATT.

8. Discrimination in government purchasing was recognized as an economic barrier when the GATT was written, but it was clearly less important than tariffs and quotas. Thus it did not get close attention until the Tokyo Round, some 30 years later. Government purchases that are not for commercial resale (e.g., where the government acts as the consumer and not as a state trading agent) were originally exempt from nondiscrimination provisions in GATT Article III.

9. The GATT Agreement on Government Procurement requires that specifications for government-procured goods be drawn in a nondiscriminatory manner; that bid opportunities and rules for tendering bids be published; that adequate time be allowed for response from foreign suppliers; and that losing bidders be entitled to information about the winning bidder and the reason the winner was selected. The agreement still has its limitations. For example, it applies only to procurement of goods (services are covered only to the extent that they are incidental to the supply of products and cost less than the products themselves), and only to purchases by certain government agencies specified by each nation in the agreement. In addition, the agreement applies only to purchases worth at least 150,000 Special Drawing Rights (equal to approximately $162,500 in January 1983). The agreement also permits governments to invoke the general exceptions (Article XX) and the national security exception (Article XXI) of the GATT.

10. Formally known as the Agreement on Interpretation and Application of Articles VI, XVI and XXII of the GATT. The most relevant article in the GATT, Article XVI, does not prohibit export subsidies. Instead, it imposes two obligations on GATT members—that they notify the GATT of subsidies likely to increase exports or reduce imports, and that an injured party be offered an opportunity to consult when serious prejudice is caused.

11. For example, it can be difficult to draw a distinction between government-financed programs to achieve legitimate economic and social policies (such as public schooling, worker training, and transportation systems) and those that have the effect of distorting trade (such as research grants or low-cost loans primarily benefiting a particular industry).

12. The United States Trade Representative's office (USTR) maintains computerized inventories of barriers to trade. As of September 1982, the list for the service industries alone included the following amounts of subsidies granted or projected by several European governments to their domestic service industries: France (1980–85)—$500 million; W. Germany (1980–83)—$540 million; Italy (1979–81)—$355 million; Sweden (1979–82)—$111 million; and Great Britain (1979–83)—$550 million.

13. GATT, Article XXI.

14. GATT, Article XIX.

15. GATT, Article XII.

16. GATT, Articles XXII and XXIII.

17. The various GATT dispute-resolution procedures are exclusively designed to handle disputes between member states. No forum has been provided for private parties to resolve their disputes. The GATT only obligates governments, and only through the intermediary of their governments can private citizens, business organizations, and other groups complain. *See* JACKSON, WORLD TRADE AND THE LAW OF GATT 163–89 (1969).

18. For example, the CENEL system, proposed in Europe some 10 years ago, purported to establish uniform engineering standards for electronic products, but the standards had very discriminatory effects because they made it more difficult for non-European electronic components to attain certification of compliance with the standards.

19. Americans brought up in the tradition of the Commerce Clause, and those who studied the multitude of Supreme Court cases involving state regulation of interstate commerce, do not find this concept of international regulation of standards very unusual. *See, e.g.,* Dean Milk Co. v. City of Madison, 340 U.S. 349 (1951). But it appears to represent a very substantial advance in the practices of many foreign countries.

20. The recent United States countervailing duty cases against the European steel industry illustrate the extent to which European governments have involved themselves in attempts aimed at improving competition and modernizing their steel industries. *See, e.g.,* Department of Commerce, International Trade Administration, Final Affirmative Countervailing Duty Determinations, Certain Steel Products from Belgium, France, Italy, Netherlands and West Germany, 47 Fed. Reg. 39,304; 39,332; 39,356; 39,372;

39,345 (1982).

In a well-publicized recent case, Houdaille Industries, an American machine tool company, claimed that a Japanese government program for stimulating competitiveness and for reorganizing its tool industry along more efficient lines was an unfair practice. As a result of that activity by the Japanese government—a kind of activity in which the United States government would not normally engage—Houdaille asked for certain relief from the U.S. government that would have made the Japanese products less competitive in the United States. The U.S. government denied Houdaille's request, but pledged to take up the issue with the Japanese in negotiations. *See* Office of the United States Trade Representative Release No. 83/14 (Apr. 22, 1983); Trade Restrictions—Receipt of Petition Regarding Machine Tools from Japan, 47 Fed. Reg. 20,411 (1982).

21.   Another element importantly affecting world trade practices, which was not considered when the Trade Agreements Program was designed, is large multinational enterprises. These companies can take advantage of opportunities available in various countries by virtue of their speed and flexibility in utilizing resources and entering markets. Thus, they may feel less aggrieved than other companies by differences in national government practices, so long as they can enjoy the benefits afforded by each government. On the other hand, if a government discriminates among enterprises based on their ownership, favoring locally-owned ones over foreign-owned ones, the effect is to create unfair competition.

22.   To a very limited extent, GATT has concerned itself with particular services incidental to trade in goods. As early as 1953, a report was prepared on issues involved in the question of discrimination in transport insurance, culminating in a recommendation adopted in 1959 to the effect that member governments should consider any detrimental effects on trade when formulating national policies of insurance. More recently, in certain agreements concluded during the Tokyo Round, limited aspects of the service trade were addressed. These included the Agreement on Government Procurement (applies to services incidental to the supply of products), the Code of Customs Valuation (excludes from value certain charges or costs paid for various types of services when distinguished from the price actually paid or payable for imported goods), the Code on Subsidies and Countervailing Duties (prohibits, among other things, transport, insurance, and export credit subsidies), and the Agreement on Trade in Civil Aircraft (extends the GATT Agreement on Technical Barriers to Trade—which covers only goods—to repair and maintenance procedures, and eliminates tariffs levied on repairs).

23.   Today, however, services, which include the telecommunications and computer services industries, are said to represent the fastest-growing sector of international trade, a market that has grown by some estimates from $80 billion to over $400 billion during the past decade. *See, e.g.,* CENTER FOR STRATEGIC AND INTERNATIONAL STUDIES, SERVICES AND U.S. TRADE POLICY GEORGETOWN UNIVERSITY 7 (Sept. 1982).

The United States formally presented its case for an agreement on trade in services at the GATT Ministerial Conference in Geneva, November 24–29, 1982. The U.S. took the position that, at a minimum, GATT should commit itself to undertake a detailed work program on trade in services "designed to achieve a broad understanding of the type of government measures that create barriers to trade in services and the extent to which GATT concepts and negotiating procedures might provide a useful basis for future negotiations." Office of the United States Trade Representative (USTR), Preparation for GATT Ministerial—Services 1–2 (unpublished and undated working paper). This effort at launching GATT toward new talks on extending the rules fell short of U.S. expectations, however, The U.S. won only grudging agreement by the conferees to encourage "interested" GATT members to begin formal studies, under GATT's aegis, of problems involved in trade in services. This commitment is unlikely to produce any new agreement on trade in services soon. In the Tokyo Round, the last time new agreements were concluded, even after commitments were made to initiate substantive negotiations, two years of preparations and five years of negotiations were required before agreements were completed in 1979.

24.   Bilateral friendship, commerce, and navigation (FCN) treaties may apply to investment activities, and recently the United States has negotiated bilateral investment treaties with a handful of countries. But those are more difficult than the GATT to

enforce. Since the GATT is a multilateral commitment by dozens of countries, any one country is more hesitant to violate it, because the offending country sees its violation setting a precedent for any number of other countries that could adopt a comparable practice and injure the trade of the offending country. The risk of such proliferation is much less under a bilateral agreement.

25.   Brazil appears to have taken the most dramatic steps of any country to use import protection as a tool in developing domestic computer and data processing industry. In 1978, the Brazilian government began gradually banning the importation of computers and set aside the microcomputer market exclusively for its national industry. As part of its teleinformatics policy, Brazil also requires certain data processing functions to be performed within the country. International links for teleprocessing systems and imports of computers and other data communications hardware are subject to approval and periodic reviews by the government. By the end of 1981, the Brazilian computer industry supplied 42 percent of all domestic sales. Still, the country's five largest producers reported losses totalling more than $100 million in that year, the equivalent of roughly one-third of the domestic industry's total sales. And certain domestic users of data processing and computer services have complained about the additional costs imposed by the requirements that these functions be carried out locally. *See Brazil Catches Computer Wave*, J. COM. Aug. 26, 1982, at B-1, col. 4; *Brazil's Ban on Small-Computer Imports Aids Domestic Firms but Drives Prices Up*, Wall Street Journal, Oct. 4, 1982, at 38, col. 3; *Brazil Says Computer Market Stays Closed*, J. COM. Mar. 14, 1983, at A-3, col. 3.

26.   An Italian proposal to discourage new private leased lines and to transfer existing traffic on leased lines to the public networks for tariffing on a volume-sensitive basis was rejected by the International Telegraph and Telephone Consultative Committee (CCIT) in May 1978. CCIT Study Group III, Report on the Meeting Held in Geneva from 1-3 May 1978, Doc. COM III-No. 51-E (Working Party III/1, July 1978).

27.   *See, e.g.*, Agreement for Facilitating the International Circulation of Visual and Auditory Materials of an Educational, Scientific and Cultural Character (concluded in Florence, 1948), which eliminated duties and other barriers to the international exchange of scientific materials.

28.   *See, e.g.*, address by Joubert de Oliveira Brizida, executive secretary of the Brazilian Special Secretariat of Informatics, at the 1980 Intergovernmental Bureau for Informatics (IBI) Conference on Transborder Data Flow Policies in Rome (June 23, 1980), *printed in* 3 TRANSBORDER DATA REP., no. 3/4, at 32–33, (1980) in which he said:

> It is a fact that the information process threatens the cultural identity of peoples. Informatics is not neutral. It bears within itself the culture that produced it. The language, in its syntactic and semantic aspects, will receive extraordinary influence from the automatic retrieval systems and information services. Such an effect will be one of the results of producing information through structures of thought alien to the culture that uses it. Consequently, the use of a universal access to computers can and will affect our habits in their most common details.

Similar fears have been expressed by other government officials and in government-sponsored studies of the industry. In 1977, Louis Joinet, then a magistrate of the French Ministry of Justice, coined this phrase: "Information is power and economic information is economic power." Statement by L. Joinet at the OECD Symposium on Transborder Data Flows and the Protection of Privacy in Vienna, Austria (September 20–23, 1977). *See also* S. NORA & A. MINC, L'INFORMATISATION DE LA SOCIÉTÉ (1978), a report submitted to the French government, expressing the concerns about the role of the United States in computers, data processing, and telecommunications, and advancing the idea that France must regain control of its own destiny in this area or suffer serious social, economic, and cultural consequences; and the CONSULTATIVE COMMITTEE ON THE IMPLICATIONS OF TELECOMMUNICATIONS FOR CANADIAN SOCIETY, DEPARTMENT OF COMMUNICATIONS, TELECOMMUNICATIONS AND CANADA (1979) [hereinafter cited as the Clyne Report], submitted to the Canadian Government, and expressing the need for Canada to avoid reliance on American information resources. The Clyne Report concludes with the statement that "informatics [computer-communications] poses possibly the most dangerous threat to Canadian sovereignty, in both its cultural and commercial aspects." Clyne Report, at 57. "The government should act immediately to regulate transborder data flows to ensure that we do not lose control of information vital to the maintenance of national sovereignty." Clyne Report, Recommendation 24 at 64.

29.   The Intergovernmental Bureau for Informatics (IBI) defines "informatique" or "informatics" as "the rational and systematic application of information to economic, social and political development." Informatics: Its Political Impact 2 IBI Doc. DG 1-04 (1980). Countries that have pursued or proposed "informatique" plans (e.g., France, Brazil, Canada, and India) impart different meanings to the term. In general, however, it conveys the notion of a plan to coordinate the computer and telecommunications industries to serve nationalistic goals.

30.   The Japanese and French, who are seeking to enter the satellite-remote-sensing business, no doubt consider LANDSAT, the U.S. government-financed satellite-remote-sensing program to be a subsidized information service. This is so notwithstanding the bilateral cooperation agreements that the U.S. has entered into, to share use of the information received from its satellites. The debate over whether this is a service that can be economically pursued in a market-oriented manner, or whether it should be treated as a defense rather than a commercial program, typifies the problems faced when attempting to apply the trading rules to government-sponsored commercial projects. See House Sub-comm. on Space Science and Applications Report on Civil Land Remote Sensing System, 97th Cong., 1st Sess. (Comm. Print 1981).

31.   See Glenn, Financing of United States Exports of Telecommunications Equipment (Washington, D.C.: International Law Institute, Georgetown University, Aug. 1982) (monograph).

32.   Global Newspaper Put Out in Boston Begins to Catch On, Wall Street Journal, Oct. 14, 1982, at 1, col. 4.

33.   Motion pictures are dealt with partially under Article IV of the GATT. This article permits screen quotes under certain conditions, and favors "negotiations for their limitation, liberalization or elimination." So far no negotiations have taken place.

34.   J.R.: The Man 86 Countries Now Love To

Hate, Ad Age, May 31, 1982, at 25.

35.   Almost no crossborder trade in equipment occurs among the European Economic Community members, even though there are no tariffs or other restrictions on shipping such equipment from one of the EEC member countries to another. The PTTs have used their positions as monopoly customers to favor national manufacturers for supply of the equipment they need. The French "télématique" program, an industrial plan that outlines broad areas of authority for the government with special emphasis on the telecommunication aspect of the new information technologies, incorporates this strategy as a tool for improving French competitiveness in the global equipment market.

Since these national PTTs are, for the most part, government-owned or controlled agencies, their purchasing activities could be covered by the GATT Agreement on Government Procurement, which requires non-discrimination by designated government agencies in their purchases from domestic or foreign suppliers. See GATT Agreement on Government Procurement 7 and nn.9–10. Unfortunately, most of the subscribing nations to the procurement code have refused to allow the code to be applied to PTTs' purchasing activities.

By contrast, the British, Japanese, and Australian telecommunication authorities, which for many years had followed this same pattern, recently began amending their nations' telecommunications laws to open monopoly-telecommunications services to the private sector. They are considering and implementing actions ranging from the deregulation of terminal equipment to transferring control of their government-controlled domestic telephone monopolies to private hands. For some years United States manufacturers and the United States government have accused Japan of obstructing imports of U.S.-made telecommunications equipment. The Americans have pointed to national-purchasing policies of the government-owned telephone company, and to excessively technical product standards and inspecion procedures which appear to be administered in a discriminatory fashion. See, e.g., U.S. Still Questioning Entry Procedures for Japan's Telecommunications Market, Wall Street Journal, Jan. 4, 1985; Telecommunications Talks in Japan Fruitless Again, Washington Post, Mar. 16, 1985.

36. *Cf.* the U.S. dairy industry, the Japanese tobacco and salt monopoly, and much of European agriculture.

37. The USTR's computerized list contains over 100 separate international impediments to international trade in telecommunications, data processing, and information services. *See also International Data Flows, Hearings Before the Subcomm. of the House Comm. on Government Operations,* 96th Cong., 2d Sess. (Mar. 10, 13, 27, and Apr. 21, 1980); *Trade and Services and Trade in High Technology Products, Hearings Before the Subcomm. on Trade of the House Comm. on Ways and Means,* 97th Cong., 2d Sess. (May 24, 1982).

38. *See* FCC WEEK, Oct. 18, 1982, at 3.

39. *See* FCC WEEK, Nov. 8, 1982, at 4. See also the Canadian Banking Act, enacted in 1980, which prevents banking transactions from being processed outside Canada unless processing is done domestically as well. Prior approval before financial data can be sent out of Canada is also required.

40. Access can be denied either directly by, e.g., refusing use of leased lines necessary for more sophisticated needs, or indirectly by, e.g., charging prohibitive fees for use of the services.

41. GATT, Agreement on Technical Barriers to Trade (Standards Code), Articles 2.1, 7.1.

42. *Id.* at Article 2.2. This obligation is partially offset by a broad escape provision in cases where "such international standards or relevant parts are inappropriate for the Parties concerned, for *inter alia* such reasons as national security requirements; the prevention of deceptive practices; protection of human health or safety, animal or plant life or health, or the environment; fundamental climatic or other geographical factors; fundamental technological problems." In contrast, however, Article 2.3 obligates nations to "play a full part within the limits of their resources in the preparation by appropriate international standardizing bodies of international standards for products for which they either have adopted, or expect to adopt, technical regulations or standards."

43. *Id.* at Articles 2, 5, 7.

44. *Id.* at Articles 3, 4, 6, 8.

45. At least seven countries in Western Europe have enacted data protection laws: Austria (1978), Denmark (1978), France (1978), West Germany (1977), Luxembourg (1979), Norway (1978), and Sweden (1973). The English versions of their data protection acts (except Luxembourg) have been collected in one source. See 2 AMERICAN FEDERATION OF INFORMATION PROCESSING SOCIETIES TRANSBORDER DATA FLOWS (1979). Other countries contemplate legislation based on recommendations contained in reports or prepared by commissions, e.g., Great Britain, Belgium, Netherlands, and Spain. In addition, the European Parliament and the OECD have discussed and prepared international agreements on this subject.

46. In contrast, most U.S. data protection legislation is narrowly directed at potential abuses in a particular sector. Some of the U.S. statutes protects individuals from potential government abuses while others address problems in particular industires, e.g., banking.

47. For example, most data protection laws are directed at protecting personal privacy and do not encompass restridtions on the flow of business data of a nonpersonal nature.

48. See, e.g., the statutes in Denmark (creates a Data Surveillance Authority whose members are appointed by the Ministry of Justice); France (creates a Data Protection Commission whose members are appointed by various state organs); Sweden (appeals from decisions of the Data Inspection Board are decided by the Ministry of Justice); and Norway (same as Sweden). *See also* Burkert, *Institutions of Data Protection—An Attempt at a Functional Explanation of European National Data Protection Laws,* 3 COMPUTER L. J., Winter 1982, at 167, 176–80.

49. For this reason, commentators have questioned the purpose behind data protection legislation. *See, e.g.,* Address by Mark S. Fowler, Chairman, Federal Communications Commission (FCC) before the International Communications Association, New Orleans (May 4, 1982), in which he said: "As you know, some nations are using the word 'privacy' to mask what are clearly non-tariff barriers."

50. *See* Remarks of George W. Coombe, Jr., Executive Vice President and General Counsel, Bank of America, at the American Bar Association 1982 Annual Meeting, Section of International Law, Panel on Legal and Business Implications of Restrictions on Transnational Data Flow (Aug. 10, 1982).

51. *See* OECD doc. C(80)58 (final), *reprinted in Symposium on Transborder Data Flows and the Pro-*

tection of Privacy, Information, Computer and Communication Policy Series (ICCP/OECD) (1979).

52. *Id.* at para. 16. The code does permit exceptions if other countries do not observe the guidelines or provide equivalent protections. *Id.* at para. 17.

53. *Id.* at para. 18.

54. Many governments of developing countries regard the mass media and information as a tool to be carefully manipulated in the process of state-building. "To many in the Third World, 'free flow' is a self-serving concept devised in 1948 by the West, and particularly by the two U.S. news agencies, to ensure their domination of world news channels." Tartarian, *News Flows in the Third World: An Overview,* in 1 THE THIRD WORLD AND PRESS FREEDOM 12 (P. Horton ed 1978).

55. *See* Feldman, *Commercial Speech, Transborder Data Flows and the Right to Communicate Under International Law,* 17 INT'L LAW. 87 (1983). See also Article 19 in United Nations, Universal Decla-

ration of Human Rights (1948).

56. *See supra* note 29.

57. E.g., some countries prohibit firms from offering local data communication and other processing services unless a significant ownership share of the business (usually greater than 50 percent) belongs to nationals. And some countries prohibit use of computer and communication equipment that was not produced domestically.

58. For examples of how macroeconomic policies benefiting industry are not made subject to countervailing duties, see Department of Commerce, International Trade Administration, Final Negative Countervailing Duty Determinations: Certain Softwood Products from Canada, 48 Fed. Reg. 24,159, 24,167-74 (May 31, 1983); Final Affirmative Countervailing Duty Determination: Carbon Steel Wire Rod from Belgium, 47 Fed. Reg. 42, 403, 42,419 (Sept. 27, 1982).

CHAPTER 25

THE STRUGGLE FOR COHERENT INTERNATIONAL REGULATORY POLICY

ALEXANDER D. ROTH

For some time the U.S. policymaking process has been criticized as ineffective at developing a cohesive U.S. international informatics policy, thereby failing to capitalize on its technological leadership to ensure U.S. strategic, political, and economic interests in the field.[1] While U.S. efforts have faltered, countries throughout the rest of the world have identified their interests and positioned themselves accordingly.[2] A congressional committee report has found that the U.S. stands alone in not having developed "comprehensive plans and policies which deal with the full range of information flow questions (as well as many others) in an integrated manner."[3] It is not clear that a single omnibus policy is appropriate for the U.S. Whether or not a single policy should be developed, it has not been clear to many why the U.S. has such difficulty achieving such a unified position when compared with other countries.

THE ROLE OF TECHNOLOGICAL DEVELOPMENTS

It is frequently observed that technological change is driving private institutions to pressure the federal government to formulate a U.S.-oriented international communications policy strategy.[4] But technological change is no novelty of the 1980s. For at least 300 years, Western society has experienced repeated shocks from technological developments as those developments have been applied in private industry, warfare, and government administration.

Nevertheless, the dramatic developments in semiconductor-device technology[5] (and the much slower but equally important breakthroughs in computer systems design and development) have not been the sole cause of U.S. policy instability. True, communications technology has become increasingly digitized, and many communications users who come from the data processing disciplines see most telecommunications facilities and issues as specialized aspects of information systems and issues.[6] In some contexts, digital communications equipment is considered in the same category as all other computer equipment, of which it is estimated that almost three million systems were sold during 1982.[7]

Technological changes have certainly been catalysts, if not the sole cause, for policy change, on numerous occasions.[8] A technological breakthrough has no effect until it is sold—until a place is found for it in an existing or new market. While the major technological developments rose from military-supported basic research, their specific market incarnations—such as ENIAC, the transistor, and the integrated circuit—came from mavericks at Bell Labs, MIT, and other academic institutions. At the same time, the marketing breakthroughs have generally emerged by efforts of smaller entrepreneurs—from Univac to DEC to Apple—as new suppliers have emerged to create and satisfy new demands not previously targeted by then-dominant organizations. Then these market breakthroughs (combined in some cases with the demands of military research)—not the existence per se of new technology—have fueled demand for applica-

ALEXANDER D. ROTH ● Mr. Roth is an attorney and computer consultant in Fairfax, Virginia and Washington, D.C. Formerly he was special counsel and director of the Washington office of the American Federation of Information Processing Societies.

tions of new technology to improve competitive positions in existing products (or, in the case of national security, improved weapons and strategic systems).

In summary, new technology has appeared as a factor in the policy arena because private and public[9] organizations are ready to exploit it, and demand the perceived benefits. They are not entirely innocent bystanders, but they themselves supply the primary foci and resources injecting these changes into society.[10] The readiness to exploit the new technology demonstrates that enough is known about it to plan effectively for its use at the level of individual organizations, as well as at the national industrial level. In turn, the market adjustments—not merely the existence of the technological developments themselves—have rendered obsolete regulatory principles that had served the telecommunications arena for decades.

STRENGTHS IN THE SYSTEM AS WEAKNESSES IN POLICYMAKING

In numerous U.S. governmental bureaus and private organizations, efforts have long been underway to attempt to establish U.S. roles in aspects of international communications policymaking.[11] At the international level, other nations are considering the political, economic, social, and military implications of new communications technologies and services to satisfy export trade concerns, to regulate the openness of domestic or foreign access to information considered sensitive, to stem loses in the indigenous data processing employment base, to preserve technological advantages of military value, and to improve their national positions in the international struggle for access to or control of the sources of vital information.[12] From the point of view of the exploitation of information flows for productive or for military purposes, communications facilities are a critical resource in providing a superior channel for new capital, for expertise and technical information, and as a means of access to the sophisticated and economical administration of locally placed facilities for production, marketing, or distribution.

The same uniqueness that makes it so difficult for the U.S. to develop a unified strategy makes other countries apprehensive about the role of the U.S. as the leader in computer/communications technology and regulatory change—the enormous depth and diversity of our economy and natural resources, our reliance on market-place mechanisms for the allocation of resources and economic activity, and the dispersion of authority among our many economic and social constituent groups.

Those differences might be summarized as follows:

1.   The U.S. is economically diverse, and the authority for overall planning and management is dispersed among many interests, joined together only by the presumed action of marketplace principles. Even in the telecommunications arena, our interests and economic structure are significantly more diverse than that of any other nation.

2.   The U.S. government and those in close contact with it are not inclined toward analyzing and predicting future trends. By contrast, the general pattern elsewhere is for centralized, government-controlled entities that take charge of all national telecommunications planning and handle procurement and management of the nation's telecommunications equipment, facilities, and services.[13]

3.   The managerial stratum in the U.S. is diverse in background and goals. In most other countries the entire leadership are alumni of a handful of schools, and interact in the same social milieux. To acquire a critical mass of leadership support in the U.S. requires a great deal more effort and communication, often among individuals who do not regularly deal with—or often even know—each other.

4.   Though both government and industry in the U.S. are generally well-informed about where the technology is going, neither knows how their power interrelationships will change as new markets are created, or as new international arrangements are made.

5.   While Europeans and others depend for their survival on the strategies and planning of their governments, the U.S. private sector generally does not view the U.S. government as an appropriate forum for such activities. Indeed, many view the federal government as a hindrance to productive enterprise and would fear the power the government would have if it could command such cooperation and initiative. The federal role is consequently limited to the negative process of regulation, using sometimes massive public proceedings in an unwieldy approach to balancing conflicting interests.

At stake are new forms of information flows as important as those resulting from the international development of telephone or aeronautical technology in their effect on the economies and societies of all countries, including our own. Attempts to obtain the attention and commitment of the leaderships of Congress and of the administration have been unsuccessful thus far, apparently because no short-term crisis—or perceptible electoral advantage—has stimulated action to date. It appears that constructive progress will require further intellectual development of telecommunications and international information flow issues and a reason for political officials to put resolution of these issues on their active agendas.

NOTES

1. E.g., DOMESTIC COUNCIL COMMITTEE ON THE RIGHT OF PRIVACY, NATIONAL INFORMATION POLICY, (ROCKEFELLER COMMISSION REPORT) (Washington, D.C.: National Commission on Libraries and Information Science, 1976) [hereinafter cited as ROCKEFELLER COMMISSION REPORT].
Kirchner, *Subcommittee Raps Reagan Global Info Policy,* COMPUTERWORLD, Dec. 7, 1981; HOUSE COMM. ON GOVERNMENT OPERATIONS, INTERNATIONAL INFORMATION FLOW: FORGING A NEW FRAMEWORK H.R. REP. NO. 1535, 96th Cong., 2d Sess. (1980) [hereinafter cited as FORGING A NEW FRAMEWORK); SENATE COMMITTEE ON COMMERCE, SCIENCE, AND TRANSPORTATION, LONG-RANGE GOALS IN INTERNATIONAL-TELECOMMUNICATIONS AND INFORMATION: AN OUTLINE FOR UNITED STATES POLICY, 98TH CONG., 1ST SESS., (Comm. Print 1983).
N.B.: The present chapter confines itself to consideration of the regulatory process itself, from the perspective of an observer from the computer industry. Discussion of particular policy concerns or alternatives may be found in other chapters in this volume.
For a more in-depth discussion of the communications regulatory process itself, numerous references are available as of early 1983, including most of the publications cited in these notes, and also the following:
G. ROBINSON, COMMUNICATIONS FOR TOMORROW—POLICY PERSPECTIVES FOR THE 1980s (New York: Praeger, 1978); Dunn, *Developing Information Policy,* 6 TELECOM. POL'Y, March 1982, at 21; Novotny, TRANSBORDER DATA FLOWS AND INTERNATIONAL LAW: A FRAMEWORK FOR POLICY-ORIENTED INQUIRY, 16 STAN. J. INT'L L., Summer 1980, at 141; F. Grad, *Government Regulation of International Telecommunications,* J.

TRANSNAT'L L. (1976).

2. E.G., *Canada*—CONSULTATIVE COMMITTEE ON THE IMPLICATIONS OF TELECOMMUNICATIONS FOR CANADIAN SOVEREIGNTY, TELECOMMUNICATIONS AND CANADA (Ottawa: Information Canada, Mar. 1979). *France*—S. NORA & A. MINC, REPORT ON THE COMPUTERIZATION OF SOCIETY (Paris: Board of Financial Examiners, Dec. 20, 1976); *France*—Commission on Transborder Data Flows, Economic and Legal Aspects of Transborder Data Flows, OECD Doc. DSTI/ICCP/80.26 (Sept. 1980).
Developing Countries—e.g., the concluding resolutions of the SPIN Conference, IBI NEWSLETTER no. 27 (1978); NTIA, INTRODUCTION TO TRANSBORDER DATA FLOWS 41 (Mar. 1980); J. Bortnick, *International Information Flow: The Developing World Perspective,* 14 CORNELL INT'L L.J., Summer 1981, at 333.
Generally—FORGING A NEW FRAMEWORK, *supra* note 1, at 32–36; Feldman, *National Regulation of Transborder Data Flows,* 7 N.C.J. INT'L L. & COM. REG., Winter 1982, at 1.
3. FORGING A NEW FRAMEWORK, *supra* note 1, at 55.
4. Pelton, The Global Electronic Communications Environment 5 infra, ch. 1; Yurow, ISSUES IN INFORMATION POLICY 2, 38 (Washington, D.C.: GPO, Feb. 1980); John M. Adams, DBS Radio and International Broadcasting: An Overview of Legal and Policy Issues Confronting the U.S. (Mar. 23, 1983) (unpublished draft for ABA International Information Networks Project). See also other references from other papers in this volume.
5. One typical recent description of semiconductor developments may be found in Blume, *Semiconductor Device Technology,* in ELECTRONIC MAIL AND MESSAGE SYSTEMS: TECHNICAL AND POLICY PERSPECTIVES, PROCEEDINGS OF THE AFIPS WORKSHOP ON TECHNICAL AND POLICY ISSUES IN ELECTRONIC MAIL AND MESSAGE SYSTEMS 127–37 (Kahn et al. eds. Arlington, Va.: American Federation of Information Processing Societies, 1981) [hereinafter cited as AFIPS].
6. *Cf.* Kobayaski, *The Japanese Computer Industry: Its Roots and Development,* in PROCEEDINGS OF THE THIRD USA—JAPAN COMPUTER CONFERENCE ix (Montvale, N.J.: American Federation of Information Processing Societies, 1979) (keynote speech). Kobayashi, chairman of the board and chief executive officer of Nippon Electric Company, makes the following observation *inter alia* (p. xiv):

This is the key to future development. The loci of development of the computer and communications have intersected, and with the addition of the semiconductor, these three are being united into a single entity, and are poised on the threshold of the next stage of development.

7. Bulkeley, *Microcomputers Gaining Primacy, Forcing Changes in the Industry,* WALL STREET JOURNAL, Jan. 13, 1983, at 33. ("International Data Corp. estimates there are 56,000 mainframe computers in the U.S. and 570,000 minicomputers. It says 2.4 million microcomputers were sold last year alone."); Libes, *Market Share for the P.C.,* BYTE, Apr. 1983, at 458. ("It appears that close to 3 million personal computers were sold last year [based on statistics from International Data Corporation].").

8. *E.g.,* regarding electronic fund transfers *see* NATIONAL SCIENCE FOUNDATION, THE CONSEQUENCES OF ELECTRONIC FUNDS TRANSFERS, NSF-RA/X-75-015, at 218 (Cambridge, Mass.: Authur D. Little, Inc., June 1975).

9. Regarding the effect of FCC regulation on innovation in telecommunications, see Lukasik, *The Impact of FCC Regulation on Innovation in Telecommunication,"* in AFIPS, *supra* note 6, at 105–25.

10. *Cf.* A.M. Rutkowski, Emerging International Information Transport Barriers 1 (Dec. 10, 1981) (presentation before International Institute of Communications, Symposium on Communications and International Trade, Washington D.C. ("It is also apparent that information technology, facilities, and user demands are symbiotically progressing at an exponential rate of development towards an integrated information services environment.").

11. *E.g.,* the OECD Guidelines effort, which resulted in Draft Guidelines Governing the Protection of Privacy and Transborder Flows of Personal Data, DSTI/ICCP/79.40 (2nd revision) Scale E (subsequently adopted by the OECD), *reproduced in* INT'L LEGAL MATERIALS, March 1980, at 318.

See also, e.g., ROCKEFELLER COMMISSION REPORT, *supra* note 1, at 182 *et seq.,* U.S. DEPT. OF COMMERCE, LOWERING BARRIERS TO TELECOMMUNICATIONS GROWTH 1923 (D. Crombie ed. Nov. 1976); FORGING A NEW FRAMEWORK, *supra* note 1, at 8–9, 41–53.

12. For more comprehensive reviews of the issues that have arisen in the area of international information flows (also known as transborder data flows), *see An Overview of Transborder Data Flow Issues,* in R. TURN, 1 TRANSBORDER DATA FLOWS: CONCERNS IN PRIVACY PROTECTION AND FREE FLOW OF INFORMATION, REPORT OF THE AFIPS PANEL ON TRANSBORDER DATA FLOW (1979) [hereinafter cited as TDF REPORT]; and FORGING A NEW FRAMEWORK, *supra* note 1, at 12–27.

13. J. Yurow, infra. chap. 20; AFIPS TDF Report, *supra* note 12, at 24–30; Markoski, *Telecommunications Regulation as Barriers to the Transborder Flow of Information,* 14 CORNELL INT'L L.J., Summer 1981, at 287, 289–296; FORGING A NEW FRAMEWORK, *supra* note 1, at 36, 38, 40; CERNI, THE CCITT: ORGANIZATION, U.S. PARTICIPATION, AND STUDIES TOWARD THE ISDN (NTIA Report 82-101, (U.S. Dept. of Commerce, Ap. 1982).

CHAPTER 26

MULTINATIONAL CORPORATIONS AND NATIONAL SOVEREIGNTY

SOL GLASNER

INTRODUCTION

The multinational corporation (MNC) has emerged as one of the industrialized world's primary engines for economic growth. It is uniquely positioned for pursuing a global business strategy aimed at maximizing productivity and return on investment.

The MNC's key to success is its ability to process transactions quickly. As such, operational efficiencies are realized through the rapid manipulation of information. Data flows over national boundaries therefore constitute an integral and essential part of the MNC's performance. Serving as the source of the MNC's vitality, transborder data flows (TDFs) have freed it from traditional limits to its growth and in the process have become a basic part of the world's economic machinery.

Attempts to understand the concerns often associated with the proliferation of TDFs have usually concentrated on issues of trade, privacy, and economics. But, fundamental to all is the notion of national sovereignty. Using the term in its colloquial sense, the MNC has been viewed as a challenge to the power of nation-states. Seen this way, data flows allow the MNC to operate as a closed universe, notwithstanding national boundaries. Feelings of vulnerability, uneasiness, and loss of control have been articulated by some nations in response to the phenomenon of TDFs within the MNC context.

The same is true when considering national sovereignty in its narrower, legal sense. Here too, TDFs may appear to cut against the classical concept of territorial-based control.

Against this background, the rallying cry of "free flow of information" appears weak. From the perspective of nations concerned about their sovereignty, one must question whether the "free flow" banner is credible. An appreciation of the national sovereignty aspect of TDFs adds a new dimension to the search for an optimum U.S. policy.

THE MULTINATIONAL–TRANSBORDER DATA FLOW CONNECTION

The cost of telephoning long distance has declined to the point that Americans alone place upwards of 100,000 overseas calls daily. Add to this the ability of computers to transmit and regroup large quantities of data rapidly and the basic elements of a complex, international information system are assembled.[1] At this system's center are the manufacturing, industrial, financial, and administrative operations of the MNCs[2] whose viability as geographically dispersed enterprises rests on their ability to move information rapidly.[3]

Most conventional data flows are those that circulate among the subsidiaries and headquarters of multinational organizations.[4] The government of Brazil, for example, has identified 27 out of 29 transnational computer–communications links established in that country as having been created by MNCs.[5]

SOL GLASNER • Mr. Glasner, a member of the District of Columbia Bar, manages government relations issues for the Sperry Corporation, dealing extensively with telecommunications and information flows issues.

Even more significant is the quality of the relationship between transborder data flows and the spread of multinational corporations. It is best described by a boastful Hewlett-Packard advertisement of several years ago:

> Today we make 4,000 different products at 40 divisions around the world and have offices in 65 countries. This rapid financial and geographical expansion in a highly technical field made the distribution of our data processing an absolute necessity.
>
> As we continued to grow, we connected our widespread sales offices with the factories. Today we have 130 high-speed communications systems in 94 locations, sending compressed data via satellite and phone lines. About 12 million words a day come into our California headquarters.[6]

Driving the MNCs' craving for information are the volatility and complexity that characterize modern economic interaction. Gyrating exchange rates and commodity prices require the MNCs to assimilate large volumes of time-sensitive data.

The bond between MNCs and data flows is integral and mutually reinforcing. Central control over decentralized operations, made increasingly more workable by TDFs, has fueled the impressive expansion and geographic dispersion of business enterprises since World War II.[7] Thus, TDFs have allowed multinationals to pursue what some have called an "integrated global strategy."[8] By inference, the global networks forged through TDFs enable the world's modern economies to function.

THE SOVEREIGNTY OF NATIONS

International law explains sovereignty as a principle fundamental to nationhood—"an inherent and unimpeachable attribute of the state."[9] Judge Anzilotti of the Permanent Court of International Justice defines it with elegant simplicity: "The state has over it no other authority than that of international law."[10] He distinguishes this from the equally fundamental "domestic jurisdiction," the freedom to exercise sovereignty within a state's territory in the absence of overriding international law principles. Finally, the practice of national sovereignty is made possible by widespread adherence to nonintervention, a principle now enshrined in the 1975 Helsinki Agreement.[11]

More pertinent to the fears sparked by MNC-generated data flows, is sovereignty's economic dimension. Invariably, this is expressed in terms such as control over growth, pace of industrial development, access to economic power, and knowledge of available alternatives.[12]

The movement of information has been imbued with economic value. That perception is reflected in the famous equation of Louis Jionet, secretary-general of the French Commission on Data Processing and Liberties:

> Information is power and economic information is economic power. Information has an economic value and the ability to store and process certain types of data may well give one country political and technological advantage over other countries. This in turn leads to a loss of national sovereignty through supranational data flows.[13]

The link between sovereignty and economic interest makes it no surprise that political sovereignty is often measured by the extent of control over local resources.[14] Thus, in the case of information, sovereignty has been measured by national control over its collection, storage, analysis, manipulation, and transmission.[15] Seen either as a commodity for sale and purchase, or as the cutting edge of technological advancement, information is increasingly viewed as the key to economic growth.

Characterized as "the epitome of the trend toward interdependence,"[16] the MNC has spawned higher levels of international trade, increased flows of technical service, and expanded movements of international capital. At its core, the fear of an MNC threat to national sovereignty may be the inevitable byproduct of interaction between two powerful systems, each of which responds to different principles and operates within a dissimilar framework. Each system strives to generate wealth by manipulating vast resources, yet neither could truly discharge the other's functions.[17]

Sovereignty's broad sweep makes it difficult to pinpoint the specific components of the conflict between MNCs and states. The precise characteristics of MNC activity that give rise to apprehensions of eroding sovereignty elude analytic precision, lending themselves instead to rhetorical flourishes. A systematic approach to the friction which often characterizes the MNC–state relationship would help give substantive form and a more focused urgency to these fears. Sovereignty-related concerns span a range of issues beginning with abstract and traditional notions of the nation-state's role in the international system, and culminating with the material impact on national economic prosperity.

The Nation-State's Role: Preserving Tradition

Traditionally, national sovereignty has been defined with reference to physical boundaries. These represented the inviolable source and protector of national expression. Contrary to the self-image of most MNCs, they are often viewed as a serious challenge to the integrity of those boundaries,[18] a perception heightened by modern communications technology.

The advent of Satellite Business Systems, Inc.,[19] founded as a provider of advanced communications capabilities to large multinational business enterprises, has been described as the ultimate step toward the obliteration of borders: "A new scheme for the merger of two information technologies—the computer and the satellite— ... eliminates, once and for all, spatial boundaries which have been the last line of defense for national governments."[20] The nervousness is echoed in the Canadian report of the Clyne Commission: "Recent technological advances have eliminated the need to consider national borders in the planning and development of complex informatics systems."[21]

The feeling that borders have been rendered obsolete has sparked alarm for the consequences of such obsolescence. According to Alain Madec, the "present vigor of the nation state" is under siege. Madec argues that TDFs promote the "decay of the nation-state." In this view the new information technologies allow state territories to be used merely as platforms for fragments of supranational activities.[22]

Madec's point echoed the earlier Nora–Minc study which articulates an apocalyptic despair of the borderless world forged by MNC data flows:

> Once a manufacturer of machines, soon to become a telecommunications administrator, IBM is following a strategy which will enable it to set up a communications network and to control it. When it does, it will encroach upon a traditional sphere of government power, communications.[23]

Nora–Minc should be criticized for its polemics, but it does accurately reflect the insecurity experienced by states in dealing with the pairing of MNCs with advanced communications technologies.

Issues of Control

Issues of control arising in the context of corporate data flows are multifaceted. They encompass questions of legal jurisdiction, extraterritoriality, and reliance on outside sources. Their significance lies, of course, in the fact of perception, not necessarily in its accuracy.

INFORMATION. Control over information, in its broadest sense, is deemed a critical attribute of sovereignty. TDFs have been linked to the potential for slippage of that control. This prospect is invariably seen as a threat to national sovereignty having profound consequences.

> [An] increasing number of nations worry that the loss of control over information about internal functions can jeopardize their sovereignty and leave them open to possible disruptions ranging from uncontrollable technical failures to political sabotage.[24]

The Canadian response to TDFs illustrates the sensitivity on this point. Loss of control over information is ascribed to TDFs and is depicted as the initial step in the total degeneration of decision-making capacity: "This migration of key decision-making functions could seriously erode Canadian control over future social and economic development."[25]

EXTRATERRITORIALITY. MNC networks, no matter how complex their role, are often suspected of simply functioning as conduits for the projection of a sovereign's power into another's territory.[26]

These suspicions were inadvertently bolstered in mid-1982 when the Reagan administration sought to enforce sanctions against the trans-Siberian pipeline project. For reasons of foreign policy, the U.S. government sought to preclude foreign subsidiaries of U.S.-based companies from servicing the pipeline. In the case of at least one major American company, the desired result was achieved by pulling the plug on data flow: "'Somebody in Pittsburgh,' where Dresser's data base was then housed, 'flipped the switch, and suddenly Dresser-France was cut off,'"[27] The fears of those who have long cautioned against reliance on foreign computer services suddenly seemed credible. In the Dresser case, TDFs became the vehicle for achieving political objectives through the extraterritorial application of home country law.

The pipeline incident may have also strengthened other misgivings about corporate citizens who store and process data overseas.[28] Intracorporate data flows travelling outside the medium of state-owned PTTs are usually regarded as beyond a state's normal access, perhaps causing a diminution in the practical reach of a state's law enforcement leverage.[29] Government's ability to assure compliance with its laws and regulations is inevitably questioned.[30] Fears of eroding jurisdiction have contributed to the view, expressed in some quarters, that data flows, such as those facilitated by Satellite Business Systems, are responsible for "removing the last link in their [MNCs] activities susceptible to government scrutiny and action."[31]

ECONOMIC. Concerns dealing with loss of national "control" usually resolve themselves into questions of economic benefit or detriment. Though the "information age" is lauded as the key to economic prosperity, nations are most responsive to their more immediate pressures. Lost jobs, for example, have been attributed to remote processing activities. Canada has estimated that by 1985 it will import $1.5 billion in computing services, chiefly rendered from foreign headquarters to Canadian subsidiaries. For Canada, this translates to a loss of 23,000 directly related jobs.[32] Though often expressed in philosophical terms as an abhorrence of "dependence on foreign computing staff, which would result in turn in lower requirements for Canadian expertise," clearly the problem is one of tangible consequences.[33]

Canada's director-general for communications has provided a graphic portrayal of the Canadian perception.

> This is an era when even the sale of individual hamburgers may be considered important enough to be registered on a computerized cash register and transmitted hundreds of miles to another location for analysis .... [We] must avoid the scenario where our young people might find jobs cooking and selling them, but are precluded from any attendant data processing, systems analysis, market research or corporate decision making functions.[34]

Less susceptible to measurement than employment levels is the movement of financial data itself. The SWIFT network, for example, is used by banks to carry hundreds of thousands of transactions daily, outside the direct control of any nation or international agency. The worldwide flows of money that are managed through SWIFT have been characterized as a destabilizing force of great magnitude. Similarly, the ability of MNCs to shunt large sums of money electronically from one point to another and to convert assets quickly from one currency to another has been criticized as a distortion of local markets.[35]

ECONOMIC DEVELOPMENT. Control over economic destiny assumes a more complex, politically charged dimension when considered in context of the relationship between developed and developing countries. Corporate data flows have been blamed for reinforcing the split

between the relatively menial industrial jobs performed in the developing nations and the intellectual, decision-making responsibilities centered in the data-rich developed countries. This rather stark view of the North–South friction over TDFs was labeled in typically caustic fashion by Alain Madec as the "terminal society," in which a centralized brain directs less significant operational activity from a distance and sales are executed via terminals located in medium-size powers.[36]

From the perspective of the developing countries, the international data market and the application of TDFs for corporate purposes, is almost exclusively the province of the developed market economies. In this model, the developing nations are exploited as suppliers of raw data and as buyers of finished information but are not involved in the lucrative intermediary steps.

Among the developing countries, Brazil has set the pace in linking its development problems to TDFs, and in devising a comprehensive strategy for dealing with them. Having recognized and articulated the challenges, principally economic, to its sovereignty, Brazil has embraced a philosophy of overt protectionism.

> From the perspective of these [multinational] corporations, such [TDF] strategies are certainly understandable because they are normally meant to increase corporate efficiency. From the point of view of Brazil, however, the potential impact of these strategies on the development process ... also have to be taken into consideration ... Brazil's transborder-data-flows policy is aimed at orienting the usage of links in a manner that contributes to the development prospects of the country.[37]

WHITHER "FREE FLOW"?

American policy regarding international communications issues has been widely criticized as fuzzy in concept and chaotic in implementation. The low esteem for U.S. international telecommunications policy has been a regular theme of official U.S. pronouncements. It was the central point of the first major congressional study on the subject, published in 1980.

> It [U.S. government] has developed neither comprehensive plans or policies nor a coherent strategy for responding to the policies of other nations which may damage U.S. interests. The U.S. Government does not have even the organizational structure to develop such policies, coordinate its actions and effectively protect U.S. interests .... it is incapable of providing the coordination of government action and the development

of policy necessary to anticipate and respond to the rapid change in international communications and the growth of barriers to the flow of information.[38]

Three years later, the gap in U.S. policy provided the impetus for a major government study of international telecommunications.

Policy has evolved in piecemeal fashion. Problems have been aggravated by inadequate high-level attention and insufficient coordination among the diverse departments and agencies involved. The net result too often has been confusion, needless jurisdictional disputes and consequent lack of adequate preparation—all of which place the United States at a serious disadvantage.[39]

Despite the overall disarray that has been ascribed to U.S. international telecommunications policy, it is distinguished by remarkably steadfast adherence to promotion of the "free flow of information." Imbued with the aura of the First Amendment, the principle of "free flow" commands unswerving American loyalty. As a goal and statement of philosophical commitment, "free flow" is laudable. Its universal implementation would surely serve American interests so long as the U.S. retained its telecommunications dominance.[40]

However, as the *strategic* pillar of American policy, "free flow'" is inadequate. It fails for at least two reasons. First, it does not address the fear of eroding sovereignty that lies at the root of states' antipathy to MNCs and their use of TDFs. Second, though "free flow" appeals to international law for its legitimacy, it does not account for the sovereign prerogatives that the same international law grants to states.

States' perception that TDFs challenge their sovereignty can be expected to elicit measures aimed at shoring up state control, i.e., restricting TDFs. In the context of sovereignty-based concerns, the chant for a worldwide commitment to "free flow" is almost beside the point, skirting the essential issues. The recently-issued National Telecommunications and Information Administration (NTIA) study alluded to this fundamental flaw in U.S. strategy:

U.S. strategists have been forced to recognize that in an area such as telecommunications and information processing, in which a "national capacity" is widely viewed as being of strategic importance to a country's economic well-being and security, attempts to dissuade governments from taking restrictive measures based on argu-

ments of "optimization" of global resources may not be adequate.[41]

The extent to which the prerogatives of sovereignty are embedded in international law also inspires skepticism of "free flow's" role as the cornerstone of policy.

The claim that free flow is a fundamental human right, while appealing to Americans steeped in the Bill of Rights tradition, is inconsistent with the ambiguity of international law on this point.[42] Article 19 of the Universal Declaration of Human Rights is often used to substantiate the human rights claim. Article 29, however, limits the exercise of rights granted elsewhere in the Declaration for reasons of "public order," an exception that conceivably could be used to restrain the flow of computer communications.

The drumroll for "free flow" based on international law principles glosses over the international law authority for the right of states to restrict information flows. The International Telecommunications Union Convention, for example, has been interpreted by some to allow states to stop private telegrams and to interrupt other private telecommunications on national security grounds.[43]

CONCLUSION

Transborder data flow is foremost a phenomenon associated with multinational corporations. Efforts by states to confine the movement of data and information are therefore an aspect of the interaction between states and MNCs.

Statehood is characterized by the exercise of sovereignty, a concept best defined in terms of political and economic control. Feeling that their control is undermined by MNCs' pursuit of supranational activity, states perceive a threat to their sovereignty posed by MNCs' extensive use of TDFs.

Recognition that state-imposed restrictions on TDFs are motivated in large part by fears of eroding sovereignty calls into question the strategic reliance on promotion of the "free flow of information" as the primary U.S. policy focus. Appeals for "free flow" are not persuasive for countries preoccupied with preserving their sovereignty. Similarly, the use of international law to substantiate the universality of the "free flow" principle may be misplaced. International law grants prerogatives to sovereign states which arguably may be inconsistent with "free flow."

NOTES

1. P. VERNON, STORM OVER THE MULTINATIONALS, 2 (Cambridge, Mass.: Harvard University Press, 1977). *See* R. TURN, COMPUTERS IN THE 1980s 53–59 (New York: Columbia University Press, 1974).

2. K. NORDENSTRENG & H. SCHILLER, NATIONAL SOVEREIGNTY AND INTERNATIONAL COMMUNICATION, 22 (Norwood, New Jersey: Ablex, 1979). *See* Mowlana, *The Multinational Corporation and the Diffusion of Technology,* in THE NEW SOVEREIGNS: MULTINATIONAL CORPORATIONS AS WORLD POWERS 77 (A. Said & L. Simmons eds. Englewood Cliffs, N.J.: Prentice-Hall, 1975).

3. *See* Rappaport, Allen, & Turn, *TDF-Dependent Organization Enterprises,* in TRANSBORDER DATA FLOWS: CONCERNS IN PRIVACY PROTECTION AND FREE FLOW OF INFORMATION 35 (R. Turn ed. Arlington, Va.: American Federation of Information Processing Societies, 1979).

4. *See* Canada Department of Communications, *Questions Before Answers,* 9 INTERMEDIA, March 1981.

5. BRAZIL SPECIAL SECRETARIAT OF INFORMATICS, TRANSBORDER DATA FLOWS OF BRAZIL: THE ROLE OF TRANSNATIONAL CORPORATIONS, IMPACTS OF TRANSBORDER DATA FLOWS AND EFFECTS OF NATIONAL POLICIES (1982) [hereinafter cited as BRAZIL SPECIAL SECRETARIAT].

6. Advertisement in *Fortune* (Jan. 30, 1978), cited in Jacobson, *Satellite Business Systems and the Concept of the Dispersed Enterprise: An End to National Sovereignty?* MEDIA CULTURE SOVEREIGNTY 235, 248 (1979).

7. Rappaport, Allen, & Turn, *supra* note 3. For a detailed description of TDF's impact on multinational corporations, see C. ANTONELLI, TRANSBORDER DATA FLOWS AND INTERNATIONAL BUSINESS: A PILOT STUDY 50–53 (Expert Group on Transborder Data Flows, Organization for Economic Cooperation and Development, 1981).

8. United Nations Center on Transnational Corporations, *Transborder Data Flows,* 10 INTERMEDIA, May 1982, at 48 [hereinafter cited as U.N. Center].

9. Jessup, *Equality of State as Dogma and Reality,* 60 POL. SCI. Q. 527–30 (1945).

10. Gross, *Some International Law Aspects of the Freedom of Information and the Right to Communicate,* in NORDENSTRENG & SCHILLER, *supra* note 2, at 198.

11. *Id.* at 199.

12. *See* CONSULTATIVE COMMITTEE ON THE IMPLICATIONS OF TELECOMMUNICATIONS FOR CANADIAN SOVEREIGNTY, TELECOMMUNICATIONS AND CANADA (1979) [hereinafter cited as CONSULTATIVE COMMITTEE; U.N. Center, *supra* note 8 P. VERNON, *supra* note 1.

13. Quoted HOUSE COMM. ON GOVERNMENT OPERATIONS, INTERNATIONAL INFORMATION FLOW FORGING A NEW FRAMEWORK, H.R. Rep. No. 1535, 96th Cong., 2d Sess. 20 n.49 (1980).

14. *Id.* at 21; CONSULTATIVE COMMITTEE, *supra* note 12, at 1–5.

15. Jacobson, *supra* note 6, at 251.

16. P. VERNON, *supra* note 1, at 193.

17. *Id.* at 177.

18. *See Id.* at 211–12.

19. Satellite Business Systems (SBS), a partnership of International Business Machines (IBM), Communications Satellite Corp. (Comsat), and Aetna Life Insurance Co., formed in 1975 to provide private satellite communications services.

20. Jacobson, *supra* note 6, at 236.

21. CONSULTATIVE COMMITTEE, *supra* note 12, at 63.

22. Alain Madec, a French government official who chaired a special commission on TDFs, appointed in late 1979 by French President Valery Giscard d'Estaing. Madec, *The Political Economy of Information Flows,* 9 INTERMEDIA, March 1981.

23. S. NORA & A. MINC, REPORT ON THE COMPUTERIZATION OF SOCIETY 3–4 (1978) (NTIA version). Despite Nora-Minc's shrill tone, it is a useful reflection of widely held feelings.

24. HOUSE COMM., *supra* note 13, at 22.

25. Robinson, *Strategic Issues Related to Transborder Data Flow,* 1979 TELECOMMUNICATIONS 85. Canada's minister for science and technology, Hugh Faulkner, makes a similar point: "There is the danger of loss of legitimate access to vital information and the danger that industrial and social developments largely will be governed by the decisions of interest groups residing in another country," quoted in Jacobson, *supra* note 6, at 250.

26. P. VERNON, *supra* note 1, at 177.

27. N.Y. Times, Mar. 13, 1983, § 3 (Business), at 1 (quoting E. Luter, Dresser vice president for finance).

28. The Canadian "Clyne Commission" cited this issue as a basis for its recommendation that data processing related to business operations be per-

formed in Canada. Consultative Committee, *supra* note 12, at 64–65.

29. Jacobson, *supra* note 6, at 249.

30. E. Kriegler, luncheon address, Symposium on Communications and International Trade proceedings published by U.S. National Committee of the International Institute of Communications, at 51 (1982).

31. Jacobson, *supra* note 6, at 237.

32. Robinson, *supra* note 25, at 85.

33. Consultative Committee, *supra* note 12, at 64.

34. E. Kriegler, *supra* note 30, at 55–56.

35. Jacobson, *supra* note 6, at 250.

36. Madec, *supra* note 22, at 22.

37. Brazil Special Secretariat, *supra* note 5, at 2.

38. House Comm., *supra* note 13, at 2.

39. National Telecommunications and Information Administration (NTIA), Long Range Goals in International Telecommunications and Information 9, 98th Cong., 1st Sess. (Comm. Print 1983) [hereinafter cited as NTIA].

40. *See* Spero, *Information: The Policy Void*, 48 Foreign Pol'y 139 (1982).

41. NTIA, *supra* note 39, at 33.

42. The extent to which international law grants a "right to communicate" is unsettled. Some of the literature reconciles the apparent ambiguities in favor of an explicit right. *See, e.g.,* Feldman, *Commercial Speech, Transborder Data Flows and the Right to Communicate Under International Law,* 17 Int'l Law. 87 (1983) infra, chap. 27. My intention here is not to choose sides, but rather, by noting the ambiguities, to highlight the limitations of "freeflow" as an instrument of policy.

43. Article 19, International Telecommunications Union, International Telecommunications Convention, Malaga-Torremolinos, 1973.

> 109 1. Members reserve the right to stop the transmission of any private telegram which may appear dangerous to the security of the State or contrary to their laws, to public order or decency, provided that they immediately notify the office of origin of the stoppage of any telegram or any part thereof, except when such notification may appear dangerous to the security of the State.
>
> 110 2. Members also reserve the right to cut off any other private telecommunications which may appear dangerous to the security of the State or contrary to their laws, to public order or to decency.

See Novotny, *Transborder Data Flows and International Law: A Framework for Policy-Oriented Inquiry,* 16 Stan. J. Int'l L. 141, 166 (1980).

CHAPTER 27

THE RIGHT TO COMMUNICATE UNDER INTERNATIONAL LAW

MARK B. FELDMAN

For several years now, proponents of a "new world information order" have challenged the free flow of news, data, and advertising across national frontiers. One result of this clash between democratic values and, primarily, Third World concerns about the social, economic, and political implications of the new information technologies has been debate about the need for a newly defined "right to communicate" under international law. The author believes a right to communicate already exists under international law that embraces commercial speech and transborder data flows.

The issue can be framed by reference to two brief texts: The first is Article 19 of the Universal Declaration of Human Rights, which was adopted unanimously by the General Assembly of the United Nations on December 10, 1948:

> Everyone has the right to freedom of opinion and expression; this right includes the freedom to hold opinions without interference and to seek, receive and impart information and ideas through any media and regardless of frontiers.

The second text is Paragraph 10 of the Declaration of Mexico on Informatics, Development and Peace, adopted by the Intergovernmental Bureau for Informatics (IBI) on June 23, 1981:

> The right to information such as it is recognised by the Universal Declaration of Human Rights and international

treaties has acquired, due to the technological revolution, a scope which is qualitatively and quantitatively different from that which prevailed when they were adopted. The concept of the "right to information" needs to be re-interpreted in the light of changes due to informatics.

The latter statement reflects the concern of the leadership of some developing countries that Western domination of the new technologies of the information era will increase the gap in economic development between the rich and poor nations and influence unduly the cultural and political life of the Third World. A number of industrial countries have concerns of their own about the economic and social implications of transnational information flows. These concerns range from the protection of personal privacy to the protection of emerging high-technology industries. One result of the LDC concerns has been efforts in the United Nations to project a new international information order. Another result of concerns in various countries has been the proliferation of obstacles to the free flow of information; these take a variety of forms ranging from privacy legislation to discriminatory pricing of telecommunications services.

All countries have a legitimate interest in enjoying a fair share of the benefits of the new technologies. In my view, these interests are poorly served by attacks upon the freedom to impart and to receive information, which is recognized in the Universal Declaration of Human

MARK B. FELDMAN ● Mark B. Feldman is a partner at Donovan Leisure Newton & Irvine in the Washington, D.C. office, and Adjunct Professor of Law at Georgetown University.

Rights. That freedom is not absolute in any country, and it is scarcely realized in many. But it remains an essential element of man's aspirations to self-government. It is my view that any effort to restrict the principle of the free flow of information should be firmly resisted by the United States and by like-minded countries. We must also resist protectionist economic measures if the international community is to derive the full benefit of the new technologies.

On the other hand, there may be an interest shared by a great many countries in developing a new set of internationally recognized rights and responsibilities relating to transborder information flows that would encourage technological innovation and economic growth by facilitating the free flow of commercial information and the development of informatics industries wherever they can serve the public. In fact, elements of such a legal regime are beginning to emerge from the actions of national authorities and international organizations. I would go so far as to suggest that we can now outline a general principle of international law that can be the basis for the elaboration of an international legal regime by negotiation on various levels and by reciprocal national rule-making. It is unlikely that this process will result in agreement on a general treaty on the right to communicate under international law. It is more likely to produce a number of agreed points arising out of the accommodation of specific interests in particular economic and legal contexts. I shall attempt to identify the present sources of a right to communicate under international law and those areas where substantial work is needed in the future.

At the outset, I should like to mention a number of interests that need to be accommodated in any meaningful international regime for transborder data flows:

1. the right to establish and to operate data-processing, information, and other computer services within states and across international boundaries;
2. the right of access to foreign databases and data-processing facilities and to international communications links at reasonable rates and without discrimination;
3. the diffusion of new technologies on reasonable commercial terms;
4. the recognition of proprietary interests in new forms of intellectual property and technology such as computer software and satellite signals;
5. the protection of personal privacy; and
6. the interests of all states in national security, economic development, and the public health and safety.

Any legal regime that encompasses these interests, if it is to be broadly acceptable, will have to reflect a balance of rights and responsibilities. It will have to allow sovereign states a measure of discretion in the implementation of the regime, and it must represent a broad mutuality of economic interests. With these aims in mind I shall now address the basis of a legal right to communicate under international law that is becoming discernible in existing texts and practices.

The starting point is Article 19 of the Universal Declaration of Human Rights.[1] A strong argument can be made that the right stated there to receive and to impart information is an international legal norm that applies to commercial speech and to transborder data flows. Although resolutions of the General Assembly of the United Nations do not have the force of law, the Universal Declaration was adopted unanimously and is widely regarded as being declaratory of general principles of international law.[2] Moreover, 69 countries have accepted the principle of freedom of information as a matter of treaty obligation, by adhering to the International Covenant on Civil and Political Rights.[3] Article 19 of the covenant is nearly identical to Article 19 of the Universal Declaration except for its omission of a specific reference to the freedom to hold opinions. Both texts state expressly that the freedom to receive and to impart information and ideas applies to "any media" and "regardless of frontiers."

The fact that this freedom is severely restricted in many countries does not mean there is no international norm. If observance were the sole criterion, most of the basic human rights recognized in the Universal Declaration would have to be deemed premature. The recognition of these norms as law is important, even if they are implemented imperfectly. Under Chapter IX of the United Nations Charter, states are responsible internationally for the treatment of their own nationals, as well as aliens, as regards basic human rights and fundamental freedoms.[4] The abuse of human rights is now an appropriate subject for diplomatic representations and for action by international organizations.

At the same time, it must be recognized that the right to receive and to impart information is not absolute. It has limitations and it implies responsibilities. In our own society we accept the prohibition of defamation. We punish the unauthorized reproduction of copyrighted works. We impose limits on obscenity and, in the case of a clear and present danger, we sometimes restrict political speech.

At the international level, Article 29 of the Universal Declaration recognizes that governments may restrict certain rights, including the freedom of information, "for the purpose of securing due recognition and respect for the rights and freedoms of others and of meeting the just requirements of morality, public order and the general welfare in a democratic society." Article 19 of the International Covenant on Civil and Political Rights refers to national security as well as public order, health, and morals.[5] Each state has the responsibility to permit the free flow of information but it also must protect other human rights and freedoms. The way states balance these interests when the interests compete determines the legal and political environment in which we live.

In the context of such a balancing process, it can be argued that the international right to freedom of information extends to commercial speech and data flows "through any media and regardless of frontiers." Support for this position can be found in the jurisprudence of the United States Supreme Court respecting the First Amendment; in various international agreements; in scholarship; and in the recent work of international organizations relating to the protection of privacy in the context of transborder data flows. All of these developments flow from the recognition that the free flow of information is essential to the public and private decision making that is necessary for economic activity.

The Supreme Court addressed this fundamental fact in 1976 in the case of *Virginia State Board of Pharmacy v. Virginia Citizens Consumer Council*,[6] where it held unconstitutional as an infringement of the First and Fourteenth Amendments a state law forbidding price advertising for prescription drugs. The Court said:

So long as we preserve a predominantly free enterprise economy, the allocation of our resources in large measure will be made through numerous private economic decisions. It is a matter of public interest that these decisions, in the aggregate, be intelligent and well informed. To this end, the free flow of commercial information is indispensable.[7]

This rationale has been applied by the Supreme Court in other cases holding invalid state or local regulations barring the posting of "For Sale" signs,[8] barring adver-

tising of contraceptives,[9] and barring advertising prices of routine legal services.[10]

The Court has made clear, however, that the right of commercial speech under the First Amendment is not absolute. To be protected, commercial speech must concern lawful activity and it must not be misleading. Even protected commercial speech can be restricted by law when the government is seeking to promote a substantial public interest, the regulation directly advances that interest, and the restriction imposed is not more extensive than necessary. The Court developed this analysis in 1980 in the case of *Central Hudson Gas & Electric Corp. v. Public Service Commission*,[11] where it struck down a regulation banning all promotional advertising by electric utilities because it believed the state could promote the conservation of energy by less intrusive means.

In July 1981, the Court reviewed an ordinance of the City of San Diego prohibiting, for esthetic reasons and for traffic safety, most billboards except certain campaign posters and commercial billboards advertising goods manufactured and services rendered on the premises.[12] The ordinance was held unconstitutional because of its effects on noncommercial speech, but a majority of the Justices indicated they could have approved that particular restriction of commercial speech. It may be too soon to determine whether this dictum represents a change of emphasis, but the Court continues to strike down overly broad state regulations of commercial speech. In a recent case, decided on January 25, 1982, *In re R.M.J.*, the Supreme Court held that the states could not prescribe the precise wording of lawyers' advertisements absent a showing that the prescribed phrases are the only means of avoiding deception.[13]

Thus, the Supreme Court has recognized that the importance of informed decision making in the marketplace gives rise to a First Amendment right to communicate truthful information concerning commercial transactions. However, government may restrict that right to protect other public interests, provided the regulation directly serves that interest and is not more intrusive than necessary.

It is interesting to consider for a moment how this test would apply to the recommendations adopted by the World Health Organization in 1981 in the Code of Marketing of Breastmilk Substitutes.[14] The code recommends that states enact legislation to prohibit all advertising to the general public for those products and to regulate in great detail the contents of their labels and other promotional materials. The code's goal—promoting infants' health by encouraging breastfeeding—is surely a substantial one. Nevertheless, there are less restrictive means of achieving that goal than a total ban upon the communication of truthful information. Public attention has focused on the serious problems of malnutrition in the Third World, but I have seen very little comment on the serious implications of legal measures prohibiting speech.

There is no specific authority extending the First Amendment principles adopted by the Supreme Court to international law, but the Court's decisions have influenced the development of international law in the past.[15] In this case, the Court's rationale—the requirements of informed decision making—applies with equal force to Article 19 of the Universal Declaration, which is the counterpart in international law of the First Amendment. We cannot expect the international community to follow the United States example precisely, but there are shared interests in recognizing that states must consider the public interest in the free flow of information when regulating commercial speech and data flows. It should not be assumed, for instance, that national regulation of international information flows are valid, if they are intended to subvert, or have the effect of subverting, international agreements or standards relating to trade, telecommunications, or transportation. Some regulations of information may violate the GATT or bilateral commercial treaties. Others may contravene regulations or recommendations under the International Telecommunications Convention.

Moreover, recent international acts concerning transborder data flows have applied the same kind of standard to national regulation in the interest of privacy as the Supreme Court has applied to commercial speech. This issue has been addressed by the Organization of Economic Cooperation and Development in the *Guidelines on the Protection of Privacy and Transborder Flows of Personal Data* adopted on September 23, 1980[16] and by the Council of Europe in the Convention for the Protection of Individuals with Regard to Automatic Processing of Personal Data, signed at Strasbourg on July 28, 1981.[17] The two instruments promote the same basic principles of personal privacy and individual liberty: (1) that personal data should be collected by legitimate means for limited economic and commercial

purposes; (2) that the information collected and stored should be relevant to those purposes and used for no other; (3) that such personal data should be accurate and confidential; and (4) that an individual should have access to data concerning him or her, the right to challenge the relevance and accuracy of those data, and the right to have it erased or corrected, if the challenge is successful.[18]

Both instruments contemplate government regulation to protect these interests. The OECD guidelines recommend that member states take account of these principles in their national legislation. The Council of Europe Convention obligates states that become party to it to enact legislation to enforce these principles. However, both instruments recognize that the free flow of personal data across frontiers is essential to economic activity[19] and both incorporate limitations on government regulation of transborder data flows in the name of privacy.

Specifically, the guidelines state that "member countries should avoid developing laws, policies, and practices in the name of the protection of privacy and individual liberties, which could create obstacles to transborder flows of processed data that would exceed requirements for such protection."[20] This sounds very much like the the standard applied by the Supreme Court to state regulation of commercial speech. In the same vein, Article 12 of the convention provides in effect that no state party to the convention shall restrict "transborder flows of personal data going to the territory of another party . . . for the sole purpose of the protection of privacy . . . where the regulations of the other party provide an equivalent protection." Restriction in that circumstance would be excessive for the purpose.

Support for this type of analysis also can be found in a thoughtful paper prepared for UNESCO in 1981 by Desmond Fisher, an Irish broadcasting official.[21] Although I cannot accept Fisher's premise that Article 19 of the Universal Declaration needs to be restated, and I find his formulation of the right to communicate so general as to be lacking any normative content,[22] his analysis is often helpful. For example, Fisher argues that society's right to limit freedom of expression can be exercised only in the interest of protecting other equal or superior human rights such as the right to life, to religious belief, to the free choice of government and, perhaps, another individual's right of expression.[23] Again, this analysis is similar to that developed by the

Supreme Court in the commercial-speech cases. Commercial speech and data flows are protected but they can be restricted by reasonable measures necessary to protect other public interests.

Having stated the broad principle, the next question is whether international law and practice provide any guidance for practical arrangements among states to balance competing interests and to facilitate the introduction and utilization of new technologies in the informatics industries. It is generally recognized that the regime established under the General Agreement on Tariffs and Trade does not apply as well to trade in services as it does to trade in goods. The Administration hopes to remedy that situation in the GATT. Legislation enacted by Congress in 1984 encouraged that program,[24] but we know this will continue to be a complex effort and cannot expect quick results.

On the other hand, the FCN treaties entered into by the United States with such states as France, Germany, and Japan generally provide rights of establishment, national treatment, and most-favored nation treatment for most economic activities. They also recognize the right to gather information for dissemination abroad by the print and electronic media, and they further provide that nationals of either party shall be permitted within the territory of the other party "to communicate freely with other persons inside and outside such territories by mail, telegraph and other means open to general public use."[25] If nationals of a treaty party have the right to participate in trade and commerce on a nondiscriminatory basis, and if they have a flat right to use the means available to the public for domestic and international communications, there is a clearly implied right to offer computer-based information and data-processing services from inside and outside the host country.

This right to communicate is not to be confused with a right to operate communications facilities. The United States FCN treaties generally include an exception from national treatment for certain sensitive sectors, including domestic communications. Further, international communications services are established pursuant to the International Telecommunications Convention. Ironically, an effective right to communicate that would embrace transborder data flows may depend on the exclusion of data-processing and information services from the definition of "communications." The same distinction will be necessary to maintain an open inter-national market for computer services outside the scope of the state monopolies that operate communications services in most foreign countries. Fortunately, this distinction has been recognized thus far by the Federal Communications Commission (FCC), in the consultative bodies of the International Telecommunications Union and, to a lesser extent, by Japanese and European regulatory authorities.

In the proceedings that have become known as Computer I and Computer II, the FCC struggled with a number of working definitions of communications services and computer services that may be useful to other national and international regulatory bodies. I have in mind, particularly, the competition authorities of the European community as they address the scope of state monopolies of communications and the consultative committees of the International Telecommunications[26] Union as they address such issues as the availability of leased lines.[27] It is doubtful other authorities will follow the FCC so far as to draw the line between "basic communications services," on the one hand, and all "enhanced services" on the other.[28] But "data processing" is not the same thing as "message switching"[29] and some test will be necessary to distinguish various types of hybrid services.

This is clearly one of the areas where substantial further work is necessary to develop the elements of a right to communicate under international law. Up to now most companies wishing to provide computer services in Europe and Japan have been able to work out their problems through ad hoc negotiations. These negotiations often have been difficult, but there still is no groundswell of support for new international legal standards. My own guess is that the continuing advance of technology will make it even more difficult and, yet, more important to develop such standards at the intergovernmental level. I am confident we shall have the opportunity to return to this subject frequently in the years ahead.

NOTES

1. Universal Declaration of Human Rights, G.A. Res. 217, U.N. Doc. A/810 (1948).

2. See Filartiga v. Pena-Irala, 630 F.2d 876, 883 (2nd Cir. 1980).

3. International Covenant on Civil and Political Rights, G.A. Res. 2200, 21 U.N. GAOR Supp. (No. 16)

at 52, U.N. Doc. A/6316 (1966). President Carter signed the convenant on behalf of the United States in 1977, eleven years after its adoption. However, the Senate has not yet given its advice and consent to ratification. *See* Henkin, *Rights: American and Human*, 79 COLUM. L. REV. 405, 423–24 (1979).

4.   U.N. CHARTER arts. 55, 56; Filartiga v. Pena-Irala, 881.

5.   The International Telecommunications Convention, done at Malaga-Torremolinos, Oct. 25, 1973, T.I.A.S. No. 8572, contains a similar parallel statement of rights and qualifications. In article 18, members of the I.T.U. "recognize the right of the public to correspond by means of the international service of public correspondence. The services, the charges and the safeguards shall be the same for all users in each category of correspondence without any priority or preference." Articles 19 and 20, however, reserve the rights of the members (1) to stop transmission of any private telegram on such grounds as security, public order or decency, and (2) to suspend the service indefinitely for all or certain kinds of correspondence.

6.   425 U.S. 748 (1976).

7.   425 U.S. 765 (1976).

8.   Linmark Assoc. v. Township of Willingboro, 431 U.S. 85 (1977).

9.   Carey v. Population Serv. Int'l, 431 U.S. 678, 701–02 (1977).

10.   Bates v. State Bar of Arizona, 433 U.S. 350 (1977).

11.   447 U.S. 557, 566 (1980).

12.   Metromedia Inc. v. City of San Diego, 453 U.S. 490 (1981).

13.   445 U.S. 191 (1982).

14.   Resolution WHO 27.43, II HANDBOOK OF RESOLUTIONS & DECISIONS OF THE WORLD HEALTH ASSEMBLY AND THE EXECUTIVE BOARD 58 (1981). 4th ed.

15.   The Trailsmelter Arbitration (U.S. v. Can.) 3 R. Int'l Arb. Awards 1905 (1938, 1941).

16.   Guidelines on the Protection of Privacy and Transborder Flows of Personal Data, OECD Doc. No. ISBN 92-64-12155-2 (Mar. 1980) [hereinafter cited as Guidelines].

17.   Convention for the Protection of Individuals With Regard to Automatic Processing of Personal Data, *opened for signature* Jan. 28, 1981, Euro. T.S. No. 108 [hereinafter cited as Convention].

18.   Guidelines, *supra* note 16, pt. 2, para. 7–14; Convention, *supra* note 17, arts. 5–8.

19.   Guidelines, *supra* note 16, Preamble & Recommendation 2; Convention, *supra* note 17, Preamble.

20.   Guidelines, pt. 3, para. 18.

21.   D. FISHER, THE RIGHT TO COMMUNICATE: A STATUS REPORT (1981).

22.   "Everyone has a right to communicate. Communication is a fundamental social process which enables individuals and communities to exchange information and opinions. It is a basic human need and the foundation of all social organization. The right to communicate belongs to individuals and the communities which they compose" (*Id.* at 38).

23.   *Id.* at 22.

24.   International Trade and Investment Act, Pub. L. No. 98-573, § 304, 98 Stat. 3000, 3002 (1974) (amended 1984).

25.   *E.g.*, Art. II (6), Treaty of Friendship, Commerce and Navigation, Oct. 29, 1954, United States-West Germany, T.I.A.S. 3593, 273 U.N.T.S. 3.

26.   *See* Treaty Establishing the European Economic Community, Mar. 25, 1957, 298 U.N.T.S. 11, arts. 85–94; Ramsey, *Europe Responds to the Challenge of the New Information Technologies: A Teleinformatics Strategy for the 1980s,* 14 CORNELL INT'L L.J. 237, 273–83 (1981).

27.   The Consultative Committee International Telephone and Telegraph (CCITT) Recommendations provide that "the leased circuit service is normally authorized in international relations where telecommunications circuits remain available after the needs of the public telecommunications services have been satisfied. However, administrations should recognize the requirement for leased circuits in their planning" (Recommendation D.1.5 (1980).

28.   *See In re* Amendment of § 64.702 of the Commission's Rules and Regulations, Docket No. 20828 Final Decision, 77 F.C.C.2d 384 (Computer II), *appeal filed sub nom.* Computer & Communications Indus. Ass'n v. FCC, No. 80-1471, 81-1193 (D.C. Cir.). Essentially, the FCC defined "basic" communications services as a "pure transmission capability over a communication path that is virtually transparent in terms of its interaction with the customer supplied information," and defined enhanced services as everything else. Computer II, 77 F.C.C.2d at 420.

29.   The FCC's first attempt to distinguish between communications and data processing services resulted in a model where data processing was defined as "the use of [a] computer for operations which include, *inter alia,* the functions of storing, retrieving, sorting, merging and calculating data, according to programmed instructions." *See* Regulatory and Policy Problems Presented by the Interdependence of Computer and Communications Facilities, 28 F.C.C.2d 291 (1970) (Tentative Decision); 28 F.C.C.2d 267 (1971) (Final Decision) F.C.C.2d *aff'd in part sub nom.* GTE Service Corp. v. FCC, 474 F.2d 724, 729 (2d Cir. 1973), *decision on remand,* 40 F.C.C.2d 293 (1973). "Message switching" was defined as "computer controlled transmission of messages" utilizing communications facilities where the "content of the message" was unaltered. *Id.*

HYPOTHETICAL SITUATIONS FOR ANALYSIS

CASE 1

A small software firm in Silicon Valley, California, asks you to draw up a contract with the Instituto Nacional de Pesquisas Espaciais (INPE) in Brazil obligating them to write some software programs to process data coming to the institute from the remote sensing (RMS) satellites. What would you advise? Would your answer be different if the Soviet secret police (KGB) were seeking your client's assistance in writing decryption programs to use in the analysis of signals they are monitoring from messages sent out from embassy rooftop antennas all over the world? Consider how you would advise the INPE concerning insurability against the risk that the United States may withdraw responsibility for the remote sensing satellite system, since the institute has read recently that the Office of Management and Budget has decided to remove the appropriation from the budget for the RMS program and turn this responsibility over to the private sector.

CASE 2

The *Writer's Digest* keeps address lists of its readers all over the world in a database in Boulder, Colorado. The government of Saudi Arabia comes to you for advice about whether it can seek an injunction against *Writer's Digest* or the database company in Colorado or the entrepreneur Japanese videotape company to prevent the sale of address lists of Saudi Arabian residents for use by the Japanese company in marketing its videotape of "Death of a Princess."

CASE 3

Situation A
The parents of a Phillips Academy student come to you. They have received a bill from Dartmouth Computer Center for $25,000, covering time that their son has been accessing—unbeknown to Phillips Academy or the parents—in the middle of the night. The boy has siphoned off a mathematical database from Edifice Rex, an architectural firm in Athens, Greece, designed to assist architects and engineers to analyze structural stress. He is an honor student at Phillips Academy and has just scored 800 on the advanced-level mathematics achievement tests.

The boy also discloses that he has developed his own version of this foreign database, with value added, that he has been able to market successfully, under the business name Computech, to potential purchasers of the Greek software. His version is not only superior to the Greek version but can be sold at a much lower price.

The parents have also been told by the Massachusetts Attorney General's Office that an indictment may soon come down charging their son with an as yet undisclosed criminal action.

Situation B
The executives of a multinational company come to you for advice regarding the use by their architects of the Computech system to design a new corporate headquarters building, which has recently collapsed, killing several dozen employees and injuring hundreds of others.

It is not clear from the evidence whether the incorrect data used for the design resulted from poor design by the Greek firm, inaccurate translation by the student, or inadequate transmission of the data in transit from the Greek computer to the Dartmouth computer.

The Greek firm is also asking your advice: Does it have a right of action against somebody for piracy of data? The Greeks went to great lengths to protect their proprietary interest by imbedding deliberate errors in the database. These errors are corrected when their application software is used, by difficult-to-find subroutines buried in the object code. They point out that this method of protection provides proof positive of theft of data, for the thief's building project will go awry. When representatives of the Greek firm see the expression of shock and horror on your face, they ask whether they might be vulnerable to a suit for damages caused by the collapse of the corporate headquarters building.

CASE 4

Situation A

The Canadian Broadcasting Company (CBC) comes to you for legal advice. Channel One, a Massachusetts company, is selling backyard earth satellite receivers to ranchers all over northern Mexico. The ranchers profess to be using the "dishes" only to receive data transmitted over the Public Broadcasting System (PBS) satellite service provided by the U.S. Department of Agriculture, called Greendata. The CBC has substantial evidence that the "saucers" are also being used to receive entertainment, sports, and news programs provided by the CBC satellite programs, including a number of programs for which they have contracted for broadcast with U.S. production companies in southern California. The American companies are asking for larger royalties, considering the larger audience provided by the Mexican ranchers.

Situation B

The Secretary of Agriculture has asked you, as his General Counsel, to write a memorandum on his options in responding to a bill recently introduced into Congress that requires all research and development costs to be recovered by U.S. government installations that establish and disseminate such databases.

CASE 5

A large U.S. computer company maintains the software program for systematic diagnosis of the cause of failure in its products in a central processing unit in the United States. Computers all over the world may be tied into this system via telecommunication lines so that the diagnostic routines can pinpoint the source of the malfunction quickly. A South American country with a strategic plan to promote the development of its own computer industry refuses to permit remote access to databases outside its national boundaries. It requires all databases to be maintained locally, to be run on locally manufactured microcomputers, and to be operated by nationals. Subsidiaries are not permitted, and joint ventures must be 51% locally owned.

Would you advise the U.S. company to do business in this country? If so, would you transfer a copy of your database? Would you train nationals of the country to make the repairs? Would you seek a waiver of the database rule? If so, would you advise the country's informatics officials to grant the waiver? Why or why not?

CASE 6

The plaintiff, a U.S. national, is the widow of a Lufthansa pilot killed in a crash in the Himalayas. The alleged cause of the crash was a garbled transmission from a weather data processing firm located in the United Kingdom that maintains its data base in Jamaica. The data were relayed to the aircraft via an anti-Clarke orbiting satellite run by a consortium of Indian Ocean nations including Sri Lanka, India, Nepal, Afghanistan, Pakistan, and the oil emirates. It is not clear whether the erroneous weather data were garbled because of transponder interruptions, a "glitch" in the software on which the system was running, or a "brownout" of the electric generator in the Central Processing Unit (CPU) in Jamaica.

Who should the widow sue? For what?

CASE 7

You are awakened at 2:00 a.m. by a wealthy advertising executive who is on a business trip. It is 10:00 a.m. at the Dubai Hilton, where he is staying, and his bedside computer terminal has disclosed a shortage of several million dollars in his cash accounts. These are deposited for convenience in a sophisticated electronic funds transfer system (EFTS) account maintained in Hong Kong, to which receipts from his advertising agencies in the major capitals of the world are deposited automatically at the end of each working day. The funds are placed in the currencies of whatever capital markets are most attractive on a 24-hour basis, according to the electronic wisdom of a computer program designed by a Chinese mathematics wizard, who also designed, and is reputed to have made a small fortune from the sale of, a computerized version of, "Go."

The cash-management firm in Hong Kong claims that an excessive burst of sunspots the previous day may have affected the program, although they have received no other complaints concerning the accuracy of their records. The *Wall Street Journal*, which is delivered overnight via satellite for publication and distribution in Dubai, has not yet appeared on the streets, but the early television news, which is also delivered via satellite, has reported no news of collapsing currencies. The news show did report that the Chinese math genius had gone on an extended sabbatical in a monastery in Outer Mongolia, with the purpose of perfecting his game of "Go" by playing it with Zen Buddhists, who do not believe in communicating with the outer world.

What do you advise?

CASE 8

A group of political activists called Smaller Is Better is systematically accessing personnel and financial files in the data processing (dp) centers of several multinational companies with subsidiaries in 10 or more countries. Smaller Is Better is deliberately changing the names and job descriptions, as well as the salary levels, of employees at random; because of this, vice-presidents of some companies are receiving the paychecks of secretaries in other companies, and vice versa.

All multinational companies involved purchase their payroll programs from Reliable Software Inc., which features strong security protection. Reliable uses an encryption scheme designed by a small but highly regarded software house in Taiwan.

Unbeknown to Company B, a Smaller Is Better activist is employed in Reliable's dp center and has access to the secret documentation of the software programs, including their security features.

The bank account of the chief executive officer of Company A was overdrawn substantially last month because he received the check of the night watchman of Company B—a check that was not sufficient to cover the automatic payments of his mortgages, utilities, tax-shelter investments, and credit-card transactions. The CEO has forfeited a $250,000 equity in a hotel to be constructed in Seattle. His American Express and Visa cards have been canceled for nonpayment, which caused his wife tremendous embarrassment as the hostess of a women's club luncheon at a prestigious restaurant. She is recovering in a sanitarium in Dutchess County, New York. The CEO is stranded in Bangkok, where his company has no office to assist him.

A secretary in Company B received the CEO's paycheck. She went on a buying spree and then left for a month's vacation in Bora Bora.

To whom does the CEO turn for relief?

BIBLIOGRAPHY

BOOKS

Baker, M. A. & Westin, A. F. *Databanks in a Free Society*. (New York: Quadrangle Books, 1972).

Baranson, J. *Technology and the Multinationals*. (Lexington, Mass.: Lexington Books, 1978).

Barnet, R. J. & Muller, R. E. (eds.). *Global Reach: The Power of the Multinational Corporations*. (New York: Simon and Schuster, 1974).

Bigelow, R. P. & Nycum, S. H. *Your Computer and the Law*. (Englewood Cliffs, N.J.: Prentice-Hall, 1975).

Bigelow, R. P. (ed.). *Computers and the Law*. (Chicago: Commerce Clearing House, 1966).

Bing, J. & Selmer, K. S. (eds.). *A Decade of Computers and Law*. (Oslo: Norwegian Research Center for Computers and Law, 1980).

Bowers, R., Hershey, C., & Lee, A. M. (eds.). *Communications for a Mobile Society*. (Beverly Hills: Sage, 1978).

Bradley, H. G., Dordick, H. S., & Nanus, B. *The Emerging Network Marketplace*. (Norwood, N.J.: Ablex, 1981).

Brown, C. J. & Chamberlain, B. F. *The First Amendment Reconsidered*. (New York: Longman, 1982).

Byrne, R.B., Gerbner, G., & Haigh, R. W. *Communications in the Twenty-First Century*. (New York: Wiley, 1981).

Charles River Associates Research Study (ed.). *The Economics of Competition in the Telecommunications Industry*. (Cambridge, Mass.: Oelgegeschlager, Gunn & Hain, 1980).

Chorafas, D. N. *Interactive Videotext*. (New York: Petrocelli Books, 1981).

Codding, Jr., G. A. & Rutkowski, A. M. *The International Telecommunication Union in a Changing World*. (Dedham, Mass.: Artech House, 1982).

Dertuozos, M. L. & Moses, J. (eds.). *The Computer Age: A Twenty-Year View*. (Cambridge, Mass.: MIT Press, 1979).

Dickinson, Jr., W. B. (ed.). *Editorial Research Reports on the Global Community*. (Washington, D.C.: Congressional Quarterly, 1972).

Didsbury, Jr., H. F. (ed.). *Communications and the Future*. (Bethesda, Md.: World Future Society, 1982).

Dizard, Jr., W. P. *The Coming Information Age*. (New York: Longman, 1982).

Haight, T. R. & Sterling, C. H. *The Mass Media: Aspen Institute Guide to Communication Industry Trends*. (New York: Praeger, 1978).

Holmes, J.C. (ed.). Computer-Based National Information Systems. (Washington, D.C.: OTS, 1981).

Inose, H. *An Introduction to Digital Integrated Communications Systems*, (Tokyo: University of Tokyo Press, 1979).

International Telecommunications Union. *From Semaphore to Satellite*. (Geneva: ITU, 1965).

Lambert, R. D. (ed.). *The Annals of the American Academy of Political and Social Science*. (Philadelphia: The American Academy of Political and Social Science, 1974).

MacBride, S. (ed.). *Many Voices, One World*. (New York: Unipub, 1980).

Madsen, A. *Private Power*. (New York: Quill, 1982).

Masuda, Y. *The Information Society*. (Tokyo: Institute for the Information Society, 1980).

Nanyena-Takirambudde, P. *Technology Transfer and International Law*. (New York: Praeger, 1980).

Neustadt, R. M. *The Birth of Electronic Publishing*. (White Plains, N.Y.: Knowledge Industry Publications, 1982).

Pelton, J. N. *Global Talk*. (Rockville, Md.: Sijthoff and Noordhoff, 1981).

Robinson, G. O. (ed.). *Communications for Tomorrow*. (New York: Praeger, 1978).

Salz, J. (ed.). *Computer Communications: Increasing Benefits for Society* (Proceedings of the Fifth International Conference on Computer Communication). (Kingsport, N.Y.: The Kingsport Press, 1980).

Sigel, E. *The Future of Videotext*. (White Plains, N.Y.: Knowledge Industry Publications, 1982).

Smith, A. *The Geopolitics of Information*. (New York: Oxford University Press, 1980).

Smith, D. D. *Space Stations, International Law and Policy*. (Boulder, Colo.: Westview Press, 1979).

Wedemeyer, D. J. (ed.). *PTC '82: Pacific Telecommunications Conference*. (Honolulu: Pacific Telecommunications Council, 1982).

Wedemeyer, D. J. (ed.). *PTC '83: Pacific Telecommunications Conference*. (Honolulu: Pacific Telecommunications Council, 1983).

Wedemeyer, D. J. (ed.). *Pacific Telecommunications Conference Proceedings*. (Honolulu: Pacific Telecommunications Conference, 1980).

Westin, A. F. (ed.). *Information Technology in a Democracy*. (Cambridge, Mass.: Harvard University Press, 1971).

Whiteside, T. *Computer Capers*. (New York: The New American Library, 1978).

Williams, F. *The Communications Revolution*. (Beverly Hills: Sage, 1982).

JOURNAL ARTICLES

Aldrich, R. F. "Privacy Protection Law in the United States." NTIA Report 82–98. U.S. Department of Commerce. May 1982.

Avent, J. & Harms, L. S. (eds.). "Communication at the Crossroads." Communication in Hawaii Series; Report No. 3. The University of Hawaii at Manoa, 1977.

Bancilhon, F., Chamoux, J. P., Grissonanche, A., & Joinet, L. "Study on Data Security and Confidentiality." Commission of the European Communities. January 1980.

Becker, J. "Rifkin, A Documentary History." *Computer Law Journal* 2, no. 3. Summer 1980. (Reprinted by the Center for Computer Law, 1980.)

Bell, D. "The Matching of Scales." Louis G. Cowan Lecture. The International Institute of Communication. London. 1979.

Bing, J., Forsberg, P., & Nygaard, E. Report on "Legal Issues Related to Transborder Data Flows." OECD. Paris. May 1981.

Bortnick, J. "International Data Flow Issues." Issue Brief No. IB1040. The Library of Congress Congressional Research Service. January 1983.

"Brazilian Experience in Informatics." Transnational Data Report Supplement.

Brussels Mandate. "Minutes of the London Meeting-Summary Report and Findings." June 1978.

Cohen, S. & Kroloff, G. "The New World Information Order." The Committee on Foreign Relations, United States Senate. November 1977.

Commission of the European Communities. *European Society Faced With the Challenge of New Information Technologies: A Community Response*. Brussels, Belgium. 1979.

Commission on New Information Technology. *New Views, Computers and New Media—Anxieties and Hopes*. Stockholm, Sweden. 1979.

Deudney, Denis. *Space: The High Frontier in Perspective*. Worldwatch Paper 50. August 1982.

Epperson, G. Michael. *Implications for the Communications Industries of Proposed Amendments to the Webb-Pomerene Act*. Program on Information Research Policy. Harvard University. Cambridge, Mass. September 1981.

Glenn, Robin Day, *Financing of United States Exports of Telecommunications Equipment*. The International Law Institute: Georgetown University Law Center. Washington D. C. 1983.

Green, Jr., P. E. *Computer Network Architectures and Protocols*. IEEE Transactions on Communications. Special issue published by the IEEE Communications Society. Vol. Com-28, no. 4. April 1980.

Groshan, Robert M. "Transnational Data Flows: Is the Idea of an International Legal Regime Relevant in Establishing Multilateral Controls and Legal Norms?" Law/Technology World Peace Through Law Center. Part I published 4th quarter, 1981. Part II published 1st quarter, 1982.

Hearings Before the Subcommitte on International Operations of the Committee on Foreign Relations, United States Senate, 95th Cong., 1st Sess., on the Implications of International Communications and Information. Washington D.C. U.S. Government Printing Office, June 1977.

Hogrebe, M. E. *Legal Persons in European Data Protection Legislation: Past Experiences, Present Trends and Future Issues*. Report prepared for the OECD. Paris. 1981.

Horowitz, Andrew, and Thomas, Wes. *The Unexplored Option, Critical Choices for Public Telecommunication 1977–2000*. Prepared under the auspices of The Public Interest Satellite Association. 1977.

Information Policy: Public Laws From the 95th Congress. United States House of Representatives, Committee on House Administration. Washington D.C. U.S. Government Printing Office. January 31, 1979.

International Free Trade—The Computer Industry. Computer Law Association Inc. 1980.

International Chamber of Commerce. *The Liberalization of Telecommunication Services—Needs and Limits*. Paris. March 1982.

The International Communications Committee of the American Bar Association, Section of International Law and Practice and The Transnational Communications Center. Vol, 1, *Communications in a Changing*

World; Vol. 2, *Issues in International Information*. Washington D.C. The Media Institute. 1983.

The Research Institute of Telecommunications and Economics. *A Vision of Telecommunications Policy in the 80s*. 1982.

Issues on Transborder Data Flow Policies. Intergovernmental Bureau for Informatics. September 1979.

Lambert, Richard D., ed. "The Information Revolution." *The Annals of the American Academy of Political and Social Science* 412. March 1974.

Long-range Goals in International Telecommunications and Information, An Outline for United States Policy. For the use of the Committee on Commerce, Science, and Transportation, United States Senate. Washington D.C. U.S. Government Printing Office. March 1983.

National Academy of Sciences, National Academy of Engineering, Institute of Medicine. *Scientific Communication and National Security*. Washington D.C. National Academy Press, 1982, vols. 1 and 2 appendixes.

National Commission on Libraries and Information Science. *National Information Policy*. Report to the President of the United States. Domestic Council Committee on the Right of Privacy. Washington D.C. 1976.

National Commission on New Technological Uses of Copyrighted Works. *Final Report*. Washington D.C. Library of Congress. 1979.

National Security Council of the Presidency of the Republic of Brazil, Special Secretariat for Informatics. *Transborder Data Flows and Brazil: The Role of Transnational Corporations, Impacts of Transborder Data Flows and Effects of National Policies*. Report to the U.N. Center on Transnational Corporations. 1982.

Network New Zealand. A summary report by the CFF Communications Policy Research Group. Wellington, England. Commission for the Future. August 1981.

Nora, Simon and Alan Minc. *Report on the Computerization of Society*. To Valery Giscard D'Estaing, President of France. January 20, 1978.

OECD. *Information Activities, Electronics and Telecommunications Technologies, Impact on Employment, Growth and Trade*, Vol. 1. Information Computer Communications Policy. Paris. 1981.

OECD. *Guidelines on the Protection of Privacy and Transborder Data Flows of Personal Data*. Paris, 1981.

OECD. *Handbook of Information Computer and Communications Activities of Major International Organisations*. Information Computer Communications Policy. Paris. 1980.

OECD. *Information Activities, Electronics and Telecommunications Technologies*. Vol. II. Expert Roberts. Paris. 1981.

OECD. *Policy Implications of Data Network Developments in the OECD Area*. Information Computer Communications Policy. Paris. 1980.

OECD. *The Usage of International Data Networks in Europe*. Information Computer Communications Policy. Paris. 1979.

OECD. *Transborder Data Flows and the Protection of Privacy*. Information Computer Communication Policy. Paris. 1979.

OECD. *Transborder Data Flows and International Business*. Report prepared by C. Antonelli. Paris. May 1981.

Office of Technology Assessment. U.S. Congress. *Computer-Based National Information Systems: Technology and Public Policy Issues*. Washington D.C. October 1981.

Pelton, Joseph N., Marcel Perras, and Ashok Sinha. *Intelsat, The Global Telecommunications Network*. Honolulu, Hawaii. Intelsat. January 1983.

Pool, Ithiel de Sola, and Arthur B. Corte, *Implications of Low Cost International Non-Voice Communications*. A Report to the Department of Commerce and the Office of Telecommunications Policy, Vol. 1. Executive Summary. Center for Policy Alternatives. Cambridge, Mass. Massachusetts Institute of Technology. 1975.

Practising Law Institute. *After the AT&T Settlement, The New Telecommunications Era*. Patents, Copyrights, Trademarks and Literary Property Course Handbook Series, No. 155. 1982.

Radio Frequency Use and Management. Impacts from the World Administrative Radio Conference of 1979. United States Congress, Office of Technology Assessment. Washington D.C. January 1982.

Recommendations for a U.S. Strategy Regarding Transborder Data Flow Issues. Module on International Data Communications. Yale School of Organization and Management. April 7, 1981.

Report of the Vulnerability Committee (SARK). Stockholm, Sweden. 1982.

Report Prepared by the Congressional Research Service, Library of Congress, for the Subcommittee on Science,

Research and Technology, Transmitted to the Committee on Science and Technology. U.S. House of Representatives, 97th Congress. Washington D.C. U.S. Government Printing Office. June 1982.

Report to the Subcommittee on International Operations of the Committee on Foreign Relations. *The Role and Control of International Communications and Information*. United States Senate. Washington D.C. U.S. Government Printing Office. June 1977.

Robinson, Glen O. "Regulating International Airwaves: The 1979 WARC." *Virginia Journal of International Law* 21, no. 1. Fall 1980.

Scientific and Technical Information (STI) Activities: Issues and Opportunities. Prepared for the Subcommittee on Science, Research and Technology of the Committee on Science and Technology, U.S. House of Representatives, 95th Congress, by the Science Policy Research Division. Congressional Research Service, Library of Congress. Serial XXX. December.

Selected Readings: Transborder Data Flow Issues. Module of International Data Communication, February 24–April 9, 1981. Yale School of Organization and Management. Yale University. New Haven, Ct.

Solomon, Richard J. *World Communications Facts*. The Annenberg School of Communications. 1980.

"Symposium on Transborder Data Flow." *Stanford Journal of International Law* 16. Summer 1980.

"Symposium on the New Technology in the Communications Industry: Legal Problems in a Brave New World." *Vanderbilt Law Review*. Spring 1983.

"Symposium on Print Culture and Video Culture." *Daedalus*. American Academy of Arts and Sciences. Fall 1982.

"Symposium on International Satellite Communications and the New Information Order." *Syracuse Journal on International Law and Commerce* 8, no. 2. Syracuse University College of Law. Summer 1981.

"Symposium on Teleinformatics." *Cornell International Law Journal* 14, no. 2. Summer 1981.

Telecom Australia, *Public Policy Making and Telecommunications Planning*. Vol. 1, Pre-Seminar Papers; Vol. 2, Proceedings Seminar. August 1980.

Turn, Rein, ed. *Transborder Data Flows—Concerns in Private Protection and Free Flow of Information*. Vol. 1, Report of the AFIPS Panel on Transborder Data Flow; Vol. 2. Supporting Documents. 1979.

U.N. Center on Transnational Corporations. *Transnational Corporations and Transborder Data Flows: A Technical Paper*. New York. United Nations. June.

U.S. National Commission for UNESCO. *Toward an American Agenda for a New World Order of Communications*. January 1980.

UCLA Communications Law Program and the International Bar Association. "The Third Biennial Communications Law Symposium, International Satellite Television." University of California. Regents. 1983.

UNECOSOC. Commission on Transnational Corporations. *The Role of Transnational Corporations in Transborder Data Flows and Their Impact on the Home and Host Countries, Particularly Developing Countries*. June 1982.

Yurow, Jane H., ed. *Issues in International Telecommunications Policy: A Sourcebook*. The Federal Communications Bar Association and The International Law Institute of Georgetown University. 1983.

JOURNALS

Computer Law Newsletter. Published by Bigelow & Saltzberg.

Computer Law Journal. Published by the Center for Computer Law.

Computer Networks. Published by the North-Holland Publishing Co.

Computers and Security. Published by North-Holland Publishing Co.

Federal Communications Law Journal. Published by the UCLA School of Law and the Federal Communications Bar Association.

Information Privacy. Published by IPC Science and Technology Press.

Intermedia. Published by the International Institute of Communication.

Intug News. Published by the International Telecommunications Users Group.

Journal of Communication. Published by the Annenberg School Press.

Jurimetrics. Published by the American Bar Association.

Keio Communication Review. Published by the Institute for Communications Research, Keio University, Japan.

Law/Technology. Published by the World Association of Lawyers of the World Peace Through Law Center.

Privacy Journal. Published by Privacy Journal.

Rite Review. Published by the Research Institute of Telecommunications and Economics, Tokyo.

Satellite Communications. Published by Cardiff Publishing Co.

Telecommunications Policy. Published by the IPC Science and Technology Press.

Telematics and Informatics. Published by Pergamon Press Inc.

The CTC Reporter. Published by the United Nations Center on Transnational Corporations.

The Futurist. Published by the World Future Society.

The Information Age. Published by Butterworth.

The Information Society. Published by Crane Russak.

The International Lawyer. Published by the Section of International Law, American Bar Association.

Transnational Data Report. Published by North Holland in association with Transnational Data Reporting Service.

Pacific Basin Law Journal. Published by the UCLA School of Law.

INDEX